Nico B. Rottke (ed.)

Handbook Real Estate Capital Markets

Handbook
Real Estate Capital Markets

– an international perspective on functionality,
subprime crisis and future developments

Prof. Dr. Nico B. Rottke MRICS (ed.)
Aareal Professor of Real Estate Banking
European Business School
International University Schloss Reichartshausen, Germany

under collaboration of Fabian Brämisch, research assistant
European Business School, International University Schloss Reichartshausen, Germany

Rudolf Müller

Bibliografische Information der Deutschen Nationalbibliothek

Die Deutsche Nationalbibliothek verzeichnet diese Publikation in der
Deutschen Nationalbibliografie; detaillierte bibliografische Daten
sind im Internet über http://dnb.d-nb.de abrufbar.

ISBN 978-3-89984-165-7
© Immobilien Manager Verlag
   IMV GmbH & Co. KG, Cologne 2008

Umschlaggestaltung/cover design: corporate design cologne gmbh & co. kg., Cologne
Satz/composing room: text grafik konzeption Sylvia Wienpahl, Cologne
Druck/printing: Media-Print Informationstechnologie GmbH, Paderborn
Printed in Germany.

This book is printed on environment-friendly paper made from chlorin-free bleached cellulose.

Preface of the editor

About the book

After finishing a handbook on "real estate private equity" in fall 2006, I realized that I had covered the "private side" of modern real estate; however still missing was the possibly more challenging side of the public real estate markets and their interconnections to "the real estate game": the idea of a handbook on real estate capital markets came to my mind.

My first conceptual data file dates back to October 2006. Nothing at that time contradicted the idea to proceed with the aforementioned idea. But I soon discovered that German experts on real estate capital market topics were either hard to identify or preferred not to write in English. This gave birth to the idea to setup a real "global" handbook written by international authors from the industry and academia.

In the middle of the project, the US subprime crisis burst onto the global real estate markets. Dealing with the question, to what extent such a (hopefully) temporary phenomenon should be integrated into a textbook covering fundamentals, I think one board member of an international bank put it clearly to me: "You do not have to rewrite the story of the capital markets because of the subprime crisis". Therefore, the current market distortion is covered, but is not the crucial point of interest in this handbook.

The next hurdle to circumvent was the fact that authors have different mother languages and own styles of writing, so language needed harmonization. The same holds true for the use of technical terms and the synchronization to American English. To keep the text simple to read, I chose not to refer to both the male and female gender what shall not be misunderstood as discrimination against female readers.

Organization of the book

When I contacted a US publisher, I was first asked, whether this was a finance or a real estate book. As it is really both, the book connects the two worlds. Being divided into six sections, this compendium looks at the important fields of real estate capital markets:

After discussing the relationship between physical and capital markets in an international context in the fundamentals section A, section B deals with equity capital markets: the (E)REIT and other indirect real estate products are covered. Next, section C analyzes the debt capital markets: CMBS, RMBS, CDOs, covered bonds and hybrid products are discussed in detail.

Section D explains the synthetization of real estate via derivatives as well as products such as interest and currency derivatives, commercial and residential real estate derivatives or certificates on indices.

Finally, section E serves as an application-oriented practice section: case studies of products described in sections B through D are provided which apply the afore-learned knowledge using existing real-life cases. Case studies 1 through 5 thus cover equity products, case studies 6 through 10 deal with debt products. Case study 11 is tied to secondary products and case studies 12 through 13 discuss going public or private from both perspectives.

As the diction of capital markets' language is sometimes hard to understand for the "outsider", section F provides a glossary with over 150 explanations of the most frequently used capital market terms used of this handbook.

Should you have any feedback which may help to optimize future editions of this book, please do not hesitate to contact the editor directly (RECM.ebs@ rem-institute.org).

Acknowledgements

The assembly of this handbook would not have been possible without the help of many colleagues, mentors and friends.

First of all, I would like to thank all 55 authors for their valuable contributions. Without their efforts despite time constraints in a volatile market environment, this book would not have been possible at all.

I would also like to thank Dr. Wolf Schumacher, CEO of Aareal Bank, for his ongoing support and promotion. As major sponsor of my professorship, Aareal Bank sets a very positive framework which allows projects like this one. I also want to thank Dr. Alexander Goepfert, partner at Freshfields Bruckhaus Deringer in Germany who proved once again to be a prudential counsellor.

Next, I would like to say thank you to two individuals from the Immobilien Manager Verlag in Germany: Mr. Olaf Hütten, the publishing director, for his ongoing help, enthusiasm and friendship and Ms. Elke Rudolph, the director of print media, who dared to execute this venture with me.

My colleague Prof. Dr. Dirk Schiereck from EBS was a very valuable partner to discuss the structure and authors of this book. My former assistant Fabian Brämisch organized the communication with the authors; thus, this book is published under his collaboration.

I would also like to thank Dr. Christoph Holzmann, Berenberg Bank, for his very valuable and unconventional help as well as my Ph.D.-candidates Mr. Alexander Reichardt and Mr. Nicolai Striewe and my student Mr. Torsten Jahn who reviewed several articles of non-native speakers and helped establishing the index of the book. Also, my thank goes to my office manager Ms. Carmen Grahn for organizing merely everything else.

Last and most important, my biggest thank you goes to my wife Melanie who has to cope with the fact that she is married to an academic with everything but a 9-to-5-job as well as my children Janina, Patrick and Michelle who try to understand that doing research and writing books is a worthwhile activity. This book is therefore dedicated to them.

Wiesbaden, March 2008   *Nico B. Rottke*

Authors

After successfully completing his degree in Economics in 1997, Sven Andersen **Andersen**
began a graduate trainee program with Deutsche Bank in the Corporate Client
and Commercial Real Estate Department. During his time at Deutsche Bank,
he was responsible for major real estate transactions. In 2006, he moved to
NIBC Bank N.V. to set up and lead the German real estate activities. In 2007,
he joined Lehman Brothers Global Real Estate Group. As Executive Director,
he leads the "Frankfurt based real estate team".

Jeffrey A. Barclay is Managing Director and Head of Acquisitions at ING **Barclay**
Clarion Partners. Clarion is the US arm of ING Real Estate, one of the world's
largest real estate investment managers. Mr. Barclay directs the firm's private
market real estate investments throughout the United States and Mexico, in all
property types, including operating properties, ground-up development and
re-development. Prior to ING Clarion, he was a partner at Hamilton Securities,
and a director of investment sales at Jones Lang LaSalle. He also serves as
Adjunct Professor at Columbia University's Graduate School of Business,
where he earned his MBA in Finance and Accounting. Mr. Barclay is Chairman
of the Institute Committee of the Pension Real Estate Association (PREA), a
member of the board of directors of the National Association of Real Estate
Investment Managers (NAREIM) and Vice Chairman of the Industrial and
Office Product Council of the Urban Land Institute (ULI).

Diplom-Kauffrau Verena Bentzien, MScRE, studied Business Administration, **Bentzien**
majoring in Real Estate Economics and Entrepreneurship, at the European
Business School (EBS) and earned a postgraduate degree in Science of
Real Estate at the University of Hong Kong. During her time in Asia, she
participated in a case study tour where she worked closely with well-known
real estate companies and gained insight into the Chinese, Singaporean and
Japanese real estate markets. She then joined the Morgan Stanley Securitized
Products Group in August 2006 and has since been contributing to the real
estate commercial loan origination and securitization efforts of the Frankfurt
based team. In her affinity for real estate as an asset class as well as the capital
markets, she contributes to the academic and research efforts of the Real Estate
Management Institute.

Diplom-Kaufmann Fabian Brämisch studied Business Administration at the **Brämisch**
European Business School (EBS), majoring in Banking, Finance and Real Estate
Management. He spent two semesters abroad at the Universidad Católica de
Argentina and at the University of Sydney and gained practical experience
by doing several internships in the financial and real estate sector. After his
graduation, he was accepted as a doctoral candidate at the Endowed Chair
of Banking and Finance at the European Business School (EBS) and started
working as a Research Assistant at the Real Estate Management Institute of
the EBS. His research interest is primarily focused on the IPO performance of
European real estate companies.

Butz   Dr. Patrick Butz studied Chemistry in Freiburg and Basel and completed his Ph. D. in Molecular Physics at Oxford University. After a period of post-doctoral research in medical sciences, Mr. Butz decided to work in the financial market, initially in the area of exotic equity derivatives. He now works in the London office of Chatham Financial on structuring and executing fixed income derivatives. Mr. Butz advises institutional investors predominantly from the real estate industry in all aspects of interest rate and foreign exchange hedging.

Damaske   Martin Damaske studied at the Universities of Göttingen and Maryland, USA, gaining diplomas in both Business Administration and Physics. After several marketing and IT consultancy projects, he specialized in numerous mortgage market focussed projects. He has written various publications on mortgage origination, risk based pricing, funding and securitization in the real estate industry. In 2001, he joined Freie Hypo AG in Berlin (later Hypoport AG) as Director of the Institutional Clients Business Unit. Currently he is a member of the Hypoport AG Executive Board and sits on the board of directors for Hypoport Capital Market AG and Dr. Klein & Co. Capital AG. Recently, he has been responsible for developing and setting-up the ABS reporting platform "EUROPACE for issuers", and with "EUROPACE for investors" he set up an information and analysis portal for 90 % of all European public ABS transactions across all asset classes.

Daric   Christine Daric, tax lawyer, partner, joined Baker & McKenzie Paris in 2004 after a six year experience at Landwell and Ernst & Young. She was closely involved in the design and the creation of the tax regime applicable to French REITs (SIIC) and in the drafting and the negotiations with the French tax authorities of the text governing the SIIC regime as the advisor of the Federation des Sociétés Immobilières et Foncières (FSIF). She is specialized in general taxation, tax optimization and international taxation for corporations within the real estate industry. She mainly advises French and foreign clients with respect to their real estate transactions and in particular tax structuring, tax planning and tax assistance within real estate transactions, French REIT's regime (SIIC) or to set up French real estate collective investment scheme ("OPCI"), design and implementation of real estate investment funds for French and foreign investors of SIIC. Ms Daric received a postgraduate diploma in town planning law and a second one in tax law.

Duemke   Gavan Duemke is a member of the Hedge Analysis & Execution Team at Chatham Financial's London office. Prior to Chatham, Mr. Duemke worked in analytical and project-based consulting roles in corporate and real estate finance in Germany and the United Kingdom. He received a BA in Business Administration from the University of Cologne, and an MBA from the University of Oxford.

Ertl   Thomas Ertl is Executive Director at Morgan Stanley Bank AG and has more than 15 years experience in real estate finance. Before he joined Morgan Stanley to become Head of Real Estate Finance Germany, he worked in various positions with Lehman Brothers, Munich Hypo and West Hypo. In addition to his Business Administration studies, majoring in Banking, English and French at the Friedrich-Alexander University of Erlangen-Nuremberg (Diplom-

Kaufmann), he also gained an "Immobilienoekonom" at the European Business School (EBS). He shares his practical and academic knowledge by giving lectures at the Real Estate Management Institute.

Jeffrey D. Fisher, Ph. D., CRE is Director of the Center for Real Estate Studies and Professor of Real Estate at the Indiana University Kelley School of Business. He is currently on the board of directors of the Pension Real Estate Association (PREA) and is a member of the faculty and board of directors of the Weimer School of Advanced Studies in Real Estate and Land Economics, Homer Hoyt Advanced Studies Institute. He is also a Director of Hoyt Advisory Services and the Paul I. Cripe Company, Inc. Mr. Fisher has served on the board of directors of the National Council of Real Estate Investment Fiduciaries (NCREIF) and is a consultant to NCREIF. He is also on the board of the Real Estate Research Institute (RERI) and he is a Research Affiliate of the MIT Center for Real Estate (CRE). Mr. Fisher served as President of the American Real Estate and Urban Economics Association (AREUEA) in 1990, and is currently a member of the editorial board for Real Estate Economics. He has been on the board of directors of the Real Estate Research Institute and is currently a Fellow of the Real Estate Research Institute. Mr. Fisher has a doctorate in Real Estate from Ohio State University. **Fisher**

Dr. Bernhard Funk is Managing Director of Metzler North America GmbH. Metzler North America Corporation was founded in 1976 to create and manage North American real estate portfolios for private and institutional clients. After his graduation from business school, Mr. Funk did postgraduate work at the Center of Real Estate of MIT in Boston and at Georgetown University in Washington DC. He earned his doctorate in business administration in Germany and continued working in various management responsibilities in real estate investment and real estate finance. He is member of "gif" (German Society of Real Estate Researchers), Erich Gutenberg society and of DVFA (Society of Investment Professionals in Germany). His research is focused on REITs and US real estate markets. Mr. Funk was session chair for REITs at European Real Estate Society's London conference in 2007. He has published numerous articles in German and English on REITs and US real estate investments and is a regular conference speaker. **Funk**

Dr. David Geltner is the George Macomber Professor and Professor of Real Estate Finance in the Department of Urban Studies & Planning, and Director of the Center for Real Estate at the Massachusetts Institute of Technology (MIT). Prior to MIT, he was the REEAC Professor of Real Estate at the University of Cincinnati, and has been teaching graduate level real estate investments and finance since 1989. Mr. Geltner also served from 1998 to 2004 as a Visiting Professor in the Department of Land Management of the Faculty of Urban and Regional Science at the University of Reading (England), a research appointment. He served since 1999 as the External Academic Member of the Real Estate Investment Committee of the State Teachers Retirement System of Ohio as well as the Academic Advisor to the National Council of Real Estate Investment Fiduciaries (NCREIF), and as co-Director of MIT's Commercial Real Estate Data Laboratory. Mr. Geltner received his Ph. D. in 1989 from the Massachusetts Institute of Technology in the field of infrastructure finance & economics. He also has degrees in Urban Studies from Carnegie-Mellon **Geltner**

University and the University of Michigan. Mr. Geltner is also co-author of the graduate real estate investments textbook "Commercial Real Estate Analysis & Investments", published by Cengage Learning.

Gentgen   Dr. Julia Gentgen's professional career started in 2004 when she joined the European Business School (EBS) Department of Real Estate as a Research Assistant focusing on real estate investment, finance and valuation. In 2007, she relocated to London to join the real estate investment team of a leading US investment bank. Dr. Gentgen studied real estate and corporate finance at the European Business School (EBS), Oestrich-Winkel, Germany as well as at the San Diego State University, San Diego, California and the CERAM, Sophia-Antipolis, France. In 2004, she graduated from EBS. In 2007, she received a doctoral degree in Real Estate for her thesis on non-performing real estate loans.

Giest   Sascha Giest is an Associate Director at the Real Estate Group of Barclays Capital in London, focusing on large real estate related transactions, predominantly in Germany. He is involved in the entire process from origination to syndication, and securitization. Prominent public transactions he completed include the multi-family residential CMBS transactions Centaurus (Eclipse 2005-3) PLC and Grand PLC. Prior to joining Barclays Capital in early 2005, he worked in various departments of JP Morgan in London, including M&A, structured products, and capital advisory. After studying business administration in Berlin and completing a trainee program at Deutsche Bank he joined JP Morgan in 2000.

Glascock   John Glascock is Grosvenor Professor of Real Estate Finance at Cambridge University and Consulting Director of the National University of Singapore Institute of Real Estate Studies. Mr. Glascock has served as an expert to the UK, China, South Korea and Taiwan on REITs and has published extensively on REITs and listed real estate companies.

Goepfert   Dr. Alexander Goepfert is a partner of the international law firm Freshfields Bruckhaus Deringer and works from the Düsseldorf office in Germany. He studied law and history of art at the universities of Göttingen and Heidelberg, and earned a Doctor of Laws (Dr. jur.) degree in private international law from the University of Cologne. He joined the law firm in 1986 and has been advising international investors and project developers in major real estate projects in Germany and Europe for many years now. He specialises in the structuring of complex real estate transactions, in particular with a view to financing, tax and planning aspects. He acted as an adviser in a number of significant Private Equity Investments, inter alia in Blackstone's acquisition of the Deutsche Bank portfolio and the WCM residential portfolio, Merrill Lynch's acquisition of Brune's retail portfolio and also in the sale of Viterra AG by E.On.

Grassinger   Dr. Robert Grassinger studied Economics and holds a Ph.D. in Economics. He joined Württemberger Hypo in 1997 as Head of Strategy, Planning and Controlling where he was responsible for the bank's first public securitization WürttHyp 2000-1. He was Deputy Head of the Foreign Department of Württemberger Hypo from 2000 to 2002, where he was responsible for the underwriting of international loans and the securitization group of the bank.

He was Head of Financial Markets from 2002 to 2004, responsible for treasury, capital markets, securitization and MBS. He was a member of the Board at Hypo Real Estate Bank International (former: Württemberger Hypo), from 2004 to 2007, responsible for financial markets. Since 2007, he has been a member of the board at Hypo Real Estate Bank and a member of the management board at Hypo Real Estate Holding, Munich.

Helms

Volker Helms joined Deutsche Bank in 1989. He worked in various departments such as corporate banking, credit and international business before being transferred to Mexico in 1997. Mr. Helms was in charge of Deutsche Bank's global trade finance business in Mexico until 2005, he was then promoted and took on the responsibility for structured trade finance for the US and Latin America out of New York. In 2007, he accepted an offer from Landesbank Baden-Wuerttemberg where he is now the chief representative and managing director of the Mexican branch. Mr. Helms holds a Global MBA from Thunderbird University.

Herfurth

Ralf Herfurth is Managing Director/Head of Investment Banking for Germany and Austria at Barclays Capital, based in Frankfurt. He was appointed as Managing Director in December 2002. Prior to this, he held positions with Barclays Capital in structured and acquisition finance and also in corporate finance advisory. Mr. Herfurth graduated with Honours from Lehigh University, USA, with a Bachelor of Science in Business (major in Accounting/Finance). After an initial training period with Deutsche Bank AG in Munich, Germany, he joined the Barclays Multinational Corporate Group in New York. He then moved to Frankfurt as Vice President and developed the group's acquisition and corporate finance activities. Following that, he was Director of the Bank´s power and infrastructure advisory business, being responsible for various markets in continental Europe.

Hester

Julian Hester, a Director at Barclays Capital in London, has a Bachelor in Economics (Catholic University Rio de Janeiro) and an MBA from the University of Manchester. After 10 years as a consultant in IT and controlling in Brazil he joined Barclays Capital in 2002. In 2003, he joined the Corporate Securitisation team in London, started work on the Hallam transaction, the first securitization of multi-family housing in Germany, which was completed in 2004. During his time with the team, now called the Real Estate Group, he helped to develop Barcap's European franchise with transactions in several real estate sub-sectors, such as non-performing loans, large scale commercial real estate and hotels, having recently taken part in some of Europe's largest hotel acquisition financings. Since 2004, he completed some of the more notable transactions on the multi-family real estate sector in Germany including the largest one to date, the Grand transaction.

Kaiser

Bernhard Kaiser has been a partner of the international law firm Freshfields Bruckhaus Deringer since 1998 and works in our Frankfurt office. He has joined the firm in 1994. He is a member of our finance practice group, specialising in securitization, derivatives and other structured finance transactions. Mr. Kaiser was born in 1959 in Ludwigshafen, Germany. He completed his legal education at the universities of Mannheim, Heidelberg and Columbia University (New York). He earned his Master of Law (LL.M.) degree from Columbia University in 1991. Since 1992 he has been admitted to the New York Bar and since 1993 to the German Bar. Before joining the firm he worked with a major New York City law firm for two years.

Keisers   Dr. Maximilian Keisers is a member of Morgan Stanley's German M&A advisory group in Frankfurt, Germany. He works mainly on large cap M&A transactions, but also has experience with both real estate and capital markets transactions. Prior to joining Morgan Stanley in 2006, he worked as a research assistant at the Chair of Banking and Finance at the European Business School (EBS) located in Oestrich-Winkel, Germany. In addition to his primary research efforts of capital market reactions to M&A transactions, Mr. Keisers was a teaching assistant in several postgraduate finance courses and supervised numerous seminar and masters theses. In early 2007, he received a doctoral degree in finance for his thesis on wealth effects of banking and REIT M&A. Prior to his research tenure, Mr. Keisers received a degree in Business Administration, with majors in both information systems and finance, from the EBS. He also participated in postgraduate study programs at Stellenbosch University, South Africa and Melbourne University, Australia.

Klug   Walter Klug played a key role in the development of the Morgan Stanley Real Estate Investment GmbH. As a member of the management board he is responsible for the corporate strategy and communications as well as for sales and marketing, liquidity management, and since 2007, for fund management and acquisitions in Asia. He has more than 30 years experience in the real estate industry, especially in the areas of real estate financing and asset management. He has been active in the upper management ranks for over 18 years, of which he spent 10 years as a member of the executive board at the Deutsche Bank Bauspar AG, 5 years as Managing Director at the DB Real Estate Investment GmbH. For the past three years he has been a member of the board at Morgan Stanley Real Estate Investment GmbH. Mr. Klug is a graduate of the Advanced Management Program at the Harvard Business School, and author of the book "Open-End Real Estate Funds".

Laudenklos   After his banking education with the Bayerische Hypotheken- und Wechselbank, Frank Laudenklos studied Law at the University of Frankfurt am Main. He joined the Frankfurt office of Freshfields Bruckhaus Deringer in 2000 and has been a partner since 2005. He is a member of the company's finance practice group and a specialist in acquisition and real estate financing as well as leveraged financing.

Leibold   Stefan Leibold has been Managing Director of the German bank Ellwanger & Geiger (E & G) Funds Sicav. Since 2000 he became fund manager of the E & G Funds Immobilienaktien Europa. In 2006, he helped set-up the E & G Funds Property stocks Asia Pacific. He is Chairman of SEE Real Estate AG and actively helped to set up this company. He is regularly contributing articles and speeches to issues of listed real estate companies, and is lecturer at the FH Nürtingen-Geislingen. In 2000, he edited the book "European Property Stocks" and in 1999 created the European Property Stock Index E & G Epix. From 1989 to 1998, he worked for international banks in Germany, France and Russia. Mr. Leibold received a Masters degree in Management Science (Diplom-Kaufmann) from the University of Mannheim and also studied at Passau University and at ESSEC, Paris.

Dr. Peter Linneman is the principal of Linneman Associates and also serves **Linneman**
as the Albert Sussman Professor of Real Estate, Finance, and Public Policy at
the Wharton School of Business, at the University of Pennsylvania. A member
of Wharton's faculty since 1979, he served as the founding Chairman of
Wharton's Real Estate Department, and was the Director of Wharton's Zell-
Lurie Real Estate Center for 13 years. He is the founding co-editor of "The
Wharton Real Estate Review". His teaching and research focuses on real estate
and investment strategies, mergers & acquisitions, and international markets.
He has published over 60 articles during his career. Mr. Linneman holds both
Masters and Doctorate degrees in Economics from the University of Chicago.
He has provided strategic and financial advice to leading corporations,
including: American Asset Corp, Sunbelt Management, Lubert-Adler Realty
Funds, Paramount Group, General Electric and IBM for more than 25 years.

After her Abitur (graduation), Michaela Lorenz studied Mathematics at the **Lorenz**
University of Dortmund, with economics being her subsidiary subject. Having
gained her degree, she joined Depfa Deutsche Pfandbriefbank AG in February
1997 as a derivative specialist. In 2000, she moved to Luxembourg where she
was involved in building up a Banque d´Emission de Lettre de Gage (Mortgage
Bank under Luxembourg Law) named Pfandbrief Bank International S.A. (now:
Hypo Pfandbrief Bank International) which was part of the Hypovereinsbank
Group (now Hypo Real Estate Group). In 2002, she assumed the role of Head
of Treasury. In February 2004, she joined Aareal Bank AG as Head of ALM
and is currently responsible for the asset and liability management and tactical
asset allocation of the real estate financing group.

Marc Louargand is a Principal of Saltash Partners LLC, a firm he founded **Louargand**
in 2007 to make Angel round investments in startup companies. From
1994 to 2007 he was Co-Founder, Managing Director and Chief Investment
Strategist at Cornerstone Real Estate Advisers LLC, headquartered in
Hartford, Connecticut. Cornerstone is a registered investment advisor with
US$ 10 billion in North American real estate equity under management.
Mr. Louargand's responsibilities at Cornerstone included the development
of investment strategy, the oversight of real estate research and Cornerstone's
securities investment practice. Prior to co-founding Cornerstone, he was a
faculty member at MIT's Center for Real Estate. He is also Chairman of Mile
Square Farm Inc, parent of Vermont Only, a leading web-based retailer of
Vermont made products, and an Advisory Board member of Doran Capital
Partners headquartered in Seoul, Korea.

Dr. Bodo Marr studied law in Bonn, Geneva, and Cologne, where he graduated. **Marr**
During his Ph. D. in Business Law he spent 10 months doing research in
Warsaw, Poland. After passing the bar exam, Mr. Marr started his career in 1999
as an analyst in the Capital Markets Division of HypoVereinsbank, Munich
with a special focus on securitization and structured credit. In 2003/2004, he
completed an MBA with Leipzig School of Management. From 2005 to 2007,
he worked for Hudson Advisors/Lone Star Funds as Vice President Acquisition
Finance, responsible for the financing of large distressed portfolios and the
acquisition of distressed corporates. Since 2007, Mr. Marr has been working
for EquityGate AG in Wiesbaden as an Assistant Director where he provides

corporate finance advisory to midsized corporates with regard to structuring equity and debt, for example, in the paper or healthcare sector.

Meiwirth   Dirk Meiwirth studied Business Administration at the University of Münster, Germany. After a trainee program at Henkel-Group (Düsseldorf), he continued working as a Project Manager for industrial adhesives. In 1999, Mr. Meiwirth joined the real estate investment company DEGI of the Dresdner Bank AG, Frankfurt, first as an Assistant to the Chief Executive Officer in charge of product development and institutional sales. Since January 2003, he has been working as Head of Client Portfolio Management & Product Development at CSAM Immobilien KAG.

Mietzner   Diplom-Kaufmann Mark Mietzner studied Business Administration at the University of Frankfurt am Main. From 2004 to 2008 he worked as a Research Assistant at the University of Münster and at the European Business School (EBS). His research interests center around the fields of finance and capital market theory with particular emphasis on private equity and hedge fund activities. Apart from devoting his efforts to research, Mr. Mietzner has supported several university courses at the universities of Frankfurt, Münster, Lichtenstein, and EBS.

Mitropoulos   Dr. Stefan Mitropoulos is currently working as a Senior Real Estate and Equity Strategist in the Investment Strategy Group of Private Asset Management of Deutsche Bank AG in Frankfurt. He holds a degree in Economics. In 1994/95 he was a Research Assistant at the Institute for Economic Policy Research at the University of Mainz, where he completed his Ph.D. In 1996 he became a member of the sector analysis team of DB Research with the main focus on real estate, the construction sector and regional economics. Before he joined Deutsche Bank again in January 2005, he worked for three years in the Equity Research & Sales department of Bankgesellschaft Berlin AG as Equity Strategist.

Moritz   Gundolf Moritz joined Brunswick in February 2007 from ThyssenKrupp AG, where he was Head of Corporate Investor Relations and drove forward the internationalization of the IR function. After studying economics at the Universities of Bochum and Dortmund, he started his professional career as Business Editor at the Frankfurt based VWD (Vereinigte Wirtschaftsdienste) news agency in 1991. Mr. Moritz was Financial Editor at the financial newspaper Börsen-Zeitung from 1992 to 1996. In 1997, he moved to SAP AG in Walldorf where he was appointed Head of Investor Relations, placing him in charge of a global team located partly in New York. In this position, Mr. Moritz was involved in SAP AG's listing on the New York Stock Exchange in August 1998.

Nass   Diplom-Ökonom Patrick Nass studied Economics at the University of Hohenheim, majoring in International Accounting & Finance, Public Finance and International Economics. Following his graduation in 2006, he joined Bankhaus Ellwanger & Geiger KG, Stuttgart, as part of the fund management team of the E&G Fonds Immobilienaktien Europa. He was also co-responsible for setting up the E&G Fonds Property Stocks Asia Pacific in 2006.

Abraham Park has degrees in Economics (BA) and Law (J. D.) from U. C.   **Park**
Berkeley, Public Policy (MPP) from Harvard, and Real Estate Finance (Ph. D.)
from Cambridge University. He has worked in law and business in the US,
management consulting in Korea, and business development and real estate
research in London. He currently serves as an Assistant Professor at Pepperdine
University's graduate school of business.

Dr. Daniel Piazolo studied at the London School of Economics and at Yale   **Piazolo, D.**
University. From 1995 to 2002, he worked as a researcher at the Institute
of World Economics in Kiel and published numerous articles to economic
and financial issues. Three of his publications received international awards.
From 2002 to 2005, Daniel Piazolo worked as Senior Economist and Project
Manager for Feri Rating & Research, Bad Homburg. He was responsible
for the development of a forcast-based system for the derivation of market
values and ratings for real estate objects and real estate funds. Daniel Piazolo
joined IPD Investment Property Databank GmbH (then called DID Deutsche
Immobilien Datenbank), Wiesbaden, as Managing Director in October 2005
and is responsible for the overall management and the strategic direction
of the company. The IPD Investment Property Databank GmbH provides
independent, reliable information to the German property market and
publishes the Deutsche Immobilien Index DIX, the established German
property performance index. Since February 2008 Dr. Piazolo serves on the
Board of Directors of the Investment Property Databank London.

Dr. Katrin Piazolo is a specialist for Asset Backed Securities (ABS) and is   **Piazolo, K.**
responsible for the analysis of the Collateralized Debt Obligations (CDO)
at the Landesbank Hessen-Thüringen (Helaba) in Frankfurt. Her activities
include the assessment of tranches of various structured financial products
and the monitoring of ABS and CDO transactions. Katrin Piazolo joined the
Corporate Finance Department at Helaba in 2002. Before coming to Frankfurt,
she worked as a researcher at the Kiel Institute of World Economics for seven
years, examining the interlinkages between financial flows, trade and the
environment. Katrin Piazolo lived in Washington (DC) for five years and
studied economics in Berlin and in Kiel. Her Ph. D. thesis was honored with
the Bernhard Harms Award and the Faculty Award of the University of Kiel,
and she received an award from the Deutsche Studienstiftung.

Shawn Rosenthal serves as a Managing Director of The Ackman-Ziff Real Estate   **Rosenthal**
Group, which he joined in 2000. His responsibilities at the firm include all
aspects of the underwriting process including sourcing, evaluating, structuring
and negotiating investment opportunities for a broad range of property types.
He founded the mezzanine debt platform at Ackman-Ziff, and is a frequent
guest speaker and published author on the topic of mezzanine financing. Prior
to joining Ackman-Ziff, Mr. Rosenthal practiced real estate law at Thacher
Proffitt and Wood, a large New York City based firm, representing lending
institutions in real estate and corporate transactions. He also has experience
as an auditor and tax associate at KPMG Peat Marwick. Mr. Rosenthal holds a
BA in Accounting and Economics, Summa Cum Laude, from Queens College
(1991) and a J. D. from New York University Law School (1997). He is a licensed
Certified Public Accountant in New York and has been admitted to practice law
in New York and New Jersey.

Rottke   Prof. Dr. Nico B. Rottke is founder and executive director of the Real Estate Management Institute (REMI) at the European Business School (EBS), International University Schloss Reichartshausen. He holds a professorship in Real Estate Banking and as Academic Director, he ministers real estate related programs at the undergraduate, graduate, and postgraduate level. Prior to his teaching and research activities he worked in the real estate industry in the area of high-yield investment. In 2004, his study "Investments with real estate private equity" was honored with the research award by the German Society of Real Estate Researchers. Mr. Rottke is an active member of the Executive Committee of the Urban Land Institute (ULI) Germany, and on the management board of the Institute of the German Real Estate Industry (iddiw). Furthermore, he is engaged as a professional member (MRICS) of the Royal Institution of Chartered Surveyors (RICS), and also as a member of the research group of the real estate energy management initiative ENRESO 2020.

Rügemer   Robert Rügemer became partner of EquityGate AG in Wiesbaden in 2006. As managing director he is responsible for corporate finance advisory for midsized to large German and European corporates with a focus on large complex structured finance transactions with recent transactions in the utility, renewable energy, paper, real estate and chemical sector. He started his career at Deutsche Bank in 1994 training in the structured finance area with his first assignment in 1995 in the securitization and afterwards the principal finance team in London. As of 1999 Mr. Rügemer worked in the securitization and principal finance team of WestLB AG in London. End of 2003 he joined Ambac Assurance UK Ltd. as director responsible for the origination and structuring of Western and Eastern European structured finance transactions with a focus on corporate securitizations and project finance transactions in the utility, transport, telecom and infrastructure sector. Mr. Rügemer graduated in 1993 with a Maîtrise de Science Economiques from Université Panthéon-Sorbonne, Paris and in 1994 with a Diplom Ökonom from the Bergische Universität Gesamthochschule Wuppertal.

Schäfer   After receiving his Master in Mathematics and a doctorate in Business Adminstration under the supervision of Prof. Dr. Bernd Rudolph at the Frankfurt Goethe-University, Prof. Dr. Klaus Schäfer worked from 1993 to 2000 as an Assistant Professor of Finance at the Munich School of Management at Ludwig-Maximilian-University. There he did his habilitation, the German post-doctoral degree, having worked on delegation and portfolio management in 2000. From 2000 to 2006, he held positions at the Universitiy of Cologne, the Leopold-Franzens-University Innsbruck, and the Technical University Bergakademie Freiberg. Since 2006, he has been a full Professor of Finance and Banking at the University of Bayreuth where he also joined the research center in bank policy and bank regulation. He is a member of the American Economic Association, the Deutsche Gesellschaft für Finanzwirtschaft, the European Finance Association, the German Academic Association for Business Research, the German Operations Research Association, and the Schmalenbach Gesellschaft für Betriebswirtschaft. His main reseach interests are derivatives, risk management and capital market theory.

Andreas Schenk, Managing Director and Head of Funding Programs at Hypo **Schenk**
Real Estate Group, joined the predecessor of Hypo Real Estate Bank International
in 1998. In 2000, he was appointed as Head of the Corporate Office. As Head
of Securitization & MBS he was responsible for all securitization activities
from October 2001 to April 2004 in the foreign department. From April 2004
to March 2006, Andreas Schenk was Head of Capital Markets, the department
responsible for all funding, securitization and MBS investment activities at the
bank. In 2006, he joined the subsidiary of Hypo Real Estate Bank International
in New York for one year. Since 2007, he has been responsible for the funding
activities for Hypo Real Estate Group as Head of Funding Programs.

Diplom-Volkswirt Prof. Dr. Dirk Schiereck, Endowed Chair of Banking and **Schiereck**
Finance at the European Business School (EBS), studied Economics at the
University of Kiel. From 1993 to 2000, he was Research and Teaching Assistant
at the University of Mannheim, where he also earned his doctoral degree
(thesis title "Implementation Issues of Institutional Investors") and finished
his habilitation (thesis title "Guarantees as Banking Business and Borrowers'
Collateral"). From 2000 to 2002, he was Professor for Capital Markets and
Corporate Governance at the University of Witten/Herdecke. In 2002, he
joined EBS as Head of Department of Real Estate. His main areas of research
interest are Mergers & Acquisitions, real estate investment banking and
communication in financial market.

Dr. Thomas Schneider started his professional career in 2005 when he joined **Schneider**
Ernst & Young's Real Estate Transaction Advisory Group. During his time at
Ernst & Young, Mr. Schneider worked on major real estate transactions such
as the € 2.1 billion sale of the real estate portfolio from Dresdner Bank to
the Fortress Investment Group LLC. In 2007, he moved to the Global Real
Estate Group of Lehman Brothers. Activities of Lehman Brothers Global Real
Estate Group include senior, junior and mezzanine financing as well as equity
transactions. As an associate, his responsibilities include the realization of
financial analysis, real estate underwriting, due diligence, and research. Mr.
Schneider received his undergraduate degree in Business Administration and
Doctor of Economics from the University of Erlangen-Nuremberg and an MSc
in Real Estate Development from Columbia University.

As of 2008, Piet Hein Schram heads up ABN AMRO's FIG Capital Markets Asia **Schram**
team responsible for execution and origination DCM and ABS transactions
with financial institutions in the Asia Pacific region. Mr. Schram joined ABN
AMRO's Asset Securitization team in 2003. Within FIG Capital Markets Benelux
he was responsible for the origination and structuring of ABS transactions for
Dutch repeat issuers. In addition to the numerous ABS transactions he has
structured in the Benelux since then, he was also responsible for structuring
the first public Greek RMBS transaction.

In 1987, Tanja Stephan started her apprenticeship at Deutsche Siedlungs- **Stephan**
und Landesrentenbank (now Deutsche Postbank AG) in Bonn. In 1991, she
began studying Economics at the University of Applied Science in Aachen and
finished with a degree in 1995. She then joined Depfa Deutsche Pfandbriefbank
AG as a bond trader, responsible for public sector investments and Pfandbrief
issuance. In 2000, she moved to Eurohypo AG and took over responsibility for

Eurohypos securitization business at that time. After her maternity break, she worked as Capital Market Specialist reporting directly to the board member responsible for treasury and public finance and the Head of Treasury. In January 2007, she joined Aareal Bank AG's asset liablility management team with special responsibility for structured credit and public sector investments.

Streckel   After his education as a Computer Scientist, Diplom-Betriebswirt (FH) Tobias Streckel began to study real estate management at the University Nürtingen-Geislingen in 2003. During his time at the university, he worked for the former German initiator of closed-end property funds, the Falk Capital Group, as well as for the real estate investment companies UBS Real Estate KAG mbH and Catella Real Estate AG KAG. In 2007, he joined the German real estate corporation IVG Immobilien AG. His responsibilities are in the area of methodical portfolio and risk management consulting for IVG's institutional fund management arm.

Striewe   Diplom-Kaufmann Nicolai C. Striewe studied at the European Business School (EBS), Oestrich-Winkel, and graduated in 2007 majoring in Real Estate and Finance & Banking. Mr. Striewe spent semesters abroad at Bond University, Australia, and at the University of Illinois at Urbana-Champaign, USA. He has done internships in the real estate industry with Jones Lang LaSalle and Ernst & Young Real Estate and gained experience in the banking sector during internships at Commerzbank and Deutsche Bank. He has been Research Assistant and Ph.D.-student at the Real Estate Management Institute of the European Business School since 2007. As Head of the Colonia Real Estate AG Competence Center Real Estate Investment he is responsible for EBS-students and companies concerning real estate investment topics.

Swain   Cathy Swain assumed her current duties as Assistant Vice Chancellor for Commercial Development in The University of Texas System's Office of Research and Technology Transfer in September 2007. Her responsibilities include coordinating activities related to the Texas Emerging Technology Fund, and developing strategies for accessing venture capital and angel investment for U.T. System startup companies. She joined The U.T. System in 2005 as Director of Investment Oversight. She has served on institutional investment committees. She filled senior management portfolio management roles, served as CEO of a property management company and as CFO of a Community Development Corporation (CDC), taught college courses, authored several articles, and contributed in finance industry associations. She earned her BA in Economics and MS in Finance from the University of Illinois, and completed postgraduate studies at the Stanford University Graduate School of Business.

Thomas   Dr. Matthias Thomas, Immobilienökonom (EBS), studied Business Administration at the Westfälische Wilhelms-University in Münster, Germany. In 1996, he completed a Ph.D. on the development of a performance index for the German real estate market at the European Business School (EBS) in Oestrich-Winkel. Since 2006, Mr. Thomas has been holding the chair of Real Estate Management at EBS, and at the same time he is Managing Director of IPD Investment Property Databank GmbH in Wiesbaden. He is Vice President of the German Society of Real Estate Researchers and past-President of the European Real Estate Society. Mr. Thomas is a professional member of the Royal Institution of Chartered Surveyors since 2000.

Patrick Trutwein joined Deutsche Bank in 2003 after graduating from the **Trutwein** European Business School (EBS), Oestrich Winkel. Since then, he has had the opportunity to assume various international responsibilities, e.g., in London, Milan, Singapore, and currently New York. During the first years of his career, he mainly covered the Italian food sector and US automotive industry. Further, he held responsibility for DB's global chemicals credit portfolio strategy. Since 2007, he has been Executive Assistant to the Global Head of Hedge Funds Credit Risk Management. Coming from a risk perspective, his specialization includes structured financing solutions, and complex lending propositions for distressed corporations. Mr. Trutwein currently pursues a doctorate degree under the supervision of Prof. Dr. Dirk Schiereck at EBS. His research focuses on Credit Default Swaps and related capital market movements.

Axel Vespermann studied International Business Administration at the ISM **Vespermann** International School of Management in Germany, the United Kingdom, France, and the Netherlands. During his professional experience of more than 15 years in real estate, amongst others he worked for the open-end funds of DB Real Estate and Deka Immobilien before he joined CSAM Immobilien KAG as co-Head of Real Estate Investment in May 2003.

Hans Volkert Volckens is a Lawyer ("Rechtsanwalt"), Tax Adviser ("Steuer- **Volckens** berater") and Tax Licensed Lawyer ("Fachanwalt für Steuerrecht"). After his training as Industrial Manager, he had a university education at the Georg-August-University in Göttingen and at the Ludwig-Maximilians-University in Munich. In 2000, he received his J.D. at the University of Osnabrück. In 2000, he joined BBLP Beiten Burkhardt Mittl & Wegener, and became Equity Partner in 2005. He is a specialist in the fields of tax law, investment tax law as well as investment law. At present, he advises several institutions on the issuance of new tax-optimized capital market products and supports German real estate companies in their efforts to reorganize in view of the introduced German REIT structure. Furthermore, Mr. Volckens advises foreign investors with regard to investments in German real estate.

Dr. Peter Westerheide studied Economics at the Witten/Herdecke University. **Westerheide** Following his graduation in 1994, he became a Research Fellow at the Centre for European Economic Research, research department "International Finance and Financial Management". From September 1995 until the end of 1998, he was Research Fellow of the Economics Department at the University of Münster. There he received his doctoral degree in 1998 with a thesis on the objectives and effects of saving incentives within the framework of the social market economy. As of 1999, Dr. Westerheide returned as Research Fellow to the Centre for European Economic Research and the "International Finance and Financial Management" department, and since 2001 in the function of Senior Researcher and Vice Head of the department. His main fields of research currently address the areas of private old age pension funding, saving behaviour, corporate finance, real estate markets, and real estate finance.

Sam Zell is the Chairman and CEO of Tribune Company. He also chairs Equity **Zell** Residential Properties, Equity Lifestyle Properties, Capital Trust, Covanta and Anixter. Recently, he also served as Chairman for Equity Office Properties Trust, the largest office REIT in the US. Mr. Zell is also the Chairman of his private entrepreneurial investment firm, Equity Group Investments, which was the originator of three of the largest REITs in the real estate industry, and is the Chairman of Equity International, a privately held, leading investor in real estate-related businesses outside of the United States. He serves on the JP Morgan National Advisory Board, the Eurohypo International Advisory Board, the President's Advisory Board at the University of Michigan, and with the combined efforts of the University of Michigan Business School established the Zell/Lurie Entrepreneurial Center. He is a long-standing supporter of the University of Pennsylvania Wharton Real Estate Center, and has endowed the Samuel Zell/Robert Lurie Real Estate Center at Wharton. Mr. Zell has also endowed the Northwestern University Center for Risk Management.

Table of contents

C   Debt capital markets

D   Derivatives

E   Case studies

A   Fundamentals

1   Real estate between the poles of public and private debt and equity markets

Nico B. Rottke

Table of contents

1   Introduction

Real estate and capital markets grow together

All over the world, real estate markets and capital markets grow together. Real estate does no longer have only a physical dimension. Although the physical dimension is and will always be the basis for successful dealing with real estate, the financial dimension is on the increase and can hardly be negated in a more and more global market place.

Dr. James A. Graaskamp stated in 1977:

"The productive elements of real estate depend on the voids, not the solids. […] Somebody rolled a rock in front of a cave and created real estate by distinguishing the natural void from the void around it. […] Today, we start out with real estate in terms of an abstraction as a three-dimensional space with a fourth dimension – time. We always talk about real estate as a space-time unit." [1]

Dr. Graaskamp added to his understanding of real estate having two key dimensions, [2] that

"The real estate enterprise is concerned with the conversion of space-time to money-time". [3]

"Money-time principle" is key

The money-time dimension does not only play a role in directly transforming space into cash flow. Today, with the possibilities of using not only private markets but also sophisticated public markets, this idea goes further: highly complex real estate related equity and debt products as well as their derivatives can be traded worldwide in the capital markets.

Such a way of thinking has been state of the art in the United States and the UK over a long period of time, but represents a relatively new phenomenon to some parts of Continental Europe: in the last years, new European REIT markets emerged taking the US equity REIT (EREIT) as a role model; the debt capital markets boomed not only in the UK, but also, for example, in Germany. Due to the creation of new real estate indices, the trading of real estate derivatives became possible. Thus, new ways, unknown to most of the investors before, can be entered, in order to safeguard against specific forms of real estate risk. The mechanisms have been known for a long time, but now, market players are able to trade the associated risk of total return or credit default. This has not been possible before. However, the aforementioned considerations work in their entirety only partially as obstacles still exist such as the missing market liquidity, the quantity and quality of data or the question if the new indices are already able to model market risk well enough.

The introductory chapter of this handbook will pursue the classification of real estate capital markets into the context of the transaction-based real estate approach – a paradigm for interdisciplinary real estate education and research.

Classification of real estate capital markets

Furthermore, this contribution will derive the basic functionality and fundamentals of real estate public and private equity and debt markets and will provide a short overview of this complex field and its most important peculiarities. The field of real estate capital markets is fairly complex and sometimes associated with a high degree of risk. The nature of this risk is hard to understand and value by the different market players. This will finally be described with a brief analysis of the US subprime crisis and its consequences.

2 Transaction-based real estate approach

The broad discipline of real estate is taught in different ways according to different paradigms in universities in different departments throughout the world. Often, the perception of what exactly constitutes the real estate discipline has historical reasons and is caused by specific national or regional evolutions.

National and regional evolutions

For example, in transition economies with very few investment grade properties, a development approach to real estate will have more impact than in an established service economy which has already built up real estate stock to a large extent.

The two most diverging positions are the multidisciplinary and the financial management approach. The multidisciplinary approach uses a very broad definition of the discipline of real estate taking adjacent disciplines such as engineering, architecture, city planning and urban planning into consideration. The financial management approach uses a narrow conception of real estate as a subset of the discipline of finance.

"Multi-disciplinary" vs. "financial management"

These differences result in extreme finance-related positions such as David Shulman, Solomon Brothers, who stated "just show me the numbers, […], dealers don't really need to know everything about the properties they peddle" [4] to positions which promote the all knowing all-rounder as Graaskamp humorously stated in his famous quote:

"The result should be a real estate entrepreneur with the creativity of Leonardo da Vinci, the sensitivity for the natural world of John Muir, and the political humanity with cash management for profit of James Rouse. […] Of course, the graduate student should be something more." [5]

For example in Germany, there is a special country situation for real estate education: Professional real estate education at the university level began as late as 1990, when the first professionals were educated via postgraduate education. Real estate undergraduate education only started as late as 1994 at the university level at two different universities. Nowadays, the situation has changed: Schacks (2006) and Schalk (2007) show that there is a multitude of universities, universities of applied sciences and universities of co-operative education which offer undergraduate and graduate programs and consequently degrees in real estate.

Diversity of paradigms Despite the diversity of paradigms in the Anglo-American world, which are described for example by Dasso and Woodward (1981), Grissom and Liu (1994), Clapp, Goldberg and Myers (1994), Epley (1996), Black et al. (1996), Rabianski and Black (1999) or Yu (2001), the German approach to real estate has been, since the introduction of real estate as an academic field of interest at university level multidisciplinary in nature alone [6]. It has to be noted that there is a different use of the terms "interdisciplinary" and "multidisciplinary": research and teaching in the sense of a diversity of disciplines shall be called "multidisciplinary" in the context of this chapter.

Obviously, the discussion about different approaches to real estate education and research is different all over the world: For example in the US, the two positions "multidisciplinary approach" vs. "financial management approach" have been discussed for more than 30 years, however, in other countries this discussion has not yet taken place amongst real estate academics themselves or between real estate academics and the real estate industry.

Transaction-based approach to real estate In the compendium at hand, real estate capital markets are regarded as a cutout of the discipline of real estate taking a transaction-based approach (TAB-approach) as the underlying paradigm which can be placed in the middle of the aforementioned two opposite perspectives. On the one hand, the TAB-approach registers that financial management is too narrow to fully understand the different dimensions of real estate, and on the other hand, it recognizes that a multidisciplinary approach to real estate, at least for an education setup at a business school, is too unfocused given the restriction to time and resources. The danger of the later approach, if not executed correctly, results in a scholar with a superficial knowledge in many related disciplines, but without expert knowledge in the core disciplines of real estate management.

Management, institutional and generic perspective The setup for the TAB-approach takes three different perspectives (see figure below): the management perspective is the predominant one, followed by an institutional and a generic perspective.

The institutional perspective looks at the real estate discipline from the point of view of real estate corporations and companies such as real estate developers, investors, construction companies, financers, servicers, managers, agents, or users. The generic perspective covers the differences in structuring,

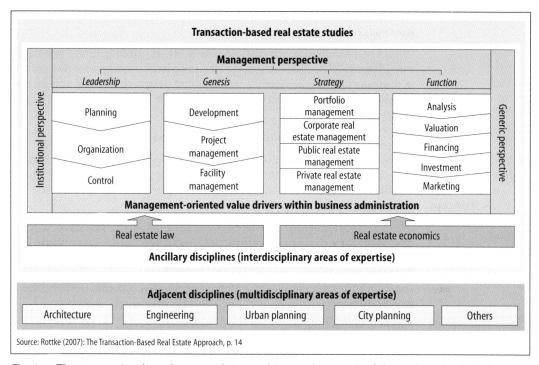

Fig. 1: *The transaction-based approach to teaching and research of the real estate discipline as an academic study field [7]*

analysis, and problem-solving ability involved with individual types of real estate assets, such as residential, office, retail, industrial or special real estate. The management perspective deals with the four different perspectives of leadership, genesis, strategy and function.

From a transaction-based point of view, what these different management perspectives all have in common, is that they have a preparing character within the area of business administration and hence are the value drivers for a later transaction.

Cradle in business administration

Next to this management core within the real estate discipline, ancillary disciplines join the management perspective as interdisciplinary areas of expertise once again serving as value drivers and preparing for a potential later transaction. The two areas of expertise within this interdisciplinary and transaction-based framework are real estate law and real estate economics.

Real estate as a discipline backed by law and RE Econ

Next to the real estate discipline consisting of real estate management backed by law and economics are multidisciplinary areas of expertise from adjacent disciplines, such as architecture, engineering, city or urban planning and others. These areas form disciplines of their own. Due to the eclectic nature of real estate, they play a basic role and should be dealt with in a real estate curriculum in the basics. As the management of real estate and its transaction stands in the foreground of the TAB-approach, these adjacent disciplines

Multidisciplinary areas of expertise

cannot be dealt with to an all-pervasive level due to philosophical, time and resource constraints.

Within this framework, the TAB-approach, the research field of "real estate capital markets" can be positioned in the functional management perspective with strong links to the strategic management perspective as well as legal real estate aspects and real estate economics.

3   Functionality of the real estate markets

Complementing the old "bricks and mortar" concept

The old "bricks and mortar" concept of directly buying privately bank-financed real estate has been complemented worldwide by the public real estate equity and debt markets, which influence physical real estate in an elusive way.

To understand the process of how private and public equity and debt markets interact, the following simple one-dimensional main sequence will be described. This description of functionality at the introductory chapter of this handbook can only be a very basic one which will serve to understand the main idea of interactions between the different markets. The following chapters will comment on the individual respective interface to the diverse real estate markets.

Four subgroups

Figure 2 provides an overview of the real estate market, dividing it into the four subgroups of private and public equity and debt markets. Together with different risk strategies (core, value added, opportunistic), this leads to diverse investment strategies and products on different levels (see figure 3 and also Chapter B1).

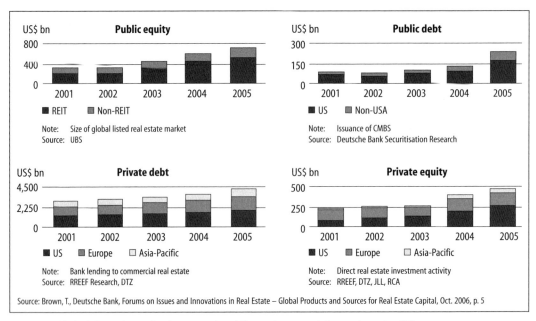

Fig. 2:   Global Overview of private and public real estate debt and equity [8]

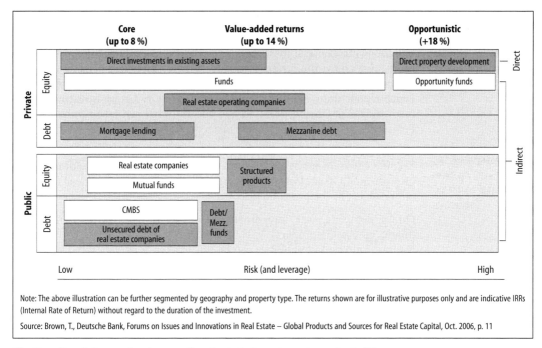

Note: The above illustration can be further segmented by geography and property type. The returns shown are for illustrative purposes only and are indicative IRRs (Internal Rate of Return) without regard to the duration of the investment.

Source: Brown, T., Deutsche Bank, Forums on Issues and Innovations in Real Estate – Global Products and Sources for Real Estate Capital, Oct. 2006, p. 11

Fig. 3:   Breakdown of universe of real estate investment products [9]

To show tendencies of development, public equity describes the size of the globally listed real estate markets dividing it into REIT and Non-REIT-products [10]. A proxy for public debt shall be the issuance of CMBS. As the dominance in this area of the US is obvious, it is divided between US and Non-US markets noting that the relevance of the Non-US markets increases which points to an enhanced ripening process within the area of public debt markets in the rest of the world over the last years. Private equity measures the direct real estate investment activity and distinguishes between the US, Europe and Asia-Pacific. Finally, as a measure of private debt, bank lending activity to commercial real estate is taken again in the US, Europe and Asia-Pacific [11].

Development of private and public equity and debt

Starting with the description of functionality, the point within the real estate process is taken when real estate is either developed, bought or (re)financed.

Starting point: development, purchase, (re)financing

On the equity side, a public or private institutional buyer is assumed who purchases a property to be put into an institutional portfolio, for instance into a portfolio of a real estate investment trust (REIT), a real estate fund or into the direct portfolio of an insurance company. REITs or direct investments serve as the basis for an index, for example the NAREIT or FTSE EPRA for listed securities or the NCREIF Property Index (NPI) or IPD Pan-European property index for direct real estate. Derivative strategies now become possible. A good current overview of real estate private and public equity as well as real estate derivatives is provided by Hoesli and Lekander (2008) in a paper on product innovation in Europe [12].

Next to the above mentioned strategies, fund of fund concepts are now also possible in order to further diversify risk.

Example of EOP The following example shows how equity markets interact: An opportunistic fund might have the strategy to exit an investment via a REIT-IPO. For example, Equity Office Properties (EOP) was born out of four Zell/Merrill Lynch Opportunity Real Estate Funds within Equity Group Investments (see case study E5). The corporation had successfully been taken public and in February 2007 EOP was profitably taken private again.

Differentiation cannot be as exact as it used to be as market players might become active in many different fields of activity: Listed corporations for instance might issue closed-end or open-end funds which again need financing on the object or the portfolio level.

On the debt side, every investment, if not bought with 100 % equity, needs financing. On the property level, this might be private debt, i. e., mortgage lending. Different possibilities can be executed such as structured or project financing. On the corporate level, financing by bond issues on the high yield (non-investment grade) or investment grade market is also a common way.

CDO-squared The financing institution itself has the possibility to refinance and securitize homogenous pools of assets into the debt capital markets, e. g., via mortgage backed securities (MBS), covered bonds (Pfandbriefe) or collateralized debt obligations (CDO). Also on the debt side, constructions such as CDO^2 ("CDO-squared") are possible, i. e. CDOs of CDOs which try to minimize risk by buying debt indirectly over other CDOs.

To point out the links between the different market segments, it is for instance possible that a bank finances a mortgage for a private house buyer. The mortgage could be part of a mortgage pool which is securitized into the capital markets in order to diversify and minimize risk. An affiliate, e. g., a conduit of the aforementioned bank might then be – as investor – the buyer of a CDO or CDO-squared and therefore indirectly the buyer of its own original loan.

Healthy property as essential requirement One essential fact in this circular flow should never be underestimated: The "problem" of the necessity of a performing underlying piece of property remains within the system: If the property is not producing cash flow, a positive leverage effect might turn to a negative one, and somewhere in the "capital markets food chain", investors lose trust or go bankrupt, for example because of buying subordinated debt associated with high risk and therefore the associated ex ante hope of high return which was never realized.

4 Public and private equity and debt markets

The dominant two players in the (indirect) real estate equity markets are non-listed real estate funds and listed real estate securities (real estate investment trusts and real estate operating companies; REITs and REOCs) which shall be briefly delineated in the following.

4.1 Equity markets

4.1.1 Non-listed real estate funds

There are several diverse investment styles and vehicle structures within the non-listed real estate universe. The term "investment style" refers to the approach a manager adopts to achieve the fund objectives. This includes the target rate of return, the degree of risk as measured by the vehicle's leverage, and the focus on return components (i.e., income versus capital growth).

Three investment styles ...

Three investment styles of real estate fund managers are widely acknowledged: core (plus), value-added, and opportunistic. These styles are defined by the target rate of return together with the level of leverage.

A core strategy is at the low end of the risk/return spectrum and is characterized by low target rates of return and little or no debt. Typical target rates of return lie between 300 to 700 basis points over government bonds for core funds and between 500 to 700 basis points for core-plus funds. This risk-averse strategy typically focuses on income return.

... Core

At the other end of the risk/return spectrum are opportunity funds whose target rates of return tend to be 1,200 basis points or more over government bonds. Opportunity funds tend to rely heavily on leverage to deliver their targets, reaching leverage often in excess of 75 % of gross asset value. The Gross Asset Value (GAV) of a fund is the gross property value plus the value of any further assets at market value as per the chosen valuation principles. Additionally, opportunity funds place as much emphasis on capital growth, sales, and intensive asset management to source their returns.

... Opportunistic

In between the core(-plus) and opportunity funds there is a group of funds using leverage ceilings ranging from 30 % to 70 % of GAV and targeting rates of return in the region of 700 to 1,200 basis points over government bonds. This fund-style is named value-added and typically focuses on deriving returns from a mix of capital value increase and income [13].

... Value added

All the opportunity funds and most of the value-added vehicles are closed-end vehicles, because they tend to require capital to be committed for a specified period to achieve their investment plans and cannot easily accommodate unplanned redemptions. In contrast, core funds tend to increasingly have open-end structures (including German open-end real estate funds).

Figure 4 presents an overview of market growth of non-listed European real estate funds with INREV's segmentation of German open-end funds as a special category, core funds, value added funds and opportunistic funds.

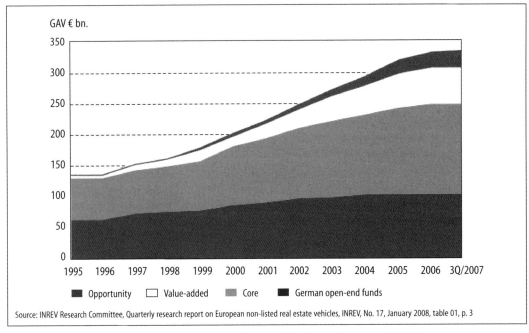

GAV € bn.

Source: INREV Research Committee, Quarterly research report on European non-listed real estate vehicles, INREV, No. 17, January 2008, table 01, p. 3

Fig. 4:   Overview of non-listed European real estate funds market growth [14]

Decreasing GAV in INREV database   Within INREV's database, the coverage of vehicles decreased from August to October 2007 to 476 vehicles representing a total Gross Asset Value (GAV) of € 336 billion. The decrease is mainly due to fund terminations but also following adjustments to the database scope in line with the INREV core definitions [15].

Regarding style, opportunity funds are finding themselves under great pressure from bankers. To the INREV research committee, who led interviews among fund managers, one interviewee reported that 85 % to 90 % loan-to-value ratios were no longer available and that they currently stood at 70 % to 75 %, but with only a slim chance of them rising to 80 % in 2008. Some interviewees thought it would result in opportunity funds rethinking business models with less value added through financial engineering and more value creation through real estate management [16].

Situation after credit crunch unclear   The INREV research committee further states that it remains too early to tell how the appetite for different types of funds and different geographies and sectors will be impacted by the current credit crunch. As a key issue, the severity of the credit crunch and its implications for real estate are identified: "only time will tell just how significant and prolonged the downturn will, or won't be." [17]

4.1.2   Listed real estate securities

Public equity means all forms of investments that are listed on a stock exchange such as Real Estate Investment Trusts (REITs) or Real Estate Operating Companies (REOCs). Since investments into the capital markets require a financial intermediary, public investment vehicles can by definition only be indirect in contrast to the private markets. A REOC is a company that invests in real estate and whose shares trade on a public exchange. They are similar to a REIT, except that a REOC will reinvest its earnings into the business, rather than distributing them to unit holders like REITs do. Thus, REOCs do not get the same benefits of lower corporate taxation which is a common characteristic of REITs. Also, REOCs are more flexible than REITs in terms of the types of real estate investments they can make. A more detailed analysis of REITs will be conducted in the following sections.

REITs and REOCs

To understand the recent development of REITs it is necessary to first provide some insight into recent developments in the real estate securities markets in general. The past decade showed a strong growth in real estate securities market. This has been driven partly by the appreciation of real estate values but more fundamentally, it is due to the increasing demand for listed real estate. In addition, the introduction of REIT legislations in many countries has also contributed to the strong growth of the global securities market. However, one must not forget that recent strong growth rates are the result of structural changes combined with the market's relatively small size which resulted in far more significant growth rates in terms of market capitalization than the broader equity markets.

Although nearly 20 countries have REIT-type structures, the size of real estate securities and REIT-markets is marginalized by the size of the global real estate market. In other words, only 12 % of the amount invested globally in real estate targets capital markets investment vehicles. However, REITs in particular have made a significant impact on the broader real estate markets in two ways:

Securitized vs. non-securitized market

- The growth of listed real estate securities has helped to increase the liquidity, efficiency and transparency of the underlying real estate since they are subject to the same rules and disclosure issues as other public companies.

- The second major benefit of REITs relates to the options they provide for investors seeking to gain access to real estate.

Particularly due to diversification benefits, investors seek investment opportunities on a global scale. Less mature markets such as central Europe make direct real estate investments cumbersome and costly due to a lack in transparency. Here, REITs and listed property companies can provide a well-proven alternative.

Global real estate securities have delivered outstanding performances over the past decade. They have been competitive in both the medium and long-term. In fact, before the subprime crisis, global real estate securities have outperformed both global equities and global bonds in each of the last 1-, 3-, 5-, and 10-year timeframes. On a 10-year period, global property shares have been slightly better than bonds and have outperformed global equities. While historical performance is not an indication of future expectations – as again the current short-term developments show – the data highlights that global real estate securities have the ability to outperform other major asset classes through various economic cycles.

Ratios as indicators of maturity level

Figure 5 shows the different distributions of global real estate securities at the end of 2006. Interesting to look at are the ratios "listed real estate vs. stock market" and "listed real estate vs. real estate market", both indications for the maturity level of the national real estate and capital markets:

The biggest real estate markets, with regard to commercial invested real estate market size, are the US, Japan, Germany and the UK. The size of the listed real estate securities market is highest in the US, Hong Kong/China, Japan, Australia, UK and France. It is amazing, that these two figures do not necessarily correlate: The US and Japan are "market leaders" in both dimensions; however, comparing listed real estate to the size of the stock market, a country such as Australia shows that it has a sophisticated market whereas a country such as Germany with a big real estate stock, has only very limited access to the capital markets.

	Listed real estate vs. stock market (in %)	Listed real estate vs. real estate (in %)	Real estate (in € bn.)	Listed real estate (in € bn.)	Stock market (in € bn.)
Germany	0.7	1.2	1,258.0	15.4	2,207.0
United Kingdom	2.3	7.6	1,240.6	94.0	4,046.9
France	2.8	8.1	955.0	77.5	2,737.1
Italy	0.6	0.9	793.0	6.9	1,106.1
Spain	3.2	6.9	505.4	35.0	1,088.2
Netherlands	2.3	4.8	281.4	13.5	574.5
Belgium	1.3	3.2	166.8	5.3	404.4
Switzerland	0.5	3.9	164.7	6.4	1,212.3
Sweden	3.2	11.2	162.8	18.3	576.9
Austria	7.0	13.8	137.4	18.9	269.4
Norway	0.7	2.3	128.8	2.9	411.7
Denmark	0.7	1.8	116.1	2.1	291.0
Turkey	–	–	101.5	0.0	282.0
Greece	0.8	2.1	101.2	2.1	262.9
Poland	3.1	6.5	97.9	6.4	208.4
Ireland	–	–	91.0	0.0	132.4
Finland	0.7	2.8	87.8	2.5	359.1
Russia	0.5	6.1	81.7	5.0	996.3
Portugal	–	–	78.6	0.0	147.2
Hungary	0.7	0.8	39.1	0.3	46.1
Czech Republic	–	–	31.7	0.0	74.5
Romania	1.0	1.5	27.1	0.4	40.6
Luxembourg	–	–	16.7	0.0	32.9
Ukraine	–	–	15.9	0.0	106.1
Slovania	–	–	11.1	0.0	28.1
Slovakia	–	–	7.6	0.0	8.5
Bulgaria	–	–	7.1	0.0	18.8
Total Europe	**1.8**	**4.7**	**6,706.0**	**312.9**	**17,669.4**

	Listed real estate vs. stock market (in %)	Listed real estate vs. real estate (in %)	Real estate (in € bn.)	Listed real estate (in € bn.)	Stock market (in € bn.)
Japan	4.3	9.7	1,996.4	193.5	4,545.9
HongKong/China	2.8	39.7	506.2	201.0	7,113.1
South Korea	0.1	0.3	329.2	1.1	1,103.3
Australia	11.6	51.1	320.7	163.9	1,413.4
Taiwan	0.7	3.7	139.1	5.1	701.1
India	0.5	7.9	121.3	9.6	1,815.0
Singapore	5.4	47.8	106.7	51.0	950.4
Indonesia	0.0	0.2	55.3	0.1	204.8
New Zealand	6.4	5.6	49.9	2.8	43.8
Thailand	1.6	8.2	42.5	3.5	212.9
Malaysia	0.2	1.8	39.2	0.7	324.5
Philippines	4.8	27.5	17.8	4.9	102.0
Vietnam	–	–	7.6	0.0	0.0
Total Asia-Pacific	**3.4**	**17.1**	**3,731.9**	**637.2**	**18,530.2**
Mexico	0.0	0.0	246.6	0.1	398.5
Brazil	0.0	0.2	245.7	0.6	1,393.5
Argentina	0.1	1.2	51.2	0.6	565.5
Venezuela	–	–	44.0	0	47.5
Chile	0.2	1.0	39.3	0.4	208.2
Colombia	–	–	27.8	0	90.6
Peru	0.1	0.5	19.3	0.1	80.3
Total Latin America	**0.0**	**0.3**	**673.9**	**1.8**	**2,784.1**
United States	2.5	8.0	5,602.2	446.6	17,663.5
Canada	2.4	8.5	502.0	42.6	1,749.1
Total North America	**2.5**	**8.0**	**6,104.2**	**489.2**	**19,412.6**
World	**2.5**	**8.4**	**17,216.0**	**1,441.1**	**58,396.3**

Source: According to Merrill Lynch Research, own calculation

Fig. 5:   Global real estate data 2006 [18]

Another major advantage of real estate securities is their low correlation with other asset classes. The correlations are lowest between real estate securities and bonds, with a negative correlation between the two asset classes in most markets around the world. Just as significant is the relatively low correlation between securities and the broader stock market. As volatility shows, real estate securities are part of the broader stock market. However, the movements of their returns differ to the broader equity market and this provides important diversification benefits for investors (see figure 6; also compare to chapter B1).

Low correlation to other asset classes

Beyond the scope for real estate securities to provide diversification benefits for broader equity portfolios, there is evidence of a worldwide factor in international indirect real estate returns. Country specific factors are found to be highly significant, which would suggest that international diversification is useful when constructing portfolios of real estate securities. The level of interest rates and the change in that level negatively impact on excess returns, whereas

The relation of beta and excess return

Total return correlations – global					Total return correlations – Europe			
	Direct RE	RE securities	Stock equities	10-year goverment bond		Direct RE	RE securities	Stock equities	10-year goverment bond
Direct RE	1				Direct RE	1			
RE Securities	0.25	1			RE securities	0.62	1		
Stock equities	0.20	0.35	1		Stock equities	0.24	0.30	1	
10-year goverment bond	−0.36	−0.28	−0.18	1	10-year goverment bond	−0.74	−0.38	−0.10	1
Source: RREEF Research, Global real estate securities – the emergence of a descrete asset class, London, January 2007, p. 14									

Fig. 6:   Global and European correlation matrix [19]

Real estate vs. stock diversification

term structure is positively related to returns. Notably, beta does not appear to be an important factor when explaining excess return on international real estate securities. Global and country-specific market risk factors are important, and a country-specific value risk factor adds some explanatory power. Correlations of real estate securities across countries are lower than cross-border correlations between common stocks. Additionally, international real estate securities diversification is more effective than international stock diversification. Since international real estate markets are segmented, benefits are to be gained from diversification, although potential gains are dependent on the exchange rate risk. With respect to the most efficient way of constructing a well-diversified portfolio of real estate securities by geographical areas, a strategy that is based on continents is more useful for Europe and in North America in contrast to the Asia-Pacific region [20].

The preceding analysis demonstrates that global real estate securities have a relatively high volatility that is in line with the broader stock market. Despite this, other performance characteristics of return and diversification generate some profound benefits particularly when considering global real estate securities within a multi-asset context.

Liquidity benefits

The intrinsic nature of real estate securities means there are significant liquidity benefits compared with other ways of investing in real estate. The liquidity ratio for real estate securities reached 79 % in Europe; 88 % in Australia and over 100 % in North America in 2006. There are two important dimensions to this. First, the trading of real estate securities can be carried out much more easily and quickly than direct real estate. In most countries it takes a number of months to complete a direct real estate transaction, whereas investing in real estate securities can take only a number of days to complete [21].

While the investors in direct real estate have the potential, with a delay, to liquidate their exposure, this is much harder for investors in private real estate funds. Within Europe and Asia, most private real estate funds remain closed-ended and fixed-life, with very little secondary market liquidity. The second important aspect of liquidity is the "divisibility" of the investments that are made. The scale and "lumpiness" of direct real estate makes it hard for investors to allocate small sums to particular markets or assets, reducing the scope to build a diversified exposure to real estate as explained in the previous section. There is greater divisibility for private real estate funds, but this is not as great as for investing in securities. The greater liquidity and divisibility of investing in securities provide investors with greater scope to change their exposure to different markets or sectors within a relatively short period of time, and this increases the scope for tactical asset allocation [22].

4.2 Debt markets

4.2.1 Convergence of real estate credit and capital markets

The convergence of real estate credit and capital markets can very well be shown taking the German example: Historically, the real estate credit market in Germany refinanced itself with covered bonds, unsecured bonds and deposits. **The German example**

Due to new requirements of international investors with high leverage ratios, subordinated real estate debt is also issued onto the capital markets, for example mezzanine or junior loans can be securitized using Commercial Real Estate Collateralized Debt Obligatons (CRE CDO) [23].

Different to the US or the UK, the German market for securitization was nearly non-existent before 2000. Over the last years, securitization activities have been fostered up until the subprime crisis set a sudden end to this trend.

Discussing the convergence of real estate credit and capital markets, the four asset classes have to be mentioned: Asset Backed Securities (ABS), Commercial and Residential Mortgage Backed Securities (CMBS and RMBS) as well as Collateralized Debt Obligations (CDO). **ABS, CMBS, RMBS & CDO**

For real estate capital markets, CMBS – securitizations which are backed by commercial property – have played the dominant role for a long time. Next to CMBS, conduit transactions are moving forward right now. Opposite to MBS, conduits buy loans based on upfront defined quality criteria and covenants. The pricing depends upon the later conditions for the notes to be placed in the capital markets.

Due to their structure, foremost the homogeneous loan election process, conduits are comparably cheaper, but restrictions are also higher: in case of impairment of performance, mechanisms of sanctions are quickly imposed on the respective loans. **Conduits**

Figure 7 illustrates how financing tranches can be exited via capital markets using the possibility of structuring them as capital markets products.

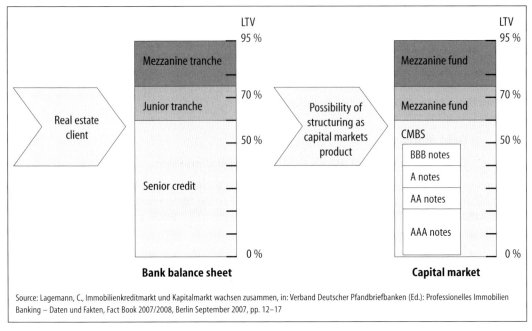

Source: Lagemann, C., Immobilienkreditmarkt und Kapitalmarkt wachsen zusammen, in: Verband Deutscher Pfandbriefbanken (Ed.): Professionelles Immobilien Banking – Daten und Fakten, Fact Book 2007/2008, Berlin September 2007, pp. 12–17

Fig. 7:   Private debt: example of financing structure and capital market exit [24]

4.2.2   Unsecured corporate debt versus secured real estate financing

Choosing a financing alternative, one can methodologically distinguish between senior financing and subordinated debt. With regard to senior financing, unsecured corporate debt and secured real estate financing are the two important areas which will be explained in this chapter as a common method of real estate debt financing.

Unsecured corporate debt
Taking a look at spread performance and corporate bond indices, unsecured corporate debt shows four peaks with regard to difference in pricing between high and low rated credits (EUR AA corp. index vs. EUR A Corp. index vs. EUR BBB Corp. Index). The spread in pricing has widened, but as of March 2008, the distortions of the Enron/Worldcom-crisis in 2002/2003 are still at a sharply higher level.

Secured real estate financing
Taking a look at secured real estate financing, at this point, European public debt development shall be representatively described as historically the most important real estate debt securitization asset class: mortgage backed securities (see figure 8).

Subprime stopped MBS trend
As shown in the figure below, the MBS issuance trend moved sharply to record highs in Europe up until mid 2007 when the US subprime crisis hit the real estate physical and financial markets. Interestingly, Germany with a figure of close to 45 % in 2007 played a bigger role in this market segment than the UK with approximately 31 %, which indicates some signs of maturity in the UK market [26].

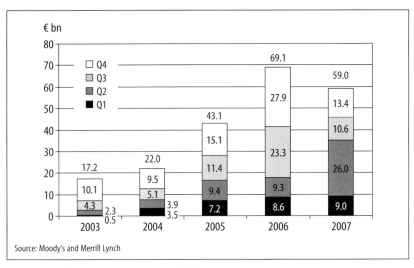

Fig. 8:   MBS issuance in Europe [25]

5   US subprime crisis: liaison of real estate and capital markets

In the following, the "vicious circle" of the US subprime crisis is drafted [27]. **"Vicious circle" of** Next to consequences for the overall economy, it is shown how a local real **the US subprime** estate non-performing-loan crisis can become global due to the liaison of real **crisis explained** estate and capital markets (see figure 9):

Step 1:   Interest rates increase: with cheap adjustable credits, US American citizens with low creditworthiness are able to afford their own homes. Due to the booming residential real estate market of the last two decades, appreciation is calculated into the payback plan. But the housing bubble bursts and interest rates nearly double within a 4-year period from June 2003 to June 2007.

Step 2:   Mostly for borrowers with low creditworthiness (subprime), interest payments become too expensive. Covenants like the Loan-to-Value ratio (LTV), the Debt Service Coverage ratio (DCR) or the Interest Service Coverage Ratio (ICR) are broken. When trying to sell their houses in order to pay back their loans, most of the time, the sales price is not adequate to pay back the loan. The borrowers have "to return their keys" and go into insolvency.

Step 3:   If this happens on a large scale, banks, as a consequence, get into **ROE problem** imbalance as well as credits are not paid back. Those credits have been securitized into the capital markets as Collateralized Debt Obligations (CDO) and many are worthless right now. Many banks have priced the risks related to CDOs incorrectly and get further into imbalance, especially if they or their affiliates have bought CDOs as investors in order to compensate for low Return on Equity (ROE) of their core business – mortgage lending.

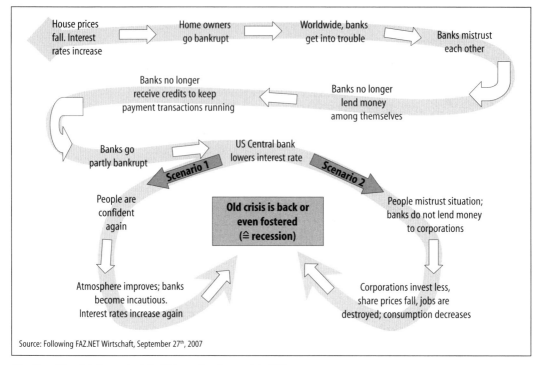

Source: Following FAZ.NET Wirtschaft, September 27th, 2007

Fig. 9:   The "vicious circle" of the subprime crisis [28]

Buy long-term, refinance short-term

What fosters the severity of the process is the fact that the affiliates buy long-term and refinance with short-term commercial papers in order to make an arbitrage gain; the parent company, the bank, provides an off-balance liquidity line to the affiliate in order to enhance the daughter's rating. The gain is received by term transformation. As the liquidity lines have to be drawn due to the panic of the market, some banks are close to insolvency. Worldwide, share prices of exposed banks fall dramatically.

Step 4:   As a consequence, banks mistrust each other, as nobody knows which bank might be the next corporation to present unexpected quarterly figures or profit warnings. Banks lose trust in each other.

Step 5:   As banks continue to mistrust each other, they no longer grant themselves credits. This affects above all short-term call money. The steady financial cycle at the money market is disturbed.

Step 6:   Even in times of prosperity, banks need loans on a continuing basis in order to keep the steady financial cycle flowing. This becomes more and more complicated.

Step 7:   Evermore banks get into difficulties: as there are no longer sufficed credits, they can no longer pay outstanding accounts and are brought to the verge of insolvency.

Step 8:   In order to get credit easily, the US central bank lowers the interest rates. Next to an amelioration of the situation, two negative scenarios might happen.

Step 9:   *Scenario 1:* If the market participants believe that the crisis is over, the situation of the banks gets better as new confidence is created and new credits are granted among each other. Share prices increase. The optimism of market participants comes back. The danger occurs that banks might react overoptimistically and lend the cheap central bank money too extensively. At some point in time, the interest rates will increase again and if the banks have granted too many loans, as a result, the crisis will come back.

Two scenarios possible

Scenario 2: The decrease in interest rate is so sharp, that market participants mistrust the situation: they think, the lowering might not be of use, the mistrust remains. The banks treasure up their funds and do not lend it – neither to other banks, nor to corporations.

Step 10: As a consequence, corporations invest less, the number of job positions decreases. Also, the share price of the corporations decreases. Both effects lead to a decreasing consumption.

Step 11: It is hard for corporations to sell their products. Evermore job positions get lost. A recession begins.

In general, debt markets particularly are growing rapidly in size and sophistication, opening a new range of opportunities to investors seeking enhanced yield and management of risk. However, successful investment in these markets requires expertise in credit assessment and financial structuring. Easily overlooked, but no less important to the investment process, are hands-on real estate knowledge and day-to-day exposure to transactions in the securitized as well as the direct real estate markets. Globalization of portfolios certainly offers diversification benefits, but investors ignore the traditional considerations of location, asset type and tenant covenant at their peril. Real estate investors therefore face a trade-off. On the one hand, the range of investment opportunities is expanding rapidly, both domestically and globally. At the same time, on the other hand, real estate investors are challenged to commit additional specialist resources to research, analysis and portfolio management.

Expertise in credit assessment and financial structuring required

6   Conclusion

A new generation of securitized products is accommodating the diverse objectives of yield, risk mitigation and capital growth from both equity and bond fund managers. Increasing market size and liquidity have facilitated new ways of packaging and securitizing conventional real estate financial instruments. The expanding range of investment products is in response to the sharp increase in the volume of funds directed towards the real estate sector in recent years. Re-rating of real estate assets and the compression of yields across the risk and duration spectrum have provided a further stimulus to financial innovation. Tighter spreads and a flat yield curve are an incentive

Expanding range of investment products

for innovation in financial packaging and fine tuning of portfolio management strategies.

The expanding range of real estate investment opportunities benefits all real estate market participants. However, the process is not without costs: investors now face greater information and analytical demands. For example, investors and portfolio managers need to consider exchange rate volatility and interest rate hedging strategies, as well as the diverse business practices, laws, taxes and regulations that apply in different countries to real estate and related financial products.

Increase of real estate weightings   Across the world, there continues to be strong demand for real estate exposure as shown by the current and target allocations to real estate. In most markets, investors are seeking to increase their real estate weightings, and countries from Scandinavia to South Korea are starting to invest in real estate for the first time (see figure 10).

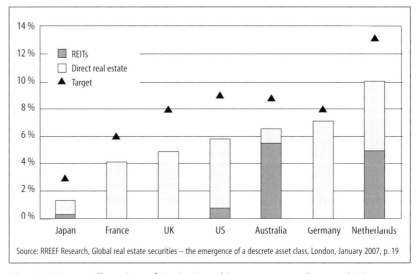

Source: RREEF Research, Global real estate securities – the emergence of a descrete asset class, London, January 2007, p. 19

Fig. 10: Target allocation of institutional investors to real estate [29]

Variations in allocations   There are, however, significant variations in the allocations to real estate across countries. The high allocations, for instance, in Australia and the Netherlands contrast sharply with the sub-2% allocations in Japan (although even in Japan the allocations have increased from 0.4% in 2003). These country-specific factors also influence the allocations of investors to real estate securities with Dutch and Australian investors having significant allocations to real estate securities. In other countries, such as the UK and Germany, there have been low institutional allocations to real estate securities as a separate asset class [30]. A new study conducted for Germany in fall 2007, in contrast, identified a total desired real estate quota of 8.9% in 2010 [31].

The strong performance of global securities markets has come with the expense of relatively high return volatility, certainly compared with bonds and direct real estate. The higher risk can be attributed to the fact that the listed real estate market is mainly dominated by small-cap and mid-cap companies that on the one hand have a greater amount of growth opportunities than larger companies, but on the other hand tend to have a more volatile business environment.

Although the volatility of securities appears to be far higher than direct real estate, academic research shows that this phenomenon can be mainly attributed to the appraisal based nature of direct real estate performance measures. The infrequency of direct real estate valuation tends to have a smoothing effect on the measurement of direct real estate performance which implies that the actual volatility is likely to be considerably higher than current appraisal based performance indexes are indicating [32]. **Appraisal-based nature of direct real estate performance**

Whether the investor will choose private or public equity or debt real estate exposure is mainly dependent on his or her preferences and thus is subject to various considerations with regard to volatility, liquidity and correlation.

That the different markets cannot be judged individually, but only in their entirety, is a mandatory postulation. That the capital markets are a catalyst for the physical real estate markets is a fact, but it should always be considered that internal rate of return, return on equity or any other return measure can only be optimized by financial engineering if the underlying cash flow has a solid basis coming from a healthy and well-positioned piece of property. **Capital markets as catalyst …**

What happens when investment decisions are not based on profound preparation work and a thorough analysis of all circumstances can be seen regarding the global consequences of the US subprime crisis for all private and public equity and debt real estate markets. **… but with due care**

Previous real estate market movements were driven by an over- and undersupply of funds from private investors and the lack of good quality data – particularly in Europe. Today, capital flows are the major factor affecting prices in real estate as well as all other investments. As positives to the public capital markets, the access to the public capital markets itself, better data and accountability have to be named; negatives to the public capital markets include price volatility, competition for capital, and unpredictability of global capital allocation. Thus, over- and undersupply of global capital is one of the major factors of false price appreciation support for real estate [33]. **Advice of caution**

Aggregating these private and public dynamics, the asset class of real estate will remain an interesting playing field to exploit arbitrage price differences.

7   Bibliography

[1] Cf. Graaskamp, J., The Failure of Universities to teach the Real Estate Process as an Interdisciplinary Art Form, speech delivered at University of Connecticut on Oct. 17, 1977, in: Jarchow, S. P. (Ed.): Graaskamp on Real Estate, Washington 1991, pp. 52–53.

[2] Cf. DeLisle, J./Graaskamp, J., A holistic perspective, in: DeLisle, J./ Worzala, E. (Eds.): Essays in honor of James E. Grasskamp: ten years after, Washington 2000, p. 63.

[3] Cf. Graaskamp, J., Redefinition of Fundamental Real Estate Concepts as a key to land use control and investment strategy, in: Jarchow, S. P. (Ed.): Graaskamp on Real Estate, Washington 1991, p. 489.

[4] Cf. Grissom, T./Liu, C., The search for a discipline: the philosophy and the paradigms, in: DeLisle, J./Sa-Aadu, J. (Eds.): Appraisal, market analysis, and public policy in real estate – essays in honor of James A. Graaskamp, Boston 1994, p. 73.

[5] Cf. Graaskamp, J., Redefining the role of University Education in Real Estate and Urban Land Economics, Speech from Dec. 1974, in: Jarchow, S. P. (Ed.): Graaskamp on Real Estate, Washington 1991, p. 44.

[6] Cf. Gondring, H., Die historische Entwicklung der Immobilien-wirtschaft – ein interdisziplinärer Ansatz (the historic development of the real estate industry – an interdisciplinary approach), in: Gondring, H. (Ed.): Immobilienwirtschaft, München 2004, pp. 15–16 or Schulte, K.-W., Real Estate Education in Germany, in: Schulte, K.-W. (Ed.): Real Estate Education throughout the world: past, present and future, Research Issues in Real Estate, Vol. 7, Norwell 2002, pp. 141–142.

[7] Cf. Rottke, N., The Transaction-Based Real Estate Approach: A Paradigm for Interdisciplinary Real Estate Education, working paper 2007, presented at the European Real Estate Society Conference, June 29th, London 2007, Great Britain, p. 14.

[8] Cf. Brown, T., Deutsche Bank, Forums on Issues and Innovations in Real Estate – Global Products and Sources for Real Estate Capital, October 2006, p. 5.

[9] Cf. Brown, T., op. cit., p. 11.

[10] It has to be noted, that this differentiation is not selective, as, e. g., mortgage REITs are debt products, but also publicly listed.

[11] It has to be noted, that other forms of private debt, e. g., debt funds, mezzanine funds or debt from institutional investors also play a role, but are not shown here. Cf. Brown, T., Deutsche Bank, Forums on Issues and Innovations in Real Estate – Global Products and Sources for Real Estate Capital, October 2006, p. 5.

[12] Cf. Hoesli, M./Lekander, J., Real estate portfolio strategy and product innovation in Europe, in: JPIF, Vol. 26, No. 2, 2008, pp. 162–176.

[13] Cf. INREV, Core definitions, Amsterdam, December 2006, p. 9–11.

[14] Cf. INREV Research Committee, quarterly research report on European non-listed real estate vehicles, No. 17, Amsterdam 2008, Table 01, p. 3.

[15] ib.

[16] Cf. INREV Research Committee, quarterly research report on European non-listed real estate vehicles, No. 17, Amsterdam 2008, Table 01, p. 10.

[17] INREV Research Committee, quarterly research report on European non-listed real estate vehicles;, No. 17, Amsterdam 2008, Table 01, p. 14.

[18] According to Merrill Lynch Research, own calculation.

[19] Cf. RREEF Research, Global real estate securities – the emergence of a discrete asset class, London 2007, p. 14.

[20] Hoesli, M./Hamelink, F., What factors determine international real estate security returns? in: REE, Vol. 32, 2004, pp. 437–462.

[21] Cf. RREEF Research, Global real estate securities – the emergence of a discrete asset class, London 2007, pp. 21–22.

[22] Cf. RREEF Research, op. cit., pp. 22.

[23] Cf. Lagemann, C., Immobilienkreditmarkt und Kapitalmarkt wachsen zusammen (convergence of real estate credit and capital markets), in: Verband Deutscher Pfandbriefbanken (Ed.): Professionelles Immobilien Banking – Daten und Fakten, Fact Book 2007/2008, Berlin 2007, pp. 16.

[24] Cf. Lagemann, C., op. cit., pp. 15.

[25] According to Moody's and Merrill Lynch.

[26] ib.

[27] The now described "vicious circle" of the US subprime crisis follows the basic remarks of Foßhaq, Bengt, The financial crisis at a glance, in: in FAZ.NET Wirtschaft, September 27th, 2007.

[28] Following Foßhaq, Bengt, The financial crisis at a glance, in: in FAZ. NET Wirtschaft, September 27th, 2007.

[29] Cf. RREEF Research, Global real estate securities – the emergence of a descrete asset class, London 2007, p. 19.

[30] Cf. RREEF Research, op. cit., pp. 19.

[31] Rottke, N., Optimal real estate vehicles for institutional investors in Germany, working paper 2008, presented at FERI institutional forum, February 27th, 2008, Königstein, p. 7.

[32] Cf. Geltner, D., Smoothing in Appraisal-Based Returns, in: JREFE, No. 4, Vol. 3, September 1991, pp. 340–342.

[33] Cf. Mueller, G., What will the next real estate cycle look like?, in: JREPM, Vol. 8, No. 2, 2002, pp. 123–125.

8   References

Black, R. et al., The role of the American real estate society in defining and promulgating the study of real property, in: JRER, Vol. 12, No. 2, 1996, pp. 183–193.

Clapp, J./Goldberg, M./Myers, D., Crisis in methodology, paradigms vs. practice in real estate research, in: DeLisle, J./Sa-Aadu, J. (Eds.): Appraisal, market analysis, and public policy in real estate – essays in honor of James A. Graaskamp, Boston 1994, pp. 107–132.

Dasso, J./Woodward, L., Real Estate Education: Past, Present, and Future – The Search for a Discipline, in: The Appraisal Journal, July 1981, pp. 413–425.

Epley, D., The current body of knowledge paradigms used in real estate education and issues in need of further research, in: JRER, Vol. 12, No. 2., 1996, pp. 229–236.

Gondring, H., Die historische Entwicklung der Immobilienwirtschaft – ein interdisziplinärer Ansatz (the historic development of the real estate industry – an interdisciplinary approach), in: Gondring, H. (Ed.): Immobilienwirtschaft, München 2004, pp. 3–17.

Graaskamp, J., Redefining the role of University Education in Real Estate and Urban Land Economics, Speech from Dec. 1974, in: Jarchow, S. P. (Ed.): Graaskamp on Real Estate, Washington 1991, pp. 40–50.

Grissom, T./Liu, C., The search for a discipline: the philosophy and the paradigms, in: DeLisle, J./Sa-Aadu, J. (Eds.): Appraisal, market analysis, and public policy in real estate – essays in honor of James A. Graaskamp, Boston 1994, pp. 65–106.

Rabianski, J./Black, R., An international perspective on the importance of real estate concepts and topics, in: JREPE, Vol. 2, No. 1, 1999, pp. 13 32.

Schacks, A., Der große Aus- und Weiterbildungsreport: Wen Immobilien-unternehmen suchen, was die Institute bieten (the big under and post-graduate education report: for whom are the corporations looking, what do the institutes offer), in: Immobilien Wirtschaft, No. 9, 2006, pp. 10–18.

Schalk, C., Weiterbildungsangebote für die Immobilienwirtschaft im Überblick (an overview on postgraduate education for the real estate industry), in: Immobilien & Finanzierung 09, 2007, pp. 311–315.

Schulte, K.-W., Real Estate Education in Germany, in: Schulte, K.-W. (Ed.): Real Estate Education throughout the world: past, present and future, Research Issues in Real Estate, Vol. 7, Norwell 2002, pp. 124–147.

Yu, S. M., New paradigms in real estate education, Pacific Rim Property Research Journal Vol. 7, No. 2, 2001, pp. 79–88.

2 The connection between capital and physical markets: drivers of real estate

Peter Linneman

Commercial real estate as major asset class
Commercial real estate is a major asset class. Every building and every piece of vacant land is owned by someone. In some cases it is a commercial interest that owns the property, while others are owned by a governmental agency or charitable organization. But in each instance, capital flows to these assets.

For commercial properties owned by for-profit enterprises, value is determined by the present value of the property's expected cash flows. But what risk is appropriate to reflect in the discount rate, and what are the future cash flows into perpetuity? This valuation exercise is typically redefined as one of evaluating the future cash flow of the property over the next five to 10 years, presuming the property is sold at the end of this period for a multiple of then expected cash flow. These expected cash streams are then discounted at a single discount rate which reflects the risk embedded in the property's cash stream and the property's illiquidity.

Starting point of forecasting are leases
When forecasting future cash streams, the starting point are in place leases. These leases are of varying length, were negotiated with a variety of tenants, at a number of different points in time, often by previous owners. Some of the markets in which these leases were negotiated were strong landlord markets, while others were strong tenant markets. In either case, the negotiated terms determine current rental payments. Some leases may be at rents below current market rates, while others may be above what the space would fetch today. But as long as the tenant is bound by the lease, and does not go out of business, it is obligated to pay the agreed upon rents and expenses for their space.

Existing leases often have bumps in their rent during the term of the lease, as landlords and tenants rarely negotiate a flat lease for the entire period of the lease. This allows rents to move upward over time, reflective of inflation. Sometimes these rental increases are gradual, perhaps 1 % to 3 % annually, while in other cases they are structured with no increases for several years followed by large rental or expense increases.

Leases, not inflation, dictate what occurs
The analysis of real estate is both simpler and more difficult than most businesses, as in place leases often determine a large portion of future income. Thus, contrary to most businesses, when analyzing real estate, one cannot simply assume that cash streams rise annually at roughly the rate of inflation, as in place leases to a large degree dictate what occurs. As a result, arduous and painstaking analysis of in place leases occurs when valuing a property. There is no shortcut. The result is that the valuation of real estate tends to be much more accurate than for most businesses, as "forward sales contracts" leases allow greater precision. However, it also means that the valuation differences among bidders tend to be smaller, as all bidders generally have access to detailed lease information. The more space that is subject to long-term in place leases, the narrower will be the bidding range [1].

Operating costs
A key element of in place leases is the extent to which operating costs are borne by tenants. This is not a matter of theoretical assumption, but rather an arduous process of reading the terms of the in place leases. Generally, tenants are responsible for the operating costs for their space, plus their pro rata share of the costs associated with local taxes, insurance, and the maintenance of common areas such as lobbies, parking lots, and general security. However, each lease dictates the precise terms. Sometimes all costs are paid by the

tenants, while at other times these costs are not paid at all by tenants. In other cases, they are paid in arrears; at other times they are paid in advance. Often they are capped in terms of how much they can rise in a particular period of time. And vacant space never pays a share of common expenses and taxes. Thus, empty space hurts real estate not only in the loss of rental income but also by not absorbing its share of the costs associated with operating a property.

A key element of in place leases are the tenant's usage and cancellation rights. For example, the tenant may have the right to cancel their lease if their business is sold or if the ownership of the property changes. Or the usage of the space may be restricted by the lease. Once again, there is no substitute for carefully examining the rights of in place tenants described in the lease. **Tenant's usage and cancellation rights**

When leased space is vacant or is expected to become vacant, one must estimate the nature of the lease that is expected to be signed for this space. This is generally done for each separate parcel of space in the building. Models such as Argus make this a relatively painless mechanical task, wherein one specifies for each currently empty or future unleased space, the length of time the property will be vacant, how much will be paid in leasing commissions, what the rent will be, what expenses will be borne by the tenant, etc. This process amounts to creating a "what will happen" lease, and modeling it as if it were an in place lease. Of course, in place leases are more certain than "what will happen" leases. By combining in place lease information with "what will happen" lease information, one constructs an expected revenue and cost structure for the property for each time period.

You must also add all sources of ancillary income, such as parking, temporary kiosks, signage, communication towers, etc. Some of the sources of income will be related to occupancy (e. g., parking), while others are not (e. g., signage income).

Total income expected for the property in each time period is the sum of in place income streams plus expected income from empty space, plus ancillary income, minus property operating costs and losses associated with poor credit. That is, not all tenants always pay their rent on time or in full. This generates a stream of expected Net Operating Income (NOI) for the property.

An important distinction to remember is that NOI and cash flow are very different things [2]. NOI does not include the costs associated with ongoing capital expenditures by the landlord. For example, lobbies have to be re-outfitted, parking decks have to be resurfaced, roofs have to be replaced, and elevators must be replaced. These capital expenditures regularly occur, though their precise timing is generally irregular and lumpy. When underwriting a property, you must evaluate when these expenses are expected to occur. In the absence of detailed engineering information regarding their precise timing, it is generally assumed that these expenses occur smoothly over time. However, it is important to remember when evaluating the risk of cash flows that while a reserve for these items may be smooth, the actual outlays are not. Thus, the riskiness of future cash flows are higher than is generally obvious when one models cash flow as NOI minus standardized capital expenditures, leasing commissions, and tenant improvements (TIs). Leasing commissions **NOI versus cash flows** and tenant improvements relate to signing new leases. Thus, when evaluating the value of a property one has to analyze these additional costs as occurring as empty space is occupied. These costs will often be quite large in the year following a lease's execution. As a result, although NOI rises as empty space is leased, cash flow will generally decline for a year or so. The link between capital markets and property markets requires one to understand these subtleties.

Property's residual value

Turning to the residual value of the property, that is the value of the property when it is sold, one typically uses the stabilized NOI five to 10 years from now, and applies a cap rate to calculate the perpetuity value of this income stream. This is equivalent to applying a valuation multiple to the stabilized future NOI. In some instances, a property's residual value is better viewed as the redevelopment value of the property rather than the value of ongoing cash streams. This is particularly the case as a building approaches the final stage of its useful life.

Choice of cap rate

Which cap rate should be used when calculating residual value? Typically one uses the cap rate for comparable buildings which prevails in the current capital market, with perhaps an upward adjustment to reflect the slope of the yield curve. Such an adjustment reflects the capital market's anticipation that alternative returns are higher (or lower) in the future. Also, the exit cap rate must be adjusted to capture the fact that the building will be older and perhaps less competitive when it is sold in five to 10 years.

Having specified the expected future cash streams, including the residual value of the property, these cash streams are subjected to a discount rate reflective of the risk inherent in the expected future cash streams. The risk reflects the tenant's credit, as well as operating risks associated with the property. It also reflects the differential liquidity of owning the property versus benchmark assets such as government bonds.

The riskiness of a cash stream, and hence the discount rate, may vary as the tenancy and the competitive circumstances of the property change. An obvious example is when a building goes from being leased by the US government to being leased by corporate tenants upon lease expiration. While the rent paid may (or may not) be higher than the rent paid by the government, the risk of corporate tenants is higher, as these tenants are inferior credit risks. Another example is that the risk associated with in place leases that have rents well below prevailing market rents is less than if leases are at rents which are well above market rates. This is because if the tenant ceases to operate, the below market rate lease sets a better floor on revenues, and rents may rise once the tenant vacates. In contrast, an above market rent is less likely to remain in place if the tenant ceases to lease the space.

Comparable risk characteristics

In assessing discount rates, it is helpful to think about the risk of the cash flow compared to assets with roughly comparable risk characteristics. For example, if the tenant is the US government, a comparable risk is a US government bond with an adjustment reflecting the differential liquidity of government bonds. Or if the property houses high-grade corporate tenants in a mid-town Manhattan office building, the comparable risk is a portfolio of high-grade corporate bonds, again adjusted for the relative illiquidity of the real estate. Remember that there is no magic to picking discount rates. In fact, markets are such that the bidder who assigns the lowest risk to cash streams tends to prevail, as they derive the highest valuation expectation.

If a property's NOI is stabilized, that is no major deviations are expected to occur, a very simple valuation model evolves as a special case of the discounted cash flow model. This is the "Gordon" model [3], which notes that the value of a perpetuity stream of stabilized cash flows (CF) growing at a rate of g and a risk discount rate of r, is equal to:

The "Gordon" model

$$V = \frac{CF}{(r-g)} .$$

That is, the value of a property is equal to its cash flow in the first year of ownership divided by the cap rate, where the cap rate for a perpetuity cash flow stream is equal to the discount rate minus the cash flow growth rate. The Gordon model only works if cash streams are such that the discount rate is significantly higher than the perpetuity cash flow growth rate. It also applies only if the cash streams grow relatively smoothly at the rate of g.

The Gordon model highlights the theoretical underpinnings for the valuation of real estate. That is, it depends upon current cash flow, the discount rate (assuming it is constant over time), and the perpetuity cash flow growth rate. For example, if the discount rate is 8 %, and the growth rate is 2 %, then the cap rate is theoretically 6 % (that is, $r-g$). This provides a powerful, yet simple, mechanism for approximating cap rates. The Gordon model is much easier to use than conducting a full discounted cash flow analysis. But it must be used with care, as it is only applicable if the discount rate and growth rate are basically constant and the property is stabilized.

The discount rate is equal to the government bond rate, plus the additional risk increment associated with the building's cash flow risk, plus an illiquidity premium associated with the property relative to government bonds. In general, one expects the cash flow growth rate into perpetuity to be equal to, or slightly less than, the economy's general rate of inflation. This is because as the building ages, its cash stream should increase at approximately the rate of inflation, with perhaps a modest reduction due to the fact that as the building ages, ever larger capital expenditures will be required to keep it competitive.

The Gordon model underscores the fact that as the base rate of interest falls, so too should the cap rate. Similarly as tenant credit risk or the liquidity of the real estate improves, the discount rate falls. Finally, as the sustainable growth rate of cash flows rises, the cap rate also falls.

In sum, a disciplined approach to the valuation of real estate is an intersection of the characteristics of the property and capital markets: leases, operational conditions, the local market, property liquidity, tenant quality, and the returns on alternative investments. Of course, actual markets at any point in time will deviate from theoretical pricing constructs. In particular, markets are always right at the moment, though over the long run they will gravitate to theoretical norms. A vivid example of prolonged mispricing relative to theoretical norms was the market valuation of dot-com companies. Ultimately, theory proved

Property and capital markets

correct, but not until several years of bizarre pricing prevailed. So too is the case in real estate.

< 1990: US real estate as debt financed business

Real estate in the US, the most transparent and liquid real estate market in the world, was substantially underpriced from 1990 through early 2006. This reflected a prolonged capital market adjustment following the meltdown of US real estate which took place in the very early 1990s. Up to that time US real estate was almost totally a debt financed business. When debt sources evaporated, pricing was far out of line with risk metrics. Instead, market pricing was established by distressed sales conducted by distressed sellers to a very limited set of buyers who possessed the requisite equity. This condition prevailed well into the 1990s. As debt capital returned to the real estate, the tech bubble caused equity investors to lose sight of the appropriate pricing of cash streams. As a result, real estate (like all other cash flow businesses) saw cap rates rise irrespective of the fundamentals of risk and cash flow growth.

This led to a long period of underpricing of US real estate, which began to end when the tech bubble burst. After the bubble burst, cap rates fell. Yet it took approximately five years of falling cap rates to finally get real pricing in line with risk. Finally, in early 2006, US real estate pricing was approximately in line with risk. Interestingly, when market pricing is about correct, it means that approximately half of the real estate is overpriced, and approximately half is underpriced.

CAPM to evaluate pricing

A simple way to evaluate correct risk pricing is to apply the Capital Asset Pricing Model (CAPM) [4]. For example, the beta for real estate is roughly 0.5, so for a risk-free rate of 4.8 %, and a market expected return of 8.8 %, the total expected return for real estate is 6.8 %. Since the cash stream of real estate is expected to increase at about the rate of inflation in the US (approximately 2.5 %), this means that the current cash flow yield for a typical piece of real estate should be approximately 4.3 %. That is, the total return expectation of 6.8 % for real estate is achieved by 4.3 % current cash flow, and a 2.5 % annual appreciation at a constant cap rate [5].

At this pricing, the cash flow yield is less than the risk-free rate. This reflects the fact that with a beta of 0.5 and a 2.5 % growth rate, real estate serves to improve portfolio diversification while also providing income growth. It also reflects that while a government bond realizes 100 % of its return through its coupon, real estate achieves approximately one third of its return through appreciation.

Comparison to bonds and equity

Another way to consider real estate pricing is to compare the expected return for real estate with the expected return on corporate bonds and equity. Specifically, BBB corporate debt generally prices at a return of approximately 180 basis points in excess of government bonds [6]. Corporate equities have an expected return of approximately 8.8 % in an environment of 2.5 % inflation. But the return expected for real estate must be lower than that for corporate equities, as the risk of lease payments is less than that of an equity claim for the corporate tenants. That is, the leases and the equity claims are being paid by the same corporations, as are the debt obligations on corporate bonds. Thus, real estate occupied by a pool of BBB credit tenants, which is approximately the typical tenant quality in a major US corporate real estate portfolio, should have an expected return much less than the equity returns expected of those tenants.

The lease claims are also safer than the debt claims, as the vast majority of the time both debt and lease claims will be paid by tenants. And when the tenant only has enough resources to pay one of these claims, they are more likely to pay their lease claim than their debt claim. This means that the total expected return of the lease claim, that is real estate, should be modestly lower than that of the debt claim. As a result, real estate pricing over the long run should move in relation to the returns on corporate equities, as well as government bonds.

My study of the relative underpricing of commercial real estate in the US based on a very simple CAPM for 1994 to 2007 demonstrates that until early 2006 commercial real estate was massively underpriced, reflective of the collapse of real estate debt markets and the tech bubble. However, today pricing is generally in line with risk (see figure 1).

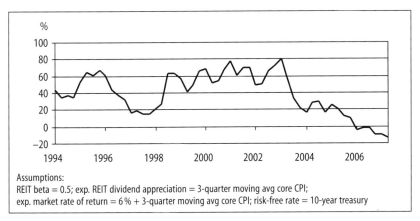

Fig. 1: *Real estate under (over) pricing with CAPM*

Real estate pricing is becoming more integrated across major real estate markets as capital flows between borders. More importantly, real estate pricing is integrating with other global assets. Increasingly, real estate is just another type of cash stream with associated risks. In this regard, multifamily buildings are just high quality consumer credit receivables, higher quality than credit card or auto receivables as tenants are more likely to pay their rents than to pay these other credits. Similarly, a portfolio of shopping centers is basically a pool of retailers' debt claims, while a portfolio of major office properties should be priced roughly similar to the claims on corporate debt [7]. **Real estate pricing to become more integrated**

Capital now moves around the world, as more and more investors move their money quickly and with relative transparency into real estate across borders. This money comes in the form of REITs, real estate private equity funds, high wealth investors, and investments by institutions such as banks and pension funds. On the debt side, Commercial Mortgage Backed Securities (CMBS) have provided transparency and risk pricing that links the pricing of real estate debt to comparable credit on corporate and government instruments. While banks and life companies continue to be major sources of direct real estate lending, their pricing is now intimately linked to the transparent pricing on CMBS. And real estate in markets in Western Europe and Japan are less and less priced on the basis of "who once slept here" or its architectural uniqueness, but rather based on cash flow potential and risk.

Markets better priced than ever

While markets remain far from prefect, they are massively more integrated and better "pricers" of risk than has ever been in the case. Every day, major investors wake up with trillions of uncommitted dollars in search of risk arbitrage. This footloose money compares risk, liquidity, and cash flow growth opportunities across a vast array of investments of different structure, geography, and sector. Increasingly, real estate is just one more asset category they examine.

Interest in German apartment portfolios

The recent interest in German apartment portfolios underscores this linkage. These portfolios had for a long time been poorly managed by both government and corporate owners. They were privatized via sales dominated by non-German private equity funds, who receive their money from university endowments, foundations, pension funds, and high wealth individuals. These private equity investors invested their money in apartments resided in by working class Germans.

The debt for these purchases was provided by CMBS offerings and global bank syndications, involving investors from across the globe. The pricing for these portfolios reflected the fact that the risk of the underlying German apartment cash streams is extremely low, as the tenants have lived in these properties for many years, and there are few viable alternatives for them to move in to, particularly given the fact that their current rents are well below market rents due to rent controls. Thus, in an environment where German government bonds yield 3.5%, a 150 basis point total return premium for such a low risk consumer receivable is a healthy premium. This implies the total return expectation needs only be roughly 5%, of which 3% comes from current dividends, and 2% from expected appreciation as the cash streams grow by approximately inflation.

Properties as high-grade consumer receivables

A 5% total expected return may seem absurd by historical standards. But upon reflection, these properties are nothing more than very high-grade consumer receivables. From this perspective, and given alternative returns, the pricing seems rock solid. This is why billions of dollars of global debt and equity gravitated from around the globe to these humble German properties. The miracle of capital market integration has taken extremely localized real estate assets, and moved them into the pricing of liquid and transparent cash streams. Welcome to the wonderful world of modern real estate!

Bibliography

[1] Linneman, P. D., Real Estate Finance and Investments: Risks and Opportunities, 2nd edition, Linneman Associates, Philadelphia, PA, 2004.

[2] ib.

[3] ib.

[4] Linneman, P. D., The Equitization of Real Estate. Wharton Real Estate Review, Vol. X, 2006, No. 2.

[5] Linneman, P. D., The Linneman Letter, first quarter 2007, Vol. 7, Issue 1.

[6] Linneman, P. D., The Linneman Letter, second quarter 2007, Vol. 7, Issue 2.

[7] Linneman, P. D., The Linneman Letter, fourth quarter 2007, Vol. 6, Issue 4.

3 Cointegration of real estate stocks and REITs with common stocks, bonds and consumer price inflation – an international comparison

Peter Westerheide

Table of contents

1   Introduction

Extensive debate on risk-return characteristics

Investment in securitized real estate is frequently considered as an instrument for participating in the long-run development of the real estate market without suffering from its typical disadvantage – its illiquidity. However, there is an extensive debate on the risk-return characteristics of Real Estate Investment Trusts (REITs) and other real estate stocks. The main question is whether real estate security returns primarily reflect real estate market developments and provide a corresponding potential for portfolio diversification, or whether their returns are dominated by the general stock market or – in the case of high leverage – even by bond market movements. Empirical studies yield diverging results, depending on the research methodology applied as well as on the country and the time period under consideration.

In the following, at first an overview on this debate in the literature is given. Secondly, additional empirical evidence on the performance of real estate securities and their relationship to other asset classes as well as to consumer price inflation is presented, based on a broad sample of countries over the 15-year period from 1990 to 2004. In contrast to many existing studies, this analysis focuses on the long-run relationships between real estate securities and other asset classes, which are particularly important for the long-term oriented buy-and-hold investors. For this purpose, the econometric concept of cointegration is used to test for long-run equilibria among different national asset categories.

The analysis covers the US, Australia, Japan, the Netherlands, Belgium, France and Germany. The real estate security markets in this sample are heterogeneous regarding their experience with highly specialized, exchange traded real estate investment vehicles like REITs or similar instruments. Furthermore, the countries differ with respect to the importance of stock markets for corporate finance and private wealth accumulation.

The detailed outline of the chapter is as follows: After reviewing the existing literature in the second part, the third part describes the characteristics of the market places under consideration and the data. The fourth part focuses on the historical performance of REITs and real estate stocks. In the fifth part short-term correlations with the bond and the general stock market are discussed. The sixth part of the chapter looks at the long run relationships between REITs and real estate stocks on the one hand and the general stock market and the bond market on the other hand. As an important characteristic of real estate investment, the ability to hedge against consumer price inflation is scrutinised as well. The seventh and final part summarizes the main findings.

2 Literature review

Studies on the relationship between real estate stocks, particularly publicly traded REITs, and the common stock market are numerous. Some former studies have also analyzed the inflation hedging ability of real estate securities. However, most of the previous studies analyze short-term correlations or other indicators based on periodical returns. Cointegration techniques have rarely been applied in the past. The majority of studies refer to the US market, particularly to exchange traded US REITs. This review highlights only some of the important studies. For a broader overview, the reader is referred to the survey by Zietz, Sirmans and Friday [1], for the older literature to the review by Corgel, McIntosh, and Ott [2].

Many previous studies find a significant positive correlation between common stocks and real estate stocks. Myer and Webb compare the return properties of REITs, common stocks and unsecuritized real estate for the period from 1978 to 1990 and conclude that the return characteristics of REITs are in the short-term similar to stocks, but in the long-term REIT returns seem to be a good predictor for the returns of unsecuritized real estate [3]. In another study, Myer and Webb scrutinize the relationship between retail stocks, retail REITs and retail real estate in linear regressions with contemporaneous and lagged variables and in VAR models during the period from 1983 to 1991 [4]. They find a positive contemporaneous correlation among retail stocks and retail REITs, but not among retail real estate and REITs or among retail real estate and retail stocks. Eichholtz and Hartzell analyze the relationship between real estate shares and common stocks in the UK and the US from 1977 to 1993 and in Canada from 1985 to 1993 [5]. They find evidence for a strong contemporaneous relationship between common stocks and real estate stocks, though differing across the countries. Mull and Soenen analyze the correlations between US REITs, domestic stocks, domestic bonds and domestic CPI inflation for the time period from 1985 to 1994 in the G7 countries [6]. They find a positive correlation with stocks, low – mostly negative – correlation with bonds and rather small, mostly positive correlation with consumer price inflation. They conclude that due to the positive correlation with stocks, the diversification potential of US REITs is limited. By comparing a three-asset model portfolio consisting of domestic bonds, domestic equity and US-REITs

Positive short-term correlation with common stocks

with a two-asset portfolio without REITs, they show that the inclusion of REITs does not improve the risk-adjusted return in most cases. However, these results depend heavily on the time period under consideration. Ling and Naranjo test for integration of common stocks and real estate stocks in multifactor asset pricing models for the period from 1978 to 1994 in the US [7]. They find evidence for (short-term) integration between both markets, based on the hypothesis that risk premia in the returns are identical for both asset classes. Brounen and Eichholtz analyze the diversification potential of property shares for the UK and the US for the period from 1986 to 2002 [8]. They find decreasing correlations between the asset classes and calculate that even in a worst case scenario efficient portfolios should contain a real estate share of around 10 %. Lizieri, McAllister and Ward study the convergence of real estate equities in the European Monetary Union in comparison to the stock markets, applying correlation analysis, principal component analysis, Granger causality tests and VAR analysis [9]. They conclude that commercial real estate equities are much less integrated than wider equity markets. Hamelink and Hoesli analyze the determinants of real estate security returns in a cross-country analysis on company level for 10 countries during the period from 1990 to 2003 [10]. They find that country-specific effects dominate returns, but also property type, size, value and growth characteristics of the company are important. Lee and Stevenson compare multi-asset portfolios with and without REITs for the US market and conclude that REITs provide substantial diversification potential, particularly by increasing the performance of low risk-return portfolios and by decreasing the risk in high risk-return portfolios [11].

Mixed evidence on inflation protection   A number of existing studies has been concerned with the question, whether real estate securities can provide protection against consumer price inflation. The evidence is mixed: A common result is that inflation hedging capabilities of real estate stocks seem to be limited. In an early study on the inflation-hedging characteristics of equity REITs, Murphy and Kleiman find for the period from 1972 to 1985, that REIT returns do not provide inflation protection [12]. Yobaccio, Rubens and Ketcham test, with linear regressions, for the inflation hedging characteristics of US REITs during the period from 1972 to 1992 and find that REITs provide some hedging against expected, but not against unexpected inflation [13]. In total, inflation hedging capabilities of REITs are therefore poor. Liu, Hartzell and Hoesli evaluate inflation hedging properties of property trusts in Australia, France, Japan, South Africa, Switzerland, the UK and the US for the period from 1980 to 1991 [14]. They find that property trusts are not a better inflation hedge than common stocks and in some countries returns are like those of common stocks – but even stronger than those – inversely related to inflation. Reverse causation between property return changes and inflation changes – i.e., that property return changes are predictors for inflation rate changes – is also tested and some evidence for this relation is found. Maurer and Sebastian analyze inflation hedging characteristics of real estate securities in France, Germany, Switzerland and the UK for the period from 1980 to 2000 [15]. They find that only German investment funds provide an inflation hedge, but real estate stocks in Germany and the other countries do not.

Only a few studies explicitly apply cointegration tests to test for long-run equilibrium relationships of real estate securities with other asset classes: Okunev and Wilson test for cointegration of US REITs with the stock market for the period from 1979 to 1993 and find no cointegration when using standard Engle-Granger tests [16]. They test a nonlinear model to describe the relationship between REITs and wider stock markets and conclude that there is evidence for a nonlinear dependency. The link, however, seems to be very weak and divergences between both markets decrease slowly over time, therefore diversification potential remains. Chatrath and Liang test for cointegration of US REITs with inflation [17]. They find evidence for cointegration in the period from 1972 to 1995 when using Johansen tests, but no evidence with other cointegration tests. Glascock, Lu and So analyze cointegration of US REIT returns with bonds, equities, unsecuritized real estate and consumer prices in the US [18]. They apply Engle-Granger tests and error correction models for the time period from 1972 to 1996. They find cointegration between stocks and REITs after the 1993 tax reform in the US and cointegration between bonds and REITs in the time period before the reform. They also find evidence for cointegration of REITs with unsecuritized real estate, measured by the NCREIF indices, and with consumer price inflation.

Cointegration studies

3 Empiricial analysis

3.1 Descriptive characteristics of the market places

The following analysis covers the US, Australia, Japan, the Netherlands, Belgium, France and Germany. While in all of these countries real estate stocks are traded, not all of them have extended experience with REITs or similar specialized vehicles for indirect real estate investments. REITs are characterized by their obligation to derive most of their income from real estate business activities (i.e., owning and operating income producing real estate such as apartments, shopping centers, offices, hotels and warehouses). REITs usually do not pay taxes on the company level, but are obliged to distribute nearly all of their income to their shareholders. REITs in the US and similar real estate investment vehicles in other countries are frequently regarded as driving forces for the indirect real estate investment market: On the one hand, they provide an opportunity for liquid investments in particular segments (property types, regions) of the real estate market. On the other hand, their regulation usually warrants a high degree of transparency and investor protection. In this respect, the occurrence of REITs or similar instruments can be assessed as an indicator of a mature real estate securities market.

With respect to their REIT history, the countries can be broadly arranged in two groups: While in some countries REITs or similar vehicles have a comparatively long tradition (US, the Netherlands, Australia), other countries only recently introduced REITs (Japan, France). In Germany, REITs were introduced in the course of 2007 (for an overview of the years of introduction of REITs in different markets, see figure 1). The countries differ also with respect to the type of their financing systems: While both, the European countries in the sample and Japan, have a bank based financing system, Australia and the US are known as countries with a more capital-market-oriented financing system.

Classification of markets

Figure 2 shows a graphical representation of countries ordered according to the market capitalization of domestic equities in relation to their gross domestic product on one axis, and their experience with REITS or similar instruments on the other axis.

With a view to both criteria, one can recognize a weak link between the maturity of the equity markets and the experience in REITs: Most of the countries in the sample with a long history of specialized real estate stock investment vehicles also have mature capital markets in terms of their relative market capitalization (quadrant IV). In another group of countries, specialized real estate stock investments are available only for a comparatively short period of time, and public equity markets are, at the same time, comparatively immature (quadrant I).

Country	Year of introduction
US	1960
Netherlands (NL)	1969
Australia (AU)	1985
Belgium (BE)	1990
Japan (JP)	2000
France (FR)	2003
Germany (DE)	2007
Source: EPRA, ZEW, 2007	

Fig. 1:   Introduction of REITs

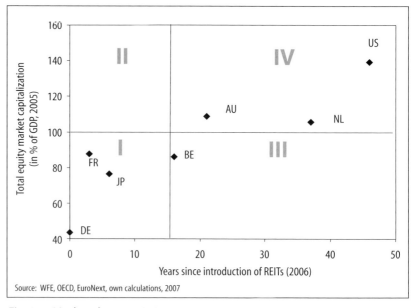

Fig. 2:   Market characteristics

3.2   The data

The real estate security market is represented by the indices of the NAREIT (the US National Association of Real Estate Investment Trusts) and the EPRA (the European Public Real Estate Association). The NAREIT data cover all REITs tradings on the New York Stock Exchange, the NASDAQ National Market System and the American Stock Exchange. Aside from REITs (or their national pendants, respectively), the EPRA indices include also other listed stocks. EPRA provides not only European indices, but also indices for Australia and Japan.

Real estate security market indices

The inclusion of a company in the EPRA indices requires a minimum free float and turnover as well as a minimum share of revenues from relevant real estate activities (ownership, trading and development of income-producing real estate, see figure 3). Therefore, the EPRA indices mainly include large companies and cover only a part of the market. According to EPRA estimates, their indices represent on average around 85 % of the total market capitalization. The EPRA indices are capitalization weighted with free float adjustment (meaning that only tradable shares are counted to calculate the respective capitalization of a company).

All NAREIT and EPRA indices are calculated as performance indices. For Germany, alternatively the DIMAX (Deutscher Immobilienaktien-Index) is applied. The DIMAX is a capitalization weighted but not a free float weighted index, calculated on the basis of 45 publicly quoted German real estate companies (as of end of December 2004; 2007: 76 companies) by the German private bank Ellwanger & Geiger. For the inclusion in the DIMAX, 75 % of turnover and revenues have to come from real estate activities, defined as rent and lease business, real estate management, trading in real estate, project development, and consulting.

In terms of bonds, government bond indices with maturities from seven to 10 years are used, calculated by Thomson Financial Datastream. For Germany, the REX (Deutscher Rentenindex), calculated by the Deutsche Börse AG, is used instead. All indices are performance indices. As stock market indicators MSCI equity performance indices are used for all countries, except Germany,

	Free float market capitalization	Annualized trading volume in a 3-month period	Share of EBITDA* originating from real estate activities
Australia	US$ 200 million	US$ 100 million	60 %
Belgium	€ 50 million	€ 25 million	75 %
France	€ 50 million	€ 25 million	75 %
Japan	US$ 200 million	US$ 100 million	60 %
Netherlands	€ 50 million	€ 25 million	75 %
Germany	€ 50 million	€ 25 million	75 %

*Earnings before interest, depreciation and amortization
Source: EPRA

Fig. 3:   Requirements for the inclusion in EPRA indices

where the DAX 30 performance index, calculated by the Deutsche Börse AG, is used. All time series consist of month end values for the period 1990 to 2004.

4   Risk and return profiles

High performance of REITs and real estate stocks in most countries
A first look into the average annual rate of return reveals that for the whole 15-year period 1990 to 2004 real estate stocks and REITs have performed well in most countries. However, the differences between the countries are substantial: Real average rates of return, calculated as nominal rates of return minus consumer price inflation, amount to more than 10 % each year on average in the US and Australia. With 9 % real rate of return p. a., French real estate has also performed very well. Comparatively low are the long-term average profits in the other European markets (Belgium, the Netherlands and Germany). In Germany, marked differences exist between the broad DIMAX index (with only 0.4 % annual real rate of return) and the EPRA index, which only consists of three large companies (with 3 % p. a.). Japan is a special case, where the burst of the real estate market bubble in 1990 induced a long lasting decline of the whole stock market. Real estate stocks – like the general stock market – had on average a negative nominal and real yield of around 4 % p. a., over the whole period.

A look at subperiods shows some further heterogeneity across countries and some interesting tendencies as well: In most of the countries, real estate stocks performed poorly in the first half of the 1990s, but in the second half of the 1990s the situation improved remarkably. Exceptions include Australia, where the performance continuously has been extraordinarily high and rather stable, and the US, where the real performance was stable and substantial as well. During the years 2001 to 2004, the performance of real estate stocks improved drastically again in all countries except Germany, where the situation deteriorated, and Australia, where performance declined a bit, albeit coming from a high level.

Comparison of risk-adjusted returns
A comparison of returns of real estate securities with other asset categories requires a transformation on the same level of risk. Therefore, risk-adjusted returns have been calculated (RAP, following Modigliani/Modigliani] to compare real estate stock performance with the general equity market performance and the bond market performance [19]. RAP is defined as

$$RAP_i = \sigma_m / \sigma_i (r_i - r_f) + r_f \tag{1}$$

with

σ_m = standard deviation of benchmark
σ_i = standard deviation of asset i
r_i = return of asset i
r_f = risk free rate of return

RAP can be compared directly among investment alternatives, because all asset returns are adjusted to the risk σ_m of the benchmark.

The RAP relative to bonds (i. e., the difference of RAP for real estate stocks, using bonds as the benchmark, to the rate of return on bonds) is positive for the whole period only in the US and Australia. For different subperiods the picture is as follows: In the first half of the 1990s there was no country with a positive value except Germany, using the EPRA index. Also in the second half of the 1990s, the bond market performed better in most countries or at least nearly as good as the real estate market (except the US and Australia) on a risk-adjusted basis. During the years 2001 to 2004, real estate stocks usually performed better than bonds, except in Japan and Germany.

With respect to the stock market, differences in risk-adjusted returns (calculated again against bonds as the benchmark for comparable figures) are higher. This is true particularly for the period from 2001 to 2004 because real estate stocks did not suffer as much from the burst of the technology bubble. In turn, the risk-adjusted return in the second half of the 1990s was usually lower than on the general stock market. Over the whole 15-year period, real estate stocks performed better than general stocks on a risk-adjusted basis in the US, Australia, Japan and France.

	US	AU	JP	NL	BE	FR	DE[1]	DE[2]
Annual return								
1990–2004	13.3 %	15.7 %	−3.9 %	5.9 %	3.4 %	10.8 %	2.7 %	5.2 %
1990–1995	11.0 %	15.1 %	−11.6 %	−5.7 %	−4.4 %	0.6 %	−0.4 %	13.1 %
1996–2000	9.7 %	17.6 %	−1.7 %	9.2 %	6.0 %	15.3 %	13.2 %	4.0 %
2001–2004	20.9 %	13.2 %	6.0 %	19.3 %	13.5 %	21.1 %	−4.9 %	−4.1 %
Real annual return								
1990–2004	10.4 %	13.1 %	−4.0 %	3.4 %	1.4 %	9.0 %	0.4 %	3.0 %
1990–1995	7.7 %	12.0 %	−12.5 %	−8.3 %	−6.9 %	−1.7 %	−3.8 %	9.7 %
1996–2000	7.2 %	15.5 %	−1.6 %	7.0 %	4.3 %	14.1 %	11.8 %	2.6 %
2001–2004	18.5 %	10.4 %	6.6 %	16.9 %	11.6 %	19.2 %	−6.4 %	−5.5 %
RAP bonds (diff.)								
1990–2004	0.6 %	1.4 %	−4.9 %	−3.1 %	−4.9 %	−1.8 %	−3.9 %	−2.8 %
1990–1995	−2.2 %	−1.7 %	−7.0 %	−8.6 %	−7.3 %	−5.4 %	−5.7 %	1.0 %
1996–2000	0.8 %	1.4 %	−5.0 %	−1.6 %	−3.1 %	0.4 %	−0.1 %	−3.5 %
2001–2004	5.7 %	4.5 %	−1.9 %	1.3 %	1.3 %	1.0 %	−7.8 %	−5.7 %
RAP equity (diff.)								
1990–2004	1.4 %	4.0 %	0.8 %	−0.7 %	−1.6 %	1.4 %	−1.2 %	−0.2 %
1990–1995	−1.4 %	4.1 %	0.2 %	−7.9 %	−3.1 %	−1.1 %	−3.3 %	3.3 %
1996–2000	−2.6 %	3.4 %	0.7 %	−2.5 %	−2.2 %	−0.5 %	−1.5 %	−4.8 %
2001–2004	11.9 %	3.1 %	2.0 %	8.7 %	6.7 %	8.0 %	−1.0 %	1.1 %

[1] DIMAX index Germany
[2] EPRA index Germany
Real annual return = annual return minus CPI-inflation
RAP bonds (diff.) = RAP with benchmark bonds market, difference to annual return on bonds
RAP equity (diff.) = RAP with benchmark bonds market, difference to RAP on equity (calculated with benchmark bond market)
Source: Datastream, EcoWin, EPRA, NAREIT, own calculations

Fig. 4:   Performance of real estate stocks/REITs

5   Correlation analysis

Substantial positive correlation with stocks – low correlation with bonds

Correlations are measured on the basis of monthly rates of returns for different time periods (see figure 5). The correlations between the general stock market and real estate stocks are positive and range from 0.26 to 0.74 for the whole period from 1990 to 2004. In the first half of the 1990s the correlations have, on average, been higher than later. Particularly high correlations can be observed in the Japanese market, which declined most of the time. But also the Netherlands and Australia show substantial positive short-term correlation of real estate stocks and general stock markets.

The correlation with the bond market is slightly negative or positive in almost every country over the whole period form 1990 to 2004. The only exception with a substantial positive correlation on average is Australia. Similar to the correlation with the general stock markets, the correlations with the bond markets tend to decrease in time. In the first half of the 1990s the correlations with the bond market have been higher in almost all countries.

	US	AU	JP	NL	BE	FR	DE¹	DE²
Stocks								
1990–2004	0.34	0.59	0.74	0.51	0.45	0.45	0.42	0.26
1990–1995	0.51	0.66	0.90	0.50	0.63	0.60	0.48	0.25
1996–2000	0.23	0.62	0.54	0.61	0.46	0.28	0.33	0.03
2001–2004	0.36	0.38	0.55	0.58	0.28	0.46	0.47	0.49
Bonds								
1990–2004	0.14	0.44	−0.03	0.10	0.27	0.26	−0.01	−0.10
1990–1995	0.38	0.58	0.11	0.34	0.35	0.55	0.21	0.19
1996–2000	0.06	0.48	−0.14	0.08	0.31	−0.07	−0.25	−0.28
2001–2004	−0.02	0.07	−0.32	−0.14	0.03	−0.03	0.03	−0.19

¹ DIMAX index Germany
² EPRA index Germany
Source: Datastream, EcoWin, EPRA, NAREIT, own calculations

Fig. 5:   Correlation of real estate stocks/REITs with general stocks and bonds

6   Cointegration analysis

The potential for portfolio diversification by investment in real estate securities depends not only on their short-term correlations, but also on their long-run relationships to other asset categories. Long-run relationships are particularly important for investors who regard indirect real estate investments as an alternative to direct investments, which is usually long-term oriented. If the performance of real estate securities does not differ from either bonds or common stocks in the long run, their long-run diversification potential would be limited.

The econometric concept of cointegration takes this into account. Its focus is not on the correlation of the first differences of a performance indicator series

(i. e., the returns), but on the relation of the levels of the variables to each other. While traditional regression analysis assumes that time series are stationary (i. e., in a short definition, they are reverting to a constant mean value, have a constant variance in time and the covariance with other values of the same series does not depend on time), the concept of cointegration implies that two time series follow the same trend and the difference between both time series is stationary. If the latter is true, a long-run equilibrium relationship between the two series can be assumed [20].

Therefore it is analyzed whether real estate stocks and REITs are cointegrated with the general stock market and the bond market. While – from an investor's point of view – cointegration with other asset classes is not wanted, it is wanted to prove cointegration with the consumer price index. This would be an indication that real estate securities would provide inflation protection.

6.1 Methodological issues

It is tested for cointegration by applying three different procedures, going from limited to more general models [21]. In the first step, Engle-Granger tests (EG) for cointegration have been carried out. In the second step, single equation Error Correction Models (ECM) have been estimated to account for short-run dynamics. Finally in the third approach, the Johansen procedure has been applied to take endogeneity of all variables in the system into consideration.

For the EG tests the linear regression (2) is estimated:

Engle-Granger test

$$RE_t = \alpha + \beta^* X_t + \varepsilon_{1t} \qquad (2)$$

with

RE_t = real estate stock index or REIT index
X_t = stock market index, bond market index or CPI
ε_{1t} = residual
α, β = estimated constant and coefficient

It has been tested with ADF tests whether the ε_{1t} is stationary (which proves cointegration), applying the Akaike criterion to determine the appropriate lag length, and using the MacKinnon values as critical values [22].

The ECMs are specified according to equation (3), assuming weak exogeneity of X_t for the cointegration vector:

Error Correction Model

$$\Delta RE_t = \gamma + \sum_{i=0}^{n} \Phi \Delta X_{t-i} + \sum_{i=1}^{n} \Gamma \Delta RE_{t-i} + \delta(RE_{t-1} - \beta X_{t-1} - \alpha) + \varepsilon_{2t} \qquad (3)$$

The symbols have the same meaning as in equation (2), with Φ and Γ as matrix of coefficients for the short-term dynamics in the model, ε_{2t} = residual and γ, δ as estimated constant and coefficients. The lag length n of the ECM was determined using the Akaike criterion, for critical values of δ (proving cointegration) it was referred to Ericsson/MacKinnon (2002).

Johansen test   The Johansen models are specified as the two-equation system 4 (a, b)

$$\Delta RE_t = \gamma_1 + \sum_{i=1}^{n} \Phi_1 \Delta RE_{t-i} + \sum_{i=1}^{n} \Gamma_1 \Delta X_{t-i} + \delta_1 (RE_{t-1} - \beta X_{t-1} - \alpha) + \varepsilon_{3t} \qquad (4a)$$

$$\Delta X_t = \gamma_2 + \sum_{i=1}^{n} \Phi_2 \Delta RE_{t-i} + \sum_{i=1}^{n} \Gamma_2 \Delta X_{t-i} + \delta_2 (RE_{t-1} - \beta X_{t-1} - \alpha) + \varepsilon_{4t} \qquad (4b)$$

The symbols have again the same meaning as in equations (2) and (3), the coefficients now being indexed to assign them to one of the two equations in the system. The lag length of the VAR is again determined by the Akaike criterion.

All series have been tested for their degree of integration by Augmented Dickey Fuller tests, using different criteria (Schwarz, Akaike and Modified Akaike) for the appropriate lag length specification. Usually all series are I(1) (meaning that they can be transformed into a stationary series by taking its first differences), except the CPI series in the US, France, the Netherlands and Germany in specifications with the Modified Akaike criterion, that recommends very long lag lengths for the unit root tests of these series. These results indicate, that the series could be I(2) as well. Further exceptions are real estate stocks and general stocks in Japan, that are I(0). For details on the empirical results the reader is referred to the appendix tables in [23].

6.2   Results of the cointegration analysis

No cointegration   Cointegration between the general equity market and real estate securities is
with stocks   unobservable in almost every country in any test procedure (see figure 6). One
and bonds   exception is Australia, where the EG tests indicate an equilibrium relationship between the general stock market and real estate stocks. Cointegration is indicated in the Johansen specification as well, but the results imply (implausibly) that the general stock market adjusts to the real estate stock market instead of the reverse. In Japan, EG results indicate stationarity of the residuals for the regression of the general stock indicator on the real estate stocks. However, due to the Japanese recession in the 1990s, both indicators are stationary in levels; therefore, stationarity of the residuals does not really prove cointegration. Consequently, the ECM and the Johansen results do not support the results of the simple EG.

For real estate stocks and bonds almost no evidence of cointegration exists as well. The US, Australia and Japan show no indication of cointegration between real estate stocks and bonds in all three procedures at all. For the European countries in the sample, only a few results point to cointegration between bonds and real estate. In Belgium and the Netherlands, the EG and ECM results are not significant on a satisfying level, however, in both cases the test statistics point at least weakly to cointegration. In France, Johansen results indicate cointegration between bonds and real estate stocks on at least the 20 % significance level – which is, however, usually not applied. In Germany, only the ECM results for the model with the EPRA index weakly point to cointegration of real estate stocks with the bond market. It might be interesting to analyze to what extent these cross country differences in the relationship between real estate stocks and bond markets depend on the average gearing of real estate companies. Unfortunately, average figures over the whole period of time are not available, and available data for single years do not show any congruence between the cointegration pattern with the bond markets and the average gearing of real estate companies.

The tests for cointegration of real estate securities with the CPI yield some significant results. In most countries, at least some weak evidence for long-run equilibria between the development of consumer price indices and real estate stock/REIT indices exists.

Some evidence for inflation protection

In the US, the ECM indicates cointegration only on the – usually not applied – 20%-level, but the Johansen results show significant cointegration on the 5%-level. In Belgium, France and the Netherlands, at least the Johansen tests indicate cointegration, which is, however, not supported by the simpler ECM and EG tests, with the partial exception of Belgium. Significant cointegration on usual levels cannot be observed in Germany. Only EG results point to weak cointegration in the specification with the DIMAX index. In Australia and Japan, however, no evidence for stable long-run relationships between the price level and real estate stock performance exist.

Summarizing the findings on cointegration of real estate stocks with the general equity market, the results let us conclude that – contrary to their positive short-term correlations – almost no evidence exists for a tight long-run relationship between real estate securities and the development of broader stock markets. With respect to bonds, there is also little evidence for a stable long-run relationship to real estate securities. Some indication for cointegration of real estate stocks with the CPI is observable in five out of seven countries, indicating that real estate stocks could basically serve as an inflation hedge in many markets.

	Equity			Bonds			CPI		
	EG	ECM	J	EG	ECM	J	EG	ECM	J
US	N	N	N	N	N	N	N	(Y)	Y¹
AU	Y¹	N	Y	N	N	N	N	N	N
JP	Y²	N	N	N	N	N	N	N	N
NL	N	N	N	N	N	N	N	N	Y²
FR	N	N	N	N	N	(Y)	N	N	Y¹
BE	N	N	N	N	N	N	Y²	N	Y¹
DE DIMAX	N	N	N	N	N	N	(Y)	N	N
DE EPRA	N	N	N	N	(Y)	N	N	N	N

¹ Significance on 5%-level
² Significance on 10%-level
(Y) Significance on 20%-level
Source: own calculations

Fig. 6:   Cointegration of real estate stock indices with equity market,
bond market and consumer price indices

7   Conclusion

Real estate securities with high performance in most countries

The analysis has shown that real estate securities in most countries had a remarkably high performance in nominal and real terms. The average performance over the whole period from 1990 to 2004 has been particularly high in the capital-market-oriented countries in the sample (US, Australia), but also in France. Real estate securities have outperformed the bond markets on a risk-adjusted basis only in the US and in Australia, while outperformance of the stock markets can be observed also in Japan and France. Particularly during the period 2001 to 2004, real estate security markets have soared in most countries with the notable exception of Germany, where average returns have been negative.

Despite the rather high short-term correlation of monthly returns with the wider stock markets in most countries, usually no cointegration with the stock markets and the bond markets exists. In general, therefore, real estate securities seem to represent an asset class distinct from bonds and stocks in most countries, providing potential for long-run diversification of asset portfolios. Additionally, real estate stocks provide a (weak) hedge against consumer price inflation in most countries.

The overall picture indicates that the existence of specialized, tax-transparent vehicles like REITs is not always correlated with a high long-run performance of securitized real estate. Belgium and the Netherlands are counter examples in this respect. On the other hand, the evidence shows that real estate securities can perform extraordinarily well in countries with mature capital markets, as the US and Australia demonstrate.

The German situation might be going to change

In the light of the international comparison, the poor performance of the German real estate stock market during the period under consideration can potentially be attributed to a couple of problems: Aside from fundamental problems of the German real estate market, the stock market capitalization in relation to GDP is still very low in international comparison, indicating that share based corporate finance is still not very widespread in Germany. Furthermore, no dedicated real estate investment vehicles have been offered on the German exchanges in the past. This combination has obviously not provided a good breeding ground for a vibrant real estate stock market. The experience in the years 2005 to 2007 has indicated that the German situation might be going to change. The prospect and introduction of German REITs has attracted foreign investors and induced a boom on the commercial real estate markets: The future will show whether this was the beginning of a structural change or the emergence of a temporary phenomenon.

8   Bibliography

[1] Zietz, E. N./Sirmans, G. S./Friday, H. S., The Environment and Performance of Real Estate Investment Trusts, in: Journal of Real Estate Portfolio Management, vol. 9 (2), 2003, pp. 127–165.

[2] Corgel, J. B./McIntosh, W./Ott, S. H., Real Estate Investment Trusts: A Review of the Financial Economics Literature, in: Journal of Real Estate Literature, vol. 3, 1995, pp. 13–43.

[3] Myer, F. C. N./Webb, J. R., Return Properties of Equity REITs, Common Stocks and Commercial Real Estate: A Comparison, in: The Journal of Real Estate Research, vol. 8 (1), 1993, pp. 87–106.

[4] Myer, F. C. N./Webb, J. R., Retail Stocks, Retail REITs and Retail Real Estate, in: The Journal of Real Estate Research, vol. 9 (1), 1994, pp. 65–84.

[5] Eichholtz, P./Hartzell, D. J., Property Shares, Appraisals and the Stock Market: An International Perspective, in: The Journal of Real Estate Finance and Economics, vol. 12, 1996, pp. 163–178.

[6] Mull, S. R./Soenen, L. A., U.S. REITs as an Asset Class in International Investment Portfolios, in: Financial Analysis Journal March/April 1997, pp. 55–61.

[7] Ling, D. C./Naranjo, A., The Integration of Commercial Real Estate Markets and Stock Markets, in: Real Estate Economics, vol. 27 (3), 1999, pp. 483–515.

[8] Brounen, D./Eichholtz, P., Property, Common Stocks, and Property Shares. Increased potential for diversification, in: The Journal of Portfolio Management, Special Issue 2003, pp. 129–137.

[9] Lizieri, C./McAllister, P./Ward, C., Continental Shift? An Analysis of Convergence Trends in European Real Estate Equities, in: Journal of Real Estate Research, vol. 25, No. 1, 2003, pp. 1–22.

[10] Hamelink, F./Hoesli, M., What Factors Determine International Real Estate Security Returns?, in: Real Estate Economics, V32 3, 2004, pp. 437–462.

[11] Lee, S./Stevenson, S., The Case for REITs in the Mixed-Asset Portfolio in the Short and Long Run, in: Journal of Real Estate Portfolio Management, vol. 11, No. 1, 2005, pp. 55–80.

[12] Murphy, J. A./Kleiman, R. T., The Inflation Hedging Characteristics of Equity REITs: An Empirical Study, in: Quarterly Review of Economics and Business, vol. 29, No. 3, Autumn 1989, pp. 95–101.

[13] Yobaccio, E./Rubens, J. H./Ketcham, D. C., (1995): The Inflation Hedging Characteristics of Risk Assets: The Case of REITs, in: Journal of Real Estate Research, 10, 1995, pp. 279–298.

[14] Liu, C. H. L./Hartzell, D. J./Hoesli, M. E., International Evidence on Real Estate Securities as an Inflation Hedge, in: Real Estate Economics, V 25 (2), 1997, pp. 193–221.

[15] Maurer, R./Sebastian, S. P., Inflation Risk Analysis of European Real Estate Securities, in: The Journal of Real Estate Research, vol. 24, No. 1, 2002, pp. 47–78.

[16] Okunev, J./Wilson, P. J., Using Nonlinear Tests to Examine Integration between Real Estate and Stock Markets, in: Real Estate Economics, vol. 25 (3), 1997, pp. 487–503.

[17] Chatrath, A./Liang, Y., REITs and Inflation: A Long Run Perspective, in:
      Journal of Real Estate Research, vol. 16 (3), 1998, pp. 311–326.

[18] Glascock, J. L./Lu, C./So, R., Further Evidence on the Integration of
      REIT, Bonds, and Stock Returns. Journal of Real Estate Finance and
      Economics, vol. 20 (2), 2000, pp. 177–194.

[19] Modigliani, F./Modigliani, L., Risk Adjusted Performance. How to
      measure it and why, in: The Journal of Portfolio Management, winter
      1997, pp. 45–54.

[20] Greene, W. H., Econometric Analysis, 5th edition, Upper Saddle River
      N. J. 2003.

[21] Ericsson, N. R./MacKinnon, J. G., Distributions of error correction
      tests for cointegration, in: Econometrics Journal, vol. 5, 2002,
      pp. 285–318.

[22] MacKinnon, J. G., Numerical distribution functions for unit root and
      cointegration tests, in: Journal of Applied Econometrics, vol. 11 (6),
      1996, pp. 601–618.

[23] Westerheide, P., Cointegration of Real Estate Stocks and REITs with
      Common Stocks, Bonds and Consumer Price Inflation – an
      International Comparison, ZEW Discussion Paper No. 06-057,
      Mannheim 2006.

4 Dynamic forces reshape global risk-return relationships: fiduciary governance standards

Cathy Swain

Table of contents

1   Introduction

Human, natural, and market dynamics are shifting global risk-reward relationships in financial and property markets. Practitioners of professional disciplines that comprise and serve the investment management community are rising to daunting challenges to communicate with clear and comparable standards. Each discipline has its own "language" that is being translated across different cultures to allow investment professionals to make more informed decisions. Information is instantly available in staggering quantity and detail; however, the complexity of diversifying investments across cultural, political, and economic boundaries requires that multi-disciplinary teams communicate like never before, to translate, verify, sort for relevance, assimilate, compare, and evaluate it.

Regulations and education related to corporate governance, including fiduciary duties of directors, are in the spotlight in today's world. This chapter will highlight resources for global standards and practices that govern the investment management process for fiduciaries and professionals serving in key roles. The chapter at hand will attempt to:

Investment management governance

- identify some of the forces that are changing risk dynamics in global financial and property markets;

- characterize decision makers among major institutional pools of investment capital that are expanding global investments;

- reference global standards and practices for investment fiduciaries evolving as the financial services industry attempts to self-regulate and promote a "culture of compliance" and

- discuss key risk management challenges for investment stewards.

2   Dynamic global forces and associated risks

Topics identified below merely scratch the surface of an impressionistic context for governance challenges that face investment fiduciaries who are addressing their charge of long-term preservation and accumulation of assets by expanding commitments in global securities and property markets. These dynamic forces are rendering obsolete traditional investment management assumptions and analysis tools for developing strategies to optimize benefits of global diversification. And they will dramatically influence global property development and investment risks and opportunities.

Other factors combine with these dynamic forces to pose grave challenges for responsible governance on the part of institutional investment fiduciaries. Concerns relate to conflicts and integrity of market participants, jurisdiction and enforceability of contract remedies, nuances and potential vulnerability of property ownership rights, fiscal consequences, and financial incentives for individuals to take risks without penalty to themselves.

2.1   Human forces

The spread of democracy, private ownership of property, and capitalism is resulting in redistribution of wealth and shifts in consumption patterns globally, the implications – risks and opportunities – of which are wide open to active analysis imaginations. "[…] the BRICs (Brazil, Russia, India, and China) could become a very important source of new global spending in the not too distant future […] India's economy, for instance, could be larger than Japan's by 2032, and China's larger than the US by 2041 (and larger than everyone else as early as 2016). The BRICs economies taken together could be larger than the G6 by 2039." [1]

Shifting wealth, consumption

Although the term "geopolitics" may mean many things in different contexts, in global investing it often refers to perceived risks due to political instability related to energy resources (particularly in the Middle East) and to emerging markets, the dynamics of which are constantly changing. As the BRIC countries

Geopolitics

move from emerging to developing market status, more attention is focusing on emerging African nations where natural and human resources abound.

Aging population Aging of the world's population will also profoundly impact the global economy, property use patterns, and investment opportunities. According to the results of a survey published by the United Nations Department of Public Information in June 2007:

"The older population is growing at a considerably faster rate than that of the world's total population. In absolute terms, the number of older persons has tripled over the last 50 years and will more than triple again over the next 50 years. In relative terms, the percentage of older persons is projected to more than double worldwide over the next half century." [2]

2.2   Natural forces

Natural resources While the world strives to emulate the life style (consumption) standards that exist in the United States, natural resources pose limitations that cannot be ignored. The inevitability of global warming threatens our natural environment and further complicates responsible management of the planet that supports us. Renewable, environmentally friendly energy sources and conservation must become the global norm.

Infrastructure Physical infrastructure (roads, water lines and purification systems, bridges, utilities, transportation, communications, etc.) in the developed world is aging, and demands in the developing world will stress capacity to create it. Raw materials needed for development and replacement of residential, commercial and industrial facilities must be shepherded and alternatives must evolve to meet demands.

Leadership, collaboration As world citizens, we must each take personal, professional, and political responsibility to provide the global leadership and collaboration necessary to avert imminent crises.

2.3   Market forces

Asset allocation modeling Long-term strategic asset allocation modeling is becoming more artistic than scientific. It could be described as "Monet" portfolio theory. Definitions of asset classes and the data that support asset allocation modeling tools to devise strategies to diversify and manage risk are seriously challenged. Correlations do change over time. Asset classes are "converging" and global financial and property markets are becoming more accessible and "efficient" in tandem with the information explosion and globalization of commerce. So the robustness of defining, benchmarking, and comparing asset classes in a rear view mirror is questionable. Creativity is being exercised in classifying specific investments in re-defined asset classes, and in selecting appropriate data and time frames to measure returns, volatility, and correlations among markets.

Hedge funds Hedge funds have gained popularity among institutional investors, applying modern "financial engineering" tools and creativity to mine data and capture opportunities, at the same time posing challenges for investment management governance and traditional analytics. Estimates of hedge fund assets vary widely among credible sources. In November 2007, Institutional Investor News and HedgeFunds.net's 2008 Hedge Fund Asset Flows & Trends Report stated that "[…] The total assets managed by hedge funds, excluding double counting of assets in funds of funds, increased by 24.4 % to an estimated $ 2.8 trillion in the first three quarters 2007." [3]

At least as relevant as the growth in total assets managed by hedge funds are their presence in institutional portfolios managed by fiduciaries and their dominant representation in US equity trading volume:

"[…] the SEC's best estimate (in July 2006) is that there are now approximately 8,800 hedge funds, with approximately $ 1.2 trillion of assets. If this estimate is accurate, it implies a remarkable growth in hedge fund assets of almost 3,000 % in the last 16 years. Much of this growth is attributable to increased investment by institutions. This includes not only investment companies and investment banks, but also private and public pension plans, endowments, and foundations […] Although hedge funds represent just 5 % of all US assets under management, they account for about 30 % of all US equity trading volume […]" [4].

A clear definition of hedge funds is illusive, but it is safe to at least conclude that they are private investment vehicles with broad investment authority. Their incentive management fee structure, uses of leverage and shorting are also widely acknowledged. Although sophisticated investment professionals agree that hedge funds are not an "asset class", they typically treat hedge funds as an asset class for modeling purposes due to a lack of robust alternatives. This despite the incredibly broad range of hedge fund investment styles, returns, volatilities, correlations with other asset classes, lags in mark to market valuations, survivorship bias in benchmarks, and flexibility to shift strategies, exposures and leverage.

Liquidity, leverage

Liquidity and leverage are often mistaken for each other, because liquidity is highly dependent on the cost and availability of credit to facilitate exchange. Expanding types and uses of derivative instruments are believed to enhance liquidity in global markets by effectively exchanging among the parties risk exposures to specific markets, credits, securities, companies, governments, currencies, hard assets, events, interest rates, etc. Because derivatives create exposures that are multiples of the cost to hold them, they effectively increase financial leverage in the system.

Derivatives

The proliferation of derivative instruments and transactions is strikingly evident in the global financial market place, with expanding uses as common practice by institutional investors for both hedging and speculative purposes. Derivative instruments have become so complex that many policy-level decision makers openly acknowledge their limited understanding of underlying exposures and associated risks. Assuming that adequate skills, models, and experience do exist to effectively measure, decompose, and monitor derivative risks, many institutional investors do not have adequate resources to access these skills, models, and experience.

As with all investments, fiduciaries are responsible to know what they are doing, why they are doing it, and how well each investment is achieving its reason for being in the portfolio. Managers and traders with delegated co-fiduciary responsibility and authority often actively trade offsetting exposures for hedging or repositioning, and full transparency is simply not feasible. So it is easy – inevitable? – for overseers to lose the crucial ability to measure and monitor underlying risks and how well each investment is performing.

2.4   Berkshire Hathaway case with Gen Re Securities

Berkshire Hathaway's experience with Gen Re Securities trading operations illustrates concerns about liquidity, leverage, and derivatives as a case in point best articulated from the "horse's mouth". Warren Buffet said in his letter to Berkshire Hathaway shareholders in February 2005: "Investors should understand that in all types of financial institutions, rapid growth sometimes masks major underlying problems (and occasionally fraud). The real test of the earning power of a derivatives operation is what it achieves after operating for an extended period in a no-growth mode. You only learn who has been swimming naked when the tide goes out" [5]. In his February 2006 chairman's letter, Buffet described the wind up of Gen Re Securities:

Warren Buffet's letter

"Long ago, Mark Twain said: 'A man who tries to carry a cat home by its tail will learn a lesson that can be learned in no other way.' If Twain were around now, he might try winding up a derivatives business. After a few days, he would opt for cats.

We lost $104 million pre-tax last year in our continuing attempt to exit Gen Re's derivative operation. Our aggregate losses since we began this endeavor total $404 million.

Originally we had 23,218 contracts outstanding. By the start of 2005 we were down to 2,890. You might expect that our losses would have been stemmed by this point, but the blood has kept flowing. Reducing our inventory to 741 contracts last year cost us the $104 million mentioned above.

Remember that the rationale for establishing this unit in 1990 was Gen Re's wish to meet the needs of insurance clients. Yet one of the contracts we liquidated in 2005 had a term of 100 years! It's difficult to imagine what 'need' such a contract could fulfill except, perhaps, the need of a compensation-conscious trader to have a long-dated contract on his books. Long contracts, or alternatively those with multiple variables, are the most difficult to mark to market (the standard procedure used in accounting for derivatives) and provide the most opportunity for 'imagination' when traders are estimating their value.

Small wonder that traders promote them. A business in which huge amounts of compensation flow from assumed numbers is obviously fraught with danger. When two traders execute a transaction that has several, sometimes esoteric, variables and a far-off settlement date, their respective firms must subsequently value these contracts whenever they calculate their earnings. A given contract may be valued at one price by Firm A and at another by Firm B. You can bet that the valuation differences – and I'm personally familiar with several that were huge – tend to be tilted in a direction favoring higher earnings at each firm. It's a strange world in which two parties can carry out a paper transaction that each can promptly report as profitable.

I dwell on our experience in derivatives each year for two reasons. One is personal and unpleasant. The hard fact is that I have cost you a lot of money by not moving immediately to close down Gen Re's trading operation. Both Charlie and I knew at the time of the Gen Re purchase that it was a problem and told its management that we wanted to exit the business. It was my responsibility to make sure that happened. Rather than address the situation head on, however, I wasted several years while we attempted to sell the operation. That was a doomed endeavor because no realistic solution could have extricated us from the maze of liabilities that was going to exist for decades. Our obligations were particularly worrisome because their potential to explode could not be measured. Moreover, if severe trouble occurred, we knew it was likely to correlate with problems elsewhere in financial markets.

So I failed in my attempt to exit painlessly, and in the meantime more trades were put on the books. Fault me for dithering … When a problem exists, whether in personnel or in business operations, the time to act is now.

The second reason I regularly describe our problems in this area lies in the hope that our experiences may prove instructive for managers, auditors and regulators. In a sense, we are a canary in this business coal mine and should sing a song of warning as we expire. The number and value of derivative contracts outstanding in the world continues to mushroom and is now a multiple of what existed in 1998, the last time that financial chaos erupted.

Our experience should be particularly sobering because we were a better-than-average candidate to exit gracefully. Gen Re was a relatively minor operator in the derivatives field. It has had the good fortune to unwind its supposedly liquid positions in a benign market, all the while free of financial or other pressures that might have forced it to conduct the liquidation in a less-than-efficient manner. Our accounting in the past was conventional and actually thought to be conservative. Additionally, we know of no bad behavior by anyone involved.

It could be a different story for others in the future. Imagine, if you will, one or more firms (troubles often spread) with positions that are many multiples of ours attempting to liquidate in chaotic markets and under extreme, and well-publicized, pressures. This is a scenario to which much attention should be given now rather than after the fact. The time to have considered – and improved – the reliability of New Orleans' levees was before Katrina.

When we finally wind up Gen Re Securities, my feelings about its departure will be akin to those expressed in a country song, 'My wife ran away with my best friend, and I sure miss him a lot.'" [6]

3   Institutional investment fiduciaries

Institutional investors are fiduciaries who manage and advise investments of corporate and public pension and retirement plans, charitable institutions (endowments, foundations, trusts), private trusts, and mutual funds. Individual fiduciaries include trustees, investment committee members, bankers, consultants, custodians, and money managers. The Foundation for Fiduciary Studies categorizes institutional fiduciaries as stewards, advisors, and managers [7].

Fiduciary Standard of Care   Investment decision makers in the United States are bound by legal standards of fiduciary loyalty and care, with comparable principles in place among practitioners globally. A fiduciary is a person who acts legally on behalf and in the best interests of another person who is managing the assets of that person and stands in a special relationship of trust, confidence and/or legal responsibility. The Fiduciary Standard of Care means that by law the client comes first. This is the highest standard of care possible. Laws that govern institutional investors have evolved from a "prudent person" standard to a higher "prudent expert" standard. Fiduciary liability can be shared but not fully delegated.

UPMIFA   New legislation with broad applicability for fiduciaries who govern charitable funds (endowments, foundations, trusts) is sweeping the United States. As of this writing, 12 individual states have enacted similar forms of the Uniform Prudent Management of Institutional Funds Act (UPMIFA), with legislation pending in seven additional states [8]. UPMIFA offers greater clarity in defining standards of prudent practice for institutional fiduciaries.

3.1   Stewards

Investment stewards with legal responsibility for managing investment decisions include trustees, directors, and investment committee members responsible for the investment of assets on behalf of the ultimate beneficiaries. They set investment objectives and policies, allocate assets, and select or direct the selection of "prudent expert" advisors and investment managers to advise and execute investment strategies consistent with objectives and policies. Investment stewards must be able to demonstrate that portfolio assets are being prudently managed and that sound investment practices are being followed.

Investment committee duties   Investment committee members must represent the client's interests, also with "independent" representatives with investment, legal, and accounting expertise. They must have adequate information and authority to act, within a defined set of by-laws and explicit code of conduct. They must understand and acknowledge their fiduciary role; understand client mission, goals, resources, and constraints; set investment policies; monitor performance, actions, and compliance of staff and prudent experts; monitor costs and risks; and avoid conflicts of interest. In short, they must know what they are doing, why they are doing it, who is doing it with/for them, how much it is costing, how well it is working, what questions to ask, and when and how to change course.

3.2   Advisors

Professionals who provide comprehensive and continuous investment advice include financial advisors, brokers, investment and financial consultants, wealth managers, trust officers, financial planners, and fiduciary advisers. These professionals advise investment stewards without discretion to choose individual investments. No specific regulations are designed for the investment consultant's co-fiduciary role; advisors have no oversight by any one regulatory body; and no practice standards, advanced education, or training requirements are mandated.

3.3   Managers

Investment manager organizations that make investment decisions to implement a specific investment mandate include organizations that have discretion to make direct investments for separate accounts, mutual funds, unit trusts, commingled trusts, partnerships, hedge funds, and other private pooled investment funds.

4   Self regulation

4.1   Global professional collaboration

Professional organizations around the world in diverse disciplines that provide crucial support to the investment management industry are collaborating actively to standardize governance and best practices.

The Foundation for Fiduciary Studies is a not-for-profit organization, independent of any ties to the investment community, established to develop and advance practice standards of care for investment fiduciaries [7]. The tangible result of the Foundation for Fiduciary Studies' mission is the "Prudent Practices for Investment Fiduciaries" handbook series that defines precepts and practices as the Global Fiduciary Standard of Excellence, with sound basis in legislation, case law and regulatory opinion letters and editorial assistance from the American Institute of Certified Public Accountants (AICPA). These prudent practices are organized as a Fiduciary Quality Management System, analogous to the Quality Management Systems covered by ISO 9000 [9].

Foundation for Fiduciary Studies

The affiliated Center for Fiduciary Studies provides training and research focused exclusively on investment fiduciary responsibility and portfolio management.

The Centre for Fiduciary Excellence (CEFEX) [10] is an independent global assessment and certification organization that works closely with investment fiduciaries and industry experts to provide comprehensive assessment programs to help mitigate risk of fiduciary breach for institutional and retail investors. CEFEX has tailored the international auditing standard ISO 19011 (Guidelines for quality and/or environmental management systems auditing) [11], developed with the primary intention of guiding Quality Management System (ISO 9000) audits, to apply to assessments of investment fiduciary programs, and assess conformity of an organization's investment fiduciary practices to the Global Fiduciary Standard of Excellence.

Centre for Fiduciary Excellence

The CFA Institute is also tackling the challenge of standardizing investment management practices for their membership globally on several fronts. The CFA Institute's mission is: "To lead the investment profession globally by setting the highest standards of ethics, education, and professional excellence. [...] The Chartered Financial Analyst® (CFA®) charter has become known as the gold standard of professional credentials within the global investment community. Investors recognize the CFA designation as the definitive standard

CFA Institute

for measuring competence and integrity in the fields of portfolio management and investment analysis." [12]

The CFA Institute binds its 95,000 plus members in 132 countries to a strict professional Code of Ethics and Standards of Professional Conduct, and promotes the adoption of an Asset Manager Code of Conduct by investment management organizations. It also maintains and promotes Global Investment Performance Standards (GIPS) for rigorous and consistent measurement and reporting investment performance and offers training and certification in the use of these standards.

Centre for Financial Market Integrity As the CFA Institute's research and policy authority on global capital markets issues, the Centre for Financial Market Integrity advocates for efficient, ethical, and transparent, capital markets, and promotes investor protections and high professional standards. The Centre promotes Trade Management Guidelines and Soft Dollar Standards, and recently submitted for public comment a draft Code of Conduct for Members of a Pension Scheme Governing Board. The Centre also supports an active Standard of Ethics Policy Group, Capital Markets Policy Group, and a Financial Reporting Policy Group. Guiding principles of the Centre are:

"Investors come first. The interests of the investing client must always take precedence over the interests of investment professionals and their employers. Investment professionals must act ethically and in accordance with the highest professional standards. They must:

- *act with integrity in all their dealings;*

- *maintain independence and objectivity;*

- *continuously strive to maintain and improve their professional knowledge and competence.*

Investors need complete, accurate, timely and transparent information from securities issuers." [13]

Other global investment professions Following are just a few examples of other organizations that are also committed to global collaboration to standardize "best practices" in their respective professional disciplines:

- The Bank for International Settlements (BIS), based in Basel, Switzerland, fosters international monetary and financial cooperation, serves as a bank for central banks, and employs 562 staff from 49 countries. The Bank's Financial Stability Institute fosters the dissemination of standards and best practices to financial system supervisors worldwide [14].

- The International Accounting Standards Board (IASB), based in London, UK, with Board members from nine countries, is committed to developing a single set of high quality, understandable and enforceable global accounting standards that require transparent and comparable information in general purpose financial statements, to achieve convergence in accounting standards around the world [15].

- The International Valuation Standards Committee's (IVSC) principal objective is to formulate and publish valuation standards and procedural guidance for the valuation of assets for use in financial statements, and to promote their worldwide acceptance and observance. The second objective is to harmonize standards among world states, and to make disclosures of differences in standards and/or applications of standards, with particular goals that international valuation standards be recognized in statements of international accounting and that valuers recognize what is needed from them under the standards of other professional disciplines [16].

- The International Association of Insurance Supervisors (IAIS) represents insurance regulators and supervisors of some 180 jurisdictions. The IAIS issues global insurance principles, standards and guidance papers, provides training and support on issues related to insurance supervision, and organizes meetings and seminars for insurance supervisors [17].

- The Global Association of Risk Professionals (GARP) is a not-for-profit association consisting of 70,490 individuals around the world who are involved in financial risk management. Members come from over 100 countries, and work in regional and global banks, asset management firms, insurance companies, central banks, securities regulators, hedge funds, universities, large industrial corporations and multinationals [18].

- The Royal Institution of Chartered Surveyors (RICS) sets worldwide standards for the property profession. Its role is to regulate and promote the property profession, maintain the highest educational and professional standards, protect clients and consumers through a strict code of ethics and provide impartial advice, analysis and guidance. RICS members offer the advice on a diverse range of land, property, construction and related environmental issues. RICS has 140,000 members who operate out of 146 countries, supported by an extensive network of regional offices located in every continent around the world [19].

- The World Intellectual Property Organization (WIPO) is a specialized agency of the United Nations with a mandate from its 184 member states to promote the protection of intellectual property throughout the world through cooperation among states and in collaboration with other international organizations. Headquartered in Geneva, Switzerland, WIPO is dedicated to developing a balanced and accessible international intellectual property (IP) system, which rewards creativity, stimulates innovation and contributes to economic development while safeguarding the public interest [20].

4.2   Global fiduciary precepts

Fiduciary practice standards documented by the Foundation for Fiduciary Studies follow seven precepts [7]:

- Know standards, laws, contractual provisions.
- Diversify assets to client's risk-return profile.
- Prepare written Investment Policy Statement (IPS).
- Use "prudent experts" and document due diligence in selecting them.
- Control and account for all investment management expenses.
- Monitor activities of "prudent experts".
- Avoid conflicts of interest, prohibited transactions.

4.3   Global fiduciary practice standards

The Global Fiduciary Standard of Excellence requires that fiduciaries organize to understand their client(s); then formalize that understanding, implement and monitor their strategy, policies, and fiduciary practices [7].

4.3.1   Organize

Organizing to understand the client means reviewing and analyzing all relevant laws and documents; setting goals consistent with resources, needs, and constraints; clarifying the delegation of authority, decision making process, and roles and responsibilities of all parties; and defining and documenting policies and procedures to manage all potential conflicts.

4.3.2   Formalize

IPS and SRI   Stewards are responsible to prepare a written Investment Policy Statement (IPS) to formalize and document the investment time horizon; expected modeled return and risk tolerance; diversification strategy/asset mix consistent with the fund size, available expertise, and reasonable and appropriate costs; and roles and responsibilities of all parties. The IPS should have sufficient detail and criteria to define and implement the investment strategy, select service providers, and monitor compliance. The IPS should also define any Socially Responsible Investment (SRI) strategies that are required to be consistent with the client's mission, regulations, and/or policies.

4.3.3   Implement

Implementation in compliance with the IPS, with compensation incentives in alignment with client interests, includes documenting due diligence in choosing appropriate internal staff, service providers, third party advisors and managers, and investment vehicles.

4.3.4   Monitor

In addition to monitoring compliance and investment performance versus IPS objectives, benchmarks, and peers, stewards should monitor risks (including operational changes in service provider organizations), conflicts, and fiduciary practices. Efforts should also be made to monitor "best execution" soft dollars, and proxy voting practices.

Finally, stewards have a legal responsibility to monitor investment management costs including fees, expenses, transaction costs, and all forms of compensation paid to all parties. To monitor costs, institutional fiduciaries must identify, measure, and benchmark them, and then negotiate. Managers should be required to report all fees and expenses, including those that are "netted" from asset values. Stewards should compare total costs of active management to passive alternatives to assess whether the value added justifies the cost.   **Legal responsibility**

4.4   Culture of compliance

A culture of compliance will "[…] link specific people, to specific documents, to specific control points, to specific risks, and ultimately, to specific strategic control processes. In a good culture of compliance, this will be seamless web, from the lowest level of detail, to the broadest level of strategic direction […]" [21].

Fiduciary duty of loyalty requires that the client's interest must come before the fiduciary's personal interest. In a culture of compliance, specific risks are identified within a strategic vision, each with established control points that are transparent and well documented, with specific people accountable for managing each one. A culture of compliance is evident from the top down, at all levels of an investment management organization. It consistently demonstrates reflexes for doing the "right thing" even when no one is looking, for putting the client's interest ahead of profits.   **Fiduciary duty of loyalty**

Competent, experienced compliance professionals must have respect at all levels of management and staff, direct access to the governing authority, adequate resources, and appropriate authority to fulfill their responsibilities. An excellent compliance program will operate like an excellent manufacturing plant safety program, with procedures and incentives to report potential and actual breaches (conflicts), correct them immediately, and adjust protocol to avoid them in the future. Transparency, broad-based training, communication, and documentation will be highly valued. Authority will be delegated to competence and accompanied by adequate supervision, oversight, incentives, procedures, enforcement, and follow-up.

5   Risk management for stewards

Institutional investment fiduciaries are charged with managing investments in line with the resources and needs of the institutions they represent. Stewards worry about funding ongoing spending for current and expanding needs while maintaining purchasing power, and for those who operate in the public arena, "headline risk" is a consideration. To accomplish these goals and avoid taking excessive risks, stewards and their advisors need to be able to rely on investment managers who have:

- culture of integrity and compliance;

- fund structure, accountability, and compensation incentives aligned with investor interests;

- strong tactical business management and operational skills;

- disciplined investment processes;

- comprehensive risk management systems and oversight; and

- sophisticated client interface.

Since the steward's primary risk management tool and legal mandate is diversification, he or she should be especially concerned about monitoring concentrations of investments/risks in a single company, security, currency, country, and so on.

5.1   Risk measurement

Investment stewards are increasingly comfortable addressing the "R" word directly, acknowledging that "volatility" statistics do not measure their risk tolerance very well, since they are delighted when swings are upward. Downside risk, on the other hand, is what they really want to understand and anticipate.

Judgment   Risk measurement, like asset allocation modeling, involves at least as much judgment (art) as science (math/engineering). And sophisticated models have always been vulnerable to the quality of input assumptions ("garbage in = garbage out"). That said, however, rigorous thinking, disciplined professional training, and analytical tools to measure risk have evolved significantly over the past 20 years. As one small example, stress testing is commonly used to simulate how a portfolio might perform under extreme positive or negative market conditions. This and other tools can be combined with informed professional judgment to employ and monitor the effectiveness of hedging and positioning tactics to help manage risk.

Transparency   The capacity of modern tools to simulate and monitor portfolio risk is vastly improved with real-time full transparency of actual holdings. Without transparency, it is impossible to monitor unintended concentrations, leverage, offsetting positions, etc. Investment stewards, however, typically do not have direct access to full transparency or to sophisticated tools to measure risk at the aggregated portfolio level, and much of their data (for private investments in particular) is reported only monthly with some lag time. Some very large sophisticated stewards use "proxies" to simulate risk profiles of these managers and aggregate them to the total portfolio, testing the results over time to develop confidence in the robustness of their proxies.

5.2 Operational risk

Operational risk has been identified as a leading cause of investment manager failures around the world, yet it cannot be modeled. And one might argue that it is the only investment risk for which there is no reward. Assessment of operational excellence encompasses the following:

- experience and supervision of operations personnel;
- compensation incentives aligned with client interests (see below);
- compliance procedures, independence, oversight, and enforcement;
- internal controls and segregation of duties for investment, trading, cash management, and protection of investor funds;
- consistent and independent portfolio pricing, valuation and performance reporting;
- quality and oversight of service providers; and
- investment due diligence with independent oversight.

5.3 Valuation

Alternative investments

Valuations are crucial to accurate measurement of performance and management fees. Institutional investors in the US are increasing allocations to "alternative investments" which include investment vehicles and/or underlying investments that are illiquid because they are private or thinly traded. Valuations of alternative investments may be largely subjective and difficult to verify. Venture capital, private equities, and direct investments in real estate are classically vulnerable to these concerns.

Audits

Auditors are placing greater scrutiny on valuations of alternative assets, and may limit their audit scope or simply decline to audit them. The American Institute of Certified Public Accountants (AICPA) addresses the issue as follows:

"Over the past several years, certain not-for-profit organizations, healthcare entities, pension plans and investment companies - including funds of funds; have dramatically increased their investment in financial instruments that do not have a readily determinable market value [...] commonly referred to as alternative investments [...] The continued increase in the percentage of alternative investments to both net assets and total investment portfolio subjects these entities to complex fair value accounting and has exposed their investment portfolios to greater risk and volatility.

Due to the increased risk of misstatement inherent with these investments, the Audit Issues Task Force of the Auditing Standards Board established the Alternative Investments Task Force [...] charged with providing additional guidance to auditors of investor entities as to how the auditor may obtain sufficient appropriate audit evidence in order to conclude that the financial statements are free of material misstatement [...] the Alternative Investments Task Force has developed and issued a practice aid for auditors 'Alternative Investments – Audit Considerations'." [22]

Best practices   Due diligence procedures should closely examine the methodology and timing for valuations and their impact on fees and performance. Best practices for valuation methods, processes, and assumptions are evolving and require transparency, pricing consistency over time, and independent verification.

5.4   Incentives

Misaligned financial incentives can have unintended consequences of excessive risk taking. Most incentive compensation plans offer mainly or only upside for individual participants, with no "give back". Stewards who peg employee compensation and manager fee incentives solely to portfolio returns should "Be careful what you wish for!" "Risk adjusted" performance, for example, is a better benchmark.

Financial compensation for risk managers and compliance professionals especially should be mainly independent of absolute investment performance. Non-financial incentives for compliant behavior include respect of colleagues, supervisors, and clients; increased supervisory responsibility and client interaction; and opportunities for professional development.

Stewards should receive full disclosure regarding compensation of all parties, and must understand their managers' compensation incentives in order to assess motivations for excessive risk taking. Part of the manager selection due diligence process will be to assess evidence as to whether compensation of individual portfolio managers with authority to select investments is aligned with investor interests.

Considerations for fiduciary due diligence   High hedge fund and private equity fees in particular take a large portion of the returns generated by underlying investments (e.g., 2 % ongoing management fee, 20 % participation in performance above a "high watermark" or a "hurdle rate" over a specified period (e.g., a year)). A few considerations for fiduciary due diligence to evaluate a manager's fee and compensation structures follow:

- Is the ongoing management fee charged on gross or net assets? If gross, how are incentives to leverage managed? Is leverage created by derivative exposures monitored constantly, and does it remain at consistent levels – daily, intra-day?

- Are fees and expenses charged to your organization identical to all other participants in the fund? What is the basis for any preferential arrangements in place?

- How are key employees of the manager compensated (e.g., firm profitability, investment performance, individual contributions)? Do they have money at risk in the fund?

- What expenses are covered by the base management fee? What "administrative costs" (legal, accounting, printing, marketing, etc.) are charged to the funds in addition to management fees? Are these audited and reported to clients?

- What incentive does the manager have to keep trading and other expenses "appropriate and reasonable"? Can the manager provide evidence of close tracking of trading and other transaction costs and monitoring of "best execution"?

- How are assets valued to calculate base and participation fees? Is there an opportunity to manipulate results?

- Is the hurdle rate realistic in light of the risk profile of the manager's strategy (e.g., some fund managers participate in all returns greater than 0%)? Are participation fees charged for performance after all other fees and expenses? Is there a "claw back" provision to balance subsequent losses against participation fees earned?

6 Conclusion

Natural forces, human forces, and market forces are dramatically re-shaping risk and reward relationships in global financial and property markets in ways that challenge institutional investment fiduciaries to constantly re-evaluate and stress test their global diversification strategies.

Summary and outlook

The Global Fiduciary Standard of Excellence is helping to guide the investment management process for fiduciaries. And conspicuous collaborative efforts to standardize "language" and best practices for key disciplines that serve the investment management industry are in process to facilitate communications, informed decision making, and risk management.

The most sophisticated financial models in the world involve at least as much art and judgment as math and science. Sustainable integrity of relationships and operations cannot be modeled, and derivatives represent a "zero sum game" minus underwriting fees and transaction costs; i.e., risks do not go away, they are exchanged. To quote the venerable veteran investor, Peter Bernstein: "Derivatives have become quite complicated, and there are a lot of inexperienced players using them. Here I worry." [23]

We would be foolish not to study the past and learn from its lessons. Fiduciaries cannot afford to allow the paradigm shifts occurring in global markets to overwhelm and tempt them to turn up their I-pods and hum along with the country chorus "Shut up and drive", as they might find themselves driving over a cliff:

"Shut up and drive
Don't look in the mirror
Turn the radio on
Get out of here
Shut up and drive" [24]

At the end of the day, integrity of participants and effective governance will most influence confidence in financial and property markets, across geographic, economic, political, and cultural boundaries globally.

Advice for global asset allocation strategies, tactics and timing may be expressed quite simply in some of the lyrics to one more country song "The Gambler" about Texas Hold 'em poker:

"You got to know when to hold 'em, know when to fold 'em,
Know when to walk away and know when to run.

You never count your money when you're sittin' at the table.
There'll be time enough for countin' when the dealin's done.

Now ev'ry gambler knows that the secret to survivin'
Is knowin' what to throw away and knowing what to keep.
'cause ev'ry hands a winner and ev'ry hands a loser,
And the best that you can hope for is to die in your sleep [break even]." [25]

7   Bibliography

[1] Wilson, D., /Purushothaman, R., Goldman Sachs GS Global Economics Website, Global Economics Paper No. 99: Dreaming With BRICs: The Path to 2050, October 1ˢᵗ, 2003, www2.goldmansachs.com/insight/research/reports/99.pdf.

[2] United Nations Department of Economic and Social Affairs, Population Division, World Population Ageing: 1950–2050, chapter 1 page 6, published by the United Nations Department of Public Information – DPI/2460B – June 2007, www.un.org/esa/population/publications/worldageing19502050/.

[3] Laurelli, P. H., CFA, Asset Flow Trends Reveal Stuttering Growth, Institutional Investor News and HedgeFunds.net's 2008 Hedge Fund Asset Flows & Trends Report, November 2007, www.iialternatives.com/AIN/fundflows08/sample.pdf, www.iialternatives.com/AIN/fundflows08/.

[4] Testimony by SEC Chairman Christopher Cox before the US Senate Committee on Banking, Housing and Urban Affairs Concerning the Regulation of Hedge Funds, US Securities & Exchange Commission, July 25ᵗʰ, 2006, www.sec.gov/news/testimony/2006/ts072506cc.htm.

[5] Buffett, W., Berkshire Hathaway 2004 Annual Report Chairman's Letter to Shareholders, February 28ᵗʰ, 2005, p. 11, www.berkshirehathaway.com/letters/2004ltr.pdf. The quotation is copyrighted and used with permission of the author Warren Buffet.

[6] Buffett, W., Berkshire Hathaway 2005 Annual Report Chairman's Letter to Shareholders, February 28ᵗʰ, 2006, pp. 10–11, www.berkshirehathaway.com/letters/2005ltr.pdf. The quotation is copyrighted and used with permission of the author Warren Buffet.

[7] Foundation for Fiduciary Studies, www.fi360.com.

[8] Uniform Prudent Management of Institutional Funds Act, www.upmifa.org/.

[9] ISO 9000, www.iso9000-standard.com.

[10] Centre for Fiduciary Excellence, www.cefex.org.

[11] ISO19011, www.iso14000-iso14001-environmental-management.com/
iso-19011.htm.

[12] CFA Institute, www.cfainstitute.org.

[13] CFA Institute's Centre for Financial Market Integrity,
www.cfainstitute.org/centre/overview/pdf/what_stand_for.pdf.

[14] Bank for International Settlements (BIS), www.bis.org.

[15] International Accounting Standards Board (IASB), www.iasb.org.

[16] International Valuation Standards Committee (IVSC),
www.ivsc.org.

[17] International Association of Insurance Supervisors (IAIS),
www.iaisweb.org.

[18] Global Association of Risk Professionals (GARP),
www.garp.com/about/mission.asp.

[19] Royal Institution of Chartered Surveyors (RICS), www.rics.org/
Aboutus/spotlight.htm and www.rics.org/Aboutus/Whatwedo/
Spotlight.htm.

[20] World Intellectual Property Organization (WIPO), www.wipo.int/
about-wipo/en/what_is_wipo.html.

[21] Speech by Richards, L. A., Director, Office of Compliance Inspections
and Examinations, US Securities and Exchange Commission, "The
Culture of Compliance" Spring Compliance Conference: National
Regulatory Services, Tucson, AZ, April 23rd, 2003, www.sec.gov/news/
speech/spch042303lar.htm.

[22] American Institute of Certified Public Accountants, Inc., New York,
NY, "AICPA Issues Practice Aid for Auditors on Alternative
Investments", Copyright 2006, www.aicpa.org/Professional+Resources/
Accounting+and+Auditing/Accounting+Standards/pract_aid_alt_
invest.htm.

[23] Bernstein, P., Chat with Business Week Contributing Editor
Christopher Farrell, April 9th, 2007, "Philosopher of Risk",
www.businessweek.com/print/magazine/content/07_15/b4029094.
htm?chan=gl.

[24] Written and recorded by Wright, C., 1999, http://lyrics.rare-lyrics.com/
C/Chely-Wright/Shut-Up-And-Drive.html.

[25] Written and originally recorded by Don Schlitz, and later made famous
by Kenny Rogers in 1978, www.lyricsfreak.com/k/kenny+rogers/
the+gambler_20077886.html.

B   Equity capital markets

1   Indirect real estate as a strategic investment

Stefan Mitropoulos

Table of contents

1   Real estate as part of the asset allocation

An important asset class

Real estate has considerable economic significance, with more than half of the wealth in the world estimated to be only in residential properties. Investor interest in real estate has increased in the past few years due to its favorable risk-return characteristics. Additionally, real estate is being viewed more and more as a separate asset class apart from equities, bonds and alternative investments like hedge funds, private equity or commodities.

Characteristics of real estate

Real estate has a number of characteristics which differentiate it from other types of investments and make it an essential part of any investment strategy to manage a diversified portfolio. These characteristics include a long investment period, the fixed location of the investment and the distinctiveness of individual properties, resulting in an attractive risk-return profile and a low correlation with other major asset classes. However, compared to equities and bonds, real estate markets are very heterogeneous with relatively low transparency. This is due to the fact that each property must be viewed individually in light of its location, occupants and physical condition. Additionally, real estate markets are fragmented and differ significantly over regions and sectors.

Income return

Many real estate investments – and especially directly held property – typically have relatively stable income returns resulting from rents from the underlying properties. The income return component in the form of high dividend yields plays a more prominent role with the liquid types of real estate investment than with the equity market as a whole. This is especially true for Real Estate Investment Trusts (REITs), which are required by law to distribute a large part of their profits to shareholders.

The safety argument

The long investment period and the relatively stable property values are the essential reasons why real estate investments are generally considered to be "safer". But these tangible assets are also subject to cyclical fluctuations. Because of the existing inherent value of the properties and the fairly stable rents, real estate prices do not, as a rule, decline as rapidly as equity prices sometimes do. Nevertheless, asset bubbles and corrections are not unknown on the real estate markets. Consequently, it is important to diversify into different property investments, regions or sectors within the asset class based on a real estate investment strategy.

Real estate has traditionally been considered a useful investment for hedging against high inflation. Investments qualify as an inflation hedge if their returns increase in times of high inflation in proportion to the general price level, keeping real returns constant. In a series of studies it was shown that real estate had provided a hedge against high inflation in the past decades – at least in comparison to other asset classes. This is a result of the rent indexation existing in many countries. While direct investments in real estate have the characteristics of an inflation hedge – at least partially – this argument holds not true for real estate equities, which tend to be negatively affected by high inflation just as is the general equity market [1].

Real estate as inflation hedge?

2 Variety of indirect real estate investments

Real estate as an asset class offers a wide range of different investment possibilities, which should be considered within an investment strategy. Fundamentally, real estate investments can be divided into two classes depending upon whether the property is held directly or indirectly, whereas there are several important categories of indirect real estate investments. Furthermore, real estate investments can be differentiated according to their geographic focus as well as their sectors. Finally, it is common to categorize real estate investments by their risk-return profiles.

Direct investment in real estate usually requires large investment sums because the investment cannot be divided into smaller denominations. For many private investors, the price of an apartment as an investment in residential real estate is acceptable, whereas the capital requirements for an office building are usually much too high for most. Since direct investments involve individual properties, risk diversification can only be achieved by buying several different real estate objects. Although the investment horizon for direct real estate investments is usually of long duration, an advantage is that the investor has complete freedom to decide about the investment. Other considerations in direct investing include tax considerations, transaction and information cost and finding the right manager to administer the property. However, for portfolio management purposes, indirect real estate investment vehicles are much more appropriate than direct investments.

Direct real estate investment

2.1 Main investment categories of indirect real estate

The most important types of indirect real estate investments are real estate securities, including REITs, as well as open-end and closed-end funds. The exact characteristics of investments falling into these categories, however, differ substantially from one country to another.

Closed-end funds Closed-end real estate funds are usually private partnerships established with the purpose of buying or developing one or a small number of real estate properties for a certain period. Much like direct investments, closed-end funds have only a small degree of diversification and are close to direct investments concerning their tax treatment. The minimum investment amount for closed-end funds varies considerably depending on the specific fund product. In Germany, for example, the market for these investments is very developed and the minimum investment amount is usually about € 10,000. There is no market valuation of the fund shares. A valuation only takes place when called for by the fund investors or on sale of the property. Despite the existence of secondary markets in some cases, a premature sale of shares in a closed-end real estate fund is difficult for investors.

Open-end funds Open-end real estate funds are primarily found in Germany and are not limited in their subscription volume or life. Since these funds are much larger in size compared to closed-end funds and have a greater number of individual properties, a wider diversification according to location or property sectors can be achieved. The determination of the fund's share price takes place through the regular appraisal of the assets in the fund. In Germany, open-end funds have a significantly lower volatility than real estate equities while being subject to the same capital market regulatory requirements as mutual funds. The redemption of the shares is usually possible on a daily basis, but sometimes certain notice periods have to be observed. Open-end real estate funds are suitable for medium- to long-term investment horizons and the minimum investment amount is low.

Real estate equities and REITs The most liquid property investments are real estate equities. These are usually shares of exchange-listed corporations which invest in real estate assets but which also could be involved in real estate development and other real estate related services, e. g., property management. The so-called Real Estate Investment Trusts (REITs) have developed to the preferred type of real estate equity in more and more countries following the example of the US. REITs have to fulfill certain requirements in order to be eligible for tax treatment. Depending on the country, there are also significant differences in details of REITs, but the essential requirements are that its main business purpose has to be the ownership and administration of properties and that a large part of profits has to be paid out as dividends to shareholders. In this case, profits are not taxed at the company level, but rather shareholders pay taxes on the dividends they receive.

Since real estate equities and REITs can be sold at any time on the stock exchange at the existing market price, they also qualify as short-term investments. The minimum investment amount is the price of one share. Investor protection is guaranteed by the relevant legal requirements for listings, audits and information publications by corporations. The price of real estate equities reacts both to the factors which generally influence the equity market and to those which affect the underlying real estate markets. Real estate equities have the largest volatility of all real estate investment types. The risk of the individual equities depends on the real estate portfolio and its diversification. Actively managed real estate securities funds or certificates on real estate equity indices offer a higher degree of diversification than individual real estate equities.

2.2 Diversification argument

Real estate investments in a portfolio should always be diversified in order to spread risk. This means that investments should not be in one property, location, region or property type only. Since real estate markets do not develop in a synchronized manner across regions or sectors but are subject to differing, time-displaced cycles, the risk in a portfolio can be reduced by diversification across different regions and segments [2].

2.2.1 Diversification across regions

Despite a certain amount of convergence of the international real estate markets in the past years, differences still remain, which can be explained primarily by the growth differentials between the countries. However, there is still a significant home bias in most real estate portfolios. This bias results primarily from the vague knowledge many investors have of foreign markets and from related tax questions or regulatory hurdles. Because of this, investors do not often make use of valuable diversification advantages. Hence, it is reasonable to pursue a global approach within a real restate investment strategy. There is evidence, however, that there is marked increase in the volume of cross-border transactions and that globalization of real estate is making good progress.

Increased volume of cross-border investments

According to Jones Lang LaSalle [3], global direct investments in commercial property totalled US$ 759 billion in 2007, with the percentage of cross-border transactions rising from almost 43 % to 46.5 %, confirming that more and more investors are diversifying their real estate portfolios internationally. During the past few years, many real estate investors extended their investment universe to include other developed regions but globalization on the real estate market does not end there. Today, North America accounts for about 39 % of the investable commercial real estate market, Western Europe for approximately 36 % and Japan for almost 12 % [4]. In the future, the real estate markets in the emerging markets of Asia, Eastern Europe and Latin America – which currently account for less than 17 % – will increase significantly and therefore come more sharply into the focus of investors.

Globalization of real estate business

	Asia	Australia	Euro zone	UK	USA
Asia	1.00	0.62	0.65	0.62	0.52
Australia		1.00	0.55	0.51	0.44
Euro zone			1.00	0.52	0.43
UK				1.00	0.51
USA					1.00

FTSE EPRA/NAREIT total return indices, monthly data in €, January 2000 to August 2007
Sources: Deutsche Bank Private Asset Management, T. F. Datastream, 2007

Fig. 1: Correlation between regional real estate equity indices

Correlation analysis   Real estate equity indices of different regions [5] are positively correlated with each other but to varying degrees. This is an indication of the globally non-synchronized movements of the real estate cycles. For example, REITs in the US have developed largely independent of real estate securities in the euro zone since the beginning of 2000 (as evidenced by the correlation coefficient of 0.43). The correlations between the regional real estate indices are all below 0.7 in this period, indicating a significant diversification potential for the investor. Correlations of the overall equity markets indices [6] to each other are much higher, meaning that the regional real estate security markets are more independent of each other than are the corresponding stock markets. For example, in the period under consideration, the correlation of the MSCI US with the MSCI for the euro zone was 0.77. This reflects the increasing economic integration of large companies worldwide in many sectors while real estate has remained a more regionally distinct sector.

2.2.2   Diversification across sectors

Different property types   Investments in various segments of the real estate market which are subject to differencing influences also promise diversification effects. The most important sectors of the real estate market are office buildings, retail, industrial and apartments. Besides these, there are a number of special property types, such as hotels, leisure and health care. Each of these property types is influenced by factors unique to their specific use, thus resulting in the development of individual cycles.

Office versus retail   For the office market, for example, the main influencing factor is the labor market, and especially the number of office employees. This sector is very cyclical as characterized by movements in vacancy rates primarily because of the long development times for large office buildings. The office sector reacts with a lag to the business cycle as well as to the labor market. In contrast, retail properties are stronger influenced by private consumption and incomes, which determine retail sales. This sector is less cyclical than office buildings. Buying frequency, regional purchasing power and in some cases zoning and planning laws are decisive. Management and the rent mix are very important, especially for shopping malls.

In view of differing cycles, investments in the various sectors can be used to diversify risk in a real estate portfolio. It should be noted that niche markets often have higher returns, but are less liquid compared to the larger market segments and thus have greater risk.

Thanks to readily available data, the US market offers a good overview of the size of the individual market segments. In the NCREIF Property Index for directly held real estate, office buildings represent the largest sector with 36 %, ahead of apartments (23.2 %) and retail (22.5 %) [7]. By comparison, the office sector is less dominant in the US REIT market. Companies that are focused on office property only account for about 14 % of the market capitalization of the US Equity REIT Index, while retail properties in contrast make up more than 26 %[8]. The example of US REITs shows that the degree of specialization of listed real estate companies usually increases with the maturity of the market. The vast majority of US REITs are specialized in one sector, while in

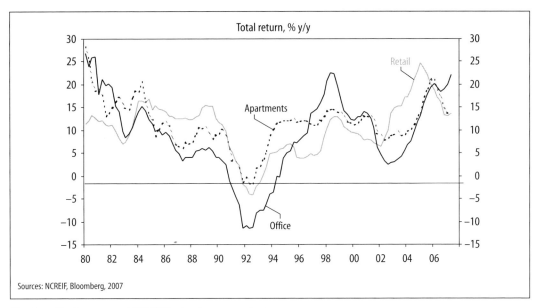

Fig. 2: Performance NCREIF Index by property type

continental Europe many larger real estate corporations can be found which are diversified over various property types.

2.3   Real estate according to investment style

Real estate as an asset class offers investors a series of different products with a wide spectrum of risk-return profiles. The various real estate investments can be classified into the investment styles "core", "value added" and "opportunistic", according to increasing return opportunities and risks. A style called "core plus" is often placed between core and the value added. The investment styles differ in the significance of their individual return components – the relatively steady income return versus more volatile capital appreciation – and the amount of debt finance.

Different investment styles

Often, investment styles are categorized according to capital leverage ratio and to the expectations of their total return [9]. It should be noted, however, that these return expectations vary over time and display regional differences to a certain extent. Core investments offer investors relatively low returns with small risks, value added investments have both returns and risks in the medium range, while opportunistic investments display the highest returns and the greatest risks.

Core investments are characterized by a high quality of the real estate properties: good locations in large, liquid real estate markets, a high occupancy rate, steady rent income thanks to long-term leases and stable property values. Core properties usually have a lower debt ratio. They are considered to be long-term investments (buy-and-hold strategy) and have characteristics associated with

Core investments

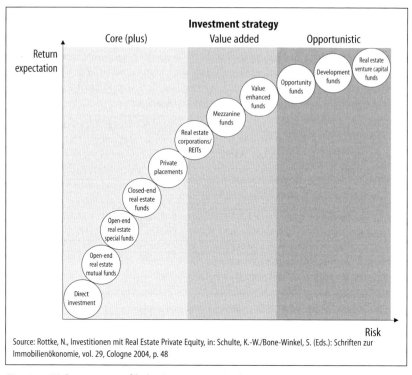

Fig. 3:   Risk-return profile by investment style

bonds owing to their low volatility. Widely diversified open-end real estate funds are considered core investments.

Value added investments
Value added investments have a greater potential for capital gains, which can be a result of modernization or of a more active building management leading to a reduction of vacancy rates and the extension of rental periods. Value added properties are often in average or below average locations, in smaller cities or belong to niche segments, indicating less liquid markets. They can also be characterized by higher debt financing ratios (up to around 70 %). The investment horizon is shorter than for core investments and extends from the purchase of the property to an exit at a favorable point in time after a successful upgrading of the property. Value added investments are as a rule less diversified and include many closed-end real estate funds.

Opportunistic investments
Opportunistic investments display high risks but also offer the highest return potential. A high debt ratio of over 70 % is used to achieve a strong leverage effect on the equity capital in a similar manner to private equity investments. Opportunistic investments are, for example, closed-end funds with distressed property in need of refurbishment, which has high vacancy rates or which is situated in development areas. Within the real estate cycle, opportunistic investments have special importance in recessionary phases. Properties in emerging markets with low market transparency and increased country risks count as opportunistic investments as well. Sectorial or regional diversification and income yields are not of prime importance with this investment style.

Real estate securities occupy the middle ground of the risk-return spectrum of real estate investments, but a classification to one of the investment styles is difficult. As a result, real estate securities can also be classified as a separate category. Total return is, on average, higher than on core investments but with higher overall risk. Value added and opportunistic investments are expected to have higher returns than real estate securities but also with higher expected risks.

Real estate securities

The specific risk-return profile of a single real estate stock depends primarily on the underlying real estate investments and the leverage (relative amount of debt financing) of the real estate company. Property owners whose main investments are in high-value properties in top locations with high occupancy rates have relatively low risk. In these cases, steady rental flows, which are passed on to the shareholders in the form of dividends, play a more prominent role than possible value increases. The majority of REITs fall into this category. Real estate securities are more risky when the main areas of business are in less attractive real estate properties or are in need of refurbishing. Project development and investments in real estate markets with lower transparency, such as in the emerging markets, are also riskier. In this case, the dividend yield is only of secondary importance to the investor compared to the potential for equity price gains.

REITs versus developer

3 Real estate as a portfolio building block

Due to their specific characteristics, real estate is an important component of asset management. A real estate allocation which would be valid for all portfolios, however, does not exist. The decision of how much real estate a portfolio should contain and how the investments should be implemented with regard to investment products, property types and geography depends on the individual preferences of the investor, including risk and return expectations, investment horizon and liquidity needs. Since many investment possibilities are coupled with certain minimum investment amounts, the size of the portfolio ultimately plays a decisive role in this regard.

No overall allocation possible

3.1 Influence of owner-occupied residential property

A large part of private real estate assets is represented by owner-occupied residential property and real estate owned by businesses. Personal and partly emotional aspects such as career planning, space for family life, the warmth and security of owning a home, rent-free accommodation in old age are at the forefront when considering owner-occupied residential property. The buying or selling of these properties does not take place primarily due to return expectations, but is often determined by personal events, such as changes of the family size, career-related moves or the development of household income.

Consequently, it is sometimes problematic to include these properties as part of a real estate allocation. Owner-occupied residential property and also business real estate are, as a rule, limited to one or only a few locations and only one property type. The fact that these real estate assets are highly concentrated from the point of view of risk management underscores the need for a broad diversification of real estate investments within the actively managed portfolio.

3.2   Limited availability of performance data

For portfolio optimization with real estate, the availability of long-term performance data is essential. Unfortunately, the availability of representative data over a long period concerning the performance of real estate is limited compared to equities and bonds.

Returns on directly hold property

For example, returns on directly held properties are only available on a yearly basis for Germany since 1996, for France since 1999 or for Spain and Italy since 2001. A positive exception is Great Britain, where monthly performance data since 1986 have been published by Investment Property Databank (IPD). In the US, the National Council of Real Estate Investment Fiduciaries (NCREIF) publishes quarterly data since 1978 based on the input of institutional investors. It is important to note that the NCREIF Property Index is calculated on an unleveraged basis.

Returns on public real estate

There are also large differences in the data situation for liquid real estate investments. While the National Association of Real Estate Investment Trusts (NAREIT) in the US already has calculated indices for listed real estate equities in the form of REITs since the beginning of the 1970s, the initial startup of the European affiliate organization EPRA (European Public Real Estate Association) was at the beginning of 2000 [10].

3.3   Need for more than one investment category

Differing risk-return profiles

When considering the optimization of a portfolio by adding real estate, it should be noted that real estate is not a homogeneous asset class. A wide range of real estate investment products with differing risk-return profiles are available to choose from. As a result, it is not sufficient to have just one type of investment to cover this asset class. Therefore, both (public) real estate equities and unlisted (private) property should be included in the investment strategy.

Public and private real estate hardly correlated

Our calculations show that there is no statistically significant relationship between the performance of directly held real estate and real estate securities, although the same assets might underlie both investments. The NCREIF Property Index provides a long time series for the returns of directly held real estate investments in the US. The original data display no significant correlation with the US REIT Index.

Explanation

There are several explanations for this. Real estate securities are not only influenced by the underlying real estate markets, but also by the general factors impacting the equity market. Empirical studies have shown that after adjustment for the specific influences of the equity market there is, in fact, a positive correlation between the two real estate categories. Furthermore, the prices of real estate securities react immediately to new information and market expectations, whereas the valuations of directly held real estate adjust

	Equities	Bonds	REITs	Direct real estate
Equities	1.00	−0.05	0.43	0.07
Bonds		1.00	0.15	−0.20
REITs			1.00	0.00
Direct real estate				1.00

In US$, based on quarterly data, Q1/1985 to Q4/2007
Equities = MSCI World; bonds = Citigroup US Government Bonds; REITs = NAREIT REIT Index;
direct real state = NCREIF Property Index
Source: Deutsche Bank, Private Asset Management, T. F. Datastream, 2008

Fig. 4:   Correlation between asset classes

only slowly over time because the valuation of these properties only takes place at longer time intervals – usually once a year – resulting in a smoothing of price fluctuations and thus a lower volatility. Another explanation is that the two forms of real estate investment represent different segments of the real estate market. In the US, for instance, REITs cover a wider spectrum of the real estate market – both geographically and in relation to sectors and risk attitudes – than do directly held real estate properties in the NCREIF Index. Additionally, the property data in the NCREIF Index have been adjusted for leverage [11].

3.4   Portfolio optimization with real estate

In order to demonstrate how the addition of real estate affects a classical portfolio of equities and bonds, we use the following simplified example for US investments – given the long historical data series available for this market. The starting point is a traditional portfolio consisting of the asset classes global equities (MSCI World Index) and US government bonds (Citigroup US Government Bonds Index) [12].

Starting point: traditional portfolio

The volatility of total returns in a portfolio can be fundamentally reduced by combining investments that have a low correlation to each other. For the US, the low synchronization of directly held property with equities and bonds illustrates such a positive effect. REITs have also had only a small positive correlation with US government bonds over the last 20 years. These listed real estate equities have a positive correlation with the total equity market, but the parallel movements are not very pronounced. The correlation coefficients already indicate that an addition of both real estate categories to a portfolio of equities and bonds should be advantageous.

Correlations of equities and bonds with real estate

Both of these real estate investments have superior return-risk profiles historically compared to equities and government bonds. The average total return of REITs from 1985 to 2007 has been 13.6 % p.a., similar to global equities. This result has been achieved with REITs having lower volatility than international equities – in other words, with less risk. The directly held properties in the NCREIF Property Index have yielded 8.9 % p.a. on average in the same period, slightly higher than US government bonds (8.0 %). The advantage of this real estate investment can be found in a significantly lower volatility compared to bonds.

Attractive risk-return profile of real estate

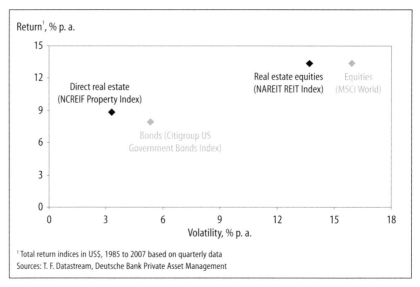

Fig. 5:   Risk-return profile of different asset classes

Efficient frontier   In a first step, the efficient frontier for a portfolio consisting of equities and bonds can be calculated. The efficient frontier indicates in which portfolio an investor should invest depending upon his individual risk preferences. The greater the readiness to bear risk, the further to the right on the efficient frontier the investor's portfolio will be. All efficient combinations of equities and bonds are on the efficient frontier. A portfolio is efficient when there is no other portfolio that offers a higher return with the same risk (volatility) or can provide a given return with lower risk.

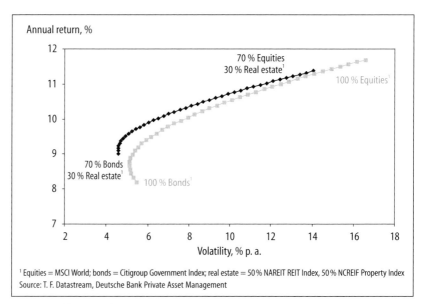

Fig. 6:   Efficiency frontier – traditional equity/bonds portfolio with real estate

In a second step, real estate is added to this portfolio of equities and bonds. In order to account for the asset class real estate as completely as possible, a simplified real estate investment that consists of 50 % in directly held US property (NCREIF Property Index) and 50 % in REITs (NAREIT Equity Index) is assumed. The addition of this real estate investment results in a shift of the efficient frontier to left and upward. This shows that higher returns and lower volatility can be achieved over the entire return-risk spectrum compared to a portfolio only of equities and bonds. The addition of real estate thus has had a positive effect on the portfolio.

Positive impact by adding real estate

4 Conclusions for investors

Real estate is an important component of a diversified portfolio. The real estate allocation depends on the market and the individual preference of the investor with regard to risk, return and liquidity. Before the question can be answered how this real estate allocation should be realized, it is necessary to know the risk preference of the investor. For investors with a higher risk preference, the share of real estate securities or opportunistic funds can be higher than for investors with lower risk preferences, where more weight should be put on core investments, such as open-end real estate funds. The structuring of a real estate portfolio is, however, not a question of all or nothing since several real estate categories have their justification. In our simplified example, a mixture of REITs and directly held property achieved better results than those cases where only one of these categories represented the entire asset class.

Allocation depends on investors preferences

For smaller amounts, investment products come into view which can be purchased in smaller denominations, which are diversified and liquid. Open-end real estate funds and real estate equity funds are a good choice here. In recent years, many new, actively managed real estate security funds as well as passive real estate index certificates have been launched [13]. There are various products which reproduce the movement of a real estate equity index or a special basket of real estate stocks selected by the certificate issuer. Index certificates directly reflect a real estate equity index, while real estate security funds could over- or underweight individual regions, sectors and individual shares vis-à-vis a benchmark. Real estate security funds can react flexibly to developments of individual companies, property types and regions depending on market conditions. Active management, however, has higher costs than passive certificates.

Smaller versus larger portfolios

Larger real estate portfolios could achieve satisfactory diversification through several direct investments or participation in various closed-end funds, which have a higher minimum investment requirement. Here, closed-end funds in the value added and opportunistic return-risk spectrum represent additional investment possibilities.

The distribution of real estate investments according to sectors and regions depends upon the respective market cycle. A concentration of the entire real estate allocation on only the home market or on single market segments is not advisable from a risk standpoint. The starting point for a regional or sectorial real estate allocation should be the overall investible universe. Depending on market assessment, corresponding under- and overweightings from this

Allocation by regions and sectors

distribution can then be decided. Besides the real estate properties underlying the investment, other aspects, such as investment horizon, liquidity, tax treatment and the track-record of the product provider, need to be considered when making investment decisions.

5   Bibliography

[1] Hudson-Wilson, S. et al., Why Real Estate?, in: Journal of Portfolio Management, Special Issue, New York 2005, p. 17 et seq.

[2] Mitropoulos, S., Various investment possibilities in real estate, in: Real estate – a versatile investment building block, Deutsche Bank Private Asset Management, Frankfurt, June 2006, pp. 8–10.

[3] Jones Lang LaSalle, Global direct commercial real estate investment reaches record levels in 2007 despite credit crunch, press release, February 18th, 2008.

[4] Based on estimates from European Public Real Estate Association (EPRA) for the end of 2006, EPRA Statistical Bulletin, June 2007, pp. 4–5.

[5] Referring to the FTSE EPRA/NAREIT Total Return index family.

[6] Referring to MSCI Total Return indices.

[7] National Council of Real Estate Investment Fiduciaries (NCREIF), NPI Snapshot, 2nd Quarter 2007.

[8] National Association of Real Estate Investment Trusts (NAREIT), as of July 31st, 2007.

[9] See INREV (European Association for Investors in Non-listed Real Estate Vehicles): definitions for core fund (overall target return up to 11.5%), value added fund (target return between 11.5% and 18.5%) and opportunistic fund (target return in excess of 18.5%), www.inrev.org

[10] For more details about real estate performance data see IPD (www.ipdindex.co.uk), NCREIF (www.ncreif.com), NAREIT (www.nareit.com) and EPRA (www.epra.com).

[11] Pagliari, J. L./Scherer, K. A./Monopoli, R. T., Public versus private real estate equities. A risk-return comparison, in: Jounal of Portfolio Management, New York, September 2003, p. 101 et seqq.

[12] Mitropoulos, S., Real estate as a portfolio building block, in: Real estate – a versatile investment building block, Deutsche Bank Private Asset Management, Frankfurt, June 2006, pp. 13–15.

[13] Hughes F./Arissen J., Top Real Estate Fund Managers go Global, EPRA, January 2006, and Bermanseder, S.: Investing in real estate security funds, in: Real Estate Securities – an attractive investment alternative, Deutsche Bank Private Asset Management, Frankfurt, September 2006, p. 18 et seq.

2 German open-end real estate funds

Walter Klug

Table of contents

1   Introduction

Development of the real estate fund market

German open-end real estate funds count among the most significant institutional real estate investors not just in Germany, but increasingly on international markets, too. Their history goes back to 1959 when Internationales Immobilien Institut was founded and launched iii-Fonds No. 1, the first fund of this kind. Interest in this type of investments began to perk up noticeably in 1969. In 1972, as many as eight open-end property funds already participated in the market. By spring 2007, 16 capital investment companies offered a total of 36 open-end property retail funds with an aggregate volume of approximately €78 billion. Moreover, a growing number of institutional real estate funds exist side by side with the retail funds today. By the end of 2005, there were 101 funds of this type whose combined fund assets totalled € 16.8 billion.

2 A brief definition

An open-end real estate fund is defined as a legally dependant property trust fund that is managed in trust by a capital investment company and invested primarily in real estate and real-estate-like rights while taking into account aspects of risk diversification and realization of profits (continuous income and value appreciation). In this context, the term risk diversification means that the fund's real estate must be diversified by region, size, types of usage, and tenancy. Open-end real estate funds subdivide either into real estate retail funds or institutional real estate funds. In common parlance, the term "open-end real estate funds" generally refers to retail funds. These, then, will be the subject under discussion.

Concept of open-end real estate funds

3 High fungibility of investment due to daily availability

The distinguishing characteristic of an open-end real estate retail fund is that it converts tangible fixed capital assets, such as office buildings, shopping centers or hotels, into mobile assets in the sense that its investors can principally dispose of their deposits on a daily basis. To this end, the fund is legally held to maintain a minimum liquidity of 5 % of its assets at all times. As it is hard to synchronize the inflow and outflow of investor capital with the fund's real estate acquisitions and sales, such funds tend to maintain a substantially higher liquidity reserve. In case the liquidity proves insufficient, they have the right to suspend the redemption of shares for a limited time, though no longer than two years. So far, just three funds have taken advantage of this possibility for a few weeks each.

Distinguishing characteristic

4 Essential legal bases

The essential legal bases for open-end real estate funds designed to prevent any arbitrary action on the part of the investment company that may be harmful to the individual investor include the German Investment Act (InvG) that entered into force on January 1st, 2004, and took the place of the German Investment Companies Act (KAGG) in the version dated January 14th, 1970, and the German Banking Act (KWG). The Investment Act, serving as framework law, contains the essential provisions to regulate the rights and tasks of the investment company and of the custodian bank, the issuance and redemption of the share certificates, the assessment of the issue and redemption price; the management of liquid assets, and the observance of investment ceilings. Supplementing these legal provisions are the fund rules that, subject to approval by the Federal Supervisory Authority for Financial Services (BaFin), regulate the legal relationship between the investment company and the investor. These contractual provisions must be handed over, together with the prospectus and the most recent annual report (and semi-annual report if the latter is more recent) to the investor prior to the acquisition of a fund share.

Legal constraints

The investor pays his or her savings capital into the so-called real estate trust fund. The investment company manages the latter in its own name, but for another's account. In other words, the real estate trust fund is kept strictly separate from the capital investment company's own assets. In return for the paid-in savings capital, the investor is issued a security that securitizes his or her claims vis-à-vis the capital investment company in regard to the investment and management of the deposit, the distribution of income, and the redemption of shares. Both private individuals and institutional investors may acquire shares in open-end real estate funds, though it must be said that in practice the overwhelming majority of shares are bought and kept by private individuals.

5   Important bodies and supervisory authorities

Tasks of the management and the investment company

Pursuant to Art. 2, Sec. 6, Investment Act, an investment company represents a financial institution and is therefore subject to supervision by the BaFin. In regard to its legal form, the company can only choose between a joint stock company and a limited liability company. The investment company is responsible for the overall management of the real estate trust fund, and acts as trustee. The management tasks include primarily the acquiring or developing, respectively, and the selling of real estate. The fund company's tasks also include the continued real estate management, that is, the portfolio development, the recruitment of tenants, the property management, the attendant marketing or research, as well as product sales. Some of these spheres of responsibility may be outsourced (Art. 16, Investment Act). Moreover, the investment company is responsible for the fund liquidity.

Function of custodian bank

The status and tasks of the custodian bank are regulated by Articles 20 et seq., Investment Act. The custodian bank handles all money transfers relating to the real estate trust fund, using separate blocked accounts, and keeps the assets that have been acquired for the fund in custody. In addition, the custodian bank is legally obligated to issue and redeem the shares, and to assess the share value in cooperation with the investment company. Moreover, it handles the distribution of dividends. Thus, the real estate held as part of the real estate trust fund cannot be disposed of with the approval of the custodian bank, and this function underlines its supervisory and controlling powers.

Responsible for appraising the value of the real estate pursuant to Art. 77, Investment Act, is a valuation committee composed of at least three members. These need to be independent, technically qualified, and experienced in the area of real estate valuations. Each property must be valuated at least once a year.

The need for a supervisory board is specified in Art. 6, Sec. 2, Investment Act, or in the German Stock Corporation Act (AktG) in the case of a public company. The purpose of the supervisory board is to monitor the company's management activities on behalf of the shareholders.

The Federal Supervisory Authority for Financial Services reviews the observation of the legal provisions of the Investment Act and the Banking Act, as well as the contractual terms of each company.

6 Assessing the share value

Pursuant to Art. 36, Investment Act, the value of the fund shares must be **Valuation** determined on each trading day. To this end, the fund's assets, i.e., its real, **of shares** liquid and other assets, are added up, whereas the liabilities and provisions are subtracted from the resulting subtotal. The resulting net amount equals the value of the fund assets. The fund assets are then divided by the number of shares in circulation. In the context of determining the share value, real estate must be assessed at its most recently appraised market value. Securities enter into the valuation at their most recently quoted price. The determined share value equals the redemption price. The issue price, by contrast, includes an additional offering premium that typically ranges between 4 % and 5.5 %.

7 Permissible investments

The entire catalogue of permissible real estate investments is compiled according **Asset allocation** to the principle of risk diversification. Accordingly, none of the properties may, **restrictions** pursuant to Art. 67, Sec. 2, Investment Act, exceed the equivalent of 15 % of the total value of the real estate trust fund. Similarly, the fund must pursue an adequate regional risk diversification, especially for investments outside the member states of the Treaty on the European Economic Area (Art. 67, Sent. 3). Following the ratification of the Fourth Act for the Promotion of the Financial Market (FMFG), the 20%-restriction was dropped, making it possible for a fund to invest to 100 % outside the European Economic Area (EEA). However, no more than 30 % of all fund assets may be subject to a currency risk.

8 Performance components

The performance of an open-end property fund is made up by two components, **Performance** to wit, the cash flow and the changes in property value. The cash dividend is **measurement** paid out of interest earnings from the liquid assets, the profits from real estate sales, and the rental income not used to cover expenses. The share performance depends on changes in the value of real estate, liquid assets and exchange rate, as well as on the extent of the distribution. Investors can realize the share performance by selling their shares.

9 Fiscal transparency

Under German tax law, open-end real estate funds are exempt from corporate **Taxation is** income tax and trade tax since they are rated as private special purpose **limited to the** funds. This means that the taxation of open-end real estate funds in Germany **investor level** is limited to the investor level. Being rated as income from capital assets, earnings from open-end property fund shares in private ownership are subject to income taxation according to the individual tax bracket. However, parts of the dividend remain income tax-free. The income tax-free share is mainly made up by earnings in connection with foreign real estate, sales profits on real estate outside the 10-year speculation period, and securities, from building depreciations, as well as from tax-deductible interest for building finance.

Dividends paid by open-end real estate funds are subject to the capital gains tax, which is set off as advance payment against the income tax to be assessed. The share value appreciation can be realized tax-free upon expiration of the 1-year speculation period. If the shares are held as corporate assets, the earnings must be taxed as operative income.

10   Essential product features

Transformation of a long-term investment into a fungible, security-like one

For an investor, the open-end real estate fund combines the benefits of a tangible fixed asset (high after-tax return and low fluctuation in value) with those of a security (daily availability). At the same time, a unique feature is that its price (quoted value) is determined not by supply and demand on the stock market, but by the net asset value. Thus, it converts a basically long-term investment form (real estate) into a fungible, security-like one. This transformation exposes the management of a property fund to special requirements.

In the past, the strict application of the income capitalization method in the valuation of building structures, the overall high tenancy quota, and the concentration on sound locations and standard market types of real estate, all caused open-end real estate funds to show a more stable performance than did the commercial real estate market seen as a whole. Compared to a direct real estate investment, the fund risk is markedly reduced due to the spread across a large number of objects, tenants, and industries, but also because of the negotiation of progressive leases. The large number of commercial and institutional tenants, the industry mix, and the different lease terms ensure a lower rent default risk than that of the commercial real estate market as a whole.

Open-end real estate funds are well suited to reduce the volatility of a given portfolio. Adding real estate assets to an existing portfolio composed of stocks and bonds permits a higher stock quota than before, without raising the overall volatility of the securities deposit.

11   Typical investment risks for open-end real estate funds

Hedging to minimize risks and the danger of a suspension of the fund's shares

Funds investing outside the euro zone are subject to a pro rata currency risk. Hedging or partial outside financing can be used to minimize the risk, but will also incur extra costs. On top of that, foreign investments are subject to risks in regard to fiscal and legal aspects. Other risks arise due to market cycles of the real estate markets, especially rent default risks due to vacancies or – to a limited degree – project development risks.

Moreover, there is the risk that investors may be temporarily unable to redeem their shares if a given investment company suspends the redemption of fund shares for up to two years because of liquidity bottlenecks. While this remained a hypothetical scenario for more than four decades, recent events have shown that this issue needs to be taken into account by the investor after all.

12 Protection against inflation-related depreciation

Real estate represents a so-called tangible fixed asset that is closely connected to the general price development. Whenever prices go up, so do the construction costs of real estate, and therefore the prices for real estate as such. Because of this (simplified) connection, real estate offers the chance to protect assets against inflation. If rent revenues are coupled to the inflation rate (rent indexing), the current revenues will also be protected against loss through inflation. Therefore, real estate ownership offers special protection against inflation. So far, open-end property funds have always more than offset the loss in spending power that was caused by inflation. In fact, the real estate performance tends to exceed the inflation rate by about 3.5 % on average.

Reduced inflation risk

13 Attractive tax breaks

The often relatively high tax-free share of open-end real estate fund dividends is largely due to the fact that rental income from foreign properties is taxed in the respective situs country, and that additional taxation in Germany is waived on the grounds of existing double taxation treaties.

Considerable parts of the annual dividend remains tax-free

Moreover, appreciations of securities (stocks and bonds) include, in addition to taxable dividend distributions or interest earnings, tax-free market profits once the 1-year speculation period has expired. Whenever real estate in Germany is sold after the 10-year speculation period, the appreciation realized will also remain tax-free.

This is the reason why considerable parts of the annual dividend of open-end real estate funds remain tax-free. In past decades, open-end real estate funds earned higher after-tax returns for investors in a high tax bracket than bond funds, and this at a markedly lower fluctuation of quoted values.

14 Target segments for investments

You can limit market risks through regional spreading of investments across more than one country, as each market, and even more so each country, will often show a very different performance. Open-end real estate funds are predominantly (to more than 70 % on average) invested in office real estate. Shopping centers, hotels and logistics real estate also play an important role as investments, but account for a much smaller share of the portfolio assets. Other diversification options include signing long-term leases for a given portfolio and selecting a mixed spectrum of tenants from a variety of industries.

Reducing market risks due to regional separation

Real estate-related risks can be controlled by mixing core properties and enhanced properties, as well as through income or value-oriented investments.

Core   = low risk (long-term leases, no vacancy, economically new buildings, no project developments)

Enhanced = higher risk (short-term leases, existing vacancy, economically older buildings, project developments)

Income   = low risk (performance depends on the realized rental income, while appreciations play a minor role)

Value   = higher risk (performance depending on realizable appreciations, while the current result is lower)

Measures, such as new acquisitions and property sales, can help to optimize an existing portfolio, as can the reshuffling of the aforementioned segments by country allocation, property group (core or enhanced), sector, etc. However, in the case of open-end real estate funds, especially of funds with a large fund volume, such optimizations will hardly impact the performance except in the long run.

15   Liquidity management

Investments in liquid assets to avoid liquidity problems

The crisis phenomena that high cash outflows within short periods of time precipitated for some German open-end real estate funds at the turn of 2005/2006 caused the significance of liquidity management to become deeply embedded in the public awareness. Article 80, Investment Act, defines the liquidity provisions pursuant to which liquid capital may be held for the purpose of implementing the individual investment policy. Accordingly, the liquidity held as part of the fund assets subdivides into minimum liquidity, spare cash, and earmarked funds.

An investment company may invest its liquid assets only in:

- cash balances,

- money market instruments,

- certain investment shares or shares in institutional property trust funds,

- ECB-approved securities (= securities identified by the European Central Bank [ECB] or Deutsche Bundesbank as collateral for loan transactions);

- beyond that, up to 5% of the fund assets may be invested in securities officially listed at a stock exchange in one of the member states of the European Union.

The investment company must ensure that the 5% minimum liquidity is available in sight deposits. The statutory ceiling for maximum liquidity is 49% of the total value of a property trust fund. This provision applies to real estate trust funds that were launched more than four years previous, meaning that newly launched open-end real estate funds may hold higher liquidity quotas during the start-up phase so as to give them opportunity to acquire a sufficient number of investments first.

Companies tend to keep higher liquid assets than the prescribed minimum liquidity in order to be able to satisfy requests for share redemptions any time. Unlike securities funds, the real estate held in fund portfolios cannot be disposed of at standard market prices on short notice. Also, a high capital inflow tends to cause a higher liquidity quota. Analogously, the amount of the earmarked capital influences the liquidity rate. Whenever there is no eligible property available for purchase, and the distribution date still months away, the liquidity quota for possible share redemptions may need to be raised.

In addition, the interest situation on the capital market influences the scope of the cash reserves. Attractive interest rates that exceed the real estate returns tend to encourage companies to stock up their cash reserves. However, in this context you should always also take a look at the after-tax performance. Inversely, low interest rates are bound to dampen the desire to keep excessive cash reserves.

Preferred securities classes in the portfolios of open-end property funds are municipal bonds and public-law mortgage bonds, as well as public loans. Customarily, these securities are held until maturity, while an important criterion for successful liquidity management is the optimized relationship of fixed term deposits to fixed interest securities. The liquidity management orients itself primarily to the obligations regarding the construction and acquisition of real estate. Decisive for a successful liquidity management is the quality of the forecasts for future developments on the capital market. Derivatives, such as futures and options, can be used to support the interest rate hedging.

Municipal bonds and public-law mortgage bonds are preferred securities

Moreover, investment companies can take advantage of the option to invest in common equity, as the latter potentially raises the long-term return on investment. Doing so, however, would imply an altered risk profile for an open-end property fund in this sub-segment.

16 Adjustment clause permits the suspension of share redemptions

If the existing liquidity proves insufficient to meet the redemption requests by shareholders, the fund company may – in addition to possibly taking out a loan of up to 50 % of the market value of the real estate held in the property trust fund – suspend the share redemption for up to two years. This rule is intended to ensure that properties will not have to be sold under time pressure and therefore below value (Art. 81, Investment Act, on the suspending of redemptions).

Suspension of share redemptions for up to two years

17 Assessment of real estate value

In conjunction with the real estate valuation for open-end real estate funds, investment companies have made the experience that the income capitalization method is the best way to assess the current market value of real estate. The income capitalization method takes all essential criteria that define value into account: the net annual income of building and land, the remaining useful life of the building, the marketability, and any factor influencing the property value.

Income capitalization method

Since such a valuation is based on sustainable income, it is not subject to short-term rental fluctuations (high points, low points). Thus, the market value so assessed comes closest to meeting the requirements of Art. 194, Federal Building Code (BauGB), because a potential real estate buyer would also calculate the purchase price of an investment property by drawing on the income likely to be realized in the years to come as basis for the decision to buy. A valuation according to the depreciated replacement cost method or the sales comparison method implies the assumption that the property could actually be constructed in the same quality at another site (in disregard of location). This would represent a purely theoretical view of things, and thus be inappropriate in practice. In order to objectify the real estate valuation of open-end real estate funds, the Investment Act prescribes the valuation by a valuation committee (Art. 67,5; 70,2; 79,1; 82,1; Investment Act).

The task of the valuation committee One of the principal tasks of a valuation committee is the assessment of market values for real estate acquisitions and sales, as well as the valuation of the real estate portfolio in order to appraise the value of the fund assets. Valuations must always be undertaken ahead of the acquisition or sale of real estate. Moreover, valuations need to be performed for the entire real estate portfolio at least once a year (Art. 70, Sec. 2 and 79, Sec. 1, Investment Act; for real estate companies in the form of a monthly "portfolio of assets" statement).

The investment company must not influence the valuation of real estate. It only provides the figures the valuation committee needs for the valuation. The activity, responsibility and composition of the valuation committee are regulated by set business terms. The Federal Supervisory Authority for Financial Services (BaFin) must be notified of, and must review, any appointment of experts to a given valuation committee. An appointment will occasion no objections if the respective expert submits proof of his or her economic independence, reliability, technical qualification, and special experience in the area of real estate valuation.

The practice of the share price assessment by expert opinion and the experts' valuation practice have been regularly exposed to criticism. However, the problem is intrinsic to the system, and an optimal method has yet to be found. In the opinion of the author, the method currently used does, in fact, do justice to the real situation. Because even in the context of stock prices, one needs to remember that the identified price merely represents a past figure with limited relevance for the future.

18   Performance components

Differentiation of real estate fund yields The fund returns of open-end real estate funds subdivide into several components. First of all, one needs to differentiate between two main components, to wit, the real estate yield and the liquidity yield. For years now, open-end real estate funds have reported the real estate yield separated by domestic and foreign values. The real estate yield table subdivides once more, vertically, into running rental income and valuation result, thus reflecting the change in real estate values. As the open-end real estate funds must apply the so-called marked-to-market method, the building reappraisals undertaken by the neutral experts enter immediately into the fund statements and result in a premium or discount for the share price, as the case may be. The balance of the appreciations and depreciations of a given year are reported in the table as one sum total, again separated into domestic and foreign figures.

19 Current developments

Open-end real estate funds used to be characterized in particular by low amplitude of fluctuation compared to corporate shares. The high share of fixed tangible assets underlying this fund set-up (being based, as it were, on real estate values) normally ensures a steady flow of income to private and institutional investors that is earned in the form of rental income from the fund properties. Moreover, the share certificate holders participate in the increase of the fund properties' value through their shares. **Low fluctuation of income**

In order to balance regional developments among the investment properties, most funds resort to a broad diversification by region or sector – this being an essential difference compared to REITs, which tend to focus on certain types of usage and regions. The broad diversification of assets practiced by the open-end real estate funds is one of the reasons why past fluctuations in value turned out to be comparatively low. In response to the growing lack of yield prospects in Germany, many fund initiators have begun to expand their portfolios to include international objects. The idea behind this approach is to take advantage of the higher yield prospects on foreign markets.

20 Increasing orientation to foreign markets

In addition to these internationally diversified portfolios, however, some initiators have entered the market who orient their investment strategy exclusively to foreign markets. Another reason suggesting a foreign investment, apart from the higher yield prospects compared to the domestic German market, are the tax breaks beckoning abroad. Rent and leasehold earnings, for instance, that exceed the often generous allowances in the situ countries are frequently not taxed at all in Germany or are subject to minimal taxation compared to domestic tax rates. As the distributed or reinvested income shares are, to a large degree, accounted for by this type of income, the implication for the investor is that a major share of the income accrues income tax-free. Not just open-end real estate funds, but closed-end real estate funds, too, have recognized this advantage and tend to invest abroad. In fact, the tendency has evolved in direct proportion to the ongoing erosion of tax benefits in Germany. **International diversification**

For decades now, the admittedly moderate, yet reliable, risk-return structure has made this product interesting for small-time investors. The investor participates in this investment model on the basis of either a one-time deposit or a savings scheme. Especially in times of falling stock markets and rising interest rates, many investors vest their hopes in this product, trying to maintain their capital value. Academic studies prove that, especially in times of rising interest rates, open-end real estate funds represent a viable alternative because of the low correlation to the bonds market.

21   In the aftermath of open-end fund crisis

Investors withdrew enormous amounts of cash

Despite these undeniable advantages, however, the open-end real estate funds underwent a severe crisis between 2004 and mid 2006. Reports on the so-called Frankfurt real estate scandal shook the faith of investors. Key words, such as tax evasion, embezzlement and graft, were making the rounds in Frankfurt's financial district, eventually reaching the ears of investors, too. As more details on the corruption scandal came to light, a significant number of investors lost their faith in the affected products and decided to pull out, causing enormous cash outflows.

In addition to the cash drains provoked by the reports, shareholders also withdrew their money for three other reasons: For one thing, the yield figures for most funds had dropped below the 3%-mark at the time. Secondly, investors began to focus increasingly on alternative forms of investment. Alternative products were integrated into the investment process in two different ways. The investors transferred their capital between different fund propositions by the same initiators. In this way, billions were siphoned off domestic funds and reinvested in more globally oriented trust funds. A case in point is Deutsche Bank Real Estate – now RREEF, where droves of investors switched from the Germany fund "grundbesitz invest" to the recently launched "grundbesitz global".

A minor group of investors lost their faith in the open-end real estate fund product altogether, and turned to traditional equity and bond values instead. Thus, asset managers were facing accelerating cash outflows, and were forced to divest themselves of assets in order to observe the statutory minimum liquidity limits, and to be able to uphold the legally mandated daily redeemablility of fund shares.

Need for transparency

Arguably, none of this would necessarily have precipitated a crisis if the open-end real estate funds had not neglected to win the confidence of investors, analysts and the media by cultivating a transparent communication in the past. For years, the author suggested that the open-end real estate fund industry set signals that would inspire investor confidence, for instance, by publishing fund market values and rents on the individual object level, and by initiating a critical dialogue with analysts. However, not until the crisis of the years 2004/2005 did the idea that confidence cannot be generated except through transparency become an accepted truth in the industry.

By the end of 2005, the increased redemption requests by investors had placed the asset managers under so much pressure that they were forced to pull the emergency brake. In order to save the special purpose fund of DB Real Estate and KanAm from a total sell-out, these funds fell back on a legal provision permitting them to suspend the redemption of fund shares for a maximum period of one year in an effort to stop the continued capital drain. This in turn triggered a panic reaction among many investors and massive cash outflows even from other investment companies. Following the record year of 2003, when nearly € 24 billion were paid into open-end funds, the year 2005 saw a net cash outflow of € 3.18 billion.

Despite the above-mentioned irregularities in the recent annals of the open-end mutual real estate funds, and the increasing number of new alternative investment products, such as the G-REIT, the crisis on the market for open-end real estate funds seems to have been overcome now. Accordingly, cash outflows clearly levelled out in the course of 2006. Increasingly, open-end real estate funds have reported net cash inflows again. Once the rumours of an imminent depreciation had been silenced, and after many voices, led by the BVI industry interest group, had called for more product transparency, investors began to regain their faith in property funds. In the interest of a long-term stabilization of the investors' faith in this asset class, BVI devised a set of measures that, while subject to some controversy, is by no means ineffective. This catalogue of measures included a general reform of the grace periods for investors, a higher minimum liquidity, and additional measures that were designed to enhance transparency.

New approaches

Always on the lookout for profitable real estate investment opportunities, fund initiators keep pioneering new approaches. Thus, 2005 saw the first investments in markets ignored for the longest times, including Mexico, South Korea and Turkey. Whether the so-called semi-institutional real estate funds, which often set investment thresholds of half a million euros and more, will stand their ground on the market remains to be seen. The question will hinge on the initiators' ability to highlight the unique sales propositions of this investment form. So far, it has been anybody's guess why an investor would want to invest in new funds rather than in the standard open-end retail or institutional funds.

The Morgan Stanley P2 Value open-end fund, launched in late 2005, represented a special innovation in the sense that it differentiated from the start between a core portfolio and a trading portfolio. While the real estate held in the core portfolio is earmarked for ownership periods of more than five years with the priority on the realization of stable rent cash flows, the real estate acquired for the trading portfolio is unlikely to remain in the portfolio for more than five years, but will be sold as soon as a certain appreciation has been realized.

22   New legal parameters

Risk management and stress tests for open-end funds in the future

In December 2007, the new German Investment Act, which means a substantial change in the legal parameters for open-end real estate funds, became effective. Now, open-end real estate funds are allowed to invest another 5% (on top of the 5% equity quota) in foreign and domestic REIT shares. This equals a maximum REIT quota of 10%.

Moreover, if funds decide to redeem the shares only once a month in case that the value of the shares returned exceeds a limit specified in the business terms, they must have mentioned it before in the selfsame business terms. Under this provision, such business terms must stipulate that the shares are redeemed subject to an irrevocable written redemption statement, and subject to a redemption period that must extend over at least one month and over no more than 12 months. Moreover, open-end real estate funds will have to set up a risk management system in the future, and will have to conduct stress tests.

No member of the valuation committee shall actively participate as main expert in the valuation of one and the same asset for more than two years. Henceforth, the appointment of an expert will presuppose that he or she substantiate adequate expertise and a sufficient amount of hands-on experience in regard to the property type to be valuated and to the regional real estate market. Representatives of the capital investment company will no longer be permitted to attend meetings of the valuation committee.

Enhancement of autonomy of the valuation committee

The new provisions will also apply to the valuation of real estate to be acquired. In this context, the law will no longer permit member experts of the valuation committee to handle such a valuation. The idea underlying the new regulation is to enhance the autonomy of the valuation committee, as it will no longer be bound to its previous expert opinion when compiling the periodic re-valuation. The issue of reporting re-measurement gains, a practice subject to frequent criticism, will be defused by requiring capital investments companies to report the purchase price of a given asset in lieu of its market value during the first 12 months following its acquisition. From now on, ancillary acquisition costs will have to be reported separately and to be depreciated in equal annual instalments throughout the time the asset is prospectively held as part of the property trust fund, though for no longer than 10 years.

23   Outlook

Pointing out the USP in the near future

With a view to the coming years, there is reason to expect the investors to keep or even intensify their interest and faith in open-end real estate in proportion to the funds' ability to position themselves as a transparent form of investment marked by stability of value, and to clearly communicate their specific product propositions, such as there are low volatility, stable performance, high liquidity and attractive tax breaks. There is hardly an industry expert and market participant who shares the occasionally articulated fear that open-end real estate funds might be dated now that REITs have been introduced in Germany. For unlike REITs, which are an equity vehicle and will most likely be used predominantly by institutional investors, open-end real estate funds have an established clientele primarily among private investors, most of whom tend to have little affinity for the stock market, at least in Germany. While substitution effects cannot be ruled out altogether, they are not to be expected to transpire on a major scale. It is not least in face of the growing importance of private pension schemes in Germany that open-end real estate funds will most likely continue to play an important, or in fact an increasingly important, role for the asset allocation of private investors.

3 Established REIT structures: the US, the Netherlands, Belgium and Japan

Bernhard Funk

Table of contents

1   Growth of global REIT market

1.1   Overview

Emergence of REITs   During the last decade, a considerable number of countries has introduced Real Estate Investment Trusts (REITs). The acceptance and use of the REIT regime is growing on a global scale. Furthermore, in countries like the United States of America, where REITs have been available for several decades now, the market development has shown that both institutional and private investor's interest has strengthened over the last decade.

Purpose of the chapter   This chapter addresses two aspects:

- It provides an overview about the emerging global trend concerning the introduction and the market growth of REIT regimes as a form of indirect real estate vehicles for institutional and private investors.

- It shows that the set-up and the structure of REIT regimes can vary from country to country. For this purpose, summarized descriptions of several countries' REIT regimes are provided. The descriptions are not considered to be comprehensive, and as fiscal and legal stipulations evolve over time, changes may already be in effect as this handbook is in print. "REIT" is mostly used as a term in an undifferentiated way. However, there are considerable differences in the REIT concept from country to country. These differences can be important: For example, exemption from corporate income tax may exist, or may not. Listing on a public stock exchange may be mandatory or just optional. It is even possible that certain countries may use other terms than "REIT" for what would be perceived as a REIT structure in a general framework of comparing real estate investment vehicles.

Definitions   A number of definitions should help to clarify the basic terms used in analyzing REITs:

Direct vs. indirect ownership   It is helpful to differentiate between direct and indirect real estate ownership. Direct real estate investment is usually understood as directly buying property and receiving rental income from the ownership. Indirect real estate ownership is taking various forms, for instance pooled funds, quoted property companies, etc. Usually, indirect real estate ownership can be listed (for example, REIT stocks) or unlisted (for example, closed-end funds).

Listed real estate ownership does not necessarily need to imply REIT (tax) status. A REIT is basically a fiscal concept, so in essence, listed indirect real estate ownership exists, which is "non-REIT". For example, one of the biggest public listed real estate companies in Germany is IVG Immobilien AG. However, as of 2007, this company has not converted to REIT status, as the German REIT legislation has only been introduced lately. However, the company plans to convert spin-offs to REIT status. In this respect, there are not only REITs, but a global market for real estate securities. The companies may, or may not, choose to elect REIT status. Furthermore, there may be countries, which do not feature REIT legislation, so listed real estate companies in these countries eventually do not feature the REIT status under domestic tax laws.

Furthermore, there are two kinds of REITs, namely public and private REITs. For example, in the United States of America, public REITs are listed companies, which file with the Securities and Exchange Commission (SEC). Private REITs are non-listed companies. To this regard, the private REIT is a structuring vehicle under domestic tax law. A fund sponsor could, for instance, employ a US corporation to hold properties. The corporation would elect REIT status. This company would not be listed on the stock exchange; however, it would be subject to the distribution requirements and to the other stipulations of the REIT legislation, and it would benefit from being exempt from corporate income tax. Not every country's REIT regime features the option to freely choose whether to list the REIT or whether to keep the REIT private. **Public vs. private REIT**

In this chapter, for the analysis of performance figures, it is anticipated that REITs are listed on a stock exchange. Furthermore, also non-REIT publicly listed companies are covered. Eventually, it could be argued that the legal concept is not the main decision making criteria for investors. For the ultimate investor it is more important to participate in an indirect real estate holding vehicle with high liquidity, benefit from the advantages of professional property management, and reap the rewards in the form of cash flows.

1.2   Advantages of investing in REIT vehicles

There are various factors investors deem important when investing in REITs:

Whereas it can take an investor, who invests into direct real estate holdings, several months to close an acquisition or to disinvest, the REIT investor can usually quickly execute sell and buy decisions via the stock exchange. This may also be considered an advantage to more traditional closed-end pooled funds. Consequently, the REIT-stocks' price movements become the dominant gauge for valuation purposes, whereas appraised property values of the portfolio become less important. **Liquidity**

REITs have, on average, demonstrated during the last decade, that they can provide attractive dividend yields between 4 % and 8 %. Real estate portfolios that are well-leased usually generate a constant cash flow stream of rents, which **Above average dividend yields** is relatively easy to predict. In addition, REIT legislation usually commands distribution requirements for companies electing REIT status. However, one caveat should be noted: Whereas the distribution requirement, which usually is an intrinsic part of the REIT regime, may support to boost dividend yields overall, it should also be mentioned that the last decade has been a period of exceptional growth patterns for REITs. Other market circumstances may exist, and the US market has historically shown that there is more than one side to the equation, which implies that strong divided yields are not granted in every phase of the real estate cycle.

Diversification and specialization REITs often have a specific geographical investment focus or a particular property segment focus, as for example office, industrial, retail or apartments. Therefore, a REIT investor or a REIT mutual fund can pick the companies that are deemed the most experienced in a certain business segment and which focus on certain geographical investment regions and/or concentrate on certain property segments. Building a portfolio of REIT securities that, as for the business strategy of the companies in the portfolio, is diversified across regions and property segments, may help to reduce risks, so investors can benefit from diversification effects.

Volatility One would expect that the volatility of REITs is higher than that of direct real estate holdings, as the share prices are influenced by the movements of the general equity markets as well as economic trends and investor sentiment. Hoesli has outlined that also conceptual issues of volatility measurements (appraisal-based versus stock index based measurements) may influence the results of these comparisons [1]. Overall, the past decade – based on empirical data from the US REIT market – has shown that risk-adjusted returns for REITs were on average quite attractive compared to other alternatives including other equities.

Transaction costs The investor will benefit from lower transaction costs for listed REITs than for direct real estate holdings. As the cyclical pace of market movements is also becoming faster in the real estate industry, this factor may become more relevant for investors in the future, as REITs support decision makers to quickly execute allocation shifts between different markets and between different property segments.

Tax efficiency and tax exemptions Taxation is an important component of many REIT regimes. However, it seems that the importance of tax efficiency and tax exemptions in REIT regimes is overestimated when discussing the reasons for the growth of the global REIT market. Liquidity, transparency, as well as superior professional management of real estate portfolios are factors that add value for the investors and contribute to the attractiveness of this indirect investment vehicle.

1.3   Market size

Size of global REIT market The market for global real estate securities has experienced a considerable growth in the past years. The market capitalization of global real estate securities including REIT and non-REIT vehicles was estimated at roughly US$ 900 billion by the end of year 2006 [2].

Between 20 and 30 countries have so far adopted "REIT-style" legislation – the precise number is pending on the narrowness of the working definition of the term "REIT". In relation to the overall universe of real estate investment opportunities, REITs still constitute a relatively small segment: Real estate securities and/or REITs make up approximately 12 % of the global real estate market [2]. Also, it is estimated that only 60 % of indirect listed ownership is actually in REIT format.

Market forces can reverse the trend towards growth of market capitalization of REIT markets. The US has seen considerable merger activities in the 1990s with market capitalization continuing to grow but the actual number of listed companies declining. The latest trend in the US is REIT privatizations, which implies delisting of formerly public quoted companies [3]. The privatization of the formerly biggest US office REIT Equity Office Properties Inc. (ticker symbol "EOP") is just one outstanding example of the current market cycle in the United States [4].

Ranked by total market capitalization, securitized forms of real estate holdings are especially important in the United States of America, in Canada, Australia, several countries in Europe (UK, France, the Netherlands), Japan and in Hong Kong. The US is estimated to make up roughly 50 % of the global market for real estate securities. Figure 1 exhibits the relative weight of global REIT markets ranked by market capitalization:

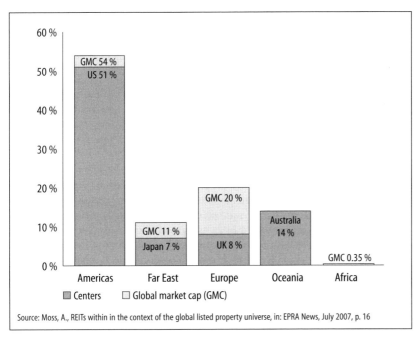

Source: Moss, A., REITs within in the context of the global listed property universe, in: EPRA News, July 2007, p. 16

Fig. 1:　Global REIT markets ranked by relative market capitalization (in % of global market cap)

2   Concepts of REIT regimes

2.1   REITs in the United States of America

The US REIT was created with the enactment of the Real Estate Investment Trust Act in 1960. The main stipulations can be found in sections 856 and 857 of the US Internal Revenue Code.

Evolvement of US REITs
The US REIT legislation was introduced to help smaller investors to participate in real estate and to "pool" investments in commercial real estate. However, in the 1960s, there existed only very few REITs in the US. From the 1960s it took a long time for US REITs to achieve the investor trust and acceptance that is established today. A few highlights from the transformation period 1960 through the early 1990s demonstrate the ups and downs [5]:

The 1970s showed a struggling economy in the US with rising interest rates. Mortgage REITs were hit by higher interest rates, and share prices plummeted. Investor trust for REITs was fading in this market environment. The early 1980s started with very healthy total returns for REITs. Then, the tax incentives for real estate in association with the passing of the Economic Recovery Act triggered a flush of private money into real estate to achieve a tax shelter. This led to overpricing and overbuilding. The Tax Reform Act of 1986 eventually reversed the tax incentives, and hit a cooling real estate market. A severe real estate recession followed, and equity REITs showed negative double-digit annual returns in the year 1990. However, this period turned out to be the basis for a very healthy recovery. Banks tried to sell off real estate portfolios with defaulting loans. REITs took their chances, and acquired quality real estate holdings at reasonable pricing. The early 1990s turned into a period, in which IPOs for equity REITs soared. Equity from IPOs capitalized real estate transactions. Major property operating companies converted to REIT status and went public. 1992 saw the birth of the Umbrella Partnership REIT (UPREIT) with the IPO of Taubman Centers Inc. This new format helped to avoid tax barriers when transferring existing portfolios into a newly formed REIT. As the market grew, more than ever before, investors could choose from a wide range of specialized REITs, with a professional management and successful track record. Public capital markets filled the gap for funding real estate investments, which banks had opened up because of very restrictive lending policies for real estate in the aftermath of the overbuilding crisis. In the 1990s, one could also witness the emergence of institutional acceptance of REITs, which was also supported by legislative changes. The Omnibus Budget and Reconciliation Act of 1993 (OBRA) eased the restriction for pension funds under the five-or-fewer rule. More and more pension funds channelled funds into REITs, and liquidity and diversity of the overall REIT market improved.

Summary
A summary of the US REIT structure is outlined in the following section [6]:

The US REIT can be any US entity which is taxable as a domestic corporation under US law ("check the box" election). It could be a corporation, partnership, business trust, or limited liability company (LLC). The entity must be managed by one or more trustees or directors.

Shares must be transferable. The US REIT stipulations require a minimum of 100 direct shareholders. Nowadays, service companies exist, which will provide to companies forming a US REIT for a fee the necessary additional shareholders necessary to satisfy this requirement. No more than 50 % of the shares may be held directly or indirectly by five or fewer individuals during the last half of the taxable year. Pension funds get the advantage of a special "look-through rule" under OBRA (see paragraph above). **Shareholdings**

Unlike many other REIT regimes, the US model allows both public (listed) and private (non-listed) REITs. Private REITs are greater in number, but smaller in size than listed vehicles. Thus by capitalization, public US REITs remain the most important segment. **Listing**

There is no legislative restriction on leverage. However, the distribution requirement must be met, which may prevent excessive leverage. Equity US REITs are on average only leveraged 40 % to 50 %. This has two major reasons: First, both equity analysts and investors have not rewarded REITs using leverage above market averages as reflected by their assessment of share prices. Second, rating agencies tend to express concern or criticism when REITs use above average leverage. As REITs are tapping the public debt markets, the ratings are an important factor in day-to-day financial US REIT balance sheet management. **Gearing**

At least 75 % of total assets must be invested in real estate, cash or government bonds. Real estate can also take the form of obligations secured by mortgages, a factor that helped to bring into existence so-called "mortgage REITs". At least 75 % of gross income must come from real estate-related income such as rents from real property and interest obligations secured by mortgages on real property. Additionally, at least 95 % of gross income must come from the above listed sources (plus certain passive sources such as dividends). A Taxable REIT Subsidiary (TRS) is an entity that is allowed to receive income from non-qualifying sources. No more than 20 % of the US REITs assets may be comprised of Taxable REIT Subsidiaries as gauged by the value of the TRS stocks. The US REIT may also invest outside the domestic US territory. **Asset and income tests**

At least 90 % of its ordinary taxable income must be distributed in the form of dividends. There is no distribution requirement for capital gains. However, a corporate income tax would be due on gains which are retained. **Distributions**

Dividends are deductible from US REITs' taxable income. For retained income, ordinary corporate income tax is due after certain tax depreciation deductions. Dividends from ordinary income are generally taxed as ordinary dividends. Income from a TRS is subject to corporate income tax. Retained capital gains are taxed as outlined before. US REITs classified as "dealing" (in contrast to "investing") are subject to 100 % excise tax on dealer sales, unless they adhere to a set of tests called "safe harbor rules". **Taxation**

Assets involved in the conversion to US REIT status are subject to corporate tax on the "built-in-gain". This is due if the company sells the assets within 10 years; it is, however, avoided, if the US REIT holds the property for at least 10 years and triggers no taxable event. All the accumulated earnings and profits generated before the entity becomes a US REIT must be distributed to **REIT transition** the shareholders no later than at the end of the US REIT's first taxable year. When bringing portfolios into an UPREIT structure, taxes can be deferred, which is a major reason why UPREITs play a major role in the formation period of new US REITs.

2.2   REITs in the Netherlands

For practical purposes of this section, the Dutch REIT is referred to as "FBI". The native name as used in Dutch legislation is "Fiscal Investment Institution" (FBI = Fiscale Beleggingsinstelling). The Netherlands is by area size a small country. Still, Dutch pension funds played an important role early on in building up global real estate allocations and were first movers in tapping the investment potential of US REITs.

Legal structure   The FBI – a pure tax regime – is one of the oldest REIT regimes worldwide and was established with its introduction in the Corporate Income Tax Act in 1969. The establishment of the FBI requires an advance ruling, which may take about two months. The FBI may elect the legal form of a Dutch public limited company (NV), a private limited liability company (BV), a mutual fund (FGR), or a comparable foreign legal entity. The minimum capital requirements are governed by the stipulations for aforementioned Dutch legal entities. The following summary gives a snapshot of the FBI structure [7]:

Shareholdings   If the FBI is listed or licensed, then a single taxable corporate investor (or group) may not hold more than 45% interest in an FBI. Individuals may not own an interest of more than 25%. If the FBI is not listed or licensed, then 75% or more of the shares must be held by individual shareholders or tax-exempt corporate investors. Furthermore, single individuals may not own a participation of more than 5%.

Listing   Both listed and non-listed vehicles can qualify for the FBI, so listing essentially is optional.

Gearing   Leverage is limited to 60% of the fiscal book value of directly held real estate and up to 20% of the fiscal book value of all other investments. In the FBI market, the actual leverage tends to be on average about 40% to 45%.

Distributions   There is a notable 100% distribution requirement on the taxable profit: By principle, the FBI is required to distribute all net current income within eight months from the end of the fiscal year. The balance from capital gains and capital losses can be credited to a special "reinvestment reserve". Capital gains or losses from dispositions are allocated to a tax free reserve and do not form part of the taxable profit/distribution obligation.

Asset and income tests   The exclusive activity of the FBI must be the passive investment into real estate. It can also invest outside the Netherlands. New legislation allows the FBI to be involved in real estate development activities through a fully owned, taxable subsidiary, which is exclusively providing services to the FBI. In this case, a restricting cap on development activities applies ("safe harbor rules").

Taxation   The FBI is neither a tax-transparent nor a tax-exempt entity. Its current income is subject to Dutch corporate income tax at a rate of 0%. As for capital gains tax, capital gains can be allocated to a tax-free capital gain reserve and will then be exempt from tax. However, remaining taxable income falls under the 100 % distribution requirement.

The Dutch stipulations require a step-up of all assets and liabilities to market value at the end of the year prior to the year the entity is converted into an FBI. The capital gain by stepping up is subject to corporate income tax at the normal rate. In contrast to the German REIT legislation, Dutch legislation does not feature special incentives in terms of favorable exit tax clauses.

REIT transition

2.3   REITs in Belgium

The structure Société d'Investissement à Capital Fixe en Immobilière (SICAFI) was established in 1995 and is for purposes of this section defined as Belgium REIT. The Belgium REIT is governed by regulatory laws and tax laws, and is supervised by the Belgian Banking and Finance Commission. The SICAFI is a limited liability company (Société Anonyme) or a limited partnership with shares under Belgian law (Société en Commandite par Actions). The companies' management must be located in Belgium. The minimum share capital is € 1.25 million.

The following summary gives a snapshot of the SICAFI structure [8]:

There are no major restrictions or requirements governing shareholders.

Shareholdings

A listing on a Belgium stock exchange is mandatory and prerequisite for receiving SICAFI status. With the Initial Public Offering, the company must include a 30 % public offering within one year from registration.

Listing

The maximum leverage is 65 % of the Belgium REITs assets at the time the loan agreement is concluded. Annual interest on the loans may not exceed 80 % of the total annual profits. The actual average leverage in the market for Belgium REITs is quite low in a range of about 34 % to 38 %.

Gearing

The main activity must be passive investments in real estate, id est immovable property. Non-real estate assets are only permitted provided the investment is temporary or secondary. A maximum of 20 % of the SICAFI's assets may be invested in one property. Developments are permitted, but have to be held in the portfolio five years upon completion before they can be sold. The SICAFI is free to invest outside Belgium.

Asset and income tests

The SICAFI must distribute 80 % of the net profit in form of dividends annually. Realized capital gains remain tax-free and are not considered under the aforementioned distribution obligation, provided that the capital gains are reinvested within four years.

Distributions

The SICAFI is subject to a 33.99 % corporate income tax, but the qualifying rental income and other business income is excluded from the taxable basis. In effect, this may result in a taxable base of zero. Income that is not received at arm's length is however taxable. For instance, this could be rental income that is excessively above market. If capital gains are received at arm's length, then they are tax-exempt from corporate income tax as well.

Taxation

In transition, the election of SICAFI requires to value properties at market value. All unrealized capital gains in REIT transition are taxed at a reduced

Exit tax

corporate tax rate at roundabout 17 % upon conversion to SICAFI status. Cash contributions are subject to 0 % capital duty. Also, a real property transfer tax may be levied.

2.4   REITs in Japan

An example of an Asian REIT regime is included in this chapter, as the Japanese REIT is a prototype of an externally managed REIT structure. The Japanese REIT regime, denoted as "J-REIT", was enacted in 2000. The J-REIT is governed by the Investment Trust and Investment Corporation Law. In addition, there are self regulating rules established by the Investment Trust Association. Set-up of the entity takes time, as several licenses have to be obtained and approvals have to be granted before the J-REIT can start operations. The J-REIT is an investment trust or an investment corporation ("toshi hojin"). In practice, the listed J-REITs up-to-date are in effect corporations. The minimum capitalization for the investment corporation is ¥ 100 million.

It is notable that the J-REIT is a structure which solely constitutes a conduit vehicle. This implies that external management is mandatory. The J-REIT has to outsource asset management and administrative functions, and is not allowed to hire employees. As this is a special feature of J-REIT, the following illustration visualizes the structure of J-REITs (see figure 2):

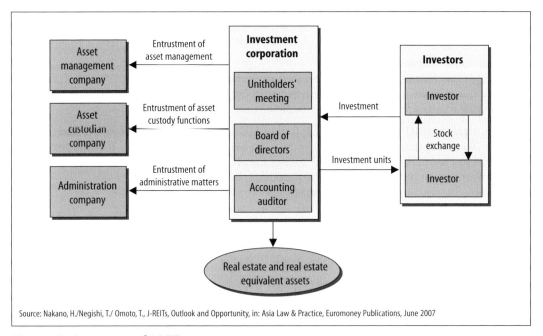

Source: Nakano, H./Negishi, T./ Omoto, T., J-REITs, Outlook and Opportunity, in: Asia Law & Practice, Euromoney Publications, June 2007

Fig. 2:   Basic structure of J-REITs

The following summary gives a snapshot of the J-REIT structure [9]:

The Investment Trust Law does not stipulate restrictions. However, if the J-REIT applies for the deduction of dividends and plans to be listed on the Tokyo Stock Exchange, this requires that various conditions are met. These include: The number of shareholders must exceed 1,000. The three largest unit holders must not collectively hold more than 50 % of the outstanding units of the J-REIT.

Shareholdings

There is the option to list on a Japanese Stock Exchange, which implies that a private J-REIT is also feasible. For listing at the Tokyo Stock Exchange, there are several conditions, including that at least 70 % of assets must be invested in real estate or trust beneficiary rights, and a minimum of 95 % of total managed assets is either real estate, trust beneficiary rights regarding real estate, real estate-related assets or liquidated assets. The listing requirements in effect also restrict the J-REIT from investing in real estate outside Japan. More flexibility on handling this restriction may come up in the near future.

Listing

There is no limit on leverage. However, the J-REIT must only borrow from qualified financial institutions to be eligible for tax deduction of dividends. The specifics are outlined in the Japanese Securities and Exchange Law. In practise, leverage is on average in the range from 35 % to 40 %.

Gearing

The J-REIT is only a conduit in the form of an asset-holding vehicle. The J-REIT must only invest in "qualified assets", including real estate and leasehold rights in real estate. The J-REIT cannot hold 50 % or more of the total voting shares of another corporation governed by the Investment Trust and Investment Corporation Law. See also details for J-REIT above.

Asset and income tests

The J-REIT must distribute more than 90 % of distributable income as defined by applicable ordinances to investors in order to qualify for tax deductions. The distribution requirement also applies to capital gains, which implies that capital gain is part of aforementioned definition of distributable income.

Distributions

The J-REIT as a corporation is subject to corporate income tax at a rate of 42 %. If the J-REIT meets all requirements, then it is entitled to deduct dividend distributions from its taxable income. Capital gains are taxed in the same way as ordinary income. Acquisition tax, registration tax, and various surtaxes may be levied with reduced rates. As outlined before, dividends are deductible with a minimum payout of over 90 %. Meeting a list of requirements and distributing full income to shareholders may result in effectively avoiding double taxation.

Taxation

Unlike other country REIT regimes covered in this book, the J-REIT regime does not include notable special provisions that apply when converting into J-REIT status.

REIT transition

3   European REIT market outlook

Future of the
European
REIT market

The five year annualized return for European property company securities as gauged by the EPRA Europe total return index stood at 20.5 % as of October 2007 [10]. At 40 % weight, Britain has the biggest index weight. France contributes 16 %, and numerous other European countries contribute 5 % or less to the index. As European REIT markets are just evolving, major shifts in these weights can be expected. Cooling equity markets in 2007 hit expected REIT-IPO-activity in a number of European countries. However, the medium and long-term growth prospects for capitalization of European REIT markets should be positive for this very fresh segment of the capital markets. For REIT analysts, rating agencies and industry groups, the challenge of the future is to establish comparable and standardized tools for analysing REIT securities that have been set-up in different country jurisdictions across the globe.

With more REIT regimes coming into existence, it would be interesting to consider the future of this market for indirect real estate vehicles. Italy is just another European country which will introduce a REIT regime in the near future. In Europe, first thoughts have been given to a pan-European REIT structure. However, this harmonization under the umbrella of EU laws is far from implementation at present, as European countries have the privilege to individually implement their tax legislations. Therefore, for the time being, a competition of European domestic REIT regimes to attract global investors is on the horizon. Furthermore, it can be anticipated, that REIT regimes will prevail and dominate in Europe, which feature the following preconditions:

- The REIT regime is by structure attractive especially for institutional investors. Historic evolvement of US REITs has shown that institutional investors are the first wave to accept widespread investments in REIT vehicles. Private investors will follow-up as market size and liquidity are growing, and if trust into the market participants in the equity markets has been established over several market cycles.

- Countries with REIT regimes, which operate in strong and efficient financial markets, will be at the forefront. Financial hubs like Frankfurt or London, where IPOs can easily be marketed to investors, will have an advantage, provided that the domestic REIT regime is attractive to domestic and international investors.

- Countries with larger commercial property markets like the United Kingdom or Germany may find it easier to attract non-domestic institutional investors. However, as the example of Luxembourg demonstrates with regards to fund vehicles (e. g., FCPs and SICAVs), not in all cases is a significant domestic commercial real estate market a precondition to attract foreign investors. A competitive edge can also be achieved by a competitive regulatory framework.

It may be concluded, that in the future we will see a trend towards a floating of REITs, which are legally set-up in one European country, but channel investments into European countries other than their domicile of residence. Drawing on the experience from the US markets, the development of REIT markets takes time, and even may take decades. However, as the impressive emergence of the Japanese REIT market in a time span of only five years shows, today's growth patterns can be more dynamic than what historically seemed to set the norm drawing on patterns in the US since 1960. This also implies that competitive shifts between various REIT markets on the global scale could materialize fast. The liquidity of the REIT vehicle will help to push the ongoing trend towards global real estate allocation of institutional investors. It will also help to trigger fast reallocations by investors: reallocations by investment region, by vehicle and by property focus.

This may bring dynamics into the transition of European real estate markets at formerly unseen pace.

4 Bibliography

[1] Hoesli, M. et al., The role of property in mixed asset portfolios, RICS and PERFRN, 2002.

[2] Chin, H. et al., Global Real Estate Securities, RREEF Research, January 2007, pp. 4, 9.

[3] Metzler North America, US-Outlook, 3rd Quarter 2007.

[4] Funk, B., Go Private – US REITs, in: Immobilien-Manager, March 2007.

[5] Block, R. L., The essential REIT, San Francisco 1997.

[6] The summary has been comprised by using the following sources: EPRA Global REIT Survey: A comparison of the major REIT regimes in the world, August 2007. KPMG: Taxation of Real Estate Investment Trusts: An Overview of the REIT regimes in Europe, Asia, the United States, and Canada, March 2007.

[7] The summary has been comprised by using sources [6] and: Clifford Chance, Global REIT Newsletter, July 2007.

[8] The summary has been comprised by using sources [6].

[9] The summary has been comprised by using sources [6] and Nakano, Harume, Negishi, Takehiko, Omoto, Taro: J-REITs, Outlook and Opportunity, in: Asia Law & Practice, Euromoney Publications, June 2007.

[10] FTSE EPRA/NAREIT: EPRA Europe total return data series as of June 30th, 2007. FTSE EPRA/NAREIT Global Real Estate Index, October 2007.

4   Recent REIT structures in Europe: France, Germany and the UK

Stefan Leibold
Patrick Nass

Table of contents

1   The rise of REITs in Europe

French aspiration, euro and globalization

The success of REIT structures in Europe started in 2002 and can be explained with the following reasons.

First, the aspirations of French real estate professionals drew attention to the new investment vehicle. The French intentions to introduce REITs were disclosed in October 2002, during a bearish state of the stock market that turned out to be amenable to adopt the REIT structure.

During the technology bubble in 1999, figures, such as dividend yield, fixed assets and profits, were of minor importance. However, in 2003 real estate investments were favored by investors because of their low correlation to the stock market.

Second, the creation of the euro currency was an important step towards greater interest for REITs from investors, who intend to build up a well-diversified pan-European real estate portfolio.

Third, global investors advocated the creation of an investment vehicle structure that suited the demands of the capital market.

2 Motives for introducing a REIT

2.1 Efficiency

The main goal of the introduction of a REIT is the creation of a liquid and transparent vehicle for investments in real estate.

Currently, many non-property companies hold large assets in property, composed of property required for operations and property deemed not necessary for use in the business. The return in the core business of those companies is in most cases higher than that from property operations. The reasons for this imbalance are a lack of expertise and missing economies of scale when managing the property portfolios. By transferring real estate assets of non-property companies into REITs, efficiency gains can be achieved by a more professional facility management and a restructuring of real estate portfolios. Additionally, the companies can use the proceeds of the REIT-IPOs for further investments into their core activities or to improve their equity ratio through debt redemption. In the past, the transfer of enterprise-owned property often failed because of an unattractive regulatory environment and unfavorable business conditions, such as high taxation of disclosed hidden reserves, an acquisition tax on real estate and discounts to net asset value.

Non-property companies

Equally, public authorities get an attractive vehicle to dispose some of their real estate portfolios. The additional revenues may be used for increasing efficiency through budget balancing (or at least for reducing new indebtedness), tax cuts or future-oriented public investments in education and infrastructure.

Public authorities

2.2 Tax revenues

From a fiscal point of view, the introduction of the REIT structure offers – at least in the first years – the prospect of higher tax revenues. Under fiscal law, properties are valued at acquisition costs less accumulated depreciation, which in most cases are clearly below the current market value. In case of a conversion into a REIT, the hidden reserves are disclosed and are subject to taxation. Therefore, the disclosure of hidden reserves means considerably higher tax revenues in the first years after the REIT introduction. In order to create an incentive for the adoption of the REIT structure, there is generally a reduced tax rate applied.

Disclosure of hidden reserves

In the long run, tax incentives may lead to reduced tax revenues from the disclosure of hidden reserves. But it is to be considered that the hidden reserves may otherwise continue to exist for decades or may be transferred to new buildings using special tax regulations (e. g., § 6 of the German Income Tax Act), resulting in a high uncertainty about the time of future tax inflows. As the attention of governments is mainly focused on short-term tax revenues rather

Tax incentives

than on tax revenues in the following decades, the fear of long-run tax deficits is not a strong political argument against the introduction of REITs anyway.

Long-term tax revenues

Furthermore, the introduction of the REIT structure also has positive effects on tax revenues in the long run. The freed-up capital and improved profitability, achieved by an efficient facility management, may lead to more investment by companies.

2.3   Competition for international investors among European financial centers

REIT structure as internationally recognized vehicle

Many international investors ask for a transparent, liquid, and tax-efficient possibility for indirect real estate investments. The REIT structure, recognized as an international and successful investment model, is particularly suited for such investments. Without the creation of the demanded structures, many foreign investors would not invest domestically, but limit their investments to countries that offer more attractive investment opportunities. Consequently, domestically invested capital would be withdrawn and no new foreign capital would be invested domestically. Therefore, the spectrum of international investors will be reduced to short-term oriented private equity funds.

If competitive investment vehicles do not exist in an economy, many real estate portfolios will be listed in other economies and on different stock exchanges, using models that are more tax-efficient and more transparent. This leads to a long-term weakening of those financial centers, as many related jobs in the areas of investment banking and financial engineering would then be transferred to other international financial centers. The banking sector takes the risk of being limited in their real estate functions to sales and marketing.

3   Structuring a REIT

3.1   Leverage

The acquisition of debt capital by a corporation is usually not restricted by legal or supervisory regulations. Instead, it is assumed that the capital market itself can efficiently regulate the leverage used by corporations.

Creditor protection

On the other hand, arguments are raised about why a REIT – in contrast to a "normal" corporation – requires an upper limit for the usage of debt capital. The first argument is based on the principle of creditor protection, for which capital maintenance plays an important role. This principle is, for example, predominant in the German commercial law. The specific characteristic of a REIT to be obliged to distribute the major part of its profit, limits the possibility to accumulate capital reserves in successful business years. Hence, a high share of debt capital is a significant danger for a REIT in recession years when payments of all interests are hindered. Thus, it can be argued that the REIT-specific rules for the distribution of profits additionally require specific regulations for financing a REIT. Furthermore, it is argued that since a REIT is a vehicle for indirect investments in existing property, a high leverage would lead to a more speculative character of the investment vehicle.

A further motive for leverage limitations is the apprehension that through high interest payments the basis for the profit distribution assessment – which actually serves in case of a REIT also as the basis for taxation – will be reduced considerably, eventually causing a lower tax revenue.

Tax revenue

One counter-argument is the fact that the capital market knows the REIT-specific characteristics. This enables the involved parties to assess for themselves the impact of the financial structure on the distribution amount and the risk of insolvency.

Self-regulation

Moreover, through the distribution obligation of a REIT, the possibility of internal financing does actually not exist. A limitation of debt financing reduces the financing options even further – especially under market conditions that impede increases in share capital. This may result in financial difficulties or could make the realization of profitable projects impossible. The latter will structurally reduce the profit potential – and thus the basis of tax revenue – which in the intermediate-term is counterproductive to the fiscal aim. Moreover, such a regulation reduces the incentive to adopt the REIT status, as many corporations are not in a position to fulfill the required equity ratio or fear, when acquiring real estate portfolios, to have a competitive disadvantage towards non-REIT entities like private equity funds which are able to pay higher prices because of their higher leverage.

Funding difficulties

3.2   Restrictions on shareholdings

Legal restrictions concerning the shareholder structure of the REIT can exist for two different reasons. First, minimum requirements concerning the free float of shares may be introduced to prevent the existence of "private REITs" like they exist in the Netherlands or the US. These non-listed REITs with a limited number of institutional investors would contradict the goals of a more liquid and transparent property market. Second, for the purpose of securing the national tax revenue, the portion of shares held by a single shareholder can be limited.

Private REIT

The reason is the privileged treatment of dividends in the existing double tax agreements. If a foreign company participates in a national company with 10 %, 15 % or 25 % – depending on the details of the double tax agreement – only 5 %, in some cases even 0 %, of the gross dividends are taxed according to Parent Subsidiary Directive. The fact that dividends are the only basis for taxation in the case of REITs means a considerable loss in tax revenue.

Double tax agreements

3.3   Dividend payments

Since REITs are tax-exempt, the major part of the operative income must be distributed among the owners. The distribution quota varies between 80 % and 100 % depending on the legal regulations of each country. From a fiscal point of view, a high distribution quota is to be preferred as the undistributed part of the REIT income is not taxed.

Distribution quota

Distribution and taxation of the accumulated income is deferred for an indefinite time. On the other hand, it makes sense to leave part of the profit within the corporations to secure a certain level of financial flexibility. Most of the operative income derives from rental income. Capital gains arising from the disposal of investment property may – partly or completely – be excluded from the distributable income in order to increase the financial flexibility for the acquisition of new property.

3.4   Restrictions on investment activities

Core business The business activities of a REIT can be limited in several areas. Since REITs have been designed as passive investment vehicles for real estate, often minimum quotas are laid down for the property share of the total assets as well as for the share of the core business income in relationship to the total revenue. In this context it must be decided whether the rental income proceeds from building sales and sale-and-lease-back transactions are also part of the core business income. Other business activities, such as property development, facility management and consultancy, can, if at all, only be provided in a limited way by enterprises which have the REIT status. Moreover, the turnover frequency of the real estate portfolio can be limited to ensure the character of a passive investment vehicle.

Regional limitations Regional limitations of the investment activities can arise when the REIT legislation prohibits or limits the acquisition of foreign property or treats such property fiscally unfavorable compared to domestic property. The latter can be the case, for example, if taxes that had to be paid in a foreign country cannot be deducted by shareholders from the taxes they have to pay on their dividends.

Sectoral limitations In addition, sectoral limitations can be defined for REITs to exclude investments in particular segments of the real estate market, for example, in residential property. Such a regulation is usually politically motivated and commercially difficult to justify. Through such measures, the attractiveness of the REIT model compared to other investment vehicles will be reduced without being guaranteed that the actual political aim will be achieved. Domestic real estate portfolios can also go public through REIT-like structures at foreign stock exchanges, which are no decisive disadvantage from an investors' point of view, but for the pertinent country it means loss of efficiency, lower tax revenue, and reduced competitiveness.

3.5   Fiscal incentives to adopt a REIT structure

Hidden reserves Tax exemption on the corporate level and the related high dividends are an attractive alternative for corporations and investors. However, as the REIT status requires the disclosure of hidden reserves from real estate assets, this alternative may be unattractive for many corporations because of the resulting high tax burden, even if the loss carried forward can be offset. To avoid a failure of this new investment form, it is – in most cases – possible to place real estate assets in a REIT by taking advantage of tax concessions for which different alternatives are offered.

Entry charge versus exit tax In alternative one, the taxation is based on the disclosed hidden reserves, using a reduced tax rate. The tax burden resulting from such an exit tax depends on the actually existing hidden reserves of each single property.

In alternative two, the complete real property transferred into a REIT is charged with a one-time tax (entry charge). This tax is based on the current market value of each single property and does not take into account any hidden reserves at the time of the conversion into the REIT status.

Depending on the exact objective, the incentives can be subject to some constraints through holding periods. If the main objective is the mobilization of company owned real estate, but to exclude, for speculative reasons recently acquired, properties from the tax concessions, a minimum holding period can be requested before a transfer into a REIT is possible. A minimum holding period after the transfer is justified with the objective to use the REIT as an investment vehicle for the existing properties, and thus to prevent a – possibly speculative – high trading frequency. A further implementation detail is the distribution of tax payments over time. After the immediate payment in the first year, the tax burden can be – to avoid problems in liquidity for the enterprises – distributed over several years.

Minimum holding periods

4 REITs in Germany

4.1 Motives for introduction

While the predominant driver of the REIT introduction in France was the establishment of tax payments for mobilizing corporate real estate assets, in Germany the introduction of REITs was lagged by the fear of melting tax revenues. Since the German real estate market is the largest in Europe, the law was finally established by the force of real estate and investment lobbies. The discussion was heavily influenced by the great investment activities of foreign institutional investors who acquired large stakes in German residential real estate companies, especially those in public ownership.

Fear of melting tax revenues

People feared that residential tenants would suffer because of pressure on earnings a REIT would receive by the capital markets. In the end this forced the politics to exclude residential real estate from REIT status. The German parliament enacted the law on March 31st, 2007 with retrospective effect from January 1st, 2007.

4.2 Ways of structuring a REIT

It turned out that the first release of the French SIIC contained loopholes in taxation. This is why the German REIT has been designed very strictly regarding these problems. Main topics to be pointed out are especially minimum share capital, minimum free float, maximum leverage level, minimum distribution of earnings, shareholding restrictions and the specialties about taxation in combination with the interstate double tax treaties.

Legal requirements

The German REIT Act requires a joint stock company, who is tradable by means of the German stock trade law. The company must have a registered office and the actual seat of management in Germany.

Share capital

The nominal share capital has to be at least € 15 million.

Shareholder diversification

At least 25 % of its shares must be widely held, where no one shareholder holds 3 % or more of the shares, at the time of stock exchange registration. Furthermore, there must be a permanent free float of 15 %, which has to be assured towards the financial supervisory agency on December 31ˢᵗ annually.

In adjustment to the double taxation agreement, the single investor's direct stake shall not exceed 10 %. If the investor exceeds the 10 % by adding indirect holdings, his rights will still be limited to 10 %.

Earning and income structure

The assets of the company must consist at least of 75 % of real property. The assets derived from REIT service companies must not exceed 20 %.

As well as to the asset relation, there will be the same regulations to revenue requirements, which must at least be 75 % from rental income, leasing and capital gains and must not exceed 20 % from revenue from REIT service companies.

As the legislator's intent is not to create a property trading company, the revenue of property disposal must not exceed 50 % of the average property portfolio within five years. REIT service companies must be 100%-subsidiaries of the REIT and are regular taxable.

Sectoral activities allowed

All tangible assets, real estate and property are basically intended to be part of the portfolio. A great exemption are the German residential properties as already stated at the beginning. Buildings constructed after January 1ˢᵗ, 2007 or if their residential area does not exceed 50 % of the total area are allowed to be acquired to a REIT portfolio.

Technically, there would be the chance of acquiring foreign residential properties, which nevertheless lacks in attractiveness because of a possible double taxation.

Leverage level

Because the definition of outside capital is very controversial, the German legislator defined the leverage limitations by limiting the minimum shareholders' equity. The equity value may not undercut the tangible assets by 45 %.

Distribution of operative income

90 % of distributable income calculated according to the German accounting principles is to be distributed. This value can be reduced by half of the capital gains if set up in reserves.

Distribution of capital gains on disposed investments

Capital gains are as in most REIT structures treated differently from general rental income. 50 % of capital gains must be included in distributable income.

The remaining 50 % can be reinvested immediately or kept as reserve for two years.

Withholding tax/distribution taxation

25 % dividend withholding tax plus solidarity surcharge whereon 1.375 % will be charged at the distribution of dividends.

Conversion into REIT status

The most important topic is primarily the legal form of a joint stock company (Aktiengesellschaft). As this approbation already takes time, existing real estate stock companies and shell companies will be the first aspirants for the REIT status. Requirements to the business model are, of course, the topics discussed earlier in this section. To ensure going early into operation, the aspiring REIT companies can get a pre-REIT status, which is not tax-exempt but benefits from the exit tax rule, which will be addressed later.

Double taxation problem

The double taxation agreements have always played a very big role in the discussion about REITs in Germany. The opponents argued that if the distributed dividends will be treated like general income from capital, it will come to reduced tax revenue regarding the affiliation privilege or Parent Subsidiary Directive. Shareholders with stakes greater than 10 % would be treated with discounts in withholding tax.

In order to avoid this, legislation forbids stakes equal and larger than 10 % through direct holdings. Including indirect holdings the limit of 10 % may be exceeded, with the constraint of just being able to execute rights below the 10 %. Although this may conflict with the basic principle of free capital flows within the European Union, it is the only way to establish a near-term investment vehicle without suffering from tax deficits.

A second problem that will come up is the double taxation itself. Properties held in certain European countries, e.g., France, will be taxed in France according to the location principle (Belegenheitsprinzip) and the shareholder will be charged again on his distribution. This puts foreign real estate to a fiscal disadvantage and lets German REITs become national investments which are hindered to diversify reasonably on a European basis. A possible answer to this problem might be an investment into foreign REITs themselves and avoid the foreign taxation through the REITs tax exemption.

4.3 Fiscal incentive to adopt a REIT structure

General tax exemption

The main advantage of a REIT structure is the general tax exemption on the corporate level. If the formal requirements concerning earnings, income and asset relations, which have been discussed earlier, are considered, then all rental income, leasing and capital gains are exempted from tax by the German law. This is especially attractive for investors, who are privileged in taxation as, for example, pension funds or non-profit organizations.

Exit tax incentives

The REIT Act contains benefits for the mobilization and the amortization of hidden reserves. If the corporate assets are sold to a REIT or pre-REIT company, real estate capital gains are tax-exempted to 50%. This incentive will only be applicable for transactions within the period from January 1st, 2007 until December 31st, 2009. In order to be able to benefit from the exit tax relief, the properties must have been a capital asset in the selling company for at least five years until January 1st, 2007. Companies applying for a change into REIT status can even benefit from real estate assets that have been acquired before January 1st, 2005.

4.4   Outlook

Exclusion of residential property

As indicated earlier, the exclusion of residential real estate was politically driven. There is no similar restriction in any other established REIT. Research has shown that residential property has never played a very significant role in REIT portfolios. For example in the US, where the REIT was established in 1960, only 17% of the REITs concentrate on residential properties, although they represent half of the national assets. It can therefore be argued whether the exclusion of residential properties from the REIT is reasonable.

Adjustment to the double taxation agreement/shareholder diversification

The requirements for a diversified shareholder structure are not a necessity in itself for a successful REIT structure. They are rather the consequence of the difficulties to quickly change existing double taxation treaties.

In order to provide a quick introduction of the German REIT, it was an easy and wise decision to avoid losses in tax revenues by the limitations and still keep up with the European REIT development. But in the long run, there will probably be adjustments in the double tax treaties. Furthermore, in acclamation to free capital flows, the restrictions in shareholder structure shall be abolished.

The incorporation of the REIT

The restriction to grant REIT status exclusively for companies that have their headquarters in Germany is likely to become a controversial subject, since opponents might argue that the free choice of location may be violated.

5   REITs in France (SIIC)

Pros and cons of early SIIC introduction

The French REIT (SIIC – Société d'investissement immobilière cotées) basically was the pioneer in the European REIT development, although it was poorly conceived in the beginning. Fortunately, the French legislation reacted and presented the fourth amendment of the SIIC (SIIC 4) in 2007. On the one hand, the French paid the apprenticeship premium for being early and for missing details, on the other hand France took great benefits and attracted real estate investments, which is indicated by the ballooning market capitalization of the EPRA/NAREIT France TR Index which has increased by almost 300% since

2003. The market capitalization of the currently 33 listed SIICs is € 42 billion, representing 23 % of the European listed property sector.

5.1   Motives for introduction

Although there had already been REITs established in the Netherlands in 1969 and in Belgium in 1995, France had a big impact on the debate about REITs especially in Germany and the UK.

In France, the industry was able to convince the Ministry of Finance that with the introduction of a REIT regime, it would actually generate a greater tax income. By giving a tax incentive on capital gains from hidden assets, companies would finally be willing to realize their hidden capital gains.

5.2   Ways of structuring a REIT

Legal requirements

In order to be able to obtain REIT status, a company must be listed on a French stock exchange and must be subject to French corporate income tax, which does not exclude foreign companies. Corporate purpose must be the acquisition or construction of real estate for investment purpose or the indirect or direct holding of shares of similar companies. The legal form can either be a joint stock company (SA) or a limited partnership (SCA).

Share capital

The nominal share capital has to be at least € 15 million.

Requirement of shareholder diversification

There is no restriction on ownership of SIIC shares for SIICs founded between January 1st, 2007 and January 1st, 2009. This created problems because of double taxation treaties and their advantages to larger shareholders. Legislation addressed these problems in the fourth amendment of the SIIC (SIIC 4). From January 1st, 2007 on, the voting rights of a shareholder or a group of shareholders owning a SIIC which is founded after this date are limited to 60 % of the share capital of that company. The second requirement is a minimum free float of 15 %, which means that a single investor out of the 15 % is not allowed to own directly or indirectly 2 % or more of the share capital. The SIIC regime can also be adapted if a company is jointly held by several SIIC companies.

Requirements to earning and income structure

The SIIC is supposed to have its main activity in (passive) real estate investment. Financial leasing may not exceed 50 % of the company's gross assets. Additional business has to be below 20 % of the company's gross assets. Furthermore, additional activities must not exceed 20 % of the total assets.

Sectoral activities allowed

In general, the corporate purpose of a SIIC is predominantly supposed to be the acquisition or the construction of rentable real estate and direct or indirect holdings of stakes in companies that have the same corporate purpose. French law does not restrict the property categories in which the company can invest. The third amendment of the SIIC (SIIC 3) even includes tax incentives for the outsourcing of buildings that are used as hotels, cafes and restaurants.

Leverage level

The SIIC actually does not require a limitation of leverage.

Distribution of operative income

The SIIC is legally forced to distribute 85 % of its tax-exempted profits, which are derived directly or indirectly from rental income and realized capital gains under certain circumstances. Dividends received by a subsidiary which has chosen the SIIC status also have to be distributed completely to the outside shareholders.

Distribution of capital gains on disposed investments

Capital gains, as in most REIT structures, are treated differently from general rental income. The SIIC must distribute 50 % of the income deriving from capital gains, real estate, real estate shares or shares in a corporate subsidiary, which is itself exempted under the SIIC regime, and from the transfer of rights in financial leases.

Withholding tax/distribution taxation

Dividends are, in general, subject to a withholding tax of 25 %. With the fourth amendment, the SIIC now has to assess the tax-exempted distributions to shareholders with stakes of 10 % and greater with a 20%-tax. This tax is a non-creditable and non-refundable corporation tax and can be avoided if the shareholder is subject to corporate tax itself.

Exceptions for SIICs as shareholders of SIICs

Shareholders that have SIIC status or a similar status of a foreign company itself are not subject to the corporation tax even when exceeding the 10%-limit. A joint holding of a SIIC also maintains the tax exemption, in case a SIIC holds at least 95 % directly or indirectly in another SIIC.

Conversion into REIT status

Publicly traded real estate companies as well as newly-founded, listed real estate companies have the option to apply for SIIC status. The application must be handed in within four months after the last tax year for which the SIIC regime will first apply.

Double taxation problem

The French tax authorities have declared the Parent Subsidiary Directive as non-applicable. Their policy shall avoid foreign companies to be taxed twice, namely in the residence and the home country.

This is why the official treaty about proceeding with withholding tax takes effect. From this it can be concluded that the withholding tax can be reduced in combination with holding sizes and double tax treaties. Germany, for example, gives a 10%-discount on withholding tax leading to an effective charge of

15 %. From stakes of at least 10 %, German companies are even exempt from withholding tax.

5.3   Fiscal incentive to adopt a REIT structure

General tax exemption

The French SIIC only exempts the rental and capital gain related income. Income from other activities, for example, management activities are not tax-exempted and have to be taxed regularly with the corporate tax rate of approximately 33 %. Gains resulting from the disposal of assets, transfer of rights in financial leases or participation belonging to the eligible activities and duly distributed are exempted.

Exit tax incentives

With the second amendment of the SIIC (SIIC 2) from November 2004, there is a tax incentive for corporate sellers. In the time from 2005 to 2007, companies can sell their properties to SIICs in exchange for shares. In case of capital gains, only half of it has to be taxed. To preserve liquidity, the selling company can pay this tax liability in four annual instalments. The SIIC then has to hold the properties at least five years.

With the third amendment of the SIIC (SIIC 3), which came into effect in January 2006, corporations are able to get the exit tax incentive of half capital gain taxation for every ordinary sale made until December 31st, 2007, provided that it is held five years by the acquiring SIIC.

Short-term gains realized by real estate brokers or property developers are excluded from the exit tax incentive.

5.4   Outlook

Adjustment of the double taxation agreement

The requirements for a diversified shareholder structure are not a necessity for a successful REIT structure. They are rather the consequence of the difficulties to quickly change existing double taxation treaties.

Since the French REIT was introduced independently from the REITs in the UK and in Germany, its main disadvantage was the poorly-conceived legislation. Fortunately, the French legislator showed high flexibility and already amended the law for the fourth time (SIIC 4) on January 1st, 2007. Thereby, problems in taxation were solved quickly. Similar to the German REIT, there must probably be changes in interstate double tax treaties in the long run in order to provide a final mature legislation.

Shareholder diversification

The objective of the SIIC 4 was the enforcement of the engagement of individual shareholders and to cut large stakes held by foreign institutional investors. That is why a single shareholder or a group acting as one may not hold more than 60 % of the shares from January 1st, 2007 on. Since currently only 7 % of the listed SIICs are in the hands of individual investors, there have to be large shiftings in shareholder structures in order to maintain SIIC status. Any new company and existing SIICs have to comply with these rules within two years.

Prolongation of SIIC law

Since the current SIIC law will only be applicable until the end of 2009, it is very likely that because of the success and the needs of the real estate industry, there will be a prolongation.

6   REITs in the UK

For centuries, the UK with London as one of the leading financial centers of the world has played a large role in global investment activities. The rising economy in the last years has also had a large impact on the British real estate market. Therefore, it seems to be a logic consequence to provide international investors with a fungible vehicle for indirect real estate investment in the UK. With the announcement of the introduction of the UK REIT, the stocks of the major property companies increased by approximately 10 % on that day. Today, there are about 13 successful UK REITs listed on the London Stock Exchange.

6.1   Motives for introduction

The UK has been faster in the introduction of REITs than Germany. The discussion about REITs has already started at the end of 2003 with the preliminary budget report for 2004. On March 22nd, 2006 the British finance minister (Chancellor of the Exchequer) announced the enactment of the UK REIT to be set on January 1st, 2007. The legislator intended to enhance the liquidity and transparency of the real estate market. The goal was to establish a vehicle that provides long-term investments and might encourage higher quality housing.

6.2   Ways of structuring a REIT

Legal requirements

There are certain legal requirements for REITs in the UK. The company must be a UK tax resident, be listed on a "recognized stock exchange" with ordinary or non-participating preference shares and provide a free float. A listing in the AIM (Alternative Investment Market) is not sufficient.

Share capital

There is no minimum share capital requirement.

Requirement of shareholder diversification

The law does not require a limitation of the shareholder structure, but provides through certain taxation an indirect limitation. According to the Parent

Subsidiary Directive of the European Union, the company will be penalized with a regular taxation of the normally exempted profits because foreign shareholders with stakes equal to and larger than 10 % might receive fully exempted dividends. This is why a 10%-shareholder of the REIT is supposed to disclose stakes equal to and larger than 10 % to the REIT.

Requirements to earning and income structure

A company must at least have three investment properties, excluding self-occupied properties. Single properties may not exceed 40 % of the total assets of all properties. Important is the perception of properties, as the existence of distinct buildings is not necessary, whereas discrete rental units, which may be in the same building, satisfy the definition. At least 75 % of the profits must derive from tax-exempt property business. Furthermore, at least 75 % of the total asset value must consist of tax-exempted property letting. An exemption from the asset test is allowed in the first accounting year.

All activities that are tax-exempted are put into ring-fenced business to keep them apart from the taxable/assessable activities. Non-ring-fenced business can, for example, be management activities and also property development. Property development, which stays in the REIT as an investment and which is not sold within three years after completion, is subject to Property Rental Business (PRB) and therefore tax-exempted.

Sectoral activities allowed

There is no restriction in the choice of investment properties.

Leverage level

Leverage is limited in the UK through the measurement of an interest cover ratio. The company will be taxed if the interest cover is less than 1.25. This can be considered to be a good way to provide a solid capital structure and avoid acquisition of low-yielding properties.

Distribution of operative income

90 % of the profit resulting from tax-exempted business must be distributed to the shareholders within 12 months of the end of the accounting period.

Distribution of capital gains on disposed investments

The UK REIT is not forced to distribute any of its capital gains.

Withholding tax/distribution taxation

Dividends distributed by a UK REIT are subject to the basic income tax rate of 22 % and are deducted with the distribution. The deduction is also dependent on the double tax treaties and can for this reason be reduced.

Conversion into REIT status, entry charge

The UK is the only country which charges an entry charge. Due to this fact, all properties imported into a REIT structure from the former company are charged with 2 % flat tax of the market value of the investment property assets. This charge will not be imposed on assets held for trading reasons. It can be paid in four instalments, but will then rise to 2.19 % of the property value.

Double taxation problem

Tax leakage was of great importance to UK treasury. In the case that shareholders have a stakes of 10 % or greater or the interest coverage rate falls below 1.25, the UK REIT is penalized with tax charges. The 10 % are subject to the withholding tax reduction for foreign investors and the interest coverage prevents foreign investors from moving profits indirectly through interest payments from the REIT.

6.3   Fiscal incentive to adopt a REIT structure

General taxation

Property Rental Business, as well as capital gains, is fully exempted from income tax. Ancillary activities are subject to regular tax legislation.

Entry charge (versus exit tax)

In the UK, there is an entry charge to the mobilized property value, namely the fair value (IAS 40). As a tax incentive, there is in most cases only a 2 % charge on the property value, which is far less than the 50 % exemption on capital gains observed in Germany and France. Optionally, the 2 % charge can be spread over four years in steps of 0.5 %, 0.53 %, 0.56 % and 0.6 %.

6.4   Outlook

Shareholder diversification

The requirements for a diversified shareholder structure are not a necessity for a successful REIT structure. They are rather the consequence of the difficulties to quickly change existing double taxation treaties.

It is very likely that in the long run, there may be adjustments to the double tax treaties, which will finally open up the REIT and may loosen shareholder restrictions. It is also likely that there will be pressure from the investment lobby to provide free capital flows. The current regulation probably also contradicts European law.

Adjustment of the double taxation agreement

With the current penalty for shareholders with stakes equal to and greater than 10 %, both the shareholder and the company have to be aware of a potential taxation. The second problem is that income deriving from non-UK subsidiaries with non-UK properties always accounts to the non-qualifying income and is therefore taxable. This will likely become a contentious issue because it discriminates foreign investment for UK REITs and leads to a reduction of diversification.

The incorporation of the REIT

The restriction of REIT status just for companies having their actual seat in the UK will probably become a controversially discussed subject, as opponents might argue that the free choice of location was violated.

An overview of the main important issues of the three mentioned REIT regimes is provided in the following two figures.

REITs in Europe	German REIT	UK REIT	French SIIC
Requirements to income and asset structure	At least 75 % of assets and income must be of rental income/leasing/capital gains; ancillary activities may not exceed 20 %	At least three properties (without self-occupied); single property may not exceed 40 %; 75 % of income and assets must be Property Rental Business	The Company's purpose must be Property Rental Business; financial leases may not exceed 50 %; ancillary activities may not exceed 20 %
Minimum free float	25 % at IPO, 15 % permanent	No minimum	15 %
Shareholding restrictions	No shareholder equal and larger 10 %, except indirect holdings, rights are always limited to 10 %	No shareholder equal and larger 10 %, penalty taxes on distributions for shareholders equal and larger 10 %	No shareholder or group more than 60 %, penalty taxes on distributions for shareholders equal and larger 10 %
Minimum distribution of operative income	90 %	85 %	90 %
Distribution of capital gains	50 % of capital gains	No minimum distribution of capital gains	50 % of capital gains
Legal form	Joint stock company, publicly traded	Joint stock company, traded on recognized stock exchange	Joint stock company, publicly traded
Minimum share capital	€ 15 million	No minimum	€ 15 million
Gearing	Minimum 45 % equity	Interest cover ratio of at least 1.25	No limitation
Tax incentive	50 % tax exemption on capital gains when sold to REIT or pre-REIT	2 % flat tax on property market value when selling or changing to REIT	50 % tax exemption on capital gains when sold to REIT

Fig. 1:   Structural outlines of European REIT structures

Treatment of Distribution	Germany REIT	UK REIT	France SIIC
Qualifying income	Capital income/dividend	Income from UK property; ancillary activities are separated and qualified as general dividend income	Capital income/dividend
Withholding tax rate	26.375%	22%	25%
Foreign shareholders and double tax treaties	Reductions in withholding tax depending on individual double tax treaty and capital stakes; no affiliation privilege if stake equal or greater than 10%; EU Parent Subsidiary Directive not applicable, since REIT-AG is tax-exempt	Reductions in withholding tax depending on individual double tax treaty and capital stakes	Reductions in withholding tax, depending on individual double tax treaty and capital stakes
Violation of shareholder restrictions	Reductions by double tax treaties are abandoned	Penalty taxes on distribution of shareholders with reduction in withholding tax	Penalty taxes (25%) on distribution of shareholders with reduction in withholding tax
Domestic corporate shareholder	Fully taxable without further tax credit on income from foreign countries or companies	Treated as profits from UK property business; UK companies can receive dividends gross from the tax-exempt business	Dividends are fully taxed at general income tax with 34.43%; qualifying parent companies holding at least 5% of the share capital of the SIIC are eligible for the parent subsidiary 95%-exemption for dividends paid out from the taxable income
Domestic individual shareholders	Fully taxable without further tax credit on income from foreign countries or companies	Withholding mechanism for the distribution of income from the tax-exempt business	Dividends benefit from a 40%-allowance at the global maximum rate of 51%

Fig. 2:   Treatment of distribution

7.   European REIT structures in the future

European REIT market still in the start-up phase Even with existing REIT structures in Belgium, Netherlands and now in France, the UK and Germany, the market is still in the start-up period. Regulations differ in the size and focus of the business models of REITs, resulting in the need for further improvements. Furthermore, reporting standards need to be harmonized. The part of European real estate that is available to investors via REITs is still small, albeit growing.

It can be expected that competition will lead to a unification of regulations through the European Union. The exclusion of residential REITs in Germany is likely to disappear. Especially in the fast growing economies of Central Europe, companies are still little focused. The shift will go to a sectoral focus. Cross-border transactions, and thus the creation of a pan-European property portfolio within a REIT will continue. But markets will be more selective. Pan-European property groups that have been created for mere fiscal reasons will lose their justification.

5   REIT portfolio management in the United States

Marc Louargand

Table of contents

1   Introduction

Why invest in REITs? Real Estate Investment Trusts (REITs), and their cousins, J-REITs, G-REITs, Listed Property Trusts (LPTs), and SIICs (Sociétés d'Investissements Immobiliers Cotées) represent a global REIT revolution in which a common form of corporate entity with a (relatively) common tax status enables investors to own interests in productive real assets in the public markets. 26 countries have REITs or REIT-like vehicles listed on public exchanges today. More are expected to follow in the near future as global capital markets become more integrated. Capital will flow to tax-advantaged opportunities wherever possible so expect firm pressure from the marketplace on reluctant governments.

REITs are attractive investments because they offer a chance to invest in the factors of production in any given economy. Real estate is an intermediate good. Firms occupy property for purposes of production, storing inventory, housing staff or offering wares to the public. Economies are more volatile at the end product – finished goods and services – than they are at the intermediate good level. Firms' production or payroll may rise and fall a fair amount without any change in their property consumption. Generally, we would expect the returns of productive real estate to be less volatile than the returns of shares in the firms that occupy the real estate. Over time, that relationship appears to be consistent with expectations. Holding shares in a single REIT that owns and operates office buildings in multiple markets offers a type of diversification since the REIT derives its income from many firms in different industries across many markets.

2   Role of REITs in a diversified portfolio

Diversification benefits REITs have several attractive characteristics to contribute to a mixed asset portfolio. Commercial real estate has qualities of both a bond and an equity. Tenants occupy for a period of years with rents that are fixed or fixed with known escalation. In that respect, lease income is much like an inflation-protected bond. At the same time, owners enjoy an equity component in their total return that arises from growth in price levels and growth in market value of specific properties. The history of REIT returns and volatility is consistent with this view that they represent both equity and fixed income return characteristics. Thus, REITs can offer diversification to both debt and equity portfolios. Further diversification benefits arise from the fact that real estate markets tend to have their own cycle, distinct from their national and regional business cycle. The overall diversification effect can be seen in figure 1, showing the REIT correlation with other asset classes.

	EPRA/ NAREIT Global	US REIT	S&P 500	MSCI EAFE	ML Corp/ Gvt Bond
EPRA/NAREIT Global Total Return Index in US$	1.00				
FTSE NAREIT-Equity TR (US Reits)	0.80	1.00			
S&P 500 Total Return (US Stocks)	0.55	0.30	1.00		
MSCI EAFE Total Return (Global Stocks)	0.66	0.33	0.83	1.00	
ML Corp/Gvt Total Return (US Bonds)	0.06	0.01	−0.27	−0.20	1.00
Source: Ibbotson, Cornerstone, 2007					

Fig. 1:   REIT correlation with other asset classes (December 1999 to March 2007)

And by examining the efficient frontiers shown in figure 2, one can see that adding REITs to a mixed asset portfolio adds convexity or lowers risk at a given level of return and increases return at a given level of risk.

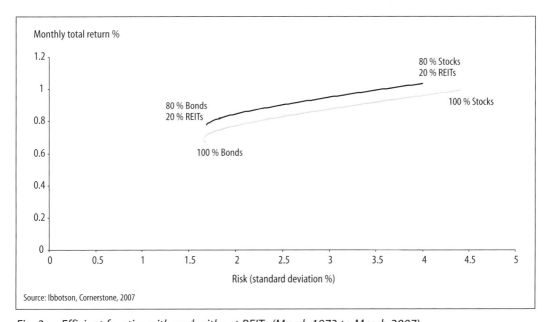

Fig. 2:   Efficient frontier with and without REITs (March 1973 to March 2007)

3   Role of REITs in life cycle funds

REITs have recently come to play an important role in a new family of investment products called life cycle funds or life style funds. These are mutual funds or similar instruments that provide a "one-stop shopping" solution. Life cycle funds are structured around the concept that investors' portfolio allocation should move from riskier to more conservative as they age. Thus, a fund labeled "20 Years to Retirement" might have 80 % equities and 20 % fixed income while a "Retirement Now" fund might have 70 % fixed income and 30 % equities.

REITs play an important role in these funds for three reasons. They are dividend instruments that offer a steady, reinvestable or spendable income stream. REIT dividends have historically grown at the rate of 5 % to 6 % per year, thus they are an inflation hedge. Real estate and REITs have low correlation with other asset classes, thus they provide diversification to the portfolio.

Dividend-centric strategies

Dividend-centric strategies are especially attractive in any vehicle designed for long-term wealth accumulation. Empirical studies have shown that a long-run strategy of reinvesting dividends is superior to a non-dividend, growth stock strategy on a risk-adjusted basis [1].

Given the value of a dividend strategy, it is clear that REITs are both an attractive long term savings vehicle and an appropriate holding for those in the wealth consumption phase of their life as opposed to the wealth accumulation years. During the accumulation phase, a steady combination of dividend reinvestment and marginal savings provides a steadily growing portfolio that can be monitored for its progress toward retirement accumulation goals. Should results be less than expected, an investor can step up the marginal savings rate to compensate. During the consumption phase, a consistently growing dividend stream hedges against inflation by allowing a larger annual payout in nominal terms while maintaining a constant percentage withdrawal.

Low volatility

Finally, REIT investment is appropriate from another viewpoint. REITs hold portfolios of commercial and residential real estate. Real estate is an intermediate good, a factor of production. Firms occupy office buildings, warehouse and retail stores as a location for doing business. The decision to lease space and the commitment it brings is a long-term decision that is costly and time-consuming to change. As a result, the expected volatility in cash flow to the real estate lessor is lower than the expected volatility of the cash flows generated by the business that occupies the real estate. Daily fluctuations in store sales or monthly fluctuations in revenues of office firms create more volatility than the multi-year lease obligations that provide real estate cash flow. A conservative investor who puts his money in these intermediate goods, like real estate, that have long duration obligations will enjoy lower volatility and will be receiving returns that are more representative of the health of the economy than the health of any single business. Hence, real estate may offer a more attractive risk exposure for investors than that of a single business enterprise.

4 Scale of REIT investment

Market capitalization

REITs were a very small part of the US capital market for over 40 years until the onset of the modern REIT era. REIT capitalization grew at approximately 9 % per year between 1971 and 1990, from US$ 300 million to US$ 5.5 billion. Between 1991 and the end of 2006, the REIT capitalization in the US grew from US$ 8.8 billion to US$ 400 billion at an average annual growth rate in excess of 22 %. During the same period, the size of the individual REITs grew dramatically as well. In 1995, there were 178 equity REITs, each with an average capitalization of US$ 280 million. At the end of 2006, there were 138 equity REITs with an average capitalization of US$ 23.9 billion each. There are currently 13 equity REITs with capitalizations exceeding US$ 10 billion each. There are also now 13 REITs in the Standard & Poors 500, an index of 500 leading large capitalization companies in the American industry. There is a considerable degree of overlap between the two groups. Finally, newly formed REITs in the mid-1990s tended to be regionally focused, sector specific operations. Today, firms like ProLogis, AMB, Brookfield and others have property interests around the globe and are well on their way to becoming truly global property companies. Worldwide, REITs and REIT-like vehicles represent over US$ 950 billion capitalization and will likely be in excess of US$ 1 trillion in the near future. Thus, a small, sleepy corner of the US capital market has grown to be a meaningful portion of global equity capitalization. Reuters estimates global market capitalization at approximately US$ 50 trillion so REITs represent about 2 % of stock market capitalization. The REIT capitalization as a share of local markets varies widely, ranging from 1 % in Japan and 2 % in the United States to 9 % in Australia, according to STBRI – the Sumitomo Trust Bank Research Institute [2].

5 Managing a global portfolio

Managing a global portfolio is significantly more complicated than managing a domestic portfolio. Some of the logistic issues involved include:

- **Trading in foreign markets**

Critical issues

A global REIT portfolio currently involves as many as 26 countries with 28 exchange-traded shares listed in 13 different currencies. These numbers are likely to grow as the REIT movement spreads to other countries. A portfolio manager must have systems and procedures in place to deal with this complexity. Consider the mechanics of trading. A US-based portfolio manager initiates a purchase order for several thousand shares of a firm listed on the Hong Kong Stock Exchange which is open for two trading sessions each trading day. Since Hong Kong is exactly 12 hours ahead of the east coast of the United States, the portfolio manager would have to trade between 10 p.m. and 12.30 a.m. or between 2.30 a.m. and 4.00 a.m. Since this is not generally feasible, the US portfolio managers need to have a Hong Kong correspondent broker who can receive an e-mail trade order and be relied upon to see that it is executed and directed toward the proper account. That is probably achieved by working with a US trading desk and a US-based broker who has affiliates in Hong Kong. Back in the US, the portfolio manager has a custodian for cash and shares held in the client accounts. The US custodian is the master custodian and needs to have a sub-custodian in Hong Kong who can hold cash and shares for the portfolio manager's clients. The trade will be executed in Hong Kong dollars (HK$) so the local custodian will need to have an HK$ balance sufficient to pay for the shares which will then be delivered within two days after the trade as T+2 (delivery within two business days after the trade is executed) is the local standard for delivery.

- **Currency translation**

The portfolio manager must debit US$ cash an amount equal to the required HK$ for settlement, requiring a currency translation in advance of settlement. The manager will most likely be relying on the local correspondent broker, the local custodian or a third party provider of foreign exchange services for currency translation so the concept of "best execution" becomes more complicated when trading across borders. Domestically, best execution refers to the efficiency of trade execution – how wide the bid-ask spread was, how quickly the trade was accomplished, and whether delivery was completed? Across borders, one is also concerned about getting the best execution in currency translation as well as stock trading. After delivery, the shares will be valued in local currency but the portfolio manager needs to have a US$ accounting of holdings in the base currency of the portfolio (US$) so that the master custodian will report a translated number to the portfolio manager.

- **Managing foreign exchange risk**

Portfolio managers or their clients must also choose whether or not to actively manage their foreign exchange (forex) exposure. While there are no hard and fast rules, it appears that the majority of investors choose not to hedge their exposure, believing that the forex risk is part of the bundle of diversification benefits. In an actively managed portfolio with many positions that might be only 1% or 2% of the total, it may be prohibitively expensive to completely hedge forex risk. A middling approach would be to execute options or futures contracts against baskets of currencies that roughly reflect the collective portfolio exposure. For example, a US-based manager with US$ 100 million exposure to the euro, the yen and the Hong Kong dollar is long those currencies and short the dollar. By buying a futures contract or an option on the dollar or by executing a more sophisticated derivative trade the manager offsets the short dollar position with a long hedge position. If the dollar declines against the other currencies, converting the local currencies will result in more dollars but the hedge will probably be out of the money. If the dollar appreciates against the local currencies, translation of the portfolio will have a negative effect but the hedge will be in the money to offset the decline. There are many different vehicles and strategies available for hedging forex exposure. Global custodial banks can offer hedging services as part of their portfolio services as can brokerage firms and third party providers.

- **Managing offshore and domestic tax obligations**

REITs have special tax status almost everywhere due to their waived or reduced corporate tax burden. In some countries REIT dividends are treated differently from other corporate dividends. Many countries impose a withholding tax on dividends paid to offshore investors. International tax treaties exist between countries that may modify or eliminate withholding tax burdens. A global custodian can also provide comprehensive tax services but they should be overseen by a tax expert periodically.

- **Managing corporate actions and proxies**

The global custodian can also be responsible for tracking corporate actions (spin-offs, buy-backs, mergers, etc.) and notifying the portfolio manager of such and seeing to it that the appropriate elections are made on a timely basis. In addition, they or a third party can manage the proxies, making sure that they are voted. Many investors hire their own third party proxy services in order to insure that certain policies are followed.

- **Custody**

Most importantly, the sub-custodians receive cash payments of dividends or other distributions, payments for trades and settlement therefrom and transmit updated accounts to the principal custodian. This responsibility further involves providing cash reconciliations and daily accounting for the Book of Record. Meanwhile, the global custodian must integrate each report into a comprehensive Book of Record for the portfolio and generate a daily report. The master custodian reports on all holdings and has oversight of the cash management process including the Short Term Investment Fund (STIF) accounts where cash is swept on a daily basis to maximize its earnings.

6 REIT portfolio strategies

Broad equity market managers tend to be classified into major style groups such as Value, Growth, or Balanced. Those categories are often further classified as Small Capitalization (Cap), MidCap or Large Cap. Thus a manager might be seen as a Small Cap Value shop or a Large Cap Growth shop or some other combination. Sector managers who invest in only one industry group like REITs, healthcare, utilities or other specialty groups may sometimes fall under these groupings, but they are more likely to cut across groups since a sector manager may invest in small, medium and large cap companies within a single sector. Within the REIT space, the emphasis on dividends tends to categorize them as Value stocks, but several REIT managements pursue a focused Growth strategy through their development pipeline and corporate M&A activities. Due to the nature of sectoral management, REIT managers are more likely to fall into the categories discussed below. **Manager classification**

The first category to mention here are the index managers. An allocation to real estate on the order of 5 % to 15 % is a common element of asset allocation models. Many asset allocators recommend a passive approach within asset classes and argue that the value is created by the asset allocation. A passive, index-tracking strategy is preferred by these investors. One problem in this approach is to determine which index is the appropriate benchmark. There are two commonly used indices in the global REIT arena, UBS Real Estate Investors and the EPRA/NAREIT Global Property Index. The UBS index represents a more traditional view of REITs in that its constituents are owners and operators of stabilized real estate and act more like investors than operators. The EPRA/ **Index managers**

NAREIT Global index constituents are more representative of the stage of maturation in their local economies. The European and North American firms are more like traditional investors while the Asian sub-index includes a larger share of development firms as well as investors.

Enhanced index Enhanced index investors stay very close to index weightings in their holdings, but are active managers nonetheless. The degree of activity varies across managers with some holding an index portfolio but managing the trades for tax efficiency at a minimum. Other index enhancers eliminate the most volatile stocks in each sector. Still others limit their rebalancing as the underlying index changes composition. But most enhanced index managers are active in some manner. A typical enhanced index manager might single out the most attractively valued stocks in each sector and then hold those stocks as proxies for their respective sectors. For example, one might hold the five highest quality apartment names from a sector of 15 companies. Choosing the names with the best quality buildings, strongest markets and/or biggest discount to Net Asset Value would be expected to bring excess return (alpha) to a portfolio that held an index weight in apartments but did not hold the weaker names.

Growth at a Reasonable Price (GARP) REITs are not generally seen as growth vehicles. They represent a mature industry and an intermediate good, thus they can be expected to grow at about the rate of economic expansion in their respective economies. In the presence of balance sheet leverage (gearing), modest growth rates in property revenue can translate into much higher operating income growth rates. For instance, if a US domiciled REIT enjoys revenue growth of 3 % per year at the property level, a 50 % debt level can translate the revenue growth into 6 % operating income growth.

Due to real estate's capital intensive nature, traditional earnings measures can be misleading since companies have to take a non-cash charge for depreciation and amortization which creates a large disparity between earnings and cash flow. Many managers prefer to use a metric known as AFFO, for Adjusted Funds From Operations. AFFO differs from earnings as shown in figure 3 below.

In addition to the adjustment for depreciation and amortization, AFFO recognizes the changes in rental income from year to year in order to better reflect actual cash flow. Unadjusted FFO includes a "straight-line" rent figure which is the average rent paid in each year of a lease contract as opposed to the actual in any given year. AFFO also adjusts for the annual capital expenditures for tenant improvements and leasing commissions as opposed to reflecting them in an amortization allowance. Thus, AFFO gives a much more comprehensive picture of the actual cash flow from operations which is available for the payment of dividends and for reinvestment in the company. Note in figure 3 that the company pays out 90 % of its taxable earnings but in fact pays out only 83 % of AFFO or actual cash flow. REIT managers that consistently get their AFFO payout ratio down into the 80 %, 70 % or even 60 % range tend to deliver superior performance over time as they have more resources available for investment. The US REIT universe achieves a payout ratio of 75 % today. If management can retain 25 % of total cash flow, they will have 2 % to 3 % of Net Asset Value (NAV) available for reinvestment. Thus, the

	Earnings (in US$ 000)	AFFO (in US$ 000)
Rental income	2,000,000	2,000,000
Operating expense	600,000	600,000
General & adminstrative expense	20,000	20,000
EBITDA	**1,380,000**	**1,380,000**
Depreciation and amortization	300,000	
Interest	400,000	400,000
Net income	**680,000**	**980,000 FFO**
Taxes	–	–
Net income available for dividends	680,000	
Taxable income X 90 %	612,000	
Adjust for "straight-line" rents		75,000
Adjust for capital improvements		170,000
Adjusted Funds From Operations (AFFO)		735,000 AFFO
Payout ratio (dividends/AFFO) 83 %		

Fig. 3:   Office America REIT

firm can grow its cash flow by 2 % or 3 % per year before raising new capital, or increasing revenue from existing assets. The history of dividend growth in the United States over the past 30 years suggests that management can grow its dividends at 5 % or 6 % per year with moderate leverage in the balance sheet as a result of reinvestment alone.

Total return

Total return strategies are those that place a roughly equal emphasis on appreciation and current income. Historically, REITs have been categorized as income vehicles, but as we have shown above they have a long history of relatively consistent moderate growth. While it is possible to pursue an income-focused strategy in REITs, it is more easily accomplished in a high yield strategy as discussed below. The total return distinction is primarily an artifact of the rest of the equity market with its distinction between growth and income. Generally speaking, if an investor holds a representative portfolio of REITs they have pursued a total return strategy.

High yield

A high yield strategy can be fashioned out of REIT common and REIT preferred stocks with attractive current yields. As of today, REIT preferred stocks yield 7 % to 8 % with some as high as 10 %. By combining these preferred stocks with high-yielding common such as mortgage REITs, a manager can create a high current yield with a modicum of growth from the common stock component. If we expect REIT common dividends to grow at 6 % per year, a portfolio consisting of 70 % preferred and 30 % common might provide 2 % per year growth in yield which is close to most central banks' targeted inflation rate. If an investor has a shorter term outlook, a preferred portfolio by itself will provide an attractive current yield but offers little in the way of principal protection unless one expects falling interest rates in the near term.

Absolute return   Absolute return strategies should not be confused with total return strategies. Absolute return strategies have a targeted rate of return which is to be achieved under all market conditions. Such a strategy requires the use of both short and long positions and typically involves the use of derivatives. Another name for an absolute return strategy portfolio is a hedge fund. There are some Real estate or REIT hedge funds in the marketplace, but many more hedge funds deploy their strategy in the REIT arena.

Hedge fund   Hedge funds are an amorphous group. In the US market they are basically unregulated relative to mutual funds. Their fee structures typically include a manager incentive on the scale of 20 % of all profits or 20 % of profits above some relatively low hurdle rate. In addition, the manager usually takes a 100 basis point (1 %) management fee annually which is above the fees of a separate account long-only manager, but not much more than a mutual fund management fee. There is not space for an exhaustive list of hedge fund strategies involving REITs, but a few will suffice to provide an understanding of how REITs can be used in this area. The distinguishing feature of most hedge funds is that they involve some form of long/short strategy in order to create market neutral returns. In other words, these are absolute return strategies not pegged to any market benchmark. Some hedge fund strategies include:

- **Long/short**

Based on sector strength expectations; i. e., short multi-family and take a long position in retail.

- **Long/short dividend balanced**

One of the difficulties in shorting REITs is that once the short sellers borrow the stock to sell they become liable for any dividend paid while the stock is on loan. One strategy is to close out a position quickly to avoid paying a dividend to the share owner. A more stable approach is to "match" the shorts and longs in terms of the dividend flow so that the long positions will pay the dividends to the owners of the borrowed shares in the short positions. Of course, the manager is giving up income at that point which may prove to be a poor choice.

- **Capital structure arbitrage**

Short the common and go long the preferred. If a REIT faces significant income declines, they are likely to suspend the common dividend before they suspend the preferred dividend. Since preferred dividends are generally cumulative, they must be paid in arrears before any common dividends can be paid so such a position can expect to receive a current yield while benefiting from weakness in the stock price.

- **Merger arbitrage**

While this strategy waned in recent years, the recent wave of privatizations and mergers has brought it back. A classic merger arbitrageur will go long the target company and short the acquiring company as history shows that those are the likely directions of the respective share prices.

- **Out-of-sector arbitrage**

Opportunities sometimes arise that allow a manager to go outside the REIT sector in a long/short strategy that is based on fundamentals. For example, during a business cycle slowdown one might short advertising and other major office occupiers while going long the office REITs. The REITs are unlikely to cut their dividend even though consumer weakness will be likely to impact the advertising agency stocks negatively. Another example would be shorting grocers while going long neighborhood retail REITs.

- **Paired trades**

A more fundamentally contrarian approach is to short the recent good performers and go long the recent underperformers on the theory that all price behavior regresses to the mean of the trend over time. In emerging markets like global REITs where transparency is not yet completely established and many firms are coming public or electing REIT status, it may be a more viable strategy than in a mature and transparent market. The strategy is to take short positions in the top performing stocks over some period, say one month, and match those with long positions in the past month's poorest performing stocks. Over time, the returns to this strategy should approach the magnitude of the sector's volatility if all goes well. Of course, if the trades go against the strategy the returns will be negatively equal to the volatility.

- **Derivative strategies**

Global capital markets are creating real estate-related derivative instruments at a rapid clip. Those that survive will be drawn into new and innovative hedging and absolute return strategies. It is sufficient to say that the clearing houses and other derivative producers will provide a steady stream of strategies involving their products.

- **Portable alpha**

The advent of robust real estate derivatives as we have seen recently in the United Kingdom will pave the way for growth in portable alpha strategies in REITs. Portable alpha strategies are popular in institutional investment circles because they separate the beta (market risk) from the alpha (active management risk). Since the derivatives tend to be built on broad indices, they offer the ability to separately trade or swap the market return while retaining the alpha created by successful active managers. This is likely to be an important growth area for managers in the next several years.

Contrarian

Contrarians have a simple worldview, namely that people are generally wrong and contrarians are often right. Much of the empirical work in the field of behavioral finance owes a debt to the contrarians. Early work in this field showed that stocks that had lagged the market in performance tended to outperform in subsequent periods. Conversely, stocks that had outperformed the market tended to lag it in subsequent periods. Hence the concepts that stocks can be "oversold" or "overbought". If oversold, they are likely to come back. If overbought, they are likely to fall back in the future. As the global REIT market matures and broadens, the opportunity for contrarians will likely grow.

7   Portfolio risk management

Portfolio managers usually manage on behalf of a client. In the institutional community the clients are sophisticated and are assisted by staff and consultants who are sophisticated. Institutional portfolios typically represent the savings of households whether they are in pension funds or mutual funds. Thus, managers have a fiduciary duty of care in executing their chosen strategy. In light of that need of care, portfolios typically have constraints on their composition and prosecution that are both absolute and relative.

Risk budgeting The portfolio has a risk budget that is a guideline for how it should relate to its benchmark and its overall market as well as the investor's objectives for the asset class. Elements of the risk budget include:

• **Portfolio beta**

Since there will be some market-based benchmark index, the index is usually taken as the beta of the asset class and the manager's portfolio is requested to be within some guidelines, perhaps that it should not exceed a beta of 1.20 relative to the benchmark. This is a straightforward calculation since the portfolio return and variance just substitute for an individual stock in the formula for beta.

$$B_{portfolio} = \frac{\text{covariance of market and portfolio}}{\text{variance of market}}$$

This type of constraint allows for active management within limits that keep the portfolio risk in some reasonable balance with the market. Analysts may also look at tracking error.

• **Tracking error**

Tracking error is the relationship between the volatility of portfolio returns and the volatility of the benchmark returns. If a manager creates excess return, alpha, but does so by taking outsized risk relative to the excess return then it is not sensible on a risk-adjusted basis. A simple formula for tracking error is:

$$TE = \text{standard deviation}_{portfolio} - B_{portfolio} \times R_{benchmark}$$

This formula essentially compares the portfolio volatility with the expected volatility given its beta. A tracking error of zero would indicate that the manager has not taken on any excess risk beyond the expected level.

• **Information ratio**

It seems logical then to put these concepts together to identify the information ratio which is essentially a modified sharpe ratio that compares the level of excess return (alpha) with the volatility of excess return which can be thought of as excess risk. It looks at volatility and return only in terms of alpha:

$$IR = \frac{R_{portfolio} - R_{benchmark}}{\text{standard deviation}_{alpha}}$$

Which is simply the ratio of excess return to excess risk. Information ratios above 1.0 are very good and rather rare.

- **Semi-variance analysis**

One problem with applying traditional stock market measures to REIT portfolios arises from the pattern of returns. Due to the steady nature of REIT dividends, there have been very few years of negative total return in the REIT sector. In the US, there have been only six such years in the past 35 years. REITs also have historically had lower price volatility than many other sectors. Market models are built on expectations of symmetrical volatility arising from an equilibrium-seeking process that moves up and down along a trend line. REITs tend to have much more volatility to the upside than to the downside. Thus, there is a nascent movement to evaluate REIT risk using semi-variance and absolute deviation techniques to isolate the upside volatility from the more stable downside scenario. As of now, there is no agreement on this approach nor is there a standard set of models in use but it is likely that this approach will gain adherents if the global REIT sector behaves in a similar fashion.

8 Portfolio concentration

- **Portfolio concentration** measures are applications of traditional diversification heuristics (sometimes called naive diversification) that set simple percentage limits on geographic and property-type exposures. There is no reason not to continue to embrace these limitations as prudent safety measures. Regional economies have regional recessions and property sectors tend to have their own property cycles so there is a valid degree of risk management in these constraints. They generally are formed in terms of relative weightings in a portfolio compared to the weightings found in the portfolio's benchmark.

- **Regional weighting** can be applied at the multi-country, country, regional or metropolitan level. For instance, if North America is 50% of the benchmark in total capitalization, the portfolio manager must decide whether to adopt an underweight, neutral or overweight position vis-à-vis those companies. Investors will want some limits on these weightings. For a multi-country region like North America or Europe, the constraint might be no more than two times the benchmark weight. For a much smaller region like a metropolitan area the constraint might be larger, such as a three times maximum weight relative to the benchmark weight.

- **Sector weighting** works the same way and would typically be limited to a two or three times weight if it is a major sector like office or retail, but for small specialty sectors like manufactured home communities or free-standing retail the constraint would more likely be stated as a maximum percent of the total portfolio, say no more than 5% for manufactured home communities which is only 1% of the US benchmark.

- **Firm weighting** can follow the same logic. For most names, a constraint of a multiple of benchmark weight, say three times, is effective. There are, however, several large capitalization names that may be 5% or even 10% of a benchmark. In those cases, a tighter limit is generally set. For example, in a US portfolio one regional mall company might be over 6% of the benchmark. In that case the limit would probably be set at 10%

of the portfolio or less. At the other end of the spectrum, there are firms whose capitalization is less than 1 % of the benchmark. In those cases, a limit of 5 % or less would be appropriate. Finally, most investors allow a small tranche of an actively managed portfolio to be invested in assets outside of the benchmark. These are typically constrained to a total of 5 % or 10 % of the portfolio. For example, there are Real Estate Operating Companies (REOCs) that do not elect REIT status but are in the same business as REITs. Most managers will want to have the ability to invest in these names as well.

9   Conclusion

REITs and REIT-like vehicles are a rapidly growing segment of the global capital market. While they are traded and managed like common stock in other industries, real estate brings some unique issues to the portfolio manager. Benchmarks may not be universally agreed upon. Traditional common equity style models may not fit the asset class well. REITs bring diversification and a dividend-centric element to broad equity portfolios. Managing equity investments on a global scale brings some complications that can best be handled by a network of cooperating banks and brokerage houses. Active management strategies for REITs follow all of the traditional models and there are a few that are unique to REITs. Active management introduces risk that may surpass the risk of the benchmark, thus there should be risk budgeting and active risk management as part of the investment process, ranging from traditional financial measures to simple portfolio constraints.

10   Bibliography

[1] See Siegel, J., The Future for investors, Crown Business, 2005 for instance.

[2] Sumitomo Trust Bank Research Institute.

6   Mergers & Acquisitions and REITs

Maximilian Keisers
Dirk Schiereck

Table of contents

1   Introduction

Concentration of REIT markets

Despite the long history of REITs since the introduction in 1960 in the US as well as the growing number of nations that have already introduced a REIT regime, empirical research on the concentration of REIT markets by Mergers & Acquisitions (M&A) has been rather limited until today, particularly if compared to research on the related industries like the banking sector [1]. The lack of knowledge about value implications becomes even more obvious as the speed of consolidation in the REIT industry experienced a significant increase since the early 1990s [2]. The numerous acquisitions raise questions on the size and direction of wealth effects for the involved REIT shareholders, which might be caused by these transactions.

In this chapter, new evidence is provided to fill this research gap, by studying REIT M&A in an international context and by including transactions until the end of 2005, which allows the authors to include all transactions of the modern REIT era – as stated by Campbell, Petrova, Sirmans (2003) [3] – from the beginning of the 1990s until today. The resulting data set consists of a total of 107 transactions.

Following the standard research design of event study methodology, the authors especially focus on two questions:

- Do bidder and target shareholders gain from M&A in the REIT industry?

- Do acquisitions of privately held targets yield more positive effects than those of public targets?

2 Prior evidence and expectations

2.1 Prior evidence

Not more than six studies that are published in academic journals deal with shareholder wealth effects of REIT M&A [4]. In the first study Allen and Sirmans (1987) [5] analyze wealth effects for shareholders of acquiring REITs with a sample of 38 completed transactions between 1977 and 1983, where both buyer and target were a REIT. The results document a significant wealth increase for acquiring shareholders. McIntosh, Officer and Born (1989) [6] extend this work by assessing the impact of REIT acquisitions on target shareholder wealth. For a sample of 27 transactions between July 1962 and December 1986 they find a small significant wealth increase for the target shareholders at the announcement event. Young and Elayan (2002) [7] confirm these findings for a more recent database of 24 mergers between 1972 and 1991.

Findings of former studies

Campbell, Ghosh and Sirmans (1998) [8] analyze also a sample of 27 completed mergers of publicly traded equity REITs between 1994 and January 1998. Shareholders of acquiring REITs lost 1.5 % while shareholders of target REITs gained 5.2 % on average over a 5-day event window surrounding the announcement date. Campbell, Ghosh and Sirmans (2001) [8] focus on the information content of the payment method in REIT mergers. Their dataset includes a large sample of 85 transactions between beginning of 1994 and end of 1998 in which the bidder is a publicly traded equity REIT. On the target side, 40 REITs were listed and 45 privately held. Acquirers of privately held targets exhibited a positive abnormal return of 1.9 % on average over a 3-day interval, whereas bidders of publicly traded targets experienced a negative abnormal return of 0.6 %. Shareholders of publicly traded targets enjoyed a 3.2 % positive abnormal return, which is consistent with McIntosh, Officer and Born (1989) [6], but is much smaller than for targets in non-REIT mergers [8]. Acquiring shareholder's wealth effects were negatively related to the acquirer's size, which is attributed to larger REITs being inclined to overpay. Similar results are presented by Sahin (2005) [2] for 35 mergers from 1994 to 1998. Bidders experienced statistically significant negative wealth effects, whereas targets earned statistically significant positive abnormal returns.

The analyses at hand will contribute to this literature by extending the geographical focus as well as to the periods covered. Both aspects are important to understand the dynamics of wealth effects in the REIT industry and the prospects of M&A on the run of consolidation.

2.2 Expectations

As long as REIT managers are acting in the best interest of their shareholders, we should expect that both target and bidder shareholders experience additional value from an M&A transaction as only in this case management will use this option to grow externally. However, not only research on REIT M&A provides a different view. Most cross-sectional studies find mixed or rather negative abnormal returns for bidders (see e.g., [9][10][11]). Prior

Expected stock price studies

research on REIT M&A yields similar results. It seems that the considerable benefits REITs gain from growing size, which were reported by Ambrose and Linneman (2001) [12], are being more than compensated by other factors. Thus, we expect the announcement to have a small abnormal negative effect on bidder share price.

Prior evidence on target shareholder abnormal returns is clearer cut. Event studies generally find large positive wealth effects for the target shareholders even in the range of 12 % to 22 % (see e. g., [13][4]). Prior research on REIT M&A suggests a positive, but rather moderate expectation on abnormal target returns compared to other industries. The authors also expect the announcement to have a moderate positive wealth effect for target shareholders.

In assessing M&A announcement effects, an important distinction can be made between acquisitions of public and private targets. If a transaction is financed with stock – this is the case in virtually all REIT transaction within this dataset –, private target firm owners often gain a large ownership position in the combined entity. According to monitoring theory, these blockholders can favorably influence the development of the company/stock [14]. In addition, the willingness of the new blockholders to hold a large position in the new entity provides a positive signal to the market. Campbell, Ghosh and Sirmans (2001) [8] present corresponding results. Faccio, McConnell and Stolin (2006) document similar findings, but conclude that "[…] fundamental factors that give rise to this listing effect […] remain elusive" [15]. In any case, the authors expect that acquirers of private targets experience more positive wealth effects compared to acquirers of public targets.

Value expectations of M&A transactions can also systematically change over time. It is assessed if there are any significant differences due to market sentiment in the first and second half of our sample period. As the first transaction took place in 1993, the 13 years from 1993 to 2005 are divided into two 6.5-year periods (period 1 from January 1st, 1993 to June 30th, 1999 and period 2 from July 1st, 1999 to December 31st, 2005).

3   Data sample and methodology

Identified transactions

To identify REIT M&A transactions Thomson Financial SDC (Securities Data Company – M&A Database) is used as the prime data source. Stock and index returns for both bidders and targets were provided by Datastream, which is a part of Thomson Financial. Relevant transactions were selected according to the following criteria:

- The transaction was announced between January 1st, 1993 and December 31st, 2005.
- In all transactions target and bidder is a REIT.
- Transaction volume exceeded US$ 100 million.
- Target or bidder was exchange listed at announcement.
- A change of corporate control has occurred during the transaction (> 50 % ownership stake only after transaction).
- Deal status is completed.

Further adjustments needed to be made as the SDC classifications also included some non-REITs. The final list consists of 107 M&A transactions where at announcement both bidder and target were a REIT and where at least one side was publicly listed (over estimation period and event window).

Following the cited literature, an event study methodology is employed to assess whether there are any abnormal value effects as a result of the M&A announcements. An event window T of 41 days: $T = [-20;+20]$ is considered, where $t = \{0\}$ denominates the announcement date of a transaction. To calculate expected returns for the event windows, the market model put forward by Dodd/Warner (1983) [16] and Brown/Warner (1985) [17] is applied and an estimation period of 160 days is used. The EPRA/NAREIT North America index as well as the EPRA/NAREIT Asia index are used for the market model regressions. To test for statistical significance, parametric tests according to Boehmer, Musumeci and Poulsen (1991) [18] are applied to explicitly account for a possible variance increase during the event period [19]. In addition, mean difference tests are used to check for significant differences between subsamples.

4   Results

4.1   Descriptives

Within the sample of 107 M&A transactions, 93 bidders and 79 targets were publicly listed. The sample composition is illustrated in figure 1 below.

Transactions incl. in sample	107		
Bidders	**93**	**Targets**	**79**
Subsamples			
Private target	23	–	–
Public target	70	–	–
US-Deal	73	US-Deal	60
Non-US Deal	20	Non-US Deal	19
First period	48	First period	37
Second period	45	Second period	42

Fig. 1:   Sample and subsample overview

Distribution of M&A transactions

Acquisitions of public targets have dominated REIT consolidation as there are only 23 bidders, which acquired private REITs. As expected from the sheer dominance of the US market in terms of size and maturity, most transactions occurred in the US. 85 of the 107 transactions in the sample had a distinct US focus. Remarkably to note, there is not a single cross-border transaction in the data set. All REIT M&A transactions took place inside national borders. The inexistence of cross-border acquisitions might be considered as an indicator for the divergences in national institutional settings which might induce high costs of integration. Besides those 85 M&A in the US, most of the remaining transactions took place in Australia and in Canada. Most of the other markets are probably still too young and/or too small, in order to consolidate via REIT M&A activity.

With regard to M&A occurrence over time, the transactions are almost equally split over the first and the second half of the period under consideration. However, the individual years were quite heterogeneous. After the real estate crisis, consolidation activity picked up slowly in 1993/1994 and then quickly rose to its peak in 1997/1998 with 16 and 15 transactions, respectively. After that the M&A market for REITs gradually declined until 2002, before it rose again remarkably in 2003 and 2004. Figure 2 illustrates the number of REIT transactions, which are included in this sample, over time.

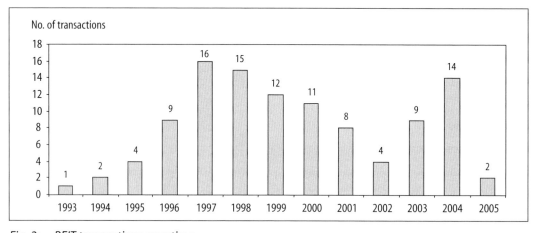

Fig. 2:   REIT transactions over time

Within the dataset at hand, acquiring REITs are on average about three times as large as target REITs. The average (median) market caps amount to US$ 1.57 billion and US$ 559 million, respectively. The median transaction value amounts to US$ 1.03 billion.

4.2   Transactions evaluation

Average stock price reactions of acquiring REITs On aggregate, a total loss in market value of US$ 1.78 billion can be found for the bidders and a value generation of US$ 3.37 billion for the targets caused by the 107 M&A announcements in this sample. For the exchange listed REITs M&A created value to an overall aggregate value of US$ 1.59 billion. The observed absolute value creation for the group of targets is almost twice as large as the value loss for the bidders.

Figure 3 illustrates the Cumulated Average Abnormal Returns (CAAR) of both bidders and targets over the entire event window. Bidders exhibit a small negative revaluation of their shares after the announcement, whereas targets yield a considerable value gain beginning at the transaction announcement.

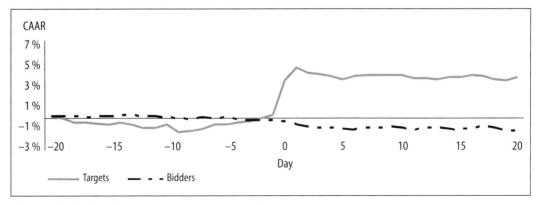

Fig. 3: CAAR development over the event window

When looking at the CAARs as depicted in figure 4 below, bidders on average experience virtually no abnormal return at announcement and small negative returns in all other event windows. Over the entire event window [–20;20], a negative return of –1.35 % can be found, which is highly significant at the 1%-level. The slightly smaller negative returns in the event windows [0;5] and [0;20] are significant at the 5%-level. For the target sample abnormal value effects are more pronounced. The CAARs are all positive and highly significant at the 1%-level. They vary between 3.39 % and 4.95 % for the event windows {0} and [–1;1], respectively.

	All bidders			All targets		
	CAAR	P-value	Sig.	CAAR	P-value	Sig.
[–20;20]	–1.35 %	0.0091	***	3.90 %	0.0008	***
[–20;0]	–0.32 %	0.1861		3.67 %	0.0001	***
[–5;0]	–0.31 %	0.2226		4.32 %	0.0000	***
{0}	–0.07 %	0.7624		3.39 %	0.0000	***
[–1;1]	–0.41 %	0.1595		4.95 %	0.0000	***
[0;5]	–0.89 %	0.0256	**	3.48 %	0.0002	***
[0;20]	–1.10 %	0.0135	**	3.62 %	0.0005	***

Notes: *** = significant at 1%-level; ** = significant at 5%-level; * = significant at 10%-level

Fig. 4: CAARs for all bidders and targets

To detect the influence of target status on bidder returns, we divide acquirers into two subgroups: acquirers of private and bidders of public targets. The two subgroups experience different CAARs, which are displayed in figure 5. CAARs of REITs bidding for private targets are almost all (insignificantly) positive, particularly in the days prior to the announcement. In contrast, bidders acquiring public targets exhibit (significant) negative abnormal returns. CAARs range from –0.24 % at announcement to –2.32 % over the entire event window. The return difference between the subsamples sums up to 3.92 % and is significant at the 5%-level.

	Bidders – private target			Bidders – public target			Mean difference		
	CAAR	P-value	Sig.	CAAR	P-value	Sig.	CAAR	P-value	Sig.
[−20;20]	1.60 %	0.3789		−2.32 %	0.0006	***	3.92 %	0.0356	**
[−20;0]	1.62 %	0.2095		−0.96 %	0.0218	**	2.59 %	0.1162	
[−5;0]	0.44 %	0.7112		−0.55 %	0.1132		0.99 %	0.2663	
[0]	0.45 %	0.3059		−0.24 %	0.5215		0.69 %	0.1920	
[−1;1]	0.66 %	0.5384		−0.76 %	0.0606	*	1.42 %	0.0819	*
[0;5]	−0.01 %	0.9259		−1.18 %	0.0147	**	1.17 %	0.2311	
[0;20]	0.43 %	0.7677		−1.60 %	0.0045	***	2.02 %	0.0524	*

Notes: *** = significant at 1%-level; ** = significant at 5%-level; * = significant at 10%-level

Fig. 5:   *CAARs of bidders of private vs. public target*

Publicly listed vs. privately held targets

To gain additional insight over time, the covered period is subdivided into two equal halves. The first period includes transactions from 1993 to the middle of 1999 and the second period includes those deals, which were announced in the second half of 1999 to 2005. Again, there are two subsamples for bidders as well as for targets. As figure 6 illustrates, there are some differences between bidder returns in the first and the second period. While returns in the first period are rather positive up to the announcement, they are slightly negative in the event windows after the announcement. However, almost all CAARs are not significantly different from zero. Bidders in the second period exhibit abnormal returns, which are all negative and large in magnitude. Over the entire event window [−20;20] the CAAR amounts significant −3.12 %, which is almost 3.5 % less than the 0.31 % of the first period bidders.

Performance over time

	Bidders – first period			Bidders – second period			Mean difference		
	CAAR	P-value	Sig.	CAAR	P-value	Sig.	CAAR	P-value	Sig.
[−20;20]	0.31 %	0.4098		−3.12 %	0.0056	***	3.42 %	0.0412	**
[−20;0]	0.63 %	0.7171		−1.34 %	0.1310		1.97 %	0.1689	
[−5;0]	−0.02 %	0.5189		−0.61 %	0.2827		0.59 %	0.4112	
[0]	0.03 %	0.7681		−0.17 %	0.8832		0.19 %	0.7355	
[−1;1]	−0.08 %	0.3797		−0.76 %	0.2749		0.69 %	0.3925	
[0;5]	−0.62 %	0.0854	*	−1.18 %	0.1495		0.56 %	0.5536	
[0;20]	−0.30 %	0.4254		−1.95 %	0.0076	***	1.65 %	0.1014	

Notes: *** = significant at 1%-level; ** = significant at 5%-level; * = significant at 10%-level

Fig. 6:   *CAARs of bidders in the first vs. second period*

Figure 7 displays the results for the two target subsamples. Again there are differences between the two, as positive returns in the second period are larger than those in the first period. The 2.45 % difference at the announcement day is significant (at the 10%-level).

	Targets – first period			Targets – second period			Mean difference		
	CAAR	P-value	Sig.	CAAR	P-value	Sig.	CAAR	P-value	Sig.
[−20;20]	3.08 %	0.0433	**	4.62 %	0.0082	***	−1.53 %	0.5197	
[−20;0]	2.10 %	0.0568	*	5.05 %	0.0007	***	−2.95 %	0.1130	
[−5;0]	3.45 %	0.0002	***	5.08 %	0.0004	***	−1.63 %	0.3069	
[0]	2.09 %	0.0045	***	4.54 %	0.0008	***	−2.45 %	0.0941	*
[−1;1]	3.89 %	0.0004	***	5.89 %	0.0001	***	−2.00 %	0.2560	
[0;5]	1.97 %	0.0694	*	4.81 %	0.0011	***	−2.84 %	0.1183	
[0;20]	3.07 %	0.0085	***	4.11 %	0.0167	**	−1.04 %	0.5959	

Notes: *** = significant at 1%-level; ** = significant at 5%-level; * = significant at 10%-level

Fig. 7:   CAARs of targets in the first vs. second period

5   Discussion

Interpretation of the results

Overall return patterns for REIT M&A follow experiences from other industries. Significant small negative returns for bidder firms can be observed. The benefits REITs gain as bidders from size are more than compensated for by other factors. For the shareholders of acquiring REITs M&A transactions do not create wealth, but instead rather destroy some value. In contrast, the abnormal returns within the group of targets are clearly positive and highly significant. There is considerable value created for the target shareholders through the transactions, which is larger compared to the findings of previous studies. This result is also an indicator for the rising wealth transfer over time. While bidder stocks in more recent transactions show increasing negative abnormal returns at the announcement of acquisitions, the target owners' CAARs become more positive. This finding can be interpreted as an increasing wealth transfer that is mainly driven by transactions in the US REIT market. Importantly, the results indicate that the gain for target shareholders exceeds the value destruction for the bidders in absolute terms implying a positive overall effect for the combined entity. REIT M&A therefore do create value on aggregate.

Lessons learned

The documented evidence shows divergences between subsamples with respect to target status and time. There are significant differences in CAARs of bidders depending on the status of the target. Bidders acquiring public targets exhibit negative returns while acquirers of private targets enjoy small positive returns. These differences are similar to those presented by Campbell, Ghosh and Sirmans (2001) [8]. The findings are in line with predictions of models on corporate governance structures. Publicly traded REITs with dispersed shareholders will not influence the overall ownership structure of the new combined entity after the merger. In contrast, former owners of privately held

REITs become new blockholders of bidder REITs and use their position to effectively monitor the management which provides a positive signal to the market.

Consistent to the evidence for more mature markets, changes in acquisition premiums over time can be observed. Value effects of M&A transactions systematically change during the period studied. Bidders experience larger negative returns in the second period, whereas in the first period returns where close to zero and rather insignificant. Target shareholders gain less in the first period. This finding might be an indication of increased competition in the acquisition of targets in the second period, which led to higher acquisition prices.

6   Conclusion

Summary   The authors presented in this chapter shareholder wealth effects of REIT M&A in an international context which includes all transactions from 1990 until 2005, globally. The broad setting enables the authors to analyze a large sample of 107 transactions. The results show that bidders experience small negative abnormal returns, whereas targets exhibit considerable wealth generation. While the overall assessment for the combined entities of bidders and targets remains rather stable over time the wealth transfers from the bidder shareholders to the target owners increase. This wealth transfers are significantly more pronounced in the US market. In addition, it appears that target status has an influence on size and direction of the observed announcement effects. Acquirers of private targets fare much better than those acquiring public targets.

7   Bibliography

[1] Kirchhoff, M./Schiereck, D./Mentz, M., Market Valuation of Real Estate Finance Mergers – A Note, in: Journal of Property Investment & Finance 24, 2006, pp. 79–86.

[2] Sahin, O. F., The Performance of Acquisitions in the Real Estate Investment Trust Industry, in: Journal of Real Estate Research 27, 2005, pp. 321–342.

[3] Campbell, R. D./Petrova, M./Sirmans, C. F., Wealth Effects of Diversification and Financial Deal Structuring: Evidence from REIT Property Portfolio Acquisitions, in: Real Estate Economics 31, 2003, pp. 347–366.

[4] Keisers, M./Schiereck, D., Wealth CREATION of Large REIT M&A – An INTERNATIONAL Assessment, Working Paper 17, European Business School, Oestrich-Winkel, 2006.

[5] Allen, P. R./Sirmans , C. F., An Analysis of Gains to Acquiring Firm's Shareholders – The Special Case of Reits, in: Journal of Financial Economics 18, 1987, pp. 175–184.

[6] McIntosh, W./Officer, D. T./Born, J. A., The Wealth Effects of Merger Activities: Further Evidence from Real Estate Investment Trusts, in:

Journal of Real Estate Research 4, 1989, pp. 141–155. NAREIT, Historical REIT Industry Market Capitalization: 1972–2005, www. nareit.com/library/industry/marketcap.cfm, accessed on May 12th, 2006.

[7] Young, P. J./Elayan, F. A., An Investigation into the Shareholder Wealth Effects of REIT Acquisitions, in: Real Estate Finance 19, 2002, pp. 27–32.

[8] Campbell, R. D./Ghosh, C./Sirmans, C. F., The Information Content of Method of Payment in Mergers: Evidence from Real Estate Investment Trusts (REITs), in: Real Estate Economics 29, 2001, pp. 361–387.

[9] Chang, S., Takeovers of Privately Held Targets, Methods of Payment, and Bidder Returns, in: Journal of Finance 53, 1998, pp. 773–784.

[10] Pilloff, S. J., Performance changes and shareholder wealth creation associated with mergers of publicly traded banking institutions, in: Journal of Money, Credit, and Banking 28, 1996, pp. 294–310.

[11] Travlos, N. G., Corporate Takeover Bids, Methods of Payment, and Bidding Firms' Stock Returns, in: Journal of Finance 42, 1987, pp. 943–963.

[12] Ambrose, B. W./Linneman, P., REIT Organizational Structure and Operating Characteristics, in: Journal of Real Estate Research 21, 2001, pp. 141–162.

[13] Huang, Y.-S./Walkling, R. A., Target Abnormal Returns Associated with Acquisition Announcements: Payment, Acquisition Form, and Managerial Resistance, in: Journal of Financial Economics 19, 1987, pp. 329–249.

[14] Shleifer, A./Vishny, R. W., Large Shareholders and Corporate Control, in: Journal of Political Economy 94, 1986, pp. 461–488.

[15] Faccio, M./McConnell, J. J./Stolin, D., Returns to Acquirers of Listed and Unlisted Targets, in: Journal of Financial and Quantitative Analysis 41, 2006, pp. 197–220.

[16] Dodd, P./Warner, J., On Corporate Governance – A Study of Proxy Contests, in: Journal of Financial Economics 11, 1983, pp. 401–438.

[17] Brown, S. J./Warner, J. B., Using daily stock returns: The case of event studies, in: Journal of Financial Economics 14, 1985, pp. 3–31.

[18] Boehmer, E./Musumeci, J./Poulsen, A. B., Event-study methodology under conditions of event induced variance, in: Journal of Financial Economics 30, 1991, pp. 253–272.

[19] Sera, A. P., Event Study Tests – A Brief Survey, Working Paper, University of Porto, 2002.

7 REITs and financial communication

Gundolf Moritz

Table of contents

1   Introduction

Communication needs

The German Real Estate Investment Trust (G-REIT) as a new investment vehicle in Germany faces specific communication needs. First of all, it is important to note that being listed on the stock exchange, REITs are owned by a heterogeneous group of many private and institutional shareholders. Their invested money constitutes the equity basis of a REIT. Equity investors want to participate in and benefit from a company's business.

Private and institutional investors have a choice in terms of what kind of corporation or which specific company they wish to invest in. Each REIT is just one option among various investment vehicles on the international capital markets. The financial communication approach should therefore focus on convincing investors to participate in the opportunities of a specific company, namely the specific REIT.

Legal framework

Legal requirements form the framework within which REITs conduct their business. In Germany, the so-called 75/75/90 rule applies, which means that a REIT has to invest at least 75 % of its total assets into real estate, to derive at least 75 % of gross income from rents from real estate property or interest on mortgages on real estate property, and to annually distribute at least 90 % of its taxable income to shareholders as dividends.

Compared to other countries such as Belgium, France, and the Netherlands, where REITs are already established as reliable equity vehicles, in Germany, the REIT market still needs to position itself in order to offer a consistent market environment for its investors and to allow comparisons at a European and a German level.

At the European level, the legal framework varies in terms of dividends and tax requirements. As already observed on a European level, in addition to the investors themselves, of which some specialize solely in REITs, a group of REIT analysts and journalists will be established in Germany. This group will examine, scrutinize and focus their expertise on REITs, and will constitute the audience for the communication of REITs.

The crucial question in this context is how to differentiate one specific REIT from another in terms of geography, legal frameworks and business models. How can an investor be convinced of the strong performance of a specific REIT? In this context, the communication of every REIT will be a decisive element in order to underline their Unique Selling Proposition (USP). A USP signifies a strict distinction from and different positioning to direct competitors. One important form of differentiation is the focusing on a specific segment. For example, REITs in Germany can mainly invest in industrial buildings, offices, healthcare real estate or warehouses, but not in buildings for residential purposes.

Differentiation among REITs

There will also be a regional differentiation between Northern, Southern, Eastern and Western Germany, as well as a differentiation according to rural, urban and peripheral regions. In addition, REITs will focus on certain activities, such as the modernization of buildings, renting and the administration of real estate.

Management credibility

Furthermore, the credibility of the REIT's management is a crucial factor. Whether or not a REIT's management is able to communicate in a credible manner will be important to its success. Questions concerning the management's track record of a successful strategy, measurable targets and ways to achieve them will be asked. What are the milestones a manager has already achieved with this REIT and in his former career positions, and how has he communicated these milestones? Equity investors will also look for a performance-related remuneration structure for REIT managers in order to give them an incentive to create shareholder value. Communicating this remuneration structure could also constitute a form of differentiation from competitors.

Key performance indicators will reflect the specialization and differentiation of the REIT. They constitute the communication vocabulary that will be used in order to explain the investment strategy of a REIT to investors and analysts. REIT key performance indicators include the EBITDA margin, the Net Asset Value (NAV), the Funds From Operations (FFO) and the dividend yield.

Communication before IPO

It is important that the investor relations department initiates sustainable communication even before an Initial Public Offering (IPO), develops it during the IPO and establishes an ongoing dialogue using the REIT vocabulary. It is crucial that the achievement of defined targets is communicated in order to develop a track record and therefore a level of valued credibility. Continuous transparency and regular communication with the main target groups using different communication tools, such as road shows, face-to-face and round table meetings, press conferences, conference calls, etc., foster relationships with journalists, investors and analysts.

It is hereby important to communicate in a manner appropriate for the specific target group. This does not mean manipulating information or news, but rather explaining it differently to the various groups, as a retail investor will obviously be looking for different information as institutional investors or journalists are. Periodical results or corporate events need to be communicated differently for each target group and without hiding any information. In addition to the "must dos", it is important to add some "should dos". As the management is the main message provider and representative of a REIT, it is crucial to remind managers of what they have said in the past.

A promise has to be made and kept in order to achieve credibility and generate trust in the investor community. Because managers often make promises and then concentrate on other issues, it is important to remind them of their promises. This is one important task of the investor relations department of a REIT.

Reduced complexity A final important point to keep in mind is the need to reduce the complexity of the information. The ideal scenario is a clear, short communication of the differentiation points, with the option for each target group to easily attain further information.

Optimal perception in capital markets If a REIT takes the above-mentioned points into consideration, it should achieve an optimal perception in the capital markets, with investors and analysts placing their trust in the management and the REIT's equity history. This also requires building up relations with journalists who understand the key messages and the history of a REIT, and who will distribute these messages to a broader audience. This optimal perception is sustainable and also valid during difficult times when a REIT knows to whom it may address the solution proposal for a problem in order to take the story to the markets.

To summarize, the clear, substantial communication of a REIT's USP and its targets, and the immediate explanation of any discrepancies before, during and after an IPO puts a REIT in the best possible light.

2 Communication requirements of a Real Estate Investment Trust

This chapter will take a look at the main characteristics of German REITs for a better understanding of their position in the European capital market and as an introduction to the current topic of this chapter: the specific requirements of a German REIT in terms of capital market communication with the aim to achieve optimum market perception.

The requirements listed in the chapter at hand are primarily based on previous experience with the communication of real estate companies listed on the stock exchange which, while not being REITs as such, can nevertheless serve as a basis for deducing communicative requirements.

2.1 Characteristics of a German REIT from an investor's point of view

German REITs as public listed investment vehicles What are the characteristics of a German REIT from the investor's point of view?

The main trait of a REIT may sound rather obvious: A German REIT is a public limited company that operates on the basis of the German Stock Corporation Act. From a potential investor's point of view, a German REIT is therefore first and foremost an equity investment vehicle much like any other listed stock corporation. In accordance with its quotation on the organized German market (entry or prime standard), a G-REIT is subject to the same publication and communication requirements as any other stock corporation. This means that REITs are often held by equity investors, which is an important factor to be taken into consideration when it comes to the REIT's communication requirements.

By their nature, equity investors wish to participate in a stock corporation's chances. As a result, this group of investors primarily makes its investment decisions by weighing up their prospects in an estimated risk-reward profile. They then choose a specific equity vehicle on the basis of this evaluation process, which itself engenders specific communication requirements. This decision-making process is based on prospects and is very different to choosing fixed-income assets, where the risks have a high priority, thus heavily influencing and shaping the communication.

Other characteristics of a G-REIT are determined by the 75/75/90 rule, which stipulates that 75 % of a G-REIT's gross income must be generated by letting, leasing and sale, 75 % of the assets must be invested in real estate and 90 % of the profit must be paid as dividends. G-REITs are entitled to invest in real estate in Germany with the exception of portfolio residential property ($> 50\,\%$ residential, built before January 1st, 2007).

Free float requirement

A further requirement is a free float quota of at least 15 %, or at least 25 % at the time of listing, and a restriction on a direct stake in a G-REIT to 10 %. In addition, shares may only be held indirectly.

These traits form the basis of a uniform market within which the individual REIT vehicles can position themselves. They also serve as a uniform basis for communication within the market.

2.2 German REIT compared to European REIT structures

Competition among REIT structures

At this point, a quick look at REIT structures elsewhere in Europe shall be taken, as the opening-up of the capital markets means that the German REIT will be in direct competition with other REITs from Europe and the rest of the world.

REITs have been an established equity vehicle in other European countries for many years now, particularly in the Netherlands, where they were introduced in 1969, albeit without having to be listed on the stock exchange. REITs have similarly been available in Belgium since 1995 and in France since 2003. In these two countries, it is required that the REITs are listed, as it is the case in Germany.

Taxation differences

The main difference between these national REITs is taxation. For example, Dutch REITs are generally not subject to corporate income tax – the full corporate income tax rate of 34.5 % is only due on the liquidation of hidden assets. In Belgium, REITs are obliged to pay corporate income tax, whereby income from rent and profits from the sale of real estate are tax-exempt. An additional corporate income tax rate of approximately 20 % applies to the sum of disclosed reserves and unrealized capital gains. French REITs are likewise subject to corporate income tax. Disclosed hidden assets are taxed at half the corporate income tax rate (16.5%) on the basis of the real estate listed in the balance sheet.

Field of activity Another difference is the field of activity of REITs in the different European countries. For example, in addition to letting and leasing activities common to all the European REITs, French REITs are also involved in other activities such as project development.

Dividend distribution There are also differences in terms of the distribution of dividends. In the Netherlands, a REIT is required to distribute 100% of its profits, a Belgian REIT is required to distribute 80% of its net profit, and a REIT in France is required to distribute 85% of its profits from letting and leasing, in addition to distributing 50% of its income from real estate sales and 100% of the income from subsidiaries. In comparison, a German REIT is in the middle with a dividend distribution requirement of 90%.

This brief comparison of European REIT structures is important, as, with the capital market being open, interested investors have the liberty to choose just the right REIT for their needs. Additionally, an investor can choose between all the different REITs and listed real estate companies on the German market, all of which are embedded in a wide array of possible German, European and international share investment vehicles.

Closer inspection of the German market for real estate shares reveals the potential this segment has. Taking the market capitalization of real estate investments in comparison to the gross national product, we can see that Germany, at around 5%, lies within the average of western industrialized nations. It is, however, also evident that four of these five percentage points represent investments in open-end funds. We can therefore assume that many real estate assets, which are currently embedded in open-end funds, will make their way onto the stock exchange, for example, through a vehicle such as a German REIT.

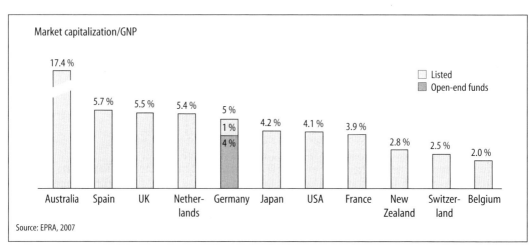

Fig. 1:   International comparison of the real estate shares sector

This straightforward derivation highlights the potential for a major market. On the demand side, this would entail requirements in terms of communication and positioning.

2.3   Communication target groups of a REIT

Groups of market participants will be formed and these will also be the main target groups for communicating with a REIT. A specific group of analysts will also be formed, which will focus on the regular examination and the analysis of the German REIT market in order to act as experts in the field. There will also be a development towards institutional investors who specifically invest in this market. Further, there will be private investors who will invest in REITs in accordance with their risk profile due to the above-mentioned free float requirement. The equity class will be completely reshaped on the German capital market and the REIT corporations will each face the question of how to stand out from the crowd and make themselves visible. The challenge lies in setting oneself apart from the competition in the G-REIT and international REIT classes to compete for capital.

Analysts, investors and journalists as main audience for the communication

Accordingly, what influence does this have on the capital market communication of a G-REIT and what differentiation options does the communication offer?

2.4   USP communication

Every REIT will need to highlight the effectiveness of its specific business model in order to win individual investors. Communication will play an important part in making a REIT attractive to investors, serving as a way of highlighting a REIT's Unique Selling Proposition (USP). The USP of a REIT will be derived from the way it specializes and differentiates itself from the competition, and from its clearly different positioning within the field.

Communication of a USP is crucial for the success of a REIT

One such USP would clearly be the focus on a specific segment within the field. REITs can differentiate themselves by choosing to invest primarily in industrial buildings, productions sites, warehouses, offices, or healthcare premises, for example. In fact, they can focus on any kind of real estate with the exception of portfolio residential property. Another form of differentiation could be the geographical distinction, e. g., within Germany between Northern, Eastern, Western and Southern Germany, or focusing on city centers or more peripheral locations. A REIT's business model could focus on letting and leasing, building modernization or management. These are merely a handful of the many aspects that could be considered in order for a REIT to set itself apart from the rest. The communication used on the capital market then needs to be in line with the individual REITs' USPs.

Focus on specific segment

Furthermore, there is another crucial means of differentiation: the credibility of the institution, the corporation and the management. This will depend on how successful a G-REIT's management is in plausibly communicating the equity history of the REIT. Analysts and investors will carefully examine whether the REIT management can show a track record of its management achievements in order to draw conclusions relating to future management performance. A REIT's vision and strategy, including the targets and strategic steps taken

Credibility of the institution, the corporation and the management

along the way will be of crucial importance. The REIT management will be expected to communicate the milestones that will contribute to the realization of the corporate strategy. In the long term, communicating these milestones and documenting them as they are successfully put into practice will lead to a kind of virtual credibility account for the G-REIT and its management. The healthier a G-REIT's credibility balance, the more attractive it will be to a potential investor.

A performance-related pay structure for the management can also contribute greatly to boosting the REIT's credibility.

2.5   REIT communication vocabulary

EBITDA margin and NAV
The way, in which REITs specialize and differentiate themselves, will be reflected in their Key Performance Indicators (KPIs). These KPIs are the communicative building blocks used by the REITs to highlight their vision and their investment case to corporate investors, analysts and private investors. Some of these KPIs do not solely apply to G-REITs and are familiar benchmarks in the equity investment market, such as the EBITDA margin, in comparison to the economic value. The EBITDA margin is a good indication of a REIT's operative success.

One specific communication term is the NAV, which stands for the net worth of the real estate investments at fair market value, i. e., the fair market value of the real estate less liabilities. The particular challenge here will be the communication of any premium that may be applied to the NAV and possible deviations later on.

FFO
The most important KPI will undoubtedly be the FFO, which is a KPI not exclusive to the real estate market that represents a company's operative earnings strength. On the basis of the net income for the year, write-offs are added and proceeds from sales subtracted. As a KPI, FFO are a transparent means of representing the effectiveness of a REIT in its core line of business, i. e., letting and leasing.

The dividend yield is undoubtedly also important for the equity investor. Thanks to minimum dividend distribution quotas, which are stipulated by law, an investor can make a very good prognosis of the distribution he will receive. This can be communicated as an advantage of this equity vehicle.

The questions which logically follow are when, where and why these communication terms should be used, or in other words, what shape the forward-looking and sustainable communication of the differentiation criteria should take.

2.6   How to use the REIT vocabulary

Sustainable communication approach
The focus should be on establishing a sustainable communication approach for the period before being floated on the stock exchange, during the IPO process and, above all, after having been floated. It is essential that a track record is developed that can be expanded upon with the goals promised and delivered ("promise and deliver" principle). Another very important aspect of such a

track record is its transparency, which should apply both to future and past statements. It is vital that the communication is coherent, both in terms of quantity and quality. In precise terms, this means that a REIT should continue to communicate with its audience in good times as well as in bad times, whilst always keeping the REIT's credibility rating in mind.

Another factor contributing to optimum market perception is reduced complexity. The differentiation criteria must be communicated lucidly. And while organizing the individual criteria as discussed above can result in highly complex structures, it is important that these are kept to a bare minimum in the communication to facilitate comprehension on the investor's side.

Reduced complexity

One aspect of sustainable communication is the maintenance of regular contact with the main target audiences, i.e., investors and their multipliers, and sell-side analysts, whilst not forgetting journalists and the media. These regular meetings should be implemented using the communication tools available. For analysts, for example, these would be one-on-one meetings, road shows, corporate presentations, a press conference on the financial statements, and conference calls. For the media, the tools used would be round tables with journalists, interviews and briefings. This can lead to a media profile that is seen not only by private investors, but also by the decision makers of institutional investors. These measures all result in a positive basic position on the market.

Maintenance of regular contact

Information should always be published in a way that is relevant to the specific target group. This shall not mean that information should be manipulated; a private investor, however, is looking for different information on a company than an institutional investor is. The same basic information, such as business transactions and operating results, needs to be edited differently to cater for the comprehension needs of the different target groups, i.e., private investors, institutional investors, analysts and the media. Otherwise, the REIT cannot maintain sustainable communication.

In addition to the communication aspects required by the regulatory bodies, it is important to also feature a wide array of optional communication aspects in order to achieve optimum capital market perception. In this respect, the REIT's main ambassador to its investors, the capital market and the public is its management.

Optional communication aspects

One of the main tasks of a company's investor relations department is to keep the management informed on how the company is perceived on the capital market and to steer the corporate message and communication in such a way that discrepancies between the general perception and reality are kept to a minimum. The investor relations department is also charged with making sure that the REIT's credibility account is well topped up at all times, thus addressing the promise and deliver principle and reinforcing the credibility of the REIT and its management. This credibility is the consequence of the discipline invested in the capital market communication by the management and the investor relations department.

3   Conclusion

Following these steps to establish a sustainable communication structure should result in an optimum perception of a REIT on the capital market. This has been achieved when the REIT has investors and analysts which understand the REIT's equity history and are willing to trust the REIT management, and when it has found itself a permanent position in the market and has stood its ground there, unscathed by difficult market periods. This also calls for solid relations with journalists as well as a close contact to the media, which a REIT should begin to foster as early as possible.

To summarize, a focused, target group-specific and sustainable communication of a REIT's differentiation criteria and an adequate and speedy explanation of possible deviations both before and after an IPO will result in the optimum perception of the corporation in the capital market, thus making it an attractive investment vehicle for investors within the segment of German REITs.

8   Non-REIT indirect real estate products: special funds, real estate corporations, closed-end funds

Nicolai Striewe
Tobias Streckel

Table of contents

1   Introduction

Investors seek for variety in investment opportunities. The availability of different investment products improves the chances to meet demands of investors with different strategies and risk attitudes. Some investors may prioritize different characteristics for their investments, such as tax transparency, liquidity, fungibility, leverage, degree of regulation, disclosure requirements or others. It shows transparency and professionalism of a real estate market if investors can realize their needs and find an appropriate investment vehicle.

In Germany, investors can invest in real estate directly and indirectly via closed-ended, open-end funds, open-end special funds, real estate corporations and Real Estate Investment Trusts (REITs).

2   German open-end real estate special funds

Open-end real estate special funds (Immobilien-Spezialfonds or Immobilien-Spezialsondervermögen) have a long tradition in Germany. The DekaBank was the first initiator of an open-end real estate special fund in 1976. This type of fund is a variation of the German open-end real estate fund which was introduced on the German market in 1959. This type of fund had been originated in Switzerland in 1938 and it has been highly demanded ever since.

Fig. 1:   History of open-end real estate funds in Europe

2.1   Definition and regulative terms

In general, open-end real estate funds are classified as non-listed investment vehicles and are subject to the restrictions of the German Investment Act (Investmentgesetz or InvG). They invest capital, contributed by investors, in commercial buildings and other types of real estate. The initiator offers and redeems units on a daily basis. Therefore, the pricing of the units will be calculated on the basis of the Net Asset Value (NAV) of the fund's properties [1]. Often the initiator suspends the redemption of shares of the fund for one year or longer after the issuance. If investors want to give back their units within one or two years, they have to consider in their calculation that they already paid an agio. The agio mostly amounts to 5 % and has negative effects on the IRR. Institutional investors tend to have a long-term view and so this issue is of lower importance.

The number of investors who can participate in German open-end real estate special funds are no longer restricted as § 91 No. 1 of the Investment Act was removed in the course of the deregulation of the special fund sector in late 2007. The target group for open-end real estate special funds is restricted to institutional buyers, such as   **Institutional investors**

- insurance companies,
- pension funds,
- superannuation funds,

- foundations,
- family offices.

German insurance companies and pensions funds in particular prefer to invest in German open-end real estate special funds.

Conservative investment

The German Insurance Supervision Law (Versicherungsaufsichtsgesetz or VAG) regulates the terms of investments for German insurance companies and pension funds. According to § 54 No. 1 of VAG, the reserve stock (Deckungsstock) of insurance companies must "be invested in a way which ensures maximum security and profitability, while maintaining its liquidity at all times, through adequate diversification and spread". Thereby, the initiator has to bear in mind which structure, risk-return profile and strategy in view of its target group has to be selected. This approach reflects a relatively conservative investment strategy which these funds mostly have. The funds, therefore, can be categorized as a relatively low volatility investment.

Public open-end real estate funds vs. open-end real estate special funds

Open-end real estate special funds have a supervisory board of investors, which public open-end real estate funds do not have. This can influence the fund managers directly on strategic investment decisions as well as on the acquisition or sale of assets. The fund targets institutional investors; however, it was created as a public open-end real estate fund with similar conditions.

Terms of contract and prospectus

The administration effort is less for special funds, as the terms of contract do not need the approval from the BaFin (Bundesanstalt für Finanzdienstleistungsaufsicht), the Federal Financial Supervisory Authority in Germany (§ 93 No. 1, Investment Act). Instead, a cumulative report of the special separate asset has to be submitted to the BaFin semi-annually (§ 93 No. 2). Many of the investor information obligations for public open-end funds are not applicable for open-end special funds according to § 93 No. 3. A prospectus (§ 42) for the marketing of the fund is not necessary, neither are investor information as required for open-end funds (§ 121).

IFRS

Investors also prepare their balance sheet according to IFRS and classify open-end real estate special fund units as securities. The value equals the price of the units and the current value, respectively. The asset side of an IFRS balance sheet, especially the financial instruments, is difficult to derive. Many investment companies have been given the possibility to report according to IFRS to investors.

Finally, open-end real estate special funds combine on the one hand the characteristics of direct real estate investments like stable cash flows, and on the other hand the characteristics of fungible stocks [2]. But the fungibility may be limited as the liquidity is generally low. Usually, there has to be a reallocation of the share to another investor in case of an exit. Therefore, shareholders early indicate their intent to sell a share in order to make a coordination of the transaction possible [3]. It is specified in § 92 of the Investment Act that an investment company has to ensure that the shares may only be transferred to another investor with the approval of the investment company.

2.2   Legal restrictions

The former German Investment Companies Act (Gesetz über Kapital-gesellschaften or KAGG) was superseded by the Investment Act which came into effect on January 1st, 2004. In order to make open-end real estate funds more international in the course of globalization, this German legislature has permitted investment companies to invest worldwide and has given them the opportunity for a larger diversification within real estate portfolios.

In 2007, the federal cabinet enforced an amendment to the Investment Act (InvÄndG). The foundation pillars were liberalization and internationalization of the German open-end fund vehicles without expenses on protection for investors. The most important changes were the following: **Amendment to the Investment Act**

- deregulation,
- modernization,
- promotion of product innovations,
- improved protection of investors, and
- corporate governance.

Rules for special funds have become less strict and more simplified. This is due to the fact that the investor groups are composed of institutional investors only, and therefore, there is no need for extensive protection. Double regulations on the demand and the supply side are eliminated with the amendment. Furthermore, in contrast to public open-end funds, institutional investors are enabled to participate in development, refurbishment and construction phases of infrastructural projects of PPP-project companies via the open-end special fund (§ 91 No. 3, § 90 a–k).

The entire asset has to be invested by taking the principle of risk spreading into account (§ 1). Investment companies of open-end real estate special funds have to place at least 51 % of their capital into the following real estate categories (§ 80 No. 1):   **Assets**

- residential, commercial or mixed-used buildings,
- plots,
- developments,
- unbuilt plots (for planned developments),
- emphyteusis.

Furthermore, open-end real estate special funds are not required to maintain a minimum liquidity of 5 % of assets under management unlike public open-end real estate funds (§ 80 No. 1).

Investment companies are supervised by the German Federal Financial Supervisory Authority (BaFin) (§ 6 No. 1). The reason for this is not just the high requirements of the investment companies, but also the fact that investment companies classify as financial institutions. They act on their own behalf but also on account of a third party, the open-end real estate fund (§ 2 No. 6 InvG). Generally, they can be established as a limited company or corporation (§ 6 No. 1).   **Investment companies**

Depository bank   Chapter 3 of the Investment Act contains the legal restrictions and functions of the depository bank. § 26 regulates accounting transactions that are subject to authorization, i. e., the purchase of properties for the fund. A further central task is the management of the fund's assets, including the issuance and redemption of shares (§ 23).

2.3   Structure

German open-end real estate funds consist of the below-mentioned key elements:

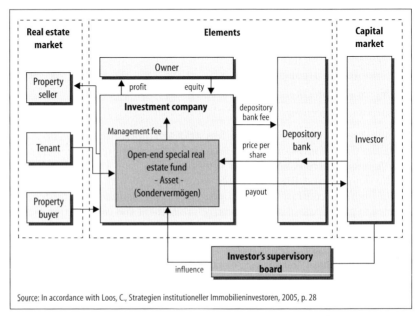

Fig. 2:   Structure of a German special open-end real estate fund

Assets   The asset is called separate asset (Sondervermögen) because it is not taxed on fund level. As soon as the dividend is distributed by the investment company, the investor derives its balance and the tax that is payable by shareholders. A characteristic and an essential part of a special fund is the supervisory board which has an impact on the investment strategy and therefore on the assets. This offers investors the possibility to bring their demands into the portfolio and allows the pursuit of the investment philosophy. The assets must be valued by an independent committee of experts annually and on every purchase of a piece of property. One of the most significant features is that the price of the units will be calculated on the basis of the Net Asset Value in contrast to real estate corporations which prices reflect the demand and supply on the stock market.

The investment company is mainly responsible for the fiduciary management of the assets which consists of the following tasks [4]:

Investment company

- portfolio management,
- tenant acquisition,
- property management,
- marketing,
- research,
- sale of shares,
- cash management,
- risk management.

Specifically, the depository bank has the role of a trustee with monitoring and controlling functions and receives a fee. All transactions concerning the units are managed by the depository bank. This can either be a German or a foreign bank.

Depository bank

The owner of the investment company, mostly a bank, has the intention to make a profit and to get a return from his invested equity. Real estate funds have the intention to let, purchase and sell properties. Furthermore, the investor's relationship as well is a crucial factor. The increasing demand for German open-end real estate special funds of institutional investors is elaborated in the next section.

Other parties and surrounding environment

2.4   Market overview

In Germany, the investment volume of open-end real estate special funds has soared to €20.4 billion in December 2006. This trend shows a positive development based on the low volatility and long-term stable investment returns which institutional investors see in this investment class. The total investment volume, including the public open-end real estate funds, amounts to approximately €95 billion. In December 2005, the Deutsche Bank suspended redemption of the units of its public open-end real estate fund GrundbesitzInvest followed by Kan-Am with its US-Grundinvest fund in January 2006. Due to this fact, investors wanted to give back their units to the respective investment companies, but as those could not liquidize the properties immediately, the funds had been closed for a certain period of time for cash buildup and revaluation purposes. While confidence in the public open-end real estate funds could be recovered, it appears that investors of open-end real estate special funds are reluctant to further investments. Open-end real estate special funds even showed a net capital outflow in the beginning of 2007. A reason for this development could be the introduction of the REIT and the current trend of insurances to invest capital directly into real estate [5].

Confidence crisis

The OGAW-Guideline of 1985 is no longer in charge for the European fund sector which had been restructured. Due to the rising establishment, presently a group of experts of the European Union is working on an EU-Pass for transborder distributions [6].

Harmonization in Europe

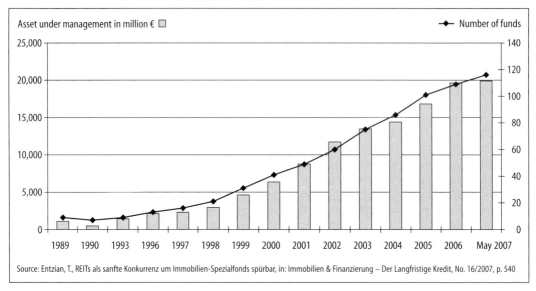

Fig. 3:   *Growth of German open-end real estate special funds*

3   German closed-end real estate funds

"The tax drive is bigger than the sexual drive", is often kidded by Germans about their investment mentality regarding closed-end real estate funds. In the past, German legislation put the kibosh on tax privileges which real estate had. Around 2005, the initiators had restructured their funds with the primary objective to gain an attractive risk-return profile instead of aiming primarily at tax savings.

3.1   Definition

Closed-end real estate funds are indirect real estate investment vehicles which are closed after achieving the planned equity. The investors normally put their money into commercial real estate, such as offices, retail buildings, logistics or residential properties. Many of the German investors used to focus on investments in Germany only.

3.2   Prospectus

BaFin supervision   Very often a fund consists of just one property. This is described in detail in the prospectus together with all accompanying chances and risks. It is not only the purpose of the prospectus to give the prospective investors information on the investment, but to protect the initiator against later possible claims for compensation. Since July 1st, 2005, the Federal Financial Supervisory Authority (BaFin) checks prospectuses for compliance with all issues before the initiator introduces its product into the market. This verification concerns only the completeness but not the correctness. Nevertheless, the initiator is liable and takes responsibility for the published contents which are subject to the terms of the contract. As an instrument of supervision the standard for a prospectus according the German Institute of Auditors (IDW) IDW S4, which will be replaced by IDW ES4, is generally accepted for closed-end funds in Germany.

3.3 Legal restriction and taxation

Closed-end real estate funds are not subject to any specific law and supervision in contrast to open-end real estate funds. Therefore, this investment vehicle is assigned to the "grey" capital market. The legal structure of these funds is designed in partnerships and not capital companies like a limited partnership, often with a limited liability company as general partner (GmbH & Co. KG). These types of companies are subject to the German Civil Code and the German Commercial Code. Compared to open-end real estate funds, which are subject to the Investment Act, closed-end real estate funds are not required to comply with a specific law.

No specific law or supervision

Closed-end real estate funds are tax transparent, meaning that income taxes are levied on the investors, who obtain rental income and capital gains from the fund. Internationally investing closed-end real estate funds usually reduce the tax burden on investor's level by means of Double Taxation Agreements. To reduce the administrative expenses, a trustee is representatively registered in the company register. Otherwise, all shareholders of the fund company would have to be registered. The flat withholding tax (Abgeltungssteuer) that will come into effect from 2009 on will not be applicable to closed-end funds. Therefore, closed-end funds will continue to benefit from the half-income system and the tax-free returns after the speculation period.

Taxation

3.4 Fungibility

Participations in closed-end real estate funds are usually long-term investments over 10 or more years. The possibility to liquidize participations was a problem in the past. Principally, the investors take back the units only in case of unemployment or death, etc.

Over the recent years, a secondary market for the shares has grown and helped to increase the fungibility. Examples are the "Fondsbörse Germany" and "Fondsbörse Hamburg". However, the smaller the volume of the funds is the lower the trading volume and liquidity tends to be. Furthermore, there are in many cases terms of contracts which allow the sale of the participation only upon approval by the initiator.

Secondary market

3.5 Liability and total loss

Closed-end real estate funds are not compensated from a depositor's guarantee fund in case of insolvency. The initiator's liability used to be limited to the equity. Meanwhile, the legal situation has changed and in specific cases the initiator is personally liable for the debts, liabilities and obligations of the fund.

Reserve liability In case of any financial difficulties of the funds the investor can have a reserve liability. This depends on the kind of participation. Especially, if the fund is in the legal form of a company constituted under civil law (GbR) the company members are liable with their personal wealth.

3.6   Case study: IVG Euroselect 14 "The Gherkin"

Many German funds have changed their investment behavior and have started to invest outside of Germany as well. Targets are beneath others European countries, the United States and Asia. Therewith, the prospective investors have the opportunity to participate in the growth of the international real estate markets and additionally benefit from alternative investments having less risk by means of higher diversification.

In 2007, IVG Immobilien AG launched one of the biggest closed-end single-property funds in Germany. The property fund EuroSelect 14 acquired in cooperation with Evan Randall the office building 30 St Mary Axe ("The Gherkin") in the city center of London. The purchase price was roughly £600 million which IVG Private Funds took an interest in to the amount of about £300 million.

3.6.1   Investment concept

The IVG Private Funds division has indirectly acquired a 50% stake in the target company 30 St Mary Axe (Bermuda) LP which is the legal owner of the property "The Gherkin". This means that the investor indirectly participates via a holding vehicle, which represents the joint venture level on the performance of the building.

Property dimensions The property, The Gherkin, consists of one office tower (30 St Mary Axe) with a rental office area of 502,518 sq. ft. (equal to 46,684 sq. m.) and the adjoining building (20 Bury Street) with a rental office area of 5,672 sq. ft. (527 sq. m.). The building is located in the center of London's financial district and sets a landmark through its remarkable design.

Investment volume 50% of the total buying price of £600 million is deducted for the share of the indirect purchase of the property, resulting in £300 million. According to the valuation the value of the property, if it had been sold in February 2007, would have amounted to £ 615 million. As of June 20th, 2007, the current market value of The Gherkin, according to Savills, increased to £635 million. For that reason, IVG could acquire The Gherkin at the current market value. The total investment volume of the trust adds up to about £347 million and venture capital to £156.3 million (excluding a 5% premium). The placed equity was raised in just eight weeks.

Minimum investment and deposit The minimum outlay amounted to £10,000, plus 5% premium. Deposits as well as payouts are made in sterling pounds. Additionally, the trust fund offers the service, subject to the declaration of enrollment, to transact the deposit and also the payouts in euros. Therewith, the German investors take the currency risks but also chances depending on the currency development of the pound sterling.

The forecasted payouts (6-monthly disbursements) are not guaranteed, but stem from the property's business control results. According to forecast calculations, the capital distribution will amount to an estimated 5.5 % p. a. on the equity capital (without premium). **Return and payout**

The investors may decide at the first corporate meeting on the acceptance for trade of the EuroSelect 14 on the appropriate unlisted securities market. **Disposability**

Currently, 94.1 % of the total area is let to 21 tenants, mainly to global companies, active in the financial and insurance industries. Occupying 43.5 % of the total floor space, Swiss Re Services Limited is the building's main tenant. Swiss Re is the world's largest reinsurance company and holds a tenancy contract until 2031 and pays the rent in Swiss franc. As the loan is also in Swiss franc, the credit will be retired directly with the rental income. This allows participating in low interest rates of the Swiss franc. **Tenant**

Kirkland & Ellis LLP, an international law firm, resides on 12.6 % of the floor area.

3.6.2   Legal and tax structure

The fund company (IVG EuroSelect Vierzehn GmbH & Co. KG) acquired indirect roughly 50 % of the property. The property is in the beneficiary ownership of the Special Purpose Vehicle (SPV) 30 St Mary Axe (Bermuda) LP. Owner of the SPV is again the holding 30 St Mary Axe LP, based in Scotland, and the management company 30 St Mary Axe Management LP Inc., based in Guernsey, one of the British Isles. The fund company is in each company the holding and the management company, taking an interest of 49.999 %.

The Double Taxation Agreement makes Great Britain particularly attractive for German investors. Currently, annual incomes of £ 5,225 solely for the financial

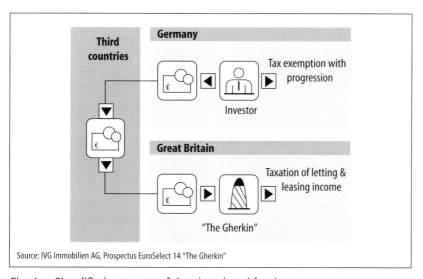

Source: IVG Immobilien AG, Prospectus EuroSelect 14 "The Gherkin"

Fig. 4:   Simplified structure of the closed-end fund

year 2007/2008 are tax-free in the UK. This is equivalent to around € 7,629 and ensures almost tax-free incomes up to an investment value of £ 80,000.

3.7   Market overview

In 2006, 73 companies initiated 135 closed-end real estate funds on the German market, consisting of 63 single-property funds, 55 multi-property funds, eight fund-of-funds, six development funds and three §6b-funds [7]. §6b of the German Income Tax Act states that a company does not have to pay taxes on its profit if the profit is invested immediately.

Higher risk-return profiles In the past, pure letting closed-end funds dominated the market. A change towards fund-of-funds and development funds began. Those funds are mostly designed as blind pools with only fixed investment criteria but no predefined concrete investment objects. At the same time, the tax-oriented changed to return-oriented closed-end fund concepts. Higher risk-return profiles were established through project development funds and fund-of-funds, which invest again into opportunity funds that have an investment focus on project developments. Despite the increase in risk-return profiles, the closed-end fund initiators try to broaden their target group to address smaller private investors by decreasing minimum subscriptions and offering saving plans [8].

Closed-end real estate funds face difficulties in the current market situation. Savings banks as well as cooperative banking associations are less committed in the marketing of closed-end real estate funds [9]. Funds with office and retail spaces in Germany were rare in closed-end funds in recent years. The high vacancy rates made investors shirk. But analyst expectations forecast a trend of decreasing vacancy rates.

The advantage that the flat withholding tax (Abgeltungssteuer) of 2009 will not be applicable for closed-end funds may further boost the vehicle's attractiveness [10].

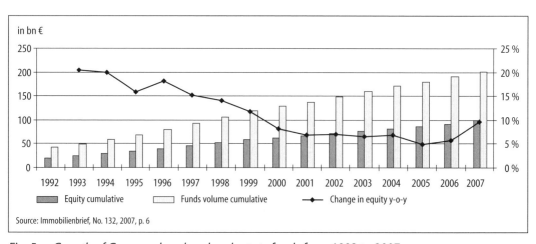

Fig. 5:   Growth of German closed-end real estate funds from 1992 to 2007

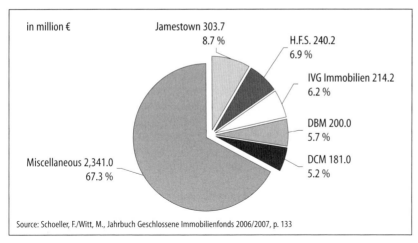

Fig. 6:   Market share of the placed equity in 2006

4   German real estate corporations (Immobilien-AG)

4.1   Definition

Public real estate corporations are exchange-listed corporations with the corporate objective of real estate investment. The price of a share in the company is determined on the stock exchange and is influenced by the value of the property in ownership by the company. The corporation is the proprietor of real estate assets which are either directly or indirectly held. The differentiation of the real estate corporation from a regular corporation is usually seen in the core business of real estate. Real estate corporations are accordingly companies which core business and main source of earnings is the development and management of real estate. But there is no uniform definition [11].

4.2   Regulatory framework

The real estate corporation in Germany is not legally defined and its legal framework and tax rules do not differ from the framework for corporations in general [12].

Regulation

The applicable law is the German Stock Corporation Act (AktG) as the real estate corporation is in the form of a corporation. This means that a board of directors, a supervisory board and a general meeting are required and annual reports and ad hoc notices have to be published. Accordingly, the investor protection and prospectus liability are high. The participation of the investor is limited to the share of participation [13]. There are no mandatory diversification requirements and limitations in which real estate to invest. Furthermore, there are no restrictions for the raising of debt capital [14].

Taxation

Corporation and trade tax are payable for any corporation and real estate corporations do not have a special regulation (§ 1 No. 1 Corporation Tax Law or KStG). There is a corporation tax of 15 % (§ 23 No. 1 KStG) and a trade tax that is fixed by the related community (§ 2 No. 2 Gewerbesteuergesetz – GewStG).

On shareholder's level there is taxation on capital income. For private investors the half-income system is applied (§ 3 No. 40 Income Tax Act, EStG) and capital gains from shares held longer than the speculation period of one year are tax-exempt until 2008. The privileges of the half-income system and the speculation period will be abolished in 2009. Instead, there is a flat withholding tax introduced that taxes capital gains with 25 % (plus solidarity surcharge and church tax) for all investors [15].

There is no property transfer tax on the purchase of the share. The stamp tax is applicable for the purchase of real estate by the real estate corporation [16].

Double taxation on level of the corporation and the investor compared to the tax transparency of investment funds reveals a main disadvantage of the real estate corporation. The principle of tax transparency means that on level of the separate asset there is no corporation and trade tax [17].

4.3   German Property Stock Index (DIMAX)

The performance of real estate corporations is reflected in the German Property Stock Index (DIMAX) by Ellwanger & Geiger.

Calculation   The index is calculated as a performance index and consequently adjusts at capital increases and dividend payments. The weighting of the companies is based on their market capitalization. The admission and cancellation of companies take place at every turn of the year. Every day, the value of the index is calculated based on the quotation of the covered real estate corporations [18].

Criteria   At least, 75 % of their revenues and earnings have to origin from real estate operations for a company to be accepted. These operations include rent and lease, real estate management, development and real estate consulting. The companies are required to be officially traded on the regulated or open market.

Performance   Since the first calculation of the DIMAX in December 1988, the performance has increased 284 % in value compared to 508 % of the DAX [19].

Market correlation   The correlation of the DIMAX representing the German real estate corporations to the DAX representing German 30 largest stock corporations is relatively high, which may be attributed to the listing of these real estate companies on the exchange (see figure 7). The correlation values for the DIMAX to the DAX are 0.40 for a 5-year period and 0.39 for a 10-year period. This means that around 40 % of the dependencies of the DAX are also reflected in the DIMAX. Open-end real estate funds in contrast show even a negative correlation of –0.06 for a 5-year period and –0.18 for a 10-year period. The betas for DIMAX and open-end real estate funds show the same pattern. The DIMAX has a beta of 0.36 for a 5-year period and 0.26 for a 10-year period, while open-end real estate funds show –0.0013 for a 5-year period and –0.0042 for a 10-year period. This means that there is a significantly lower risk observed for the

Source: Bankhaus Ellwanger & Geiger, Reuters January 31st, 2008

Fig. 7:   E&G-DIMAX vs. DAX, indexed from 1988, Dec. 31st

DIMAX compared to the DAX, which is even underbid by the open-end real estate funds [20].

Indices that represent real estate corporations on a European level are the European Property Stock Index (EPIX) by Ellwanger & Geiger and the index of the European Public Real Estate Association (EPRA).

European indices

4.4   Valuation

Real estate corporations are usually valued on the basis of the NAV. The valuation method is regarded as being closely related to the market value of the real estate and therefore decreases the risk of over- or undervaluing the real estate. In case the real estate corporation does not mainly derive directly from rental income, the DCF valuation method is recommended. Deviations from the market value of the real estate corporation from the NAV of the portfolio properties can be explained by factors not considered in the valuation like quality of the management, strategic alignment, business plan, concentrated portfolio management, focus on shareholder value, balance strength, etc. [21].

4.5   Market overview

The index currently consists of 71 real estate corporations with a total market capitalization of € 21 billion [22], a relatively small amount compared to German blue-chip corporations listed in the DAX like Siemens AG (€ 99 billion), Deutsche Telekom AG (€ 66 billion) and Volkswagen AG (€ 46 billion). The dominating companies in the index are IVG Immobilien AG (€ 3,02 billion), GAGFAH (€ 2,82 billion), Deutsche Euroshop AG (€ 885 million) and Deutsche Wohnen AG (€ 580 million) [23].

Market capitalization

Domination of open-end real estate funds The low free float and low liquidity of real estate corporations is problematic [24]. Consequently, the open-end real estate funds (market capitalization of open-end funds: € 82.59 billion [25]) dominate the market (market capitalization of real estate corporations: € 21 billion [26]) [27].

Discount to NAV Although not currently the case for German real estate corporations on an average level, a discount to NAV is a typical characteristic of many real estate corporations and makes them possible candidates for takeovers. As the NAV bases on the sum of all isolated market values of the objects in the real estate corporation, other factors have to be found as an explanation for the deviation of the company value from the NAV. These factors may be, on the one hand, a too high debt portion, a too risky real estate mix and a missing attractive strategy and investment story. Furthermore, there is the quality and the cost for the management influencing the value of the company. Additionally, investors may calculate with different discount factors than those applied for the individual properties. Especially opacity in the real estate corporation market indicates a lower professionalism and inefficiencies that make investors shirk [28]. On the other hand, the vehicle offers low transaction costs, is a relatively safe investment and may be suitable to diversify a real estate portfolio.

5   Future of non-REIT investment vehicles in Germany

Preference of investors It is often argued that the high degree of attractiveness of the separate asset would make the fund structure superior to listed real estate investments and that there would be no reason to invest via real estate corporations. In Germany, the investment into real estate on the stock market has no tradition and the fund concept seems much more familiar to the domestic private investors which are more risk-averse, conservative and interested in stable cash flows [29]. Next to the German REIT, introduced in 2007, there used to be only one listed vehicle form for real estate investments: the real estate corporation.

Market cap of real estate corporations The German real estate corporation meets the demands of the capital market perfectly [30]. But still real estate corporations (market capitalization: € 21 billion [31]) did not gain a market share comparable to open-end real estate investment funds (€ 83 billion [32]). This may be due to inconsistency in the segment, missing standardization and no focus of the investment.

Target group of real estate corporations As real estate corporations reveal many characteristics in practice that are only relevant for a certain target group, the conclusion can be drawn that there is a need for an alternative. The target group of real estate corporations consists of rather institutional investors like insurances as well as investment and pension funds [33]. Furthermore, low volumes, low degree of fungibility, few free-float shares, and a general opacity challenge private investors and makes the vehicle rather comprehendible for professional investors.

Real estate corporations vs. REITs There are many reasons why real estate corporations may want to adopt the REIT status. But this does not necessarily mean cannibalism so that real estate corporations will vanish from the market. Even though REITs are in principle tax transparent, real estate corporations with a limited scope of business and an investment focus, may offer an attractive investment opportunity for investment ideas that are not realizable due to the regulatory framework of the

REIT. REITs can therefore also be seen as a subtype of a real estate corporation, as they are both subject to the German Stock Corporation Act (AktG). The REIT is equipped with additional specifications and limitations which can be perceived as advantages, as they create transparency and taxation benefits, and disadvantages, as they limit the flexibility of a REIT, e. g., in its operations, financing and distribution of profits [34].

Real estate corporations can diversify their operations and supplement their core business with real estate related businesses and project developments. Further, they may be active in the residential real estate sector and can adjust their risk-return profile easily as they have no debt financing limitations. The recent IPOs of the real estate corporations GAGFAH, GWB Immobilien AG, DIC Asset AG or Patrizia Immobilien AG support that argument. The exclusion of residential property from the REIT will also prohibit real estate corporations that have a residential real estate portfolio from converting. This problem that presently is one of the major disadvantages of the current German REIT Act will in the long-term be reduced as only residential properties which were constructed before January 1st, 2007 are excluded [35]. In contrast, the REIT is an internationally known and standardized real estate investment vehicle which foreign investors are familiar with and trust in. The limitations on that vehicle let it obtain tax advantages, while creating transparency. This could mean that REITs offer a risk-return relationship that could be lower than that of real estate corporations (e. g., that it involves less risk while offering higher expected returns). This opinion is supported by factors like transparency issues, i.e., less information asymmetries and a higher predictability and comparability to benchmarks, resulting in a risk decrease of REITs.

Open-end real estate funds

Open-end real estate funds will certainly have an importance in the future further on, regardless of the bad news concerning valuation problems and the introduction of the REIT. Most properly the opposite will happen, the REIT may supplement the portfolios of open-end funds, as it could reduce the risk of illiquidity because of its closed and traded structure.

Closed-end real estate funds

The closed-end fund structure is not threatened by the REIT. In contrast to REITs, closed-end real estate funds mainly focus on single objects and only invest smaller volumes, whereas REITs consist of several properties and therefore are on average larger. In case of an introduction of a private REIT to the German market, there could be some competition for large closed-end funds that invest in a theme-oriented real estate portfolio [36].

Uncertainty about the REIT introduction

The long-lasting discussion and the delayed introduction of German REIT as well as the repeating amendments to the REIT Act created an engrained uncertainty among investors that causes them to hesitate with their optimistically announced plans involving REITs. Involved and partially responsible for the lagging discussions are the lobbies of real estate investment funds which fear a crowding out of investors from their products into REITs. This fear is only partly justified. Even though the REIT concept shows many similarities with the present investment vehicles on the German investment market, it will certainly not replace any of those, but will rather be a further differentiation and supplement to the existing vehicles [37].

Low securitization in Germany

The value of German real estate is estimated at US$ 1,075 billion ranking third (behind the US and Japan) in the international comparison. This attractive figure is clouded by the low securitization of real estate in Germany of only 0.49 % ranking Germany 23rd among the FTSE EPRA/NAREIT countries. A global average is around 6 %. It is expected that the introduction of the REIT could change this underdeveloped situation [38].

Support for the REIT

The German government states that there is a need in Germany for an internationally known and recognized indirect real estate vehicle that provides tax transparency. This means that there is a gap to be filled. The consequence of the REIT introduction should therefore be a strengthening of the German investment market, a contribution to a higher professionalism of the real estate industry and an enabling of Germany to compete with European finance and real estate centers [39]. The German Federal Ministry of Finance (Bundesministerium der Finanzen or BMF) sees the great need to push the REIT structure with an "exit tax" in order to attract interest from investors that have large hidden reserves which would become taxable in case of a transfer. Pursuant to the exit tax only half of the profits from hidden reserves are taxed until 2009 and only for properties that are owned for at least five years. This move is not only for the purpose to increase acceptance but also to optimize the tax income of the state [40].

Pressure from REIT countries

International investors will not wait long for investment opportunities in Germany, but invest in countries in which the framework develops and advances faster [41]. There is pressure from fast-evolving real estate investment markets that have successfully introduced the REIT like France, Luxembourg, etc. [42].

Lobbyism

The lobbies of the different investment vehicles and other advocacy groups have a considerable influence in the real estate industry which becomes obvious especially in the REIT discussion. The fear of being replaced or displaced drives the lobbies to impair the success of the REIT and advocate for a restricted introduction of the REIT structure. The government is advised to find an independent decision that is led by market principles and investors' demands.

No competition for special funds

The exclusion of private-REITs means that the special open-end real estate fund does not experience further competition in the near future.

Investors' perception and amendments to REIT Act decisive

The regulatory framework cannot absolutely define the boundaries of the various investment vehicles and separate one perfectly from another. Even though the real estate corporation could have been provided more investment opportunities in terms of its regulatory boundaries it was positioned by the investors and the real estate corporations themselves in a way that made the introduction of REITs especially necessary.

The behavior of the investors and the way the market will exploit the regulatory framework will reveal how the REIT is to be positioned in the German investment vehicle portfolio. But still, the future amendments to the REIT Act will lead the evolving perception by the market participants of the REIT and the other existing investment vehicles. The weak market position of the real estate corporation leads to the conclusion that in the long run, the REIT construction might be dominant. Practical experience from France shows a successful introduction that caused all real estate corporations to convert into REITs [43]. This leaves the investment market with many open questions and uncertainty on the reaction of REITs, real estate corporations and open-end real estate funds.

6   Bibliography

[1] Falk, B., Fachlexikon Immobilienwirtschaft, 3rd edition, Cologne 2004, p. 441.

[2] Klöppelt, H./Kulke, M., Internationale Immobilien-Spezialfonds, in: Schäfer, J./Conzen,G. (Eds.): Praxishandbuch Immobilien-Investitionen, Munich 2005, pp. 60–78.

[3] Alda, W./Lassen, J., Kapitalanlagegesellschaften, in: Schulte, K.-W./ Bone-Winkel, S./Thomas, M. (Eds.): Handbuch Immobilien-Investition, Cologne 2005, p. 112.

[4] Klug, W., Offene Immobilienfonds, Frankfurt/Main 2004, p. 9.

[5] Entzian, T., REITs als sanfte Konkurrenz um Immobilien-Spezialfonds spürbar, in: Immobilien & Finanzierung – Der Langfristige Kredit, No. 16/2007, p. 539.

[6] Bundesverband Investment und Asset Management (Ed.), Jahrbuch Investment 2007, Frankfurt/Main 2007, pp. 57–63.

[7] Schoeller, F./Witt, M., Jahrbuch Geschlossene Immobilienfonds 2006/2007, Berlin 2007, p. 134.

[8] Kunath, A., Aktuelle Trends im Markt der Geschlossenen Fonds, in: Immobilien & Finanzen, No. 21/2007, p. 762; Gerber, J., Geschlossene Immobilienfonds–Transparenz und Service lohnen sich, in: Immobilien & Finanzierung, No. 23/2007, p. 836.

[9] Rullkötter, S., Geschlossene Fonds – Aufstrebende Gewächse, in: Euro Finanzen, No. 2/2008, p. 138.

[10] Boutonnet, B., Riskante Rendite – Geschlossene Fonds, in: Capital, November 22nd, 2007, p. 120.

[11] Rehkugler, H., Die Immobilien-AG – Chancen für Unternehmen und Investoren, in: Rehkugler, H., Die Immobilien-AG – Bewertung und Marktattraktivität, Munich 2003, pp. 5–6; Rehkugler, H., Die Immobilien-AG als attraktive Kapitalanlage – Chancen für Unter-nehmen und Investoren, in: Finanzbetrieb, No. 4/2000, pp. 230–239.

[12] Rehkugler, H., Die Immobilien-AG – Chancen für Unternehmen und Investoren, op. cit., p. 5; Maurer, R./Sebastian, S. P., Inflation Risk Analysis of European Real Estate Securities, in: Journal of Real Estate Research, Vol. 24, No. 1/2002, p. 51.

[13] Rehkugler, H., Die Immobilien-AG – Chancen für Unternehmen und Investoren, op. cit., p. 5.

[14] Maurer, R./Reiner, F./Rogalla, R., Return and risk of German open-end real estate funds, in: Journal of Property Research, 2004, Vol. 21, Nr. 3, p. 210.

[15] Bundesministerium der Finanzen (Ed.), Ausführungen für Jedermann zur Abgeltungssteuer, www.bundesfinanzministerium.de/cln_03/lang_de/nn_302/DE/Steuern/Veroeffentlichungen__zu__Steuerarten/Einkommensteuer/006.html#1, date issued October 17th, 2007, accessed on December 16th, 2007.

[16] Cadmus, A./von Bodecker, M., Immobilien-Aktiengesellschaften und REITs, in: Schulte, K.-W./Bone-Winkel, S./Thomas, M. (Eds.): Handbuch Immobilien-Investition, Cologne 2005, pp. 146–147.

[17] Hickl, T., Vergleich von offenen Immobilienfonds und Immobilien-Aktiengesellschaften, in: Rehkugler, H., Die Immobilien-AG – Bewertung und Marktattraktivität, Munich 2003, p. 179.

[18] Beck, M., Die geeignete Benchmark für die Performancemessung, Indices deutscher und europäischer Immobilien-AGs, in: Rehkugler, H., Die Immobilien-AG – Bewertung und Marktattraktivität, Munich 2003, pp. 143, 152.

[19] Ellwanger & Geiger (Ed.), DIMAX vs. DAX, www.privatbank.de/web/webneu/cmseug.nsf/0/2F5F768CB67407A9C1257310003E1460/$file/DIMAXCH1(zitelmann).XLS?OpenElement, accessed on December 20th, 2007.

[20] Correlations and betas calculated from monthly data until January 31st, 2008. Open-end real estate funds data source: Thomson DataStream; real estate corporations data source: Ellwanger & Geiger (Ed.), DIMAX vs. DAX, op. cit.

[21] Cadmus, A., Zur Bewertung von Immobilien-Aktiengesellschaften, in: FinanzBetrieb, Vol. 2, February 1st, 2000, pp. 96–106

[22] Ellwanger & Geiger (Ed.), E&G DIMAX, www.privatbank.de/web/webneu/cmseug.nsf/0/2F5F768CB67407A9C1257310003E1460/$file/Zusammensetzung.pdf?OpenElement, accessed on December 13th, 2007.

[23] Comdirekt (Ed.), Market Capitalizations, www.comdirect.de, accesssed on December 13th, 2007.

[24] Cadmus, A./von Bodecker, M., op. cit., pp. 145.

[25] BVI (Ed.), Fund volumes and number of German public real estate funds, inclusive foreign funds with German origin and foreign investment funds with sales in Germany – 1988–10/2007, www.bvi.de/de/statistikwelt/fondsvermoegen_mittelaufkommen/zeitreihen/fv_dt_pubf_inkl_auslf_dt_pro/zr_fv_fondsgrup_1950-102007.pdf, accessed on December 17th, 2007.

[26] Ellwanger & Geiger (Ed.), E&G DIMAX, op. cit.

[27] Naubereit, P./Gier, S., An Institutional Economic Analysis of
      Securitization in Real Estate, www.prres.net/Papers/Naubereit_An_
      institutional_economic_analysis_of_securitization.pdf, date of issue
      January 21st, 2002, date retrieved December 12th, 2007, p. 1.

[28] Rehkugler, H., Die Immobilien-AG – Chancen für Unternehmen und
      Investoren, op. cit., pp. 20–22.

[29] Weber, M., Fünf vor zwölf für die Einführung deutscher REITs, in:
      Börsenzeitung, April 7th, 2006, p. 8.

[30] Cadmus, A./von Bodecker, M., op. cit., p. 148.

[31] Ellwanger & Geiger, E&G DIMAX, op. cit.

[32] BVI, Development of plan assets of open-end real estate funds –
      1988–2006, www.bvi.de, updated on October 15th, 2007.

[33] Bron, J. F., Das G-REIT Gesetz – Eine Analyse auf Basis des
      Gesetzentwurfes der Bundesregierung, in: Betriebswirtschaftliche
      Diskussionsbeiträge Martin-Luther-Universität Halle-Wittenberg,
      No. 60/2006, http://wcms.uzi.uni-halle.de/download.php?down=819&e
      lem=236076&func=b85c12bd023be98341ad09e2ba9f701c, accessed on
      December 16th, 2007, p. 15.

[34] Bundesministerium der Finanzen (Ed.), Entwurf eines Gesetzes zur
      Schaffung deutscher Immobilien-Aktiengesellschaften mit
      börsennotierten Anteilen, www.bundesfinanzministerium.de/cln_03/
      nn_54/sid_D74389481FA6BA12403697022DE6667D/nsc_true/DE/
      Aktuelles/Aktuelle__Gesetze/Gesetzentwuerfe__
      Arbeitsfassungen/007__a,templateId=raw,property=publicationFile.
      pdf, accessed on December 15th, 2007, p. 26.

[35] Bundesministerium der Finanzen (Ed.) Entwurf eines Gesetzes zur
      Schaffung deutscher Immobilien-Aktiengesellschaften mit
      börsennotierten Anteilen, op. cit., p. 3.

[36] ZEW/ebs (Ed.), Real Estate Investment Trusts (REITs), Internationale
      Erfahrungen und Best Practice für Deutschland, Mannheim 2005,
      pp. 125–126.

[37] ZEW/ebs (Ed.), op. cit., p. 166.

[38] Huges, F./Arissen, J., Global Real Estate securities – Where do they fit
      in the broader market?, www.epra.com/media/Size_of_the_Total_
      Real_Estate_Markets.pdf, date of issue, 9/2005, accessed on December
      17th, 2007, pp. 2–5.

[39] Bundesministerium der Finanzen (Ed.), Entwurf eines Gesetzes zur
      Schaffung deutscher Immobilien-Aktiengesellschaften mit
      börsennotierten Anteilen, op. cit., p. 1.

[40] Bundesministerium der Finanzen (Ed.), Gesetz zur Schaffung
      deutscher Immobilien-Aktiengesellschaften mit börsennotierten

Anteilen, Ein international anerkanntes Finanzmarktprodukt für Deutschland, in: Monatsbericht des BMF, May 2007, www. bundesfinanzministerium.de/cln_05/lang_de/nn_17844/DE/Aktuelles/ Monatsbericht__des__BMF/2007/05/070522agmb008,templateId =raw,property=publicationFile.pdf, accessed on December 13th, 2007, p. 67.

[41] Voigländer, M., Der deutsche REIT, Grundzüge und steuerpolitischer Anpassungsbedarf, in: IW-Trends 2006 – Vierteljahresschrift zur empirischen Wirtschaftsforschung aus dem Institut der deutschen Wirtschaft, Cologne, No.1/2006, www.iwkoeln.de/data/pdf/content/ trends01_06_1.pdf, accessed on December 16th, 2007, p. 15.

[42] Weber, M., op. cit., p. 8.

[43] Dietz, D., REITs in Frankreich – Ein Erfolgsmodell seit 2003, in: Sonderbeilage der Bank, No. 7/2007, www.die-bank.de/special/ reits-pdfs/04_frankreich.pdf, accessed on December 17th, 2007, p. 6.

C Debt capital markets

1 Asset Backed Securities

Robert Rügemer
Bodo Marr

Table of contents

1   Introduction

In the past 25 years, global credit capital markets experienced an explosive growth of both financial instruments and a shift in risk transfer, starting with the advent of the High Yield Bond market in the 1980s, over the introduction of structured credit products such as securitization to the most recent large scale employment of credit derivatives, themselves employed in multitude of other instruments. Asset-backed securitization as a trend is fuelled by various developments, e. g., the explosive evolution of IT calculation power, technological developments, standardization, deregulation and integration of capital markets (e. g., European Union), the desire of financial institutions to recycle their balance sheet to free up capital and to transfer risk and ultimately the evolvement of a sophisticated investor base interested to diversify their investments away from traditional investments such as government or corporate bonds [1].

Securitization – an explosive growth story and …

Alongside the rapid growth and increased sophistication of the securitization development, the structured finance market has reached a size and complexity that became increasingly difficult to monitor since transparency and information standards are not uniform for this global industry. As a result, a looming crisis in the US subprime mortgage market has lead to a lack of confidence by investors and, thus, a liquidity crisis of the entire structured finance market, which resulted in liquidity crisis of the global financial market as a whole. The industry has now set a list of measures to increase transparency, unify standards and quality and availability of data requirements in order to restore investor confidence. Since the merits of securitization to both the originators and the capital markets are substantial, it will only be a question of time until the current liquidity crunch in the structured finance market will be overcome and most likely will return to its former strength.

… a healthy bump in the road

The following should provide particularly newcomers to the topic with a short overview of the major aspects involved in a securitization transaction.

2   What is securitization?

2.1   Concept and definition

Disinter-mediation – the bank's balance sheet is no longer needed

Securitization as a modern financing technique is the outcome of the so-called disintermediation, i. e., the substitution of the financing bank in order to gain straight access to the capital markets. Whereas banks previously have worked as the sole capital allocation centers by collecting deposits and lending to corporations and individuals, the application of securitization techniques makes the use of the bank's balance sheet practically obsolete [2].

A debt financing technology transformed into a global risk transfer system

Securitization is a form of debt financing technology, developed 20 years ago and actively used in a variety of forms to raise off-balance and alternative financing for companies and banks. In practice, the majority of transactions are undertaken by financial institutions, which use their balance sheets as "warehouses" for a subsequent risk transfer of the underwritten loans to the capital markets in form of securitization. In its most recent modification, synthetic securitization is used as a risk transfer rather than financing mechanism [3][4].

In more general terms, securitization comprises the sale, transfer or pledge of the specified assets (e. g., receivables, loans, bonds) to a Special Purpose, bankruptcy-remote Vehicle or trust (SPV – a shell company), which in turn issues Asset Backed Securities (ABS) to capital market investors. Investors (banks, insurance companies and specialized funds) generally rely on those underlying assets and associated pledges for the redemption of these securities, either from the cash flows generated by the assets or from the assets' sale/liquidation under adverse conditions [5].

2.2   Basic structure and parties

Originators are able to obtain higher ratings for their assets than their own and …

The originator (or sponsor), a company or bank originates assets (e. g., loans, receivables, etc.) in the normal course of its business and holds them on its balance sheet. Since the originator needs financing, it can sell them to another entity, (the SPV), established solely for the purpose of that financing. The SPV (the issuer) issues ABS to investors and uses the issuance proceeds to purchase the assets from the asset originator [2].

After the purchase, the SPV's balance sheet consists of assets acquired from the originator and liabilities in the form of the security issued. The SPV is a shell company, which holds the assets for the benefit of the bond investors. The SPV has no personnel to take care of the underlying assets, thus a servicer is required to collect cash and maintain those assets (which in practice typically remains with the selling company). In order to achieve the desired credit quality of the securities issued based on the assets, there is a need for additional support, so-called credit enhancement (which can be credit, structural and legal enhancement). Credit enhancement is of paramount importance for any securitization since it is to protect the ABS bondholders against credit, legal, liquidity, interest rate, currency or other risks and constitutes the basis to receive a marketable rating for the ABS.

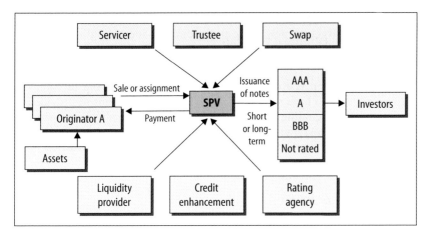

Fig. 1: Generic overview of a securitization structure

The investor typically takes comfort in the credit assessment which the rating agencies provide for each transaction in form of ratings assigned to the individual tranches of notes issued by the SPV. A fundamental principal of securitization is the division of the asset pool's inherent cash flows and risks into subordinated tranches. The most senior tranches of a securitization transaction generally receive an AAA rating, the highest rating a debt instrument can get.

... a much better fund spread

And this is one of the most crucial aspects in securitization: The rating of the ABS is delinked from

- the originator, which typically has a lower rating, and
- the underlying individual assets.

By pooling of the assets and by adding various means of credit enhancements, originators are able to issue AAA rated securities. To put it differently, the originator obtains a better funding spread than he would have obtained if he borrowed money on its own credit worthiness. It is the legal separation of its assets, combined with credit and structural enhancement techniques which create a financing structure delinked from the rating of the originator [6][7].

2.2.1 Originator/sponsor

The originator is the company selling its assets to receive financing. In the majority of cases the originator is a bank or financial institution, but can also be a corporation, a trust or a government, or more generally, any entity which avails oneself of securitizable assets on its balance sheet. These assets need to generate predictable and stable cash flows. The assets must be clearly defined (separable) and legally transferable (e. g., free of any third party rights).

Reliable cash flows – condition precedent for any deal

The sponsor's origination (i. e., underwriting) standards play a critical role in the ultimate performance of the securitized portfolio. Rating agencies and investors pay particular attention to the standards employed by sponsors to underwrite new business which is later used as collateral for the securitization transaction. Particularly changes in the business strategy of a sponsor by, for example, targeting new customer groups or increasing sales volume by lowering underwriting standards can lead to significant changes in the performance of an ABS.

Securitization does not work without state-of-the-art IT systems

Since securitization is strongly dependant on the processing of data, the originator needs to have state-of-the-art IT and data systems to provide the arranging bank and rating agencies with consistent data quality (i. e., historical performance and loss figures). In complex transactions, it can be advisable to use specialized IT companies to take over the preparation of historical asset data.

2.2.2   SPV or issuer

Special purpose means single purpose in reality

The issuer is a specially created vehicle or company for the purposes of the securitization (SPV) or a trust under Anglo-Saxon jurisdiction and needs to be bankruptcy remote from the originator. This can be achieved by creating a new legally separated entity, which is completely organizationally independent from the originator. The SPV is solely established for the purpose of raising funding through the issuance of ABS [2].

To ensure insolvency remoteness, the SPV is not allowed to have any other substantial obligations or incur other debt outside the securitization. In practice, SPVs are set up in countries with dedicated securitization laws or in jurisdictions which provide for a tax-neutral treatment and are administered by specialized international law or accountancy firms [8].

2.2.3   Arranger/underwriter

Deal maker and numbers alchemist – the arranger has many roles

The arranger (mostly an investment bank) is the main initiator and transaction manager of the securitization process and advises the originator in setting up a securitization transaction and through the rating process of the securities. It calculates and structures the securitization cash flows and waterfall (i. e., cascade of payments to investors of the ABS). Typically, the arranger will offer underwriting for the transaction, i. e., will give the originator certainty over the placement of the ABS. However, it is not unusual to separate the arranging and underwriting functions in a transaction. The arranger's task it to carefully balance the conflicting interests of a transaction: the originator's desire for a less costly funding on the one hand, and the marketability of the resulting securities on the other hand.

Arranging securitization transactions provide arrangers with a variety of fee opportunities:

* upfront in form of a structuring fee for arranging the transaction and a underwriting fee for placing the ABS in the money or capital markets and

* ongoing through the provision of support facilities in form of liquidity lines or Letter of Credits (LoC), secondary trading services and funding management services (agency fees) [2].

2.2.4 Servicer

Servicing is a fundamental aspect in any securitization. The servicer is responsible for the assets, i. e., monitoring the generation of cash, its collection, developing and adhering to a credit policy (e. g., standards how to deal with delinquent and defaulted borrowers), for pursuing delinquent and defaulted borrowers. Usually, the originator remains the servicer but could also be an external party. The servicer's role is crucial since he is ultimately responsible for the orderly transfer of the cash flow to the SPV. If the servicer is the originator, investors are exposed to any negative corporate changes associated with the originator (liquidity or creditworthiness problems). Rating agencies very much focus on how the originator has organized its internal procedures and on which fall-back means he has implemented to guarantee the smooth operation even in the case of problems [5].

The servicing role – often underestimated but crucial for investors

2.2.5 Liquidity provider

The liquidity provider is usually a bank which backs the transaction by a bridge financing, which is required to address timing mismatches between the cash flows generated by the asset pool (e. g., receivables) and the outgoing cash flows to pay down the ABS. In other words, the liquidity line covers the risk of later inflows into the SPV than outflows to investors. These timing mismatches may arise due to delays in transferring the money, due to technical problems or market disruptions (e. g., market standstills due to external shocks). The liquidity line bridges those timing mismatches but does not cover any shortfalls in cash if the underlying asset pool experiences delinquencies or losses.

Liquidity bridge but no credit coverage for shortfalls

2.2.6 Rating agencies

Rating agencies play a pivotal role in the securitization process since almost every transaction is rated (usually by one or two of the Big Three – Moody's, Standard & Poor's or Fitch). The rating agencies review the transaction primarily with a view on credit risks, but also take into account legal, currency and liquidity aspects. As a result of its review it will assign a rating for each tranche of a transaction based on the required credit enhancement, i. e., the protection that the security comprises to protect investors against losses according to the desired rating levels. Typically, rating agencies also provide ongoing rating services to a transaction by monitoring the performance over the life of the ABS. For its services, rating agencies usually charge an upfront and a yearly monitoring fee [5][9].

Pivotal deal analysts – now under fire from capital markets investors and supervisors

2.2.7 Swap provider

Swap providers are usually financial institutions which hedge the interest and currency risks of the underlying assets in relation to the ABS (e. g., a transaction backed by Japanese consumer credit receivables funded through the issuance of EURO denominated ABS). The incorporation of sufficient hedging arrangements is a condition precedent to receiving the desired rating assignment.

2.2.8   Trustee, lawyers and other parties

Specialized law firms indispensable

In most transactions, there is a trustee (often an accountancy firm or a specialized bank) whose role is to process payments to security holders, enforces the indenture provisions and often provides backup to other third parties. Specialized law firms are vital to any securitization transaction since they need to have a thorough understanding of capital markets law, of general credit and corporate as well as regulatory laws of various jurisdictions (e. g., underlying French, American, Dutch and Slovenian assets with ABS issued under English Law). Complex, multi-jurisdictional deals require substantial legal due diligence and is advisable to undertake a cost benefit analysis before the inclusion of assets from a particular country at the outset of a transaction [5].

The role of accountancy firms is to advise on the desired accounting treatment of a transaction, e. g., they need to certify, for instance, whether or not a transaction is off-balance sheet. Furthermore, transaction services departments will review the transaction cash flow models to testify compliance with the agreed deal structure.

2.3   Transaction process

2.3.1   Due diligence

A thorough due diligence is half the battle and predicts the outcome of the rating

A company (originator) attempting to accomplish a securitization starts with the due diligence. During the whole process the originator usually takes advice from several consultants for various aspects, to arrange the debt, to create the transaction structure and to place the issuance of ABS. The due diligence sets the base for outcome of the transaction and every originator is well advised to pay particular attention to the completeness and accuracy of this process. The results of the due diligence and the final structure are submitted to the rating agencies in the form of an information memorandum [2].

To give an example, the following items comprise the key issues of a due diligence catalog for a real estate securitization:

- originators corporate structure,
- equity structure of the real estate property,
- register of real estate entries,
- tenancy agreements.

Further quantitative and qualitative aspects are:

- market information for real estate markets related to the underlying assets,
- vicinity, grade and actual condition,
- real estate appraisal by external parties,
- analysis by the trustee of the real estate,
- particular information related to the cash flow, e. g., basic rent, occupancy rate, other income, administrative expenses;
- tenants market,
- environmental aspects.

The more detailed and comprehensive the given and evaluated database is the more exact the structural elements, such as credit enhancement, capital tranches and reserves, can be arranged. Particularly, the rating agencies apply more conservative assumptions the less informative the database is. Due to the cyclicality of markets, rating agencies pay special attention to periods of recession to derive the behaviour of the underlying asset. The longer the time series and therefore the more business cycles to be portrayed the better and hence more reliable the forecast is [10].

2.3.2 Offering Circular

To place the ABS with capital investors, an Offering Circular (OC) is issued which basically contains the information memorandum and the transaction structure in a term sheet version with all the different participants. The OC is an official document submitted to the stock exchange if the issuance is listed and therefore includes the bond indentures as well as representations and warranties of the ABS issuer. ABS investors pay a lot of attention to the OC since it is their primary information source if a transaction is marketed. The sale of ABS to investors is executed by the placement agent which is often the arranging bank. The placement agent thereby determines the final price of the individual tranche of the ABS depending on the relevant rating, maturity, complexity of the structure and involved sponsors and ultimately the risk appetite of investors [10].

Primary information source for investors

2.3.3 Documentation

The documentation of a securitization is in principle comparable to other financial market transaction but more complex due to

More complex documentation than in traditional transaction

- the establishment of one or more SPVs in other jurisdictions,
- the bankruptcy remoteness of the SPVs, and
- the true sale requirement of the underlying assets to the SPV, to name a few.

Hence, ABS documentations are more time consuming and costly than standard bond transactions. By the signing of transaction contracts (e. g., sale and purchase agreement, intercreditor agreement or servicing agreement) the transaction is legally "closed" and it follows the subsequent funding (i. e., financial closing) and payment of the raised monies to the originator [10].

2.4 Asset classes

There is a multitude of underlying asset classes of which the most important distinctions are the following.

Securitization is as diverse as the multitude of underlying assets

2.4.1 Asset and Mortgage Backed Securities (ABS and MBS)

ABS and Mortgage Backed Securities (MBS) are the predominant categories of securitization and involve the issuance of ABS/MBS debt, secured by a homogenous pool of assets. Securitized assets could include assets such as credit cards, auto loans, equipment leases and corporate loans, or corporate assets like trade receivables, vendor financing (in practice summarized under ABS) or mortgages for residential lenders (so-called Residential Mortgage Backed Securities or RMBS) and mortgages for commercial lenders (called Commercial Mortgage Backed Securities or CMBS) or cash flows from real estate assets (called real estate securitization) [11][12][8].

2.4.2   Future flow financing

The distinguishing feature of future flow securitization is the fact that the asset being transferred by the originator is not an existing claim against existing obligors, but the right to receive cash flows under a future claim against future obligors. In other words, the claims are yet to be created, against obligors who are yet to be identified. Examples can be: emerging market export receivables (normally crude exports), future royalties, hotel revenues, sports receivables, worker remittance payments, etc. [6].

2.4.3   Whole Business Securitization (WBS)

WBS is typically employed for companies with a strong and stable cash flow profile with low operating risk. The issued debt is based on the company's free cash flow, not on single assets alone. Typically, WBS securities are backed by the core operating assets of a company and often have a strong real estate element. As such, WBS is a merger of corporate bond with securitization technique. WBS has specific legal requirements which are stricter than in traditional corporate bond transactions, and are most frequently employed in a creditor-friendly legal environment like the UK.

2.4.4   Synthetic securitization (CDO, CBO, CLO)

Synthetic securitization means that the underlying assets are not transferred via a true sale but their inherent default risk via credit derivative techniques. Synthetic securitization was mainly developed to address a banks' need for transfer of risk associated with given assets without the transfer of the assets

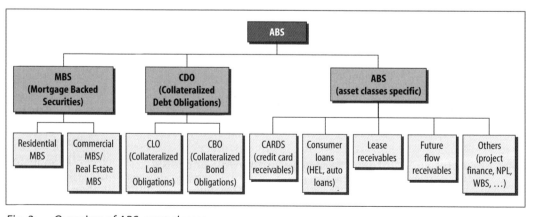

Fig. 2:   Overview of ABS asset classes

themselves (due to legal restrictions). It can be executed as partially or fully funded securitization [13].

2.5 Factoring and covered bonds

The concept of backing financing transaction with a dedicated pool of assets has been employed for many years in form of factoring of receivables and refinancing of commercial mortgages through covered bonds.

2.5.1 Factoring

Factoring resembles in its concept the securitization of trade receivables in three aspects:

- Receivables are sold to a third party at a discount;
- the legal transfer (true sale) is definite and the receivables are off-balance;
- illiquid working capital is transformed into cash.

Similar concept but very different in practice and more expensive

However, there are fundamental differences. There is no SPV involved but a specialized factoring company which is in most cases taking over the servicing of the portfolio by collecting the outstanding claims against a servicing fee. The typical batch size for factoring is much smaller starting from hundreds of euros up to approximately € 30 million maximum, whereas ABS programmes favor minimum transaction volumes in excess of € 30 million. In addition, factoring companies have a slightly different risk approach. Whereas securitization credit evaluation is focused on a pool analysis, factoring companies will accept receivables based on an individual credit quality analysis. In terms of seller risk appetite, they do not refrain from purchasing receivables from lowly rated originators, whereas securitization programs usually require a certain originator rating. Moreover, factoring does not comprise a rating by a rating agency but go through an in-house due diligence by the factoring company. Thus, factoring transactions will typically require less time to execute and are less complex. On the other hand factoring is usually more expensive than securitization transactions [14].

Conclusion: Factoring has a different goal and client focus. Whereas securitization is set up as a long-term alternative funding source, factoring is a rather quick and uncomplicated liquidity instrument for smaller portfolios. It needs to be mentioned that securitization and factoring are not mutually exclusive. A seller could employ both at the same time.

2.5.2 Covered bonds (Pfandbriefe)

The German Pfandbrief (which was a blueprint for a covered bond in other countries [14]) has some similarities with the MBS concept since a distinct pool of assets (mortgages or municipal loans) is separated from the mortgage lender's balance sheet and transferred to an insolvency remote estate to be used as collateral for the issuance of so-called covered bonds (the Pfandbriefe) [15]. However, the German Pfandbrief Act, for example, only permits the issuance of bonds backed by a restricted list of underlying assets, i. e., mortgages and

The Pfandbrief – a German success story – blueprint for other jurisdictions

municipal loans, whereas securitization covers a much larger universe as suitable assets. In addition, Pfandbrief issuance is limited to a 60% Loan-to-Value of a mortgage loan, whereas in a securitization there are typically no restrictions on Loan-to-Value levels. Finally, the rating of the Pfandbrief will depend on the rating of the issuing bank – a fundamental difference to an ABS structure.

2.6   Transaction size and costs

Transaction size matters

The efficiency of a securitization strongly depends on the volume (economies of scale), the quality of the portfolio of assets, the servicing quality of the originator and not at least on the market conditions at the time of issuance. As a rule of thumb, the higher the underlying asset volume the lower the overall transactions cost for the originator, since upfront transaction costs will in comparison to the overall transaction size be smaller.

To illustrate how the financing costs of an ABS transaction could be calculated (under normal market conditions), the following should serve as a close to reality example:

A company has a working capital line of € 50 million and a term loan of € 90 million. The working capital line margin is priced at 2%, the term loan at 1.8%. The company has annual sales of € 250 million, monthly trade receivables outstanding of € 60 million and a monthly inventory of € 20 million. Its internal bank credit rating is BB. On a weighted average basis, the company has annual funding costs of 1.9% over EURIBOR. The company wishes to expand and invest but the banks react rather restrictive and require higher asset collateral/higher equity injection and a higher margin (0.5%). The company's ability to tap the capital markets directly is limited.

And do your math!

A standard Asset Backed Commercial Paper (ABCP) program of a bank could, for example, offer the following funding conditions for the securitization of the trade receivables portfolio with an advance rate of assumed € 50 million: Arrangement fee upfront € 300,000, legal fees upfront € 100,000, rating fees and other fees upfront € 20,000. In addition, the bank would charge – on an annual basis – 1% for Letter of Credit and Liquidity line costs and another € 50,000 p.a. for miscellaneous administration costs. Altogether, this would make up around 1.94% costs in the first year. However, since ABCP programs are set up to run for at least three to five years, the costs would be spread over five years: The all-in costs decrease down to approximately 1.3%.

Thus, from a pure cost perspective, the cost savings is 1.9% – 1.3% = 0.6% on € 50 million for five years = approx. € 1.8 million. Next to the improved funding spread, securitization offers other advantages, too (liquidity, improved capital structure ratios, transfer of default risk, independency from bank financing – a more detailed overview on benefits and drawbacks is shown under section 4).

2.7   Key legal considerations

Given the number of parties involved in a transaction, securitization typically requires extensive documentation to establish the mechanics of cooperation between them. The key considerations of any securitization structure are the following.

2.7.1   True sale

The assets are transferred from the originator to the SPV and thus are removed from the bankruptcy estate of the originator who retains no legal and equity interest in those assets (no risk and rewards). If the removal is definite, a true sale is perfected. True sale indicators are the degree of transfer of "risk of loss" away from the originator (does the originator still bear some risk if the receivable cannot be collected?); the degree of retention of ownership benefits by the originator (does the originator still have certain economic ownership rights?); the degree of control over the assets and the like. It is of paramount importance to achieve a full separation between the assets and the originator to obtain the desired top rating for the ABS securities, so that the assets (and subsequently the bond investors) are not affected negatively by a potential originator bankruptcy. As mentioned above, the assets need to be transferred free of third party rights (e. g., liens and encumbrances) and need to be owned by the originator [13].

A true sale is needed – free of any third party rights

2.7.2   Bankruptcy remote SPV

The SPV is structured to be a bankruptcy remote entity whose assets are deemed to be fully separated from the estate of the originator in case of an originator's bankruptcy. So, the SPV's activities are restrained to the purchase of assets and the issuance of ABS only. Therefore, the risk that some third party could file for bankruptcy of the SPV is limited. Often, ingoing and outgoing cash flows are swapped to hedge against interest rate and currency risk of the notes issued by the SPV. If there is hedging in place, it is important to determine what the potential termination payment is (the payment that the SPV owes to the swap counterparty (usually a bank) in case of a termination event), and how this payment obligation to other creditors (the termination payment is mostly senior to all other creditors in the waterfall) is disclosed [7].

SPVs need to be legally waterproof in stress scenarios

2.8   Credit enhancement

An indispensable feature of all types of securitization transactions is the use of credit enhancement, i. e., a layer of protection put in place as a buffer against expected losses. The credit enhancement is sized to reflect an expected loss level determined under a series of adverse scenarios that could affect the asset pool during its life.

Credit enhancement is key in any securitization

There are various ways to structure credit enhancement. The main distinction is the provision of credit enhancement within the asset pool ("internal" credit enhancement) or through a third party ("external" credit enhancement). Most popular forms are the following: Bank Letter of Credit (LoC), insurance company surety bond, financial assurance company guarantee, subordinated loans from third party, reserve account/refunded or build up from excess spread, originators guarantee, senior-subordinated structure, excess spread, overcollateralization, cash diversion triggered through minimum required Debt Service Coverage Ratio (DSCR) and other trigger events. The first three examples represent external credit enhancement, whereas the remainder represents internal credit enhancement mechanisms.

Usually, the credit enhancement for a specific deal is a combination of several forms of credit enhancement mechanisms and reflects the specific characteristics of the securitized assets, the goals of the securitization sponsor and the requirements of the rating agencies. The level of credit enhancement is determined by the rating agencies and depends on the desired ratings for the securitized notes. The higher the desired rating is the higher the required credit enhancement [9].

2.8.1   Credit tranching (subordination)

The originator's primary goal typically is to receive access to cheaper funding through the improvement of the credit quality of the separated asset pool for a securitization. The credit quality of the underlying assets may be B or BB and the desired rating of the ABS, AAA. Now, the credit enhancement for this specific pool is sized to absorb the expected loss of a BB pool during its life time in order to push it up to AAA.

Credit tranching is the most popular method in term securitizations

Let us take an example. After an in-depth analysis of the historical loss and dilution (rebates or discounts) data, the originator's underwriting policy, the macroeconomic environment and other important risk factors, the rating agency phrases the structural requirements as follows: Average asset quality of the pool is BB as well as the hypothetical corporate rating of the originator. That means, without a securitization it would be fairly expensive for the originator to sell BB securities based on its own rating into the market. In order to reach an AAA issuance level, the rating agency proposes the following credit enhancement requirements: AAA = 15 %, A = 11 %, BB = 8 %, which is provided through the equity tranche = 8 % (first loss piece). In other words, the transaction has a subordination level (cushion) of 15 % (4 % + 3 % + 8 %), i. e., AAA-tranche investors are protected by losses up to 15 % in the pool, the A-tranche investors up to 11 % and so on. Usually, the equity tranche is non-rated and often remains on the balance sheet of the originator [9].

Throughout the transaction, the incoming cash flows from the asset pool will amortize (pay down) the senior debt tranches first (i. e., AAA, then A, then BB, then equity, which is called sequential amortization). This principle or payment cascade is called the waterfall and is a key element in almost any structured finance transaction (see figure 3) [16].

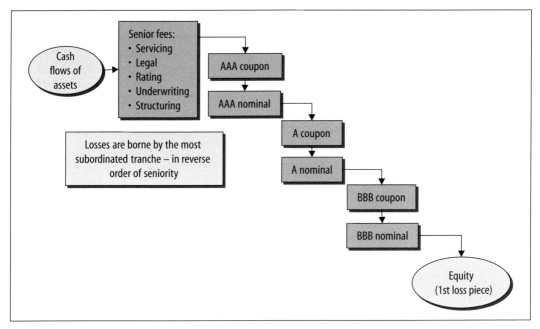

Fig. 3:   Waterfall or cascade of payments

In turn, this means that AAA investors are more protected, the longer the transaction amortizes since their downward protection (the tranches below AAA) remains the same (see figure 4).

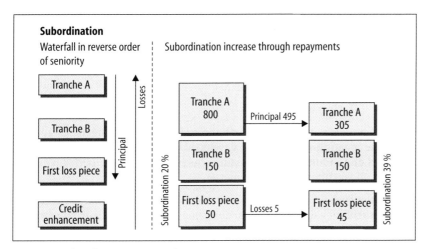

Fig. 4:   Subordination principle

2.8.2 Overcollateralization

Overcollaterali-
zation – the SPV
gets more assets
than it pays for

Similar to the concept of subordination (tranching) outlined above is the technique called overcollateralization which means that the value of the assets exceeds the face value of the notes (the underlying asset pool is worth 100, whereas only, e. g., 95 of ABS securities are issued). For instance, the assets can be purchased at a discount, say at 95 %. The level of the 5 % discount reflects the level of expected losses multiplied by a buffer for additional risk to be potentially incurred by the assets, as well as the level of deal expenses.

2.8.3 Other forms of credit enhancement

The above-mentioned external credit enhancement techniques (LoC, monoline surety bond or any other guarantee) have a direct link with the rating of the credit enhancer. For this reason, the external credit enhancer needs to have a very good (prime) rating, typically at least A. Any volatility in the quality or performance of the respective credit enhancer, which would impact on the credit enhancer's external credit rating, will have a direct impact on the performance or the rating of the insured securitization bond. This also means that the rating of the pool cannot be higher than the rating of the external credit enhancer (so-called weak link approach).

Securitization transactions often use so-called trigger events to provide protection to investors against adverse transaction developments. For example, when employing a minimum Debt Service Coverage Ratio (DSCR) concept, the decrease of free cash flow will typically lead to a cash trap or sweep mechanism. In this case, the free cash flow has deteriorated to a low level to cover merely the financing cost (interest and principal of the transaction after reduction of all other costs). The cash trap secures that future potential excess free cash flow from prepayments will be trapped in a reserve account to protect senior investors. The levels set as triggers will vary by transaction and are normally set at levels representing a downside scenario against the initial base case [9].

2.8.4 Rating assumptions

Ratings are
driven by
scenario analysis
and probability
distribution

In order to calculate the credit enhancement, the rating agencies apply a multitude of rating valuation sets, developed over decades and across various countries and industries. Their main focus is to predict the performance of the pool under different stress scenarios.

One of the best predictive tools available is the scenario analysis based on either probability distribution of scenarios or on certain extreme (stress) scenarios. The stress scenarios are generally related to the bankruptcy of the originator on day one of the transaction and assume that the asset pool incurs excessive losses. If the originator is also the servicer, further losses due to the transfer of the servicing function to an external party are assumed [9].

2.9   Basic structure types

Securitization structures vary strongly depending on asset class, cash flow profile, legal restrictions or objective by the originator. The most important categories are the following [5]:

- revolving structures,
- pass-through structures,
- synthetic structures (vs. true sale),
- multi-seller structures (vs. single-seller).

2.9.1   Revolving structures

Generally speaking, revolving structures are used if the underlying assets have a short-term maturity (trade or credit card receivables). The ABS security may either be short-term (i. e., ABCP) or a medium to long-term bond (i. e., one to five years). For example, a pool of credit cards or trade receivables, which have a maturity until payment of between 30 and 120 days, is used to back 3-year credit card or trade receivables ABS security. The principal collections generated on the asset pool are used to purchase new receivables during a specified period (i. e., the revolving period) whereby the interest of the asset pool pays interest due on the ABS notes (mostly in conjunction with specially created reserve accounts). After the revolving period which, e. g., ends six months before the ABS securities expires, the principal collections are used to repay the securities. To protect investors against the bankruptcy, those transactions often feature amortization events or triggers which stop the purchase of new receivables in case of deterioration of the credit quality of the Originator [6].

Revolving structures replenish the pool constantly with assets

The cash flow profile of a revolving structure is depicted in figure 5. During the revolving period, the principal of the ABS remains outstanding in full and the investors receive only interest payments. The revenue or the yield generated by the underlying assets is used to pay interest to investors and all the other expenses (e. g., servicing fee, LoC fees, swap fees or losses). This mechanism is applied during the revolving period in figure 5 for four years. Throughout this period, principal payments of the asset pool can either be accumulated in a special reserve account, or after the revolving period has finished, used to pay down the ABS security step-by-step through its maturity. This is called soft bullet payment in contrast to a hard bullet payment (i. e., full redemption in one payment). In a controlled amortization, the principal is not accumulated on a reserve account but paid out in regular instalments to investors after the revolving period. Investors therefore receive their principal back in several regular equal instalments [12].

Hard and soft bullets make a difference for investors

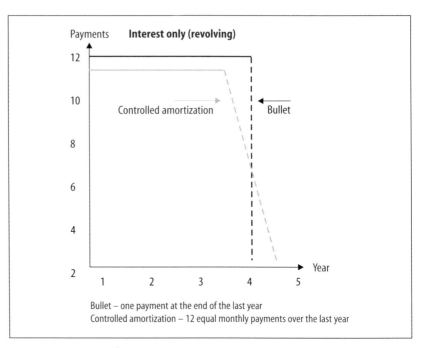

Fig. 5:   Overview of a revolving structure

2.9.2   Pass-through structures

Pass-through structures have become quite rare

In a pass-through structure, the principal payment is passed through to investors to repay gradually the outstanding amount of the ABS security, i. e., the principal is not deposited on a reserve account [6]. This structure has been applied to address the amortization profile of assets with longer maturities (mortgages or auto loans). However, investors generally prefer securities with a predictable pay-back profile to calculate their own return on investment. Pure pass-through structures therefore have become quite rare.

2.9.3   Synthetic and CDO structures

CDO structures – long time on vogue but now under special scrutiny

Synthetic securitization means that legal ownership of the asset is not transferred from the originator to the SPV but the inherent credit risk of the underlying asset is transferred to the SPV. Since there is no true sale, this kind of transaction is called synthetic. Synthetic structures are used if it is legally not permitted to transfer assets (e. g., certain bank loans) or the technical or legal separation of the assets is too costly (e. g., IT infrastructure or stamp duties or transfer taxes). The synthetic transfer of risk is generated by credit derivatives, e. g., Credit Default Swaps (CDS) or Total Return Swaps (TRS). The synthetic ABS is also-called Credit Linked Notes (CLN). When only the risk is transferred via a CDS and no notes are issued, the transaction is called unfunded. If, for instance, the major part of the default risk is transferred via CDS and the remainder is issued via CLN, the transaction is called partially funded (i. e., the issuance of notes) [4].

Until recently, synthetic structures were predominant in Germany among bank originators since it was legally not permitted to sell bank loans without further approval of the customer (so-called syndication clause). Nowadays, banks have adopted syndication clauses in most contracts and legislation has changed so that synthetic structures have become less common for bank loan securitizations.

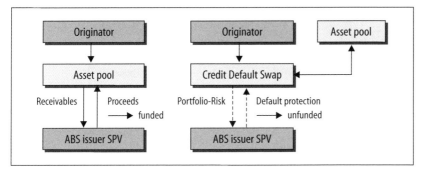

Fig. 6:   Overview of a synthetic structure

More important, however, is the explosive growth of the CDO (Collateralized Debt Obligation). In its most generic form, a CDO is a pool of securities (also ABS) or loans which are bundled into a new structure (sold into a new SPV) and then re-tranched into new CDO notes (AAA, AA and so forth). If the CDO itself consists of various CDO notes, it is called CDO squared or CDO cube.

Synthetic structures do not need a true sale of assets

The American subprime mortgage crisis of July 2007 is closely linked with the rise of the CDO market. One of the major drivers of the extensive growth of the US and UK subprime mortgage market was the use of securitization techniques. By employing the securitization or CDO technique, banks were able to lend heavily to subprime mortgage lenders (i. e., low quality borrowers) since they effectively could sell the default risk associated with those borrowers into the securitization market.

2.9.4   Single-seller vs. multi-seller structures

Another important category in securitization structures is the differentiation between single-seller and multi-seller transactions typically employed in the short to medium-term funding markets. In principal, single-seller structures are used for larger transactions with one originator (e. g., multinational corporate issues ABCP securities with an outstanding volume of over € 1 billion). In contrast, multi-seller structures are used when different sellers sell their diverse assets into one SPV (also-called conduit) which issues ABS notes. Multi-seller conduits are mostly used in the short-term Asset Backed Commercial Paper (ABCP) market (maturity from 9 to 270 days) which is part of the money market. The ABCP market is the largest segment of the ABS market since it allows originators to securitize also smaller transaction sizes (from € 10 million to € 1 billion) into a predefined established structure and

Multi-seller ABCP conduits – the largest and most liquid segment – until the crunch

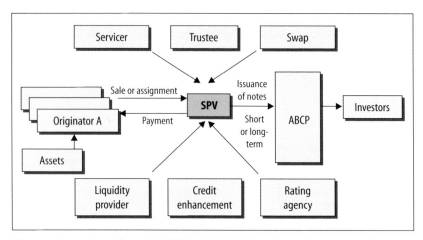

Fig. 7:   Overview of a multi-seller structure

benefit from the low short-term refinancing spread of ABCP (mostly rated A-1, the highest short-term rating) [5].

3   Real estate securitizations

3.1   Residential mortgage-backed securitization

Real estate – by far the largest asset class
Real estate is by far the most important asset class, both from the originator as well as from the investor's perspective. Residential and commercial-backed securities combined account for almost 75 % of the overall European securitization market (thereof RMBS 62 % and CMBS 12 %). The most important originators in this segment are banks and specialized real estate financing institutions which underwrite mortgage loans to private individuals. Due to the homogenous asset and cash profile (standardized evaluation methodologies by banks, constant annuity payments, and predictable prepayment rates), RMBS have become the standard asset class of ABS issuances [17][10].

3.2   Commercial mortgage-backed and
real estate securitization

CMBS tend to be more complex than RMBS
Due to the more diverse asset nature, Commercial Mortgage Backed Securitizations (CMBS) are typically more complex. CMBS comprise both the securitization of a loan by a bank to a commercial real estate developer as well as securitization of rental cash flows by the property to the owner himself (hereinafter called real estate securitization) [17].

Whereas bank originators have optimized their portfolios by transferring residential and commercial mortgage-backed loans into the market via securitization, many corporate or real estate companies have not done so. One reason for this is that arranging a real estate securitization for an asset holder typically raises more obstacles than an RMBS because of the less standardized nature of the underlying asset with typically lower diversification. The basic assumption in structured finance is that the more diversified a pool of assets is the lesser the default probability and expected loss of the entire pool. A company owning a property with only a few tenants faces a higher risk of non-payment than with hundreds of borrowers distributed over various regions.

Thus, the credit quality of the tenants of the underlying properties plays a key role and the analysis of a CMBS resembles in this respect a traditional corporate credit analysis. In a second step, the quality of the asset is analyzed (vacancy costs, restructuring and marketing costs in order to re-let the property). Although real estate securitization is more complex than traditional bank funding it is worthwhile to consider this alternative funding source once the transaction size exceeds € 100 million. Depending on the status of capital or banking market at the time of issuance, it can be more efficient for property holding companies to generate funding through the sale of the income streams of their properties in form of a real estate securitization. Examples of properties used as underlying in real estate securitization transaction are, e. g., industrial sites, hotels, gas stations, amusement parks, nursing homes, pubs or shopping malls [10].

Real estate securitization resembles rather a classical corporate analysis

Transactions backed by properties will always require a certain degree of management of the assets in order to generate rental income. Once this performance aspect of a transaction – as in the case of securitizing a pub estate – becomes more pronounced, rating agencies will classify such a transaction as whole business or company securitization.

4 Benefits and potential drawbacks for individual originators

The reasons for securitization are manifold and depend on the particular situation of an originator. However, the most common benefits may be summarized as follows: the ability to raise financing less costly by tapping markets with a higher then its own corporate rating and to diversify funding sources (capital markets instead of bank loan). Further benefits for an originator include

Securitization provides different benefits for different originators

- a soft approach to capital markets and rating agencies (rating the asset pool versus corporate rating),

- an independent review of its origination and servicing as part of arranging the transaction, and

- a means for active balance sheet management [8].

On the other side of the spectrum, investors benefit from a diversification of investment forms combined with a yield pick-up compared to traditional debt instruments along with credit enhanced, well-diversified asset pools. The higher yield on ABS derives from the higher complexity and additional work involved an investor has to undertake to analyze the specific ABS structure. However, securitization can have drawbacks for both issuers and investors if not properly executed or not fully understood. One of the major drawbacks of the ABS markets lies in the less liquid secondary market, which will make it more difficult to trade or exit securities for investors.

4.1 Benefits

4.1.1 Banks

Usually, financial institutions benefit most from securitization

Banks have been the most active players in the market due to the requirement of making the best use of their balance sheets and the permanent need for efficient funding sources. Typical loans employed in securitization were consumer loans (e.g., car or mortgage loans) or corporate loans (e.g., unsecured term loans or commercial mortgage loans). Since bank assets provide the estimated qualities in ABS (large homogenous asset pools with substantial historical data), many banks started off with arranging in-house securitizations before providing agency services to clients, which offers them substantial fee generation opportunity. With respect to the first, the transfer of risk associated with these assets through their sale or synthetic risk transfer was very often a driver for these transactions. Ultimately, banks seek to release regulatory capital they are required to hold against those assets (Basel II). The use of securitization allows banks and companies to access alternative sources of liquidity and diversify their funding sources, thereby reducing the correlation between the bank's own financial risk and the risks of the assets (active portfolio management) [18].

Securitization also allows banks and companies to remove illiquid assets from their balance sheets, as is the case with non-performing or sub-performing loans (NPL), and sub-performing real estate (which has become popular in Germany since 2004). Securitization is often the solution for banks burdened by NPL and an urgent need to sanitize their balance sheet. Companies that have accumulated large amounts of real estate may want to focus on their core businesses, but retain use of their real estate assets without burdening their balance sheets. They can transfer those assets through securitization by selling real estate and leasing it back to their own rise.

4.1.2 Corporations

The second largest group making use of securitization are corporations. Companies have short-term or long-term assets in the form of trade receivables, export receivables, inventory or any other assets (real estate) that could be used in securitization transactions, for the purposes of financing and streamlining their balance sheet. One additional driver for corporates to use securitization is the possibility to tap the capital market and its cheaper funding without the requirement for a corporate credit rating (e.g., in case of a receivables' securitization).

Certain companies with a very stable cash flow profile (e.g., due to monopolistic positions or state guarantees) and backed by hard asset collateral (mostly commercial real estate) could be subject to securitization in a Whole Business Securitization. Typically, these structures are used by financial sponsors to optimise their acquisition financing costs compared to other available financing sources [10].

4.1.3   Projects

After the completion, a project generates stable cash flows. In certain circumstances, these projects could be refinanced through a securitization, which would generate substantial cost benefits. Securitization is also possible early in the construction phase to leverage the cash flows to be generated post completion. Examples for suitable projects include, e. g., sport stadiums, power plants, toll roads, ports, airports, etc. These transactions in its profile closely resemble whole business securitizations after the erection of the assembly itself.

4.1.4   Real estate holders and developers

A growing group of securitization users are companies based on real estate. Real estate holders and developers have commercial real estates, offices, shopping malls, hotels that generate rental and capital income. Many banks also hold on their balance sheets respective real estate assets. Such assets can be subject to Commercial Mortgage Backed Securities or commercial real estate securitizations [10].

4.1.5   Municipalities, states and countries

The use of securitization by public issuers varies strongly by country, even though its overall potential is substantial. Countries have export credits, different assets that they may want to privatize. These assets could be securitized or the purchase of these assets by another entity, privatization could be financed through securitization. It needs to be mentioned that the major obstacles to employ securitization techniques for public issuers are regulatory constraints.

4.1.6   Numerical example

To illustrate the benefits of securitization for a bank, a numerical example is presented below (see figure 8). By removing certain loan assets from its balance sheet, substantial effects on the bank's ROE can be observed.

Securitization is able to improve ratios substantially

This very simplistic example assumes a yield of a portfolio of 50 basis points over the reference rate EURIBOR. It is obvious that the asset-backed funding may be slightly more expensive than the bank funding. On the other hand, the securitized portfolio results in a substantially higher ROE than the traditional bank funding: 17 % versus 7 %. Similar effects can be achieved for a corporate originator.

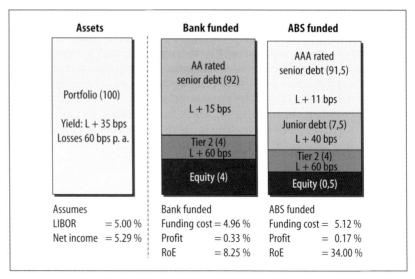

Fig. 8: Numerical example

4.2 Drawbacks

It needs to be noted that securitization is not a superior financing technique per se but contains pitfalls, too.

4.2.1 Complexity and costs

Securitization is not a panacea but a complex financing technique

Setting up a securitization may be complex, time-consuming and sometimes costly. Whereas a bank loan may require a standard credit procedure, securitizations require tailor-made process management between many parties for months (often at least three months until closing). A potential originator needs to be aware of whether the total upfront costs and work effort (mostly uncounted) amortized over a period of three to five years, is justified versus a simpler bank loan transaction.

4.2.2 First loss position

Originators and investors – beware of the first of loss piece!

In many securitizations the originators retain the equity piece on their balance sheet. As outlined above, cash flows generated by the pool are distributed from the top, from the senior tranche downwards, whereas the losses are absorbed from the bottom, from the junior tranche upwards (waterfall principle). An originator retaining the junior equity piece is in a first loss position which comprises the concentrated loss of the large pool of assets it has sold. When an entity relies heavily on securitization by retaining more equity tranches, it increases its effective leverage of the balance sheet. One of the best ways to avoid that is to find a way to sell the equity piece to investors willing to assume the associated risks. However, this might be very costly and could outweigh the benefits [9].

Increased leverage risk also applies to the world of investors in the search of higher yielding assets: The inherent equity risk of a pool cannot be "structured away", regardless how sophisticated the structuring and tranching technique might be. Securitization spreads the risk over more, and more sophisticated participants than traditional bank funding could achieve but obviously does not minimize the risk per se. On the contrary, buying a lot of higher yielding subordinated tranches of various complex (and difficult to analyze) underlying asset pools can be a perilous strategy if the behaviour of underlying assets of the various subordinated tranches are correlated and the rating experience on those assets limited [19].

4.2.3   Liquidity risks

Securitization is a capital markets financing technique and implies transparent liquid money or structured bond markets. However, there have been times where investors withdrew from these markets due to external shocks like the Asian or Russian Crisis in 1998 or, quite recently, like the US subprime mortgage market crisis in July 2007. Since structured finance products are complex, their intrinsic value is harder to calculate, particularly in cases of distress of the underlying assets. For instance, investors have shunned the short-term asset-backed commercial paper market entirely during the subprime crisis in July 2007 worldwide and turned to classic money market funds. Corporations which relied on the ABCP market had to tap bank funding again which in turn left the banks exposed with more exposure to company risk and their balance sheets used up.

Liquidity has never been really an issue – until July 2007

5   ABS market overview

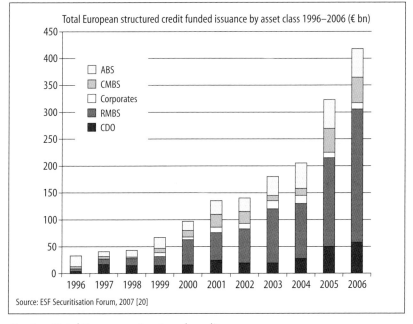

Source: ESF Securitisation Forum, 2007 [20]

Fig. 9:   Total European structured credit

Market update – historical ABS volume development

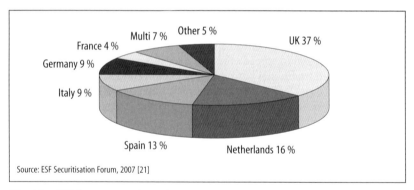

Source: ESF Securitisation Forum, 2007 [21]

Fig. 10: ABS issuance volume by country

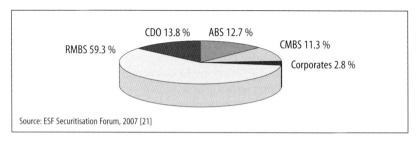

Source: ESF Securitisation Forum, 2007 [21]

Fig. 11: Issuance volume by asset class

6   Bibliography

[1] Fabozzi, F. J., Bond Markets, Analysis and Strategies, 5th edition, New Jersey 2004, pp. 1–12.

[2] Achleitner, A.-K., Asset Backed Securitites, in: Handbuch Investment Banking, 2nd edition, Wiesbaden 2000, pp. 413–437.

[3] Goodman, L. S./Fabozzi, F. J./Douglas J. L., Cash-Collateralized Debt Obligations, in: Fabozzi, F. J., The Handbook of Fixed Income Securities, 6th edition, New York 2001, pp. 669–694.

[4] Prince, J. T./Cifuentes, A./Bakalar, N., Synthetic CDOs, in: Fabozzi, F. J., The Handbook of Fixed Income Securities, op. cit., pp. 695–730.

[5] Kretschmar, T./Damaske, M., Securitization, in: Rottke, N. B./Rebitzer, D. W., Handbook Real Estate Private Equity, 1st edition, Köln 2006, pp. 575–593.

[6] Fabozzi, F. J., Bond Markets, Analysis and Strategies, op. cit., pp. 307–328.

[7] Fahrholz, B., Asset Backed-Finanzierungen, in: Neue Formen der Unternehmensfinanzierung, München 1998, pp. 213–239.

[8] Breidenbach, M., Real Estate Securitization – Asset-Backed Security Financing for the Property Industry, Köln 2005.

[9] Silver, A. A., Rating Asset Backed Securities, in: Fabozzi, F. J., Investing in Asset-Backed Securities, New Hope 2000, pp. 17–41.

[10] Rügemer, R./Siemes, M., Property Securitization – eine Kapitalmarktfinanzierung für Immobilien, in: Schulte, K.-W./ Achleitner, A.-K./Schäfers, W./Knobloch, B., Handbuch Immobilien-Banking, Köln 2002, pp. 757–788.

[11] Bhattacharya, A. K./Berliner, W. S., An Overview of mortgages and the mortgage market, in: Fabozzi, F. J., The Handbook of Fixed Income Securities, op. cit., pp. 487–512.

[12] Edens, L. M., New Mortgage Designs: Tiered Payment, Balloon, Two-Step And Fixed/Adjustable-Rate Hybrid Mortgages, in: Fabozzi, F. J., The Handbook of Mortgage Backed Securities, 3rd edition, New York 1992, pp. 31–56.

[13] True Sale International Initiative, www.true-sale-international.de/index.php?id=345.

[14] Erster Pfandbrief der Bank of America gefragt, in: Handelsblatt, March 28th, 2007.

[15] Fabozzi, F. J., Bond Markets, Analysis and Strategies, op. cit., pp. 195–210.

[16] McElravey, J. N., Securities Backed by Credit Card Receivables, in: Fabozzi, F. J., Investing in Asset-Backed Securities, op. cit., pp. 45–60.

[17] Snaders, A. B., Commercial Mortgage-Backed Securities, in: Fabozzi, F. J., The Handbook of Fixed Income Securities, op. cit., pp. 615–628.

[18] Fabozzi, F. J., Bond Markets, Analysis and Strategies, op. cit., pp. 411–450.

[19] Goodman, L. S./Ho, J., Analyzing Mezzanine Tranches of CBOs, in: Fabozzi, F. J., Investing in Asset-Backed Securities, op. cit., pp. 289–298.

[20] ESF Securitisation Forum, ESF Securitization Market Outlook, 2007, www.europeansecuritization.com/ESFMrktOutlook0207.pdf.

[21] ESF Securitisation Forum, ESF Securitization Data Report, Autumn 2007, www.europeansecuritization.com/ESFDataRprt1107.pdf.

2 Commercial Mortgage Backed Securities

Thomas Ertl
Verena Bentzien

Table of contents

1   Introduction

A fairly old concept The principle of securitization, by means of which illiquid assets such as receivables are turned into tradable securities, is a fairly old concept. During the 1970s and 1980s, it had already been applied to residential mortgage pools in the US. In order to reduce an individual bank's exposure and provide investment opportunities in diversified real estate pools, bonds were issued on the capital markets backed by purely residential mortgage pools and called "Residential Mortgage Backed Securities" (RMBS). Investment banks were then the first to apply securitization framework and legal structures to commercial mortgages during the savings and loans crisis in the US in the mid-1980s, which had caused commercial real estate prices to fall by more than 50 % and delinquency rates to soar at all-time highs.

The packaging of commercial mortgages into CMBS developed At first, issuers securitized only a few loans on single properties into "Commercial Mortgage Backed Securities" (CMBS). In the mid-1990s, when the Resolution Trust Corporation (RTC) pooled non-performing loans from failed institutions, the packaging of commercial mortgages into CMBS developed. Since the RTC transactions were successful and some even larger than US$ 1 billion, CMBS gained acceptance among investors and non-government issuers. Increased demand for the product caused issuance in the US to grow steeply in the mid-1990s. By the end of 2006, US CMBS had grown to a market capitalization of US$ 700 billion. Outside the US, Europe with a market capitalization of US$ 161 billion and Japan with US$ 50 billion are worth mentioning. Even though both markets are relatively small, compared to the US, growth rates were significant in the past. While Europe lagged the US nine years until 2004, with an issuance of US$ 23 billion, it is now close to just two years behind; European issuance volume in the first half of 2006 was at € 161 billion [1] compared to US$ 170 billion realised in the US in 2005. Regardless of its brief history, a favorable real estate market, economics and legal environment has promoted the German market such that it accounted for roughly a third of European CMBS at the end of 2006.

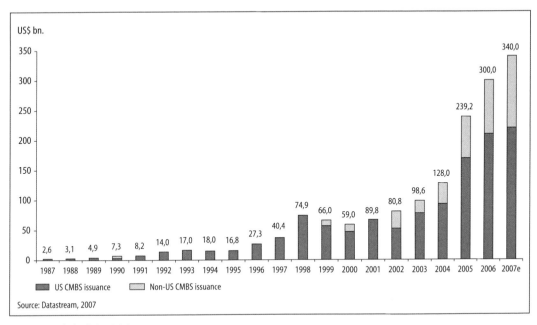

Fig. 1:   Global CMBS issuance

At times of a rising the number of delinquencies and defaults on the US subprime mortgage market, however, not only RMBS but also CMBS attract attention. On the residential mortgage side in the US, the number of loans, which are 60 days or more delinquent, in foreclosure or held for sale, currently accounts for approximately 7% of all 2006 originations, a vintage as bad as the worst experienced to date in the year 2000. In order to better understand CMBS, a product that looks back onto 20 years of strong performance in light of the current market environment, its historical development as well as the basic concepts and theories shall be outlined first. Afterwards, a brief overview over securitization fundamentals will be given, with special focus on a typical CMBS transaction. Following an overview over the major reasons for the success of CMBS on the German market, the main value drivers of CMBS and the rating agencies' view will be explained. All major findings will be summarized at the end, to round up the reader's understanding of the subject. Additionally, a future outlook will be given. The clear focus on an investment banker's perspective on the product will be maintained throughout and an investor's point of view will only be taken where expressly mentioned as such.

An investment banker's perspective

2   Commercial Mortgage Backed Securities

2.1   Definition, concepts and theories

CMBS   "CMBS are bonds backed by pools of mortgages on commercial and multifamily real estate" [2]. As shown in figure 2, the term refers to a number of loans which are backed by commercial real estate, pooled and then passed on to capital market investors through the issue of bonds. CMBS can be viewed as a sub-class of "Asset Backed Securities" (ABS), which include all kinds of receivables, i. e., not only those related to real estate, but also consumer loans, credit card receivables, etc. "Mortgage Backed Securities" (MBS) classify as ABS, but only as part of a broader definition. MBS relate to all bonds backed by collateral, the security of which is a mortgage and as such by a tangible asset. "Collateralized Debt Obligations" (CDOs), however, are backed by pools of company loans and/or bonds which are thus viewed very differently than any sub-class of MBS [3].

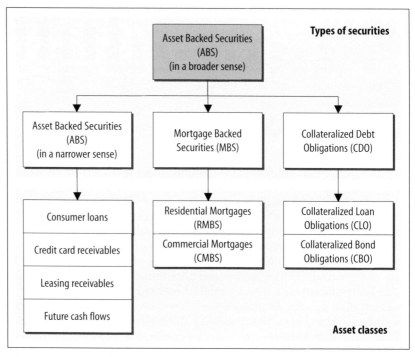

Fig. 2:   Asset classification

2.2   Development of CMBS in Germany

The German lending landscape   The German lending landscape, which had been hit by the real estate recession in 2000, changed significantly after the introduction of securitization. Not only under the introduction of the Basel II Capital Accord, which assigned higher risk to the majority of German real estate loans and as such forced banks to allocate more underlying equity to the aforementioned, but also due to the fact that a number of major traditional lenders had pulled out of the market abruptly. Because the balance sheets of traditional lenders had been extended continuously, the credit risk became overwhelming at some point during the crisis. The resulting constraints on the volume of available financing as well as the increased prices real estate companies had to pay, raised demand for an alternative. Securitization was very attractive in this respect because, under certain conditions which will be dealt with in a later section, it allows the removal of loans from the lender's balance sheet. This practice was supported by the introduction of favorable legislation as well as the foundation of the "True Sale Initiative" in Germany [4].

Introduction of CMBS

After more than five years following an increasing trend of money flowing into German real estate, more than € 80 billion of direct investments by new platforms were recorded at the end of 2006; sellers were not only open-ended funds and corporations, but also the public sector in need of debt reduction. In combination with a changing investor environment and more and more private equity firms acquiring large German real estate portfolios, an attractive niche opened up for international investment banks which had previously not been present on the German lending market. Securitization experiences from more mature markets such as the US, as well as established relationships with international investors, offered an attractive platform for the introduction of CMBS in Germany. As the market has shown by its exponential growth rates, there was significant demand for the product until the 2007 subprime crisis which will adjust an overheated market trade.

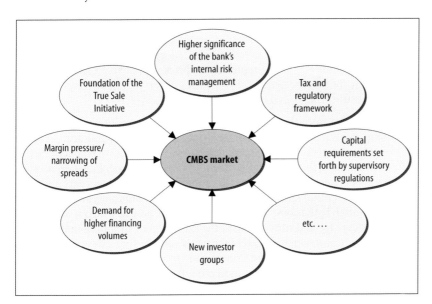

Fig. 3:   Reasons for CMBS

Advantages

CMBS have established themselves today as a means for investment banks to not only participate in the lending market without the otherwise required large amounts of equity, which typically only a traditional lender would have on its balance sheet, but also shaped the commercial real estate financing landscape. As single-borrower risk was almost eliminated and capital markets determine the loan quality, large financing volumes required for portfolio transactions can be made available. Because all loans are divided into credit classes, allowing investors to buy classes ranging from AAA to single B and even unrated, with different returns and according risk exposures, financing has in many cases also become cheaper. From a capital market investor's perspective, CMBS offer a number of advantages over commercial whole loans. Due to attractive relative spreads and call protection stronger than that of RMBS, CMBS are suitable for a wide array of investment strategies. While RMBS are backed by a large number of individual homeowner loans, CMBS benefit from economies of scale in that the asset class of residential property is also included, but only in packaged portfolio deals, where ideally all assets securing the loan are cross-collateralized.

3   Fundamentals of asset securitization

3.1   Asset classes

Commercial loans   Commercial real estate has traditionally been looked at as either property which is income generating, or with a commercial use. The fact that residential property/portfolios above a certain threshold such as € 50 million are also included in CMBS asset pools, however, emphasizes another important aspect. Because life insurance companies were historically the dominant long-term lender to the real estate industry, loans were structured such that they could be matched against long duration liabilities. Commercial loans can unlike some single-family loans, not be prepaid at the borrower's option. This is defined as "Call Protection" and an important feature of US fixed-rate CMBS collateral. Additionally, an increasingly investor oriented perspective in the definition of real estate asset classes is being taken: professional real estate investors buying solely for income generating purposes versus private investors seeking personal use of the acquired property.

Differences among the asset classes   Even though the number of transactions secured by multifamily housing is increasing, the European market share is only at 16 %. Still office and retail are the two largest asset classes with market shares of 33 % and 27 % respectively [5]. Differences among the asset classes mostly stem from a cash flow perspective. In office properties, typical lease terms range from five to seven years and each tenant can be identified. Particularly where landmark buildings are concerned, tenants are often listed companies the credit worthiness of which is assessable. Retail assets are treated similarly with the exception of shopping malls, where particular indicators such as catchment area, purchasing power, tenant mix and pedestrian flow have to be considered. In multifamily assets, however, assumptions are based on factors indicating the attractiveness of the location such as GDP per capita, respective population development and quality of life. While accessibility of the asset by car and public transport is important for all asset classes, closeness to major highways, train lines and airports are of the essence when it comes to logistics and warehouse assets.

Challenging asset classes   In line with the above cash flow perspective, hotels and nursing homes can be challenging asset classes because operating companies usually run them and cash flow security thus depends on the aforementioned. In such cases, the respective company valuation and terms of the operating agreement may become just as important as the asset itself, particularly when an established hotel or nursing home operator has not entered into a lease agreement for the asset on conventional terms. Transactions secured by non-traditional CMBS asset types are also on the rise, backed by, for example, holiday parks, car parks, bingo halls and public houses [6].

3.2   Securitization process

While there is a large array of set-ups available, a typical conduit structure can be summarized as shown below.

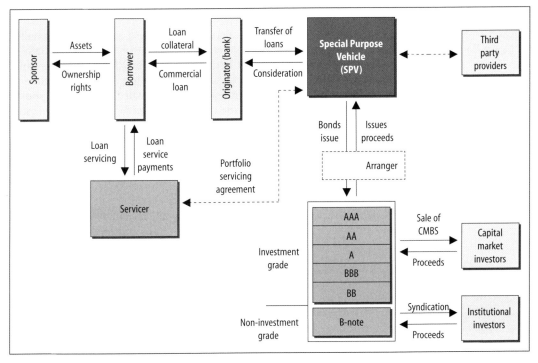

Fig. 4:   CMBS transaction structure

The client seeking financing can either be a private individual or any kind of real estate company (sponsor). Depending on whether the acquisition of the subject asset(s) will take place by means of an asset deal or a share deal, the existing property company will be bought and kept, or a new one will be set up for the acquisition. The property company can only be directly used as the borrowing entity (borrower), if it fulfils certain requirements necessary for securitization. Typically, it should be free of any existing and future liabilities, not have any employees and be of a clear structure. Because of financial reasons and economies of scale in structuring, faster and easier procedures and "re-usability" of the property company, share deals have become more common than asset deals.

Sponsor/ borrower

Security package When entering into the loan agreement, the borrower will give a standard security package. This includes a first ranking mortgage over the property, a pledge over all shares of the company, a negative pledge (meaning that the borrower cannot pledge any of its assets to anyone else), an assignment by way of security over all rent receivables and insurance policies, as well as control over all operating accounts. In cases of a portfolio acquisition with more than one asset, cross-collateralization throughout is preferable; this is to say that in the event of default of one borrower, the remaining ones will be held liable and usually continue to service the loan. Upon satisfactory valuation, legal and environmental due diligence, the loan will be funded.

SPV Since procedures and legal documentation necessary for securitization are very complex, it seems sensible to standardize the aforementioned as much as possible in order to facilitate and speed up the process, as well as to capitalize on economies of scale. Most large market players, such as Morgan Stanley (world market leader in terms of issuance volume in 2006), Deutsche Bank, Credit Suisse and the Royal Bank of Scotland, have thus established a conduit platform for their loan program transactions. The issued loans will be pooled until a desired volume is reached and then transferred to the "Special Purpose Vehicle" (SPV) for securitization. For stand-alone transactions, the SPV will be set up only for that particular transaction and not be used otherwise. Since the legal title is transferred, i.e., all rights to and liabilities from the loans, these are not part of the bank's insolvency estate any longer. As such, it is not only ensured that the SPV is an insolvency remote vehicle, independent of the economic situation of the originator, but the loans are also removed from the bank's balance sheet (true sale). This is beneficial since regulatory capital is freed up, which can be used for new transactions and the loan principal is returned to the originator for refinance.

Conduit With the increasing acceptance of the CMBS product in Europe, several investment banks have also established their brand on the conduit market, the past performance of which may generate potential upside for the pricing and selling of new product via the same platform. Similarly, the servicer takes care of loan handling issues throughout the term of the loans, such as collection of rents and recoveries in case of default, has also established itself as a service provider at the point of interaction with the individual borrowers. A number of third party providers ensure a smooth process without any potential adverse impacts for the borrower brought about by the securitization of the loan.

Subordination After a structuring phase of the new issue by the arranger, which is usually an investment bank, the CMBS product will be presented to the rating agencies. Depending on their view, a varying percentage of the overall balance, the investment grade portion, will be sliced into several tranches with increasing risk of default and return from AAA to BB (subordination) and sold as CMBS to capital market investors. According to this structure, AAA investors will always receive their proceeds first, then AA and so on until BB (cash waterfall). The non-investment grade portion, called B-note, will usually be syndicated in its entirety to an institutional client, who is comfortable with the risk of being the first to assume all potential losses and receiving extraordinary returns for it. By means of overcollateralization or third-party guarantees, a credit rating such as AAA can be achieved (credit enhancement). After the bonds have been issued successfully, investors will bear the risks associated with the loans and are compensated by the returns generated through the aforementioned. Because of the division into several risk-return tranches, CMBS not only cater to a wide range of investors, but also allow the tighter pricing of credit risk upon issue of the loans.

Credit enhancement

3.3 Types of CMBS

In light of the age of the market, a classification of CMBS types common in the US shall be explained in the following – the current European product is not classified as strictly. Since in the early stages of the US CMBS market, only large trophy assets were securitized on an asset-by-asset basis, these were called stand-alone large loans. The term large loan typically refers to mortgages of over US$ 50 million on commercial properties with an institutional borrower. Most large loan CMBS are single-asset or single-borrower transactions issued on a small number of commercial mortgages above the given size; single-asset transactions may even be as large as US$ 500 million.

Stand alone large loans

In the 1990s, however, when the CMBS market evolved, large pools of small-to-medium-sized loans became more popular. Of 200 or more of such loans with respect to geographic regions and property types, a well diversified pool is packaged to back up a conduit transaction. Especially after the terrorist attacks of September 11th, 2001, investors have become more in fond of conduit transactions, as risks associated with the individual property are spread out better. As a result, single-asset transactions and fixed rate large loan deals have become less numerous on the marketplace, even though they tend to not only have more creditworthy borrowers, but also lower leverage than conduit loans.

Conduit transactions

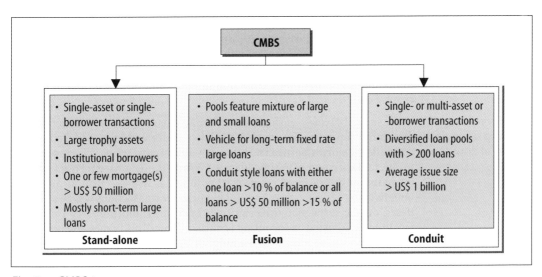

Fig. 5: *CMBS types*

Fusion transaction   The fusion transaction has become the new vehicle for the securitization of fixed rate large loans, while short-term large loan transactions continue to be issued as usual. Fusion transactions are characterized by a mixture of larger and smaller loans pooled together. Definitions vary, but commonly a transaction that features conduit style loans as well as either one loan accounting for more than 10 % of the overall balance, or all loans above US$ 50 million accounting for at least 15 %, would be classified as a fusion transaction.

4   Main value drivers of CMBS

4.1   Real estate and credit analysis

The underlying real estate   Even though loan structuring issues significantly impact the outcome of any rating analysis, a detailed review of the underlying real estate assets is the starting point of any European CMBS transaction rating. As mentioned above, the non-recourse loan structure means that investors get hurt if the assets default, regardless of the respective sponsor's situation. This, of course, makes both volume and sustainability of the property's cash flows vital to meet debt service and investor's return requirements. Since typically, there may be a vacant portion yet to be rented out or leases up for re-letting during the loan term, respective asset quality is of great importance. While across all asset classes, the classification A, B, C and D summarizes aspects, such as location, state of maintenance and third-usability, asset class specific factors as mentioned above ought to be considered in particular.

This holds especially true in light of the fact that typically less than 50 % of a property's investment value are recovered by contractual rental income over a 10-year period. On a cumulative basis, it is therefore usually less than the loan amount. In order to ensure the possibility of refinance or asset sale upon expiry of the loan term for repayment of the outstanding debt, real estate quality and future income producing potential are essential. Similarly, cash flows and values are assumed to decline in a stress case scenario, in order to determine up to which level investors would be hurt by potential losses. The base case scenario also accounts for potential downsides by taking a so-called "haircut" – likewise a reduction in values and cash flows, but to a lesser extent [7].

Underwriting of rating agencies   While single-borrower or single-asset transactions are rated very conservatively due to the concentration of risk, the latter is deemed to be reduced by the diversification of properties and leases in pooled transactions. This is mirrored in the underwriting of rating agencies: While the Standard & Poor's sample for loans in the pool of conduit transaction is usually around 30 %, the underwriting of single-asset and single-borrower transactions will be at 100 %. Based on the respective underwriting, cash flows and property valuations will then be adjusted by the rating agencies. Typically, a higher leverage and a lower net operating income in the range of 10 % to 20 % are assumed. Because adjustments are made for collateral quality, rating agencies state that an AAA-rated conduit transaction is as risky as an AAA-rated stand-alone large loan deal. Following this concept, the credit risk of a AAA-rated corporate bond should theoretically be the same as that of a AAA-rated CMBS.

Regardless of the aforementioned, investor preferences can be very different. **Investor**
Companies which have a larger number of employees taking care of the **preferences**
underwriting may prefer to use their real estate expertise and as such re-
underwrite stand alone large loans. Alternatively they may prefer to buy the
lower investment grade classes such as the BBB class as long as they match
closely the yield on whole loans, which would have been the investment
alternative. Other investors feel that they have to rely on rating agencies to
evaluate commercial mortgage credit risk and to be comfortable with an
originator's general underwriting guidelines because their real estate expertise
is not sufficient. Typically, they see more a call-protected fixed-income asset
in CMBS than a direct investment in real estate. The latter are not very fond of
single-asset deals, where they find diversification and liquidity to be lacking
and might thus buy half of the AAA bonds from conduit deals, but no more
than a third of AAA-rated securities from stand-alone large loan transactions.
As a result, both types of CMBS have historically traded very differently,
with converging tendencies brought about by the introduction of fusion
transactions.

Real estate loans are typically structured such that the probability of appropriate **Financial**
servicing and repayment of the loan are maximized. For this reason, financial **covenants**
covenants such as "Loan-to-Value" (LTV) ratio, "Interest-Coverage Ratio"
(ICR) and "Debt Service Coverage Ratio" (DSCR), as well as amortization,
interest payments and interest hedging are included in the loan contract.
All of the aforementioned enhance a plain structure and reduce the need for
subordination, whereas the trend towards bullet loans with no amortization
during the loan term increases refinance risk.

Generally speaking, CMBS bonds are in most cases sequential pay and of **Bond structure**
a much simpler structure than their RMBS counterparts. Amortization,
prepayment penalties and recoveries from defaults always go to the most
senior remaining class, while the lowest-rated one absorbs the losses. An
important structural difference between RMBS and US fixed-rate CMBS is the
fact that due to the nature of commercial loans, the CMBS are call protected.
As mentioned above, the borrower is either prevented from prepaying the loan
before maturity by certain contractual provisions or economically penalized
for doing so. The four main call protection categories for such CMBS are yield
maintenance, fixed percentage points, defeasance and hard or legal lockout,
with the latter two providing the greatest average life stability for investors.
Defeasance, which is also the mainstay of the municipal market, has also
established itself on the US CMBS market. The mechanism implemented is
such that the borrower has to replace the payment stream of the mortgage loan
with a series of US treasury strips upon exercise of his defeasance option, in
which case investors actually benefit from the improved credit quality without
a decrease in return. Even though the allocation of prepayment penalties to the
different bond classes differs significantly across deals, it is a very important
determinant of relative value.

4.2   Other loan level issues

Various other aspects to consider   Especially at times of an uprising real estate market, investors start to increasingly look for opportunities to add value to acquired property by means of management and asset re-positioning. In line with the aforementioned, the trend towards non-traditional CMBS collateral requires rating agencies to consider the peculiarities of each asset class. As mentioned in the section about asset classes above, assets such as shopping malls or self-storage require active management. Rating agencies would therefore expect to see an experienced sponsor. Extraordinary initial expenditures are not assumed, unless a cash reserve for this purpose has been set up deliberately. The more sponsor equity is committed to the transaction, however, the less subordination is required. Generally speaking, the purchase price is deemed to be equal to the property market value and thus the basis of the LTV calculation. In order to ensure fast and efficient recoveries upon an event of default, a first-ranking land-charge and a full share pledge is essential. Otherwise, enforcement procedures may be unfavorable and lengthy, with an adverse impact upon recoveries. Various other aspects to consider, such as substitution of assets, development works and robustness of a swap, will be assumed in a worst case scenario, so as to cushion any potential obstacles.

Additional debt   In cases in which the borrower wishes to take on additional debt, potential disputes between a senior and a junior lender should be avoided by means of comprehensive inter-creditor agreements. Increased leverage does, however, always bring about an increased probability of default and adversely affects recoveries under circumstances of disputes between the different lenders. Higher subordination levels are therefore commonly required. Only where inter-creditor agreements are drafted clearly and no embedded control rights are granted, subordination levels are reduced again.

5   Conclusion and future outlook

The product can be deemed to develop in line with the market   While the US commercial real estate sector is estimated to range from US$ 6 trillion to US$ 8 trillion [8], European commercial property stock is valued at around € 5.5 trillion, with residential assets adding a further € 14.5 trillion [9]. Ernst & Young Real Estate forecasted investments into German real estate to reach € 70 billion in 2007. If realized, this would even surpass the record 69.7 billion realized in 2006. Of the before mentioned, € 44 billion were invested in commercial real estate (approximately 63 % of overall turnover), of which approximately 88 % were generated by office and retail assets. Developments on the hotel and residential were similar: Hotel transactions reached a volume of € 2.3 billion in 2006 compared to € 800 million the year before. Residential portfolios are also expected to reach the same level as achieved in 2006 at € 11 billion. Roughly two thirds of overall investment volume was generated by international investors [10]. Since CMBS are not only a feasible way of financing for the major asset classes traded on the German market, but also meet the needs of an international investor clientele, the product can be deemed to develop in line with the market. More traditional investors turning to securitized financing products, may potentially generate additional upside in this respect.

The current disturbance of the market, however, is yet to fresh to interpret. In the US, Moody's decision to implement stricter subordination requirements for new commercial mortgage bonds from the beginning of April onwards, points in that direction. While the two other rating agencies, Standard & Poor's and Fitch, kept rating models the same, Moody's now requires subordination levels of around 14 % compared to the former 11 % for an Aaa rating of a junior CMBS conduit transaction class. CMBS spreads movement as shown in figure 6 indicate similar tendencies. The continuous trend of tightening spreads, which the market had seen for the past five years, has been offset by a significant deflexion of as much as 20 bps in two weeks. There had been increasing concerns about loans underwritten on increasing future cash flows including, for example, planned improvements rather than on its historical net operating income, as done typically in the past. Such tendencies were mostly brought about by the increasing share of hotel and condominium conversion deals, for both of which historical income data is hard if not impossible to obtain [11]. Even though underwriter's and analyst's consent seemed to have been that the situation had stabilized and deal quality was improving, such uncertainty in the market may have contributed to the impact of the US subprime crisis.

US subprime crisis

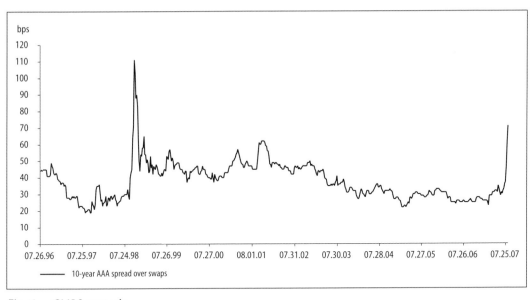

Fig. 6: CMBS spreads

On the fundamentals side, the increasing integration of the capital and real estate markets can be deemed to have been mutually beneficial. Not only has the German real estate market gained in terms of transparency and professionalism, but also the financing landscape has changed significantly. Securitization in general and CMBS in particular have established themselves as a complementary way adding to what traditional balance sheet lending had originally offered to investors. With solid real estate fundamentals, economic growth, 20 real estate company IPOs in 2006 and the G-REIT Act just passed in

CMBS as a sustainable way of alternative financing

2007, there should be further upside potential in the market. Ultimately, CMBS live in 2007 and die from capital market investor's sentiment for the product, which usually enforces discipline fast – future developments of the German securitization market will allow inference upon CMBS as a sustainable way of alternative financing.

6   Bibliography

[1] Standard & Poors, Ratings Direct – European CMBS Performance Review H1 2007: Signs of Weakness Despite Robust Performance?, New York 2007.

[2] Esaki, H., European CMBS, in: Morgan Stanley (Ed.): Transforming Real Estate Finance – A CMBS Primer, 6th edition, New York 2006.

[3] Breidenbach, M., Real Estate Securitisation, in: Schulte, K.-W./Bone-Winkel, S. (Eds.), Schriften zur Immobilienökonomie, Vol. 34, Cologne 2005.

[4] Emse, C., zeb Themen, Competence-Center Kreditrisiken, Forderungsverbriefungen und ihre regulatorische Erfassung, November 2005.

[5] Morgan Stanley (Ed.), Securitised Products: US CMBS, New York 2007.

[6] Standard & Poors, op. cit.

[7] ib.

[8] Standard & Poors (Ed.), Framework for Credit Analysis in European CMBS Transactions, London 2007.

[9] Just, T., Property Derivatives Marching Across Europe, in: Deutsche Bank (Ed.): Deutsche Bank Research, Frankfurt 2007.

[10] Früend, H., Neue Trends am deutschen Immobilienmarkt, in: Ernst & Young Real Estate (Ed.): Real Estate Trends, Eschborn May 2007.

[11] O'Leary, C., Credit Enhancement on the Rise, in: Asset Securitization Report, www.asreport.com, June 11th, 2007.

3   Residential Mortgage Backed Securities in Germany

Bernhard Kaiser
Frank Laudenklos
Alexander Goepfert

Table of contents

1   Introduction

1.1   Basics

Residential Mortgage Backed Securities Residential Mortgage Backed Securities (RMBS) are securities backed by a pool of mortgage loans (grundpfandrechtlich gesicherte Darlehen) that finance residential property. RMBS are employed by banks primarily for two purposes: First, as a refinancing technique, enabling banks to refinance the residential mortgage loans for their customers through the capital markets. Second, as a risk transfer tool, for the purpose of transferring the credit risk associated with the mortgage loan to the capital markets. Consequently to such a transfer, the bank may be entitled to regulatory capital relief under the applicable capital adequacy rules.

In terms of securitization techniques, one may distinguish between true sale securitizations and synthetic securitizations. Synthetic structures have been dominating the German RMBS market since 2000. In contrast, internationally the market share of true sale RMBS is significantly larger than that for synthetic transactions. Moreover, the term RMBS used in an international context, typically refers to true sale RMBS.

While true sale RMBS transactions so far have not played a large role in Germany, there are expectations that they might do so in the future. Due to the industry's lobbying efforts by the True Sale Initiative (TSI), most of the legal and tax obstacles that were regarded to impede the development of true sale Mortgage Backed Securities (MBS) in Germany were removed. Nevertheless, despite of the abolishment of the trade tax for MBS in 2003 and the introduction of the refinancing register in 2005, there have not been many true sale RMBS transactions as of yet in the German market. **Future relevance of RMBS transactions**

Worldwide, the volume of MBS in general and RMBS in particular grew rapidly until the beginning of 2007, when defaults on subprime mortgages (i. e., mortgage loans with a lower initial credit quality, see section 3.1.2) accelerated in the United States. The development was due to a change in macro-economic conditions in the US that let real estate prices drop and long-term interest rates increase simultaneously. As a result, the market values of RMBS structures, especially those including subprime loans plunged [1]. The ensuing global financial liquidity crisis affected the worldwide market for Asset Backed Securities and caused severe difficulties for the primary and secondary RMBS markets, even for those securities which were unrelated to subprime mortgages. It is probably still too early to judge whether that crisis will have an enduring impact on the development of the RMBS market in general and the German RMBS market in particular. This chapter will not engage in speculations on the consequences of the crisis, but rather take a look at the status of recent true sale RMBS.

1.2 Residential Mortgage Backed Securities defined and distinguished

1.2.1 Basic transaction structure

An RMBS is a special form of the Asset Backed Security [2]. The term "Asset Backed Security" (ABS) describes a security that is backed by a pool of assets, receivables in particular. Typically a Special Purpose Company (SPC) or Vehicle (SPV), established solely for the purpose of the securitization transactions, will purchase the assets, or mortgage loans in case of an RMBS transaction, from the bank holding the mortgage loans. The SPV will finance the purchase of the mortgage loans by issuing bonds on the capital markets. The cash flows generated by the mortgage loans will be used by the SPV to satisfy the payment obligations of bonds [3]. **Structure of RMBS transactions**

The transaction will be structured in a way that the bond investors are only exposed to the credit risk of the borrowers of the mortgage loans, and not to the credit risk of the originating bank (the originator), the SPV or any other **Role of Special Purpose Vehicles** transaction participant. One element used to achieve this is the involvement of a security trustee to whom the mortgage loans are transferred as security for the obligations of the bond's SPV [4]. Additionally, the SPV typically employs the originator, who has the business relationship with the borrowers, collects payments for the loans or receives payments as a result of the enforcement of the mortgage and forwards them to the SPV. In this function the originator is called the servicer.

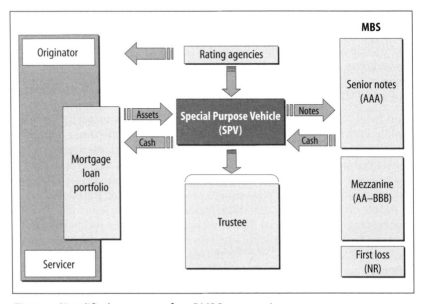

Fig. 1:   Simplified structure of an RMBS transaction

1.2.2   True sale and synthetic structures

True sale vs. synthetic transactions ABS transactions (including MBS transactions) can be subdivided into true sale transactions and synthetic transactions. In true sale transactions the assets are physically transferred to the SPV, whereas in a synthetic transaction they remain on the originator's balance sheet. The originator enters into a credit default swap, a credit linked note, a guarantee or a similar instrument that buys protection against the credit risk associated with the pool of mortgage loans. As a result, the credit risk associated with the pool of mortgage loans is transferred to the entity selling the protection.

Subject to certain requirements being met, the transaction has the purpose to relieve the protection buyer (the originator) from the capital adequacy requirements under its regulatory regime. While synthetic structures are used if regulatory risk transfer is the underlying motive of the transaction, true sale securitizations are predominantely employed in situations where the originator seeks funding in addition to regulatory risk transfer.

1.2.3   RMBS and CMBS

In RMBS transactions, the underlying mortgage loans are granted to finance the acquisition, the construction or the refurbishment of residential property. The borrower of the mortgage loan is typically the home owner who is using the mortgaged property for private purposes. This differentiates RMBS from Commercial Mortgage Backed Securities (CMBS) where the borrower is a person or an entity that uses the property commercially. Typically, such a commercial borrower would offer the property (retail or office space, hotels, industrial or other commercial sites, apartment or multi-family buildings, etc.) to tenants who are using the property on the basis of lease agreements with the borrower. The focus in a CMBS transaction is the securitization of the income generated by the commercial use of a property.

Separation of RMBS and CMBS

In CMBS transactions, the loans are typically rather large (exceeding € 10 million), whereas the asset pool in an RMBS structure is normally quite granular and diversified. The potential default of an individual single borrower compared to the insolvency risk of a borrower in a CMBS transaction has typically lesser of an impact on the repayment of the notes issued with the securitization [5]. In RMBS transactions, rating agencies and investors evaluate the portfolio, which may comprise several thousand loans, by using statistical models. In RMBS transactions, typically neither a single loan nor the corresponding real property is assessed individually.

2   Market overview and development

The first securitization of residential mortgage loans in Germany was performed in 1995 by Rheinische Hypothekenbank AG. A pool of residential and commercial loans was transferred and refinanced through an SPV called German Mortgage Securities B.V. (GEMS). In 1998, an RMBS transaction arranged by Deutsche Bank AG followed (HAUS 1998-1 Limited) with exclusively residential loans.

The origination of the German MBS market

Both transactions highlighted an issue that has been viewed as an impediment for the development of the German true sale MBS market: Due to the fact that in Germany it is legally and administratively quite onerous to transfer registered mortgages (Buchgrundschulden), the mortgages in both transactions were not transferred to the SPV; rather the SPV was granted merely a right to have the mortgages transferred to it, upon the breach of certain triggers that are related to the credit risk of the originator. Therefore transactions did not achieve a true disengagement from the insolvency risk of the originator.

On top of that issue, beginning in 1999, there was a concern that SPVs established for the purpose of securitization could become subject to German trade tax. The application of such tax would have increased the costs of these transactions to a level which would be prohibitive. The tax issue was due to the fact that the mortgage loans were held by the SPV which, as opposed to the originating bank, is not trade tax exempt, and were serviced by an agent (the servicer) in Germany. Consequently, the SPV was deemed to have an establishment for tax purposes in Germany.

Development of synthetic transactions

German banks thus tended to synthetic securitizations, and most of the securitizations of mortgage loans occurring during the first years of this decade were done synthetically. In October 2001, the KfW (Kreditanstalt für Wiederaufbau – KfW) established its synthetic securitization platform "PROVIDE", which offered banks a standardized infrastructure for securitizing mortgage loans.

In 2003, the German legislator addressed the trade tax issue described above by enacting an amendment to the commercial tax ordinance (Gewerbesteuer-durchführungsverordnung – GewStDV), making true sale securitizations of bank loans ever since exempt from German trade tax.

A further important development for the true sale securitization market occurred in 2003, when KfW together with a number of German commercial banks, which were subsequently joined by other banks, including five public-sector banks, established the True Sale Initiative (TSI). The TSI is devoted to the promotion of the German securitization market. As a result of the TSI's efforts, the German legislator introduced the refinancing register in 2006, addressing the issues related to the transferability of mortgages. A loan or mortgage for which a right to transfer is registered for the benefit of an SPV gives the right to segregate the loan or mortgage. This SPV, together with the relevant mortgages and loans, is registered in the refinancing register and will be treated in case of insolvency of the originator as if the mortgage and loans had been transferred to it prior to insolvency.

Despite these developments, true sale RMBS, as a securitization asset class, have not yet played a major role in the German securitization market. The traditional refinancing tools of German banks, such as tapping the covered bond market, directly issuing bonds or taking deposits from customers – at least in the more recent past – seem to have been able to largely satisfy the banks' refinancing needs.

The German mortgage market

The German mortgage market traditionally was a purely prime market with fairly standardized mortgage products. However lately, there have been signs that the German mortgage market will further diversify and further explore new market segments of mortgage lending. The target customers in this market (referred to as "near prime") are those who may not necessarily comply with those traditionally rather strict loan underwriting criteria (see section 3.2.1).

In the recent past, two banks, GMAC-RFC Bank GmbH (GMAC-RFC) and Deutsche Bank, have built platforms to refinance their origination activities in that market through the RMBS market. The GMAC-RFC's platform, called "E-MAC", has executed four transactions so far. The latest transaction under Deutsche Bank's platform "Eurohome Mortgages" (Eurohome Mortgages 2007-1 P.L.C.) involved German and Italian mortgage loans and may serve as an example for an innovative legal structure. While in Germany there was a direct sale and transfer of the loan claims and the corresponding mortgages from the originator to Eurohome Mortgages 2007-1 P.L.C., an indirect way was chosen for the Italian leg of the transaction. Therefore, at the level of the SPV, the portfolio consisted of German mortgage loans on the one hand, and notes representing an interest in Italian mortgage loans on the other hand.

3 The loan level: loans and mortgages in German RMBS

3.1 Loans

3.1.1 Types of loans

Most German residential mortgage loans have fixed interest rates and fixed repayment characteristics for a certain period of time. The length of the fixed rate period (Zinsfestschreibungsperiode) varies from one to 15 years, but is most commonly set at 5 to 10 years. Upon expiration of the fixed rate period, the lending bank is obligated to provide a new offer for the next fixed period. The offer is typically only for a new interest rate, but some lenders renegotiate the amortization features as well. Mortgage payments are usually directly debited monthly, but quarterly, semi-annual, and annual payments can also be arranged [6].

Repayment profile of residential mortgage loans

In terms of their repayment profile, residential mortgage loans can be divided into the two main categories of amortizing loans (Tilgungsdarlehen) and so-called bullet loans (Festkredit or Darlehen mit Endfälligkeit). The amortizing loan seems to be prevailing in the market.

Amortizing loans vs. bullet loans

Amortizing loans are characterized by the borrower either paying a fixed amount of principal each period (ratierliche Tilgung) or making a fixed payment each period. The amount is comprised of both interest and principal (annuitätische Tilgung), with the portion of interest becoming smaller each period (and thus the principal portion becoming larger) due to the periodical reduction of the outstanding principal through the principal payments [7].

Bullet loans are characterized by the fact that they are payable in full on the final maturity date.

Pursuant to the German Civil Code, the bullet loan is the typical form of a loan (see § 488 No. 1 sentence 2 of the German Civil Code). If the underlying residential mortgage loans are bullet loans, the whole outstanding principal is due and payable only upon the final maturity date with no periodic partial repayments during the term of the loan [8]. Unless borrowers accrue this principal payment from another source, e.g., home loan and savings contract (Bausparvertrag) or capital life insurance policy (Kapitallebensversicherung), bullet loans, which are also referred to as interest-only loans, are subject to refinancing risk.

The borrower's interest in their alternative repayment schemes, according to which they accrue the principal payment from another source, are normally assigned to the lenders to serve as an amortization surrogate (Tilgungsersatzleistung) and are used to redeem the residential mortgage loan at maturity. Whenever the lender accepts the assignment of rights and claims under capital life insurance policies it has to ensure that the disbursement under the capital life insurance policy, i.e., the maturity payment (garantierte Ablaufleistung), at least covers the whole outstanding loan amount on the final maturity date. Any difference between the outstanding loan amount on the final maturity date and the maturity payment needs to be covered by other means. In respect of capital life insurance policies and the prepayment of the residential mortgage loan, the maturity payment becomes less important compared to the surrender value (Rückkaufswert) [9].

Construction loans Another type of loan is the construction loan: Residential mortgage loans for the construction of new houses or for home improvements are often considered to be riskier than loans for purchasing existing houses. The amount granted under a construction loan is usually based on the appraised value after the construction or refurbishment is completed and therefore involves additional risks, since the project still has to be completed at the time the funds are disbursed [10]. Moreover, one has to take into consideration that the borrower might be faced with the situation of having to pay both the rent on his residence and the loan installments until the construction work is finished. Such risk may be mitigated by granting an initial lockout period in which interest-only payments may be made.

3.1.2   Types of borrowers

Three categories of credit quality In an international context, mainly based on practices in the US, RMBS and the underlying pool of mortgage loans can be classified into three main categories according to credit quality [11]:

- Prime residential mortgage loans with prime borrowers, full documentation (e. g., verification of income and assets), and strong credit scores, etc. Prime mortgage loans are characterized by a high credit quality at the time the loan is granted. The borrowers have strong employment and credit histories.

- Between the prime and the subprime sector is a somewhat nebulous category referenced to as "Alt-A" residential mortgage loans with generally prime, but non-conform borrowers [12].

- Subprime residential mortgage loans are loans of lower initial credit quality which are likely to experience significantly higher levels of default. The borrowers in this segment often have lower income levels and blemished credit histories resulting in weaker credit scores. After issuance, these loans must be serviced by special units designated to closely monitor the payments by the borrowers.

Compared to other jurisdictions, especially the US, the German residential loan market traditionally commands high loan underwriting standards. The borrower is usually required to have a significant amount of equity. There are programs subsidized by the state under which potential home owners are encouraged to build up equity, in particular through the wide spread building associations (Bausparkassen).

Against that background it is an interesting development that recently banks in Germany have begun to explore and develop a market segment for customers who may not necessarily be able to comply with those rather strict underwriting standards that have prevailed in the German market for a long time. These customers are, e. g., young families with little or no equity, older customers, self-employed customers, foreigners, etc. [13]. In this market segment, which is sometimes referred to as "near prime", banks underwrite loans much above the traditional 60 % LTV limit. Even financing up to LTVs of 100 % and above is offered.

3.2 Collateral

3.2.1 Different types of mortgages

German law distinguishes between two types of security interests in land: the land charge (Grundschuld) and the mortgage (Hypothek). Their main difference is that the "Hypothek" is necessarily linked to a certain claim and automatically reverts to the owner in the form of an owner's mortgage (Eigentümergrundschuld) if and to the extent such claim has been settled or is non-existent. This link is commonly referred to as the mortgage being accessory (akzessorisch) to the claim. In contrast, the "Grundschuld" remains with the creditor independently of the actual existence of a claim until it is retransferred to the owner. This means, in particular, that once the debtor has repaid a certain obligation (e.g., a loan), the "Grundschuld" securing such claim will survive and may again be used as collateral for other claims of the same creditor or, after assignment of the "Grundschuld", of another creditor. Thus, a "Grundschuld" may even be used as security for multiple obligations vis-à-vis the same creditor. The "Grundschuld" is independent of the secured claim and, consequently, can be transferred independently. For these reasons the "Grundschuld" is much more common in the German residential mortgage practice than the "Hypothek". Accordingly, most German RMBS have the "Grundschuld" as collateral rather than the "Hypothek".

Two types of mortgages

The "Hypothek" and the "Grundschuld" can be in certificated or registered form. A registered mortgage is created and transferred by mutual consent of the owner of the property and the holder of the mortgage and the registration of the mortgage [14] and its holder in the land register. Thus, a registered mortgage can only be transferred by the registration of the new holder of the mortgage in the relevant land register [15]. Any such registration will trigger notarial and registration costs. Given that in an MBS context a large number of mortgages needs to be transferred to the SPV, which could be prohibitive in considering an MBS transaction at all, the German legislator has introduced the refinancing register (Refinanzierungsregister) in 2006 (see section 5.1) [16]. By employing the register, the mortgages do not need to be transferred to the SPV. Even without the transfer, the SPV will have a segregation right in case of insolvency of the originator and accordingly, will have the same insolvency protection as if the mortgages had been transferred.

Certificated and registered mortgages

The certificated mortgage is created by mutual consent of the owner of the property and the holder of the mortgage, the registration of the mortgage and the holder of the mortgage in the land register, and the requirement that the owner of the property handed over the mortgage certificate (Grundschuldbrief) to the holder of the mortgage. Subject to being recorded in the deed of mortgage (Grundschuldbestellungsurkunde), the land registry (Grundbuchamt) is authorized to hand over the mortgage certificate directly to the holder of the mortgage. The certificated mortgage is transferred by mutual consent of the assignor and the assignee and the transfer of the mortgage certificate from the assignor to the assignee [17]. The certificated mortgage can be transferred without the new holder of the mortgage being registered in the relevant land register [18].

A disadvantage of the certificated mortgage is the cost and long duration of the cancellation proceedings (Aufgebotsverfahren) in case the mortgage certificate is lost [19]. If the mortgage certificate is lost, the lender may not be able to enforce the mortgage and foreclose on the real property [20].

3.2.2   Submitting to immediate enforcement

On the basis of the prevailing market practice in Germany, the lending bank will require the borrower and owner of the property to submit the immediate enforcement of the mortgage. Such submission will provide the lender with enforceable title against the borrower and owner of the real property. With such a submission the lender, in an enforcement scenario, saves time and court costs. Rating agencies in MBS transactions typically require such a submission to be granted.

4   The securitization level: underlying motives, structural features and selected legal issues

4.1   Underlying motives for the originating bank to enter into a securitization transaction

Motives for securitization A mortgage originator may have various motives [21] to refinance its pool of mortgage receivables through an RMBS transaction. These motives are primarily the following:

- RMBS may offer a lower-cost source of financing in comparison to other bank and capital market financing alternatives [22] due to the disengagement of the credit risk associated with the pool of mortgage loans from the bank's credit risk. The bank can obtain a financing that is based on the credit risk of the pool; if the pool's credit quality (rating) is higher than the bank's credit quality (rating), the bank may be able to raise funds at more favorable financial terms than through straight debt issuance;

- RMBS are more flexible than German covered bonds (Pfandbriefe) [23] due to the relatively rigid statutory provisions applicable to the latter [24];

- RMBS allow originators to replenish their funds which – subject to the capital adequacy requirements of the German Solvency Regulation (Solvabilitätsverordnung) – they can invest in additional or other more profitable origination activities [25];

- RMBS allow for balance sheet risk management by reducing credit risk from certain borrowers, markets, regions, etc. which may lead to more diversification in the remaining loan portfolio held by the bank [26]; and

- RMBS allow originators to remove assets from their balance sheet which – if they reduce their debt exposure with the cash they receive from the purchase price – may improve their financial ratios [27].

4.2 Rating implications in RMBS transactions

4.2.1 The importance of rating agencies

The feasibility of any RMBS transaction, as of any ABS transaction, depends on whether the notes issued by the SPV will receive the required ratings. Without ratings, RMBS could normally not be placed in the public bond market. Investors buying RMBS base their investment decision to a large extent on the ratings assigned to the relevant securities.

Ratings as a condition for the placement of RMBS

Given the importance of the rating, the structuring of an RMBS transaction is substantially influenced by the requirements of the rating agencies. The rating agencies involved in the transaction will review the structures in a number of aspects. In particular they will analyze, among other things,

- the soundness of the originator's underwriting policies,

- the legal robustness of the structure, especially if a true sale has occurred and the mortgage loans are fully transferred to the SPV without an insolvency of the originator;

- the loan and mortgage portfolio, including the granularity and diversification of the loans, the historical losses and recoveries, the size of the individual loans, concentration issues, etc.;

- the servicing standards applied by, and the credit quality of, the loan servicer [28].

Depending on these and other factors, the rating agencies will determine in particular the credit enhancement required for the transaction and the tranching (see section 4.2.2) of the securities issued by the SPV.

4.2.2 Tranching

In RMBS transactions, the bonds issued by the SPV to finance the acquisition of the pool of mortgage loans are typically issued in more than one class or tranche. The various classes or tranches of notes typically differ in

Dividing mortgage loan portfolios in different tranches

- the amount of interest they pay,

- the ratings they carry, and

- their entitlements to the cash flow generated by the assets (i. e., the mortgage loan pool).

The tranche with the highest rating and the lowest interest entitlement is referred to as the most senior tranche. The tranche with the lowest rating and the highest interest entitlement is referred to as the most junior(-rated) tranche. Depending on their ranking, the various tranches have different entitlements to the cash flows the SPV receives from the assets. These cash flows are distributed to the note holders on the basis of a prescribed order of priority ("waterfall"). All payments are first allocated to the most senior tranche and thereafter to the more junior tranches in the order of their seniority. As a result of such a distribution, realized losses on the assets will be allocated from the bottom to the top, i. e., they will first be borne by the most junior tranches and only thereafter by the more senior tranches. The most senior tranche, carrying the highest rating, will be the last one to suffer from any such losses. Accordingly, investors in the most senior tranche will have the highest security for the recovery of their investment and the interest payable thereon.

Typically, in addition to the rated tranches of securities, there may be unrated tranches, ranking from regular junior to the most junior rated tranche. The most junior of these unrated tranches, to which losses in the portfolio are allocated first, are referred to as "first loss piece" or "equity piece". Many times, the first loss piece is subscribed by the originator who has selected the asset pool, who is charged with the servicing of the asset pool and as such should be the one who is in the best position to evaluate the risks of the portfolio. The fact that he is subscribing to the riskiest piece of the capital structure and therefore will be hit by any losses first serves as a selling point and means of building trust with third-party investors which are subscribing to the more senior tranches.

By the same token this fact should operate as an incentive for the originator, acting as servicer of the sold residential mortgage loan receivables: Its quality of servicing may influence the losses allocated to the first loss piece – the better its servicing, the lower its losses and the higher its potential profit [29].

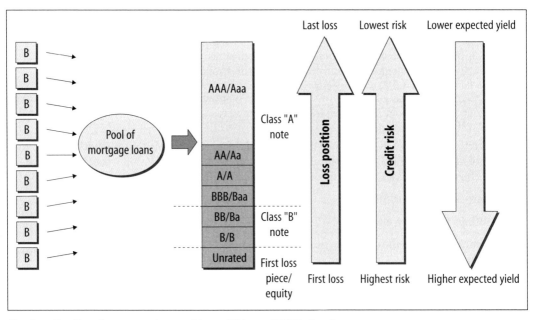

Fig. 2:   Credit enhancement: tranching within an RMBS structure

4.2.3   Credit enhancement

In order to achieve the economically desired size and rating of the most senior tranche, the rating agencies will determine the amount of the necessary enhancement of the pool's credit quality. Examples of credit enhancement techniques typically employed in RMBS structures and the terminology used in that respect are as follows:

Enhancement of the credit portfolio quality

- Overcollateralization refers to the face value of the underlying asset portfolio being larger than the security (Wertpapier) it backs. Because of this, even if some of the payments from the underlying assets are late or default, principal and interest payments on the notes can still be made.

- Excess spread means in an ABS transaction with interest-bearing assets (such as loans) the difference between the interest received on the underlying asset pool of mortgage loans and the interest payable under the notes. Such excess income may be used to cover losses in the portfolio.

- Tranching as described above will also operate as credit enhancement, as the tranches will suffer losses only after the capital provided by the junior tranches has been extinguished.

- External guarantee or sub-loan: A third party, which may be an entity within the originator's group, or an external entity, e. g., a monoline insurance company, can be employed to provide a guarantee for losses to the SPV. A similar effect will be achieved with a sub-loan extended to the SPV which will be redeemable only after the rated notes and senior expenses have been paid.

- A reserve account may be created to reimburse the investors for realized losses up to the amount allocated for the reserve. The reserve account can be funded by various means, e. g., at initiation directly by the originator or an entity of the originator's group; alternatively, it can be built up over time funded by an excess spread.

4.2.4   Insolvency issues

A key principle that lies at the heart of ratings assigned by the leading rating agencies is that the assets that fund the rated obligations are isolated from insolvency risk, in case of the insolvency of the originator, the SPV or any other transaction party.

Reducing the SPV's insolvency risk

With respect to the insolvency risk associated with the SPV, rating agencies require the SPV to be "insolvency remote", i. e., the likelihood of an insolvency of the SPV must be reduced to the largest extent possible. To that end, the rating agencies have developed a number of criteria with which the SPV must comply, e. g., the SPV must be newly established and not have a history, its articles of incorporation must limit the purpose of the company to activities related to the transaction, it shall not have any employees, etc.

Further, all contractual agreements the SPV enters into shall contain limited recourse and non-petition clauses. Limited recourse clauses limit the claims and entitlements a transaction creditor may have against the SPV to the SPV's assets, subject to the distribution rules prescribed by the priority of payments. Each transaction creditor will waive any claims and entitlements it may have in excess of what is due to it pursuant to the application of that rule.

Non-petition clauses stipulate in the creditor's agreement of the relevant transaction that it will not make a filing for insolvency [30] against the SPV until the lapse of a certain time period after the last maturing obligation of the SPV vis-à-vis any transaction creditor under any transaction document that has been fulfilled.

With respect to a potential insolvency of the originator, rating agencies in particular require the pool of assets to be transferred to the SPV as a true sale; this means in essence that the transfer causes the SPV to be exclusively entitled to these assets and the payments that are to be made under the pool. These rights of the SPV must not be affected by an insolvency of the originator. The fact that such a true sale has occurred will be required to be confirmed in a legal opinion given by the arranger's counsel.

5 Recent legal developments in Germany affecting RMBS

5.1 The introduction of the refinancing register

Difficulties in transferring registered mortgages

As pointed out above, the fact that registered mortgages in Germany are onerous to transfer in large numbers, in terms of costs and administrative procedures, was believed to constitute a significant impediment to the further development of the German MBS market. Such transfer is generally necessary in order to enable the SPV to have unrestricted access to the mortgages securing the residential loans, even in case of an insolvency of the originator, as it is required by the rating agencies. In the light of the difficulties associated with the transfer of large pools of mortgages, the early RMBS structures (e. g., "GEMS" and "HAUS") left the mortgages with the originators, but had to employ complicated rating triggers, which would not work in environment today, inter alia given the different rating levels of German banks today.

Introduction of the refinancing register

As a reaction to that issue, the German legislator enacted an amendment to the German Banking Act (KWG), introducing the refinancing register. Under the amended KWG an actual transfer of the mortgages and the loans to the SPV is no longer necessary to afford the SPV the insolvency-remote position required by the rating agency in securitizations. An originator may now register the loan receivables and the mortgages, or the claim to have these receivables transferred to the SPV, in a refinancing register. If the originator is a credit institution, it may establish and maintain the refinancing register itself. Registration of the assets or the claim for transfer has the legal effect that the SPV is, in case of insolvency of the originator, entitled to claim segregation of such registered assets. The position of the SPV is further protected so that the originator may neither set off against nor assert any rights of retention over the claim to have the registered assets transferred to the SPV.

The application of the refinancing register is not limited to assets which are subject to German law. Assets subject to a non-German jurisdiction are registrable, provided that the originator has the legal capacity to transfer the title to them. Assets may be registered despite the fact that their assignability has been restricted by oral or implicit agreement. In case of a written restriction on assignment, such assets may not be registered unless the receivables debtor is a merchant and the further requirements of § 354 a of the German Commercial Code apply.

The refinancing register may be operated in physical or electronic form. Each refinancing register is to be monitored by a neutral registered administrator appointed by the German Federal Financial Supervisory Authority (BaFin).

In case of insolvency of the originator, the relevant insolvency court may, if requested by the BaFin, replace the register administrator (Verwalter) with a special administrator (Sachwalter). It is regarded as one of the main responsibilities of the special administrator to ensure that the cash flows from the registered assets to the SPV are not interrupted.

Insolvency of an originator

Although the refinancing register has been welcomed by the financial community as constituting a substantial step forward in fostering the German true sale securitization market, it has not been used much in practice yet with the primary reason that the MBS structures, in particular CMBS conduits, that are currently dominating the German market are set up for securitization from the outset and are using certificated mortgages where no transfer issue exists. It may be a further reason that the refinancing register needs quite some explanation as far as offering circular, rating agencies and investors in an international transaction are concerned.

The two RMBS platforms by GMAC-RFC and Deutsche Bank mentioned above (see section 2) do not employ a refinancing register. Instead, they provide for certificated mortgages, which can easily be transferred to the SPV, as they were set up for a securitization exit.

5.2 The amendment of § 108 of the German Insolvency Statute (InsO)

Before § 108 of the German Insolvency Statute (InsO) was amended, it was disputed in legal literature whether § 103 of the InsO, in the event of insolvency of the originator, would be applicable to fully-disbursed mortgage loans [31]. § 103 deals with executory contracts in case of insolvency and gives the insolvency administrator the right to either terminate or to continue executory contracts. In either case, any payments made under the receivables originating from such contract, i.e., the mortgage loans in an RMBS transaction, would fall into the insolvency estate and would not be available to the assignee. An executory contract within the meaning of § 103 of the InsO is a contract which – at the time of the institution of insolvency proceedings – has not yet been fully performed by either party. One might think that in case of a fully disbursed loan at least the bank acting as a lender would have fully performed its duty under the contract. This approach, however, has been drawn into question by some authors who argue that the bank, after disbursing the loan, still owes to the customer the obligation to leave the loan outstanding. According to this argument, the contract would not have been fully performed by either party. For RMBS transactions this would mean that the SPV would

Amendment of § 108 InsO

not be entitled to the cash flows out of the mortgage loans in case of insolvency of the originator.

Neither the legal securitization community nor the rating agencies seem to have shared this view, but, nevertheless there was some undesired legal uncertainty surrounding the issue. In order to resolve the legal uncertainty, the legislator enacted § 108 subsection (2) of the InsO of 2007 [32]. Pursuant to this provision, any loan agreement shall be continued with effect against the insolvency estate to the extent that the loan has been made available to the borrower. Accordingly, the loan receivables to the extent they relate to the already disbursed tranches can be validly assigned. In an RBMS transaction they would belong to the SPV despite of the insolvency of the originator [33].

On the other hand, a loan that has not been fully disbursed yet, for instance a construction loan for which progress disbursements have been agreed upon, the insolvency administrator of the originator in its capacity as a lender has the right to terminate any non-disbursed tranches of the loan according to § 103 of the German Insolvency Statute. The provisions of § 108 subsection (2) of the German Insolvency Statute do not apply with respect to those loan tranches that have not been disbursed yet [34].

5.3   Data protection and secrecy issues

Disposition of receivables In principle, receivables governed by German law are freely assignable on the basis of §§ 398 et seq. of the German Civil Code, unless their assignment is excluded

- by mutual agreement,
- by the nature of the relevant receivable, or
- on the basis of legal restrictions applicable.

Nevertheless, the collection, processing, use and transfer of personal data must comply with the requirements of the Federal Data Protection Act (the Act). According to the Act, the transfer, processing and use of personal data is only allowed if so permitted by the Act or any other legal provision or if the relevant person has consented to such a transfer, processing or use and such a declaration of consent fulfills the requirements of the Act.

In cases in which the borrower did not explicitly consent to the transfer of its personal data, it was in dispute whether the lack of the borrower's consent to transfer personal data to a third party, e.g., the purchaser of the loan receivables, would represent a violation of the bank secrecy or German data protection law and would cause such an assignment to be null and void.

Against that position, the Federal Supreme Court (Bundesgerichtshof) [35] and the Federal Constitutional Court (Bundesverfassungsgericht) [36] recently ruled that neither the bank secrecy nor the German data protection law causes the non-assignability of receivables and the invalidity of such an assignment. This view is supported by the provisions set forth in § 22 d of the German Banking Act [37]. Notwithstanding, a violation of data protection or banking secrecy rules may trigger contractual claims for damages. In addition, under the Act the protected customer might have a right that the transferred data be extinguished in certain circumstances, if the requirements of the Act are violated.

Given these consequences, it is advisable to obtain the authorization of the customer to transfer its personal data for refinancing purposes. Any such consent needs to comply with the provisions of § 4 a of the Act. But one has to bear in mind that any such consent given in general business conditions such as standard form credit facility agreements is subject to further restrictions based on §§ 305 et seq. of the German Civil Code [38].

Given these difficulties, it is practice to employ a data protection trustee and the procedures as suggested by circular 4/97 of the German BaFin [39]. On the basis of that circular, customer consent to the data transfer is not required if the personal data is transferred to the purchaser in encrypted form only and the encryption key is deposited by a data trustee. Qualified to act as a data trustee are, on the basis of the examples given by the circular, a notary or an EU credit institution.

6 Bibliography

[1] Risk Glossary, Mortgage Backed Security, www.riskglossary.com/ articles/mortgage_backed_security.htm, accessed on October 2nd , 2007.

[2] Kern, C., Die Sicherheit gedeckter Wertpapiere, Tübingen, 2004, pp. 38 et seqq.

[3] Pursuant to circular (Rundschreiben) 4/97 released by the former Federal Banking Supervisory Office (Bundesaufsichtsamt für das Kreditwesen) now replaced by the Federal Financial Supervisory Authority (Bundesanstalt für Finanzdienstleistungsaufsicht) on March 19th, 1997, the term "Asset Backed Securities" means securities or debentures (Schuldscheine) with payment claims (Zahlungs- ansprüche) against a special purpose entity. Such payment claims are backed by unsecuritized receivables that have been transferred to the special purpose entity and primarily serve as a liability base (Haftungsgrundlage) for the investors, the holders of the asset-backed securities. Pursuant to another interpretation closely related to the aforementioned circular, the payment claims are secured by a pool of similar unsecuritized or securitized, secured or unsecured receivables (see Jahn, in: Schimansky, H./Bunte, H. /Lwowski, H., Bankrechts- Handbuch, 3rd edition, 2007, § 114 a marginal note 1).

[4] UBS Bankfachwörterbuch, Asset Backed Security, www.ubs.com/1/g/ about/bterms/content_a.html#AssetBackedSecurity, accessed on October 2nd, 2007.

[5] This issue must not be confused with the fact that in CMBS the lease agreements which the borrower might enter into may also provide for an element of granularity and diversity from a rating perspective, as it is especially applicable for multi-family housing RMBS.

[6] Standard & Poor's, Criteria for Rating German Residential Mortgage
     Backed Securities, http://www2.standardandpoors.com/portal/site/sp/
     en/eu/page.article/2,1,14,0,1145817706240.html, released on
     August 31st, 2001, accessed on December 11th, 2007.

[7] For further guidance see Früh, in: Hellner, T./Steuer, S., Bankrecht und
     Bankpraxis (as of April 2007), marginal note 3/221.

[8] Regarding the risks related to bullet loans from a lender's perspective,
     see Früh, op. cit., marginal note 3/220.

[9] See Eckstein/Wilhelm, in: Hellner, T./Steuer, S., op. cit., marginal note
     3/813 et seqq. for further general details of amortization surrogates.

[10] Fitch in RMBS/Germany Criteria Report "German Residential
     Mortgage Default Model 2004", www.fitchratings.com/corporate/
     reports/report_frame.cfm?rpt_id=228248&sector_flag=
     5&marketsector=2&detail=104, accessed on December, 18th, 2007, p. 13.

[11] Common to all three is that the loan is secured by a first-ranking
     mortgage, i. e., a mortgage first in the ranking of Section III of the
     relevant land register. See Fabozzi/Bhattacharya/Berliner, Mortgage
     Backed Securities, 2007, p. 5 regarding the classification of mortgage
     loans by credit quality.

[12] An alternative A (Alt-A) loan is defined by what it is not. An Alt-A loan
     is a first-lien residential mortgage loan that generally conforms to
     traditional prime credit guidelines, although the Loan-to-Value (LTV)
     ratio, loan documentation, occupancy status, real property type, or
     other factor causes the loan not to qualify under standard
     underwriting programs. Less-than-full documentation is typically the
     reason for classifying a loan as Alt-A.

[13] See also section 3.1.2.

[14] In this respect the mortgage amount, the interest in rem and any one-
     time ancillary costs (einmalige Nebenleistungen) need to be registered
     next to the holder of the mortgage. The interest in rem would typically
     be between 12% and 18% per annum. In respect of heritable building
     rights interest in rem of 15% per annum may also be in line with the
     rules of a proper business (Regeln einer ordnungsmäßigen Wirtschaft)
     within the meaning of § 7 No. 2 of the German Ordinance Regarding
     Heritable Building Rights (Verordnung über das Erbbaurecht) (see
     District Court (Landgericht) of Munich I, ruling (Beschluss) of
     February 13th, 1973 – 13 T 179/72 in DNotZ 1973, pp. 554 et seq.); von
     Oefele, in: Münchener Kommentar zum Bürgerlichen Gesetzbuch,
     4th edition (2004), § 7 ErbbauVO marginal note 12.

[15] See § 1154 No. 3 in connection with § 873 No. 1 third alternative of the
     German Civil Code.

[16] See §§ 22 a et seq. of the German Banking Act. See Fitch, CMBS/RMBS/
     Germany Criteria Report, Criteria Regarding the Application of the
     refinancing register in German CMBS and RMBS Transactions,

released August 28th, 2007 for remaining uncertainties not addressed by the refinancing register (summary on p. 7).

[17] See § 1154 No. 1 sentence 1 of the German Civil Code.

[18] See Gaberdiel, Kreditsicherung durch Grundschulden (2004), marginal note 439.

[19] As a mere indication, cancellation proceedings take between 7 to 12 months. The cancellation period (Aufgebotsfrist) already is at least six months (§ 1015 in connection with § 1192 No. 1 of the German Code of Civil Procedure (Zivilprozessordnung)). In addition to these six months, the facts need to be gathered and presented in court to the satisfaction of the competent registrar (Rechtspfleger). Thereafter the cancellation ruling (Ausschlussurteil) needs to be pronounced and obtained in writing. Within any such timeframe one has to bear in mind that only the lost mortgage certificate has been declared null and void. The lender has then to consider whether he would like the certified mortgage to be converted into an uncertificated mortgage or whether he would want a substitution mortgage certificate to be issued. To the extent the mortgage shall be deleted, the lender can directly consent to the deletion of the affected mortgage.

[20] The holder of the mortgage might have to present the mortgage certificate in court if it seeks to enforce the mortgage pursuant to the provision §§ 1160, 1155 of the German Civil Code in connection with the provisions of § 16 No. 2 of the German Act on Forced Sale and Forced Administration (Gesetz über die Zwangsversteigerung und die Zwangsverwaltung). But usually such a presentation requirement is excluded in the deed of mortgage.

[21] See, in general, authorless, Asset-Backed Securities in Deutschland, Die Veräußerung und Verbriefung von Kreditforderungen durch deutsche Kreditinstitute, in Monatsbericht der Deutschen Bundesbank, July 1997.

[22] Wiese, in: BB 1998, pp. 1713, 1714.

[23] The major difference lies in the Loan-to-Value which for a German Pfandbrief is limited to a maximum of 60 %. Regarding the refinancing by means of the issuance of German Pfandbriefe versus Mortgage Backed Securities see Lorenz/Stephan, in chapter C4 of this book.

[24] Koscielny, M., Mortgage Backed Securities – Konkurrenz für den Hypothekenpfandbrief?, 2006, p. 90.

[25] Jahn, op. cit., § 114a marginal note 3; Kümpel, in: Bank- und Kapital-marktrecht, 3rd edition, 2004, marginal note 14.68; Caliebe, in: BB 2000, pp. 2369, 2370.

[26] Hey, in: Gondring, H./Zoller, E./Dinauer, J., Real Estate Investment Banking, 2003, pp. 431, 435. While on the face of it the same appears to also be achievable by syndication, Residential Mortgage Backed

Securities offer the possibility of disposing of the full credit risk in specific investments (see sub-clause for further details).

[27] Hey, op. cit., pp. 431, 435 et seq.; True Sale International, www.true-sale-international.de/index.php? id=345, accessed on October 2nd, 2007. The capital ratio (Eigenkapitalquote) can be improved if the funds raised by the sale of the residential mortgage loan receivables are used to pay down debt, simultaneously leading to a reduction of the balance-sheet total (Verkürzung der Bilanzsumme).

[28] Arbeitskreis "Finanzierung" der Schmalenbach-Gesellschaft Deutsche Gesellschaft für Betriebswirtschaft e.V., in: zfbf 44 (6/1992), pp. 495, 501 et seq.

[29] Arbeitskreis "Finanzierung" der Schmalenbach-Gesellschaft Deutsche Gesellschaft für Betriebswirtschaft e.V., op. cit., pp. 495, 506.

[30] Geiger, in: Habersack, M./Mülbert, P./Schlitt, M., Unternehmens-finanzierung am Kapitalmarkt (2005), § 16 marginal note 2; Wagenknecht/Iffland, in: Kronke, H./Melis, W./Schnyder, A., Handbuch Internationales Wirtschaftsrecht, 2005, pp. 842, 846 et seq.

[31] Denying the applicability to fully disbursed loans see Huber, in: Münchener Kommentar zur Insolvenzordnung, 1st edition, 2002, § 103 marginal note 69; Jahn, op. cit., § 114 a marginal note 36; Laudenklos/Sester, in: ZIP 2005, 1757, 1762; Fleckner, in: ZIP 2004, pp. 585, 596; different view, Kübler/Prütting/Tintelnot, InsO (as of August 2006), § 103 marginal note 19; Berscheid, in: Uhlenbruck, Insolvenzordnung (2003), § 103 marginal note 21; Lind, in: ZInsO 2004, pp. 580, 582.

[32] See BR-Drucks 549/06, p. 36.

[33] Hess, H. in: Hess, H./Weis, M./Wienberg R., InsO, 2nd edition, 2001, § 103 marginal note 126.

[34] The impact on the borrower who depends on the disbursement of the tranches which have not been disbursed at the time of insolvency of the lender shall not be further analysed in this chapter. But in the light of any borrower's claims for damages in that respect pursuant to § 103 No. 2 sentence 1 of the German Insolvency Statute, the full disbursement of the residential mortgage loan should be one of the eligibility criteria under the RMBS, and the rating agencies need to be comfortable with the fact that the residential mortgage loan has been fully disbursed or that the rest of the outstanding commitments were cancelled at the end of the availability period.

[35] Federal Supreme Court, judgment of February 27th, 2007 – XI ZR 195/05 in: NJW 2007, pp. 2106, 2107 et seqq.; so already Federal Supreme Court, ruling of January 27th, 1998 – XI ZR 208/97.

[36] Federal Constitutional Court, ruling of June 11th, 2007 – 1 BvR 1025/07 in: WM 2007, pp. 1694, 1694 et seq.

[37] Jahn, op. cit., § 114 a marginal note 18.

[38] See Gola, P./Schomerus, R., Bundesdatenschutzgesetz, 9th edition, 2007, § 4 a marginal notes 5 e et seq., 8 and 10 et seqq.; Simitis, S., in: Simitis, S., Kommentar zum Bundesdatenschutzgesetz, 6th edition, 2006, § 4 a marginal notes 42 et seqq. and 81; Gehrlein, S., Die Veräußerung und Übertragung eines Kreditportfolios unter Berücksichtigung der Übertragungsstrukturen, des Bankgeheimnisses und des Datenschutzes, 2007, p. 170 et seq.

[39] Gehrlein, S., op. cit., pp. 175 et seq.

4   German Pfandbrief versus MBS

Michaela Lorenz
Tanja Stephan

Table of contents

1   German Pfandbrief

1.1   History and legal environment

A brief description of Pfandbriefe   Pfandbrief, the German covered bond, is a special type of security with a very long history in the German market. Mortgage bond like papers find their roots in the year 1769 under King Friedrich II. Originally they were planned as an instrument for the landed aristocracy to finance and cultivate the rural area. The first issuers were the so-called "Landschaften/landscapes". The first mortgage bank, Frankfurter Hypothekenbank, was established 1862 in Frankfurt, and by 1875 the volume issued by mortgage banks was higher than the volume issued by these "Landschaften".

A real estate depression at the end of the 19th century showed the deficiencies of the system: incongruent refinancing, real estate speculation and risky credit policy.

Having these experiences in mind, the Mortgage Banks Act of 1900 was launched. On the basis of this law private mortgage banks, as specialist banks in Germany, have issued Pfandbriefe for more than hundred years. The main intention of the law was to establish a robust legal framework to preserve the rights and claims of the Pfandbrief investors. The word "Pfandbrief" can only be used for covered bonds issued under the Mortgage Banks Act. Besides, private mortgage banks, ship mortgage banks and several public sector credit institutions (i. e., Landesbanken) were allowed to issue covered bonds as Pfandbriefe under three different legal frameworks – mortgage banks under the Mortgage Banks Act, the public sector credit institutions under the Public Pfandbrief Act and the ship mortgage banks under the Ship Mortgage Banks Act.

Additionally, the confidence in the German Pfandbrief was strengthened by a series of amendments to the Mortgage Banks Act. The latest amendment came into effect in April 2004. With this amendment the mandatory over-collateralization comprising excess cover of 2 % and clarified rules concerning the privileged position of a Pfandbrief holder in case of the issuer's insolvency were introduced. In addition, the net present value regulations were set out.

Amendment in the Mortgage Banks Act

Several developments especially those with regard to the European Union and the creation of the Internal Market with fair competition rules, obliged Germany to introduce a general legal framework to abolish the advantageous status of the public credit institutions, which so far were also profiting from specific state guarantees. To avoid these credit institutions losing one of their most important funding sources a general Pfandbrief Act as a uniform legal basis for all Pfandbrief issuers. The Pfandbrief Act was launched on July 18th, 2005.

Now, any bank can issue the Pfandbrief because with the Pfandbrief Act, Pfandbrief business was defined as banking business in terms of §1 of the German Banking Act (KWG). To conduct this business a special license is needed. The German Federal Financial Supervisory Authority (Bundesanstalt für Finanzdienstleistungsaufsicht – BaFin) assigns this license under particular preconditions:

- The minimum core capital needed by a Pfandbrief issuer is € 25 million.

- Pfandbrief issuers must have professional risk management in place and an adequate organizational structure to conduct the Pfandbrief business.

- Pfandbrief banks are permanent issuers who tap the capital markets regularly and not in an opportunistic manner.

The Pfandbrief Act safeguards the high quality standards of the German Pfandbrief even though mortgage banks do not operate any longer as specialist banks and the state guarantee mechanism for public sector credit institutions has been abolished.

High quality standards of Pfandbrief maintained

To maintain the high quality of the Pfandbrief, many principles from the original Mortgage Banks Act were incorporated into the Pfandbrief Act, for example,

- separate cover pools for each type of Pfandbrief
  - mortgage Pfandbriefe,
  - public sector Pfandbriefe,
  - ship Pfandbriefe.

- Matching principles, i.e., outstanding Pfandbriefe, must be secured at all times by cover assets equivalent to both their nominal amount and their net present value. Additionally, the interest coverage ratio of cover assets and all related Pfandbriefe has to be at least one and the currencies of cover assets and outstanding Pfandbriefe must match (including derivatives).

- Every Pfandbrief Bank is obliged to appoint a cover pool monitor (trustee) and at least one deputy. They must possess the necessary expertise and experience to meet their duties, i. e., to ensure that only cover pool eligible assets come into the cover pool and that all legal measures and procedures are fulfilled to warrant all rights and claims of the Pfandbrief holders.

- A Pfandbrief investor's preferential claim in case of insolvency of the Pfandbrief issuer as well as detailed regulations about insolvency procedures and installation of the cover pool administrator.

- Mandatory over-collateralization of 2 % (including stress scenarios).

- Special supervision of the Pfandbrief business including regular audits by the BaFin.

- High quality demands and eligibility criteria for cover assets

    - conservative mortgage evaluation – the mortgage lending value ("Beleihungswert") principle,

    - regional business restrictions.

Quarterly reports as measure of transparency Additionally, the Mortgage Banks Act provided for transparency and therefore detailed transparency provisions regarding the cover pools were included in the Pfandbrief Act. Pfandbrief banks are obliged to publish quarterly publicly accessible reports. These reports shall inform investors and facilitate comparison of the pools of different issuers. Most issuers publish these reports on their homepages under the investor relation section. The Pfandbrief bank reports on each cover pool separately and the reports comprise the following:

- **Mortgage business** (analogue mortgage shipping business)

    - aggregate amounts of cover assets, and of mortgage Pfandbriefe issued,

    - maturity structure of mortgage Pfandbriefe issued, and fixed-interest periods of related cover assets,

    - breakdown of assets used as cover (based on their nominal value) by their amount,

    - breakdown of assets used as cover for mortgage Pfandbriefe (based on their nominal value) by the country where the properties selling as collateral are located,

    - notice about overdue loans of at least 90 days during reporting period, if applicable.

- **Public finance business**

  - aggregate amounts of cover assets, and of public sector Pfandbriefe issued,

  - maturity structure of public sector Pfandbriefe, and fixed-interest periods of related cover assets,

  - breakdown of assets used as cover assets for public sector Pfandbriefe (based on their nominal value), by borrower's/guarantor's country of domicile,

  - notice about overdue loans of at least 90 days during reporting period, if applicable.

1.2   Collateral pools

The license may be given for all types of Pfandbriefe as there are mortgage Pfandbriefe, public sector Pfandbriefe and ship Pfandbriefe or a mixture of the above.

A detailed explanation of different types of Pfandbriefe

1.2.1   Mortgage Pfandbriefe

As described above, the original mortgage Pfandbrief was the prototype of today's Pfandbrief. The cover pool consists of mortgage loans secured by first lien mortgages. The first lien of a mortgage must not exceed 60 % of the mortgage lending value. The mortgage lending value principle already known from the former Mortgage Banks Act is a very conservative mortgage evaluation principle focusing on the long-term and enduring value of a mortgage. Normally, it will differ to a certain degree from the market value and will usually be below it. A real estate appraiser needs to have adequate professional experience and specialized knowledge to determine the mortgage lending value. Every mortgage needs to have a valuation in the form of a mortgage lending value to specify the mortgage cover pool as eligible part of the loan.

According to the Pfandbrief Act, the group of countries eligible for mortgage Pfandbrief covering purposes comprises the EU, the European Economic Area, Switzerland, USA, Canada and Japan.

The collateral pool comprises residential and commercial mortgage loans. Almost all Pfandbrief banks have already diversified collateral pools regarding their regional distribution.

Diversification outside the European Union is restricted by law to a maximum of 10 % of the collateral pool. The reason for this restriction is that the legislator sees a potential risk in the fact that insolvency legislation outside the European Union might not acknowledge the preferential claims of the Pfandbrief holders.

1.2.2   Public sector Pfandbriefe

The cover pool consists of claims to public sector authorities or claims fully and unconditionally guaranteed by such authorities. A public authority may be a central or local government or other public entities with a risk weighting under Basel I of not more than 20% which has been set by a relevant supervisory authority. 100% of the loan qualifies as cover pool assets.

According to the Pfandbrief Act, the group of countries eligible for public sector Pfandbrief covering purposes comprises the EU, the European Economic Area, Switzerland, USA, Canada and Japan.

Like the mortgage Pfandbriefe, diversification outside the European Union is restricted by law to a maximum of 10% because of the uncertainty of the preferential claims of the Pfandbrief holders in case of the insolvency of the issuer.

To follow the investors' and to a certain degree the rating agencies' demands for higher diversification of cover pool assets to mitigate concentration risks, Pfandbrief banks try to find a solution of this issue.

1.2.3   Ship Pfandbriefe

Ships and ships under construction quality

To qualify as cover for a ship Pfandbrief, assets must be backed by a registered first-ranking ship mortgage. In order to guarantee the protection of investors, the Pfandbrief Act determines certain eligibility criteria, such as only ships and ships under construction which are recorded in a public, domestic or foreign shipping register, may be used. Additionally, the lending is limited to a maximum of 60% of the ship mortgage lending value. A ship mortgage

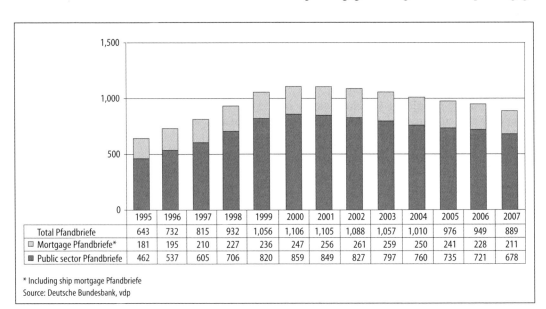

	1995	1996	1997	1998	1999	2000	2001	2002	2003	2004	2005	2006	2007
Total Pfandbriefe	643	732	815	932	1,056	1,106	1,105	1,088	1,057	1,010	976	949	889
▢ Mortgage Pfandbriefe*	181	195	210	227	236	247	256	261	259	250	241	228	211
▪ Public sector Pfandbriefe	462	537	605	706	820	859	849	827	797	760	735	721	678

* Including ship mortgage Pfandbriefe
Source: Deutsche Bundesbank, vdp

Fig. 1:   Total volume of German Pfandbriefe outstanding 1995 to 2007 (in € bn)

appraiser needs to have adequate professional experience and specialized knowledge to determine the ship mortgage lending value. The maximum loan maturity is 15 years. The ship or the ship under construction must be insured throughout the duration of the loan at least in the amount of 120 % of the loan claims.

1.3   Reasons, motives of the issuer

The reason for the Pfandbrief bank to issue Pfandbriefe is to obtain funding for the related cover pool. Funding by Pfandbrief is cheaper than unsecured funding and allows the Pfandbrief bank to create a certain funding mix on their liability side and to diversify its investor base. Efficient issuance of a Pfandbrief calls for considerable asset volumes. The license to issue Pfandbriefe also demands its permanent use. Therefore, Pfandbrief banks are permanent issuers who tap the capital market regularly and not in an opportunistic manner. Under the provisions of the Pfandbrief Act, which require that Pfandbrief business to be conducted on a lasting basis, a one-off transaction is out of the question. The collateral pool of a Pfandbrief is a dynamic pool. The Pfandbrief bank continually focuses on diversification and optimization of the cover pool. Therefore, efficient asset liability management and risk management is required. This combined with the above strict quality measures set by the Pfandbrief Act made Pfandbriefe one of the highest quality covered bonds in Europe.

Pfandbriefe are one of the highest quality covered bonds in Europe

1.4   Recent developments, market share

By the end of 2006, the outstanding volume of Pfandbrief issues was almost € 1 trillion. Around one quarter consists of mortgage Pfandbriefe and three quarters of public sector Pfandbriefe.

Jumbo Pfandbriefe suffer decrease of prominent role while structured Pfandbriefe increase

Since 1995, Jumbo Pfandbriefe have played a very prominent role within the Pfandbrief market. Before, the German Pfandbrief market tended to be a fragmented, illiquid and difficult to penetrate market especially from a foreign investor's viewpoint. To achieve the Hypobanks' aim to broaden and internationalize the investor base for the German Pfandbrief, they started-up the new Jumbo Pfandbrief market segment. Key factors were liquidity, market making and standardization.

These factors are documented in the "Minimum Standards for the issuance of Jumbo Pfandbriefe" launched by the "Association of German Pfandbrief Banks (vdp)" the latest version dated August 2006. To qualify as a Jumbo Pfandbrief in brief, the following criteria need to be met:

- **Minimum issue size**
  The minimum issue size of a Jumbo Pfandbrief is € 1 billion. The volume of the initial issue must be at least € 750 million. The issuer must then tap the issue to € 1 billion within 180 calendar days after the initial offering.

- **Format**
  Only Pfandbriefe of straight bond format (i. e., fixed coupon payable annually in arrears, bullet redemption) may be offered as Jumbo Pfandbriefe.

- **Stock market listing**
  Jumbo Pfandbriefe must be listed not later than 30 calendar days after the settlement date on an organized market in Europe.

- **Market making**
  Each Jumbo Pfandbrief must have at least five market makers who pledge to quote bid/ask (two-way) prices simultaneously for lots of up to € 15 million during usual trading hours (at least 9 to 17 hrs. CET). The function of a market maker may also be performed by the issuing house itself. The market makers undertake to quote prices as long as there is sufficient outstanding volume to maintain a liquid market in the Jumbo Pfandbrief. The market makers undertake not to exceed specified spreads between the bid and ask prices when quoting two-way prices dependent of the residual life to maturity of the particular Jumbo Pfandbrief. In the exceptional event of market making being suspended which might be, e. g., in the event of substantial rating changes or of a considerable deterioration of a Jumbo issuer's financial situation, this must be immediately communicated to the market in an appropriate manner by the market maker.

- **Add-ons**
  In the event that a Jumbo Pfandbrief is tapped, the amount of the increase should not be less than € 125 million per add-on.

- **Transfer and buyback**
  A subsequent transfer to the name of an investor is inadmissible ("Vinkulierung"/restriction on transferability). It is admissible to buy back securities for redemption purposes or trustee administration ("Treuhänderverwahrung"/custody by the trustee) if the outstanding volume of the issue is not less than € 1 billion at any time. Furthermore, buybacks are limited to half of the outstanding issue volume.

- **Loss of status**
  If one of the aforementioned provisions is not met, the issue will lose its Jumbo Pfandbrief status.

Around one third of the outstanding Pfandbriefe in Germany are issued in the Jumbo format. In Europe, the German market share in the Jumbo market has shrunk over the last number of years to one third of the whole market due to growing new covered bond markets in Europe, especially Spain.

Figure 2 shows the evolution of the European covered bond markets over the last years.

Structured Pfandbriefe Another very important Pfandbrief type in Germany are the structured Pfandbriefe. Generally speaking, structured Pfandbriefe are issues that can only be valued in connection with a derivative financial instrument. By linking a derivative instrument to Pfandbriefe, it is possible to tailor Pfandbriefe which meet investors' needs regarding their interest rate views, interest rate risk appetite and capital market circumstances. Since the beginning of the 1990s, the market for structured bonds, in which Pfandbriefe have played a large role, has increased steadily. The majority of the issues are private placements, and for this reason official figures about the definite share of structured

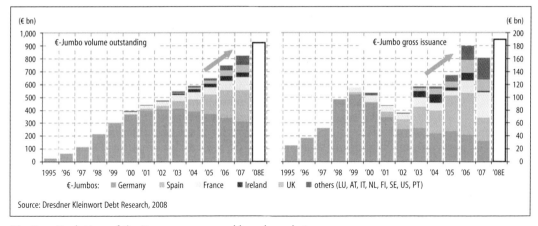

Fig. 2:   Evolution of the European covered bond markets

Pfandbrief cannot be presented. The size of the structured Pfandbrief market is estimated to be roughly between one quarter and one third of the total issuance. Structured Pfandbriefe can have various features, such as interest rates step-ups, interest rate limits, links to certain indices or rates, embedded call rights, trigger options and many more features. Pfandbrief banks show a considerable flexibility to meet investors' demands. In this way, investors can take an interest rate position without taking an appreciable credit risk because a Pfandbrief is a bond product with a triple-A credit quality. The credit quality of Pfandbriefe also sets certain limits to the apparently unlimited possibilities of structuring with derivative financial instruments. First, the legislator has explicitly forbidden the issuance of Pfandbriefe with an embedded put option in favor of the investor. Additionally, it is prohibited to issue Pfandbriefe with an unclear redemption price at the time of issuance. The BaFin monitors the legal compliance of Pfandbriefe. The Pfandbrief issuers themselves aim for clearness regarding the development of structured Pfandbriefe to avoid structures which dilute the high credit quality of the product. This is the main reason why Pfandbriefe with links to stocks and stock indices are out of the issuers' scope.

2   German MBS market

2.1   History

Real estate finance banks, in addition to Pfandbrief issuance, use other capital market instruments with regard to funding and/or managing their loan portfolio. Such instruments include syndication, true sale and synthetic securitization. With securitizations, the main focus is on the management of credit risk and risk capital or equity. For other non-bank issuers, the focus is on funding.

Development of MBS in Germany since their introduction in 1995

Relative to Pfandbriefe, Mortgage Backed Securities (MBS) have a very short history in Germany. The first securitization transaction on a mortgage portfolio was realized in 1995. This was the GEMS-1 transaction by Rheinische Hypothekenbank (one of the predecessors of Eurohypo), a bank operating under the Mortgage Banks Act. The transaction was launched as a true sale. Because of several problems regarding legal, regulatory and tax issues, securitization techniques only made moderate progress in Germany compared to other European countries, such as Great Britain and Spain. Hence, synthetic securitization techniques were developed to circumvent these problems. The first synthetic transaction on a commercial real estate portfolio was launched in 1999. In the following years, many synthetic transactions were issued, in particular via the KfW securitization platforms "Promise" for the transfer of credit risk related to SME loans (small and medium enterprises) and "Provide" for the purpose of securitizing private residential loans. There was a clear trend towards the securitization of small-scale retail businesses (Residential Mortgage Backed Securities – RMBS). From 2000 to 2005, RMBS dominated the German market with a share of close to 70 % of the total volume. Germany advanced to become one of the largest securitization markets in Europe. The largest market is still Great Britain.

True sale and synthetic securitization techniques facilitate credit risk transfer to the market. To avoid losing market share in Europe, a handful of German Banks initiated, in 2003, the so-called "True Sale Initiative". The initiative focuses on resolving the main problems of true sale securitization in Germany. It became obvious that several amendments of laws and tax regulations were needed as it was unlikely that Germany would implement a special securitization act as Spain, Italy and some other countries did.

The legal and tax framework was adjusted and since 2004, a number of true sale ABS and MBS transactions has been launched subsequently.

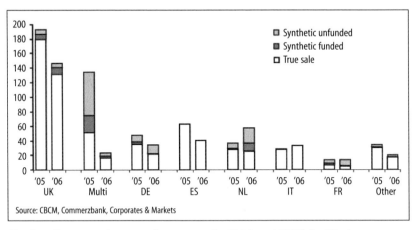

Fig. 3: European issuance by country in 2006 and 2005 (in € bn)

2.2   Synthetic vs. true sale

As mentioned above, both securitization techniques allow for the transfer of credit risk to the market. Since synthetic securitizations transfer the credit risk by means of credit derivatives, they are often technically easier to perform than true sale transactions. This is even permissible for receivables that have already been funded through Pfandbriefe. Synthetic transactions are often more suitable for securitizing "old business" and cross-border transactions because the assets remain on the bank's books. In order to ensure that there is a reduction in capital requirements following a synthetic transaction, the securitized portfolio must reflect the overall portfolio. In this way, BaFin seeks to prevent a situation in which only a certain, marketable quality of balance sheet assets are securitized. Regulatory changes can have far-reaching implications for synthetic securitizations. To keep this risk as low as possible, a forward-looking examination and, if needed an adjustment of the structures is necessary from one transaction to the next. Basel II in particular needs to be factored into the capital relief calculation at the beginning of the transaction. As outcome some issuers put "regulatory calls" in their deals so that they can call them for regulatory reasons, i. e., if a change in the regulatory environment makes the deal uneconomical.

Synthetic securitizations are easier to perform, while true sale securitizations create funding

The greatest advantage of a true sale securitization compared to a synthetic transaction is that it creates funding. This funding is independent of the originator's own rating. Additionally, balance sheet management and improvement of balance sheet ratios may be a key driver for true sale transactions when the assets are sold.

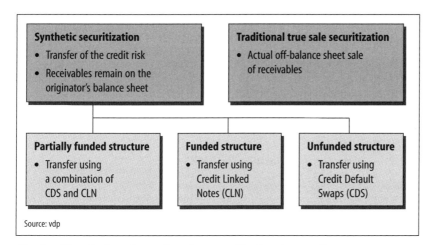

Fig. 4:   Structuring alternatives for securitization transaction

2.3   Collateral

As can be seen in figure 5, mortgage related securitization business has always been the biggest share of the whole securitization market over the years. RMBS constantly account for of approximately one half and the CMBS portion has increased significantly since 2004.

Differences in collateral across different types of securitizations

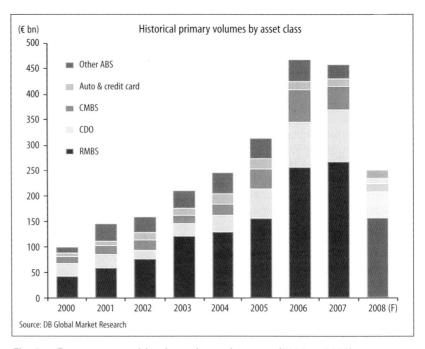

Fig. 5:   European securitization primary issuance (2000 to 2008)

The range of collateral in Mortgage Backed Securities (MBS) differs from transaction to transaction. Nevertheless, the market has developed certain unbinding standards to make comparability between similar transactions a little easier for investors.

Regarding the portfolio selection, one can identify two cases: In the first case, the assets are originated solely for securitization, an arbitrage deal which is the most common case for CMBS transactions. In the second case, a bank originator aims to securitize parts of its existing loan book, what can be described as a balance sheet deal.

2.3.1   Some particularities for RMBS

Apart from the legal and regulatory issues mentioned above, the market has set certain parameters it considers acceptable for eligible assets for different types of securitization. Regarding the maximum size of a loan, no single residential mortgage loan should generally exceed € 1.5 million. In Germany, mortgage loans are commonly structured with annuity redemptions which causes comparatively long weighted average maturities. Bullet loans without any amortization until maturity are rare to find and are commonly transacted with an endowment policy. If the inclusion of those loans into an RMBS transaction is planned, all claims on the endowment policy need to also be pledged as additional collateral.

The LTV of a mortgage loan has a significant impact on the pricing of the transaction. In this context, both the average LTV of the portfolio as well as the LTV of each single loan is of interest. Single mortgage loans with an LTV higher than 80 % drastically increase the risk profile of a transaction. However, its inclusion into a transaction is possible but will result in higher level of credit enhancement to reflect the increased risk in the mortgage portfolio.

A high share of owner-occupied properties has a positive effect on the level of credit enhancement. The provision of normal household insurance is generally a condition of the mortgage.

2.3.2   Some particularities for CMBS

Data provision for a commercial securitization is very detailed and goes down to individual loan, tenant and property details, whereas in an RMBS transaction the data is based on portfolio averages. For any single loan in a CMBS transaction above 10 %, very detailed information on the mortgage is required from both rating agencies and investors.

Regarding LTVs, the majority of the CMBS transactions have an average LTV of around 60 % to 80 %. If single loans with higher LTVs form part of the pool, this will result in a higher level of credit enhancement to reflect the increased risk in the loan portfolio.

The key figures for commercial mortgages are Interest Coverage Ratio (ICR) and Debt Service Coverage Ratio (DSCR). These ratios explain the relation between (rental) revenues of the property and the interest and repayment obligations of the mortgage loan. They allow comparison of different transactions and have significant impact on credit enhancement.

Due to the increased probability of environmental disasters and possible terrorist attacks, commercial properties need to be insured adequately against these events and these policies need to form part of the securitization transaction.

3   Pfandbriefe versus MBS

3.1   Issuers' motives

While the main driver for the issuance of Pfandbriefe is to get attractive funding for assets on the own balance sheet, the reasons for issuing MBS are more diverse. In the capital markets, one issuer may appear as an issuer of both instruments but with different or complimentary aims as the driver of the issuance. To give an overview of the decision making process, different objectives which have to be taken into account are listed below:

A number of different objectives drive the issuers' motives

- Funding

Both Pfandbriefe and true sale transactions generate 100 % funding. A synthetic transaction transfers risk by the use of credit derivatives particularly by Credit Default Swaps (CDS) and by Credit Linked Notes (CLN). If a CLN is issued, the investor's liquidity will be used by the issuer to invest in adequately rated collateral for each tranche. This means that by the use of credit derivatives no nominal cash flows occur. Synthetic transactions often combine CDS and CLNs and the latter are commonly issued only for the non-senior portion of the portfolio.

- **Type of assets**

The Pfandbrief refinancing may be used for residential, commercial and ship mortgages as well as public sector assets. ABS in general offer a greater flexibility but MBS are usually issued for residential and commercial mortgages. Mortgage Pfandbriefe only allow for 60 % of the mortgage lending value. MBS basically permit higher LTVs, but, of course, higher LTVs have a significant impact on the pricing of the transaction.

- **Volumes**

The Pfandbrief is an instrument for permanent issuers in the capital markets. As described, a license is necessary and the authorities request expertise in the business concerned. The Pfandbrief bank has to tap capital markets regularly and not in an opportunistic manner. Therefore, the issuance of Pfandbriefe requires considerable asset volumes and a long-term issuance horizon.

In general, one-off transactions are possible in the MBS market even though market entrance costs are substantial. Due to internal and external costs, volumes of several hundred million euros are needed if a securitization transaction is to be viable. However, there are many issuers on the market who regularly conduct securitizations through established programs and product names. Furthermore, the use of standardized platforms is becoming increasingly important.

- **Regulatory relief and credit risk management**

Assets remain on balance sheet of issuer

Regulatory capital relief can only be achieved by transferring the credit risk to an investor. In the case of Pfandbriefe, the assets although pledged to the cover pool remain on the balance sheet of the issuer. To achieve capital relief, MBS transactions are the appropriate instrument. Either assets are explicitly sold to investors in a true sale transaction or credit risk is transferred using credit derivatives like credit default swaps. MBS transactions are often used for the diversification of ones portfolios from a credit point of view. Furthermore, big exposure limits can be managed using securitization techniques. This is even permissible for receivables that have already been funded through Pfandbriefe. In order to ease the capital requirements by synthetic transactions, it must be ensured, however, that the securitized portfolio reflects the overall portfolio. In this way, BaFin seeks to prevent a situation in which only a certain, marketable quality of balance sheet assets is securitized to avoid "cherry-picking" from a bank's portfolio.

- **International diversification**

Pan-European transactions emerge

The regional distribution of the loans is of great importance. According to the Pfandbrief Act, the group of countries eligible for mortgage Pfandbrief covering purposes comprises the EU, the European Economic Area, Switzerland, USA, Canada and Japan. True sale transactions had traditionally been restricted to single country portfolios due to the different treatment and legislations relating to the sale and enforcement of loans in each country, however, this is changing and pan-European transactions emerge as a new asset class. Synthetic transactions have fewer restrictions and can cover several jurisdictions on the loan portfolio side because documentation of credit derivatives is flexible and can be easily adopted. Therefore, synthetic transactions are often used for "old business" i. e., business with a longer seasoning because the assets remain on the bank's books. These loans might not fulfill the rigid documentation standards that are essential for true sale MBS.

- **Cash flows and confidentiality**

With MBS – in particular with true sale transactions – the predictability of the cash flows from the individual properties and the transferability of the loans are essential aspects. Close cooperation between the securitization department and loan acquisitions is crucial in order to meet these criteria. By reason of confidentiality and protection of data privacy, securitization via a true sale transaction under German law is subject to the borrower's consent which can be included into the loan documentation.

Another aspect to be considered is whether the bank is prepared to put up with the often negative impression the borrower may have, i.e., that the bank apparently no longer appreciates his loan and wants to sell it. MBS pools are therefore very often static pools, which are determined once in the structuring phase, whereas all Pfandbriefe of a German Pfandbrief issuer are based on one cover-pool that is managed by the issuer on an ongoing and regular basis. Assets that do not fit the criteria any more are taken from the pool and are substituted.

- **Costs**

Beside the explicit cost of funding, both instruments produce other types of costs for the issuer. Pfandbriefe as well as MBS will usually be rated by at least one external rating agency which will charge for their rating service. Placement of Pfandbriefe as well as of MBS is usually done through investment banks which collect fees for the placement of the bonds. The Pfandbriefe as such have no further structuring costs other than the setup for the Pfandbrief business (collateral pool administration, legal documentation, issuance programs, etc.). MBS issues have higher costs during the structuring phase, especially for legal, accounting and tax advise, the setup of SPVs, trustees, etc. Apart from these external costs, internal costs, may also be significant because a lot of processes need to be established, e. g., for the issuance and furthermore to meet the reporting requirements fixed in the transaction. Additionally information technology developments may be very cost intensive as well.

MBS are more expensive than Pfandbriefe in terms of cost of funding and cost of issuance. Nevertheless, MBS are designed to free up capital and reduce risk limits for the issuing banks and enabling them to transact more business. These savings have to be considered when comparing the costs of both instruments.

Thanks to its standardization, the Pfandbrief is the preferred means of obtaining favorable funding conditions in the capital markets for existing Pfandbrief eligible assets, particularly compared with unsecured funding. The Pfandbrief market is capable of absorbing large volumes of debt and has proven itself to be a reliable source of funding for issuers, especially in times of crisis. The highly optimized internal processes of inclusion of loans into

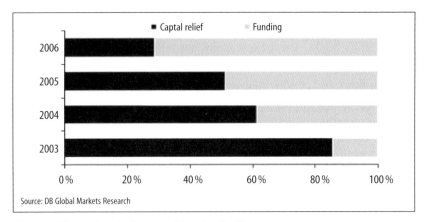

Fig. 6: The rationale for securitization in Germany

the cover pool and the Pfandbrief issuance keep transaction costs for the deal at very low levels.

With securitization, in contrast, issuers pursue other objectives. If the main focus of the issuer is on diversifying, managing and optimizing an asset portfolio, particularly with a view to improving balance sheet ratios, such as the large-exposure limits or capital ratios, and funding is of lesser importance, then securitization is the right instrument. However, securitizations are always based on the current legal and regulatory environment at the time of issuance and adjustment of the structure is indispensable from one transaction to the next.

3.2   Investors' perspective

Decisions by an investor are mainly driven by its risk appetite

MBS and Pfandbriefe have built themselves a global investor base over the recent years. Typical investors are real money accounts like insurance companies or pension funds, money market or fixed income funds, central banks, bank treasuries, as well as retail clients. MBS was originally set up in the United States to allow the transfer of credit risk and granular loan portfolios to the capital markets. Therefore, the US was the original investor market for MBS, being popular in Europe for roughly 15 years now. However, as the growth in European issuance has exceeded the growth in US issuance, the European investor base has become firmly established and it has developed into a well diversified investor base. The Pfandbrief had its start in Germany and has gained a well diversified investor base all over Europe over the last decade. An Asian and US investor base has developed over the last years.

Looking at investors' decision making process, the first investment criterion is the investor's own risk appetite. Several other criteria will apply after this fundamental choice:

- **Risk appetite/rating**

Whereas the Pfandbrief is a product with a high credit quality, as is reflected in consistently top ratings, MBS transactions are issued in different rating tranches. The triple-A rated tranche is the largest and often the most liquid. But tranches with ratings of BBB or lower or unrated equity tranches are also on offer. If an investor seeks to invest in lower rated paper which represents real estate risks, this is only possible with MBS. The reason for this is that with MBS, the risks involved in the underlying assets are distributed differently in contrast to Pfandbriefe. In MBS transactions, only the creditors of one tranche rank equally and the claims of the lower class are satisfied only once all the creditors of the higher classes have been satisfied in full, whereas all the Pfandbrief creditors rank equally.

High risk investments with MBS only

- **Asset portfolio**

Issuers of Pfandbriefe are required by law to maintain a high asset quality, and seek to fund their Pfandbriefe on permanently favorable conditions. Active management and the dynamic nature of the cover pools enable them to set and pursue a risk profile, whereas many MBS transactions are fixed until maturity on a certain portfolio that is assembled. Changes in the portfolio are unusual or strictly limited to avoid a worsening of the underlying portfolio after the transaction once has been launched.

- **Limits/underlying risk**

The rules set down in the Pfandbrief Act concerning creditor protection are to ensure that in the event an issuing bank defaults, all the interest and redemption payments will be effected in a timely manner until the Pfandbriefe mature, notwithstanding the bankruptcy of the bank. Thus, only in the case of a bank's bankruptcy does the underlying real estate portfolio become the sole safeguarding instrument. This is why Pfandbrief investors also pay attention to the issuers' business model. Investments in Pfandbriefe use up the credit lines of the issuer, reducing lines for other products of the same issuer, such as uncovered bank bonds. In contrast to Pfandbriefe, the issuer of an MBS transaction is usually not a bank but a Special Purpose Vehicle (SPV) to which the loans in question are passed. The investor in MBS purchases a direct, defined real estate exposure of which the credit analysis of which is therefore more extensive than in the case of the Pfandbrief.

- **Regional diversification**

The Pfandbrief Act allows issuers to build up regionally diversified coverpools: By buying a mortgage Pfandbrief, the investor can purchase exposure to different real estate markets. The real estate portfolio underlying the Pfandbrief is actively managed by the Pfandbrief bank's specialists. With investments in MBS, loans from only one country are usually securitized although this is changing. Traditionally cross-border securitization was only possible via a synthetic transaction by passing the credit risks to the SPV via derivatives. Although it is more complex to include different countries in true sale transactions this model is about to develop with several pan-European deals having been issued todate.

- **Issuance format (size, documentation, coupon, maturity)**

Unlike MBS, which are almost exclusively issued as fungible securities and in large-volume transactions, Pfandbriefe are a highly flexible instrument. The Pfandbrief issue volume may range from only several million to amounts of one billion and more, and the structures offered also vary widely. Pfandbrief structures range from tailored structured and registered Pfandbriefe to large volume and highly liquid Jumbo Pfandbriefe that have an active primary and secondary market. Jumbo Pfandbriefe command great respect among international investors due to their first-rate credit quality and the size of the market segment. Jumbo Pfandbriefe feature a market making pledge, fulfill – like all Pfandbriefe – European Central Bank (ECB) eligibility criteria, are traded on different electronic platforms and offer a functioning repurchase agreement market (repo market). Hence Pfandbriefe, especially Jumbo Pfandbriefe, are often considered as surrogate for government bonds. In contrast, many European triple-A rated MBS transactions are also eligible as collateral for ECB tenders. However, the repo market in these instruments is still underdeveloped. Jumbo Pfandbriefe, like government bonds, are fixed-income securities. Investors are not only interested in the yield markup versus government bonds but can also, by investing, position themselves and allocate their portfolio according to their interest rate expectations. Asset Backed Securities (ABS), on the other hand, are for the most part issued as floating rate bonds. Regular and premature repayments of the underlying receivables can often result in AAA rated tranches in particular showing sizeable repayments. For this reason, many investors use AAA tranches of ABS as money market paper or as an alternative to bank floaters. Many issuers offer investors their own Jumbo curve of the same credit quality. Moreover, when demand for a certain bond increases, Jumbo issuers are in a position to serve the market by tapping the issue. ABS issuers do not offer such a flexibility. Thus, Pfandbriefe as a general principle offer investors a level of flexibility that securitizations, with a different specific objective and transaction structure, cannot match.

- **Currencies**

In the key liquid currencies such as the euro, US dollar and pound sterling in particular, MBS provide a wide investment universe. Whereas the largest volumes in Pfandbriefe are still issued in euro, diversification to other stable and tradable currencies is possible, notably by diversifying the assets and including derivatives in cover. In the large-volume segment, US dollar Pfandbrief issues and issues in Swiss francs are especially popular among international investors.

4   Summary and outlook

Pfandbriefe and Mortgage Backed Securities are well established in the capital markets and provide many interesting features.

Pfandbriefe and MBS are complementary products
Despite their different histories, Pfandbriefe and Mortgage Backed Securities are accepted on the international capital markets and offer considerable market liquidity. Investors and issuers alike make use of both instruments and look upon them as complementary products. The different purposes they serve and

their different structures make them appear as alternatives rather than rivals to pursue different strategies.

Many banks invest in or issue both financial instruments. Market trends and regulatory circumstances may provide the products with different degrees of support, but both products are well established in the capital markets and provide many interesting features and opportunities for issuers and for investors. Hence, none of them will be squeezed out of the markets.

The new Pfandbrief Act on the one hand and a better environment for securitization on the other hand offer banks in Germany great potential to use both products in a flexible and economic manner as part of their funding strategy and to conduct their business. This lays the ground for being prepared to face increasing competition and consolidation in the banking sector.

5 References

Bundesverband Öffentlicher Banken Deutschlands (Ed.), The new German Pfandbrief Act, VÖB, Juli 2005.

Commerzbank Corporates & Markets Research, various research publications.

Dresdner Kleinwort Debt Research, various research publications.

Deutsche Bank Global Markets Research, various research publications.

KfW Research, various research publications.

True Sale International GmbH, various research publications.

vdp (Verband Deutscher Pfandbriefbanken), The Pfandbrief, Facts and Figures about Europe's Covered Bond Benchmark, 1995–2006, various articles, particulary.

Lorenz, M., Pfandbriefe versus MBS – Rivals, or Complementary Instruments, in: The Pfandbrief 2006, vdp (Verband Deutscher Pfandbriefbanken), Berlin 2006.

Schulte, M., Structured Pfandbriefe as an alternative investment, in: The Pfandbrief 1999, vdp (Verband Deutscher Pfandbriefbanken), Bonn 1999.

5   Collateralized Debt Obligations

Katrin Piazolo

Table of contents

1   Introduction

Important product innovation One of the most significant developments in the evolution of the capital markets in the 1990s was the emergence of Collateralized Debt Obligations (CDOs). Aside from serving as a mean for risk-transfer for banks, they also represent a vehicle for buy-and-hold investors to participate in the underlying collateral markets. CDOs are one of the main drivers in the worldwide securitization market. In Europe CDOs are after Residential Mortgage Backed Securities (RMBS) the fastest growing sub-sector in the structured credit market. CDO issuance was growing in 2006 by 48 % in Europe and even by 80 % in the US. CDOs have become an established part of the real estate capital market. The credit and liquidity crisis that was triggered by the weak performance of US subprime ABS in 2007 due to housing recession and mortgage meltdown has led to a market reshaping for securitization especially affecting the CDO sector.

Although the nature of the CDO issuance mix and structures of CDOs are changing constantly in response to changing market conditions, this chapter focuses on the main characteristics of CDOs, describes the basic structures, and gives a brief overview of the CDO market. In the second part, it concentrates on CDO structures particularly for the real estate capital market.

2   CDO market

2.1   Characteristics of CDOs

Definition of CDO CDOs are the outcome of structured, leveraged transactions backed by a variety of assets. They securitize the credit risk of debt. A great variety of CDO types exists. CDOs can be classified using three criteria:

- asset type,
- motivation, and
- form of risk transfer [1] (see figure 1).

Criteria	Characteristics	CDO type
Asset type	• Bonds • Loans • Entities, mixed portfolios • Structured finance securities	• Collateralized Bond Obligation (CBO) • Collateralized Loan Obligation (CLO) • Collateralized Debt Obligation (CDO) • CDO of ABS/MBS; CDO of CDO; Commercial real estate CDOs
Motivation	• Arbitrage • Risk management	• Arbitrage CDO • Balance sheet CDO
Risk transfer	• True sale • Synthetic • Combination of true sale and synthetic	• Cash flow CDO • Synthetic CDO • Hybrid CDO
Source: Own compilation based on Fitch, 2003 [1]		

Fig. 1: Classification of CDOs

CDOs are Asset Backed Securities (ABS) where the underlying portfolio can be classified as bonds (Collateralized Bond Obligation – CBO) or loans (Collateralized Loan Obligation – CLO). The term CDO is also used for portfolios combining both bonds and loans, portfolios of structured finance products, such as consumer related ABS, Mortgage Backed Securities (MBS) or other CDO tranches. CDOs refer also to transactions, where the underlying portfolio does not reference specific debt obligations, but rather entities, as, for example, corporate or financial institutions. **Asset type**

The underlying Portfolio of CDOs can include various types of debt obligations or focus only on one class of debt. The main types of debt, i. e., bonds or loans, can appear in various forms with unique characteristics.

Bonds are fixed income, tradable, and therefore relatively liquid debt obligations issued by an entity like a sovereign, a corporate, a financial institution, or a specific funding entity in structured finance transactions. Depending on the credit rating of the issuer, bonds are classified as Investment Grade (IG), i. e., ratings equal or above Baa3 from Moody's or BBB– from Standard & Poors (S&P) or Fitch, or as High Yield (HY), i. e., ratings below Baa3 or BBB–. Bonds, whether IG or HY, are mostly unsecured obligations of the issuer. **Bonds**

Compared to bonds, loans are less tradable and, hence, less liquid debt obligations which are usually hold by a smaller group of investors. The relationship between a debtor and a creditor on a bank loan is often much stronger than it is with a bond. Also loans can be divided in IG and HY loans depending on whether the borrower is an IG or an HY issuer. The characteristics of bank loans vary with IG and HY loans because of the different credit risk profiles. Hence, IG loans are normally unsecured while sub-IG borrowers usually have to assign a dedicated collateral or asset security as is the case with Leveraged Buy Out (LBO) transactions or highly leveraged issuers. **Loans**

Though fungible instruments, ABS assets are generally less liquid than bonds. ABS investors benefit from the direct access to dedicated collateral in the **ABS assets** case of a default of an ABS obligation. In case of default the allocation of the proceeds from the collateral is quite clear, i. e., sequentially from the senior to the junior notes and the equity. It is important to note that liquidity of ABS assets has much increased in the last years until the liquidity crisis in the second half of 2007.

Motivation CDOs, differentiated by the motivation, can be divided into balance sheet and arbitrage transactions. Balance sheet CDOs remove assets or the risk of assets off the balance sheet of the originator. They are primarily used by financial institutions to transfer credit risks into the capital market in order to manage their credit exposure and/or improve returns on economic or regulatory capital. Arbitrage CDOs attempt to capture the positive spread between the average yield on the assets (underlying CDO portfolio) and the financing cost of the generally higher rated liabilities (CDO notes or swaps).

Risk transfer Depending on the way the credit risk is transferred into the capital market, true sale or synthetic transactions can be distinguished. With true sale the CDO issuer actually purchases initially the credit risk debt obligations and becomes their legal owner. The credit risk is then transferred from the CDO issuer to the investor in CDO notes. In these cash flow CDOs liabilities are paid off with the interest and principal payments of their collateral. Synthetic CDOs combine the CDO securitization technique with the credit derivative technology. Here, the risk transfer happens synthetically by using credit derivatives, mainly Credit Default Swaps (CDS). That means, debt obligations are referenced for loss determination without being purchased by the CDO issuer. Hybrid CDOs combine the funding structure of cash and synthetic CDOs.

2.2   History of the CDO market

Development of issuance volume Although the first CDOs were issued in the late 1980s, annual issuance remained below US$ 1.5 billion until 1996 when issuance jumped to US$ 15 billion of funded and unfunded volume [2]. Funded volume comprises all notes that are actually sold to investors while unfunded means that risk has been transferred in form of a swap, guarantee or insurance policy without an initial payment. Since 1996, CDO issuance has experienced tremendous growth with a preliminary peak of US$ 556 billion of funded volume (see figure 2) added by US$ 404 billion of unfunded volume in 2006. CDO funded issuance 2006 showed again a record year-by-year increase of 75 % compared to 63 % growth in 2005 before it decreased by 7 % due to the subprime crisis in 2007. 2002 had a stagnation in CDO issuance volume caused by a weak credit environment.

Regional distribution The main origin of CDO issuance lays in the US with 71 % funded issuance volume, followed by Europe with 25 %, and a new market developing in Asia with 4 % in 2006 (see figure 3). Since 2004, the growth in CDO funded issuance was again higher in the US than in Europe. While in Europe the CDO issuance grew again, the US issuance suffered already from the crisis in 2007 (see figure 4).

Balance sheet vs. arbitrage in Europe and the US Although the growth picture is the same for the US and Europe, the motivation of the transactions differs. Balance sheet driven regulatory Collateralized Loan Obligations (CLOs) were the most active issues between 1996 through 1999 [2]. While balance sheet driven CDO transactions are of minor importance in the

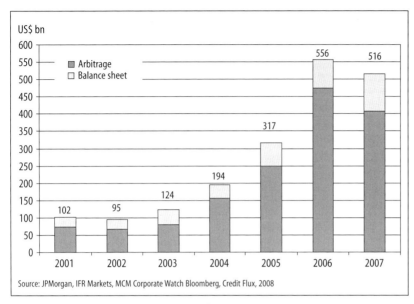

Fig. 2: *Global CDO funded issuance by year*

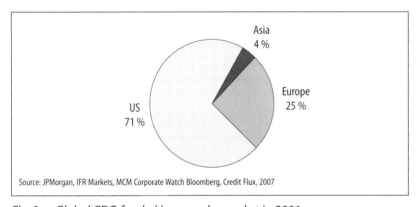

Fig. 3: *Global CDO funded issuance by market in 2006*

US since 2001 as changes in the accounting rules have removed much of the incentives, the situation is different in Europe. Balance sheet transactions account for almost half of all CDO transactions in Europe throughout time (see figure 4). For the last two years, Basel II has focused attention on economic capital, i.e., the amount of risk capital that is realistically needed to cover all the risks a firm is running, helping to drive the growth in balance sheet CLOs in Europe. 2006 balance sheet CLOs issuance recorded a 163 % year-on-year increase and account more than 49 % of the entire CDO issuance in the Europe, Middle East and AFRICA (EMEA) region [3].

The structure of CDO collateral also differs strongly between the US and Europe. While in the US the market for Structured Finance CDOs is quite mature, it is in its infancy in Europe. Therefore, in the US the Structured Finance CDOs take the largest share of total CDO funded issuance with

Collateral mix in the US and Europe

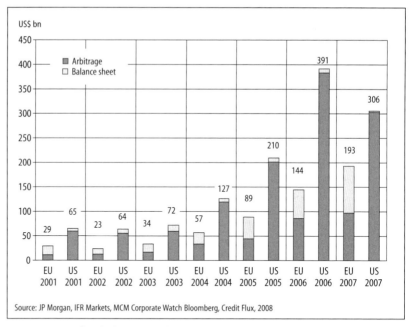

Fig. 4:   *CDO funded issuance by region*

58 %, comprising High Grade Structured Finance CDOs (HG SF), Mezzanine Structured Finance CDOs (Mezz SF), Commercial Real Estate (CRE) CDOs, and CDO of CDOs (CDO Squared), followed by the asset class of High Yield (HY) Loans with 29 %, and IG Debt with 7 %. For a further breakdown of the Structured Finance CDOs see section 3. In Europe the High Yield Loan CDOs capture the lion share of total CDO issuance with 80 %, followed by IG Debt with 10 %. The Structured Finance CDOs altogether account only for 6 % of total CDO funded issuance in Europe in 2006 (see figure 5).

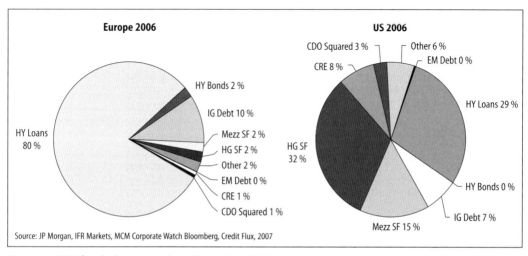

Fig. 5:   *CDO funded issuance by collateral in 2006*

Across all sectors the increase of synthetic vs. cash CDO transaction continues. **Synthetic vs. cash**
According to Moody's, the rated mix was 30 % cash and 70 % synthetic CDO **transactions**
transactions in 2006 for the EMEA region, compared to 37 % and 63 % in
2005 respectively [3]. Standardized Credit Default Swap (CDS) contracts for
Commercial Mortgage Backed Securities (CMBS) and ABS securities have
led to rapid growth in synthetic issuance in the US market. Hence, CRE and
Mezzanine Structured Finance CDOs have grown around 100 % annually in
2005 and 2006 by notional amount [4].

2.3   Basic CDO structure

Whether CDOs are to be used as financing vehicles or for transferring risk **Cash structure**
off a bank's balance sheet, the basic CDO structure is the same. A bankruptcy **of CDOs**
remote Special Purpose Vehicle (SPV) is set up to acquire pools of either bonds
or loans (or a combination of these). The purchase price of the portfolio is
funded by issuing notes to investors. These CDOs, where assets are purchased
by the SPV, are known as cash structures and were the first types of CDO
structures in the market [5].

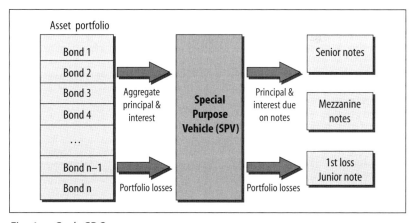

Fig. 6:   Cash CDO structure

The notes issued by the CDO represent undivided interest in the asset portfolio, **Liability side**
but are divided or "tranched" into classes with decreasing priority of claims
on the principal and interest flows from the collateral. Each class of notes is
subordinated to the notes above it in the right to receive principal and interest.
Hence, the senior notes stand first in line to receive first interest and principal
from the asset pool followed by the mezzanine notes and so forth. The junior
notes are the last to be paid or the first to lose and therefore are often called the
first loss or equity tranche. Investors bear the financial losses of any obligor in
the asset pool being unwilling or unable to meet the terms of debt obligation.
Therefore, the investor's return is directly related to the performance of the
pool.

CDOs are structured such that there is a "buyer" and a "seller" of credit **Motivation of**
protection on a specified asset portfolio. The investors in CDO notes are the **CDO participants**

ultimate protection sellers. Usually one or more financial institutions are the protection buyers. These institutions are either looking for economic and/or regulatory capital relief by shifting exposure off their balance sheets, or trying to take advantage of a perceived arbitrage situation in the market.

Credit tranching The financing efficiency of the CDOs is created by the credit tranching. Each of the issued tranches is assigned a credit rating based upon the likelihood that the tranche will receive principal and interest. The higher the likelihood of payment, the higher the rating and the lower the required coupon payment on the tranche.

2.4 Synthetic CDOs

Synthetic CDO structure In a synthetic CDO structure, the SPV, instead of directly purchasing assets, enters into a portfolio credit default swap with the protection buyer, i. e., typically the arranging bank. The aim is to synthesize the credit risks of buying a referenced portfolio of assets using derivatives. The proceeds of the SPV's note issuance are invested in low-risk collateral, i. e., high quality, highly liquid, AAA-rated government obligations or Pfandbriefe (German mortgage-backed securities). The protection buyer in the Credit Default Swap (CDS), i. e., the arranging or originating bank, usually pays a premium to the SPV to cover the expenses of the SPV and the difference between the coupon due on the performing notes and the income received on the collateral (see figure 7).

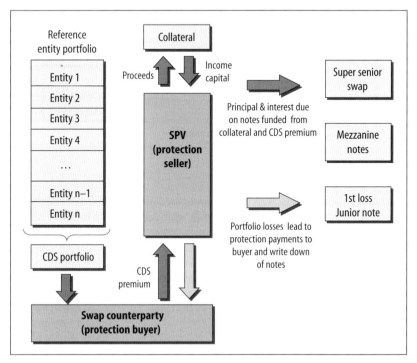

Fig. 7:   Synthetic CDO structure

Credit derivatives are tools that facilitate the isolation and management of credit risk from all other components of risk. CDS are by far the most widely used type of credit derivatives. A CDS is a contract in which one party agrees to compensate the other party for the financial loss it may incur following a credit-related event (e. g., a default) with respect to an underlying obligation. In case of the synthetic CDO it means, if a credit event affects an obligor in the reference pool, the protection seller, i. e., the SPV, pays the protection buyer an amount according to the loss incurred on the reference entity asset, i. e., normally a bond or a loan of the entity. This loss is passed on to the investor by writing down the notes by an equal amount beginning with the most junior note. The protection payment requires a corresponding sale of the collateral. On maturity of the transaction the remaining collateral is liquidated to repay principal to the note holders on a priority basis.

Credit Default Swap (CDS)

A credit event in a synthetic CDO may be considered a proxy for the default of an asset. The definition of the credit event depends on the underlying reference obligation in the portfolio, i. e., whether it is a corporate, a sovereign, or a structured finance reference obligation. Most transactions refer to the International Swaps and Derivatives Association (ISDA) credit derivatives definitions where the documentation for CDS contracts is standardized. For corporate reference obligations a credit event usually occurs with failure to pay, bankruptcy, and restructuring.

Credit event

If a credit event occurs, two mechanisms of settlement can be employed to establish the recovery value: physical or cash settlement. With physical settlement the investors (the protection seller) buy through the SPV the defaulted asset for a price equal to the par value of that asset from the protection buyer. The protection seller will establish the recovery of the delivered asset either by selling the security or holding on to it for workout. Far more common is the cash settlement, where the investors pay a cash amount equal to the difference between the par value of the assets and their post default market price. The value will typically be established by requesting bids from various market participants. Therefore, this process directly influences recoveries achieved. Important factors are the timing of valuation following default, the size of the bids, the number of bids, the identity of bidders, and the selection of bids, i. e., whether the highest or average highest of bids is taken [6].

Settlement mechanisms

Another risk of synthetic transactions is that the reference obligation, which determines the credit risk, can be different from the deliverable obligation, which determines the recovery value. Even when the reference entity, seniority and security of the obligation is determined, there still may be obligations that trade more cheaply than others. If the deliverable security is not pre-specified, the protection buyers will seek to use those cheaper credits, like, e. g., convertible securities, as valuation obligations (cash settlement) or as deliverable obligations (physical settlement) to maximize the loss and hence the protection amount payable by investors. This is called the "cheapest-to-deliver" option.

Cheapest-to-deliver option

Within the last decade the synthetic CDO market emerged, grew in size and sophistication, and has attained maturity. Its development has been characterized by constant innovations. An early driver for synthetic transactions were the

Development of synthetic CDOs

problems arising with the transfer of loans/bonds from the originator to the SPV in the cash structure. Particularly in the case of loans many borrowers expressly restrict their lender's right to sell the loan for confidentiality or client reason. Hence, in the beginning (1997 to 2000) the balance sheet driven synthetic CDOs were predominant. Balance sheet CDOs were executed as very large size transactions with or without replenishment features. The importance has declined since the year 2000 but has been revived in the Basel II context. Static synthetic CDOs, i. e., CDOs with non-managed portfolios, made a brief appearance on the market during 2000 to 2001, but vanished again due to the weak credit environment in 2001/2002 and subsequent spread tightening. Later on, static synthetic CDOs in a single-tranche format were used in more advanced CDO structures. Static deals were replaced by managed synthetic CDOs in order to protect investors from negative events in a weaker credit environment [7]. Hence, the manager performance and experience has become a very important criterion to assess a CDO transaction.

Funded, partially-funded, single-tranche CDO

If all tranches are sold to investors, the CDO is fully-funded. It is partially-funded if the most senior tranche, i. e., the super senior, is un-funded in the sense that an investor does not pay cash upfront but rather enters into a default swap with the SPV. In a single-tranche CDO only one (or few) tranche of the structure, in general at the mezzanine level, is sold to investors. Therefore, although the reference portfolio is, e.g., US$ 1 billion, the issued tranche may be only US$ 10 million, and can be tailored to the investor needs regarding rating, maturity, underlying, etc. Single-tranche technology can be used to transfer the risk of any type of underlying asset. These trades typically use multi-issuing SPVs rather then setting up new SPVs each time a new tranche is issued. Compared to traditional synthetic CDOs, the main difference of single-tranche CDOs is that only a portion of the risk of the reference portfolio is being transferred. Sponsors have developed techniques to dynamically hedge the remaining risk (also called delta hedging). A number of single-tranche CDOs can be combined in a pool, building a new transaction, referred to as CDO squared. The new CDO is further tranched in one or multiple tranches.

New structures

Spread tightening as well as diversification requirements led in the last few years to the development of new structures by applying internal leverage (like with CDO squared), external leverage (e. g., leveraged super senior), or using new types of exposure to create the reference pool (e. g., ABS, Equity Default Swaps, insurance obligations). CDOs backed by credit derivatives are known as Collateralized Synthetic Obligations (CSO). Usually the SPV enters into CDSs to sell protection and will receive a premium but has to make payments in case of a credit event. The SPV can also enter into a CDS to buy protection, in which case it has to make premium payments but will receive payments upon the occurrence of credit events. This is also called as having "short" positions in synthetic CDOs. The combination of long and short positions has become a common structure in synthetic CDOs over the last two years.

Cash vs. synthetic CDO

Compared to cash CDOs, synthetic CDOs allow to transfer the credit risk of some assets more easily. Another main advantage of synthetic transactions is the flexibility and timing provided by the derivative products. A CDS can be tailored to meet specific needs of the originator and/or provide customized risk-returns profiles to investors. A synthetic CDO differs from a cash CDO also in the payment structure. In a cash CDO the investor pays via the SPV the value of the assets upfront and takes ownership of the assets and their risk. However, in a synthetic CDO the investor buys an obligation via the SPV to pay a protection amount if defined credit events occur. Depending on the definition of the credit event and the settlement mechanism the investor's credit risk exposure can be increased or decreased.

3 CDOs and real estate

Structured Finance CDOs have been one of the fastest growing sub-components of the CDO market in recent years. They have emerged since 2000. Transactions issued between 2000 and 2002 were collateralized by a variety of assets, ranging from tranches of consumer related ABS, Residential Mortgage Backed Securities (RMBS, i. e., debt obligations that represents claims to the cash flows from pools of mortgage loans on residential property), Commercial Mortgage-Backed Securities (CMBS, i. e., debt obligations that represents claims to the cash flows from pools of mortgage loans on commercial property), and even Real Estate Investment Trusts (REITs). Since 2002, the market has gravitated towards structures that rely extensively on RMBS in a consumer related collateral mix (ABS) on one hand and on commercial real estate (CRE) on the other hand. These two categories, i. e., CDO of ABS and CRE CDOs, are shortly discussed in the following sections.

Development of CDO of consumer related ABS and CRE CDO

3.1 CDO of consumer related ABS

Both in the US and Europe the dominant cash asset class and dominant referenced assets for CDOs of consumer related ABS (in the following called CDO of ABS) are real estate-backed Home Equity Loan (HEL) and UK RMBS transactions respectively. Although the CDO-of-ABS market was a fast growing segment of the overall CDO market until 2007, the importance is by far larger in the US. In the US the segment of CDO of ABS has increased its share over the year 2006 and is with 47 % by far the largest of the overall CDO market. In the beginning of the CDO-of-ABS-market in 2000, the share was 10 % of the global CDO volume [2]. In contrast, the share of CDO of ABS of the overall CDO market in Europe was much smaller with 4 % in 2006. Although US CDO of ABS were the flagship of structured credit, deterioration in mortgage credit has brought CDO of ABS issuance to a halt in 2007.

Importance of CDO of consumer related ABS in the US and Europe

The motivation for CDOs of ABS is similar to that of other CDO types. That is, fund managers are using CDO of ABS as an asset acquisition vehicle to earn management fees as well as arbitrage the spread between asset and liability costs. Hence, there is always a development in the composition of the collateral as well as in the structure of CDOs of ABS. Since 2004 high grade CDOs of ABS have emerged and represent around two thirds of the overall CDO-of-ABS-market in 2006. The average collateral composition of CDOs of ABS in the US differentiated for mezzanine and high grade CDOs is shown in figure 8.

Collateral mix of CDO of ABS

For high grade CDOs of ABS the share of HEL transactions is much lower although they constitute the main part of the collateral. High grade CDOs of ABS are backed by higher rated collateral, i. e., assets are rated single-A or

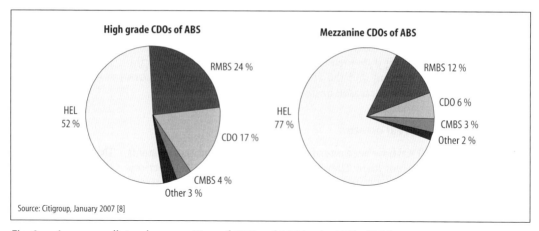

Fig. 8:   *Average collateral composition of CDOs of ABS in the US in 2006*

better. Prior to 2004, most high grade CDOs of ABS were backed exclusively by AA-rated RMBS floaters in the prime mortgage sector and other plain vanilla ABS structures. Due to a spread tightening environment, the collateral mix has shifted to higher yielding alternative products which were highly rated securities, such as CDOs, fixed-rated collateral, or papers backed by fixed rate non-prime mortgage pools which are swapped to floating. According to these trends, credit risk tended to be replaced by interest rate and pre-payment risk. Furthermore, since most of the CDOs serving as collateral for CDO-of-CDOs structures are in fact other CDOs of ABS, this has increased the levered exposure to residential borrowers [8].

Leverage of high grade and mezzanine CDOs of ABS
Compared to mezzanine CDOs of ABS, high grade CDOs of ABS rely on considerably greater levels of leverage in order to generate sufficient returns. While a typical mezzanine CDO of ABS backed by triple-B RMBS would have a 4 % equity tranche (25 times leverage), a high grade ABS could have an equity tranche of 1 % to 0.5 %, i. e., a leverage of 100 to 200 times [9].

Trends in CDO of ABS market
Trends seen in the CDO of ABS market were the increase in hybrid structures, i. e., the asset side contains cash as well as synthetic components. Synthetics enable vintage, and collateral diversity. Hence, the diversity within each CDO as well as amongst different CDOs can be increased. While the CDO of ABS market was just packed at the beginning with new issue HELs, the market was evolving into different product types by collateral (e. g., focusing on other CDOs of ABS, seasoned HELs, special categories of non-prime, or prime residential mortgage loans) allowing to express different strategies for extracting value.

Other trends seen in the market were a surge in static synthetic CDOs of ABS with single-tranche or full capital structure, or with automatic reinvestment attached to an index, and the inclusion of short positions in the underlying portfolio of CDO of ABS (see also [8]).

3.2 Commercial Real Estate CDO

The first CDO backed solely by Commercial Real Estate (CRE) assets came out in 1999. While in 2003 the CRE CDO issuance still was as low as US$ 5 billion, in 2006 the issuance increased dramatically by 87 % on a year-to-year basis and reached US$ 33 billion (including the funded proportions of synthetics) [8]. The first CRE CDOs consisted of static pools of CMBS. But over time, more pure mortgage loans as well as subordinated loan interests and mezzanine loans have been added to these transactions.

Development of CRE CDOs

Both CMBS as well as CRE CDOs involve the pooling of real estate loans for repackaging as bonds. For borrowers, loans destined for securitization are attractive because they typically cost less than loans originated by banks, pension funds or insurance companies. However, CMBS transactions are fairly standardized, concentrate on first lien mortgage collateral and are subject to highly developed rating agency criteria. With time, products have emerged in the commercial real estate market such as mezzanine loans, subordinated participations and preferred equity as means of offering mortgage loan borrowers increased leverage. In contrast to CMBS, which do not allow the investment in such products, CRE CDOs give originators of this collateral and investors on the subordinated level the ability to securitize this product.

CMBS vs. CRE CDO

A further difference between CRE CDOs and CMBS is the fact that CRE CDOs are not limited to static pool transactions. With managed CRE CDOs, the collateral manager has the ability to reinvest principle proceeds of the current pool of collateral for additional collateral. The manager may even sell current collateral and invest in additional collateral. This can not only increase the returns for equity investors, but can help to manage down side risks related to distressed assets as in the aftermath of the subprime crisis. For borrowers this dynamism of CRE CDOs means that an exit strategy can be established much more easily and that CRE CDOs can be considered as a good source of short-term financing a project.

Before 2007 the CRE CDO market was evolving into two somewhat distinct product types, that were on one hand the re-securitization of CMBS bonds, CMBS first loss positions or subordinated pieces (B-pieces), and REIT debt, i. e., the "resec-type" CRE CDO, and on the other hand the securitization of whole loans, B-notes, and mezzanine loans, i. e., the loan CRE CDOs [8].

Product types of CRE CDO

The resec-type of CRE CDOs show two variations. In the first one, the CDO is used to finance the activities of CMBS B-piece buyers and are therefore backed by the non-investment grade tranches of CMBS. The leverage on such CDO equity is typically low, such as three to one, and the CDO manager takes all below investment grade liabilities of the CDO. In the second variation, investment grade CMBS bonds are repackaged into the CDO, often achieving higher leverage. These CDOs were typically issued by larger managers or investment bank ABS correlation desks.

Re-securitization CRE CDO

Loan CRE CDOs are first time securitizations of whole first mortgage loans, A-notes, B-notes, mezzanine loans, or any other yielding commercial mortgage loan type. Loan CRE CDOs differ widely by the mixture of loan types and real estate sectors covered. However, many assets pooled in these transactions

Loan CRE CDO

are deeply-discounted short-term floaters, often containing some element of real estate development risk. The short-term nature of the collateral implies that the CDO portfolio will revolve extremely rapidly. For a more detailed introduction to the CRE CDOs see also [10].

CRE CDOs in the European market   Until now the CRE CDO market is a domain of the US. The first two European CRE CDOs have come to market only in 2006. The collateral pools backing the European CRE CDOs consist of a mix of subordinated or mezzanine portions of loans (named B-loans), tranches of European CMBS transactions, undivided commercial real estate loans, and senior portions of these loans (also named A-loans). Although this is similar to the US, the main difference is the small size of the European CMBS market with a high concentration of the activity in the UK and Germany. This generates a considerable overlap between the CMBS tranches and the B-loan collateral in the European CRE CDO pools, since a substantial portion of the B-loan collateral has its senior portion already included in the collateral backing the CMBS notes which are also part of the CRE CDO pool. This leads to high credit enhancement levels in the European transactions, because such overlap increases the probability of joint default scenarios [3].

4   Outlook

Further de-risking in the liquidity and credit crisis aftermath   With so much uncertainty in the market, outlooks for structured credit products range from the assessment that no form of structured credit will ever again be issued to the idea that at the end of the first half of 2008 everything should return to normal. However, the truth will be somewhere in between. The primary issuance volumes of CDOs in 2008 will sharply decline, most outlooks predicting a decline by 50 % from 2007 issuance level. Repacked structures like CDO of ABS, and, to a somewhat lesser extent, CRE CDOs will suffer most due to their extreme vulnerability to relatively modest changes in the underlying.

Back to basics, defensive structures, greater collateral diversity   The coming primary market vintage will have better quality borrowers and assets reflecting the tightening of credit standards. Additionally, greater collateral diversity can be expected. There will be more defensive structures in terms of, e.g., hedging, substitution requirements, collateral eligibility, credit enhancement. Furthermore, a greater simplicity to capital structures, especially in the synthetic transactions, is likely in order to improve transparency.

5   Bibliography

[1] Fitch Ratings, Global Rating Criteria for Collateralised Debt Obligations, Criteria Report, July 14th, 2003.

[2] Bear, Stearns Co. Inc., Collateralized Debt Obligations: A Primer, September 2002, p. 11.

[3] Moody's, 2006 Review and 2007 Outlook: EAMA Collateralised Debt Obligations: An Increasing Appetite for Corporate Credit with Economic Capital driven Volumes, January 29th, 2007.

[4] JPMorgan, US Fixed Income Markets 2007 Outlook: Collateralized Debt Obligations, November 24th, 2006.

[5] Moody's, Collateralised Debt Obligations: A Moody's Primer, March 7th, 2005.

[6] Standard & Poors, Structured Finance Ratings: Criteria for Rating Synthetic CDO Transactions, September 2003.

[7] Merrill Lynch, Synthetic CDO Guidebook: Pushing the Boundaries of Innovation, September 26th, 2005.

[8] Citigroup, CDO Outlook 2007, Global Structured Credit Strategy, January 8th, 2007.

[9] Deutsche Bank, High Grade ABS CDOs – Market Update and Modelling Considerations, July 26th, 2006.

[10] Wheeler, D./Roy, R., Commercial Real Estate CDOs, Chapter 13, in: Rajan, A./McDermott, G./Roy, R., The Structured Credit Handbook, February 2007.

6   Real estate hybrid products in the United States

Shawn Rosenthal

Table of contents

1   Introduction

Outline of this chapter The following chapter will focus on hybrid financing products utilized in the United States by various buyers and developers of real estate. Specifically, it will discuss the use of mezzanine debt and preferred equity and the reasons why these products have become so popular in today's environment. Advantages and disadvantages of using these structures will be discussed and contrasted with alternative financing structures, including the use of additional common equity. A short case study will be utilized to monitor the economic returns to the buyer under various scenarios followed by a discussion of the types of investors who seek mezzanine loans or preferred equity investments.

2   Types of products – mezzanine debt

Mezzanine debt as a secondary loan Various hybrid products have developed over the years to allow borrowers to raise additional financing beyond traditional first mortgage borrowing. The most popular products include mezzanine debt and preferred equity.

What is mezzanine debt? The phrase mezzanine debt can take many forms and can mean different things for different people. Typically, mezzanine debt refers to a secondary loan made by an investor beyond a first mortgage loan. It is subordinate in all respects to a first mortgage loan and carries a higher yield to account for the additional risk. Mezzanine loans can increase the leverage from standard first mortgage financing of 65 % to 75 % of the value of a property, to as high as 80 % to 90 %. From 2004 through 2007, the cost of mezzanine debt has ranged between 7 % to 22 % per annum. This return may include a set pay rate, an accrual feature, origination fees, exit fees and perhaps even in some cases, a participation in the profits of a transaction. The loans are typically non-recourse to any individuals and rely on the value of the property for repayment. Pricing of mezzanine debt is dependent on the leverage level, debt service coverage ratio, the strength of the borrower, the asset type, the rights and remedies available to the lender in the event of a default, the risk of a transaction, and the particular geographic market. Mezzanine financing is used for traditional cash flowing investment properties such as office, industrial, hotel, retail, apartments and other asset classes. Ground up construction projects can also utilize mezzanine financing. Generally in these types of transactions, an interest reserve is set up to pay currently some portion of the mezzanine return, with an accrual for the balance.

Uniform Commercial Code (UCC)

Since most senior loan documents in the United States prohibit second mortgages, a pledge of the partners' equity interest in the borrowing entity generally serves as security for the mezzanine loan, as opposed to a security interest in the real estate directly. Such pledge of collateral is usually memorialized through the filings of Uniform Commercial Code (UCC) statements and filed in the personal property records of the appropriate states. Some senior loan documents allow a pledge of 100 % of the equity interests in the borrowing entity as collateral for a mezzanine loan, while other documents allow a pledge of less than 50 %. Generally, a mezzanine lender will negotiate a specific set of loan documents with the borrower, similar to a senior lender. These documents specify the responsibilities of all parties, and what will constitute a default. In the event of a default under the mezzanine loan, the mezzanine lender will be entitled to exercise its rights under the pledge, and foreclose on its security interest (which is the partnership shares of the borrower). Through this UCC foreclosure, the mezzanine lender steps into the shoes of the borrower and takes over the property. What is most important to the mezzanine lender is the ability to quickly be put on notice of any defaults under the senior loan, and potentially cure the situation. The mezzanine lender can then make specific decisions on how to best protect its investment.

Inter-Creditor Agreement

Mezzanine lenders and senior lenders will typically negotiate an "Inter-Creditor Agreement". This agreement specifies the rights and remedies of the senior lender and the mezzanine lender. Among other things, it establishes priority of payments and subordination, establishes cure rights, grants a purchase option to the mezzanine lender, and may restrict transfers of the mezzanine loan. Prior to 1999 to 2000, mezzanine debt in commercial real estate transactions was not as common. In the commercial lending markets of 2001 to 2007, mezzanine investments have become more commonplace and a part of most transactions. Wall Street lenders in many instances have taken on the role themselves of committing to the mezzanine layers of financing, and then selling off these strips later in the process to various investors.

3   Types of products – preferred equity

Similar characteristics to mezzanine debt, but without any pledge

Preferred equity has similar characteristics to mezzanine debt. It is generally found within the same leverage level within a capital structure, and is generally priced at the same levels or close to the same levels as mezzanine debt. One important distinction in a preferred equity structure is that there is no "security" or pledge of ownership interests in a borrowing entity, as is typical in mezzanine debt. The preferred equity investor has its rights and remedies upon a default specifically set forth in the partnership agreement of the borrower. Typically, in the event of a default under a preferred equity investment, the partnership agreement triggers a change in control of the borrowing entity from the original sponsor to the preferred equity investor. There may also be provisions in the partnership agreement that could trigger a buy-sell or put option between the preferred equity and the common equity. Often investments need to be structured as preferred equity to avoid stringent provisions in senior loan documents that prohibit secondary debt.

4   Why do borrowers use mezzanine debt?

Reasons for dramatic increase of mezzanine debt use

The use of mezzanine debt has increased dramatically over the last decade for several reasons, including:

- continued stringent underwriting by first mortgage lenders leading to lower first mortgage leverage;

- increased competition and pricing for buyers of real estate, leaving a larger amount of equity to be raised on each transaction;

- a significant demand from hundreds of domestic and international investors who seek the risk-adjusted returns available for mezzanine debt as compared to direct real estate equity investments, thus driving down the cost of the mezzanine financing; and most importantly;

- the ability for buyers to increase their equity yields by leveraging their transactions higher at favorable mezzanine pricing.

Specifically, buyers analyze their projected Internal Rate of Return (IRR) on investments without the use of mezzanine debt and the increased return available through the use of this additional debt. If the overall cost of the mezzanine loan is less than the projected leveraged equity IRR, then the buyer will create positive leverage by using the mezzanine loan and increase the equity returns. Refer to the case study below for an analysis of the positive impact of mezzanine debt.

5   Unique situation requiring mezzanine debt

Another situation that often requires mezzanine debt or preferred equity is when a purchaser acquires a property that is encumbered with a longer-term Wall Street or life insurance mortgage, that is at a lower leverage point than a new buyer would prefer. The loans typically have locked out prepayment or defeasance clauses, where the cost for the buyer to prepay the loan is prohibitive. To fill the large gap of equity needed to purchase these assets, mezzanine capital is often utilized. In some instances, the cost of the existing senior debt to be assumed is more favorable than the current debt pricing. In these situations, the new buyer must analyze the cost of the existing first mortgage loan that is being assumed, blended with the cost of secondary mezzanine debt or preferred equity pricing as compared to the cost of a new first mortgage. Considerations such as prepayment fees or defeasance costs also must be analyzed.

6 Case study

A simple case study will be used to show the impact of mezzanine debt on equity returns. This model will then be adjusted to show the changed equity returns in two different disposition scenarios. These examples will also be used to expand on the various advantages and disadvantages of using mezzanine financing as compared to all equity.

Description of the basic setup

The case study assumes a simple example of a buyer who purchases an office building for US$ 97 million and incurs US$ 3 million of additional expenses for closing costs and capital expenditures. The first buyer utilizes a 70 % of cost senior loan, and utilizes 30 % equity. The second buyer utilizes a 70 % of cost senior loan, 15 % mezzanine debt and 15 % equity. The senior debt carries a cost of 7 %, interest only, and the mezzanine debt cost is 10 %. Net Operating Income (NOI) is assumed to be US$ 6.4 million in Year 1, US$ 7.6 million in Year 2, and US$ 8.4 million in Year 3. The buyers sell the asset at the end of Year 3 at a 7 % capitalization rate, based on Year 3 NOI.

See figure 1 for the two alternative capital structures utilized to purchase an office building.

	All equity structure		Mezzanine debt structure	
Uses				
Purchase price	97,000,000		97,000,000	
Closing costs	2,000,000		2,000,000	
Capital improvements	1,000,000		1,000,000	
Total uses	**100,000,000**		**100,000,000**	
Sources				
First mortgage debt	70,000,000	70 %	70,000,000	70 %
Mezzanine debt	0		15,000,000	15 %
Total equity	30,000,000	30 %	15,000,000	15 %
Total sources	**100,000,000**	**100 %**	**100,000,000**	**100 %**

Fig. 1:   Sources and uses (in US$)

Buyer 1 will invest US$ 30,000,000 of equity and generate a leveraged 3-year IRR of 25.46 %. Cash-on-cash returns over the 3-year period will be 5 %, 9 % and 11.67 % (before the sale of the asset), respectively.

		Year 1	Year 2	Year 3
Net Operating Income/cash flow	(100,000,000)	6,400,000	7,600,000	8,400,000
Sales proceeds at seven cap rate				120,000,000
Total cash flow	(100,000,000)	6,400,000	7,600,000	128,400,000
Unleveraged yield		**6.40 %**	**7.60 %**	**8.40 %**
Unleveraged IRR	**13.24 %**			**128.40 %**
First mortgage debt service (7 %)	70,000,000	(4,900,000)	(4,900,000)	(4,900,000)
Cash available for equity	(30,000,000)	1,500,000	2,700,000	3,500,000
Proceeds of sale				120,000,000
Pay first mortgage				(70,000,000)
	(30,000,000)	1,500,000	2,700,000	53,500,000
Cash-on-cash return		**5.00 %**	**9.00 %**	**11.67 %**
Leveraged IRR	**25.46 %**			**178.33 %**

Fig. 2:   *Equity IRR – no mezzanine debt (in US$)*

Buyer 2 will invest US$ 15,000,000 of equity and generate a leveraged 3-year IRR of 37.09 %. Cash-on-cash returns over the 3-year period will be 0 %, 8 %, and 13.33 % (before the sale of the asset), respectively.

		Year 1	Year 2	Year 3
Net Operating Income/cash flow	(100,000,000)	6,400,000	7,600,000	8,400,000
Sales proceeds at seven cap rate				120,000,000
Total cash flow	(100,000,000)	6,400,000	7,600,000	128,400,000
Unleveraged yield		**6.40 %**	**7.60 %**	**8.40 %**
Unleveraged IRR	**13.24 %**			**128.40 %**
First mortgage debt service (7 %)	70,000,000	(4,900,000)	(4,900,000)	(4,900,000)
Cash available for equity	(30,000,000)	1,500,000	2,700,000	3,500,000
Mezzanine debt (10 %)	15,000,000	(1,500,000)	(1,500,000)	(1,500,000)
Cash available for equity after mezzanine debt	(15,000,000)	–	1,200,000	2,000,000
Proceeds of sale				120,000,000
Pay first mortgage				(70,000,000)
Pay mezzanine debt				(15,000,000)
Cash available to equity	(15,000,000)	–	1,200,000	37,000,000
Cash-on-cash return		**0.00 %**	**8.00 %**	**13.33 %**
Leveraged IRR after mezzanine debt	**37.09 %**			**246.67 %**

Fig. 3:   *Equity IRR – with mezzanine debt (in US$)*

7 Advantages and disadvantages of mezzanine debt – summary

The decision for borrowers on whether to use mezzanine debt is not only a function of the potential equity returns in each scenario, but is also a function of various other non-economic factors. Set forth below are some advantages and disadvantages of utilizing mezzanine debt followed by a more detailed explanation on each point.

Decision is a function of various non-economic factors

The advantages of the mezzanine loan as compared to a full equity raise are:

- it lowers the overall equity required to close the transaction (in the case study, US$ 30,000,000 vs. US$ 15,000,000);

- the mezzanine lender generally limits and fixes its total return requirement and does not share in the profits of the transaction;

- less day-to-day interference and reporting required from the mezzanine lender than an equity partner;

- generally the mezzanine lender will have no governance rights over the property or major property decisions; and,

- the structure can increase equity yields.

Disadvantages of the mezzanine debt include

- the full subordination of all equity current returns and return of capital to the mezzanine debt;

- generally shorter term horizon than equity partners;

- more difficult and challenging closing process, including the need for an Inter-Creditor Agreement between a first mortgage lender and the mezzanine lender; and,

- limited patience and flexibility by the mezzanine lender if cash flow declines or if the asset has problems.

8 Advantages mezzanine debt – detail

- **Lowering the overall equity raise**

The impact of mezzanine debt on this case study

Using mezzanine debt of US$ 15,000,000 in this example will leave the buyer with a more manageable equity requirement of US$ 15,000,000, as opposed to US$ 30,000,000. This equity most likely could be syndicated or raised from private investors. Without the use of mezzanine debt, it is a much larger equity raise for the buyer, and most likely would require an institutional equity investor.

- **Capped return**

A mezzanine lender generally requires a stated return without a share of the equity profits. In a situation where there is large value creation and profits, a buyer would rather pay a fixed coupon then share a percentage of the profits. However, in a situation where there is little value creation, a high priced mezzanine loan will negatively impact (and in some cases, completely erase) the equity returns.

It is also fairly typical for buyers, who are raising equity from third party private or institutional investors, to obtain a disproportionate share of the profits when certain return hurdles are achieved. The disproportionate share, or "promoted interest" as is it sometimes referred to, can be extremely valuable as value is created. The use of mezzanine debt at its stated return decreases the amount of equity dollars that needs to share in the profits, leaving more available cash to the buyer for his hard work.

- **Day-to-day interference**

A mezzanine loan generally will not involve the day-to-day interference and reporting requirements that an equity partner would require. Typically, a mezzanine lender's involvement in the asset is minimal, provided the loan payments are current and there are no major events occurring at the property level. An equity partner would require more reporting and disclosure.

While mezzanine lenders are not generally as involved in the day-to-day decisions at the property level, they often have specific rights that are built into loan documents, including major lease approvals, or approvals of major capital expenditures. Borrowers are typically able to negotiate these provisions such that they are consistent with the senior lender requirements, and are limited to truly significant events.

- **Governance rights**

A mezzanine lender typically has no governance rights over the property with respect to major property level decisions including refinancing or sales. The buyer would have the sole right to make these decisions. An equity partner, would in most instances, have these rights, and may even have the right to block a proposed refinancing or sale. If the use of mezzanine debt allows a borrower to utilize his own internal equity, as opposed to third party equity, he can greatly improve his control over his property. Decisions can be made without protracted conversations with third party equity partners.

- **Increase of equity yields**

In situations where the cost of mezzanine debt is less than the leveraged IRR to equity for a transaction, the mezzanine debt is accretive to the equity and has the impact of increasing the overall returns. In the example noted above, the owner increased his IRR from 25.46 % (in the case of no mezzanine debt) to 37.09 %, with the use of mezzanine debt. It is important to note that in situations where the equity investment does not meet its intended returns, the mezzanine loan can have the impact of greatly reducing or eliminating equity returns.

9 Case study – adjusted for lower sales price

Assume that in the case study mentioned previously, there is a drop in the market and capitalization rates on office assets increase. Assume that instead of selling the asset at a 7% capitalization rate on Year 3 net operating income for US$ 120,000,000, the owner can only sell the asset for a capitalization rate of 9%, or for US$ 93,333,333.

The impact of a lower sales price

Buyer 1, who utilized the full US$ 30,000,000 of equity, will manage to squeeze out a very low IRR of approximately 1.21%. He will barely recoup his initial principal investment.

		Year 1	Year 2	Year 3
Net Operating Income/cash flow	(100,000,000)	6,400,000	7,600,000	8,400,000
Sales proceeds at nine cap rate				93,333,333
Total cash flow	(100,000,000)	6,400,000	7,600,000	101,733,333
Unleveraged yield		6.40%	7.60%	8.40%
Unleveraged IRR	5.32%			101.73%
First mortgage debt service (7%)	70,000,000	(4,900,000)	(4,900,000)	(4,900,000)
Cash available for equity	(30,000,000)	1,500,000	2,700,000	3,500,000
Proceeds of sale				93,333,333
Pay first mortgage				(70,000,000)
	(30,000,000)	1,500,000	2,700,000	26,833,333
Cash-on-cash return		5.00%	9.00%	11.67%
Leveraged IRR	1.21%			89.44%

Fig. 4: Equity IRR – no mezzanine debt (in US$)

Buyer 2, who utilized the US$ 15,000,000 of mezzanine debt will lose a portion of his original equity investment and earn a negative IRR of –8.66%.

		Year 1	Year 2	Year 3
Net Operating Income/cash flow	(100,000,000)	6,400,000	7,600,000	8,400,000
Sales proceeds at nine cap rate				93,333,333
Total cash flow	(100,000,000)	6,400,000	7,600,000	101,733,333
Unleveraged yield		6.40%	7.60%	8.40%
Unleveraged IRR	5.32%			101.73%
First mortgage debt service (7%)	70,000,000	(4,900,000)	(4,900,000)	(4,900,000)
Cash available for equity	(30,000,000)	1,500,000	2,700,000	3,500,000
Mezzanine debt (10%)	15,000,000	(1,500,000)	(1,500,000)	(1,500,000)
Cash available for equity after mezzanine debt	(15,000,000)	–	1,200,000	2,000,000
Proceeds of sale				93,333,333
Pay first mortgage				(70,000,000)
Pay mezzanine debt				(15,000,000)
Cash available to equity	(15,000,000)	–	1,200,000	10,333,333
Cash-on-cash return		0.00%	8.00%	13.33%
Leveraged IRR after mezzanine debt	–8.66%			68.89%

Fig. 5: Equity IRR – with mezzanine debt (in US$)

10   Disadvantages mezzanine debt – detail

Potential disadvantages by using mezzanine debt

- **Subordination of returns to equity**

A mezzanine loan gets fully repaid before any equity and requires a full subordination of returns from the equity. This has a major impact on initial cash-on-cash returns to the equity. In an environment of low cap rates and high asset prices, mezzanine debt has the effect of grabbing cash flow in the early years, leaving little to the equity. As seen in the original example, the cash-on-cash equity returns without the use of mezzanine debt are 5 %, 9 %, 11.67 %, respectively. With the use of mezzanine debt, the cash-on-cash returns to equity are 0 %, 8 %, and 13.33 %, respectively. The first two years' cash-on-cash return is lower with the use of mezzanine debt because all available cash flow from the property is used to pay the current 10 % return on the mezzanine debt. To the extent that the buyer is not successful in increasing the net operating income, the returns to the equity could stay low for future years.

These types of concerns are extremely important to equity investors. While IRR is one way of analyzing equity returns, equity investors are also concerned about current cash-on-cash yields. Some investors would even settle for a lower IRR, if the going in cash-on-cash returns are enticing.

Additionally, in the case of a sale or refinancing, the mezzanine debt gets fully repaid before any of the equity is returned. In the second example of the lower sales price in Year 3, the net sales proceeds of US$ 93,333,333 must first repay the US$ 70,000,000 first mortgage, then repay the US$ 15,000,000 mezzanine loan, leaving only US$ 10,333,333 for the equity (less than the US$ 15,000,000 initial equity contribution).

- **Shorter term horizon**

Mezzanine debt typically has a term of between two and five years. Equity investors typically have longer-term views, and may hold a property for as long as 10 years. More importantly, the mezzanine lender's set and rigid term for its investment may lead the buyer to certain forced decisions, which may not be in the best interest of the property. Often, major property decisions such as sales or financings may be forced by an expiring mezzanine loan, at un-opportunistic times. A flexible equity partner avoids some of these concerns. There are some exceptions to the shorter-term mezzanine lenders, and the market of seven-to-10 year mezzanine lenders has grown dramatically.

- **More difficult closing process**

The use of mezzanine debt from a practical standpoint has the impact of making the closing process more difficult. An Inter-Creditor Agreement is usually required in these transactions. The negotiation of this agreement can be a difficult and time-consuming process. Many transactions get bogged down at this point. Borrowers often speak with potential mezzanine lenders to ascertain with which first mortgage lenders they have previously closed deals. If agreements have already been negotiated between these parties, it can help the closing process tremendously and lower the buyer's execution risk.

The use of mezzanine debt on a transaction may increase the pricing on the senior loan and impact a senior mortgage lender's desire to make the loan.

Generally, a senior lender will prefer 30 % percent cash equity to a capital structure that includes mezzanine debt up to 85 % of cost, with only 15 % cash equity. In some cases, however, an extremely strong mezzanine lender can make a senior lender more comfortable. These situations generally involve a buyer whose experience in a specific asset class or project is not as strong as the mezzanine lender's. Since the mezzanine lender will take over the asset in the event of a default under the mezzanine loan, and since their financial strength and experience is greater than the original borrower, the senior lender feels more secure. This has happened in recent years in major United States office markets, where publicly traded Real Estate Investment Trusts (REITs) have often made mezzanine loans.

Lastly, in an environment where transactions are extremely difficult to locate, and timing and speed of closing are paramount and necessary to win transactions, the use of mezzanine debt adds a layer of complexity to the transaction. A buyer is forced to negotiate with three parties (first mortgage lender, mezzanine lender and equity investor) instead of two parties. This also can increase legal and due diligence costs significantly.

- **Limited flexibility**

Another important disadvantage of high leverage mezzanine debt is the limited flexibility for buyers and developers if there are any short-term reductions in cash flow, or significant issues at the property. A loss of one tenant can impact the ability of a developer to pay its mezzanine debt service, and potentially lose its equity interest in the property to a mezzanine lender. If the gap over the first mortgage is filled with all equity, there is greater flexibility to make longer-term decisions for the property, and wait out a bad cycle or negative incident.

11   Who are mezzanine lenders and investors?

Who are the mezzanine lenders and preferred equity investors in the market today? The amount of lenders and investors in this market has increased dramatically over the past five years. Investors include life insurance companies, private equity funds, publicly traded REITs, private individuals and investors, pension funds and foreign investors.

The amount of lenders increased dramatically

Some of the new, longer-term mezzanine lenders in the market are the veteran wealthy real estate families and real estate operating companies, who see an opportunity to invest in mezzanine transactions that generate a return that is most often higher on a current basis than equity returns. This higher return is also coupled with a true preference in payment to the equity, which is subordinate to the mezzanine debt in all respects. This is a way for seasoned real estate investors to generate solid returns at preferred positions. As a downside, the investors look at their exposure as a function of leverage and determine that in a worse case scenario of a default under the mezzanine debt, they would step into the ownership of a property at 80 to 90 cents on the dollar. This type of financing is often seen in large New York office acquisitions, including the General Motors Building.

Investors in mezzanine loans often use leverage to bolster their returns even further. Traditionally, funds have utilized lines of credit to finance the mezzanine loan investments. As an example, an investor may make an unleveraged 10 % mezzanine loan, and borrow anywhere from 50 % to 75 % of the principal via a line of credit, at a cost below 10 %. This helps increase yields to that investor even further.

12 Collateralized Debt Obligation (CDO) market

Investments collectively pooled in a CDO

Another recent trend to finance the mezzanine loan and preferred equity business has been the explosion of the Collateralized Debt Obligation (CDO) market. In these cases, investors in mezzanine loans and other investments collectively pool the investments and create a CDO. This vehicle, which is rated by the various rating agencies, is split into various tranches and sold to investors. The cumulative effect of these transactions allows mezzanine lenders to effectively lower their cost of financing on the mezzanine loans, and generate significantly more leverage. Borrowing costs of mezzanine lenders in some cases dropped from LIBOR plus 150 to 200 basis points, to LIBOR plus 40 to 75 basis points. At the height of the market, it also allowed these lenders to finance close to 90 % of their loan instead of 50 % or 60 %. This phenomenon during 2005, 2006 and early 2007 had the impact of pushing mezzanine loans pricing down for borrowers. The lenders' overall returns were similar, however, achieved through the very aggressive leverage afforded through the CDO market. Borrowers were the beneficiaries since the coupon payments were significantly lower than ever before. As of late 2007, these structures have slowed dramatically due to the credit concerns of bond buyers and CDO investors world-wide.

13 Wall Street as source for mezzanine debt

Wall Street lenders often became a source of mezzanine debt

As the commercial lending market heated from 2004 through 2007, Wall Street lenders often became a source of mezzanine debt for borrowers. Lenders offered commitments to borrowers for 85 % or 90 % financing, and were responsible for selling various tranches of the specific loan. Large loans on major assets were often split into five or six different classes. The rights of each of these classes were determined, and various investors across the world purchased the specific loan that met their risk and return thresholds.

The benefits to borrowers of this high leverage commitment from Wall Street were avoiding the time-consuming process of locating and negotiating with separate mezzanine lenders and instead receiving a "one-stop-shop" bid. On the flip side, Wall Street lenders typically priced into the loans a potential profit component from the sale of each subordinate class leading to higher overall pricing for borrowers.

14 Conclusion

The use of mezzanine debt on transactions can be a cost effective way for buyers to reduce their equity needs, increase yields, and purchase larger and more costly assets. The increased leverage, however, brings additional risks and complications into deal structures and transactions. Buyers must decide if the increased returns are justified by the additional risk. They must also analyze the down side, in order to understand the economic impact in a worse case scenario. Many factors should influence these decisions including the cost of the mezzanine debt, the ability to raise additional equity, the hold period for the asset, the time available to close a transaction and the risk tolerance of the buyer.

Cost effective way, but also additional risks

D Derivatives

1 Interest and currency derivatives

Klaus Schäfer

Table of contents

1   Introduction

Individuals and corporations are affected by increasing volatilities on interest rates and foreign exchange markets. One response to this development was the creation of financial instruments, so-called derivatives. To understand the included risks and to take correct decisions, it is necessary to get a fundamental insight into interest rate and exchange rate risk management. First, it is the aim of this chapter to systemize and describe the components of the interest and currency derivative instruments. Second, the motivation in using interest and currency derivatives and risk management applications will be analyzed.

Derivative instruments A derivative is a financial instrument whose value is derived from the value of an other basic variable. Such underlyings are often the prices of traded assets like interest rates, bonds and currencies. Derivatives can be categorized as unconditional or conditional instruments [1]. Instruments whose completion is not bound to constraint conditions are defined as unconditional instruments like forwards, swaps and future contracts. Options are conditional instruments because their completion is to a large degree subject to specified contractual conditions. The broad range of risk management applications is typically identified by three categories of traders: hedgers, speculators, and arbitrageurs. Hedgers use derivatives to reduce the risk from potential movements in the underlying variable, speculators try to profit from such potential future movements, and arbitrageurs profit from price inefficiencies between two ore more instruments with an identical risk-return profile. For the following, the attention will be turned exclusively to hedging motives.

2 Markets for interest and currency derivatives

The markets for derivatives are dominated by interest and currency derivatives. Both, the over-the-counter and the exchange-traded market for derivatives, are of great importance although the over-the-counter (OTC) market is obviously much larger than the exchange-traded market. OTC markets do not operate in a specific fixed location. Trading on OTC markets implies that the terms of the contract are not specified by an exchange. Exchange-traded derivatives involve a high grade of standardization, i.e., regarding the underlying asset, the quantity of the asset per contract, where delivery will be made and when, and the clearing and margining process.

The Bank for International Settlements (BIS) collects data in both markets. In figure 1 it can be seen that swaps play the most important role in the OTC market for both interest and currency derivatives. Indicated by the turnover statistics in figure 2, futures are dominating the exchange-traded market [2].

Instruments	Notional amounts outstanding		Gross market values	
	Dec 2005	Dec 2006	Dec 2005	Dec 2006
Interest rate contracts	211,970	291,987	5,397	4,834
Forward rate agreements	14,269	18,689	22	31
Interest rate swaps	169,106	229,780	4,778	4,166
Options	28,596	43,518	597	636
Foreign exchange contracts	31,364	40,179	997	1,262
Forwards and forex swaps	15,873	19,828	406	467
Currency swaps	8,504	10,772	453	599
Options	6,987	9,579	138	196
Equity-linked contracts	5,793	7,485	582	851
Commodity contracts	5,434	6,938	871	667
Credit default swaps	13,908	28,838	243	470
Others	29,199	39,755	1,659	1,610
Total contracts	**297,670**	**415,183**	**9,749**	**9,695**

Over-the-counter derivatives

Fig. 1: *Amounts outstanding of Over-the-counter derivatives (in US$ bn)*

Instruments	Amounts outstanding		Turnover	
	Dec 2005	Mar 2007	2005	2006
Interest rate				
Futures	20,708.8	28,737.5	939,590.2	1,169,320.7
Options	31,588.3	48,533.5	328,778.9	446,103.8
Currency				
Futures	107.6	48,533.5	328,778.9	446,103.8
Options	66.1	82.8	943.7	1,119.9

Exchange-traded derivatives

Fig. 2: *Derivative financial instruments traded on organized exchanges; notional principal (in US$ bn)*

3   Interest derivatives

3.1   Interest rate options

Hedging is characterized by all measures taken to achieve protection towards existing exchange rate risks. These actions include the creation of positions that offset the effects of exchange rate changes on already existing or anticipated exposures as well as the matching of exposures to minimize these effects. Hence, the motivation for hedging can be seen in the wish for security and risk avoidance, respectively. Speculation can be defined as all measures taken that aim on the realization of profits by departing from the obtainable risk minimizing position.

If a corporation's hedging actions are assessed from a utility viewpoint, hedging specifies measures that maximize the expected utility of a decision maker in such way that the amount of expected cash inflows denominated in home currency will not be influenced. In this context, speculation is characterized by actions taken on foreign exchange markets aiming at increasing expected positive payments.

Options on interest rates Caps and floors are basic OTC option contracts on interest rates. A cap contract, or for short a cap, is an option that provides a payoff when a specified interest rate is above a certain level (strike, cap), a floor provides a payoff when the rate is below a certain level (strike, floor). The specified interest rate is a floating rate like the London Interbank Offered Rate LIBOR or the Euro Interbank Offered Rate EURIBOR that is reset periodically. The component of a cap (floor) that refers to one period is called a caplet (floorlet). Caps and floors are purchased for a premium and typically have expirations between one and seven years. They may make payments to the holder on a monthly, quarterly or semiannual basis. Each period, the payment is determined by comparing the current level of the reference interest rate with the certain level (cap respectively floor). If the reference interest rate exceeds respectively falls below the cap respectively floor rate, the payment is based upon the difference between the two rates:

$$\text{(reference interest rate} - \text{cap rate)} \cdot \text{(notional amount)} \cdot \frac{\text{actual days}}{360}$$

$$\text{(floor rate} - \text{reference interest rate)} \cdot \text{(notional amount)} \cdot \frac{\text{actual days}}{360}$$

The relevant parameters of a cap (floor) contract are therefore the reference interest rate, the strike level, the notional amount, the time to maturity divided in a fixed number of periods with a specified length and the premium that the holder of the option has to pay.

Caps A cap might be purchased by an issuer of a floating rate debt note who wishes to protect from the increased financial costs that would result from a rise in interest rates. If the reference interest rate lies below the cap, no payment is made for this period (see figure 3). Obviously, a cap has some similarities to a call option. The cap is in-the-money above and out-of-the-money below a specified strike level and can be used to hedge against the rise in the underlying variable. In figure 4 the payoffs of three basic positions (spot, derivative, and

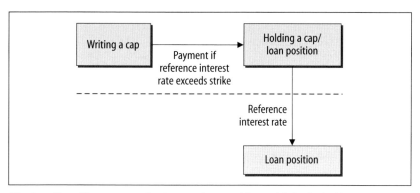

Fig. 3: *Payoff structure of a borrowing position with included interest rate cap*

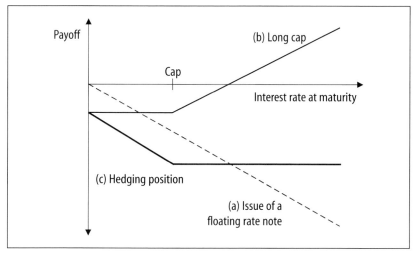

Fig. 4: *Payoffs from the positions of (a) issuing a floating rate debt, (b) buying a cap, and (c) the resulting interest rate hedge*

resulting hedge) of a standard interest rate hedge are given in dependence of one interest rate fixing date, the maturity date.

Floors

Interest rate floors compare to interest rate caps in the same way that puts compare to calls. Consistently, floors might be used by purchasers of floating rate debt notes who wish to protect themselves from the loss of income that would result from a decline in interest rates (see figure 5).

Collars

End users may also short one interest rate option against another to reduce the premium costs of the above discussed protections against interest rate risk. The combination of such two options results in the position of an inexpensive collar contract. A long collar is the result of the combination of a long cap with a short floor, just as a short collar is the result of the combination of writing a cap and buying a floor (see figure 6).

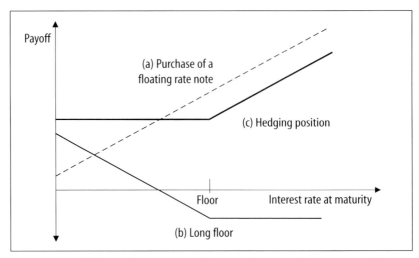

Fig. 5:   *Payoffs from the positions of (a) purchasing a floating rate debt,*
           (b) buying a floor, and (c) the resulting interest rate hedge

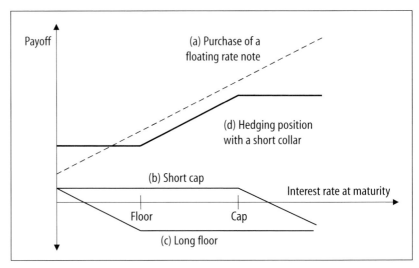

Fig. 6:   *Payoffs from the positions of (a) purchasing a floating rate debt,*
           (b) writing a cap, (c) buying a floor, and (d) the resulting short
           collar hedge

Zero cost collars   In the case that the parameters of the cap and floor can be chosen in a way
that their premiums are identical, the resulting collar position requires no
premium. For short, one speaks of a costless collar position, the so-called
zero cost collar. In figure 7 the "long-"version of such a zero cost collar is
illustrated.

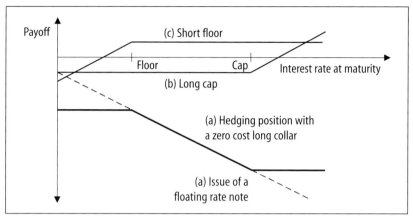

Fig. 7:   *Payoffs from the positions of (a) issuing a floating rate debt,*
(b) buying a cap, (c) writing a floor, and (d) the resulting zero cost
long collar hedge

3.2   **Forward rate agreements**

A forward contract is an agreement between a buyer and a seller to buy or sell
a prespecified amount of an asset at a certain future time for a certain price.
Thus, a forward rate agreement (FRA) is a cash-settled forward contract on a
short-term loan. For example, a 3×9 FRA is a 3-month forward on a 6-month
loan. The interest rate on the loan, called the FRA rate, is set when the contract
is first entered into. Contracts settle with a single cash payment made on the
first day of the underlying loan, which is called the settlement date (maturity
or delivery date).

On the settlement date, the party that is long on the FRA, called the borrower,
receives from respectively has to pay to the lender the amount

Payoff of an FRA

$$(\text{notional amount}) \cdot \frac{(\text{reference interest rate} - \text{FRA rate}) \cdot \dfrac{\text{days}}{\text{basis}}}{(1 + \text{reference interest rate}) \cdot \dfrac{\text{days}}{\text{basis}}}$$

Although they are traded over-the-counter, forward rate agreements have fairly
standardized contract provisions. As a hedging vehicle, they are very similar
to futures but have the advantage that they can be traded for any maturity
date. In contrast to the option positions above, forward rate agreements are
unconditional derivatives with a so-called symmetric risk-return profile (see
figure 8)

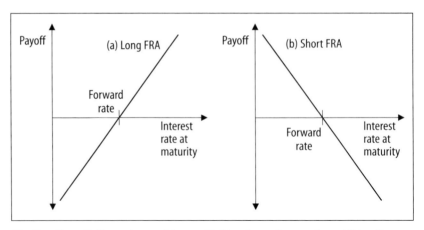

Fig. 8:   *Payoffs from the positions of (a) buying a forward, and (b) selling a forward*

3.3   Swaps

Interest rate swaps are one of the most widely used financial derivatives for managing interest rate risk. Swaps are unconditional risk management instruments, too. A swap is a contract between two counterparties to exchange (or "swap") the cash flows of one security for the cash flows of another security. The swap contract contains specifications of the applicable rate of interest to each such payment. The most common swap is a plain vanilla interest rate swap. By this swap, a party agrees to pay cash flows equal to interest at a predetermined fixed rate on a notional amount for a number of periods. In return, it receives interest at a floating rate on the same notional amount for the same period of time. By that, a swap can be seen as a series of forward contracts combined into one contract. Therefore, the payoff pattern of a swap is identical to forward contracts.

Plain vanilla interest rate swaps   The party that pays the fixed interest rate is called the payer, the party that receives the fixed rate is called the receiver of the swap contract. The floating rate in most agreements is the LIBOR or the EURIBOR. A plain vanilla interest rate swap may be used to transform liabilities from one party to another. In figure 9 a typical situation is illustrated: A company (the "payer") uses a swap to transform a floating rate loan into a fixed rate loan. In exchange, the receiver realizes the effect of transforming a fixed rate loan into a floating rate loan.

Comparative advantages   A popular argument to explain the huge market for swaps concerns comparative advantages. Some companies might have advantages when borrowing in fixed rate markets, whereas others have advantages in floating rate markets. If these advantages are of a comparative style, it makes sense for the companies to go into these markets and to use a swap to transform their loans. An opposite position and criticism of the comparative advantage argument is that the swap market is established for a long time and is of high liquidity and informational efficiency so that such price inefficiencies and arbitrage opportunities really can not exist anymore [3].

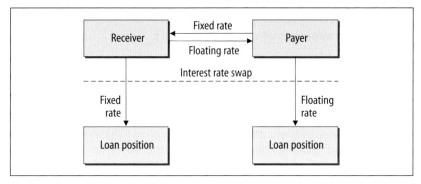

Fig. 9:   Transforming liabilities by an interest rate swap

3.4   Futures and options on futures

Like a forward, a futures contract is an agreement between a buyer and a seller to buy or sell a prespecified amount of an asset at a certain future time for a certain price. Futures contracts are traded on an exchange. Therefore, they are standardized unconditional instruments and are integrated in the clearing and margining system of an exchange.

Interest rate futures refer to short-term interest rates or bonds respectively long-term interest rates. Succesful interest rate futures are traded in the US at the exchanges in Chicago. In Europe, the London exchange offers a broad range of short-term futures, whereas the trade in the popular German Bund Futures is concentrated at the European exchange EUREX. At these exchanges, market participants also have the opportunity to take on an option position that insures the right to buy or sell a future contract during a specified time period.

Long-term interest rate futures offer the seller of the contract to deliver any of the eligible issues on any date during the delivery month, a so-called delivery option. To remove the effects of different bonds having different parameters, the exchanges are prepared to have a system of conversion factors. In practice, however, one of the eligible delivery bonds is cheapest to deliver because the system of conversion factors is not exact. Only in the case that the term structure of interest rates is flat, all bonds will be equally desirable for delivery. These problems in relation with the cheapest to deliver CTD bond has received a great deal of attention in the relevant literature, also because bond futures are one of the most widely traded derivatives at exchanges [4]. The hedge ratio, i. e., the number of futures contracts that must be sold in hedging the interest rate risk of a long bond portfolio, regarding the duration of the underlying portfolio and the cheapest to deliver bond, can be calculated as follows:

Cheapest to deliver CTD

$$
\text{Hede ratio} = \frac{\text{Market value of bond portfolio}}{\text{Spot price of CTD bond} \cdot \text{Contract value}} \cdot
$$
$$
\frac{\text{Duration of bond portfolio}}{\text{Duration CTD bond}} \cdot \text{CTD conversion factor}
$$

4   Currency derivatives

4.1   Components of exchange rate risk

Currency risks for corporations arise from all those activities of a corporation that are carried out outside the firm's currency area. Currency risks are a result of exchange rate fluctuations as well as the unforeseeable extent of exchange rate changes. The inability to predict exchange rate changes as well as the extent of these changes create uncertainties for corporations in regard to potential losses. In line with these findings, currency risk can be defined as the uncertainty regarding future movements of exchange rates. The exchange rate is the price of one currency measured in terms of another currency. Direct quotation displays the number of domestic currency per unit of foreign currency. Indirect quotation displays the number of foreign currency units per unit of domestic currency.

Exchange rate risk   The term "exchange rate risk" (ERR) is defined in many different ways [5][6]. One possible definition describes ERR as the probability distribution of future uncertain exchange rates that affect the value calculated in home currency of certain financial positions. This definition emphasizes the fact that future exchange rates typically are not known for certain in advance. In addition, it states that the knowledge of corporations as to future exchange rates is limited to a probability distribution of future exchange rate changes. A requirement for exchange rate risk and currency risk in general to arise is the existence of a financial position that is affected by possible exchange rate changes. Such a financial position is called currency exposure or, for short, exposure. An exposure represents a target for exchange rate risk. It is a result of real business and the financial activities of a corporation.

Price and quantity risk   Based on these statements, two parameters can be identified that affect the financial positions of a corporation:

- Price risk results from unexpected changes in future exchange rates. This risk is determined by the maturity of planned cash flows as well as the currency of denomination. The longer the maturity the longer is the duration in which possible exchange rate changes can affect cash flows.

- Quantity risk refers to the uncertain size of cash flows. It is the risk that actual exposures are different from expected exposures [7]. It is determined by the volume of exposed financial positions denominated in foreign currency.

Furthermore, it is important to differentiate between nominal and real exchange rate changes. The nominal exchange rate is defined as the price of a unit of foreign currency measured in domestic currency. The real exchange rate is defined as the nominal exchange rate corrected for relative prices [8].

Convertibility and transfer risk   Other types of currency risk are the convertibility risk and the transfer risk. Convertibility risk arises when currency regulators restrict the conversion of currencies. These restrictions can limit volumes and conversion dates. An additional source of risk facing an internationally operating corporation is transfer risk. Transfer risk arises from official restrictions on transferring funds from one currency area into another.

The two basic concepts of quantifying exposure are translation exposure and economic exposure [9]. Translation exposure results from the need to convert the financial statements of foreign subsidiaries from the foreign currency to the home currency of the corporation, for the purpose of reporting and consolidation. If the translation of a financial position, such as assets, liabilities, revenues, expenses, gains and losses in the future, will be carried out with the spot rate then prevailing, which is not known for certain in advance, the value of that position in the home currency will be uncertain as well. The possible extent of the gains or losses of reported financial positions due to an exchange rate change is measured by the translation exposure.

Translation and economic exposure

The concept of economic exposure focuses on cash flows. It includes already booked receivables and payables denominated in a foreign currency as well as all potential future cash flows which have, at the time of assessment, uncertain volumes that depend on the development of the exchange rate. Hence, the economic exposure represents possible fluctuations of future cash flows in home currency that are caused by changes in the exchange rate. The economic exposure concept extends the measurement of risk to the long run. Therefore, it also intends to describe the consequences of exchange rate changes on the competitive position of a corporation. Thus, it includes both parameters of exchange rate risk, price risk and quantity risk.

The economic exposure concept embodies all cash flows of a corporation. These cash flows can have differing characterizations that make it necessary to further subdivide economic exposure. Contingent exposure, for example, arises when a corporation takes part in invitations to tender and makes a contractually binding bid for a contract that will create cash flows denominated in foreign currency at some later date. The outcome of the tendering procedure will only be known at a future date. Therefore, a position that is exposed to exchange rate risk is created only when the corporation obtains the contract. Operating exposure originates from the effects of currency fluctuations on a company's revenues and costs and therefore on the operating cash flows. The operating exposure is a long-term measure of the effect of exchange rate changes on a corporation's cost and price competitiveness. A corporation is exposed to operating risk when it is engaged in a market that is subject to foreign competition or when it sources inputs in a foreign market. If transactions take place at several future dates, rather than at one date in the planning period, the transaction exposure of a corporation includes these certain, future foreign currency cash flows. Thus, the transaction exposure has a temporal structure. This characteristic of the transaction exposure can be recorded and presented by a system, that shows the balance of foreign currency cash inflows and outflows, called exposure report. This presentation of the transaction exposure is similar to a liquidity or a financial plan.

Components of economic exposure

4.2   Currency options – plain vanilla and exotic

Currency hedging with external instruments has become more popular in industrial companies in the last years [10]. Derivatives like forwards, futures, swaps, vanilla and exotic options offer a wide variety of possible strategies to hedge against the economic exposure, i. e., transaction and contingent risks.

Corridors Currency options are contracts that give the holder the right, but not the obligation, to buy or sell an underlying currency at a prespecified price for a specified time period. In return for the possibility of not having to exercise a contract, an option premium has to be paid to the seller by the contracts' buyer. In combining plain vanilla call or put options once again it is possible to construct inexpensive low-cost strategies like collars and zero-cost collars. Another example of an inexpensive option combination is the corridor strategy. The corridor is the result of the combination of two calls or two puts with different strike prices. Opposite to the collar strategy, the corridor is a position where the exposure is hedged between the two strikes. If the exchange rate at maturity lies below the lower strike price or exceeds the higher strike price, the holder of the corridor does not enter into an exchange rate hedge (see figure 10).

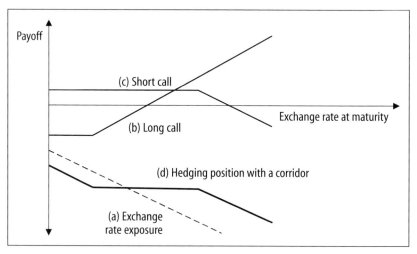

Fig. 10: Payoffs from the positions of (a) the exchange rate exposure,
(b) buying a call, (c) selling a call, and (d) the resulting corridor hedge

Plain vanilla vs. In addition to plain vanilla calls and puts, a number of non-standard, or exotic,
exotic options options have been created for exchange rate risk management. In general, these products have been designed to meet specific needs of buyers which plain vanilla products could not satisfy. Exotic options are applied by corporations in situations where a standard derivative cannot hedge the corporation's exposures as efficiently. Exotic options are a further development of plain vanilla options. The creation of exotic options brings about a modification of basic elements of plain vanilla options:

- The assessment of whether to exercise a plain vanilla option involves the examination of the market price of only one underlying asset. By contrast, exotic options can have several underlying assets that influence the decision to exercise.

- The payoff of a plain vanilla option is a linear function of the market price of the underlying when the option is exercised. This implies that when the option is exercised, the payoff of a standard option will be higher by one currency unit when the market price of the underlying is higher by one currency. Exotic options can have a payoff that is a non-linear function of the underlying when the exotic option is exercised.

- The payoff of an exercised standard option is determined solely by the market price of the underlying asset at maturity. By contrast, the payoff of an exotic option can be determined by the market price of the underlying at several dates or time periods.

- The right of a holder of a long position in a plain vanilla option to exercise the option is limited solely by the exercise date. Exotic options can put additional constraints on the holder by linking the right to exercise to specific conditions, such as the performance of the underlying asset.

Examples of exotic options

Based on these possible modifications to standard options, a large number of different exotic options have been created, especially for the case of currency options [11]. Average rate options, for example, fall into the category of so-called path-dependent exotic options. Contrary to a plain vanilla option, the payoff from an average rate option is determined by the difference between the average price of the underlying asset over a certain time period and the price at maturity. There are several possibilities for the averaging process: The averaging sample can be taken weekly, monthly or over any other prespecified time period, the averaging period can cover the entire life of the option or another prespecified subperiod, or either an arithmetic or a geometric average can be calculated. Which method will be used is generally determined by the specifications of the exposure of the average rate option purchaser. Since most exotic options are created to closely match the needs of the option buyers, they are almost exclusively traded on OTC markets.

An advantage of exotic options is that they allow to hedge complex cash flow structures requiring lower premiums than plain vanilla options. Academic literature on derivatives proposes the application of average rate options in exposure situations, e.g., where a corporation receives cash inflows at previously determined dates throughout a year and the corporation's management attempts to participate in favorable exchange rate developments. The advantage of average rate options over plain vanilla options in such case is that average rate options are cheaper. Premiums of average rate options are lower, because the average of the underlying asset price is less volatile than the underlying price on a specific date [12].

4.3   Currency forwards and swaps

Covered interest rate parity   Currency forwards can be characterized in the same way as forward rate agreements. A currency forward (FX forward) locks in the price at which an entity can buy or sell a currency on a future date. The forward rate for currencies is determined by the covered interest rate parity

Forward exchange rate =

$$\text{Current spot exchange rate} \times \frac{\left(1+\text{interest rate in the quoted currency} \times \dfrac{\text{days}}{\text{basis}_{\text{quoted}}}\right)}{\left(1+\text{interest rate in the base currency} \times \dfrac{\text{days}}{\text{basis}_{\text{base}}}\right)}$$

Forwards are the most important exchange rate risk hedging instruments for non-financial corporations. Forwards on the most important currencies are available at all over-the-counter markets and can be entered into with most major national and international banks, without requiring additional agents as intermediary. A disadvantage is that the secondary market for these products might be small, if it does exist at all. Therefore, once a currency forward is entered into, it generally cannot be sold to close the position. Nevertheless, a closing of the forward contract can be achieved by entering into another forward contract that offsets the original position. However, the terms of the offsetting contract are subject to the then prevailing market conditions. This implies that the offsetting position is likely not to completely match the original position.

Counterparty and country risk   In taking positions in forward contracts, corporations accept the risk that the counterparty will not fulfill its obligations from the contract. A common reason for this to happen is that the counterparty becomes financially distressed or has to file for bankruptcy. An implementable way of assessing the pre-settlement risk inherent to forward contracts for corporations is to evaluate the counterparty's liquidity and creditworthiness by its rating. Country risk is the risk that a country will impose restrictions on the transfer of currencies and thereby makes it impossible for two banks to carry out the terms of their forward contract.

Currency swaps   In the academic literature currency swaps are proposed to hedge exposures to currencies in certain situations. In fact, empirical research on the use of derivatives reports that swaps are the second most applied derivative for currency risk management for non-financial corporations. Currency swaps can daily be entered into with banks as an intermediary, which assumes the role of the counterparty to the swap. The general framework of entering into swaps with a bank is set by the international master agreement of the International Swap and Derivatives Association. By entering into a swap agreement with a bank, the financial institution takes over the risk of counterparty default.

A basic form of a currency swap involves exchanging a principal payment and interest payments on one currency for principal and interest payments in another currency. The principal amounts are specified for each of the two currencies in the contract. The amount of the interest payments is based on the principal. The procedure of applying currency swaps with a bank typically includes three steps:

- First, the principal amounts, which are agreed at the commencement of the contract, are exchanged between the two parties in two different currencies at the prevailing spot rate.

- During the term of the contract, interest payments on the principal amounts are exchanged at prespecified dates.

- Finally, principal amounts are re-exchanged at maturity at the forward rate prevailing at initiation of the swap.

This procedure shows the main field of application of a currency swap, which is to manage temporal liquidity needs arising in two different currencies.

4.4   Futures

Futures contracts also fall in the category of unconditional external instruments for exchange rate risk management. Futures contracts have the same payoff structures as forward contracts. The difference between the futures and the forwards contract can be seen in the markets they are traded on as well as in the standardization of futures contracts. Futures exchanges provide mechanisms which guarantee that the contract will be honored by futures sellers and buyers. The risk of the counterparty defaulting for a futures seller or buyer is eliminated by the interposition of an exchange clearinghouse, also called clearinghouse. The clearinghouse acts as an intermediary in futures transaction by creating offsetting positions to every contract. If a contract is entered into, the clearinghouse of the futures exchange takes the counterparty position for the futures buyer as well as the seller. It guarantees both parties that the contract will be honored. That way, the clearinghouse takes over the risk of counterparty default from market participants. The clearinghouse in turn takes measures to minimize the risk of default by setting margins.

Liquidity risk

Euro-Dollar futures contracts can be bought and sold, e. g., at the International Money Market or the New York Cotton Exchange. Trading futures contracts is conducted through a futures broker, with a membership in the futures exchange. These brokers can be contacted through intermediaries. Despite the general possibility of conducting a transaction exposure hedge with futures, specific features of this instrument can be identified that make it disadvantageous for most non-financial corporations. Implementing a futures hedge creates liquidity risk for a corporation, due to the margin requirements of the futures exchange. If, for example, one currency appreciates, the value of the expected cash inflows from one party increases. Thus, the party gains on this position. If this exposure is hedged with a futures contract, the corporation simultaneously loses on the futures position by the same amount. The crucial difference is that losses on the futures position have to be levelled out at the same day by adding additional funds to the margin account, whereas gains in the value of the expected cash inflows might be accounting profits. Therefore, these gains do not necessarily result in cash flows that can be used to balance losses on the futures position prior to the delivery date. Hence, by entering into a futures position, a company needs to take the impact of marking-to-market on cash funds into consideration. As a consequence, the corporation needs to keep funds available to meet margin calls or have the prearranged capability of financing these cash flows.

Basis risk and cross-hedging

Other questions and resulting problems in hedging exchange rate risk exposures must be considered [13]:

- Does the volume or a multiple of the volume of the futures contract fit exactly to the existing spot position?

- Does the maturity date of the future fit to the time horizon of the exposure position or is there any time incongruence?

- Does the exchange even list futures contracts with the requested currency underlying?

Therefore, a basis risk might occur in hedging a currency exposure with currency futures. Cross-hedging occurs if the currency underlying the futures contract differs from the currency exposure. In some sense, thus, by cross-hedging one can speak of an indirect hedge against ones foreign exchange risk exposure. When cross-hedging is used, the hedger should have in mind the correlation between the two currencies, i.e., he or she should choose a value for the hedge ratio that minimizes the variance of the value of the hedged position [14].

5   Bibliography

[1] Rudolph, B./Schäfer, K., Derivative Finanzmarktinstrumente, Berlin et al. 2005, p. 15.

[2] Bank for International Settlements BIS (Ed.), International Banking and Financial Market Developments, Quarterly Review, June 2007, p. A 103, A 108.

[3] Hull, J. C., Options, Futures, and Other Derivatives, 6th edition, Upper Saddle River, New Jersey 2006, pp. 157–159.

[4] Stoll, H. R./Whaley, R. E., Futures and Options, Cincinnati, Ohio 1993, pp. 144–148.

[5] Breuer, W., Unternehmerisches Währungsmanagement, Wiesbaden 2000, p. 117.

[6] Pfennig, M., Optimale Steuerung des Währungsrisikos mit derivativen Instrumenten, Wiesbaden 1998, p. 11.

[7] Stulz, R. M., Risk Management & Derivatives, Mason, Ohio 2003, p. 224.

[8] Copeland, L., Exchange Rates and International Finance, Essex 2000, p. 70.

[9] Adler, M./Dumas, B., Exposure to Currency Risk: Definition and Measurement, in: Financial Management, vol. 13, pp. 41–50.

[10] Gebhardt, G./Ruß, O., Einsatz von derivativen Finanzinstrumenten im Risikomanagement deutscher Industrieunternehmen, in: Gebhardt, G./ Pellens, B. (Ed.), Sonderheft 41 der Zeitschrift für betriebswirtschaftliche Forschung, Düsseldorf/Frankfurt 1999, pp. 23–83.

[11] Adam-Müller, A. F. A., Merkmale und Einsatz von exotischen Optionen, in: Franke G. (Ed.), Bewertung und Einsatz von Finanzderivaten, Sonderheft 38 der Zeitschrift für betriebswirtschaftliche Forschung, Düsseldorf/Frankfurt 1997, pp. 89–125.

[12] Galitz, L., Financial Engineering: Tools and Techniques to Manage Financial Risks, London 1995, p. 296.

[13] Shapiro, A., Multinational Financial Management, New York 2003.

[14] Hull, J. C., Options, Futures, and Other Derivatives, 6th edition, Upper Saddle River, New Jersey 2006, pp. 56–60.

2 Commercial real estate derivatives

Jeffrey D. Fisher
David Geltner

Table of contents

1   Introduction

Growing interest in derivatives   Despite the tremendous growth in the use of derivatives for commodities, stocks, interest rates, currency and other applications, the availability of derivatives for commercial real estate has been limited. When you consider that real estate assets comprise over one-third of the value of all of the underlying physical capital in the world, the potential for real estate derivatives is impressive. It is therefore not surprising that in recent years real estate derivatives have begun to develop, as market participants have realized the role that derivatives can play, investment banks have been willing to offer derivatives, and new indices have been developed that are designed to meet the needs of the evolving real estate derivatives market.

Methodology   This chapter discusses the type of derivatives now being offered for commercial real estate including total return swaps, forward contracts, and structured notes. Such products address several of the classical problems that have been raised regarding real estate investment, including: high transactions and management costs, lack of liquidity, inability to sell short, and difficulty making well-diversified property investments whose returns are measured in a manner comparable to those of stocks and bonds. This chapter also discusses the fundamentals of real estate return indexes used to support derivatives including the both appraisal-based and transactions-based indexes.

2   Uses and users of commercial real estate derivatives

There are a myriad of potential uses of real estate derivatives by different market participants. Examples are exposure to the real estate asset class, hedge existing exposure, harvesting alpha, portfolio balancing, real value investing, and efficient leverage.

Real estate market participants

2.1   Exposure to the real estate asset class

Derivatives provide a way for investors to get exposure to the commercial real estate asset class relatively quickly, with relatively low transaction or management costs and relatively high diversification. This can be particularly useful for investors who lack the expertise to either purchase and manage individual properties directly, or find and manage specialized investment managers or real estate property funds. For example, a foreign investor who wants immediate, well-diversified exposure to the US real estate market may want to take a long position on a real estate derivative such as a forward contract or a swap that is based on a national real estate index. Purchasing the derivative results in the equivalent of exposure to a well-diversified portfolio of properties and hence very little if any unsystematic risk without incurring the costs of purchasing and managing properties. Similarly, a small pension fund may want exposure to a well-diversified portfolio of real estate but lacks the scale to purchase enough individual properties to be well-diversified by property type and location, and lacks the expertise to choose among property funds with their various investment management and transaction fees.

Advantages of derivatives in real estate

Investment managers who find they are over exposed to the real estate asset class, perhaps because real estate has performed well compared to their stock and bond portfolio, or because they have a relatively bearish outlook for real estate, may want to take a short position in a derivative to reduce their exposure to real estate without the need to sell properties, or until transactions can be completed on the sale of properties (which can take time to market and close). Shorting the derivative can also lock in profits made in the real estate market so the investment manager does not risk a drop in value before the properties can be sold. Lenders and originators of Commercial Mortgage Backed Securities (CMBS), exposed to either "warehouse" or portfolio risk, can hedge using a short position in forwards or swaps, or by purchasing a put option, based on real estate indexes. Credit default swaps can also be designed that result in a payoff to the party purchasing the swap that is triggered by the index declining below a certain level.

Short position

2.2   Harvesting alpha

Real estate investment managers who have the expertise to acquire, manage, and sell properties so as to persistently outperform the real estate market can monetize such positive alpha without selling properties, and produce profitable returns even when the real estate market turns down, by using the short position in the derivative to effectively "cover" their real estate market exposure, a "risk management" tool that acts effectively like real estate market value "insurance". This allows the investment manager to focus on his area

Risk management tool

of specialized expertise and comparative advantage, dealing and managing in the real estate market, regardless of the current ebbs or flows in the capital markets.

2.3   Portfolio balancing

Property type diversification

Real estate portfolio managers may also feel that their allocation to different property types or geographic locations has gotten out of balance. For example, they may feel that they are over exposed to office properties and under exposed to retail properties. They may enter into a swap with a counterparty where they pay the office returns on an index of office properties and receive the return on an index of retail properties. Similarly, an investor could swap returns on an index of properties in the east with an index of properties in the west.

2.4   Relative value investing

Capture of perceived mispricing

Hedge funds and other more opportunistic investors may feel that they can identify which property sectors or geographic locations will outperform others. Thus, they may enter into different long and short positions on derivatives to try to capture the perceived mispricing. They would not necessarily have any desire to own and manage the physical real estate.

2.5   Efficient leverage

Lower-cost method of leverage

As forward and futures contracts do not in themselves require up-front cash investment, such derivatives can be used in effect to take levered positions in real estate if the investor does not fully cover the derivative position with bond investment. Depending on circumstances, this may present a lower-cost method of levering the investment, compared to traditional real estate debt.

3   Examples

3.1   Example 1: Forward contract

Diversification across countries

Suppose a foreign investor wants to quickly get exposure to the real estate market in a foreign country that has index-based derivatives. To take a specific example, suppose a European investor wants immediate exposure to the US real estate market, for diversification purposes, but does not have the time and expertise to identify individual properties and be sure he is also diversified within the United States. He enters into a long position on a 2-year forward contract based on a national real estate index. The index is currently at 100. He has seen forecasts for the index ranging from 105 to 115 in two years. He agrees on a forward price of 105 that he will pay at the end of the two years in order to receive a payment based on the actual change in the index. The contract pays US$ 500,000 times the index value. No cash payment is made today although a margin or bond may be required. The magnitude of the required margin or bond posting is relatively small, and may earn interest. The required posting would normally be related to the likely magnitude of change in the value of the index over the relevant derivative contract period, rather than to the magnitude of the overall notional amount of the trade, and thus allows the investor to obtain very high effective leverage unless the notional amount of the trade is otherwise covered by up-front cash investment (e.g., in bonds).

Suppose that at the end of the two years the index is 115 (upper end of forecast). The investor will receive US$ 500,000 · (115 – 105) = US$ 5 million. On the other hand, if at the end of the two years the index is 95 (bad forecast!) the investor will pay US$ 500,000 · (95 – 105) = US$ –5 million.

There will also be a counterparty to the above transaction, who has the short position, the other side of the position the foreign investor took. The short position receives the opposite cash flows in the previous example, receiving US$ 5 million when the index is 95 and paying US$ 5 million when it is 115. The short might be, for example, a CMBS issuer who wants to hedge its warehouse risk, a hedge fund that believed the low end of the forecast was more likely, or an investment manager seeking to "harvest alpha" (explained next). The CMBS issuer trying to hedge "warehouse risk" (loan pools or securities held temporarily awaiting sale) would probably prefer to use a periodically cash-settled swap rather than a 2-year forward (because "warehoused" loans are not held very long, though the CMBS issuer may typically always have some warehoused loans on hand). Swaps will be described shortly. **Counterparty of transaction**

3.2 Example 2: Harvesting alpha example

A specialized real estate asset management fund believes it can purchase, manage, and sell properties so as to consistently outperform the real estate index that underlies the derivative (and with same risk), based on the manager's specialized expertise. They want to harvest this positive "alpha" from these excess returns whether the market is up or down. Since the investment manager cannot control the market, but can (presumably) control its alpha (based on its specialized expertise), the idea is for the manager to profit from the activity they can control and are particularly good at, while laying off risk exposure to factors they cannot control. This is a classical type of "risk management" for an investment management firm. To hedge exposure on US$ 50 million worth of properties the manager owns, for example, the manager would sell (short) US$ 50 million notional value of the forward contract on the index that we described in the previous example. For that portion of the fund's property holdings, the fund is "market neutral": they have laid off their "beta" market risk exposure by their offsetting positions in the forward short and their covering property holdings. This leaves them with only their alpha, the difference between their property performance and the market (index) performance, and with any "basis risk", systematic or non-systematic differences between the ex post performance of their property holdings and the market (index) not due to the manager's actions. **Outperform the market indexes**

Suppose at the end of the two years the fund's portfolio increased in value by 20 % (including income reinvested in the fund). Suppose the index rose to 115 over the two years (i. e., the fund beats the index by 500 basis points). **Calculation**

Appreciation on portfolio	US$ 10,000,000
Loss on short futures	US$ 5,000,000
Net gain	US$ 5,000,000

Suppose at the end of the two years the hedge fund's portfolio decreased in value by 2 % while the index decreased to 95 (i. e., the fund beats the market by 300 basis points).

Loss on portfolio	US$ 1,000,000
Gain on short futures	US$ 5,000,000
Net gain	US$ 4,000,000

The fund thus gains in this example between US$ 4 and US$ 5 million whether the market increases or decreases, based purely on the positive alpha obtained on the fund's properties. In this extreme example of fully hedging the US$ 50 million amount (and with no basis risk), the fund has been turned into an "alpha machine" that makes (or loses) money purely on its differential performance relative to the index, a differential that purely reflects the fund manager's particular expertise and skill at the property and deal level relative to the index. This "disarticulates" performance based on real estate expertise from performance based on the movements and forces and flows of the broader financial capital market that may move the real estate asset market one way or another at any given time.

3.3   Example 3: Capital return swap example

Index capital in return for a fixed leg

An open end fund has funds to invest but has not identified properties they wanted to purchase. They believe that the return on an index that tracks changes in property values will be stronger over the next two years than most market participants believe. They decide to take a long position in a real estate index capital return as a swap where they receive the index capital return and pay a fixed leg each quarter. Recall that the capital return is the change in property value. Suppose they can purchase the capital return and pay a fixed leg of 50 basis points. The notional amount of the swap is US$ 100 million. Suppose the actual capital return over the next eight quarters is as shown in figure 1. In the first quarter the capital return is 2 % so the fund receives 2 % of US$ 100 million or US$ 2 million. They pay 0.5 % of US$ 100 million or US$ 500,000 on the fixed leg. Thus, they net US$ 1.5 million. Note that in the last four quarters they end up paying money because the capital return did

Quarter	Capital return	Long receives (US$ million)	Long pays (US$ million)	Net to long (US$ million)
1	2.00 %	2.0	0.5	1.5
2	1.50 %	1.5	0.5	1.0
3	1.00 %	1.0	0.5	0.5
4	0.50 %	0.5	0.5	0.0
5	−1.00 %	−1.0	0.5	−1.5
6	0.00 %	0.0	0.5	−0.5
7	0.50 %	0.5	0.5	0.0
8	−0.50 %	−0.5	0.5	−1.0

Fig. 1:   Capital return swap example

not cover the fixed leg. They end up netting zero over the eight quarters, no doubt not as well as they had hoped in this case, but this reflects the real estate market risk that is represented in the index. Perhaps the market performed worse than this investor had hoped, or perhaps they agreed to a fixed leg that was too high. (See Geltner/Fisher (2008) for the pricing principles for real estate index swaps.)

4 Real estate indexes

4.1 Introduction

Creating derivatives for commercial real estate requires the availability of indexes that are the basis for calculating the payoffs to the parties in the derivative transaction. Commercial real estate equity derivatives have taken off first in the United Kingdom and Europe, based on indexes produced by the Investment Property Databank (IPD). The oldest index for commercial real estate investment performance in the United States is the NCREIF Property Index (NPI) published by the National Council of Real Estate Investment Fiduciaries. The NPI is similar to the IPD indexes in that it is an appraisal-based index. The NPI has returns available on a quarterly basis since 1978 and as of the end of 2006 included almost US$ 250 billion in real estate. More recently other indexes have been created to meet the needs of having a viable derivative market in the United States, including indices based on real estate transactions developed initially at the Massachusetts Institute of Technology (MIT).

Overview of real estate indexes

In order to have good derivative contracts, we need good indexes underlying the contracts. A property derivative contract is no better than the index upon which it is based. It is probably impossible to have a perfect index to use for commercial real estate derivatives. Unlike stock indices that can be used for futures contracts, it is not possible to invest in all or even a few of the properties used for a real estate index because the properties are held by many different investors in different types of investment vehicles that are privately held. Furthermore, properties do not transact on a frequent basis like stocks to be able to simply measure the change in value of each property in the index based on daily, monthly, quarterly or even annual transaction prices. There are two main ways of dealing with the fact that the same property does not transact frequently. The first is to have an index based on appraisals of the property on a quarterly basis. This is the basis for the NCREIF Property Index mentioned above. The second way of creating an index is to base it on the transactions that do occur for properties and have the model control for the varying time between sales of properties.

Characteristics of real estate indexes

No single index is likely to be best for all trading purposes in all countries. The informational complementarities of different types of commercial property indexes, combined with the diversity and heterogeneity in some large markets, such as the US commercial property market and real estate industry, suggests that there can be value from having more than one type of index available in such countries. Use of derivatives in "arbitrage" trading across indexes can be a source of profit, price discovery, and liquidity.

Value of good indexes

Real estate indices, especially appraisal-based indices, tend to be more predictable than stock market indices. Derivative prices can reflect forecasts for the underlying index. Commodity futures contracts have always reflected consensus forecasts of where the corresponding commodity spot markets are headed. Because there is momentum in a real estate index, the equilibrium (or "fair") pricing of its derivatives in the derivatives market must reflect the index predictability implied by such momentum. This differs from typical stock market index derivatives in which the underlying indexes have relatively little momentum and the stock shares on which the indexes are based are directly traded in liquid cash (or "spot") markets, allowing execution of arbitrage between the futures and spot markets.

4.2   Income and capital returns

Return components and return volatility

Periodic total returns for commercial real estate that reflect overall investment performance come from both the current cash flow generated by properties (income return) and changes in the capital value of the properties between the beginning and end of each index reporting period (capital return). Compared to capital returns and to most financial series, income returns are very nearly constant over typical trading periods. This is because in long-lived assets such as real property the current income per period is at least an order of magnitude smaller than the capitalized asset value. In the NPI, the quarterly volatility of the capital return between 1978 and 2006 was 1.7% versus only 0.3% for the income return. (This compares to quarterly volatility over the same historical period of 0.8% for Treasury bills, 6.8% for REIT stocks, and 7.7% for the S&P 500 large-cap stock index.) Figure 2 shows the NPI return components (income, capital, and total) from 1978 through 2006 (quarterly unleveraged returns), revealing how the income return is essentially constant compared to the capital or total return components.

If the underlying index reports the total return (as in appraisal-based indexes such as the NCREIF or IPD indexes), then derivatives can be structured based

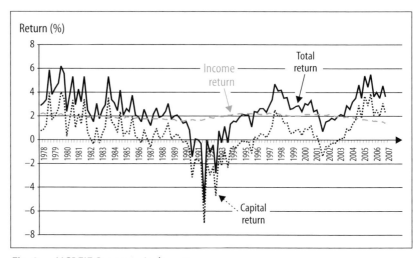

Fig. 2:   NCREIF Property Index returns

on either the total return or just the capital return. However, even if the underlying index reports only the capital return, derivatives can effectively be used to create the total return synthetically, because virtually all of the index total return volatility is in the capital return component alone. In the NPI over 116 quarters during 1978 to 2006, the capital return and total return were correlated +99%, with essentially equal volatilities of 1.7% each. For example, a structured note in which the investor funds up front the fixed leg of a capital return swap will effectively provide the investor with the index total return, as we will see later when we discuss swap pricing.

4.3   Appraisal-based indexes

The first regularly produced commercial property price indexes were appraisal-based, and designed for benchmarking institutional real estate investment manager performance. These include the NPI in the United States and the IPD Index in Great Britain, among others worldwide. In a traditional appraisal-based index all of the properties in the index population are reappraised frequently, and the index periodic returns are based on the average (usually value-weighted) of those appraisal-based returns each period. This is similar to the way many institutional real estate investment funds "mark-to-market" their asset values and correspondingly report quarterly returns to their investors. Of course, the NPI reflects property-level returns (unleveraged, and before any fund-level or management expenses and fees to which investors are subject).

Mark-to-market

While such traditional appraisal-based indexes can be excellent tools for benchmarking investment manager performance, and this in itself gives them a particular use in derivatives of interest to such managers, they do have some inherent problems from the perspective of a broader derivative support role. The appraisal process tends to be somewhat subjective and backward looking (perhaps more so in the United States than in Great Britain). This tends to impart a lag bias to the property values and the index returns. Furthermore, in the case of the NCREIF Index in the United States, not all properties are reappraised every period that the index is reported, and this adds an additional "stale appraisal" effect into the index. In the NCREIF Index, at least during some periods of its history, greater frequency of reappraisals in the fourth calendar quarter has imparted an artificial seasonality to the index (the index can tend to "spike" in the fourth quarter). It must also be recognized that, at least as of the early 2000s, the NCREIF Index represents a relatively narrow segment of the population of US properties. In 2006 the NCREIF population of properties consisted of less than 10% of the commercial properties in the United States, a much smaller percentage than the IPD Index represents in Great Britain. For example, in 2006 the NPI included less than US$30 billion of property sales, whereas the Real Capital Analytics Inc. (RCA) database recorded over US$330 billion of commercial property sales tracking only sales of greater than US$2,500,000. As of the end of 2006, the NPI was tracking some US$250 billion worth of property, whereas JP Morgan Asset Management's "Real Estate Universe" report estimated the total value of US commercial real estate at that time to be some US$6.7 trillion, or over 25 times the NCREIF population value (although this included corporate real estate and

Problems with appraisal-based indexes

small "mom & pop" properties as well as the larger properties covered by the RCA database). For smaller market segments there may be only a few NCREIF properties available in the index, and their specific identities will be known to at least some potential participants in the derivatives marketplace.

Index lag The above problems are of less concern for purposes of benchmarking institutional real estate portfolios that are marked to market using appraised values, but they can be more problematical for broader derivative support purposes. If the lag in the index causes it to still rise when the real estate market turns down (or vice versa), this can be confusing to parties trying to use the index to hedge or speculate on such market movements. Derivative pricing when the index is lagged needs to reflect the lag, and that may make price discovery more difficult, potentially hampering liquidity in the derivative market, although in principle the lag can be relatively easily reflected in the derivative price (especially if indexes that are not lagged are also available as information sources). Even if the index lag is taken into account in the derivative price, if the derivative contract expires before the lagged price movement is fully reflected in the index, then the hedge will not be complete, presenting a type of "basis risk" for the user of the derivative. Thus, for a variety of reasons, futures traders may prefer indexes that lead the appraisal-based indexes in time, and in which the true volatility is not dampened, as such volatility can be a source of potential profit that might motive some derivative traders.

4.4   Transactions-based indexes

Characteristics of transactions-based indexes An alternative to appraisal-based indexes is to have an index based on transactions (sales) of properties. In some countries (including notably the United States), the real estate transaction market is more active and more ubiquitous than is the regular and consistent appraisal of commercial properties. In such countries, transactions-based indexes can be based on the entire population of commercial properties, because all properties potentially transact (providing a random price sample of the population each period), whereas only certain specialized portfolios of properties are regularly marked to market. Where a well-functioning and independent real estate market exists, transactions-based indexes can be good bases for derivatives provided the indexes are carefully constructed based on sufficient quantity and quality of transactions observations data and state-of-the-art statistical procedures to control for "apples versus oranges" differences in properties trading in different periods and to minimize "noise" or random deviations from the property population prices. By a "well-functioning" market, we mean one that tends to have a large number of independent buyers and sellers regularly negotiating or auctioning the sale of a large number of properties in "arms-length" transactions (that is, where there is no favoritism or pre-arranged prices or side-payments).

Calculation approaches There are two major procedures to calculate transactions-based indexes in a statistically rigorous manner:

- the repeat-sales regression procedure and
- the hedonic value model.

Both procedures address the fundamental problem in the construction of a transactions-based real estate price index, the fact that the properties that transact in one period are generally not the same as the properties that transacted in the previous period, making a direct comparison of prices "apples-versus-oranges". The two procedures address this issue in different ways.

The hedonic procedure models property prices as a function of various characteristics of the properties that affect their value, such as age, size, location, building quality, etc. By regressing property transaction prices onto these "hedonic characteristics" of the properties that sell, and controlling for or keeping track of the time of the sale, one constructs a "constant-quality" price-change index or an index that tracks property market price changes controlling for differences in the properties that transact at the different points in time. The MIT Center for Real Estate began publishing the first regularly-produced hedonic index of commercial property in 2006, in cooperation with NCREIF, based on the prices of the properties sold from the NCREIF Index. This transactions-based index uses the recent appraised values of the sold properties as a "composite" indicator of the hedonic characteristics of the properties, controlling in this way for cross-sectional differences in the sold properties. Because this transactions-based index was based on the same underlying population of properties as the NPI, it can present a good "apples-to-apples" comparison of the difference between a transactions-based and an appraisal-based index. This comparison over the historical period from 1984 to 2006 is shown in figure 3. The comparison gives an indication of the typical

Hedonic procedure

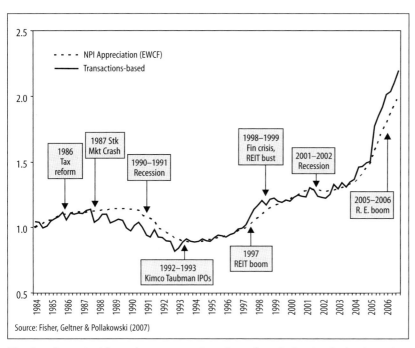

Source: Fisher, Geltner & Pollakowski (2007)

Fig. 3: Appraisal-based vs. transactions-based capital value index based on NCREIF 1984–2006

differences between a transactions-based and an appraisal-based index. Note that the transactions-based version of the NCREIF Index is a bit more volatile, and tends to slightly lead the NPI in time (in terms of the timing of major turning points in the index history).

Repeat-sales indexes

Repeat-sales indexes use a different approach to address the "apples-versus-oranges" problem. As the name suggests, repeat-sales indexes rely on individual properties selling more than once, so that the change in price between sales provides an indication of how same-property values have changed over time. The index is thus based on the type of price changes that investors in properties actually experience, and the same type of price changes that stock market indexes are based on. Stock market indexes are also based on comparing the transaction prices of stock shares in one period with the transaction prices of similar shares in the previous period. As stock shares are homogenous (a share of IBM that traded this month is the same as a share of IBM that traded last month), the result is comparable to a "same-property" price change index such as the repeat-sales transactions-based indexes. It should also be noted that stock share prices reflect the value added by the corporation not paying out all of its cash in dividends, but reinvesting some in the corporation. This is analogous to the effect of capital improvement expenditures in real estate. Thus, repeat-sales indexes aimed at tracking property prices do not generally try to remove the effect of capital improvement expenditures (although normally data filters are applied to eliminate property sale pairs that would reflect major development, redevelopment or rehabilitation of the properties). This is in some contrast to appraisal-based indexes, that may subtract capital expenditures from the appreciation return reported by the index.

The statistical process used to calculate repeat-sales indexes takes into consideration the time between the same-property sales and appropriately allocates the price change to each period that the index is reported, based on information from other repeat-sales occurring over various time frames. Repeat-sales is the approach used in widely-quoted housing price indexes such as the S&P/Case-Shiller housing index on which the Chicago Mercantile Exchange (CME) launched futures trading in 2006. A simple numerical example of how the calculation process works is presented in section 5.

First repeat-sales transactions-based index

The first regularly-published repeat-sales transactions-based index for commercial property was developed by the MIT Center for Real Estate for Real Estate Analytics LLC (REAL), based on transactions data from the firm Real Capital Analytics Inc. (RCA) and launched in 2006. This index was based on a much broader property population than the appraisal-based NCREIF Index, as the RCA database attempted to track all commercial property sales in the US of over US$ 2,500,000, whereas the NPI tracked only the NCREIF members' properties. In 2007 the publication of this index was assigned to Moody's Investor Services in New York and commenced publication as the Moody's/REAL Commercial Property Price Indices.

5   Numerical example of how the repeat-sales index works

In this section we present a simple numerical example of the mechanics of how the repeat-sales regression procedure works to construct an index of periodic capital returns based on same-property price changes. In so doing, we will also highlight some key features of the repeat-sales model that are not intuitively obvious, such as how the model can detect a downturn in the market even when all of the individual property investments are producing a positive return over their holding periods, and how no single period's return estimate is based only on the second-sales occurring in that period alone.

To understand how the repeat-sales regression (RSR) index construction process works, you must step back briefly and recall some basic statistics. You may recall that regression analysis is a statistical technique for estimating the relationship between variables of interest. In a regression model, a particular variable of interest, referred to as the dependent variable, is related to one or more other variables referred to as explanatory variables. The regression model is presented as an equation, with the dependent variable on the left-hand-side of the equals sign, and a sum of terms on the right-hand-side consisting of the explanatory variables each multiplied by a parameter that is estimated by the regression and that relates each explanatory variable to the dependent variable. For example, if the dependent variable is labeled "Y" and there is a single explanatory variable labeled "X" then a simple regression model of Y as a function of X would be expressed as:

Regression model as foundation

$$Y = aX$$

The model says that the value of the variable Y equals the value of the variable X times the parameter "a", and we would use the regression analysis of relevant empirical data to estimate what is the value of "a". This process is referred to as "estimation" of the regression, or "calibrating" the model.

Application of basic model on real estate

How can this technique enable the development of a real estate price index? Let's take a very simple numerical example. Suppose that the true returns in the market are respectively: 0 %, +10 %, and −5 %, in three consecutive periods (say, 2011, 2012, and 2013). Thus, a true price index starting out at 1.00 at the end of 2010 would remain at 1.00 at the end of 2011, jump to 1.10 in 2012, and then fall back to 1.045 in 2013 [as (1.045 − 1.10) / 1.10 is −5 %]. Now suppose we have three property repeat-sales observations involving altogether at least one sale in each of the three years, with each being consistent with the true returns but in which no one observation can directly reveal any one period's return because the properties are held across more than one period. Property #1 is bought at the beginning of 2011 for US$ 100,000 and sold after three years at the end of 2013 for US$ 104,500. Property #2 is also bought at the beginning of 2011, but for US$ 200,000 and sold at the end of 2012 for US$ 220,000 (held for two years). Property #3 is bought at the beginning of 2012 for US$ 300,000 and sold at the end of 2013 for US$ 313,500 (also held two years). This is summarized in figure 4 and 5, where figure 5 indicates both the true market price index (the solid line) and the capital returns achieved by each of the three investors in these three properties (dashed lines).

Application of repeat-sales regression model

Now, the repeat-sales regression model shall be applied to this problem. Let the dependent variable, "Y", be the natural log of the ratio of the second sale price divided by the first sale price, for each repeat-sale pair. Thus, the first repeat-sales observation, based on Property #1, has a Y value of the log of 1.045.

Similarly, the second repeat-sales observation, based on Property #2, has a Y value of the log of 1.10, and so on.

	Prices observed at ends of years			
	2010	**2011**	**2012**	**2013**
True price index	1.00	1.00	1.10	1.045
True capital return		0%	10%	−5%
Property #1	US$ 100,000	No data	No data	US$ 104,500
Property #2	US$ 200,000	No data	US$ 220,000	No data
Property #3	No data	US$ 300,000	No data	US$ 313,500

Fig. 4:   Repeat-sales index in example

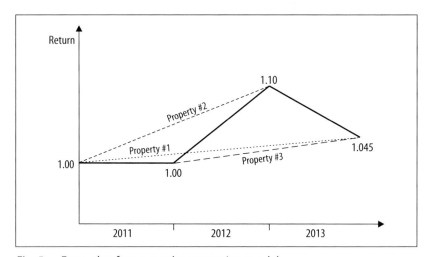

Fig. 5:   Example of repeat-sales regression model

On the right-hand-side of our repeat-sales regression, instead of just one variable, "X", let there be three variables, corresponding to the three consecutive periods of time for which we want to construct the index periodic returns. Let us label these as "X2011", "X2012", and "X2013". These right-hand-side variables are what are called "dummy variables", which means they take on a value of either zero or one. The "X2011" variable stands for the year 2011. It takes the value of one if 2011 is after the year of the first sale and before or including the year of the second sale in the repeat-sales observation (in other words, if the dummy variable's year is during the property investor's holding period between when he bought and sold the property of the observation in question); otherwise this dummy variable has a value of zero. Similarly, "X2012" takes the value of one if 2012 is after the year of the first sale and before or including the year of the second sale. Thus, the price observation data described previously gives the repeat-sales regression estimation data in figure 6. For example, for the repeat-sales observation corresponding to Property #3, US$ 313,500 / US$ 300,000 is 1.045, and the natural log of this value happens to be about 4.4 %, which is therefore the Y value for that observation in the RSR estimation database.

	Y value = LN(Ps/Pf)	X2011 value	X2012 value	X2013 value
Observation #1	LN(1.045)	1	1	1
Observation #2	LN(1.100)	1	1	0
Observation #3	LN(1.045)	0	1	1

Fig. 6: RSR estimation data

Our regression equation can now be expressed as:

$Y = a_{2011}(X2011) + a_{2012}(X2012) + a_{2013}(X2013)$.

Now recall from statistics that the estimation of a regression model, that **Calibration** is, the "calibration" of the value of the parameters in the above equation, is mathematically the solution of a system of simultaneous equations. Each equation corresponds to one "observation", one data point in the database used to estimate the regression model. Thus, in our present example, we have three equations, one corresponding to each row (each repeat-sales observation) in figure 6. The three equations are:

$LN(1.045) = a_{2011}(1) + a_{2012}(1) + a_{2013}(1)$ (EQ.1)

$LN(1.100) = a_{2011}(1) + a_{2012}(1) + a_{2013}(0)$ (EQ.2)

$LN(1.045) = a_{2011}(0) + a_{2012}(1) + a_{2013}(1)$ (EQ.3)

which equates to:

$LN(1.045) = a_{2011} + a_{2012} + a_{2013}$

$LN(1.100) = a_{2011} + a_{2012}$

$LN(1.045) = a_{2012} + a_{2013}$

We thus have three linear equations with three unknowns (a_{2011}, a_{2012}, and a_{2013}, representing the true log price ratios in each of the three periods). Such a system can always be solved, and in this case the solution can be found as follows:

Use equation (EQ.2) to derive: $a_{2012} = LN(1.1) - a_{2011}$. Then plug this into equation (EQ.3) to obtain: $a_{2013} = LN(1.045) - LN(1.1) + a_{2011}$. Now plug both of these into equation (EQ.1) to obtain:

$LN(1.045) = a_{2011} + [LN(1.1) - a_{2011}] + [LN(1.045) - LN(1.1) + a_{2011}], \rightarrow$

$a_{2011} = LN(1.045) - LN(1.045), \rightarrow$

$a_{2011} = 0$.

Now plug this result back into equation (EQ.2) and (EQ.3) to obtain: $a_{2012} =$ LN(1.1), and $a_{2013} =$ LN(1.045) − LN(1.1). The result that $a_{2011} = 0$ simply means that the estimated price index level did not change during 2011. From the definition of logarithms we have 0 = LN(1), and algebraically we can express this as LN(1/1). Similarly, we can express $a_{2012} =$ LN(1.1) as LN(1.1/1). Thus, the implied log price ratios of the price index ending values divided by its beginning values each year are:

for 2011 = a_{2011} = LN(1/1)

for 2012 = a_{2012} = LN(1.1/1)

for 2013 = a_{2013} = LN(1.045/1.1)

Exponentiating these values, we arrive at the implied straight level price index as of the end of each year as follows:

2006 = 1.000

2007 = 1.000

2008 = 1.100

2009 = 1.045,

with the resulting implied price-change percentages (capital returns):

2007 = 0 %

2008 = +10 %

2009 = −5 %.

Evaluation of results   Thus, we see that the repeat-sales model has derived the true capital return in each period, even though no single repeat-sale price change observation corresponded to any one year. The model correctly derived the negative return in 2013, even though none of the repeat-sale observations used in the estimation showed a negative price change in itself. In other words, all of the three investors made a positive resale gain over their holding periods. Note also that the estimation of the returns in each of the three periods was affected by all three of the repeat-sale observations. For example, the estimate of the negative 5 % return in 2013 was determined in part by the +10 % return obtained on Property #2, even though that property's second sale occurred prior to the beginning of 2013.

While this is a simple numerical example, the type of result shown here is general. In principle, the repeat-sales model only requires one sales observation per period (either a first or second sale) in order to be able to estimate the true return each period, even though no single repeat-sale pair corresponds to any one period. And the model uses all observations to estimate every period's return. Thus, it is not correct to think that the estimated return in the current period is determined solely or in isolation by the second-sale observations that occur only in the current period.

Of course, in the real world individual transaction prices will be dispersed randomly around the average (normalized) sale price at any given time, which makes index estimation a statistical process. The existence of more than one observation (hence more than one equation) in each period of time enables such estimation to be optimized in various ways, as is done in actual RSR indexes.

6   Summary

This chapter has reviewed the nature and mechanics of the major real estate equity index derivative products and their use and usefulness. It has also presented the fundamentals of real estate return indexes, including the important differences between the two major types of indexes: appraisal-based and transactions-based indexes.

7   References

Bailey, M./Muth, R./Nourse, H., A regression method for real estate price index construction, in: Journal of the American Statistical Association 58, 1963, pp. 922–942.

Court, A., Hedonic price indices with automotive examples, in: The Dynamics of Automobile Demand, Detroit: General Motors Corporation, 1936.

Fisher, J. D., Introducing the NPI Based derivative – New strategies for commercial real estate investment and risk management, in: Journal of Portfolio Management, Special Issue on Real Estate, 2005, p. 1–9.

Fisher, J. D./Geltner, D./Webb, R.B., Value indices of commercial real estate: A comparison of index construction methods, in: Journal of Real Estate Finance & Economics 9(2), 1994, p. 137–164.

Fisher, J. D./Geltner, D./Pollakowski, H., A Quarterly Transactions-Based Index of Institutional Real Estate Investment Performance and Movements in Supply and Demand, in: Journal of Real Estate Finance and Economics, Volume 34, #1, 2007.

Geltner, D./Pollakowski, H., A set of indexes for trading commercial real estate based on the Real Capital Analytics Database. Report by the MIT Center for Real Estate, 2006.

Geltner, D./Fisher, J. D., Pricing and index considerations in commercial real estate derivatives: Understanding the Basics, in: Journal of Portfolio Management, Special Issue, September 2007, pp. 99–118.

Goodman, L. S./Fabozzi, F. J., CMBS total return swaps, in: Journal of Portfolio Management, Special Issue on Real Estate, 2005, pp. 162–167.

Griliches, Z./Adelman, I., On an index of quality change, in: Journal of the American Statistical Association 56, 1961, pp. 535–548.

Rosen, S. , Hedonic prices and implicit markets, in: Journal of Political Economy 82(1), 1974, pp. 33–55.

Acknowledgement

Fisher/Geltner, Commercial Real Estate Derivatives,
in: Fabozzi (Ed.): Handbook of Finance, Vol. 1 (ISBN 978 047 0078143)
© John Wiley & Sons, Inc., 2008

Reprinted with permission of John Wiley and Sons, Inc.

3   Synthetization of real estate via derivatives

Daniel Piazolo

Table of contents

1   The advent of real estate derivatives in Germany

Derivative on the DIX
The first trading in derivatives on the German Property Index DIX (Deutscher Immobilien Index) at the end of 2006 was a milestone for real estate investors for two reasons. First, it was the first European trading in derivatives on a real estate index outside of the UK. Second, this derivative was the first option on a real estate index. Until then, investors could only trade derivatives as swaps. Swaps trade the return of a real estate index against an interest rate. By contrast, an option gives the asset holder the right but not the obligation to buy the underlying basis at a defined point in time. This option on an index product also shows how the market for property derivatives may react with tailored services to complex investor's demands.

Fantastic growth in other markets
Other markets demonstrate the great potential for real estate derivatives. For example, derivatives on coal exist since 1998. At that time, investors traded derivatives for nominal one million tons of that resource. Until 2003, the derivatives volume increased to nominal 250 million tons, only to grow further to 2,000 million tons of coal by 2006. Hence, the dealing in coal derivatives is five times bigger than the real physical coal trade to date. The dealing in derivatives may even increase further as some oil markets show where the trading in derivatives is 15 times as big as the real transaction volume.

Consequently, real estate derivatives might also experience a phenomenal growth in the near future. Especially, since this product opens up very promising uses: Real estate investors may use derivatives to expand or reduce the allocation in certain markets and sectors. Real estate derivatives allow investors to change synthetically and quickly country allocations in their portfolios. For example, investors may reduce the share of the German retail sector in their portfolio while they increase the share of French office properties.

Overcoming illiquidity of real estate

Derivatives decrease effectively the illiquidity of real estate as asset class. Real estate derivatives make asset classes comparable – also between national boundaries – and therefore will contribute to professional real estate portfolio management. A well-functioning market for real estate derivatives will help diversify investment markets. This contribution will set out the different types of real estate derivatives, potential underlying indices and recent developments. Furthermore, the license agreements and the perspective for derivatives will be discussed.

2 Property derivative types

The four main derivative types for the real estate world are swaps, futures, options and certificates. Of course, derivatives in other markets have developed further varieties such as forwards, collars, floors, etc. and it is likely that also the real estate world will make use of these tools in the near future. However, the four types that have been used already for real estate indices are set out in the following.

2.1 Swaps

Until now, institutional investors have only been able to influence the risk-return profile of a property portfolio through measures on property level. Now derivative swaps offer a cost-effective way to specifically change the risk-return profile. The systematic risk of a national real estate market can be encapsulated via a real estate derivative. Then the total return of a real estate index is swapped against a floating or a fixed interest rate. As a result, a construction is possible where the portfolio only carries the unsystematic risk of the individual properties.

Real estate in exchange for interest

The use of such a swap can be illustrated with an example: A swap offers a chance for real estate investor A who is confident that he can manage his properties more effectively than all market participants on average. The counterparty for this swap is bank B which will try to eliminate its own risk exposure through a second swap with investor C (see figure 1). Investor C, for example, could be a foreign real estate fund that wants to increase the weight of the German market in its portfolio. C will receive the total return and the systematic risk of the German real estate market. In return, C pays a fixed or a floating interest rate via bank B to investor A.

Consequently, for a specified time period the risk and return opportunities are traded between two parties without any change in the ownership of properties. Investor A pays, for example, the German Property Index DIX total return to bank B which passes the total return on to investor C. In reverse, C pays an

Ownership of real estate stays the same

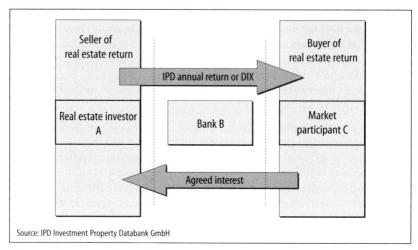

Fig. 1:   Swaps on the basis of property derivatives

interest rate to B which is passed on to investor A. In most cases, it is negotiated in advance that only the debtor is paying the creditor the resulting difference, i.e., the money streams are balanced.

The specified time period for a swap usually ranges between one and 10 years, thus both parties know the specific end of the transaction. The seller of the total return of the German real estate market (investor A) can automatically re-enter into the real estate market, once he has decided not to renew the swap. In contrast, if investor A has decided to sell directly owned properties, then the decision to re-enter into the German real estate market and build up a real estate portfolio would require substantial efforts.

Figure 2 shows how investor A, who is swapping real estate total return for a floating interest rate with bank B, is able to eliminate the overall development of the real estate market. Investor A will receive independently of the development

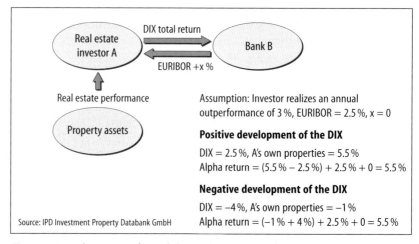

Fig. 2:   Development of an alpha real estate portfolio

of the property market a floating interest rate (e.g., the EURIBOR) and the relative return (positive or negative) earned by his own real estate portfolio compared to the whole property market.

GFI Brokers Ltd. traded the first over-the-counter UK real estate swap on the IPD All Property Index versus 3-month LIBOR in January 2004. Since then, the swap market has grown substantially and has diversified into real estate sectors and sub-sectors. In early 2007, ING Property Select and Merrill Lynch traded the first-ever central London office swap.

2.2   Futures

Futures are a standardized financial instrument that is traded at a futures exchange. The buyer of a futures contract must sell or buy a certain underlying instrument at a certain date at a specific price. Hence, both contracting parties must exercise the contract in contrast to options described below.

Locking in today's price

For example, an investor is looking to sell his property in a year from now. Futures allow him to lock in today's prices and offer him strategic income security. If actual prices have fallen by the time the investor will sell, he will lose money on his property but receive a premium for the futures. If market prices have risen by the time he wants to sell, he will lose some money on the futures but earn higher profits from the sale of his properties on the market. In times of uncertain real estate price development, future markets are good for experienced investors. However, they carry a higher risk than options.

The Chicago Mercantile Exchange (CME) offers futures based on the S&P/Case-Shiller Home Price Index (see below). Investors can trade contracts on single-family home price indices for 10 major US metropolitan areas and one composite index.

2.3   Options

A real estate index option gives the buyer the possibility to benefit from the positive performance of a real estate market without bearing the risk of a negative performance. In return, the issuer of the option demands a price in advance which reflects the potential of this right. In other words: options are conditional futures. That means, one of the contracting parties may choose on the maturity date if the transaction takes place. The buyer of an option has the right but not the obligation to buy (call option) or sell (put option) a certain amount of units of a basis value at a pre-set price. The deal may be carried out either within a certain time frame (American option) or at a specific date (European option). The seller takes the contrary position. He either buys if the option holder bought a put option or sells the underlying in case of a call option to the prefixed price and amount.

The right, not the obligation

The investment bank Goldman Sachs was the first bank to issue options on the real estate market in 2004. A British house price index, the Halifax House Price Index (HPI), which is described below, underlies this option. The investor may speculate on increasing or decreasing house prices. As for futures, Chicago Mercantile Exchange (CME) issues call and put options on

10 US metropolitan areas based on the S&P/Case-Shiller Home Price Index. This financial instrument is also available for small private investors to hedge against decreasing home prices. The Zurich Kantonalbank offers call options bound to the Zurich House Price Index (ZWEX) since 2006.

In the US, private investors can choose between several forms of derivatives to secure the value of their house against a volatile market. HedgeStreet.com offers binary options for housing prices in 10 US metropolitan areas [1]. With a binary option an individual bets on a market trend based in this case on median sales prices of existing single-family homes. If the investor believes the median sales price will stand above the strike price at maturity, he will take the "buyer" position. If he estimates that the market price will fall below the strike price, he will position himself as "seller". For the right estimate the investor receives US$ 10 per binary.

2.4   Certificates

Also for small private investors

Certificates are capital-based financial instruments: The buyer invests a certain amount and pays this to the emitter of the instrument. Barclays Bank was the pioneer in this area. Through the real estate crisis in the UK at the beginning of the 1990s, many debtors were not able to pay their mortgages. Barclays and other banks acquired through foreclosures various properties. In order to reduce the exposure to the real estate market, Barclays issued Property Index Certificates (PICs) in 1994. These Certificates ensure that the investor receives a return linked to a real estate index. For the UK, the basis for these certificates is in most cases the IPD UK Annual Index. However, IPD calculates also a quarterly and a monthly UK Index, since a considerable share of the real estate owners in the UK value their holdings on a regular basis for periods of less than a year. The PICs have frequently a maturity of three years.

Property index certificates are a form of derivative that increase also the investment universe of retail investors. Since the 1st of September 2006, it has been possible to trade real estate index derivatives at German stock exchanges starting at roughly € 15. Goldman Sachs has been offering certificates on the IPD UK Annual Index in Germany shortly after its introduction to the UK market in July 2006. Thus, a German small retail investor can participate via a derivative certificate in the development of the UK real estate market. The value of the derivative depends on the development of the UK real estate total return measured by the underlying UK Annual Index which is based on the information of more than 10,000 properties (see also below). Consequently, an investment in real estate is possible without actually directly owning any real estate or in other words, one synthetically invests in the whole UK real estate market.

3   Benefits and costs

Beware: transactions costs

Obviously, the involved bank in any derivative trade will get paid for its provided services and own risk exposure. Especially in the case of retail investors these transaction costs should not be neglected. In the case of the above mentioned certificate, the involved bank Goldman Sachs is currently adjusting the index by 2.8 % p. a., consequently reducing the return of investors. Between 2004 and 2006 the UK IPD Annual Index increased on average by 18.5 % p. a. Thus, the adjustment of the index in such profitable times can be seen as fair entrance fee. With respect to investors with an investment horizon of several years, it should be analyzed if the transaction and management costs of, for example, open-end real estate funds are for such a period favorable compared to the ones of derivative certificates [2]. Concerning large institutional investors, it should be noted that with an investment of derivatives on real estate indices an investor buys the "systematic risk", while real estate portfolios offer the possibility to buy the "unsystematic risk" which can offer further chances. The advantages, disadvantages and transaction associated with cost of direct real estate investments and derivatives on real estate indices are shown in figure 3.

Derivatives also carry certain risks. One risk of a derivative on real estate indices, which is wanted by buyers of the synthetic real estate market, is the dependence of cash flows on the development of the real estate market. If the **Wanted and unwanted risks**

	Directly held real estate	Derivatives on real estate indices
Advantages	• Full autonomy of decision and direction for real estate portfolio • Generate Alpha – Increased returns in comparison to the market as a whole possible • Long-term protection of real estate (e. g., site for headquarters)	• Enable to diversify risk across geographies • Potential to minimize risks or manage them consciously • Short-term investment in real estate feasible • Fast implementation of strategies • Low transaction costs for acquisition and sale • Low administrative costs
Disadvantages	• High transaction costs for acquisition and sale • High administrative costs • Considerable acquisiton and sale periods • Cluster risk • Always a combination of systematic (market) and unsystematic risks (e. g., tenant) • Requires relevant real estate knowledge	• If invested for a longer period, fees for derivatives exceed the saved transaction costs for direct investments • No outperformance of the market possible • Yet a new market, hence, only certain regional and sectoral investments are presentable • Danger of default of counterparty • Derivatives count as liquidity not as real estate holding, thus for some investors who are allowed only a maximum share of liquidity only of limited use • Requires financial economics knowledge
Costs/Fees	• Transaction costs for real estate acquisiton and sale range between 7 % and 8 % of the investment volume	• Institutional investors: 0.1 % to 0.2 % of the nominal transaction value for a swap per year • Private investors: 2.8 % annual index deduction as fee for certificates from Goldman Sachs UK IPD tracker (minimum investment € 15) • Costs of holding real estate indices are higher than for stock market derivatives

Source: IPD Investment Property Databank GmbH

Fig. 3: Advantages and disadvantages of directly held property versus derivatives on real estate indices

development of the DIX is positive, then the buyer of the DIX total return has a good position, because he was right with his assumptions. However, if the DIX total return is only marginal, then the buyer has to pay the seller the pre-negotiated interest payment without being over-compensated through the receipt of the DIX total return. A further risk of a real estate index derivative concerns the solvency of the counterparty. In most cases, a bank acts as a mediator between both parties and carries this risk. If, for example, the DIX total return is extremely high, it is theoretically possible that the counterparty is not able to pay its debts. Consequently, most institutional investors limit the possible amount of their exposure with counterparties or banks. With respect to derivatives, this business risk for other kinds of investments is usually reduced as all outstanding amounts are balanced and only the debtor has to make a safety deposit for all currently outstanding debts. However, as long as real estate indices are published only once per year, this kind of risk reduction is only partially possible for real estate index derivatives.

4   Underlyings

The existence of a qualified real estate index is decisive for the development of a real estate derivatives market. This index has to meet certain standards such as sufficient index size, market coverage, historical data series and compilation by an independent third party. IPD Investment Property Databank GmbH has issued such an index for Germany since 1996. Within the IPD Group indices are published for various countries. Real estate indices that are useable for derivatives – either from IPD or not IPD sources – are set out in the following.

4.1   IPD indices: the German index DIX

Representative for the German market IPD's German Property Index DIX (Deutscher Immobilien Index) is based on an extensive databank which contains about 3,000 properties with a market value of approximately €53.8 billion in 2006. Hence, the DIX covers 50% of the relevant institutional real estate market that is valued each year. This compares to 21% of all institutional properties including those that are valued less frequent than once a year. The average market value per property of the DIX is roughly €18 million. The DIX covers the performance of directly held institutional real estates from the large institutional investors in Germany. The institutional investors supply the data to IPD and receive in return a portfolio analysis relative to the benchmark of all participants. The DIX consists therefore of primary data mirroring the relevant financial accounts and business reports of the data supplier. IPD validates and double checks all the supplied information to enforce high data quality.

The DIX shows performance as total return as a product of income return and capital growth. Capital growth is the net increase of the market value of all properties in the year adjusted for expenditures. Income return is calculated as net rental income which is calculated as gross rental income minus non-allocated operating costs of the year reviewed. Both values are expressed in % of the capital invested [3]. The DIX is the only German real estate index that allows the direct comparison between different asset classes such as the

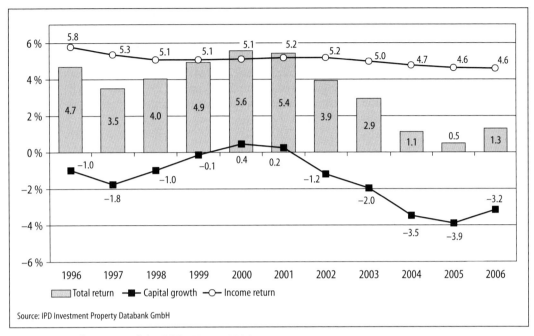

Fig. 4: Development of the DIX 1996 to 2006

German stock market index DAX or the E&G-DIMAX which lists German real estate stocks.

Figure 4 shows the development of the DIX between 1996 and 2006. The total return reached its maximum at 5.6 % in 2000. Since 2001, the DIX total return declined gradually to 2.9 % by 2003 and further to 0.5 % in 2005. Therefore, the year 2005 marks the all-time low to date. In 2006, the DIX increased again at 1.3 %. While the income return proved relatively stable at about 5 % during the last 10 years, the capital growth decreased from 0.2 % in 2001 to –3.9 % in 2005 and has a bit recovered to –3.2 % in 2006. The negative capital growth influenced mostly the performance of the DIX.

German property market: turnaround in 2005

4.2   Other IPD indices

The IPD Group issues indices for more than 20 countries and several aggregated indices such as the Global Index or the Pan-European Index. All indices are based on the assessment of properties owned by institutional investors. The indices show the total return of properties (property return before tax and financing costs). The indices rise when the total return of the precedent period was positive. They are based on primary data and enable IPD to develop indices for main market sectors and segments. Main market sectors are usually retail, office, industrial and residential. These markets can normally be further disaggregated into segments such as geographical areas, size bands, etc. The potential generation of specific indices facilitates the diversification of real estate derivatives.

Global coverage

As figure 5 shows, market coverage and historic data vary between the different national indices. For all IPD countries annual indices are available, some countries have additional quarterly or even monthly indices. The Irish index offers the highest coverage of the institutional real estate investment market at 79 % and has been calculated back to 1984. Since 1995, IPD has issued a Dutch index containing 60 % of the institutional real estate market. The UK index offers the largest time period and reaches back until 1981. It covers 45 % of the

[1] rough estimate, [2] **ready to trade**, [3] *use with caution*, [4] [not yet there]			
	Index starts	**Estimated % of market**	**Frequency, readiness**
Australia[5]	1985	25[1]	*Annual, (quarterly updated)*[3]
Austria	2004	30	*Annual*[3]
Canada[5]	1984	50	**Annual**[2], *(quarterly updated)*[3]
Denmark	2000	41	**Annual**[2]
Finland	1998	60	**Annual**[2]
France	1986	54	**Annual**[2], [6-monthly estimate][4]
Germany	1996	21	**Annual**[2]
Ireland[6]	1984	79	**Quarterly**[2]
Italy	2002	24	*Annual*[3]
Japan	2003	10[1]	[Annual][4], *monthly estimate*[3]
Netherlands[7]	1995	60	**Annual**[2], *quarterly estimate*[3]
Norway[8]	2000	47	**Annual**[2], [quarterly estimate][4]
Portugal	2000	51	**Annual**[2]
Spain	2001	48	**Annual**[2]
South Africa	1995	60	**Annual**[2]
Sweden[8]	1984	30	**Annual**[2], [quarterly estimate][4]
Switzerland	2002	35	*Annual*[3]
UK[9]	1981/86/01	45	**Annual**[2], *quarterly*[3], **monthly**[2]

[5] In Australia and Canada, funds are annually valued but at different year-ends – these are not therefore "true" quarterly services.

[6] In Ireland, all funds have had a full quarterly valuation since March 1995 (annual in preceding years).

[7] In the Netherlands, all funds are annually-valued, and some also value some properties at various stages throughout the year – but because whole funds are not quarterly-valued, this is not a "true" quarterly service.

[8] In Norway and Sweden some funds are quarterly valued, and IPD is investigating the possibility of launching quarterly indices.

[9] In the UK, 100 % of funds (by value) are at least annually-valued, approx. 67 % quarterly-valued and approx. 25 % monthly-valued.

Source: IPD Investment Property Databank GmbH

Fig. 5:   Potential of property derivatives on IPD indices

market. In Germany, the real estate index covers 21 % of the institutional real estate market and 50 % of the relevant market which includes only properties whose performance is measured at least annually.

Non-IPD indices useable for property derivatives

4.3 Halifax House Price Index (HPI)

HBOS (Halifax and Bank of Scotland) issues the Halifax House Price Index (HPI) [4]. The index provides quarterly information on UK house prices derived from mortgage approval data of UK's largest mortgage lender HBOS. The index is available in various categories sorted by house type (new or existing), type of buyer (first-time buyer or home-mover) and regional categories (12 UK standard planning regions). In order to compare only similar houses, various data, such as type of property, location or tenure, are included into the analysis. HBOS makes no statement about the exact methodology and data basis. The HPI shows prices about one month ahead of completion which is one of the main differences towards the subsequently described Survey of Mortgage Lenders. In January 2007, TFS London, one of the big inter-dealer brokers, launched an index for residential derivative trading reaching into 2030 based on the HPI [5].

UK residential mortgage data based

A future alternative basis for UK residential derivatives could also be data from the Regulated Mortgage Survey of the Council of Mortgage Lenders (CML). The UK Secretary of State for Communities and Local Governments issues indices based on this survey every month since 2005 [6]. The indices are a weighted average of prices for a standard mix of dwellings in different regions and the UK as a whole. In order to obtain the necessary information, communities and local governments collect monthly about 50,000 actual prices of residential buildings at completion from about 50 mortgage lenders in the UK. The time-lag for the indices is three months. Temporarily, the indices will not be seasonally adjusted, therefore may not be compared on month-to-month basis. Communities and Local Governments will develop the indices further in the near future. This may result in a new basis for derivative trading.

4.4 Zurich Residential Property Index (ZWEX)

The IAZI AG (Informations- und Ausbildungszentrum für Immobilien, Zürich/Information and Education Center for Property, Zurich) calculates quarterly the Zürcher Wohneigentumsindex (ZWEX) [7]. The index is based on mortgage data of 17,000 transactions and reaches back to 1980. The ZWEX is a hedonic price index that is cleared off qualitative changes over time and differences between properties to show the price development for comparable single-family homes and multi-residential units in the Zurich region. Variables for the calculation of the ZWEX are amongst others age of structure, number of rooms, number of bathrooms and location variables. Annually, approximately 1,000 transactions are added to the index' database which accounts for about 17 % of all relevant residential real estate transactions.

Residential price developments in Zurich

4.5   Case-Shiller Index

US residential price development

The S&P/Case-Shiller Home Price Indices measure the residential housing market in the USA. An Index Committee composed of Standard & Poor's, the real estate firm Fiserv Case Shiller Weiss and industry experts generates and publishes the indices [8]. They are based on the "repeat sales" method that exclusively takes into account single-family home re-sales. The index's methodology was originally developed by Karl E. Case and Robert Shiller from Yale University in the 1980s. It is considered to be the most accurate way to measure home price evolution and therefore, the US Office of Federal Housing Enterprise Oversight has also adopted the method to generate the official US House Price Index (HPI).

S&P/Case-Shiller Index Committee publishes regional indices for 20 metropolitan areas in the USA on a monthly basis. Based on these regional indices, the Committee also generates two composite indices. One index aggregates all 20 metropolitan areas and another one 10 metropolitan areas which have been originally calculated when the index was first calculated in the 1980's. Additionally, the Index Committee quarterly issues the S&P/Case-Shiller US National Home Price Index based on the nine US Census divisions. The market coverage stands at about 50 % of the US housing market which roughly totals US$ 21 trillion (2005).

Traded at the Stock Exchange

Since May 2006, the Chicago Mercantile Exchange (CME) in collaboration with MacroMarkets LLC has offered derivatives on S&P/Case-Shiller Indices. MacroMarkets LLC possesses the exclusive license and sublicensing rights for the purpose of developing, structuring and trading financial products on the indices. Currently, the CME offers futures and options on 10 metropolitan markets and composites with the most volatile, hence most promising real estate markets for derivatives [9].

4.6   NCREIF Property Index (NPI)

US Commercial Real Estate Index

The National Council of Property Investment Fiduciaries (NCREIF) has been issuing the formerly called Russell/NCREIF Property Index since 1982 [10]. The index value is set at 100 in 1977 and takes into account about 4,200 properties with a market value of US$ 150 billion which are owned by approximately 500 tax-exempt institutions such as pension funds. The calculations are based on the estimated quarterly returns before deductions of management fees. Income return and capital appreciation return compose the total return. Each property is valued by its market value which is estimated by professional property valuation methods. IPD launched a portfolio analysis service in the US in 2004, following a pilot study carried out in association with NCREIF. The service uses data that funds are already providing to NCREIF and provides managers with detailed information to optimize decisions about their portfolios. The fund managers receive comparisons on a consistent basis between their performance and a peer group as benchmark. IPD does not publish a US Index separate to the existing NCREIF product. Rather NCREIF offers different sector indices for office, retail, industrial and apartment buildings.

4.7   Hong Kong All Residential Price Index (HKU ARPI)

Since 1991, Professor K. W. Chau of the University of Hong Kong's Department of Property and Construction in collaboration with GFI Colliers has offered a monthly property index – the Hong Kong All Residential Price Index – for the Hong Kong Special Administrative Region (SAR) [11]. The index is based on a modified "repeat sales" methodology to capture changes in market value of the total stock of all residential units. The index calculations contain all actual residential real estate transactions registered with the Hong Kong Land Registry. The Hong Kong All Residential Price Index is a value weighted average of three sub-regional indices. The sub-regions are the Hong Kong Island (HKU-HRPI), the Kowloon Peninsula (HKU-KRPI) and the New Territories (HKU-NRPI). Due to data processing time, GFI Colliers publishes the indices with a six week time lag. GFI Colliers brokered the first real estate derivative deal between Sun Hung Kai Financial and ABN Amro based on the HKU HRPI in February 2007.

First real estate derivative in Asia

4.8   Valuation versus transaction-based indices

The discussion of various indices around the world shows that they are mostly residential. IPD and NCREIF are the only suppliers of indices that cover different real estate market sectors such as office, residential or retail. Generally, indices are constructed in two different ways: the transaction-based method and the valuation-based method. Transaction-based property indices generate their values from real estate transactions at actual prices paid at the market. Valuation-based indices express a total return calculated on basis of the estimated current market value and the income return. Most non-IPD indices are transaction-based excepting the NCREIF Property Index which also uses the valuation-based method.

Two different methods available

Of course, both methods have their own merits. The main difficulties of these two methods and possible solutions are identified shortly in the following, far from being conclusive. Problems of the valuation-based indices lie within the estimated property values and time-lags between valuation and calculation of the indices. Statistical methods such as Repeat Measures Regression [12] are used to diminish impreciseness. Transaction-based indices encounter problems due to the heterogeneity of property (size, quality, etc.) and low frequency of transactions. Hedonic price models and the Repeat Sales Price method [13] improve transaction-based indices.

Some researchers argue that transaction-based indices should be called real estate asset class research indices and valuation-based indices should be named evaluation benchmark indices [14]. Transaction-based indices are more research-oriented and useful for statistical means. They show the general performance of an asset class excluding external effects such as management performances. Meanwhile valuation-based indices should be rather used to set benchmarks and measure performances of specific portfolios in comparison to the market as a whole.

Valuation index preferable for benchmarking

5   Trading activities

UK: pioneer in trading real estate derivatives

To examine how a market for real estate derivatives has grown, the focus will be in the following again on IPD and particularly on the UK Index. Investors traded more derivatives on the IPD UK Index 2007 than in the three years 2004, 2005 and 2006 together (see figure 6). Between the beginning of 2004 and the end of the fourth quarter of 2007, investors traded derivatives with a notional value of £ 12.2 billion (€ 17 billion). Merrill Lynch expects for the next years that the market will continue to grow strongly [15]. The success of real estate derivatives in the UK during the last two years will presumably repeat itself in other countries. France is making the leap besides Germany at the moment. The first swap on the French office market took place at the beginning of 2007 just a bit later than the first option on the DIX, the German Property Index, traded late in 2006. Until the end of 2007 44 trades took place on the DIX with a notional value of € 400 million.

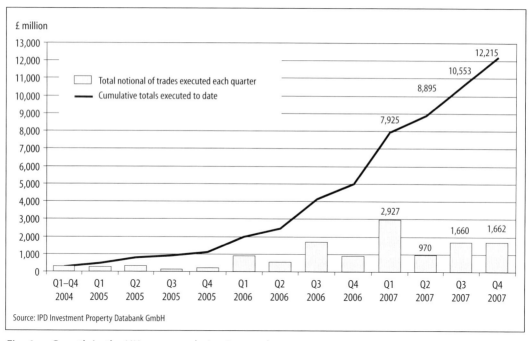

Fig. 6:   Growth in the UK property derivative market

6   License agreement for trading

Available for all institutions

IPD does not offer financial products such as derivatives. Financial institutions, who want to establish an IPD licensed derivative, have to sign a license agreement with IPD: The use of the IPD indices is non-exclusive. Thus, other institutions may use the same indices. The indices include all properties, sectors and segments available at IPD. The licensee normally agrees to five-year duration of the contract which may be cancelled after the first 12 months. The licensee will not need a new license for new sectors or segments but he is obliged to report the creation of new products to IPD. IPD is committed to provide the licensee with certified index values and index estimates and to publish the results of the indices on its own web site. Figure 7 shows the banks with a license for property derivatives based on IPD indices.

- Abbey National
- ABN Amro
- Bank of America
- Barclays Capital
- BNP Paribas
- Calyon
- Commerzbank AG
- CSFB
- Deutsche Bank
- EuroHypo
- Goldman Sachs

- HSBC
- HSH Nordbank
- Hypo Vereinsbank
- JP Morgan
- Lehman Brothers
- Merrill Lynch
- Morgan Stanley
- Royal Bank of Scotland
- Toronto Dominion
- UBS

Source: IPD Investment Property Databank GmbH

Fig. 7: Banks with license for IPD property derivatives

Standardization of derivative documentation

The bank with a license for writing derivatives on an index will act as financial intermediary between the two partners of a real estate derivative swap and will usually prepare an International Swaps and Derivatives Association (ISDA) document for the swap details. The ISDA is the world's largest organization of financial service providers with more than 750 members in 54 countries. The financial transaction document includes the underlying real estate index, the underlying payable interest rate (e. g., LIBOR, EURIBOR), the maturity date, etc. The ISDA paper also regulates that the investor may sell the swap before maturity. Then the price depends on the secondary market for swaps. Only one party of the deal has to be IPD-licensed. For example, institute X trades a derivative with institute Y through bank Z. This deal is legitimate as long as bank Z is licensed by IPD.

In general, it is difficult to prevent illegal use of the index. However, a bank usually has to participate in any deal and normally will be unwilling to act illegally [16].

7   The perspective for property derivatives

Derivatives on REITs?

The international standard product of indirect real estate investment, the Real Estate Investment Trusts (REITs), was introduced to the German market in 2007. REITs in Germany offer international investors a further investment opportunity. German REITs need to be listed at the stock market and have to meet minimum free float standards. It can be assumed that REITs will depend more on the development of the overall equity market as on the development of the real estate market. This is an experience which can be drawn from listed real estate corporations in Germany. A distinguishing difference between

REITs and listed property corporations is that REITs will need to distribute 90% of their profit and 75% of all income has to be property revenue. These profits are taxed on the investor's level according to the individual income tax rate. Similarities between REITs and listed real estate corporations concern the determination of the price by the stock exchange and not through the value of the properties owned by the corporations. In 2004, for example, listed German property corporations were traded at a 20% discount compared to the value of their properties, while in 2006, there was a premium of 20%.

The expected high volatility of REITs will make REITs derivatives an attractive speculation object for investors. However, investors who want to disengage from stock markets and pursue the strategy to diversify away from stock market risks might prefer derivatives on property indices such as the DIX composed of directly held properties. As consecutively shown, real estate indices have proven to be rather independent of the performance of the stock markets.

Negative correlation between DIX and DAX

Figure 8 shows the annual return of DAX, E&G-DIMAX and DIX between 1996 and 2006 and the correlation between the different asset classes. Looking at the return, it becomes evident that both DAX stocks and E&G-DIMAX with listed real estate corporations offered a high return in good years (DAX 1997: 47.1%, DIMAX 1997: 20.0%). However, in some years, both indices went into dark red (DAX 2002: –43.9%, DIMAX 2002: –19.9%). By contrast, directly owned properties, as shown by the DIX, usually offered a single digit return but so far never a negative one. In other words, the DIX constantly performed with a positive return while DAX and DIMAX strongly fluctuated between high profits and losses. It seems as if the DIX is exceeding the DAX when the DAX has a negative return and the DIX is below the DAX, when the DAX performs with a positive annual return. This impression is also reflected in the negative correlation between DAX and DIX of –0.27. In contrast, the correlation between DAX and DIMAX is +0.58.

High growth for real estate derivatives expected

Derivatives on a real estate index like the DIX offer a great opportunity to diversify a portfolio quickly and cost effectively. As set out, 21 banks have already purchased licences by IPD in order to trade derivatives on IPD indices. Consequently, an optimistic anticipation for the real estate derivative market in Germany builds on two aspects: First, it can be expected that the relentless search of investment banks for margins will result in an increase of real estate derivative types offered to investors and therefore to an increase in different means for portfolio optimization. Second, the German real estate market is likely to gain momentum over the next years resulting in increasing total returns comparable to other European countries that had positive double digits total returns in most recent years. If this proves true, international investors will continue to substantially increase their investments either directly or indirectly, reinforcing the demand for advanced financial engineering instruments like real estate derivatives.

Annual return in %			
	Dax	**E&G-DIMAX**	**DIX**
1996	28.2%	−12.9%	4.7%
1997	47.1%	20.0%	3.5%
1998	17.7%	37.6%	4.0%
1999	39.1%	56.5%	4.9%
2000	−7.5%	−25.4%	5.6%
2001	−19.8%	−2.3%	5.4%
2002	−43.9%	−19.9%	3.9%
2003	37.1%	−3.2%	2.9%
2004	7.3%	8.3%	1.1%
2005	27.1%	38.4%	0.5%
2006	22.0%	46.3%	1.3%
Average	**9.1%**	**6.7%**	**2.8%**
Correlation			
	Dax	**E&G-DIMAX**	**DIX**
Dax	1.00	0.58	−0.27
E&G-DIMAX	0.58	1.00	−0.41
DIX	−0.27	−0.41	1.00

Source: Own calculations based on Deutsche Börse, Privatbank Ellwanger & Geiger, IPD Investment Property Databank GmbH

Fig. 8:   Correlation DAX, DIMAX, DIX (1996–2006)

8   Bibliography

[1] HedgeStreet Inc., Binaries Description, San Mateo USA April 2007.

[2] Piazolo, D., Die Virtualisierung der Immobilien durch Immobilien-Index-Derivate, in: Immobilien & Finanzierung, Vol. 57, No. 22, Frankfurt a. M. 2006, p. 775.

[3] Thomas, M./Piazolo, D., Performance Messung und Benchmarking, in: Schulte, K.-W./Thomas, M. (Ed.): Handbuch Immobilien-Portfolio-management, Cologne 2007, pp. 207–222.

[4] Halifax and Bank of Scotland HBOS plc, The Halifax House Price Index – Index Methodology, Edinburgh 2008.

[5] Traditional Financial Services TFS, Risk & Manage – The Newsletter of the Property Derivative Market, April 2007 edition, p. 5.

[6] UK Secretary of State for Communities and Local Government, Statistical Release – House Price Index, London February 2007 edition, pp. 5–6.

[7]   Zürcher Kantonalbank ZKB, ZWEX – Der Zürcher Wohneigentums-
      index, Zürich 2007 pp. 1–3, 9–10.

[8]   Standard&Poor's, S&P/Case-Shiller Home Price Indices – Index
      Methodology, New York 2008.

[9]   Chicago Mercantile Exchange CME, CME Housing Futures and
      Options, Chicago 2008.

[10] National Council of Real Estate Investment Fiduciaries NCREIF, User's
      Guide to NIP – Frequently Asked Questions About NCREIF and the
      NCREIF Property Index (NPI), Chicago 2008.

[11] GFI Colliers, The University of Hong Kong All Residential Price Index,
      Hong Kong October 2006 edition.

[12] Geltner, D., The Repeated-Measures Regression-Based Index: A Better
      Way to Construct Appraisal – Based Indexes of Commercial Property
      Value, in: Property Finance, Vol. 12, Iss. 4, 1998, pp. 29–35.

[13] Case, K. E./Shiller, R. J., Prices of Single-Family Homes since 1970:
      New Indexes for Four Cities, in: New England Economic Review,
      Sep./Oct. 1987, pp. 45–56.

[14] Geltner, D./ Ling, D., Benchmarks & Index Needs in the US Private
      Property Investment Industry: Trying to Close the Gap, A RERI
      (Property Research Institute) Study for the Pension Property
      Association, October 2000.

[15] Merrill Lynch, Property Derivatives Handbook, Structured Finance
      Europe, January 22th, 2007, p. 3.

[16] The inidices are the intellectual property of IPD and any form of
      republication needs IPD's written consent.

4 Certificates on the German Property Index DIX

Matthias Thomas

Table of contents

1   Introduction

German real estate index certificates
The DIX Deutsche Immobilien Index is at present the only index available in Germany, which measures the ungeared performance of direct real estate investments held by institutional investors like pension funds, real estate companies, open-end funds, etc. The time series has its starting point in 1996 and the index may be segregated in varying sectors (e. g., office vs. retail) or in various segments (e. g., office Frankfurt vs. office Hamburg). As all the data of the DIX is computed on the basis of single property data, the index figure may be recalculated by the index provider IPD according to the needs of the market.

So far no real estate index certificates have yet been issued on the German DIX albeit more and more certificates on real estate indices are now available for varying European markets and thus are expanding the investment universe. Certificates may be seen as derivatives in a wider context, as the price of a certificate is derived from the price of the underlying assets, which in this case would be the German Property Index DIX. As the DIX measures the return on direct real estate investments, certificates on indices measuring the return or price development of indirect real estate investment vehicles like REITs, open-end funds, property shares, etc. will not be dealt with in this chapter. Instead, the following chapter will analyse and describe various existing certificates on European direct real estate indices which currently are or have been available for investors, as in essence these certificates could play a benchmark role in the establishment of the first DIX certificate of this kind covering the German real estate market.

Definition of derivative
A derivative is a financial instrument whose value is dependent upon, or derived from, the value of an underlying asset, index or other investment. In a narrower sense derivatives are understood to be products such as options, swaps, futures or forwards which may either be traded Over-the-Counter (OTC) or on an exchange. For these derivatives in a narrower sense there is a time spread between entering the obligation to buy or sell a certain quantity of a predefined asset at a predefined price (strike price) and the fulfillment of this transaction, which lies in the future.

Real estate is an inhomogeneous asset class. In order to create homogeneity for the difficult types of assets which is inevitable as underlying for a derivative product usually a real estate index is chosen in order to fulfill this requirement. Index certificates typically are designed as bonds (notes), where the return of the bond (note) is linked to the return of the underlying index. A certificate on a real estate index may therefore be classified as a derivative in a wider sense. An investor in an index certificate participates in any upward or downward movement of the respective index and at the same time bears the risk that the credit rating of the bond issuer might decline over time.

Homogeneity as prerequisite

In mid-1994, Barclays in London offered via its investment management arm, BZW, for the first time property index certificates (PICs). At that time Barclays had the largest exposure to real estate risk of any UK bank, as Barclays' loans to the commercial real estate sector amounted to 7 % of the overall loan portfolio of £ 70 billion. BZW believed that it would have been more expensive to either securitize those loans or sell any bad risks in the secondary market, thus Barclays was offering PICs as part of their overall balance sheet and portfolio management program [1].

UK real estate index certificates

The Barclays' certificates were aiming at institutional investors and had a minimum investment tranche of £ 250,000 with maturities between two and five years. The certificates were linked to the IPD All Property Index, which at that time was covering over £ 40 billion of real estate. An initial fee of 5 % was charged to investors, plus a quarterly fee of 0.0375 %. The return given by the certificates to the investor comprised two parts:

Investors received 88 % of the income return as quantified by IPD's Annual Index. The second part of the return was the capital growth or decrease in the UK real estate market as described by the index. From this initial starting point today various certificates are available to investors, offering instant access to the UK real estate market.

2 Property index certificates

2.1 General structure of an index certificate

Following German law, an index certificate typically is a bond ("Inhaberschuldverschreibung") according to § 793 BGB (German Civil Code). The holder of the bond in general is entitled to receive interest payments and a repayment of the notional amount of the bond at maturity. A bond may be seen as a securitized loan.

Legal structure of certificates

A certificate may be economically seen as a call option with a strike price of zero. Thus, a certificate gives the owner the right to participate in market movements. This implies that an investor in a certificate can not lose more than the original investment and at the same time, may conduct trading in the certificate through a standard equity trading account of a bank [2]. Typically, an index certificate replicates the underlying index in a predetermined ratio of 1 : 100 or 1 : 10.

2.2   DIX German Property Index as underlying

DIX composition   The DIX German Property Index is published annually by IPD Investment Property Databank. The DIX Deutscher Immobilien Index is based on an extensive databank which contains about 3,000 properties with a market value of approximately € 53.8 billion in 2006. Hence, the DIX covers 50 % of the value of properties held by institutional investors, which at the same time are valued at least on an annual basis. This compares to 21 % of all institutional properties including those that are valued less frequent than once a year. The average market value per property of the DIX is roughly € 18 million. The DIX covers the performance of directly held institutional properties from the large institutional investors in Germany. The institutional investors supply the data to IPD and receive in return a portfolio analysis relative to the benchmark of all participants. The DIX consists therefore of primary data mirroring the relevant financial accounts and business reports of the data supplier. IPD validates and double checks all the supplied information to enforce high data quality.

Capital growth and income return   The DIX shows performance as total return as a product of income return and capital growth. Capital growth is the net increase of the market value of all properties in the year adjusted to expenditures. Income return is calculated as net rental income which is calculated as gross rental income minus non-allocated operating costs of the year reviewed. Both values are expressed in percent of the capital invested. The DIX allows the direct comparison between different asset classes such as the German stock market index DAX or the E&G-DIMAX which lists German real estate stocks.

2.3   Case studies – existing real estate index certificates in Europe

Via an index certificate an investor may gain exposure to a certain market. If a certificate on the German DIX was available, the investor then could buy this product, and thus gain exposure to the risk and return characteristics of the German real estate market. The investor could either hold the certificate until redemption or sell the certificate on to other investors.

An investor might, for example, believe that the German real estate market will offer attractive returns within the next years. If the forecasted attractive returns hold true, the investor will participate in the performance of the German real estate market, as the price for the certificate will increase over time. If the reverse was true and the German real estate market would experience a downward shift with low or even negative returns, this would be reflected in the pricing of the certificate. The investor would achieve a low or even negative return. As mentioned before, at present no certificates on the DIX are available, but for other European real estate markets, e. g., the UK there are. Since 2006, it is possible for retail investors to participate in the performance of the IPD UK Index via a certificate issued by Goldman Sachs. Investors can purchase these certificates which were issued at £ 10 in sizes of one or multiples thereof, thus offering the opportunity to participate with small investment sums in the UK real estate market.

The redemption value of the Goldman Sachs IPD UK tracker is calculated at expiry according to the following procedure: At maturity, the investor receives a one-for-one exposure to the performance of the index return, subject to the fixed Annual Index Adjustment of 2.80%. The following example shows how the value of tracker will be calculated at expiry. **Case Goldman Sachs IPD UK tracker**

The closing level of the Estimate Index that was published by IPD for June 2006 was 1,456.48. As example, the following returns for each year shall be assumed [3]:

Annualized return (December 2006/June 2006) is 15%, i. e., Index (December 2006) = 1,456.48 · (1.15) ^ (6/12) = 1,561.90

Return (December 2007/December 2006) = 10%

Return (December 2008/December 2007) = 7%

Return (December 2009/December 2008) = 8%

Return (December 2010/December 2009) = 11%.

Using the assumptions above, if an investor holds the tracker until expiry, he or she will receive a single payment per tracker calculated as follows:

= £10 · (1,561.90 / 1,456.48 – 2.80% · 6/12) · (1 + 10% – 2.80%) ·
   (1 + 7% – 2.80%) · (1 + 8% – 2.8%) · (1 + 11% – 2.80%) = £13.457

The issuer Goldman Sachs provides real time liquidity for the IPD UK tracker, so investors can time their market entry and exit with a transparent bid/offer pricing published on the London Stock Exchange. The fixed Annual Index Adjustment of 2.80% which is applied to the UK IPD Index, is comparable with the total annualized cost of buying a UK commercial property unit trust and selling it after five years [4].

In 2006, Zürcher Kantonalbank issued two certificates on the ZWEX Zürcher Wohneigentumsindex, a hedonic index that tracks the price development of residential properties in the canton of Zürich, based on more than 16,000 transactions of single-family as well as multi-family housing. The index has been issued since 1980 [5]. **Case Zürcher Kantonalbank**

These structured products were named PROTEIN Zürcher Wohneigentums-index (Capital Protected Notes) and CASUAL Zürcher Wohneigentumsindex (Cash or Underlying Certificate) [6][7]. Both products are interesting for non-Swiss based investors due to a special requirement of the Swiss law, that in order to invest in Swiss residential properties, foreign investors need authorization from the appropriate cantonal authority [8]. Using these products now foreign investors can gain exposure to the price development and the associated risk of residential properties in the canton of Zürich, which in the past had been impossible due to legal restrictions.

The PROTEIN Notes offered by Zürcher Kantonalbank are protected participation notes with a guaranteed redemption of face value at 100% at the end of the life-time, which is – in this case – the February 24th, 2011. Annual interest payments take place, which depend on the performance of the underlying house price index ZWEX Zürcher Wohneigentumsindex, with an interest rate payment floor of 0% and a cap of 5.5%. If, for example, the **Case Zürcher Kantonalbank PROTEIN**

Zurich house price index shows a performance of 4%, investors receive an interest rate payment of 4%. If the annual house price index shows a negative performance, investors receive no interest payments. If the ZWEX Zürcher Wohneigentumsindex performs with, e. g., 8%, an investor would receive the maximum interest rate of 5.5%. Thus, the risk of an investor is limited to the extent of the difference between the purchase price of the product and the guaranteed redemption value of 100% face value at termination. Nevertheless, during the lifetime of the product, the price of PROTEIN on the secondary market can fall under the 100% face value [9]. The payoff structure of the PROTEIN Notes is shown in figure 1.

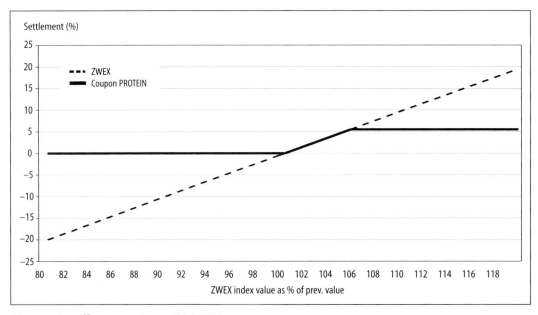

Fig. 1:   Payoff structure Immo-PROTEIN

Case Zürcher Kantonalbank CASUAL The Immo-CASUAL Cash or Underlying Certificate was designed as a product linked to the ZWEX Zürcher Wohneigentumsindex combined with selling a call on the house price index. Thus, an investor in this product would achieve superior returns in the case of a stagnating Zurich housing market. If at final fixing the ZWEX Zürcher Wohneigentumsindex was below the level of the cap, the investor would receive the current index value. The maximum return an investor in this product could achieve was 3.5%, based on a selling price of 192.19 and a cap level of 198.84 (100% of the index value at the time of issuance of the Immo-CASUAL). If the underlying house price index at termination was below 198.84, the investor would receive the house price index in CHF. The payoff structure of the CASUAL Notes is shown in figure 2.

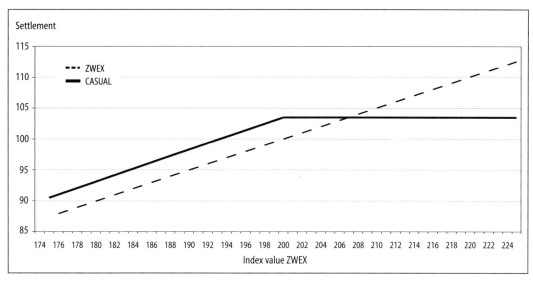

Fig. 2: Payoff structure Immo-CASUAL

2.4 German fiscal aspects for investors in real estate index certificates

For German private individuals resident in Germany and thus liable to German taxation, the following fiscal aspects result from investing in an index certificate (for cases in which the investor has held the certificate for a consecutive period in excess of 12 months).

Income from capital assets

Income from capital assets ("Einkünfte aus Kapitalvermögen") following § 20 (1) No. 7 of the German Income Tax Act (EStG) is only subject to be taxed with German income tax if a repayment of the notional amount is guaranteed and/or the investor has a right to receive interest payments for the conveyance of capital from the issuer.

Certificates with a capital guarantee

If an issuer of a certificate guarantees the full or partial repayment of the invested capital or even a repayment in excess of the invested capital, the investment is treated as a "financial innovation" in a taxation sense. Profits from selling or redeeming these certificates are treated as income from capital assets and are taxable according to § 20 (1) No. 7, § 20 (2) No. 4 German Income Tax Act. Furthermore, withholding tax ("Zinsabschlagsteuer") is applicable.

Certificates without a capital guarantee

Certificates without a capital guarantee carry neither a guarantee for repayment of the notional amount nor any interest payments. Instead, the profit or loss for an investor results from the development of the respective underlying. The redemption value of the certificate is totally dependent on the value of the underlying, which may rise or fall. A loss of 100 % of the invested capital is possible.

- The German Ministry of Finance has clarified the situation in its memos dated July 21st, 1998 (IV B - S 2251 116/98) and November 27th, 2001 (IV C 3 - S 2256 - 256/01) that profits from a capital investment are not subject to taxation, if the repayment of the invested capital is dependent on the uncertain outcome of a stock index. This even holds true, if the underlying stock index is a performance index, which takes account of dividend payments. This would be the case if the investor has had a holding period of the certificate in excess of 12 months. If the certificate had been held for a consecutive period of less than 12 months, all profits would be treated as profits from private disposition ("private Veräußerungsgeschäfte") and subject to income tax.

- Nevertheless, the German Ministry of Finance has the opinion according to its memos from July 21st, 1998 (IV B 4 S. 2252 - 116/98) and March 16th, 1999 (IV B 4 - S. 225s - 87/99) that depending on the economic content of an asset secured or probable – even partially – interest and capital repayments may leed to income from capital assets according to § 20 (1) No. 7 of German Income Tax Law. This would be the case if the repayment of the notional amount or interest payment are secured even if this is not explicitly stated in the terms document of the issued certificate (guarantee in an economic but not in a legal sense). It remains unclear when and if such an economic guarantee may arise. The Regional Finance Office of the Rhineland has followed the opinion in its decision from March 5th, 2007, that a certificate on the German notional government bond performance index REXP is carrying such an economic guarantee.

Therefore, each certificate needs to be analyzed and treated separately.

Fiscal changes effective from January 2009

The German parliament (Deutscher Bundestag) decided in its meeting of May 25th, 2007 that from January 1st, 2009 a flat rate withholding tax (Abgeltungsteuer) shall be implemented. All types of capital profits – including realized profits and profits from derivative transactions – will be subject to a flat rate tax of 25 % (solidarity surcharge and church tax will be levied extra on the 25 %). This law changes the previous system in which profits resulting from capital investments with a holding period in excess of one year had been tax exempt. This new law will be applicable for all assets, which have been purchased by an investor after December 31st, 2008. In deviation of this new arrangement, profits resulting from the sale of a certificate are to be taxed according to the new regulation if the certificate has been purchased after March 14th, 2007 and before January 1st, 2009 and the sale has taken place before June 30th, 2009.

The fiscal situation for institutional investors/corporations subject to taxation in Germany is rather straightforward in comparison to private individuals. As a certificate is basically a bond, the difference between the net selling revenues and the gross purchase price and received interest rate are subject to full taxation with the German corporate income tax plus solidarity surcharge. The wording in the German Corporation Tax Law as well as in the German trade tax regulations does not provide for any tax exemptions of certificates. As a certificate is a debt, investment, tax exemptions for interests resulting from equity investments (Beteiligungsertragsbefreiung) in accordance to § 8 b German Corporation Tax Law (KStG) do not apply.

2.5 Advantages and disadvantages of real estate index certificates

Investing into a real estate index certificate bears unique characteristics, distinguishing this investment compared to a direct property investment or investing into broadly diversified indirect products, e.g., like open-end real estate funds.

- **Low transaction costs**
  Unlike the costs generally associated with buying and selling real estate, such as legal fees, due diligence costs, the only transaction charges levied on dealing in real estate index certificates are the general commissions which typically are the same as for equity trading. For longer holding periods these transaction cost advantages will cease to exist.

- **Diversified exposure**
  Buying a real estate index certificate gives the investor exposure to a broadly diversified portfolio, which constitutes the index. In case of the DIX of nearly 3,000 properties with a market value in excess of € 50 billion, such diversification would be impossible to achieve from investing in individual properties. In contrary, index investors will not generate any excess return on the market return, which might be attributable to special managerial know-how. A buyer of a real estate index certificate will have access to a cheap beta but is unable to generate alpha with certificates.

- **Pure real estate risk and return exposure**
  Unlike open-end real estate funds, which are forced by law to have a liquidity ratio of between 5 % and 49 %, a plain vanilla index certificate would offer investors the possibility of receiving a pure real estate return and real estate risk, which is not diluted by returns and/or risks of other asset classes like bonds or cash.

- **Product structuring**
  A real estate index certificate may be structured or combined with other financial innovations in a way that it offers investors a positive return in stagnating or falling markets, enabling a more active portfolio management approach.

- **Fast market access**
  Entering new markets via a real estate index certificate allows investors a rapid implementation of their investment strategies without time extensive search cost. Thus, after gaining exposure to the general market development via a real estate index certificate an investor may build up a physical real estate portfolio.

- **Trading in any size**
  Investors are able to trade any number of certificates.

- **Liquidity**
  Typically, the issuer of an index certificate acts as a market maker and will provide liquidity on the secondary market/stock exchange.

- **Taxation**
  A real estate index certificate on the DIX could have on the one hand a structure making it very attractive for private investors, offering tax free returns if the prerequisites have been met. On the other hand, a real estate index certificate on the DIX seems less attractive for institutional investors from a taxational aspect, in comparison to a direct real estate investment or into open-end funds, as the holder loses the effect of depriciation of the buildings offset the rental income.

- **Legal aspects**
  As a real estate index certificate is not governed by the German Investmentgesetz (Investment Act), certificates allow on the one hand the issuer a high degree of flexibility in the design of their product characteristics. On the other hand, a lack of a strong regulatory framework might increase the inherent risk of such a product.

- **Lack of experience**
  As with all innovations at present no investor experience exists for a certificate on the DIX, making this product hard to market to a broad investor base in the beginning.

3   Summary and conclusion

It is interesting to note that the derivative market on the German DIX has evolved rapidly in 2007, with over 20 deals carried out, predominantly as swaps. So far, no certificate on the DIX has been issued, albeit there are no major obstacles, which would prevent investment banks moving forward and creating such a vehicle. One might see obstacles with respect to the frequency the DIX is calculated (annually at present), nevertheless the liquidity of certificates on an illiquid underlying may exist.

In general one must conclude that the fiscal aspects of an index certificate probably are for most investors less attractive than other forms of indirect real estate investments, but as the diversification and liquidity of these products may be higher, the advantages may outweigh the disadvantages. Therefore, from the author's point of view, it is just a question of time to see a first offering of a certificate on the DIX. Like all financial innovations this has to be demand driven.

4   Bibliography

[1] Roche, J., Property futures and securitisation – the way ahead, Cambridge 1995, p. 89.

[2] Goldman Sachs (Ed.), Property-linked Warrants & Certificates, no location, no date, p. 2.

[3] Goldman Sachs (Ed.), UK IPD Tracker, no location, no date, p. 2.

[4] Goldman Sachs (Ed.), UK IPD Tracker, no location, no date, p. 1.

[5] For a more detailed description of the ZWEX, please refer to chapter D3 „Derivatives: The Synthetization of Property" by Dr. Daniel Piazolo in this handbook.

[6] Zürcher Kantonalbank (Ed.), Strukturierte Produkte PROTEIN Zürcher Wohneigentumsindex (ZWEX), no location, no date, pp. 1

[7] Zürcher Kantonalbank (Ed.), Strukturierte Produkte CASUAL Zürcher Wohneigentumsindex (ZWEX), p. 1

[8] Schweizer Bundesamt für Justiz (Ed.), Erwerb von Grundstücken durch Personen im Ausland (Merkblatt), Bern 2005, p. 1.

[9] Zürcher Kantonalbank (Ed.), Strukturierte Produkte PROTEIN Zürcher Wohneigentumsindex (ZWEX), no location, no date, pp. 6.

5   Market for German residential real estate derivatives

Sven Andersen
Thomas Schneider

Table of contents

1   Residential real estate derivatives: another financial gimmick or a real breakthrough for the real estate world?

Difficulties implementing real estate derivatives   The usage of derivatives outside of the real estate world is already so trivial today that probably nobody would bother to write many lines to justify the benefits or necessity of its existence. The list of examples for the underlyings is long and includes many different areas, for example, commodity-, freight-, inflation or energy derivatives, such as coal, gas and power. The trading with derivatives can even go so far that the underlying asset has no direct value to the price, which would be, for example, the case with weather derivatives. This might now raise the question why it took so long to develop real estate derivatives. This question becomes even more evident, if taken into consideration the inherent characteristics of real estate, such as being physically bound to one location, the high transactions costs, slow ability to liquidate and high dependency on the micro- and macro-surroundings. All these limitations clearly reveal the immanent need to mitigate the risks and limitations that come along with investments into real estate. So far, there is no affordable and efficient tool in the market that offers home owners and/or professional real estate investors a possibility to hedge all or some of the risks that result from these limitations. The problem gets even more severe considering the fact that the majority of wealth within the private households is bound in real estate. Any fluctuations with regard to the value of real estate will have a considerable influence on the discipline in public spending. This is especially true for low- to mid-income households for whom real estate investments always meant a considerable cluster risk. Today, this problem is not only limited to private households due to the increasing integration of real estate and capital markets. In the last four years, many market participants heavily invested in German residential real estate portfolios, such as, for example, Fortress/GAGFAH who bought from the city of Dresden 50,000 residential units with a value of more than € 1.7 billion [1]. These investors are now heavily exposed to the German residential real estate market and so far no real efficient financial tool is available to manage their asset allocation risks and/or to deal with the situation in case of a occurring crisis in the housing market.

In this context it is surprising that the exposure of derivatives to real estate still plays a negligible role. The fact that this segment still has not yet evolved can primarily be attributed to the following main reasons:

- **Difficulty to standardize real estate**
  In contrast to commodities, interest rates or energy, it is much more difficult to standardize real estate and to achieve a market transparency in this area that is needed to create a reliable and meaningful database. These problems lead to the result that up to now most of the real estate databases are not able to fully satisfy the demands of the market players.

- **Creation of reliable databases and indices**
  Without the existence of such databases, no functional indices can be developed that are trusted and accepted by the market players. The indices simultaneously serve as the combining link and playfield that connect the market players with real estate derivatives and the real estate market. Without the existence of working real estate indices no significant real estate derivative trading can be initialized.

- **Education of the market players**
  Until very shortly the real estate industry itself was heavily neglected both by academia and the financial real estate sector itself. Both sides neither spent much effort to develop any kind of real estate derivative market nor to educate its potential market players on how to participate in the game. The first efforts in that direction took place in London in

the early 1990s, at the London Futures and Options Exchange (London Fox) but for many reasons came to a quick end. It took until 2005 before a second attempt was undertaken in the United Kingdom to revitalize an active real estate derivative market. Unlike the last attempt, it now looks like the real estate derivatives market has gained momentum and enjoys increasing attention and enthusiasm.

At the end of 2006, the total outstanding notional traded volume amounted to nearly US$ 500 trillion, which is about ten times the amount of the global GDP of 2006. Around 80 % of the total volume was traded Over-the-counter (OTC) [2]. These achievements in mind, it seems like the development of reliable and feasible indices, not only in the UK, but also in other European real estate market, such as France and Germany, is making good progress. Nevertheless, it also has to be pointed out that the attempts currently made to increase the level of education of market players has grown but is still lagging behind.

Given the promising success in the UK to establish a working real estate derivative market, this chapter will focus its efforts in the following section to analyze the potential of the German residential real estate market to achieve a similar success story.

2   Characteristics and usage of real estate derivatives

Definition of derivatives
Derivatives are financial instruments whose return and price is based on the value of an underlying asset, e. g., commodities, stocks or real estate. In practice, four types of derivatives have been relevant for the real estate market so far: swaps, futures, certificates/bonds and options. Derivatives give investors the opportunity to take certain positions in the market including:

- **long:**   to hold a position in a security with the anticipation of an increase in price;

- **short:**   to hold a position in a security with the anticipation of a decrease in price;

- **market neutral:**   to hold a position that is equally divided between long and short positions to hedge out market direction [3].

Types of derivatives
Depending on the type of the derivative used, the real estate owner can hedge many unwanted market risks and the speculator could purse different investment strategies depending on how he estimates the market will move. In the following will we briefly discuss the most common types of real estate derivatives [4][5].

- **Real estate swaps**

Real estate swap deals are up to now the most frequently used derivative in regard to real estate transactions. In these deals, the contracting parties exchange cash flows in order to mitigate their risk. One side of the party agrees to receive a floating or fixed rate of interest, which is, for example, linked in an interbank rate (EURIBOR or LIBOR) and pays, in return, the counterparty the movements in the Total Return Property Index. In order to make a real estate swap deal work, both parties with different expectations on the real estate market have to agree on a fair price for themselves at which they would agree to sell real estate return against a fixed or floating rate.

- **Real estate bonds**

Real estate bonds are based on the same concept. They are linked to a certificate which reflects the movement of a prior determined real estate index. An individual investor may purchase real estate bonds to secure payouts over the maturity which are reflected by the index. The fact that this financial instrument is linked to the index enables the shareholder to invest indirectly in real estate.

- **Real estate index options**

Options give the client the right to carry out a transaction at a later date at an agreed upon price. A call option may, for example, give the client the right to purchase a real estate index-linked product at the price previously agreed upon. Call options give the investor the possibility to benefit if the market is rising. In case of a market drop, the investor simply chooses not to exercise the option and "only" loses the premium he paid for. Conversely, an investor buying a put option can bet on a falling market, where he or she buys the right to sell an index-linked product at the price previously agreed.

- **Real estate forward contracts**

In this case, the contracting parties are committing themselves to carry out a future transaction at the conditions they agreed upon before. The products discussed are based directly on a real estate index, and are therefore linked to outright real estate investment. Alternatively, derivatives can also be exercised on real estate stocks or REITs.

- **Real estate future contracts**

Real estate future contracts are standardized, transferable, exchange-traded contracts that require the delivery of a commodity, bond, currency, or stock index at a specified price, on a specified future date. Unlike options, futures convey an obligation to buy. The risk to the holder is unlimited, and because the payoff pattern is symmetrical, the risk to the seller is unlimited as well. Dollars lost and gained by each party on a futures contract are equal and opposite (often also called zero-sum game). Futures contracts are forward contracts, meaning they represent a pledge to make a certain transaction at a future date. Futures can, for example, be used by real estate developers who fear that condominium prices in their region will fall, enabling them to look in today's prices and offering a secured financial planning reliability.

3 Advantages and disadvantages of real estate derivatives

The usage of derivatives does not only offer professional and private investors several possibilities to overcome limitations and risks that come along with direct investments in real estate, but they could also be used as a tool for active portfolio management and/or as an alternative for investments into real estate.

3.1 Reduced costs, speed, volume and ease of transactions

Easy to use The use of real estate derivatives enables investors to avoid investing directly in real estate which is always connected to relatively high acquisition costs, a tedious due diligence process and the provision of a huge amount of capital. Furthermore, direct investments in real estate require the investor to find the right property, which alone may take months. Due to the quite long and costly acquisition process, direct real estate investors are usually forced to stay in their investment for a longer period. Investment in real estate derivatives instead bypasses this long procedure and enables the investor to be invested in real estate on the same day. Furthermore, the usage of derivatives enables the inexperienced investor to be invested in the whole real estate market or sector of a country, instead of putting all of his investment into a single property. A private investor, for example, who wants to purchase a residential unit in a hot upcoming market, but who does not have the money yet to acquire it, could lock in today's cheaper prices by taking a long position investing in the real estate index that represents this area. Gaining that time advantage could be especially important during a strong bull market where the lag between future and retrospective investment financially makes a significant difference [6].

3.2 Mitigating real estate market risk

Trading real estate market risk Two further motivations to use derivatives are to either actively hedge existing risks or to speculate/bet on the market. Derivatives give the investor a unique opportunity to hedge their real estate exposure by taking a short position on the index. In the past, the only real way to avoid the negative effects of an expected market downturn was to sell the asset, which involved high transaction costs and required a considerable amount of time to close the transaction. This is especially problematic for home owners, because they in most cases do not have the possibility or the interest to sell their home quickly if they believe that house prices will fall. Through the usage of derivatives they can comfortably stay in their home, because potential value losses of their home will be offset by gains of the derivative. This might become especially important for home owners that have a substantial mortgage on their home. Derivatives allow investors to react immediately and more cost efficiently on anticipated market movements [7].

3.3 Asset class re-allocation

More efficient portfolio management Apart from hedging, derivatives can also be used for prompt reallocation between different asset classes within mixed asset portfolios. Many institutional investors, for example, have regulations on the size of their real estate exposure within their portfolio. When, for instance, due to new real estate valuations the value of the real estate portfolio increases automatically an imbalance within the target allocations occurs. In the past, the only way for portfolio managers to correct the imbalance, in order to confirm with the investment guidelines, was to sell parts of the portfolio. This often led to the result that hastily actions were undertaken. Now, with the use of derivatives, the portfolio manager can more efficiently mitigate these problems by trading parts of his real estate exposure (by going short), by paying the movements in the Total Return Property Index in exchange for LIBOR plus a fixed spread. The same, of course, would be possible if the investor wanted to increase his exposure to real estate [8][9].

3.4   Portfolio diversification

Since real estate cycles are not perfectly correlated within the different real estate sectors, investors can also use derivatives to rebalance their portfolios by short or long positions depending on the different markets. An investor, for example, who currently manages a portfolio of in total € 100 million (50 % residential and 50 % office), got offered an interesting € 100 million portfolio with a sector balance of 70 % residential, 30 % office. An investor who only wants to invest equally in residential and office properties would have a problem with such an allocation due to the existing unbalance within the offered portfolio. Here, derivatives offer a unique way to solve the problem by letting the investor go simultaneously short in residential swaps for € 20 million and long in office swaps for € 20 million. The same concept could, of course, be also applied with regard to regional aspects in order to hedge any unwanted overexposure to certain regions [10][11].

Increased opportunities through diversification

3.5   Hedge property beta exposure and retain alpha

Returns created by investors can in general be separated into two segments: Alpha (α) and Beta (β) returns, whereby β represents the projected market returns of, for example, the IPD index and α the amount by which an investor was able to outperform the index returns through above average management performance on the underlying property. If, for example, an owner of residential properties believes that the residential market will soon be bearish for a while and that his properties still will be able to outperform the market due to his superior management skills, he then could hedge his market risk by selling β (going short on the IPD index) in return for LIBOR plus a fixed spread and still earn α through successful asset management [12][13][14].

Successful asset managers can keep their alpha

3.6   Acquisition finance

Here the usage of derivatives might turn out to be especially valuable if banks, for example, feel uncomfortable financing certain parts (real estate sectors) of a large real estate portfolio. Through the usage of derivatives, the purchaser could reduce its exposure to property sectors the bank has concerns about. The ability to hedge out certain risks the banks are not willing to take, gives the

Banks may hedge out certain risks

investors the opportunity to achieve finance terms he otherwise would have never obtained [15].

Risks associated with investing in real estate derivatives

Despite of all the clear advantages that the usage of derivatives brings along, there are also risks that the two parties that are involved in the derivative deal have to bear in mind. As stated before, derivatives are mainly used either by end users who want to mitigate their risks or by speculators. The main risk that speculators face is that they misjudge the market or that they do not truly understand the index itself or the derivatives instruments they are trading. End users need to bear in mind that derivatives are a synthetic investment in real estate and because of that hold clearly different characteristics than direct real estate investments. In sharp contrast to direct investments, where the investor can personally influence the performance of his or her property, derivatives as a purely passive investment vehicle do not provide investors any opportunity to directly influence or control the performance of the index.

3.7   Mismatch risk

Selection of appropriate underlying

One major risk in any investment with derivatives is that the chosen index is composed by properties that do not reflect the portfolio that the investor wants to hedge. The German Property Index DIX, for example, consists mainly of office and retail properties in Germany and would for that reason not at all serve the needs of an investor who want to use this index to hedge his residential property portfolio risks in the UK. It is absolutely necessary that end users who want to hedge their risk very careful asses which index most closely correlates with their real estate [16].

3.8   Counterparty risk

One side of the deal fails to deliver

One main disadvantage of swaps is that both parties due to the mismatch in the timing of payments always have to be aware of counterparty risk. For that reason, both parties in a swap contract need to make sure that each side is covered for the case that they heavily misjudged the market and have to pay the counterparty. Another way to reduce counterparty risk could be to agree on more frequent payments [17][18].

4   Market overview and development in Europe

UK real estate derivative market most developed

Even though real estate derivatives are being discussed by academia and financial institutions for the last 15 years, only in the last three years a noteworthy market developed. In 1991, the IPD index was introduced on the London Fox but was unable to achieve momentum due to a scandal of false trades which were designed to manipulate the market's perception on trading volume. Although the first implementation failed in the 1990s, the UK market started to keep picking up after a phase of recovery, which laid up an auspicious foundation for a second attempt in 2005 to initialize an index in the UK. Since the UK real estate derivative market clearly sets the standard not only in Europe, but also in the world, it is only logical to start investigating developments there.

4.1   UK real estate derivative market

In the first quarter of 2007, the value of property derivatives based on the IPD index reached a cumulative notional of approximately £7.6 billion. Almost 360 transactions took place in 2006, whereby the number of deals carried out increased by a factor of five in comparison to the previous year. The volume of deals conducted in that 12 months rose more than by the sixfold [19]. The following graph visualizes the dimensions of the before mentioned growth. **Development of the UK real estate derivative market**

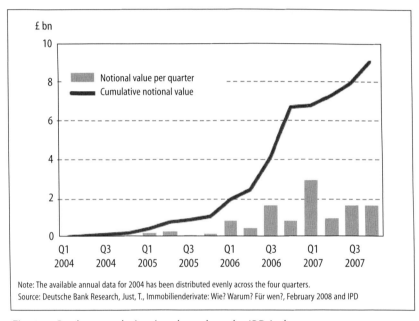

Fig. 1:   Real estate derivatives based on the IPD index

Also the UK residential real estate derivatives market experienced a considerable growth over the years. Within the last seven years over £ 2 billion of derivatives trades were executed, which were based on the Halifax house price index. The majority of counterparties involved in these trades, were retail banking institutions that offered house price index-linked investment products to their retail customers [20].

The last cycle in the UK real estate market was characterized by historically low going in yields and high transaction volumes. The majority of transactions during this cycle was mainly driven by permanent inflow of liquidity and not so much by strong market fundamentals. Only until very recently, the UK market faced a slowdown in the number and volume of transactions, which created an uncertainty within the ranks of property owners and now by return, triggers an increased interest in financial vehicles that allow for hedging their real estate exposure. This effect got reinforced by the sub-prime crises in the United States; spreading the fear within property owners that the ongoing yield compression will not only end but possibly reverse. This situation finally created even more awareness within the investor circles to consider real estate derivatives to hedge their property risk as well as to get a much quicker and affordable exposure through derivatives to a more diversified pool of real estate.

4.2   Outlook

Signals for an ongoing growth

Due to the above mentioned market conditions, it is expected that the UK derivative market will continue its strong growth. Another clear signal for an ongoing growth of the derivative sector is that now 22 financial institutions in total have acquired licenses for the IPD index (source: IPD). It is fair to assume that the growing number of banks involved in real estate derivatives will consequently lead to more trading and as a result of that create the liquidity needed to support the continuous growth of this sector. Furthermore, it can also be observed that an increasing number of advisory companies are building up expertise in the real estate derivatives sector and try to generate new businesses by educating potential market players on how real estate derivatives can help them to achieve their goals. As market education will continue to expand, more end users will get used to derivatives and create further trading volume and liquidity. By the first quarter of 2007, the total notional trading volume in the UK was approximately £6.5 billion with £2.9 billon being executed within that quarter (see figure 2). DB Research is projecting that the market volume will by the end of the decade have exceeded a volume of £100 billion [19]. It is reasonable to expect that the success story of the UK has great potential to spill over to other European countries; it currently seems that France and Germany are slowly gaining some tender momentum in the development of their real estate derivative markets.

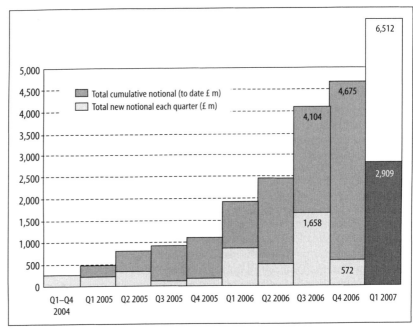

Fig. 2:   Growth in the notional value of all deals traded based on the IPD

Irrespective to the fact that the real estate derivative market within the UK is experiencing an exponential growth, it is necessary to mention some constraints that are inherent in these figures:

Note of statistical limitations of the IPD Index

- **The possibility for multiple counting**
  It is quite realistic to expect that one transaction could end up in several interbank transactions, of which all of them are reported to IPD.

- **Not a complete overview of the market**
  The IPD only considers reported transactions, but it has to be assumed that not all transactions are reported and thus some are missing in the index.

The goal of figure 3 is to provide the reader a short overview of some of the most crucial events in the history of the UK real estate derivatives market.

Milestones of the UK real estate derivative market	
1991	London FOX (UM) attempt failed
1994	Property Index Forwards (PIFs) established
1998	Real estate index market failed
1994–1999	Property Index Certificates (PICs) established by Barcleys Capital in the UK, based on IPD index
2000	Barcleys & PRUPIM create Property Derivatives User Association (PDUA)
2000–2003	PDUA addresses regulatory issues and obtains approval from UK regulators for trading on IPD index
2004	Licenses taken by various international banks to use IPD UK indices for derivatives
December 2004	British Land and Prudential trade first major contract for £ 40 million
2005	First UK OTC derivative trade took place (EuroHypo/DB) Banks acting as middlemen, not active parties
December 2005	UK derivatives trades close to £ 1 billion, seven banks with licenses
2006	UK trades over £ 1 billion, 10+ banks with licenses first sector swaps in the UK (ABN AMRO)
2007	UK market reaches over £ 7 billion
Current market conditions	Current market low yield compression, but still good transaction levels
	Investments are still liquidity driven, except further yield compression expected
	Total notional value trade Q1 2007 £ 6.5 billion
	Banks are actively warehousing risk to create liquidity
	Market conditions are triggering hedging needs for property investors
Source: Venter, J., Barriers to Growth in the US Real Estate Derivatives Market, September 2007, p. 39	

Fig. 3:   Important events in UK real estate derivatives market history

5   Market participants and motivation

Banks   So far, 22 investment banks have obtained a license for the IPD UK index in order to trade real estate derivatives. Due to the business concept of investment banks to make their income through market making by gaining the spread between the prices agreed by two opposite parties, they are very eager to avoid taking positions in transactions themselves and rather focus their efforts on identifying counterparties. Similar to investment banks, derivative brokers are also actively engaged in the market as "matchmaker" in order to sell IPD derivatives whereby their compensation mainly consists of a one-off upfront fee. Huge institutional investors, such as Prudential and Hermes, along with IPD and IPF (Investment Property Forum) are very supportive on any efforts to establish a working real estate derivative market and for that reason are sponsoring and initiating a multitude of educational and training events [21].

Other major players   Other major players involved in the derivatives market within the UK are fund managers, hedge funds, life- and pension funds and real estate companies. Their level of commitment and participation in the market depends very much on their acceptance with regard to market liquidity and general understanding of derivatives.

Institutions and major pension funds are mostly considering the usage of derivatives for asset allocation purposes, hedging and to increase their exposure. Institutions on the long side are aiming for beta gains at a very competitive pricing. Due to the fact that real estate companies are by nature already long in real estate, they mainly use derivatives solely for hedging purposes. An increasing number of real estate owners realized the benefits of trading beta and started focusing on their alpha gains. In general, developers mainly have a need for capital hedges and are not very aggressive on pricing. It is very important for them to have planning reliability. In order to secure their business plan they need to hedge the down side risk and accept a lower upside in return in order to do the hedge. Hedge funds in general tend by nature to favor more short-term speculative positions on both sides of the market. For private investors, investments in their residential properties always means, a considerable cluster risk and they are keen to improve their situation by using derivative indices to reduce their exposure.

Additional uncertainty created by the US subprime crisis   The dominating tendency, at the beginning of the derivative market in the UK, was that the vast majority of market participants chose to "go long" on real estate. This was mainly the case because of the investors' inability to hedge risk and due to a bullish real estate market where the clear majority of investors expected real estate prices to rise further. In such upbeat times, the professional investors and home owners simply saw no justification for investing capital to hedge market risks or even going short. This momentum changed due to the slow-down in the market and additional uncertainty generated by the US subprime crisis. Slowly market players are considering the possibility of negative capital value growth and reverse yield compression and as a consequence the need to hedge these potential risks, which will lead to a much more balanced real estate derivative market [22][23].

6 Barriers to growth

The following section addresses the barriers to growth in the German residential real estate derivatives market. The main hurdles that were identified to be responsible for preventing the evolution of a derivative market in Germany similar to the UK are the following:

German real estate fails to evolve similar to the UK market mainly for three reasons

- problems with the pricing;
- the implementation of reliable and compelling indices;
- lack of education of market participants.

6.1 Pricing

The existence of sufficient liquidity on both sides of the market is a crucial necessity for end users in order to be able to take positions. One main driver for the success of the UK real estate derivative market was the willingness of major banks to warehouse risks at the beginning to ensure that the real estate derivative market has the necessary liquidity to develop. The German real estate derivative market would need a similar engagement from major banks in order to create a movement that turns out to be significant enough to be self-sustainable.

Similar to the UK (but by far not as distinctive), also the German real estate market experienced increased demand, mainly from international investors which were intensely acquiring German real estate portfolios. The current subprime crisis in the US also created growing concerns about the sustainability of the German real estate boom within Germany, with the result that a growing number of investors began considering using derivatives to hedge parts of their real estate exposure.

One major disadvantage of the German real estate market in comparison to the UK is its lack of sufficient transparency, which causes illiquidity and high spreads that in turn directly impacts pricing. The lack of a functional and liquid secondary market is another shortcoming in Germany, since it leaves investors locked in their contracts until maturity. Due to the fact that the German derivatives market still is at its early development stage, it consistently has to deal with liquidity problems in general and with the lack of a secondary market, which as a consequence leaves huge room for pricing errors. The ability to ensure correct pricing is an important precondition to build trust beneath the end users and to enable them to use derivatives efficiently [24]. Figure 4 displays the main drivers that determine the LIBOR margin.

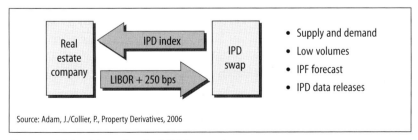

Source: Adam, J./Collier, P., Property Derivatives, 2006

Fig. 4: Main drivers for the LIBOR margin

6.2   Indices

Differences between Germany and the UK

One of the most significant differences between the German and the UK derivative market is the quality and number of indices that are available to trade on. The UK offers to both commercial and residential investors two separate indices (IPD for commercial and Halifax for residential properties) that cover their sectors sufficiently and enjoy huge acceptance within the investor community. This stands in sharp contrast to the German market, where today only the commercial real estate sector is covered sufficiently (DIX). This situation makes it especially difficult for residential property owners who are over proportionally exposed in Germany, because the German market today does not offer any residential real estate index of the quality and acceptance similar to the UK Halifax Index. Due to the fact that the residential and commercial real estate markets are highly different, the authors are confident that the success of a German residential derivative market will strongly depend on the establishment of an own meaningful residential real estate index.

Another important difference between the existing UK and German real estate indices is that the UK indices provide their date quarterly and the German

Development level of IPD property indices		
	Market coverage of index (%)	**Is the index ready for derivatives?**
AU	25	Ready to a degree
AT	30	Ready to a degree
CA	50	Ready
DK	41	Ready
FI	60	Ready
FR	54	Ready
DE	23	Ready
IE	79	Ready
IT	24	Ready to a degree
JP	10	Not yet ready
NL	60	Ready
NO	47	Ready
PO	51	Ready
ES	48	Ready
SA	60	Ready
SE	30	Ready
CH	35	Ready to a degree
UK	45	Ready
Source: Just, T./Feil, J., Property derivatives marching across Europe, 2007, p. 9		

Fig. 5:   Market coverage of index

indices only annually. Many existing and potential market players are quite concerned about the limited market coverage that the current German indices have. The German residential real estate index, for example, so far only covers 65,000 condominiums with a total value of approximately € 4.5 billion and the IPD German real estate index market coverage is less than 23 % [25]. Figure 5 provides a broad overview of the development level of IPD property lines to the reader.

Within the industry there are many discussions about which strategy and composition makes the best real estate index. The transaction-oriented indices claim, in comparison to valuation driven indices, to have the advantage of using realized and by the market verified market prices only. Figure 6 provides a good overview on the various strategies an index can use in order to create its own data pool.

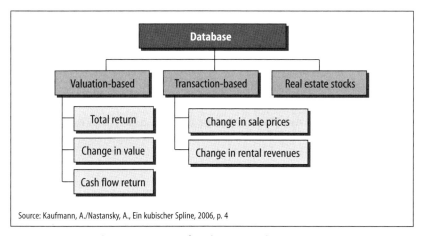

Source: Kaufmann, A./Nastansky, A., Ein kubischer Spline, 2006, p. 4

Fig. 6:   Potential compositions of real estate indices

The development of a derivative market similar to the UK will only become possible in Germany if its real estate market is able to provide similar reliable and meaningful indices. In the following overview we will briefly introduce some of the already used and established real estate indices in Germany [26][27].

- **German Ownership Property Index (DEIX)**

The DEIX (Deutscher Eigentums-Immobilienindex) was introduced for the first time in 1996, by the Institut für Städtebau, Wohnungswirtschaft und Bausparwesen (ifs). The DEIX indicates the performance of condominium units and single-family houses in West (since 1989) and East Germany (since 1995), and is based on annually registered real estate transactions of newly built and existing houses and apartments. The index itself is then calculated by using average house and apartment prices.

- **German Property Index (DIX)**

The DIX (Deutscher Immobilienindex) represents a performance index that has been published since 1996 by IPD Germany formerly Deutsche Immobilien Datenbank (which is a subsidiary of IPD in the UK). This index is based on a databank that contains close to 3,000 properties with a market value of approximately i 53 billion. The clear focus of this index is put on commercial real estate, particularly office and retail properties. The index considers in its calculations only properties that were assessed in two consecutive years. The DIX is the only real estate index in Germany that allows direct comparison with different asset classes, for example, the German stock market index DAX.

- **Index from BulwienGesa AG**

Since 1990, the performance and price index from BulwienGesa presents an annual overview about the price and rental development of residential and commercial real estate in 125 German cities. The statistical foundation of this index is based on own data collection, analysis, surveys and publications from other sources (such as broker associations, advisory committees and home savings and loan associations).

- **E&G DIMAX Ellwanger & Geiger**
  German Real Estate Stock Index

The first comprehensive stock index for German real estate companies was disposed in the year 1995 by the bank Ellwanger & Geiger. The start date of the DIMAX was calculated back to early 1989 and its construction is based on the German stock index. As a performance index the DIMAX considers changes in the capital structure and/or dividend payments only. The value of the index is determined and published on a daily basis. Currently 76 stock companies are listed in the DIMAX, with the main listing requirement being that at least 75 % of the company's total revenues are achieved through their real estate investments.

- **German residential property index**

IPD has started a new German index which is only focused on residential real estate. The index currently consists of 60,000 apartments with a market value of approximately € 4.5 billion. The data made available for the German residential real estate index so far is derived from nine contributors (Allianz, AMB Generali, AmpegaGerling, AXA, Bayerische Versorgungskammer, DEFO, MEAG Munich Ergo, REDEVCO, R+V Lebensversicherung). The performance of the index is mainly driven by the following three real estate sectors:

- Munich (35.97 %),
- the Rhineland (19.5 %) and
- the Rhine-Main area (10.4 %).

The methodology of the IPD index is to measure direct investments into real estate using time-weighted returns based on the GIPS standard.

The following figure 7 briefly summarizes the advantages and disadvantages of each index in regard of its ability to be used as an index for trading real estate derivatives.

Index	Advantages	Disadvantages
DEIX	• Value and not performance driven index • Nationwide coverage	• No commercial real estate • Contains also structural effects
DIX	• Usage of primary data • Appropriate as benchmark for real estate portfolio investments	• Residential real estate is underrepresented • Performance and no value driven index • Short-time series (since 1996)
Index of BulwienGesa Joint Stock Company	• Nationwide coverage of all real estate sectors • Publication of separate property segments • Long-time series (since 1990)	• Data collection from secondary research • No pure price index
German residential property index (IPD)	• Focus only on residential real estate • Established provider of real estate indices	• Short-time series (since 1996) • Value currently covered in the index is low • Too strong concentration on a few sectors/cities
E&G DIMAX	• Daily calculation • High market coverage	• Performance highly dependent on management performance and development of the stock market • High concentration within the index
Source: Kaufmann, A./Nastansky, A., Ein kubischer Spline, 2006, p. 6 and IPD		

Fig. 7: Comparison of German real estate indices

6.3   Education

Real estate derivatives are an important financial product that is definitely needed in the real estate industry. The currently existing lack of education in regards to derivatives has proven to be a strong barrier to growth. This hurdle definitely needs to be overcome in Germany if any serious attempt to develop a real estate derivative market is to be undertaken. The majority of real estate professionals in Germany currently does not at all or not sufficiently understand how to use derivatives. The predominantly fragmented composition of the currently existing education process is not able to close this gap. The fact that this specific market is separated by two groups of professionals with two very distinct skill sets, namely either real estate knowledge or finance know-how, does not ease the problematic situation. So far, it appears that both sides have not yet spent sufficient time and effort to learn to speak and understand each others language and for that reason too often miss each other. In order to close this gap and to make the end users and market players more comfortable with the usage of derivatives, a much broader education needs to be provided by a wider range of groups, such as banks, intermediaries and academia [28].

7   Concluding remarks

Summary and outlook

There are strong market indications that real estate derivatives within Europe will become an accepted and used capital-market-oriented real estate instrument in the near future. Although real estate is not perfectly suited for the use of derivatives due to its specific nature, as opposed to commodities, interest rates or inflation, a real estate derivative market nevertheless is to be expected to grow over the next years. This assessment gets affirmed just by considering the enormous size of the underlying real estate class: The value of commercial real estate in Europe is estimated to be around € 5.5 trillion. The specific importance of the residential real estate stock becomes evident if taken into consideration that its value in Europe is estimated to be approximately € 14.6 trillion. These statistics clearly point out that in particular the development of residential indices in Europe is a major area of growth for real estate derivatives. If theoretically only 1 % of this underlying market were hedged using derivatives, the European derivative market would have a volume of approximately € 200 billion [29].

As the market continuous to evolve, it is to assume that the importance of options and certificates will grow next to the already established swaps. One prerequisite for further growth within the German real estate derivatives market will be the successful implementation of two meaningful separate indices: one for residential and the other focused on commercial real estate. This separation is necessary because of the highly different conditions that are prevailing within these two markets. Any private home owner or professional investor who owns residential real estate in Germany can only mitigate his investment risk if the index used closely matches his portfolio. Furthermore, it would be highly beneficial if these indices were upgraded through the implementation of sub-sector indices and the introduction of monthly reporting. A noteworthy residential derivative market within Germany will only be able to occur if the above mentioned obstacles are removed and the necessary preconditions are intransigently implemented. Whether the new IPD residential real estate index will turn out to be efficient enough to serve as a starting point to create a working residential derivatives market is hard to tell. Nevertheless, it shows that the development of a residential real estate derivatives market in Germany is under way. How quickly this vision becomes reality will for a great extent depend on how the real estate markets develop, since real estate derivative in general tend to become especially en vogue during crises where investors and real estate owners are forced to take action in order to deal with their increasingly uncomfortable real estate exposure. The current volatile market conditions are working in favor of real estate derivatives because they trigger the investors' urge to acquire or divest themselves of exposure quickly which has always been one of the significant attractions of the product [30].

Figure 8 provides with a short outline to the reader of what would need to happen within the German residential real estate derivatives market, in order to create a success story similar to that of the UK residential derivative market.

Road map to a successful German residential real estate derivatives market

- German market players need to form a group similar to the UK Property Derivative Interest Group

- Identify key players to educate, warehouse risk and create liquidity

- Educate end users and market players on the specific benefits of utilizing derivatives in management and investment decisions

- Educate end users and market players on pricing methods for respective indices

- Support further development of existing indices, such as the German residential real estate index, and encourage the development of new sub-indices and to make the transition from annually to monthly reporting

- Try to initiate a significant initial trading volume and sufficient liquidity in the German real estate derivative market in order to create a substantial enough momentum to become self-sustainable

Source: Based on Venter, J., Barriers to Growth in the US Real Estate Derivatives Market, 2007, p. 103

Fig. 8:   Road map German residential real estate market

8   Bibliography

[1] Ernst & Young Real Estate GmbH, Transaction Real Estate, March 2007, p. 6.

[2] Just, T./Feil, J., Property derivatives marching across Europe, Deutsche Bank Research, June 12th, 2007, p. 2.

[3] Elkin, N./Havsey, J./Sayklay, G. T., Real Estate Derivatives – The Next Evolution, Shopping Center Business, May 2007, p. 2.

[4] Just, T./Feil, J., op cit., p. 3.

[5] Euromoney, The 2007 guide to Property Derivatives, April 2007, p. 9.

[6] Venter, J., Barriers to Growth in the US Real Estate Derivatives Market, Massachusetts Institute of Technology, September 2007, pp. 21–22.

[7] Venter, J., op cit., p. 22.

[8] Venter, J., op cit., p. 23.

[9] Lehman Brothers, Liquid Property: Commercial and Residential Property Derivatives, May 2007, p. 9.

[10] Venter, J., op cit., p. 24.

[11] Lehman Brothers, op cit., p. 9.

[12] Venter, J., op cit., pp. 26–27.

[13] Lehman Brothers, op cit., p. 11.

[14] Geldner, D./Miller, N.G., Commercial Real Estate Analysis & Investment, 2nd edition, Mason, OH, 2007.

[15] Euromoney, op cit., p. 8.

[16] Venter, J., op cit., p. 48.

[17] ib.

[18] Euromoney, op cit., p. 10.

[19] Just, T./Feil, J., op cit., p. 8.

[20] Fenlon, A., UK property derivatives – a focus on residential, Santander Global Banking & Markets, 2007.

[21] Lim, J. Y./Zhang, Y., A Study on Real Estate Derivatives, Massachusetts Institute of Technology, September 2006, pp. 21–22.

[22] Lehman Brothers, op cit., p. 14.

[23] Lim, J. Y./Zhang, Y., op cit., pp. 21–22.

[24] International Monetary Fund, Compilation Guide on Financial Soundness Indicators, July 2004, pp. 159–163.

[25] IPD, German residential property index 2006, 2007.

[26] Kaufmann, A./Nastansky, A., Ein kubischer Spline zur temporalen Disaggregation von Stromgrößen und seine Anwendbarkeit auf Immobilienindizes, Statistische Diskussionsbeiträge N. 22, Universität Potsdam 2006, pp. 4–5.

[27] IPD, German residential property index 2006, 2007.

[28] Venter, J., op cit., pp. 83–84.

[29] Just, T./Feil, J., op cit., p.10.

[30] Daley, M., Property Derivatives Update, February 2008.

9   References

Just, T./Feil, J., Property derivatives marching across Europe, Deutsche Bank Research, June 12th, 2007.

Elkin, N./Havsey, J./Sayklay, G. T., Real Estate Derivatives – The Next Evolution, Shopping Center Business, May 2007.

Venter, J., Barriers to Growth in the US Real Estate Derivatives Market, Massachusetts Institute of Technology, September 2007.

Lehman Brothers, Liquid Property: Commercial and Residential Property Derivatives, May 2007.

Geltner, D./Miller, N.G., Commercial Real Estate Analysis & Investment, 2nd edition, Mason, OH, 2007.

Kaufmann, A./Nastansky, A., Ein kubischer Spline zur temporalen Disaggregation von Stromgrößen und seine Anwendbarkeit auf Immobilienindizes, Statistische Diskussionsbeiträge N. 22, Universität Potsdam 2006.

Lim, J. Y./Zhang, Y., A Study on Real Estate Derivatives, Massachusetts Institute of Technology, September 2006.

Euromoney, The 2007 guide to Property Derivatives, April 2007.

Case, K. E./Shiller, R. J./Weiss, A.N., Index-based futures and options markets in real estate, Journal of Portfolio Management 19, 1993, pp. 83–92.

Iacoviello, M. /Ortalo-Magne, F., Hedging housing risk in London, The Journal of Real Estate Finance and Economics 27, 2003, pp. 194–209.

Shiller, R. J./Weiss, A.N., Moral hazard in home equity conversion, Real Estate Economics 28 (1), 2000, pp. 1–31.

Reiss, J., Broad Benefits of Housing Market Financial Innovation, Working Paper No. 3 prepared for the Real Estate Derivatives World USA conference, April 24th, 2007.

Adam, J./Collier, P., Property Derivatives, ICAP Securities Ltd, 2006.

Ernst & Young Real Estate GmbH, Transaction Real Estate, March 2007.

Rhode, W., Property Derivatives – Opportunity knocks, Mortgage Risk Magazin, October 2007, pp. 24–27.

Fenlon, A., UK property derivatives – a focus on residential, Santander Global Banking & Markets, 2007.

IPD, German residential property index 2006, 2007.

International Monetary Fund, Compilation Guide on Financial Soundness Indicators, July 2004.

E   Case studies

1   Development of German open-end real estate funds into an asset class: the example of CS Property Dynamic

Dirk Meiwirth
Axel Vespermann

Table of contents

1   Introduction

The first German open-end real estate fund was launched in 1959 [1]. Before, further products had been incepted by different investment companies from the mid-1960s on. The aforementioned fund was the only product in the sector for over seven years.

Development of asset class   Since German open-end real estate funds mainly invested in the German market and almost had the identical core investment strategies, they generated similar returns and got therefore noticed by investors as homogeneous products and not as a separate asset class. This might have been the reason why German real estate funds suffered a niche existence for a long time without remarkable inflows, although they produced stable and positive annual returns. At the beginning of the 1990s, more and more funds got launched which invested in other European countries next to Germany. By doing so, the products started to differ from each other, became more and more popular and the inflows into the sector increased significantly. By the enlargement of the core investment strategies throughout Europe, not only the returns, but also the volatility increased. Once the development of new European products had started and larger inflows into the sector were generated, it did not take long until the first funds with a global core investment strategy was launched at the beginning of the 21st century.

Due to the core investment strategies, German real estate funds were only addressed to retail clients. Institutional clients did not pay attention to the sector, since they had a low allocation in indirect real estate investments and were – more or less – invested directly into real estate. After the decrease of the equity markets beginning in 2001 and the consolidation of the bond market, institutional investors started to get interested in German open-end real estate funds, especially since their asset liability studies claimed a certain percentage of real estate investments. Since 2004, German open-end real estate funds have been developed for institutional investors as well as for high net worth individuals. These institutional funds differ from retail products not only by a limited liquidity, but also by the investment strategy, since most funds follow a core-plus strategy.

For a little less than 50 years, German open-end real estate funds developed from a homogeneous product for retail clients into a heterogeneous asset class for retail and institutional clients. Meanwhile – by the end of 2007 – the asset class consists of 31 funds, managed by 16 investment companies and €81.0 billion assets under management [2].

2 Real estate funds under German Investment Act (InvG)

2.1 Characteristics

Legal framework

While closed-end funds are basically not regulated, open-end real estate funds as an investment product are regulated by German Investment Act (InvG), German Banking Act (KWG) and controlled through supervision of the German Federal Financial Supervisory Authority (BaFin).

Risk limitation

As part of the regulation, the investment company managing the fund acts as a trustee and has to segregate the fund from its own assets. By doing so, the fund is not reliant on the investment company. This detail can become very important, e.g., in case of bankruptcy. The abidance by the laws is controlled by the companies' supervisory board and the internal audit as well as by external facilities, such as the committee of appraisers, the depositary bank and especially by the German Federal Financial Supervisory Authority. Besides regulations regarding the supervision of the company, the German Investment Act also prescribes regulations for risk limitation and diversification, e.g., regarding investment limits (§67), currency hedging (§67), risk diversification (§73), liquidity requirements (§80) or regarding the committee of valuers (§77).

Trading at NAV

The biggest difference between German open-end real estate funds and closed-end funds or other direct real estate investments is the liquidity and volatility of the unit value. The investment company issues units for the open-end real estate fund, which allows the investor to participate even with a modest investment outlay in a diversified stake of commercial properties – a holding that is typically not available to retail investors. Furthermore, the investment company has to allow the redemption of units on a daily basis under a regular market environment. Since the units are traded at Net Asset Value (NAV) and not listed on the stock exchange, the investor gets a fair value for his unit at any time.

2.2   Functionality

No premium
or discount to
unit value

Trading the units at NAV brings liquidity into the illiquid asset class of real estate without having the volatility of the equity market and without producing a premium or discount on the fair value as in comparison to real estate equities. To make the asset class liquid, the German Investment Act (InvG) provides a unique construction (see figure 1), which was also adopted in Austria in 2004 and in France in 2006.

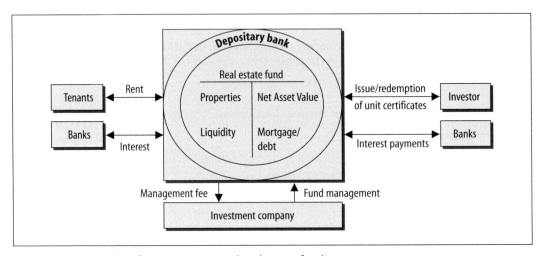

Fig. 1:   Functionality of German open-end real estate funds

Liquidity of units

The investment company invests the inflows from the units issued into direct real estate or holds the properties via real estate companies. Some portion of the inflows is kept in liquid assets to pay the funds expenses and interest payments on the one hand and to allow potential redemptions, since unit certificates can be redeemed on a daily basis on the other hand.

For this reason, at least retail products hold a higher liquidity than other direct investment vehicles, such as closed-end funds or listed real estate companies. In order to be able to continue business even in times of higher outflows, the German Investment Act prescribes to keep a minimum liquidity of 5 % of the fund's assets. If the liquidity reaches 5 % of the fund's assets due to high outflows, fund management has to temporarily suspend redemption by law to avoid bankruptcy. During this time, properties can be disposed to generate liquidity for further redemptions. So far, this happened once in the time period from end of 2005 to beginning of 2006 in nearly 50 years of fund history.

Calculation
of NAV

The unit certificates are traded at NAV, which means that every transaction of the same day is executed for the same unit value. The value of the properties is assessed at least once a year by an independent committee of appraisers. The NAV is determined on a daily basis by adding the value of the fund's assets (see figure 1) and by deducting the debt and other liabilities. The division of the total net assets of the fund by the number of units issued is the value for each unit. The calculation of NAV is controlled by the depositary bank.

This calculation method provides major advantages to the investor in comparison to closed-end real estate funds and real estate stocks. Unit certificates can be redeemed on a daily basis. In contrast, closed-end real estate funds investors usually get back their investment when the property is sold, since there is only a very limited secondary market for this type of investment. Listed real estate companies are also fungible; however, the value is much more volatile. Since the stock value depends on bid and ask, they are always traded with a premium or discount of the NAV, which can not happen with open-end real estate funds.

Advantages of NAV

3 Increasing demand on and requirements of institutional investors on real estate investments

3.1 Increasing demand of institutional investors on real estate investments

Due to the crisis of the equity markets as a consequence of September 11th, 2001, institutional investors suffered losses on their equity exposure. Also, bond investments seemed to be less attractive since interest rates were low and increasing interest rates would have caused losses on the bond exposure as well. As a consequence of such a market environment, new asset liability studies (ALM-study) claimed a higher percentage of real estate investments in the portfolio. Real estate investments are still considerably underweight in institutional portfolios even though – given their low correlation to other asset classes – they are a good way of diversifying a portfolio as they can improve the risk-return-ratio.

Underweight of real estate investments

On the one hand, direct real estate investments imply a grown structure of personnel for acquisition & sales as well as for asset/property management. On the other hand, they are illiquid assets. Although institutional investors could influence two out of three points of the "magic triangle" of investments by direct investments, most did not prefer direct real estate investments. Closed-end funds would solve the problem of personnel, but they still would have the problem of liquidity.

As a consequence, institutional investors had to meet the required quote of real estate investments by indirect real estate investments. Listed real estate vehicles would be more liquid, but due to the high correlation to equity markets, they

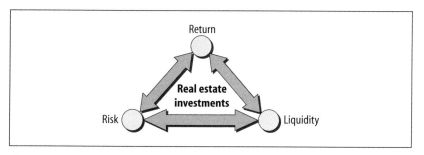

Fig. 2: Magic triangle of investments

would be quoted as equity investments and therefore would not qualify for the required quote of the ALM-study.

Because of the characteristics of the aforementioned real estate investment opportunities, institutional investors became aware of open-end real estate funds which are addressed to retail clients. Although open-end real estate funds did not match the risk-return expectations of institutional clients, the construction of a NAV-based product met their requirements regarding liquidity. This was the decisive factor to cause a strong demand by institutional investors on retail focussed open-end real estate funds.

3.2 Requirements of institutional investors on open-end real estate funds

Risk-return combinations
Within the real estate asset class, however, a number of risk-return combinations are possible. The requirements of institutional investors who consider an investment in real estate from a strategic point of view are often not fulfilled by products with a conservative core investment strategy. Instead, they look for more dynamic real estate products to structure their portfolios. On the one hand, products are expected to deliver a stable cash flow; on the other hand they take a higher volatility into account to achieve higher returns in the long run.

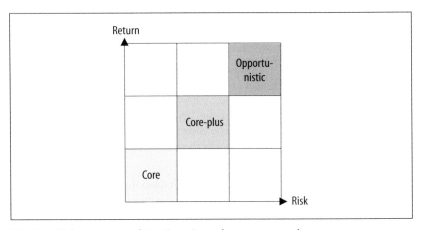

Fig. 3:   Risk-return combinations in real estate asset class

Taking into consideration that most of the existing open-end real estate funds predominantly have core investment strategies and have no dynamic component, they do not always meet the risk-return expectations of those institutional clients. But opportunistic funds are often no alternative to core products as well. Their risk-return profile would be too high and mostly opportunity funds do not offer a stable cash flow for an annual distribution.

As a consequence, investment companies developed open-end real estate funds in between core and opportunistic strategies within the "magic triangle" of investments. While ensuring that cash flow is relatively stable so as to permit distributions, the fund has to acquire also higher-opportunity investments to achieve the necessary dynamic development to provide a higher performance. However, this performance is accompanied with higher risk (volatility) which would still be below equity vehicles. Since institutional clients also do not need a daily liquidity, the funds do not need a 20 % to 30 % proportion of liquidity, which dilutes the fund performance, since liquidity returns are predominantly lower than property returns.

4 Idea of CS Property Dynamic

4.1 Characteristics of CS Property Dynamic and positioning within the asset class

CS Property Dynamic is a total return oriented open-end real estate fund under German Investment Act. Due to its minimum investment of € 3 million, it is primarily addressed to institutional investors. The fund's expected long-term target return is in-between 6 % to 8 % p. a. over a 10-year-horizon by a maximum expected standard deviation of up to 6 % p. a. To avoid a dilution of the fund's return by a high liquidity ratio, the average target liquidity is 10 %, achieved by a cash-on-demand system for inflow. Due to the low percentage of liquidity, a long-term investment of at least five years is strongly recommended. Therefore, a redemption fee of 3 % in favor of the fund's assets is charged, unless 12 months' notice of redemption is given.

The fund is aimed at experienced, primarily institutional investors who are familiar with capital investment in properties and seek a product with a core-plus investment strategy and the characteristics of the fund as mentioned above. Due to the risk-return profile, CS Property Dynamic fits in the product universe between core products, real estate equity funds and REITs and still is a NAV-based product and therefore positioned as a core-plus investment (see figure 3).

4.2 Investment strategy

4.2.1 Basic idea

Although CS Property Dynamic is permitted to invest globally due to the terms of contract, it is not based on a geographical allocation. This might sound strange at first, but is validated by taking a closer look at the reasons.

A separate look at primary and secondary effects of real estate investments points out, that it is possible to achieve positive primary effects from diversification by leaving domestic markets towards Europe without having notable secondary effects. The euro zone offers a nearly standardized level of interest rates which reaches over almost all important real estate markets except Great Britain, Switzerland and parts of Scandinavia and also provides a single currency by the euro.

Primary and secondary effects of real estate investments

Furthermore, the ongoing trend of a harmonized tax structure over the euro zone and the alignment of usages of the real estate markets can be recognized. This is completely different when leaving Europe to invest globally. The enhanced chances of diversification from primary effect are considerably higher influenced by secondary effects in either way – positive and negative. This might also be the reason why globally investing funds have not outperformed funds with a European investment strategy so far. Global real estate investments involve particular risks on the one hand, though offer attractive opportunities on the other if actively managed (see section 4.2.2). Another reason for not having a geographical allocation was the fact that the management would not have to invest in countries just because of the geographical allocation when having superior opportunities in other countries or even on other continents.

No geographical allocation Since the investor will stay in the fund when satisfied with the performance according to the risk-return profile, the fund management decided to resign from a geographical allocation in favor of the individual selection of properties by asset picking in order to achieve the desired yield target. Therefore, CS Property Dynamic was set up as a dynamic open-end real estate fund for institutional investors with a global focus and will invest outside Europe if it appears to be the right time to apply this strategic measure from a property yield, economic and legal point of view.

4.2.2 Cash flow-oriented investments and dynamic component

To meet institutional investors risk-return expectations, the fund pursues an income-oriented investment policy focusing on the achievement of property value increases and the generation of sound cash flows. CS Property Dynamic mainly invests in commercially used properties both at locations with development potential and already established locations to combine stability and dynamic development:

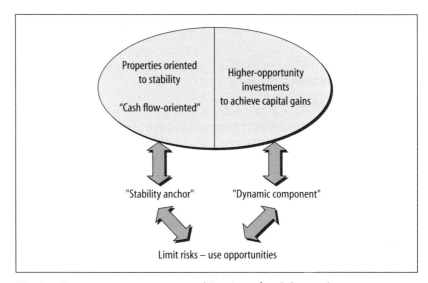

Fig. 4:   Investment strategy: a combination of stability and dynamic development

By selecting cash flow-oriented properties that generate steady income, the fund seeks to achieve stable cash flows and an inflation hedge secured by index-linked rental contracts. Investments in established locations and more "liquid" types of property, such as retail and office buildings for administration or shopping centers, are also conducive to stability. Regarding the "stability anchor", the fund's investment strategy does not differ from other core funds. What makes a difference to other core funds is the fund's dynamic component.

Steady income

By pursuing a more flexible investment policy than traditional core products, the managers have the opportunity to buy properties beyond the core strategy. Besides the types of usage mentioned above, other real estate types, which offer a higher return, but are much more volatile – such as trade and services, hotels and logistical properties, senior residences, multi-storey car park or leisure properties – can be added to the portfolio under the dynamic component.

Types of dynamic characters

Within the scope of active portfolio management (purchase, sale and re-/development of assets), the different most favorable investment times – resulting from different market cycle progressions in different countries or locations – are used and property-specific features relevant for a subsequent sale are considered in the investment decision. Due to this proactive approach, the real estate portfolio is continuously developed and adapted to the changing political, economic, fiscal and legal environment resulting in a continuous change in the composition and weighting of the portfolio. In addition to existing buildings and buildings under construction, the fund management can also purchase properties for project developments if pre-leased or not. The investment company either develops such properties itself or a suitable contractor is ordered for the development. The main criteria for the selection of the properties are either sustained earning power and/or the value increase potential resulting from property or site developments.

Within the scope of the opportunity-oriented part of the investment strategy, country specific peculiarities in financing and the expected exchange rate trends for investments outside the euro zone are also taken into account when selecting properties. A proportionate external financing in compliance with the maximum limit leverage permitted by the German Investment Act (a maximum of 50 % of the total of market value of all fund properties) is arranged if a sustained increase in the return on equity can be achieved in this way. For the determination of the borrowing ratio, both country-specific financing conditions and exchange rate risks as well as fiscal aspects are taken into account.

Exchange rate and leverage

If suitable, currency risks of real state investments outside the euro zone are hedged by way of currency futures, options, swaps or foreign currency loans. Within the scope of statutory provisions, a maximum of 30 % of all properties and other assets of the fund may have a currency risk.

For the limitation of risks, fund management ensures that the portfolio structure complies with the laid-down risk-return profile, that a sufficient diversification can be achieved and that the portfolio strikes a good balance between cash flow-oriented properties and properties with value increase potential.

4.2.3   Effects of both strategic components on total return

Stable   Although the fund's performance consists of cash flow and dynamic component
distribution   of the investment strategy, both components get treated differently due to the
construction of German open-end real estate funds.

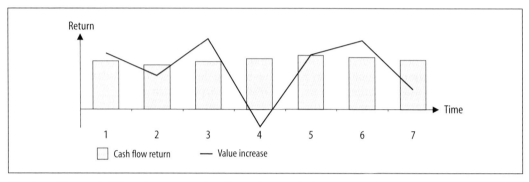

Fig. 5:   Effects of different components of investment strategy on total return

The cash flow portion of the portfolio permits a relatively stable distribution.
This is key to institutional investors, as real estate investments often rather
substitute bond investments than equity investments due to a better risk-
return profile. After the distribution, the unit value of the fund decreases by the
amount distributed. The capital gain, also included in the fund's performance,
can not be distributed unless the property is sold. The capital gain or loss in- or
decreases the value of the unit certificates. Due to the different effects of both
components of the investment strategy, the fund can still have a distribution
in times when the performance is close to zero or even negative.

4.3   Issue and redemption of units compliant with German Investment Act (InvG)

Daily liquidity   As a German open-end real estate fund, units of CS Property Dynamic can also
be issued and redeemed on a daily basis. To avoid a dilution of the real estate
yield, it is therefore necessary to keep the liquidity low and to inhibit a high
volatility of in- and outflows of the fund. This requires both an active liquidity
management (the funds in- and outflows have to be matched with the property
transactions) and a transparent methodology to call for investors capital.

Controlling   These aims are achieved by issuing the units exclusively with the use of a
inflows   subscription certificate, with which the investor makes a binding commitment,
for a period of 12 months. Thus, upon request, the investor makes available to
the fund the subscription amount he has promised at first. The funds, which
therefore have been bindingly promised, are called off (cash-on-demand) in
the sequence of receipt from the subscription list open to public, depending
on the business activity of the fund. The minimum volume per subscription
certificate is € 3 million.

Redemption fee   While the limitation of inflows is allowed, the limitation of a daily redemption
is prohibited by German Investment Act unless the fund is down to the

minimum liquidity of 5% of the fund's assets. To prevent investors from redemption without or with short notice, the investment company charges a redemption fee of 3% in favor of the fund's assets. This is supposed to keep up the investors from blindfold redemptions. In case of redemption on short notice, the investment company might have to take a high debt level into account to avoid a suspension of redemption. A negative leverage effect could occur. To prevent this, the redemption fee can be used to compensate the difference between the fund's performance and the interest rate.

In case a negative leverage does not occur, the remaining investors will benefit from the redemption fee. The redemption fee is waived, if a 12 months' notice of redemption is given in written, so that the fund management has time to dispose off properties and to generate the liquidity needed.

5 Conclusion

Over nearly the last 50 years, German open-end real estate funds have developed from homogeneous products to an own heterogeneous asset class. Even during the German open-end fund confidence crisis at the end of 2005/beginning of 2006, the funds delivered a good performance. Furthermore, they proved that the legal construction of the German Investment Act is also working in an extreme situation.

Heterogeneous asset class

After German open-end real estate funds had been addressed only to retail clients for a long time, a small number of institutional products have been launched since 2004. CS Property Dynamic as one of these products has finished its first short fiscal year successfully with a performance of 6.02% in 11 month only. Even under the effective law, the fund offers a transparent cash-on-demand method, which is already practiced in other capital investment areas, in order to achieve a primarily pure real estate yield. To reduce the danger of unexpected redemptions, a redemption fee in favor of the fund has been installed. However, the redemption fee will not apply if certain conditions such as a 12 months' notice have been fulfilled. By these arrangements, fund managements attenuate the weaknesses of the system of open-end real estate funds regarding the volatility of in-/outflows.

The German legislator had noticed these weaknesses and provided further arrangements to reduce them by the novel of the German Investment Act. Therefore, we will see a variety of funds with different issue and redemption conditions in the future. Also, the heterogeneity of the asset class will further increase. For a long time, most of the funds did only provide for a pure German investment strategy. At the beginning of the 1990s, the funds evolved to a more European strategy. More recently, funds have developed a more global focus. After institutional funds with different risk-return profiles have been launched from 2004 on, in the future, funds with special strategies, such as focussing on special segments like kind-of-use (e.g., retail funds, hotel funds or nursing home funds), will be issued onto the market. Also, the alignment of the investment strategy towards issues, such as "capitals" or "trophy" buildings, seems to be possible.

No matter which structural and legal changes will have an impact on the investment vehicle, the decisive factor for the success of real estate investments is the professional survey of the asset manager, his or her global network and his or her ability to source the right assets for his strategy.

6   **Bibliography**

[1] Jahresbericht iii-Fonds No. 1, December 31st, 2004, p. 5.

[2] Mittelaufkommen-Statistik Bundesverband Deutscher Investmentgesellschaften (BVI), September 30th, 2007.

2 First experience with the new REIT structure in Germany: tips and pitfalls

Hans Volkert Volckens

Table of contents

1   Introduction

After a long political and legal debate the German REIT was finally introduced on March 30th, 2007 when the German REIT Bill passed the German Upper House (Bundesrat). This new investment vehicle was regarded with high expectations as in the preceding years various investment banks had published calculations indicating a significant market volume for German REITs as well as a great potential for transferring German real estate into REIT structures.

Waiting for the first REIT   More than half a year later, on October 11th, 2007, the German real estate industry witnessed the first REIT introduction of Alstria Office AG. End of 2007 Fair Value REIT AG was founded and opted for the REIT status. In addition, German media still question the indicated potential for German REITs as the legal and tax environment of the German REIT do not seem to be sufficient and encouraging enough for the real estate community. In addition, the international market for real estate securities seems to be under pressure and a number of companies are therefore reluctant to IPO their real estate in the current market environment.

Nevertheless, it would be too early – and most likely even wrong – to consider the G-REIT as being a legislative failure. It may be true that the REIT development was expected to be a bit more aggressive and a few more IPOs or REIT conversions already in 2007 would have calmed the industry and skepticisms. But even with only two existing REITs today, there is a lot of activity in this respect "underneath the surface". A number of real estate companies and fund initiators are currently diligently evaluating the possibility of setting up REITs and their way of sophisticated planning reveals a great interest in this new structure.

Activities of the industry

Taking the aforementioned activities and market movements underneath the surface into account, one may be sure that the G-REIT will be a product to succeed. But the G-REIT will enter the market slowly and without haste. Such a more moderate development is advantageous for the overall goal of the G-REIT's fathers and mothers, which is to build up trust and confidence on the level of the real estate industry as well as its investors.

Whether the G-REIT will be a great success story in the near future already is difficult to predict from today's perspective. But it is almost certain that the G-REIT will find its way into the center of existing structures for indirect real estate investments in Germany. The G-REIT will develop into an important instrument to serve markets' and investors' needs and without doubt will become a success – at least in the longer run.

Important instrument

Advising these structures from a legal and tax perspective reveals the great potentials as well as existing deficiencies of the German REIT legislation (the "REIT Act"), the necessity to improve the law and the upside potentials of the REIT in comparison to other indirect forms of real estate investments. The following chapter shall provide an inside view of the aforementioned considerations, builds up on the equity capital markets part B in this handbook and shall outline the first experiences made in practice.

The chapter should not be considered as being comprehensive, but shall provide for an overview of the most important issues related to this new instrument from the perspective of a legal advisor.

2   Market evaluates the REIT concept

Even though Germany has only seen two G-REITs being implemented, a number of further candidates are currently evaluating the economic potential of the G-REIT and assessing their current business and company structure in order to determine the possibilities of using the G-REIT in their scope of business. The analysis is being carried out from different perspectives depending on the individual position in the real estate market. Real estate companies have different issues to address and evaluate in the utilization analysis as compared to, e.g., fund initiators. Whether a real estate company wants to convert into a REIT in toto or found a sub-REIT to complement its business is also a question requiring different views on the REIT Act.

Restrictions   It became obvious that the concept of the German REIT provides for significant restrictions with regard to portfolio and income structure, prohibition of real estate trade and maximum leverage. In addition, the tax system partially still lacks clarity and competitiveness. A great need exists to amend the law accordingly to promote the REIT development in Germany.

Due to the set of restrictions and still existing insecurities, almost no well-known real estate company will transform into a REIT in toto. With the exception of Alstria Office AG, which transformed into a REIT in October 2007, existing real estate companies rather seem to intend to establish a sub-REIT. These sub-REITs would provide for a special focus on real estate (asset class or regional specification) in order to differentiate the concept of the sub-REIT from the business strategy of the parent company.

Moreover, German fund initiators also focus on the REIT concept as a substitute for parts of their closed-end funds. In addition, the REIT may well be an attractive tool for acquiring shares in closed-end funds at the end of the investment period. This enables the fund initiators to expand their business concept beyond the lifetime of a regular investment and also may provide for an attractive market place for shares in closed-end funds.

Evaluation   Issues that have to be examined in order to assess the impact of the REIT structure on the existing business of the candidates are of economic, legal and tax nature. Management has to define a strategy that "sells" in the capital markets and does not leave existing investors disoriented. In addition, the legal obligations and restrictions with regard to portfolio and income as well as shareholder and capital structure of a REIT must be quantified. Tax implications may be significant not only on company level, but especially for the (current) shareholders. Management, investment bankers, lawyers and auditors are required to present their view and to reveal the upside and downside potentials. This diligent process serves as the backbone of the development strategy and needs comprehensive consideration by all parties involved. Most companies have not finished their evaluation yet and it will be interesting to follow the individual outcome.

What are the issues that are being evaluated at the moment and influence management decisions of REIT candidates? Even though every company has a unique approach and therefore qualifies and quantifies the REIT criteria from a very individual angle, the following – non comprehensive – issues are more or less always in the center of discussions.

2.1   Asset and income test (Sec. 12, REIT Act)

Even though real estate companies invest in real estate, not all companies invest exclusively in real estate that is eligible according to the REIT Act. Residential real estate, real estate related assets which are legally not real estate (such as technical equipment that is not part of the building) or even foreign real estate investments have to be examined closely. Does a Singapore strata right, for example, qualify as real estate according to Sec. 3 (8) of the German REIT Act?

In addition, real estate companies often carry out auxiliary services that do **Scope of business**
not meet the restrictions stipulated in the REIT Act. Facility management for
third parties, brokering activities or even fund initiation are services being
rendered by the REIT candidates that may have to be restructured into Taxable
REIT Subsidiaries (Dienstleistungsgesellschaften) or even be avoided entirely
in order to comply with the G-REIT rules.

Whether such restructuring of the business makes sense from an economic
point of view has to be assessed carefully. The influence on the expected yield
and tax implications of a potential restructuring of the business are important
parts of such assessment. It seems obvious that those real estate companies
with a pure business concept are in a better position to adapt the REIT status
than companies that have a differentiated business. The creation of a sub-REIT
may be an appropriate way to comply with the REIT restrictions without the
need to reorganize a successful business concept on the parent level.

2.2   Restructuring of the shareholder base (Sec. 13, REIT Act)

According to Sec. 13 of the REIT Act, no shareholder may hold 10 % or more
directly in a G-REIT. This maximum shareholding must be followed and
observed closely by management in order to avoid endangering the REIT
status.

REIT candidates have to consider whether their current shareholder base already **Shareholder**
meets the maximum shareholding requirement or whether a restructuring **limitations**
also has to be encouraged on the investor's level. Larger shareholders may
be reluctant to restructure their direct shareholding into an eligible indirect
shareholding in order to comply with the REIT regime. Especially in cases
were such restructuring of shareholdings will lead to a tax burden of the single
shareholder, either as a result of the restructuring itself or due to increased
taxes upon distribution of profits, the encouragement of the shareholder base
may become a difficult task for the management. In such cases the underlying
business concept of the prospective G-REIT must indicate the economic
benefits for the shareholders. Those benefits must reveal that the conversion
of and participation in a G-REIT is creating higher after tax returns for the
shareholder than continuing the current status quo.

2.3   Provision of distributions

The REIT is obliged to distribute 90 % of its annual income to its shareholders.
But what amount of annual income is the prospective REIT able to generate?

The business concept of a REIT on the one hand has to consider the market **Distribution**
expectations with regard to distribution yield. On the other hand, the REIT **required**
must meet the restrictions with regard to debt financing (Sec. 15) and trading
of real estate (Sec. 14). Especially new portfolios face a start-up period where
the annual income is generated almost exclusively from the letting of the real
estate. In a time of high property prices and increasing costs of debt financing
the yields decrease. Investment bankers together with the management of
the REIT candidate have to calculate whether or not the portfolio is able to
generate sufficient income to be distributed. Portfolios that have been acquired

in order to form the base portfolio of a REIT or portfolios that are envisaged to be acquired for such new REIT have to be assessed. In addition, the prospective costs of a REIT have to be determined. A number of REIT candidates currently seem to be worried with regard to the possible amount of distributions to be generated due to status of the real estate market and the legal environment.

2.4   Possible benefit of tax advantages for shareholders

Without a doubt, the REIT status is a tax regime that allows for avoidance of income taxation on the level of the REIT. Such benefit justifies the various restrictions a REIT must comply with, without such benefit it is more than questionable whether the legal restrictions are worth complying with.

Management of the REIT candidate must evaluate whether the future shareholders may benefit from the tax regime of the REIT. Who shall be shareholders of the REIT, institutionals, privates or foreign investors? Do current major shareholders face tax disadvantages from the REIT status, such as additional trade tax on distribution of profits?

Tax analysis necessary   In addition, it must be observed that the taxation of REIT distributions will be different in 2008 and from 2009 onwards. The introduction of the flat tax system for capital income of private investors will change the tax landscape from 2009 onwards significantly. This tax reform will also change the taxation of REIT distributions a private investor will receive. Analyzing the tax impacts on the shareholder level will have to take the future tax reform into account as the overall tax burden will change. Further, it must be considered that the REIT may generate income that has been subject to tax on the company's level. Foreign real estate income as well as income from Taxable REIT Subsidiaries has been taxed already and does therefore not benefit from a REIT privilege.

The necessary overall tax calculation must consider all tax aspects of the entity level and the current and future tax burden on the level of the shareholder.

2.5   External versus internal management

As only few real estate companies will convert into REITs in toto but will rather form sub-REITs, the question whether external or internal management should be implemented remains important. Fund initiators that want to benefit from the REIT as a further investment tool face that important question as well.

A German corporation (Aktiengesellschaft) requires a management (Vorstand) and therefore – at least from a legal point of view – must be internally managed. But the question of external and internal management is not only based on the civil law perspective, but on the question, whether the management of the REIT really runs the company, takes the daily decision and provides for the knowledge necessary to perform successfully. A REIT with a staff that is only formally taking the decisions but is factually fully depending on a service provider (asset manager) may not be regarded as being internally managed.

Hybrid approach?   Even though the REIT in an international context provides for both external and internal management structures, it seems that the European Market follows the US approach of trusting more internally managed companies.

Also, investment banks seem to prefer a strong management structure that provides for all the necessary expertise in order to lead the company. But management capacities with real estate as well as capital market experience are rather rare in Germany and still have to be built up. Therefore, it seems likely that the REITs of the first hour will follow a more hybrid approach: An experienced management with sophisticated personnel from the sector will work together with the management of a parent company, the expertise of a fund initiator or a third party asset manager. It is expected that over time the management will gain the experience needed to act on a sovereign and fully independent basis.

REIT candidates have to liaise with their chosen investment bankers in order to jointly determine whether their envisaged approach meets market requirements and investor's needs. Fund initiators using the REIT structures must be especially sensitive with regard to this issue.

2.6   Analysis of alternative investment products

Real estate companies and especially fund initiators have to determine whether the REIT is the appropriate investment vehicle for the investors to be attracted and the property to be invested into:

Due to the current tax regime, it is, for example, doubtful whether foreign real estate should be transferred into a G-REIT. Such assets may prove to be better positioned in closed-end or open-end funds as they may provide for a more beneficial tax treatment of the income generated. This is due to the fact that the foreign income may be tax-exempt when investing in those funds while distribution of the same profits by a G-REIT will be taxed on the shareholder level.

In this respect it is worth mentioning that open-end funds allow shareholders to benefit from the privileges of applicable Double Taxation Agreements as well as the beneficial tax treatment the flat tax system will create for private shareholders with respect to domestic real estate income. The possibility to leave foreign real estate income untaxed on the level of the German investor while granting the private investor a tax rate of only 25 % (plus solidarity charge) for income generated from domestic real estate is without doubt an attractive regime. Compared to a REIT, this is – speaking purely from a tax perspective – more competitive.

What is best?

Real estate companies with an already very attractive tax burden due to various optimizations may consider preserving their current tax status instead of converting into a REIT. Especially the reduction in Germany of corporate tax rates from 2008 onwards may increase the attractiveness of the regular corporate tax regime. Even though private investors and foreign investors benefit from a tax-exempt REIT the possibility to stay in the regular tax environment may be considered as being the best option in specific scenarios.

These are only a few of the number of issues a G-REIT candidate has to be concerned with and that require sufficient answers. The catalog of issues varies from case to case but remains equally important.

The appropriate answers may be difficult to find but such process is probably the most important phase of planning. This stage of discussion may create or destroy values, may create success or may cause failure.

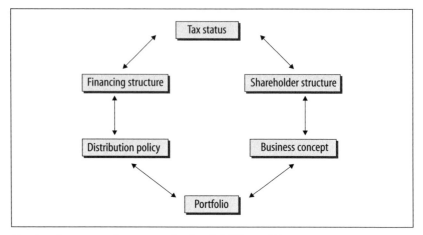

Fig. 1:   Important issues to solve for G-REIT candidates

3   Evaluation of tax and legal environment

In the recent months, on the one hand, it became obvious that the German REIT Bill leaves prospective REIT candidates with a number of legal insecurities as important questions remain unanswered. In addition, a number of regulations are unclear or even affect the development of G-REITs in an adverse way. These open issues and necessary improvements currently hinder the development of G-REITs and should be dealt with immediately. On the other hand, some aspects of the REIT law or other legal changes that influence the G-REIT have created a positive legal environment.

In the following, positive and negative issues of greater importance shall be used to outline areas of the law that must be considered insufficient or that have proven to be well drafted. The following analysis may not be seen as a comprehensive approach but shall provide a glance on the experience that could be gained over the recent months.

3.1   Portfolio

3.1.1   Exclusion of domestic residential real estate

Residential real estate excluded Without doubt, the exclusion of domestic residential real estate affects the German REIT concept in the most adverse way. Irrational political skepticism led to a solution that is difficult to understand and that lacks any rationale. Unfortunately, it seems not very likely that the German legislator will correct this matter in the near future. Opposition from tenant associations, trade unions as well as left-wing politicians seems to be too strong so far.

On one hand, the German real estate market will be able to live with this curiosity. As foreign REITs, private equity funds and German "conventional" real estate corporations continue to be allowed to acquire domestic residential real estate, enough opportunities for investors remain. The G-REIT itself is, on the other hand, cut off from an important real estate segment and is lacking one of the dominant value chains.

The hope remains that in the future the German legislator will draw back and will allow German REITs to invest also in domestic residential real estate. It must also be borne in mind that domestic residential real estate constructed after January 1st, 2007 is not excluded from a G-REIT's portfolio.

3.1.2 Exclusion of real estate corporations with domestic real estate

The German REIT is allowed to hold German real estate either directly or via partnerships. The participation in corporations holding domestic real estate is disallowed. Such exclusion is based on the argument that a corporation as subsidiary of a REIT would not be tax-exempt and thereby lead to an overall tax scenario which equals non-REIT investments.

No domestic real estate in corporations

Indeed, this argument must be considered being true from the tax perspective as an income generated in such a subsidiary would be taxed regularly. Distributions of such subsidiary would be distributed to the REIT which again would distribute the dividend to its shareholders. The structure would not benefit from the REIT privilege and would even result in higher tax burdens than a non-REIT investment.

Even though the REIT concept is a tax-driven concept, the REIT must compete with all other players in the real estate market. It should therefore also be allowed to utilize all possible investment structures in order to form a promising investment concept. The legislator narrowed the flexibility requested for no reason.

3.1.3 Required 100 % participation in foreign real estate corporation

The G-REIT may hold foreign real estate either directly, via a partnership or via a fully owned so-called foreign real estate corporation (Auslandsobjekt-gesellschaft). The REIT is not allowed to participate in such foreign real estate in case it does not hold all outstanding shares. The participation in joint ventures is therefore not allowed. It would have been preferable to allow G-REITs to enter into joint ventures when investing in foreign jurisdictions especially when the management needs assistance in the relevant local market. The legislator should consider that this measure with regard to the requirement of full ownership in a foreign real estate corporation may increase the risk for the shareholders in the G-REIT with possible influence on the share price.

No joint venture

3.2   Distribution

Distribution base   The G-REIT is required to distribute 90 % of its annual profits. The basis for determining the profits to be distributed is formed by the annual profit (Jahresüberschuss) of the G-REIT according to German GAAP. At the same time capital markets expect a specific yield with regard to distributions of a REIT. Especially newly incorporated G-REITs may have difficulties in meeting these expectations in their first years due to following reasons:

- Real estate acquisitions by such G-REITs generate income but the current real estate market and the prices paid for real estate as well as the lack of capital gains generated by sales of real estate allow only for a small profit margin. In order to meet investors' expectations, the G-REIT would have to distribute a larger amount than actually generated as profit. Nevertheless, it has to be observed that German stock corporation law does not allow a distribution beyond the annual profit unless the company provides for corresponding profit reserves. As the G-REIT has almost no possibility to built profit reserves of any significance due to the distribution requirement according to Sec. 13 of the German REIT Act, the distributions of a G-REIT will regularly directly relate to the annual profit generated.

- In order to increase the amount eligible for distribution a special provision in the German REIT Act to allow distribution also of the depreciation volume was discussed. In the end, the German legislator refrained from introducing such a provision as it would have led to inconsistencies with the German Stock Corporation Act.

Today, management and advisors structure the incorporation of a G-REIT in a way that leaves the company with a considerable amount of reserves that are eligible for distribution. Those structures cannot be implemented in all cases, but a considerable number of G-REITs can be equipped with considerable reserves and distribution volume from an accounting perspective.

3.3   Limitations on shareholdings

No investor may directly hold 10 % or more of the capital of a G-REIT. Violations with regard to this limitation may result in penalty payments and ultimately in the loss of the REIT status. Even though the articles of associations (Satzung) of the G-REIT may provide for a sophisticated set of rules urging and forcing a shareholder to meet these limitation requirements, it cannot be excluded that a shareholder violates the shareholding limitation on purpose in order to influence the stock price of the corporation or – even worse – to get rid of a competitor.

The fact that the articles of association will provide for the possibility to claim damage payments from the violator in those cases will not prevent such critical dealings sufficiently. This will most likely be due to the fact that the shareholder will be sited in a jurisdiction which will hinder or even circumvent the possibility to enforce legal rights.

The 10%-limit could also be protected by empowering the G-REIT to transfer or withdraw the shares of a shareholder exceeding this limit to a third party or itself at a price for below market value. The G-REIT's management should be enabled to execute this right of transfer or withdrawal without the prior consent of the shareholder violating the 10%-limit. This should enable the management to counteract such critical dealings.

Securing the limitations

In this context it must be noted that a violation of shareholder limitation is only being constituted when the shareholder meets the notification requirements stipulated in the German Securities Trading Act (Wertpapierhandelsgesetz – WpHG). In case of a shareholder who does not meet these requirements on the acquisition of shares that lead to a shareholding equaling or exceeding 10 %, no breach of the REIT rules occur. At the same time the shareholder – due to this lack of notification – may not exercise any rights with regard to the shares violating the limitation.

3.4   Tax

The G-REIT is exempt from corporate income tax as well as trade tax as far as the obligations stipulated in the German REIT Act are met. The tax exemptions of the G-REIT shall create the transparency which is decisive for a REIT in the international context.

Tax transparency of the G-REIT is being "financed" by abolishment of the tax-privileged half-income system (Halbeinkünfteverfahren) as well as the tax exemption according to Sec. 8 b of the German Corporate Income Tax Act on the level of the domestic shareholder. Distributions of REITs are therefore taxed fully in the hand of the German investor. Comparing the taxation of traditional real estate corporations with the taxes levied on G-REITs and their domestic shareholders, it becomes obvious that the overall tax burden remains more or less the same. The G-REIT does not serve as a tax saving entity for German investors and may not be regarded as such.

3.4.1   Withholding tax

Investors are confronted with a withholding tax on dividend distributions of 25 % (plus solidarity charge of 5.5 % thereon). The withholding tax rate is higher than the withholding tax applied on distributions of regular real estate companies which amount to 20 % (plus solidarity charge of 5.5 % thereon). For foreign shareholders, a general withholding tax of 25 % (plus solidarity charge of 5.5 % thereon) applies which is reduced to 15 % or even 10 % in case of applicability of a Double Taxation Agreement for certain foreign investors. The reduction can be claimed by the foreign shareholder as a refund from the Federal Tax Office (Bundeszentralamt für Steuern).

As the distributions received by the shareholders have not been reduced by corporate income tax charges on the level of the real estate company and have therefore been distributed on a gross basis, the REIT could be an interesting investment opportunity for foreign shareholders. No taxation on the level of the company and a withholding tax that (in most cases) may be credited against

Competitive taxation

the domestic income tax charge in the country of shareholder's residence is an attractive indirect investment into German real estate.

Even though open-end funds would allow for the same benefit, foreign investors are not acquainted to the concept of open-end funds and their regulatory specialties. For many years, the funds from foreign sources that were invested in open-end funds were insignificant. It is to be expected that the REIT investment which is broadly based on the common principles and parameters of US REITs will be a much more common and convenient investment for foreign investors.

	Open-end funds	Closed-end funds	Corporation	REIT
Earnings from real estate income	Earnings from real estate income are calculated based on regular procedures			
Trade tax	Open-end funds are exempt from trade tax	Closed-end funds as commercial partnerships are subject to trade tax but may be able to claim the extended trade tax deduction	Corporations are subject to trade tax but may be able to claim the extended trade tax deduction	REITs are trade tax-exempt
Corporate income tax	Open-end funds are exempt from corporate income tax	Closed-end funds are considered tax-transparent, i.e., income is taxed at the level of the partner	Corporations are subject to a 15% corporate income tax plus 5.5% solidarity surcharge thereon	REITs are corporate income tax-exempt
Earnings available for distribution	The open-end funds' earning are allocated to the investors according to the rules of the Investment Tax Act	The closed-end funds' earnings are allocated to the partners according to their participation level	The corporation can distribute a dividend in the maximum amount of its earnings (less taxes)	The REIT is required to distribute at least 90% of its earnings to the investors
Withholding taxes (from January 1st, 2009 onwards summary withholding tax, i.e., no further tax return necessary)	Investor's earnings are subject to a 30% withholding tax (from January 1st, 2009 onwards: 25%) which is credited against the investor's income tax burden	none	Dividends are subject to a 20% withholding tax (from January 1st, 2009 onwards: 25%) which is credited against the investor's income tax burden	Dividends are subject to a 25% withholding tax which is credited against the investor's income tax burden
Taxable income at investor's level	Earnings from real estate allocated to the investor	Earnings from real estate allocated to the investor	Dividends are 50% tax-exempt (summary WHT as of January 1st, 2009)	Entire dividend is subject to investor's income tax
Please note that this is only a summary presentation of the tax consequences involved for an investment of a private person in the companies mentioned above under German tax law. This presentation does not cover all aspects relevant for such an investment.				

Fig. 2:   *Overview of different fiscal regimes: G-REIT vs. real estate corporation vs. open-end real estate fund*

3.4.2 Flat tax from 2009 onwards

The domestic potential for REITs will increase with the introduction of the flat tax for capital income from 2009 onwards:

Private investors will be taxed on dividend income received with a withholding tax in lieu in the amount of 25 % (plus 5.5 % solidarity charge thereon). This newly introduced flat tax will apply to all dividends irrespective whether the dividend had been subject to corporate income tax or not. Such equal taxation irrespective of source was a surprise when enacted by the German legislator. Nevertheless, the application of the flat tax to REIT distributions became necessary when open-end real estate funds also became eligible for the flat tax. Otherwise, the significant open-end fund industry would have received a non-justified business advantage and the free market of capital allocation would have been influenced by the legislator.

Flat tax for private investors

With the beneficial tax treatment of German investors from 2009 onwards, the G-REIT should receive an enhancement that enables it to become a recognized investment opportunity for private investors. The after tax yield will simply be higher: Similar to the foreign shareholder described above, the domestic private shareholder will benefit from the lack of any corporate level tax without paying higher taxes for the distributions received.

3.4.3 No REIT privilege for Taxable REIT Subsidiaries

The REIT privilege applies to the REIT-Aktiengesellschaft itself but not to any of its subsidiaries.

Taxable REIT Subsidiaries which may be formed as subsidiaries of the G-REIT will be taxed according to the general rules. Taxable REIT Subsidiaries may carry out real estate related services for third parties. The G-REIT is allowed to hold such service companies as far as their value as well as their income does not exceed the threshold of 20 % of the overall assets and income of the G-REIT. Their income will be subject to corporate income tax as well as trade tax. Depending on the community where the Taxable REIT Subsidiary is situated in, the overall tax charge will amount to approximately 30 % from 2008 onwards (15 % corporate income tax, solidarity charge of 5.5 % thereon and trade tax of approximately 13 %).

Regular taxation

The Corporate Tax Reform 2008 will have a positive effect on the creation of Taxable REIT Subsidiaries as the tax burden will decrease from approximately 40 % to roughly 30 %.

3.4.4 No REIT privilege for foreign real estate companies

Foreign real estate companies will also be taxed as regular corporations. This rule applies for Germany where the foreign real estate company may have its seat and management as well as to the country were the real estate is located in. The REIT concept is a German tax benefit and no foreign country currently refrains from applying its sovereign tax rights because the investor's home country applies the REIT concept. This isolated application of the REIT benefits may become an issue in the European Union. The national tax offices

Solution on its way?

as well as the OECD are working on practical solutions in this respect and hope to come up with a concept that will be able to be implemented. It is an important mission and goal which should lead to the possibility to also apply a REIT concept in another REIT country as otherwise foreign investments of REITs will always remain lacking the tax transparency which is decisive for a REIT and its shareholders.

As far as they invest in a country where Germany did not enter into a Double Taxation Agreement, the real estate income generated may be subject to German corporate income tax. Foreign income tax may be credited according to the unilateral provisions of the German Corporate Income Tax Act. As far as Germany ratified a Double Taxation Agreement with the country of situs, the real estate income generated as well as capital gains from dispositions of real estate are regularly exempt from German tax. In a few cases (such as Spain and Korea, for example) the Double Taxation Agreements provide for the crediting method were foreign income tax is credited against the German corporate income tax charge.

3.4.5   No REIT privilege for real estate partnerships

A critical issue remains with regard to the tax status of real estate partnerships and their investments in German real estate. Even though partnerships qualify as tax-transparent vehicles with regard to income/corporate income tax a partnership may be subject to trade tax when carrying out a trade or business.

Transparent but not tax-exempt
Such trade or business is either carried out by the partnership due to its activities (production, distribution, etc.) or trade or business is being deemed to be carried out irrespective of the actual activity of the partnership due to its set-up: As far as the G-REIT acts as limited partner of the partnership and the general partner is a corporation which regularly forms a subsidiary of the G-REIT the partnership is deemed to carry out a trade or business. Due to the underlying structure, the partnership is subject to trade tax even in case of pure asset management such as holding and managing real estate. Only as far as the real estate qualifies for the so-called extended trade tax relief, trade tax will not be charged on the income generated by the partnership.

The set-up of a partnership described above that leads to the qualification of carrying out a trade or business must be considered being the standard way of establishing partnerships. This role model creates the problem that the real estate held by such partnership must qualify for the extended trade tax relief in order to avoid any trade tax burden. Real estate exclusively qualifies for the extended trade tax relief as far as the real estate does not contain any fixtures and fittings (Betriebsvorrichtungen), such as goods lifts, special air conditionings for technical equipment, etc.

In recent years, tax lawyers were engaged to assess the property to be acquired and to evaluate the risk of missing the qualifications for trade tax relief. With the rise of the G-REIT the hope arose that such analysis would not be necessary any more. With regard to real estate held in partnerships the exercise remains crucial. Even though understandable from a fiscal point of view, it would have been preferable that partnerships would have been exempt from trade tax as far as the REIT participates in.

3.4.6   Double taxation of income

G-REIT distributions have not been subject to corporate income tax on the level of the company. Therefore, the German REIT Act prohibits the application of the half-income system or the tax exemption according to Sec. 8b of the Corporate Income Tax Act (CITA). Such measure seems reasonable at first glance as the higher taxation of the shareholder is compensated by the missing corporate income tax at the level of a REIT.

Unfortunately, the income distributed by a G-REIT may also contain distributions from Taxable REIT Subsidiaries, foreign real estate, as well as foreign real estate companies. In those cases the income has already been subject to tax. With regard to Taxable REIT Subsidiaries, Germany already applied the regular tax mechanisms. Foreign real estate has already been taxed in its country of situs. For those distribution components the German REIT Act should have deemed the half-income system as well as the tax exemption according to Sec. 8b Corporate Income Tax Act for applicable. As any privileges are missing, the aforementioned income components are taxed much too high. The REIT is factually prohibited to be structured via Taxable REIT Subsidiaries or to invest in foreign real estate as such investments are penalized as far as taxes are concerned.

High tax burden to be borne

This imbalance of the current tax system has been recognized and the Federal Ministry of Germany has been requested by the Fiscal Budget Committee to find an appropriate solution. It is expected that the half-income system as well as the tax exemption according to Sec. 8b Corporate Income Tax Act will be declared applicable with regard to distribution components that have already been subject to corporate income tax on a lower level.

3.4.7   Withholding tax on distributions of domestic subsidiaries

Distributions from foreign real estate companies domiciled in a foreign country will in most cases be subject to withholding tax. This is due to the fact that the foreign country does not acknowledge the REIT status of the parent and treats the distributions no different to all other distributions effected by local corporations.

As far as the foreign real estate corporation is situated in Germany one could assume the German legislator to provide for a provision that the distributions of such a corporation would be free of any withholding as all withholding is considered as being a different form of income tax of the receiving entity creditable against its regular income tax charge. As the REIT is tax-exempt, no withholding is necessary. Nevertheless, the legislator did not introduce a provision that disallows withholding in case a domestic subsidiary distributes its profits to the G-REIT. Therefore, the regular withholding principles apply and the domestic subsidiary has to effectively withhold 10% as the distribution is affected to a tax-exempt entity. The same applies to distributions from Taxable REIT Subsidiaries.

No reason for withholding tax

As the withholding tax is not credited or refunded, the REIT becomes partially taxable with its income from domestic corporate subsidiaries. Even though not intended by the legislator, there is no indication that he wants to correct this odd and negative result. In sum, the income of Taxable REIT Subsidiaries, for example, are being taxed on the corporate level with 30 % (2008) and the withholding in the amount of 10 % is also lost. In addition, the shareholder of the REIT is being taxed with the distribution of the REIT which contains the income generated by the Taxable REIT Subsidiary. The profits are clearly overtaxed so that a correcting amendment of the REIT Act is necessary.

3.4.8   The exit tax

The German legislator wanted to incentify real estate transfers into REIT and pre-REIT structures as German companies hold great values of real estate in their balance sheets which should be disposed in order to release the funds for core investments. Therefore, the exit tax was introduced which for a limited period shall allow a tax deduction of 50 % in case German property which formed part of a business for a certain time is being sold to a G-REIT or a pre-REIT. The 50 % tax cut has been considered by real estate experts as not being sufficient especially as each transfer of real estate triggers additional real estate transfer tax in the amount of 3.5 % of the purchase price. Despite the various warnings, an even further reaching tax benefit was politically not acceptable. Already the current exit tax regime was heavily attacked in parliament hearings from left-wing democrats who argued that tax subsidies do not fit in the overall concept of budget consolidation.

Good but good enough? But not only must the remaining tax burden be considered problematic with regard to the envisaged goal of turning real estate of German corporations into a more liquid asset class. Due to a number of restrictions, the possible value of the exit tax seems to be further reduced:

Indirect transfers of real estate (such as transfer of stakes in a real estate partnership), privately held real estate as well as real estate that has not been owned by a domestic business for at least five years may not benefit from the exit tax, for example. In addition, real estate that has been acquired by deducting taxable capital gains from a previous sale of real estate (Sec. 6 b of the German Income Tax Act) from the acquisition costs may not qualify for the exit tax insofar. Finally, the exit tax may not be used when closing or selling a business by applying tax privileges stipulated in Sec. 16 and Sec. 34 of the German Income Tax Act. These restrictions make it difficult for a REIT to acquire younger properties by applying the exit tax especially. It must be observed closely whether the exit tax as currently stipulated will provide for the encouragement of real estate owners as envisaged. In case the market should prove that the current exit tax regime is to be considered insufficient, it would be recommendable to adjust the rules accordingly. But such a market oriented approach seems rather unlikely in a period where the leading parties already focus on the coming elections.

3.5 Financing of REITs

One of the goals of the current German coalition government is a reform of the tax regime regulating companies in Germany in order to increase the competitiveness of the German tax system compared to other countries within the European Union and worldwide.

On May 25th, 2007, the Bundestag, the German Lower House of Parliament, passed the bill containing the changes to income tax, corporate income tax, trade tax and other tax laws. The Bundesrat, the German Upper House of Parliament, voted on the draft bill on July 6th, 2007.

The major changes contained in the bill will be outlined below. These changes will generally enter into force as of January 1st, 2008.

The bill reduces the corporate income tax rate from 25 % to 15 % (plus 5.5 % solidarity surcharge thereon) and thereby lowers the combined corporate income and trade tax rate to less than 30 %. In order to compensate for this reduction of the tax rates, a number of changes to the computation of taxable income are provided for in the bill. In the author's opinion, the changes of highest relevance for foreign investors are the changes to the deductibility of interest expenses and the changes to trade tax.

3.5.1 Changes to thin cap regulations

One of the greatest changes concerns the treatment of inter-corporation loans and debt financing in general: Currently, expenses related to debt financing are deductible for tax purposes as far as the conditions of the thin cap rules under Sec. 8 a Corporate Income Tax Act are met.

The bill will formally replace these rules with a so-called interest deduction ceiling (Zinsschranke) which will apply regardless of the legal form (corporations, partnerships and sole proprietorships). The current thin cap rules will be abolished. This interest deduction ceiling will exclude certain amounts of interest payment/expense from deduction of taxable income in a given business year. Interest expense thus excluded from deduction shall be carried forward and be deductible in the following business years under certain conditions.

This interest deduction ceiling will disallow the deduction of a certain amount of interest expense and will apply to any kind of debt financing, whether relating to inter-company loans or true debt financing. Please note that the tax treatment of the interest payments at the level of the paying entity is not reflected correspondingly at the level of the recipient of the interest payments: Regardless of the extent of the deduction of interest as an expense, the interest payments will be considered taxable income in full at the level of the recipient. Also, contrary to the former thin cap rules, interest payments will not be re-qualified as dividend payments if the new interest deduction ceiling is triggered.

Limitation of interest deduction

The interest deduction ceiling mechanism can be summarized as follows:

Interest expenses will remain deductible up to the level of interest income of the current business year. Interest expenses exceeding the interest income will be deductible if

- the balance amount of interest expenses exceeding the interest income is not more than € 1 million (threshold); or

- the corporation is not part of or only proportionally part of a group; or

- the corporation is part of a group, but able to show that the equity-to-balance sheet total ratio of the company concerned by these rules is the same as the equity-to-balance sheet total ratio of the other group corporations (so-called "escape clause"). A lower equity-to-balance sheet total ratio of the company concerned will not be considered harmful if the difference in comparison to the equity-to-balance sheet total ratio of the other group corporations is not more than 1 %.

Equity-to-balance sheet total ratio
The equity-to-balance sheet total ratio is calculated by comparing the amount of balance sheet equity with the amount of the balance sheet total. This calculation is subject to a number of modifications, for example: Shares of other group-corporations held by the corporation in question will be deducted from the amount of equity. There are no special rules for holding corporations. Any goodwill related to the calculating company shown as part of the group's consolidated balance sheet has to be added to the calculating corporation's amount of equity.

If the above exception should not be met, the interest expenses exceeding the interest income will only be deductible to the extent of 30 % of the company's modified EBITDA (= earnings before tax plus interest expenses, depreciation and amortization minus interest earnings).

Being a group
Please note that a corporation is considered to be part of a group as soon as it could be included in consolidated financial statements under the applicable GAAP or as soon as its fiscal or business policy can be determined jointly with the policy of other corporations. A further requirement of the "escape clause" will be that the equity-to-balance sheet total ratio will be calculated on the basis of financial statements for the whole group in German language audited by an auditor admitted to practice in Germany.

Interest expense carried forward by the company will be lost in case the company is liquidated or transferred. Interest expense carried forward in case of the company being a partnership will also be lost if a partner leaves the partnership to the extent the interest carried forward is attributable to the partner leaving.

Further restrictions
For corporations certain additional conditions are required:

Non-consolidated corporations will be subject to the interest deduction ceiling if they cannot prove that not more than 10 % of the balance amount of interest expenses exceeding the interest income is paid on

- loans by shareholders holding a participation of more than 25 %,
- loans to parties related to such shareholders or
- third party loans with a right of recourse against such shareholder/ related party.

According to the statements made by the government regarding detrimental recourse, the term "recourse" will be extended in comparison to the current thin cap regime and a detrimental recourse will be assumed under the new interest deduction ceiling rules as far as the lender has any kind of recourse to the shareholder. Rather than legal recourse, factual recourse will be considered sufficient, i. e., it will be sufficient if the shareholder or related party has any kind of factual duty vis-à-vis the lender regarding the corporation's loan.

Furthermore, in order to be allowed to make use of the escape clause consolidated corporations will also be required to meet the 10 % interest expense limitation mentioned above when receiving loans from non-consolidated parties, i. e., where the loan is shown as a liability to the lender in the consolidated balance sheet. In case of a third party lender, the 10 % interest expense limitation only applies where the third party lender additionally has a right of recourse against a shareholder/related party not belonging to the consolidated group. According to the wording of the bill, the 10 % interest expense limitation has to be complied with by all consolidated corporations worldwide, e. g., interest payments of a single (domestic or foreign) group entity to a substantial shareholder/related party or third party with recourse in excess of the 10 % limitation could lead to the interest deduction ceiling being applied to the entire group without the possibility to benefit from to the equity-to-balance sheet ratio total test of the escape clause.

In case of loans granted by consolidated parties, only the equity-to-balance sheet total ratio test of the escape clause will apply without the additional restrictions mentioned above.

3.6 Local financial authorities and their expertise in IFRS accounting

Without doubt, the REIT Act presents a challenge to the local financial authorities as the tax exemption of the real estate company requires fulfillment of certain requirements with regard to asset and income structure, scope of business, financing structure as well as distribution, for example. The tests to be made in order to assess such fulfillment of conditions are broadly based on IFRS accounting principles. Especially the determination of asset and income allocation as well as gearing require in-depth knowledge in IFRS accounting.

Until today, German financial authorities had not been required to understand IFRS and therefore did not develop any visible expertise in this field of accounting. This is due to the fact that German tax laws mainly focused on German GAAP and special tax accounting principles stipulated in the German Income Tax Act.

New field of expertise

As German financial authorities will be requested to inspect whether a REIT meets the criteria of the REIT Act and applies the tax exemption correctly, knowledge of IFRS accounting principles becomes decisive.

The REIT Act provides for the right of financial authorities to request detailed confirmation of German Certified Public Accountants (Wirtschaftsprüfer) that the different criteria of the REIT Act have been met. Nevertheless, the financial authorities will have to evaluate the results of Certified Public Accountants on an autarkic basis in order to fulfill their control duties. As the new Business Tax Reform 2008 introduces the interest deduction ceiling on an IFRS basis, German financial authorities will have to learn quickly. The in-depth understanding of IFRS accounting principles by the financial authorities will be important to establish the authorities as reliable and fearless authorities that do not apply restrictive measurements due to lack of understanding and uncertainty.

3.7 Accounting of minority shareholders in real estate partnerships

The G-REIT may invest in domestic or foreign real estate either directly or via a partnership (Immobilienpersonengesellschaft). Such a partnership must limit its scope of business to holding and managing real estate as outlined in Sec. 1 (1) of the German REIT Act. Foreign real estate may also be acquired through a corporation with its registered seat in Germany or in any other foreign country (Auslandsobjektgesellschaft).

Influence on Sec. 15 of the REIT Act

As far as the G-REIT owns a controlling stake in the partnership but not 100 % of the partnership interests a problem arises that has not been considered by the Ministry of Finance when drafting the REIT Act. Minority shareholders in a partnership qualify as debt according to IAS 32. Therefore, a controlling participation in a partnership influences the amount of existing debt and may trigger the minimum equity threshold according to Sec. 15 REIT Act.

Even though not intended by the legislator, minority shareholders reduce the possibility to debt finance activities as they absorb parts of the eligible debt potential. G-REITs participating in partnerships in the amount of, e.g., 55 %, insofar already provide for a debt financing according to IAS 32 in the amount of 45 %. It is obvious that such adverse effect on the debt financing potential of a G-REIT simply due to accounting mechanisms seems inappropriate and counterproductive. It is therefore expected that the German legislator will clarify that IAS 32 will not qualify as "debt" in the meaning of Sec. 15 REIT Act.

4 Conclusion

The REIT is an internationally accepted form of indirect real estate investments. The international perception of this legal and tax format makes it very likely that the G-REIT will become a success as well. Nevertheless, not every real estate investment and not every shareholder may benefit equally from the REIT concept. Therefore, a diligent evaluation must be carried out and each

REIT candidate must assess all economic, legal and tax implications of a REIT conversion or creation carefully.

A number of open questions as well as insufficiencies of the German REIT Act remain and it is expected that only parts will be clarified timely. Nevertheless, the G-REIT benefits from a number of internationally accepted criteria and changes in the domestic tax environment. Even though a lot of work is still ahead, overall the REIT Act must be considered as being a good start to promote the REIT concept in Germany.

3 Sociétés d'Investissements Immobiliers Cotées: the French example

Christine Daric

Table of contents

1   Introduction

Development of the SIIC "Successful", "performing", "competitive"! These are adjectives which are often used to qualify the French Société d'Investissements Immobiliers Cotées (SIIC) regime. This regime was created by the Finance Bill in 2003 [1] upon the initiative of the French federation of listed real estate companies (Fédération des Sociétés Immobilières et Foncières – FSIF) and has come into effect on January 1st, 2003.

This regime is applicable, upon election, to companies which are listed on a French regulated market, which have a share capital amounting to at least € 15 million and which main activity is to purchase or build properties with a view on leasing them as well as the direct or indirect shareholding of subsidiaries having the same corporate purpose. The SIIC regime was created in a way to be very simple, flexible and adapted to the existing situation of 2002 large listed companies. It relies on a tax look through principle: The SIIC is exempt from corporation tax on certain income provided that it respects a binding obligation to distribute it depending on the type of income (85 % for rental income, 50 % for capital gains, 100 % for dividends received from qualifying subsidiaries). After the regime has been chosen, a 16.5 % exit tax shall be paid on latent capital gains from real estate properties. The Finance Bill of 2003 has defined the main general characteristics of the regime. Since it has come into effect, every year some adjustments have been made by the legislator, which were aimed either at improving it or at challenging abusive schemes.

In the first section, the development of the regime and its grounds is described; in the second section, detailed examples of the application of the SIIC regime will be given.

Methodology

2 Development of the SIIC regime

As mentioned above, the SIIC regime is a success story and has annually been extended by new provisions which have completed and ameliorated it. The main tax exemption regime applicable to SIICs and their subsidiaries was codified in Article 208 C of the French Tax Code. The measures, which have followed the initiation of the SIIC regime, have contributed to its success. This development will be analyzed below.

New provisions

2.1 SIIC 2: more flexibility and initiative measure to outsource properties towards SIICs

The SIIC regime was created with several aims. On the one hand, the regime was designed to allow the restructuring of the large French listed real estate companies which were not able to structure themselves in a way to avoid tax payments in France like foreign competitors did. On the other hand, the aim was to promote and strengthen the real estate division of the Paris stock exchange, thereby offering alternative investment opportunities for individuals. In order to do so, after the creation of the SIIC regime, two main measures were enacted in an Amendatory Finance Bill in 2004 to favour concentration operations between SIICs and to favor the outsourcing of real estate properties from corporations to companies which core business is the long-term investment in real estate properties.

Goals of the SIIC

2.1.1 Extension of the exemption regime to financial lease

Until December 31st, 2004, the tax exemption regime covered real estate properties themselves but not other rights on properties. Real estate properties which are financed through a financial lease agreement were included in the tax exemption regime of the Amendatory Finance Bill of 2004. The reason for this measure was to consider that it was not fair to make a distinction between properties held directly with a standard financing and properties financed through financial leasing. Due to the launch of this new category of assets within the tax exemption regime after its creation, it was too complex to provide for the inclusion of the existing rights relating to financial leases into the tax exemption regime. As a consequence, only rights relating to real estate financial leases acquired after January 1st, 2005 may be included in the regime. Financial leases concluded or acquired before remain outside the scope of exemption. In the scope of the exemption, this allows certain flexibility for the SIICs to include or exclude this category of assets which were already in the portfolio at the date of change of the law (for instance, the absorption of a subsidiary which owns a financial lease concluded before January 1st, 2005 will allow the SIIC to include such financial lease in the tax-exempt result since this financial lease will be considered for the SIIC as acquired after January 1st, 2005 as a consequence of the merger operation). It has to be noted that 16.5%

Broadening of the SIIC

corporation tax may be due once the option on the financial lease is levied for financial leases concluded or acquired before January 1ˢᵗ, 2005 (see section 2.1.2 below). The basis for such an exit tax is the difference between the fair market value of the property and the price of the option (usually near € 1 at the expiry of a financial lease).

2.1.2   Creation of a tax-neutral regime for restructuring operations

Restructuring operations

The Finance Bill of 2005 [2] states that the favorable provisions of the French merger regime provided for by Articles 210 A following of the French Tax Code will be applicable to SIICs and their subsidiaries having elected for the tax exemption regime of Article 208 C of the French Tax Code.

The sole condition is that the absorbing company commits, in the merger deed, to substitute the absorbed company concerning binding obligations to distributions which have not been satisfied at the date of the merger. It was very important to allow the SIICs to restructure themselves and to participate in large restructuring operations with other SIICs. Examples for this are "Gecina" and "Simco" or "Bail Investissements" and "Foncière des Régions".

The standard French favorable merger regime was in addition adapted as follows:

*   Exemption of merger bonus stated upon the restructuring operation on condition of its distribution up to the minimum of 50 % before the end of the second fiscal year after its realization; because of the accounting obligation to choose net book value for a merger between two companies placed under a common control, the bonus should only reflect profits and reserves of the absorbed company which have not been distributed yet.

*   Add-back in equal shares over a 15-year period of the capital gain realized on depreciable assets (for instance, constructions) in the exempted result subject to an obligation to distribute 85 %; the add-back in equal shares of capital gain realized upon restructuring operation is provided by the standard French merger regime applicable to companies, which are fully liable to corporation tax. This regime was adapted to allow its application to SIICs and their subsidiaries and to subject the exemption of such add-back to an obligation to distribute. In principle, in case of a sale of the property, according to the author's information, the French tax administration should admit that the amount of this capital gain, which has not been added back yet, is exempted on the condition that it is distributed up to a minimum of 50 % before the end of the second fiscal year following the sale.

*   In addition, the merger between two SIICs will not trigger the challenge of the favorable regime depending on the condition that the outstanding binding obligations of the absorbed SIIC are satisfied by the absorbing SIIC. This commitment has to be mentioned in the merger deed. The fear of the SIICs was that the absorbed SIIC would be considered as existing from the SIICs regime as a consequence of the merger. It has to be reminded that in case of an exit from the SIIC regime by a SIIC,

corporation tax at standard rate is retroactively due on capital gains which were subject to a 16.5 % exit tax upon the entry into the exemption regime. This measure helps to avoid such a consequence.

- In case of an absorption by a SIIC or one of its subsidiaries subject to Article 208 C regime of a company not subject to the regime, the exit tax will be levied on latent capital gains on properties, rights attached to real estate financial leases, certain real rights or shareholdings in real estate partnerships which become eligible to the regime.

It is worth mentioning that the favorable regime is applicable under standard conditions to the taxable sector (postponement of the taxation on latent capital gains).

An administrative guideline should specify this regime but has not been published yet.

A specific provision covers the case were some assets become eligible to the tax exemption regime. An example for this is if a SIIC or a subsidiary, which has elected for the tax exemption regime, absorbs a company, which is subject to corporation tax under standard condition and which owns a property.

Thus, Article 208 C of the French Tax Code allows the levying of exit tax at the rate of 16.5 % if subsequently to opting for the SIIC regime, properties, rights attached to a real estate financial lease or shareholdings in a partnership become eligible to the exemption. The latent capital gain is then added back in equal shares over a 4-year period, which allows the spreading of the taxation.

This provision mainly concerns properties financed through a financial lease agreement concluded or acquired prior to January 1st, 2005, which become eligible to the exemption due to the exercise of the option to buy. It also concerns cases where corporations would be transformed into partnerships or where a company which has elected the regime of Article 208 C wants to absorb a company which is not subject to that regime.

2.1.3   SIIC 2 measure: reduced rate for capital gains

Outsourcing of real estate properties

Article 210 E of the French Tax Code was created by the Finance Bill in 2005. This measure was done to favor the outsourcing of real estate properties to companies for which the owning and the managing of real estate is the core business and to allow SIICs to reach a critical size. Once the SIIC regime had been created, it was crucial to help the new SIIC companies attracting opportunities of acquisition. The model, which was pursued, is the US REIT model. In the US, the major part of the properties is held by real estate companies and not by corporates which core business is not real estate. This was not the case and still not is the case in France. The SIIC 2 regime, now called SIIC 3 regime (see below), was created in this particular context.

Levying of corporate income tax

Article 210 E of the French Tax Code allows the levying of corporate income tax (CIT) at the rate of 16.5 % – plus an additional tax of 3.3 % computed on corporation tax exceeding € 763,000 (the average reduced corporation tax is around 17.04 %) – instead of 33⅓ % standard CIT rate on net capital gains resulting from the contribution of buildings or rights attached to a financial lease agreement if the following conditions are met:

- The contributor is a legal entity liable to French CIT according to standard rules,

- the beneficiary of the contribution is a company raising funds from the public (appel public à l'épargne) or is agreed by the stock exchange authorities (Autorité des Marchés Financiers), and

- the beneficiary of the contribution performs a long-term real estate investment activity. The company acquiring or benefiting from such contribution must assure to keep the assigned property for five years. The formalism of this commitment shall be specified in a decree which has not been published yet. It has to be noted that the scope of this measure not only concerns SIICs, but also the beneficiary may be any other company which capital is open to the public, provided that it has a long-term real estate investment activity.

Non-compliance with this covenant shall entail a penalty corresponding to 25 % of the contribution value of the assigned property.

This provision was initially applied to assignments carried out until December 31ˢᵗ, 2007 but was extended and has in practice mainly concerned assignments to the benefit of the SIIC. Its purpose is to favor the transfer of the real estate patrimonial system of industrial or commercial companies to real estate companies. A sale of the shares received in exchange shortly after the contribution could be judged as an abuse of law and should therefore be subject to transfer duties (sale of listed shares are in principle outside transfer duties' scope).

Examples for this measure
The measure was a success and from the beginning large operations fell within the scope of it. Examples are the outsourcing of its real estate properties (precisely, financial leases) by "ACCOR group" to the benefit of "Foncière des Regions", by "Groupe Générale de Santé" to the benefit of "GECINA" or by "Groupe Casino" of its shopping malls to the benefit of "Mercialys" (see below).

2.1.4   Example

Benefit of measure
The following example shows the attractiveness of the measure.

Assumptions:

Fair market value of the property (out of transfer duties)	€ 150 million
Tax value of this property, equal to its net book value	€ 80 million

If the contribution falls within the scope of Article 210 E of the French Tax Code:

Capital gain realized	= m€ 70	(m€ 150 – m€ 80)
CIT (reduced rate)	= 11.9	(70 · 17.04 %) [5]
Net cash for the seller	= m€ 138.1	

The application of this regime is based on the condition that the beneficiary of the contribution commits to keep the contributed real estate property for at least five years. The SIIC 2 regime provided that such commitment needed to be included in the contribution deed. As it will be mentioned below, the formalism of such a commitment was subsequently changed in the SIIC 3 measure and precised by a decree.

If the beneficiary of the contribution does not respect its commitment, the reduced rate applied to the capital gain realized upon the contribution is not challenged.

However, the beneficiary of the contribution shall pay a penalty equal to 25 % of the contribution value of the property for which the commitment was not respected.

If the contribution is not placed under the scope of Article 210 E of the French Tax Code:

If the contribution of properties is placed under the standard regime, the amount of the capital gain realized upon the contribution is taxed at standard corporation tax of $33^1/_3$% on top of which a social contribution of 3.3 % is levied and computed on corporation tax exceeding € 763,000. The average corporation tax is around 34.43 %.

Taking the same assumption as above:

Should the contribution be placed under the standard regime:

Capital gain realized	= m€ 70	(m€ 150 – m€ 80)
CIT (standard rate)	= 24.1	(70 · 34.43 %)
Net cash for the seller	= m€ 125.9	

This amount needs to be compared to the € 138.1 million above in case of the application of the SIIC 2 regime.

It can be seen that this measure has clearly given a competitive advantage to companies which are allowed to offer such kind of possibility to sellers.

2.2   SIIC 3: how to further improve the critical size of SIICs

Extension of measure

In addition to the above-mentioned SIIC 2 measure which was created to favor corporates to outsource their properties to large listed real estate companies, it appeared that contribution operations were too heavy to be put in place for listed companies. Indeed, in order to achieve a share capital increase of a listed company, it is necessary to organize extraordinary shareholder meetings which may be expensive as well as time consuming as a specific auditor who has to provide a report on the valuation has to be appointed. In addition, sellers are more keen to get cash instead of shares, with these outsourcing operations being an opportunity for corporates to concentrate on their core business again and to proceed with new investments. The experience after this measure has been in effect for one year shows that SIIC 2 was only applied to sizable operations of several hundred million euros. It therefore appeared necessary to extend this measure to sales operations rather than only to the contribution in exchange for shares operations.

Amendatory Finance Bill in 2005

This is precisely the purpose of the commonly called SIIC 3 measure which was enacted in the Amendatory Finance Bill in 2005. As from January 1st, 2006, the temporary measure which allows the application of a reduced corporation tax to capital gains realized upon the outsourcing of properties and rights relating to financial leases is applicable to all kind of assignments, including contributions in exchange for shares or for considerations and sales.

The effect of that measure is that it has vested SIICs with an attractive and competitive advantage on deals. Some are only open to bidders that may allow the seller to benefit from the 16.5 % low capital gain tax rates.

2.3   SIIC 4: end of the abuse

Evolvement of SIIC 4

After three years in effect, the SIIC regime can be deemed a success and a role model for European countries which have followed the French initiative as, for example, the UK REIT (United Kingdom), the G-REIT (Germany) and the SIIQ (Italy). However, it appears necessary to reform the regime which was already done in the fourth part of the amendments, commonly called SIIC 4, which in principle is the last strong modification of the SIIC regime. In fact, aside from the SIICs which were created in line with the objectives of the regime, abusive situations of "tax opportunities" appeared, however, marginal but clearly contrary to the spirit of the regime: "captive SIICs, meaning controlled by a single dominating shareholder" and situation of "cumulative exemptions by foreign investors" have been noted by senator Marini [3]. To put an end to these situations is precisely one of the objectives of the SIIC 4 provisions introduced by Article 138 of the Amendatory Finance Bill of 2006 [4].

This set of measures is commonly called SIIC 4 and is aimed at restoring the free float and liquidity on SIIC shares, still avoiding situations in which a shareholder may abusively benefit from the regime in comparison to a French corporation acting in the same sort of situation.

2.3.1   Free float condition upon election for the SIIC regime

Conditions for the election

The SIIC 4 measure has established a new condition to be met in order for a listed company to be able to elect for the SIIC regime. It shall be mentioned that until SIIC 4, three conditions needed to be met:

• It was mandatory to have a share capital of at least € 15 million.

• It was mandatory to be listed on a French regulated market.

• It was mandatory to mainly pursue a long term real estate activity, i. e., the acquisition and/or the construction of properties with a view to lease them and/or the holding of shareholdings in companies having the same purpose.

New condition

For fiscal year open as from January 1st, 2007, there is a new condition: A company can opt for the tax exemption regime as a SIIC only if its share capital and its voting rights are held to at least 15 % by persons which individually own directly or indirectly less that 2 %. For companies wishing to enter into the regime, the condition is evaluated only once, namely at the first day of the FY during which the election is exercised.

It is therefore not applicable

- to existing SIICs having already elected for the SIIC regime for the fiscal year open before January 1st, 2007;

- in the course of the regime. This condition must only be met once and may not be respected by the SIIC after the election for the tax exemption regime.

2.3.2 Limitation of percentage of shareholding of the main shareholder

The direct or indirect ownership of a shareholder or a group of shareholders acting as one (action de concert) by meaning of Article L 233-10 of the Commercial Code is limited to less than 60 % of the share capital and the voting rights of the SIIC.

General principle

This new condition is both an eligible condition for the SIIC regime but also a condition for the application of the tax exemption regime. If it is not respected, even slightly, the SIIC becomes taxable at corporation tax under standard condition during the considered fiscal year.

Article L 233-10 of the Commercial Code provides for several definitions of the "action de concert". Therefore, such notion is deemed to be characterized in the situation where persons have concluded an agreement with a view to purchase or sell voting rights or with a view to exercise voting rights in a common policy vis-à-vis the company. The law therefore assumes the existence of such agreements in various situations which shall be evaluated on a case-by-case basis.

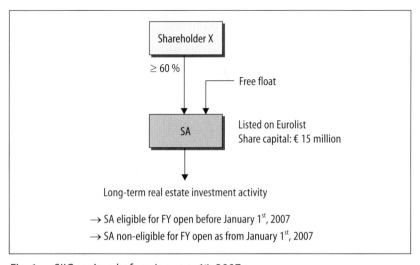

Fig. 1: SIIC regime before January 1st, 2007

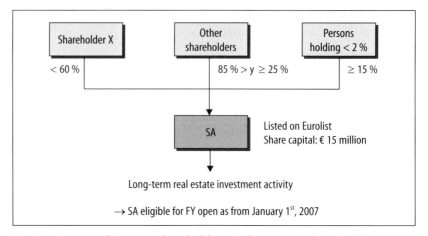

Fig. 2:   Two conditions on shareholdings to be respected on election

Figure 1 shows the situation before January 1st, 2007. Therefore, most of the first SIICs which elected for the tax exemption regime when created in 2003 had a sponsor which was not respecting this condition. Now, in order to be able to elect for the SIIC regime, it is necessary to diversify the shareholding of the concerned company. Figure 2 shows the two conditions on shareholdings which must be respected on election.

In addition, in case several shareholders invest, the condition may not be met as stated in figure 3 if the said shareholders are acting as one. This will be the case if shareholders have common directors and have agreed on a common strategy for the SIIC. Shareholder agreements may be put in place. It is therefore very important to carefully examine those kinds of agreements to check that they will not put the shareholders in a situation where they may be considered as acting as ones.

Exceptions   The 60 % threshold shall not be applicable when the shareholders are themselves SIICs. However, in the author's opinion, the shareholding threshold is not respected in the case when shareholders act as one and only one of the concerned shareholders is a SIIC but not the other.

Besides, the 60 % shareholding threshold may be temporarily not respected in case of a public offer of purchase or exchange on the stock exchange according to Article L 433-1 of the French Monetary and Financial Code or in case of a restructuring operation according to Article 210-0 A of the French Tax Code, which includes mergers, partial mergers splits or universal transmission of wealth. Such threshold may also temporarily not be respected in case of a conversion of convertible bonds and reimbursement of redeemable bonds into shares. In such situations, although the 60 % threshold may not be respected as a consequence of the operation, it is deemed to have been respected if it is actually respected before the expiry of the delay given to file the corporation tax return of the fiscal year during which the exceptional operation occurred. For instance, after a conversion operation of convertible bonds of a SIIC, which has a fiscal year closing on December 31st of each year, 70 % of its share capital becomes held by a unique shareholder on December 15th of a considered year

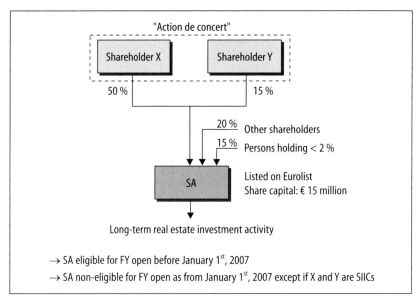

Fig. 3: "Action de concert": the case of several shareholders acting as one

(year n). The said shareholder has until April 30th of year n+1 to decrease his shareholding in the SIIC. If it is the case, the SIIC will remain within the corporation tax exemption regime during years n and n+1. If it is not the case, then the SIIC becomes liable to corporation tax at standard rate on all its income. In case of an exceptional operation, depending on the date on which such operation occurs, there is a regularization period which is provided by the texts and which may vary from four to 16 months.

This condition is applicable to the fiscal year open as from January 1st, 2007 for new companies willing to elect for the SIIC regime and as from January 1st, 2009 for SIICs having elected for the SIIC regime before January 1st, 2007. Most of the existing SIICs do not respect such a shareholding threshold, and in particular SIICs indirectly held by the French State such as "EMGP" or "Foncière de Pimonts". More than € 1.9 million shall be marketed before January 1st, 2009. The 60 % threshold will allow the existence of a sponsorship by a main shareholder but should favor a more important diversification of the share capital. **Entry into force**

The following examples illustrate the coming into effect of these new conditions and their consequences:

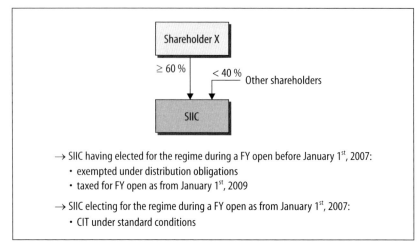

Fig. 4:   New conditions for SIICs from January 1ˢᵗ, 2007 on – scenario I

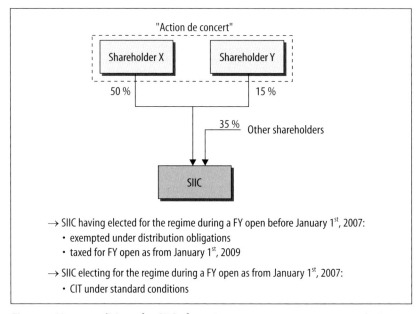

Fig. 5:   New conditions for SIICs from January 1ˢᵗ, 2007 on – scenario II

Now, in order to be exempted from corporation tax, SIICs will have to be held as follows:

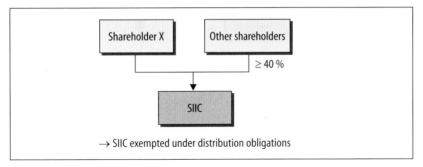

Fig. 6:   SIIC exemption from corporation tax

2.3.3   New 20 % levy

In order to avoid situations in which a shareholder would be, in addition to the tax exemption regime of the SIIC, also exempted on the dividends received by the SIIC, therefore completely avoiding corporation tax, the following measure was taken.

Scope of application

A SIIC becomes liable to a tax rate of 20 % on any distribution levied on the tax-exempt result and benefiting to shareholders, other than individuals,

- which own directly or indirectly 10 % or more of its share capital and

- which are not subject to French corporation tax or to an equivalent foreign tax on dividends distributed by the SIIC.

Dividends are not considered as subject to an equivalent tax to French corporation tax when they are exempted or subject to a tax which amount is lower than two-thirds of the French corporation tax that would have been due in the same standard conditions, i. e., effective taxation shall exceed 11.11 %. The 20 % tax concerns distributions but also deemed distributions.

The 20 % tax is not due when the beneficiary of the distribution is a company subject to a binding obligation to distribute 100 % of the dividends received and its shareholders respect the above-mentioned conditions.

Basis

The exceptional tax is equal to 20 % of the sums actually distributed to shareholders which meet the two above-mentioned conditions and is levied on the tax-exempt result of the SIIC.

Distributions levied on the taxable result of the SIIC do not trigger the payment of such a tax. When sums have already been subject to 20 % of tax, in particular when a SIIC owns shares in another SIIC, the law provides for a reduction of the basis of the 20 % tax on sums which have already been subject to this tax.

Example:

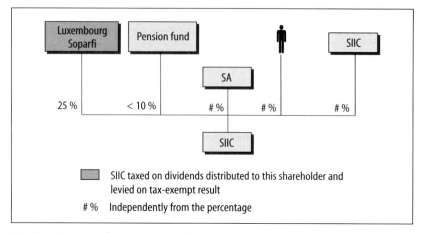

Fig. 7:   Example for avoidance of a 20 % tax payment

In this example, it has been assumed that:

- the SIIC is held
    - to 25 % by a Luxembourg corporation,
    - to less than 10 % by a Dutch pension fund,
    - to the rest of the stocks by an individual, a French corporation (SA) and a SIIC;
- the SIIC distributes a dividend amounting to 100.
  85 of which are levied on the tax-exempt result and 15 being levied on the taxable result.

Solution:

- The distribution will not trigger the payment of the 20 % tax for that part of the dividend levied on the taxable result, i.e., 15.

- It will neither trigger the 20 % tax on dividends levied on the tax-exempt result and distributed to
    - the individual,
    - the French SA, since the French SA cannot benefit from participation exemption regime on dividends distributed by SIICs and levied on the tax-exempt result;
    - the Dutch pension fund, since it owns less than 10 % of the share capital of the SIIC.

- In the present case, it has been assumed that all the shareholders of the SIIC owning the shares of the distributing SIIC were SIIC 4 compatible, i.e., any shareholder owning directly or indirectly 10 % or more of the receiving SIIC is liable to corporation tax on the dividends distributed by this second SIIC. As a consequence, the dividends distributed to the SIIC shareholder do not trigger the 20% tax. It would have been different if the shareholders of the receiving SIIC had not met the conditions to allow a 10% tax exemption. In such a case, when the receiving SIIC would redistribute the dividends received from the lower tier SIIC, it would be allowed to offset the 20% tax paid by the lower tier SIIC on the 20% tax to be paid on such redistribution as a kind of tax credit.

- 20% corporation tax will have to be paid by the SIIC on that part of the dividend levied on the tax-exempt result and distributed to the Luxembourg company:

    – Indeed, as a consequence of the current Luxembourg/French tax treaty from April 1st, 1948, the Luxembourg corporation is in principle tax-exempt on the tax result distributed by the SIIC.

    – The SIIC must pay 4.25 corresponding to $(85 \cdot 25\% \cdot 20\%)$.

    – This 4.25 will be in fact beard by all the shareholders, since it is paid by the SIIC and will impact the net equity of the SIIC.

The 20% tax is due and paid by the SIIC. Its costs are therefore beard by all the shareholders and are not tax-deductible from the amount which is paid to the „failing" shareholder. It is recovered and controlled like corporation tax, i. e., its statute of limitation is December 31st of the third year following the fiscal year during which the 20% must be paid and cannot be offset as a tax credit or refunded nor admitted as a tax-deductible expense. It is paid spontaneously the month following the payment of the dividend.

Payment and control

This provision is applicable when the company, which has elected for the SIIC regime, is French or foreign and should notably affect SIICs held by Spanish investors, in principle exempted in Spain from tax on distributions received from French SIICs. It should also affect SIICs held by foreign pension funds, in particular Dutch SIICs.

This provision is applicable to distributions paid as from July 1st, 2007. As a consequence, existing SIICs (SIIC having elected before January 1st, 2007) and new SIICs fall within the scope of such provision.

Entry into force

2.3.4 More flexibility of the SIIC regime and extension of the SIIC 3 provision

The scope of the exemption regime is extended to benefits derived from real rights such as usufructs, construction leases (bail à construction) or long-term leases (bail emphytéotique). It has to be reminded that the right of the lessor of a construction lease of a long-term lease already fell within the tax exemption regime as a consequence of the administrative guidelines which already allowed such possibility if the lessor is the owner of the constructions [6]. The rights which become eligible to the tax exemption as a consequence of this new measure trigger the add-back of the latent capital gain on such rights in four equal installments over a 4-year period, as well as the corresponding payment of the 16.5% exit tax.

Extension of the scope of the SIIC regime

In order to facilitate the creation of the joint ventures between the SIICs, the Article 208 C exemption regime is extended to subsidiaries which are jointly held, directly or indirectly, by several SIICs at least by 95% (the previous condition was to be held at least at 95% directly or indirectly by a unique SIIC).

The conditions of application of the exemption to dividends received by a SIIC from another SIIC (so-called SIIC on SIIC, "SIIC sur SIIC") are more flexible. Therefore, the tax exemption regime applies as long as the receiving SIIC owns at least 5% of the share capital and voting rights of the distributing SIIC (the previous conditions implied a dependence link) during at least two years and redistributes the whole amount of the dividends.

Finally, the SIIC 4 provision provides that the tax exemption remains applicable when a SIIC becomes held to at least 95% by another SIIC, provided that it still respects its binding obligations to distribute and remains a subsidiary of its SIIC parent company until the expiry of the 10-year period starting at its own election. It has indeed to be reminded that the exit of a SIIC from the tax exemption regime during the 10-year period following its election triggers the retroactive recapture of the taxation of the latent capital gains at standard corporation tax rate instead of 16.5%.

More flexibility for internal restructuring of SIIC

Rationalize the holding of real estate portfolios   Another provision of SIIC 4 was aimed at allowing SIICs to rationalize their holding of their real estate portfolio. Indeed, the French tax authorities refuse to consider that the owning of properties may constitute an autonomous and complete branch of business which would allow to apply a tax-neutral regime in case of a contribution. In addition, a SIIC cannot set up a tax consolidation group with its subsidiaries which would allow under French tax rules to proceed with intra-group sales operations with a postponement of the payment of the realized capital gain. The new measure allows neutralizing capital gains realized upon the sale of real estate properties, financial leases or real rights between subsidiaries of a SIIC having elected for the tax exemption regime or between a SIIC and its subsidiaries provided that certain conditions are met.

In particular, the purchaser must commit in the acquisition deed to respect the conditions set up for the standard neutral merger regime (the one applicable between companies subject to corporation tax), such as in particular the computation of the future capital gains on the non depreciable assets (land) with a reference to the tax value of the said assets in the accounts of the seller and the add-back of the over-depreciation on the depreciable assets. The add-back of the over-depreciation on the constructions (only constructions and not land may be depreciated) shall be included in the tax-exempt result subject to the 85% binding obligation to distribute applicable to rental income.

2.3.5 Precision and extension of the SIIC 3 provision

As mentioned above, the SIIC 3 regime is not only applicable to SIICs, but also to any company which shares are publicly traded. In order to avoid a scheme where such conditions would be met only for the purpose of offering the SIIC 3 regime to potential sellers, the Amendatory Finance Bill of 2006 has specified the definition of "raising funds from the public" by meaning of SIIC 3 provisions. It must be characterized by the emission of securities giving a binding access to the share capital, excluding other types of emissions (such as listed bonds). For the fiscal year open as from January 1st, 2007, this attractive tax regime is also applicable if the assignee is a subsidiary of a SIIC or a SPPICAV (sociétés de placement à prépondérance immobilière à capital variable) having elected for the tax exemption provided by Article 208C as long as they remain within the scope of this regime during at least five years as from the acquisition.

In addition, the SIIC 3 regime has been extended to transactions occurring until December 31st, 2008.

3 Comments

When the SIIC regime was created, 13 companies elected to be subject to it. There are now more than 40 companies which have elected the SIIC regime. This spectacular development was made possible through different ways. On the one hand, the advantages of the regime rapidly became obvious: flexibility, tax exemption on rental income and capital gains, the possibility to keep ancillary activities, the possibility to rely on tax treaty provisions (SIIC is a French tax resident) and the competitiveness as a consequence of the SIIC 2/3 regime. The development described above has certainly favored such a development.

In order to set up a SIIC, it is necessary to have a listed company. The IPO process is one of the ways to be listed. However, this implies that a significant real estate portfolio already exists and nobody can guarantee the success of an IPO. Thus, investors which were willing to set up a SIIC tried to find shell quoted companies, listed companies which have no longer an operational activity but are still listed. As a consequence, a market of the shell quoted companies appeared since 2003. The first of this type of companies were sold without any premium, but now there is a high premium which is paid by actors which are willing to purchase shell quoted companies (in the area of several million euros).

For instance, "Compagnie de la Lucette" (previously "Mines de la Lucette") or **Examples** "Société de la Tour Eiffel" were initially shell quoted companies which were purchased and subsequently elected for the SIIC regime.

Another significant example of the development of the SIIC regime is the creation of "Mercialys" by "Groupe Casino". "Groupe Casino" used to hold shopping malls near supermarkets. They decided to create a SIIC, dedicated to commercial assets, and to attract new investors and partners. "Mercialys" was born in October 2005 after an IPO process. The assets were outsourced by "Groupe Casino" to "Mercialys" under the SIIC 2 regime described above. Today, "Mercialys" is one of the major SIICs.

With the SIIC 4 regime, it can be anticipated that there will be cross-shareholding between SIICs and that concentration operations may arise. Indeed, the maximum shareholding of a unique shareholder will have to respect the 60 % threshold from January 1st, 2009 on (for SIICs having elected before January 1st, 2007), and it is anticipated that the critical size to attract shareholders and increase liquidity of the shares will have to be reached.

4 Bibliography

[1] Finance Bill for 2003 (no. 2002–1575) dated December 30th, 2002.

[2] Finance Bill for 2005 (no. 2004–1484) dated December 30th, 2004.

[3] Free translation of the report drafted by the Finance Commission of the French parliament.

[4] Amendatory Finance Bill for 2006 (no. 2006–1771) dated December 31st, 2006.

[5] 16.5 % on top of which a 3.3 % social contribution is computed on corporation tax exceeding € 763,000.

[6] Administrative guidelines dated September 25th, 2003 BOI 4 H-5-03 no. 8.

4 Property Investment Trusts in the UK

John L. Glascock
Abraham Park

Table of contents

1   Introduction

Swayings with UK REITs

UK REITs (listed property companies to become REITs) started off with a bang and had significant appreciation right up and until they were officially REITs. UK REITs soon after introduction seemed to begin their decline in market value and began trading at discounts to Net Asset Value (NAV) as well. What happened and how will UK REITs fair over the long term and what are the crucial issues facing the REIT market in the UK?

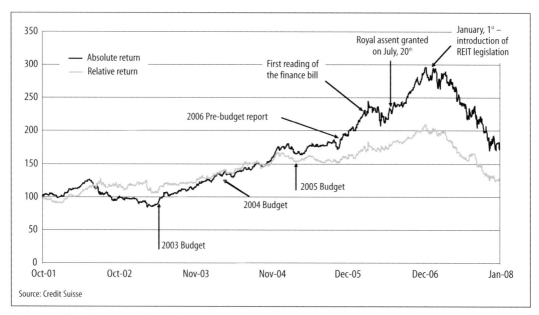

Fig. 1:   UK REITs peak with legislation

Three key factors for the future market

There seem three key factors. First, it took the USA a long time to get its REIT legislation right and it seems that the UK is following in the USA footsteps. Second, the market as a whole has not favored REITs since their introduction in the UK (e.g., real interest rates did not continue to decline and overall market conditions, including the subprime issue, do not favor increasing real estate valuations). Third, UK REITs have not yet fully become REITs in terms of market expectations.

2   UK legislation is less than encouraging

UK legislation provided for a standard REIT – that is, the REIT must own and operate real estate and earn its primary income from leases or rental values; must not have too much debt (but this was not directly limited); must have broad ownership and not too much concentration in control; and must pay out most of its defined income as dividends.

REIT standard taken from the US

Additionally, REITs must pay an entry fee that allows them to have tax transparency (no double taxation) and absolves them essentially from their accumulated capital gain tax burdens on the property held. This is a good start, but it does not solve or even encourage the overcoming of two key issues.

One, how do you grow a REIT? Two, how can you start a new REIT? The government initially stressed that it hoped that UK REITs would help solve the housing shortage, especially in affordable rental housing. But nothing in the legislation makes it easy or even clearly defines how to start-up such a REIT. The French government helped to solve this issue by their first patch to the original SIIC legislation: It introduced UPREITs as the Americans had done in the early 1990s.

Two key issues still to solve

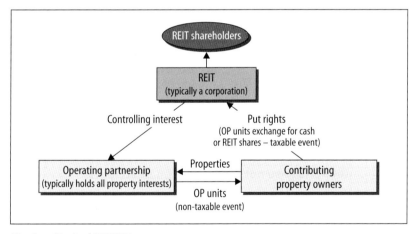

Fig. 2:   Typical UPREIT structure

The UPREIT, an umbrella REIT, allows current property owners to swap in their real estate for partnerships shares that allow the deferral of capital gains taxes until later conditions are met. This encourages the growth of REITs by giving them access to large estates of real estate without the owner having to bear the current burden of taxes. It also tends to move assets from lower levels of management to stronger management inside the REIT. Society seems to end up a winner and REITs grow. Most of the USA growth has been attributed to the UPREIT legislation there. In fact, REITs were essentially not an important

UPREIT as catalyst for REIT growth

capital market story until UPREITs were created. French REITs have done better since the introduction of UPREITS. Current legislation does not allow such an option.

3   Market conditions do not favor real estate valuations

Cap rate compression
After the general market crash of 2000/2001, real estate and particularly REITs did very well in market appreciation. Two factors seemed to drive this outcome. First, people noticed that REITs did not fall as strongly as the market as a whole – they thus discovered a good defensive stock. Second, real interest rates fell and debt became easier to use. Therefore, the good cash flows of real estate and REITs meant that values would escalate as the discount rate fell: The by-word was cap rate compression for most for the post 2001 period.

However, by 2007 capitalization rates had very little room left to compress – rates across European markets from Poland to France were very tight. In the UK, rates across industry types of real estate had seen strong compression and little room was left to improve values by lower interest rates. Higher debt levels were being structured: then came the subprime crisis and by December of 2007, it is likely that real estate values in London had fallen by 10 % (perhaps more) [1].

No longer could a deal be structured at say 85 % debt; debt now needed to be about 70 % and it is likely that the cap rate in the deal has also risen.

Deal killers
For example, while in summer of 2007, one might have completed a good industrial deal at a 5 % to 6 % cap rate with liberal debt, it was at perhaps 7 % to 7.5 % by the autumn with only 70 % debt. Thus, some deals just stopped. In such an environment, REIT shares declined in value and looked low compared to their Net Asset Values. However, it may be that temporarily NAVs are estimated as too high and thus as they adjust the market price to NAV will close.

Also, the post 2001 until the summer of 2007 was a low inflation environment; but now, inflation looks more likely to increase. Real estate and REITs do not perform as well in such an environment.

4   UK REITs have not yet become (market) REITs!

US REITs vs. UK REITs
Historically, UK property companies have behaved clearly differently than US REITs. They have tended to have more debt, less cash dividends and be involved in more development. This helps to explain why the listed UK property companies from 1989 through 2002 underperformed the FTSE All-Shares Index, while US REITs did substantially better than the USA S&P 500 [2]. UK listed real estate was about a play for capital appreciation and thus lower taxes. But REITs have clearly been cash (dividend) driven, at least in the United States.

UK REITs have not yet become cash driven nor have they shed much of their preference for development. Thus, on a yield basis, UK REITs just do not yet look like REITs. "Land securities" and others have raised their dividends greatly, but it is not enough. A good REIT must yield on a cash basis more than the 10-year safe rate. Generally, the authors would expect that the spread should be 100 to 200 basis points over the 10-year gilt (or for US REITs, the 10-year treasury).

If US REITs that are S&P 500 listed with the key large UK REITs [3] ("British Land", "Hammerson", "Land Securities", "Liberty International" and "Segro") are compared, it can be found that the US REITs have a dividend rate of 4.42 % while the UK REITs have a dividend rate of 2.88 %. US REITs have also fallen in price as their relative dividend has taken a slide against the 10-year treasury rate. However, the UK REITs are still not as cash driven as the market would prefer [4].

Differences in dividend rates

Good REITs also seemed to be focused. The UK REITs are still essential conglomerates of real estate activities – some office, some retail and some development, etc.

Land Securities and Slough (now "Segro") made a positive move toward focus with their trade of assets before the REIT regime took place and Land Securities has since announced that they will have three core divisions (retail, office, and Trillium). This is a good step, but these are still not three well defined and incentive compatible REITs. It is still one company with perhaps less agency issues than before. Time will tell if the market buys this approach to focus.

5 Moving forward in the UK

The REIT legislation in the UK clearly bifurcated the listed real estate market – today the UK REIT is over 10 times the market capitalization of the remaining listed real estate sector. The UK REIT sector seems to be reducing debt and increasing dividends and considering focus. These actions will go far in reaching the government's goal of providing a more stable listed real estate sector.

REIT penetration in the UK

But, the sector faces key challenges in terms of how to grow. If it is good to have a more stable listed (REIT) real estate sector, it would seem to be advantageous to have a larger REIT sector with more of the overall real estate market managed by this sector. But to do so, UK REITs need to grow and there need to be new REITs that provide competition and innovation.

This will require new legislation to allow something like an UPREIT and to allow ways to start up a new REIT without undue tax penalties. Perhaps a private REIT can be allowed that must eventually be turned into a public listed REIT. Thus, investors and key players can accumulate the asset base needed for a UK REIT over time and then list after a critical mass has been achieved.

New legislation required

Overall, the next few years will be challenging for UK REITs. They face strong competition in the UK from other forms of tax-advantaged structures, they need further internal reform to become more REIT-like, and they face strong competition from other European REITs and global REITs as well.

Company	Listing country	Market cap (£ million)
Westfield	Australia	16,288
Simon Property Group	USA	9,304
Unibal-Rodamco	France	8,750
Prologis	USA	7,422
Land Securities	UK	7,214
Vornado Realty	USA	6,544
Public Storage	USA	6,196
Stockland Group	Australia	4,931
British Land	UK	4,857
General Growth	USA	4,094
Source: Bloomberg, January 2008/Credit Suisse		

Fig. 3:   Global REITs in Europe

6   The next round

Strong globally oriented REITs

As figure 3 shows, there are already strong non-European and non-British REITs operating in Europe and the UK. These REITs are more global and have better financial attributes than the UK REITs. Thus, competition will be high for the REIT investor and for property. If the UK does not change its legislation to accommodate and encourage REIT competition, growth and innovation, it will be an anomaly in the world market for efficient and competitive real estate management.

UK mangers have excelled at accumulating a strong asset base that is well situated in the UK market, but that asset base needs to produce higher cash flows that end up as dividends for shareholders.

Fewer debt for more stability

Additionally, over time the balance sheet needs to be less debt driven – this provides for more stability, but also requires more efficiency in operations (otherwise dividends remain low). The authors expect that UK REITs require less overall dividend yields than US REITs primarily due to the stronger UK leasing laws that make property safer than in the USA, but current yields are too soft for a good valuation landing. UK REITs offer a strong opportunity for income and appreciation, but new legislation and quick industry adjustments are the keys to unlocking this opportunity.

7   Bibliography

[1] See GVA Grimley, A Monthly Review from Howard Cooke on Current Factors Influencing Corporate Occupiers of Real Estate, December 2007, p. 2.

[2] For details see, Glascock, J./Zhu, T., Cambridge University working paper: Performance Measures of Real Estate Portfolio Returns and the Risk Behavior Across Market Conditions: Some UK Evidence, 2004.

[3] The average market cap for the UK REITs is US$ 8.6 billion while the USA S&P 500 listed REITs is US$ 10 billion (January 2007). Thus, these are about the same size and each represent the relatively larger entities in their respective markets.

[4] Both relative positions of UK REITs and US REITs to their respective safe rates will likely improve due to re-setting of target rates in both countries. But the authors' belief is that REITs in both countries need more cash dividend to sustain capital values: The UK REITs perhaps need more growth in dividends due to being farther behind.

5 REIT history in the US: a look at Equity Office Properties Trust

Samuel Zell

Table of contents

1   Introduction

Real estate stocks have outperformed the S&P 500

Real Estate Investment Trusts (REITs) are income-producing stocks that provide among the highest dividend yields available in the capital markets. They are diversified equity products that have been stress-tested, protecting investors during times of inflation, and providing stable income during economic downturns. REITs revolutionized the real estate industry, broadening it as an investment vehicle by instilling transparency and liquidity, and by bringing real estate on par with the rest of corporate America. Real estate is now an integral part of Wall Street, and the US economy. Each year, the market has a clearer perspective of what REITs can offer, and this increased understanding has been reflected in the industry's growth.

The US REIT industry has grown from a market capitalization of US$ 1.5 billion to US$ 438 billion over the past three decades, with most of that growth, nearly 400 %, occurring in just the past 10 years. Real estate stocks have outperformed the S&P for the past 1-year, 3-year, 5-year and 10-year time periods. REITs have been successful in the US largely because they have consistently provided strong returns with transparency and accountability in their financial reporting to shareholders.

EOP – from public to private

From its initial public offering in 1997, Equity Office Properties Trust (EOP) was at the forefront of the industry's evolution. For the better part of the last 10 years, EOP was the largest REIT in the US. The company debuted in the public arena at US$ 21 per share, and sold to The Blackstone Group in 2007 for US$ 55.50 per share in the largest private equity deal in history. The story of EOP reflects the genesis of the industry as well as the market force trends that are impacting REITs today.

Equity market capitalization outstanding (millions of dollars at year end)					
End of year	# of REITs	Market capitalization	End of year	# of REITs	Market capitalization
1971	34	1,494.3	1989	120	11,662.2
1972	46	1,880.9	1990	119	8,737.1
1973	53	1,393.5	1991	138	12,968.2
1974	53	712.4	1992	142	15,912.0
1975	46	899.7	1993	189	32,158.7
1976	62	1,308.0	1994	226	44,306.0
1977	69	1,528.1	1995	219	57,541.3
1978	71	1,412.4	1996	199	88,776.3
1979	71	1,754.0	1997	211	140,533.8
1980	75	2,298.6	1998	210	138,301.4
1981	76	2,438.9	1999	203	124,261.9
1982	66	3,298.6	2000	189	138,715.4
1983	59	4,257.2	2001	182	154,898.6
1984	59	5,085.3	2002	176	161,937.3
1985	82	7,674.0	2003	171	224,211.9
1986	96	9,923.6	2004	193	307,894.73
1987	110	9,702.4	2005	197	330,691.31
1988	117	11,435.2	2006	183	438,071.1

Source: www.NAREIT.com

NAREIT is the exklusive of the National Association of Real Estate Investment Trusts®, Inc. Copyright © 2007 National Association of Real Estate Investment Trusts. All rights reserved. NAREIT documents available from this website are protected by the copyright laws of the United States and international treaties. All use subject to conditions of use. See: http://www.NAREIT.com/conditionsofuse.cfm. See our website disclaimer: www.NAREIT.com/disclaimer.cfm.

Fig. 1:   Historical REIT industry market capitalization 1972 to 2006

Period	Total return	Price
Historical (compound annual rates through end of previous month)		
1-year	29.58	24.01
3-year	23.06	16.75
5-year	23.14	16.04
10-year	14.14	6.84
15-year	14.85	7.14
20-year	11.30	2.81
30-year	13.52	4.30
35-year	11.29	2.06

Source: www.NAREIT.com

Disclaimer: The FTSE NAREIT US Real Estate Index is calculated by FTSE International Limited (FTSE). All rights in the FTSE NAREIT US Real Estate Index vest in FTSE and the National Association of Real Estate Investment Trusts (NAREIT). FTSE is a trademark of the London Stock Exchange Plc and the Financial Times Limited and is used by FTSE under license. NAREIT® is a trademark of NAREIT. Neither FTSE nor NAREIT nor their licensors shall be liable (including in negligence) for any loss arising out of use of the FTSE NAREIT US Real Estate Index by any person. All data is derived from and applies only to, publicly traded securities.

Fig. 2:   Investment performance of publicly traded REITs
(percentage change, except where noted, as of February 28th, 2007)

2   History of REITs in the US

First REIT wave   The US Congress created REITs in 1960 to provide small investors with a vehicle through which to invest in large-scale, income-producing real estate. The first wave of industry growth came in the early 1970s, bringing total REIT market capitalizations to nearly US$ 2 billion. Mortgage REITs, which, due to their penchant for development, were also called construction & development (C&D) REITs, were predominant. Their highly leveraged, high-risk model of lending long and borrowing short was no match for the energy-crisis recession. They took a beating – losing roughly US$ 30 billion in equity – and many went into bankruptcy. What remained of the industry were a few equity REITs, and these survivors became the forefathers of the REITs which are known today.

Tax Reform Act of 1986   Two factors prevented REITs from becoming a revolutionary force for the first 30 years of their life. First, REIT rules prohibited the operation and management of owned assets, leaving these functions to third parties whose economic interests often did not align with owners' interests. Secondly, and even more significantly, tax shelters were in place, which prevented the real estate industry from functioning on a truly economic basis. Investment decisions did not need to focus on yields when the goals were tax deductions and credits. Further, these tax rules encouraged risk, which spurred development, which helped lead to extreme overbuilding and a massive oversupply of real estate by the late 1980s. The pivotal change for REITs came when the Tax Reform Act of 1986 was passed. It permitted REITs to operate and manage their owned assets, and limited the deductibility of interest, lengthening depreciation periods and restricting the use of passive losses [1].

"Stay alive 'til '95"   But for the growth of the REIT industry to gather momentum, the Act's reach had to wait for marketplace equilibrium. The 1987 recession slowed job growth and end user demand for real estate, amplifying the oversupply with low absorption. Industry losses exceeded US$ 80 billion and commercial property values dropped by up to 50 %. Even tenured companies collapsed, and the motto "Stay alive 'til '95" was born. It was the worst real estate downturn since the Great Depression in the 1930s, and it ushered in the disappearance of dedicated real estate lenders, a pivotal change for the industry. To access capital, real estate investors and developers were forced to turn to Wall Street and the rigors of discipline of the public market.

Prior to 1990, developers and entrepreneurs were assuming exceptionally high leverage. Mortgages often represented more than 90 % of a property's estimated market value [2]. Bankers and investors were wagering that either inflation would deliver a margin, or the banker would sell the loan before it defaulted. It was a private club with very little liquidity, and investors were leery of REITs because of the billions of dollars that had been lost in the industry two decades earlier. Lenders had no means with which to weigh proposals, to access competitive information or to analyze market conditions.

The opening of the black box   With the shift of financing to the public market, real estate owners brought disclosure to this black-box industry. Rental rate schedules, vacancy projections and other benchmarks equalized lenders' ability to assess risk. Capital market requirements made hundreds of comparables available, and allowed lenders

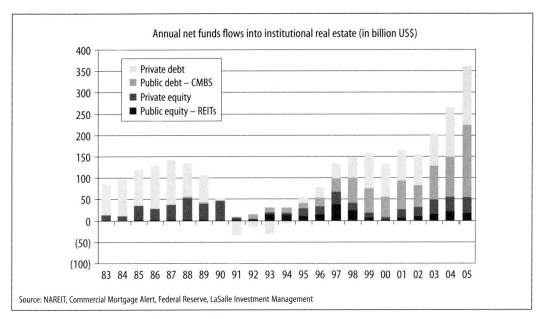

Fig. 3: Increasing capital flows to real estate

and investors to base assumptions and projections on real-time data. This made an enormous impact on increasing investor confidence in the industry.

From its onset, Equity Office set the bar for industry transparency with detailed quarterly financial supplemental reports, which included financial statements, same-store analysis, detailed debt and joint venture information, leasing activity and property statistical information. Other unique examples of EOP's transparency included detailed analyses of different types of tenant improvements and lease costs depending on lease type, and a detailed reconciliation of GAAP net income to taxable income.

Equity Office also pushed through barriers that for so long relegated real estate as a separate, uncorrelated asset class. In 2001, the company was the first REIT to be included on the S&P 500, and this was momentous validation of the real estate industry.

As the authenticity of REITs began to take hold, the successful transition of the industry from small, private owners to liquid, transparent companies was apparent. By the early 2000s, REIT dividends had been stress-tested, and REITs had earned solid standing with institutional investors. In 2004, Institutional Shareholders Services (ISS), an institutional shareholder watchdog, reported that real estate had the highest average Corporate Governance Quotient (CGQ) among the 24 industries ISS tracked at the time [3].

Most recently, the industry's success in the US has translated across the globe. REITs are fast becoming the international benchmark for real estate investment. In 1993, only four countries had REITs. Today, there are 30 countries that have REITs or REIT-like structures, or that are considering developing them. Great Britain has joined the ranks in 2007, and Germany is about to do the same. REIT has done.

Future upward potential of REITs

The US REIT structure has provided the blueprint for all of them: Australia, Bulgaria, Canada, China, France, Germany, India, Japan, Singapore, the UK and many others. Europe and Asia have seen the intoxication of liquidity. The shift to REITs is liquefying an enormous number of assets, and this is boosting stock markets around the world. Assuming the asset quality is institutional-grade, REITs overseas should have the same exponential growth as they have had in the US. Further, REITs in developing countries – where there is vast, diversified real estate ownership – provide an enormous benefit. When in a public forum, widespread wealth can be much more productive for a country's economy.

Worldwide, REIT activity is spectacular, even though it is still in its embryonic stage. Other countries are learning from the industry's evolution in the US that the more REITs they have, the higher the demand; the higher the demand, the higher the pricing; and the higher the pricing, the higher the yields.

3   Forces impacting real estate

There are momentous forces shaping the future of the US real estate industry today, namely liquidity, demographic shifts, and globalization.

3.1   Liquidity

Monetization   In the past few years, we have seen acceleration in the conversion of hard assets – to the point of imbalance. This monetization has created perhaps the greatest pool of liquidity in history, not only in the US, but across the globe. Concurrently, the population of the developed world is aging, and together, these two dynamics have created an enormous need and demand for yield.

Worldwide, this massive amount of capital has dramatically increased the number of investors who want to own bricks and mortar in the US. The developed world's graying population is increasingly taking notice of REITs, and the secure stream of income they offer.

So, how do we reconcile the value of REITs' attraction as an income stock with the recent billion-dollar private buyouts? Liquidity converged with low interest rates and unjustifiably undervalued public real estate, and together, these factors drove significant levels of real estate into the arms of the private sector.

Privatization   During the privatization trend in the US real estate industry, from 2005 through mid-2007, more than US$ 90 billion of public-to-private transactions took place. The annual increases in the number of these transactions were been staggering, going from just US$ 252 million in 2004 to over US$ 9 billion in 2005, and then jumping to US$ 31 billion in 2006 (see figure 4). The subprime market crash in the US in August 2007, brought this prolific level of deal making to a relative halt. But, the catalyst was not a credit crisis, but rather a crisis of investor confidence. The market remained awash in liquidity, but market volatility generated by lack of investor confidence restrained investors who had aggressively borrowed just one month earlier.

Year	Total transaction (in million US$)
2004	252
2005	9,090
2006	31,200
2007 (through 1Q 07)	49,891
Total transactions 2004–2007	**90,433**

Fig. 4:   Real estate public-to-private transactions

The public market offers the momentous advantage of access to the capital markets, which provides liquidity and access to a broad investor base, and, by nature of its limited leverage, low risk. Private real estate companies have the benefits of full use of the revenues, higher leverage thresholds, and fewer restrictions. REITs tend to finance their projects at 50 % debt and equity, while the private market is often leveraging upwards of 80 %. REITs' limited flexibility is exemplified by the fact that they cannot sell more than 10 % of their cumulative tax base in a year in the US. This can hinder their ability to take advantage of frothy sales environments.

3.2   Demographic shifts

Population shifts are also redefining the real estate growth markets in this country. The US Census and Bureau of Labor Statistics data report that over the next 10 to 20 years, the size of the working-age population (20 to 64) will shrink dramatically, while employer demand for office jobs will grow. Consequently, workers will be more empowered to choose where they want to live and work, and employers will have little choice but to follow.

Data also reveal a delay in the average marriage age. Younger workers are more likely to choose to live in 24/7 cities – places that offer numerous cultural activities and housing options, particularly in coastal markets. This means that

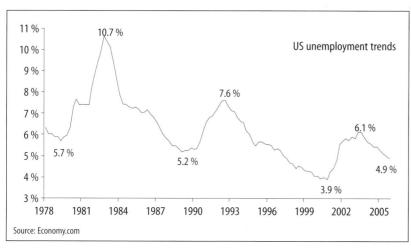

Fig. 5:   Employee labor shortage

corporations, such as Sears and Motorola in Chicago's suburbs, that built the "mega-campuses" of the 1980s in far-flung suburban areas, will be challenged to attract high-end talent, and eventually, will be forced to move back to urban areas, or to create working alternatives through technology.

3.3 Globalization

End user needs for real estate are also being impacted by globalization. Over the past 20 years, the off-shoring of assembly and manufacturing jobs has become commonplace. But within the past seven years, there has been an increasingly higher level of sophistication in the jobs moving offshore, including: call centers and other administrative support, software production and computer programming, information and data processing, and legal and other professional services. Further, studies indicate that the scope of potential jobs that could be outsourced is expanding. In theory, 11 % of today's US$ 1.5 billion service jobs could be performed remotely [4]. And trends indicate that research and development (R&D) will be in the next wave of professions to be impacted.

A recent study by Georgia Tech's College of Management revealed that nearly 40 % of more than 200 multinational corporations from the US and Western Europe plan to substantially change their worldwide distribution of R&D work over the next three years, with China and India likely to attract the greatest increase in projects. While labor costs were certainly a factor in the decision to increase outsourcing, the primary motivation was a search for talent, which, in the US, reflects the demographic trend of a workforce labor shortage [5].

The low-rise suburban office buildings that once housed call centers are more likely to remain vacant for lack of replacement tenants. Cities that primarily house high-tech centers may struggle for strong office space absorption. And, if the predictions for exporting R&D jobs take hold, the demand for R&D space may diminish.

4 Equity Office Properties Trust

4.1 Strategy

History of Equity Office Property Trust Through its history, Equity Office's strategies evolved to best respond and take advantage of these mega-trends. The company was born out of four Zell/Merrill Lynch Opportunity Real Estate Funds within Equity Group Investments. EOP began trading on the New York Stock Exchange in July 1997, priced at US$ 21, and closed that first day at US$ 27. The company had 32.2 million square feet in 90 primarily Class A office buildings in 35 markets.

The office market in the US is dependent on job growth, local market demographics, and local economies. Like the national economy, it is cyclical. Due to long-term leases, which average five years on a national basis, the office market will predictably lag the national economy up or down by two or three years. When there is a lack of new construction (supply), and office employment (demand) is growing, tenants absorb space and rents rise. When there is limited supply, rents rise and developers try to build new buildings.

Equity Office was designed to weather all points in the cycle. By focusing on Class A office buildings, EOP was able to take full benefit from the flight-to-quality trend that occurs in a soft market as businesses take advantage of lower rental rates to upgrade their office space. EOP also mitigated risk posed to Class B and C building owners from off-shoring, as tenants that occupied these types of buildings began moving their operations overseas. Further, in a strong market with solid job growth, Class A space commands the highest rents, and can dramatically out-price its less desirable counterparts.

Investment strategy of EOP

EOP's strategy was to amass scale under the premise that the advantages of size and scale leveraged by other industries could apply to real estate. Contrary to popular belief, EOP knew commercial real estate could earn a national brand. Industry leadership was the company's benchmark, and through its growth, EOP continued to surpass historical industry thresholds, including:

- Mergers & Acquisitions totaling more than US$ 26 billion, including three mergers, each of which at the time were the largest in real estate history,

- the first REIT listing on the S&P 500 in 2001,

- entrance onto the Fortune Most Admired Companies in America list in 2001 as the number one real estate company,

- the introduction in 2003 of a centralized operating model that had never before been applied to real estate,

- the largest revolving credit facility, which was obtained in September 2006,

- a US$ 1.5 billion senior convertible unsecured notes offering in 2006, which was the largest unsecured REIT debt offering of its kind at the time.

By the end of 2001, EOP had grown to be the largest REIT in the country, totaling more than 128 million square feet in 774 office buildings in 37 markets across the country. Its signature buildings defined the skylines of cities coast to coast, and Equity Office earned a national reputation with its irreplaceable portfolio of Class A assets, consistent, investment-grade balance sheet, excellent liquidity, and exceptional management team. The company also established a highly disciplined investment strategy, along with the ability to attract and execute unique, off-market investment deals.

For example, in 2004, EOP executed an investment transaction that reflected the advantages of broad geographic market position. While fielding numerous bids for an industrial portfolio, EOP had acquired as part of a merger, the company indicated to the market that to gain an edge, bidders could include Class A office properties located in EOP's markets. The company received a number of offers that included high-quality buildings in four of our target markets, and selected the best cash/asset offer from the finalists. EOP closed the sale with US$ 407.3 million in cash, and the acquisition of two office buildings in Orange County and Chicago, valued at US$ 137 million. The buildings never went to market for bid, which kept their sales prices low.

Advantages of geographic diversification

	% of total NOI	Square feet in million	Market rank by SF
Boston	14.3	11.9	1st
New York	11.4	6.3	10th
San Francisco	9.9	10.0	1st
Los Angeles	8.7	8.4	5th
San Jose	8.4	5.9	3rd
Seattle	8.2	9.6	1st
Chicago	7.2	12.0	1st
Washington, D.C.	7.2	6.6	3rd
Orange County	4.1	5.7	2nd
Portland	2.9	3.9	1st
Denver	2.8	4.4	1st
Atlanta	2.5	5.3	2nd
Sacramento	2.2	2.7	1st
Oakland	2.0	2.6	2nd
San Diego	2.0	2.2	4th
Stamford	1.7	1.7	2nd
Austin	1.6	3.4	1st
Data as of 3Q 2006			

Fig. 6:   Equity Office market concentration

EOP's national brand earned recognition within the asset investment community, as well as on Wall Street, and with customers and brokers. Size and scale, and a focus on quality, definitely had its advantages, including:

Procurement Procurement: The company centralized procurement and consolidated the number of its vendors, including waste haul, landscaping, window cleaning, elevator maintenance, and others, from 950 to 68, achieving significant savings and status for EOP as a preferred customer, which secured a higher level of service.

Retention and recruitment Retention and recruitment of top-quality professionals within and outside the real estate industry: EOP was the first real estate company to actively recruit and secure senior and executive management from outside of the real estate industry. It attracted its CFO, executive vice president of human resources, senior vice president of accounting and senior vice president of information technology, along with other positions from across industries to broaden its ability to access best practices across corporate America. EOP's board, which included trustees from the automotive, consulting, investment management, and retail sectors, also reflected this industry diversity.

Unique customer programs Ability to serve as a national landlord for premium, national tenants: EOP built a Strategic Customer Program that established partnering relationships with in-house corporate real estate executives at national and multi-national corporations. The program was designed to proactively and strategically address national tenants' needs for ongoing flexibility in managing their own national real estate portfolios. Among other benefits, this Strategic Customer Program provided a customized national lease form, which allowed a national tenant to sign a simple addendum for each new lease within EOP's portfolio. The prenegotiated terms saved tenants time and money in legal fees, and provided them with unprecedented flexibility in fulfilling their companies' changing needs for office space.

For example, in the case of Citigroup/Smith Barney, EOP executed a series of six "linked" transactions across five cities that provided the financial services firm with unprecedented flexibility in contracting and expanding their office space, while delivering a rent savings of approximately US$ 1 million. These linked transactions further helped this prestigious tenant by alleviating the financial burden of excess vacant office space, and by providing long-term real estate solutions in two challenging markets. In exchange, EOP received a larger market share of this tenant's business, and established Equity Office as an unrivaled partner in providing real estate solutions.

EOP's market drivers

To maintain these advantages, but more fully focus on a portfolio in high-performing, high-growth markets, the managing directors redefined EOP's portfolio strategy in 2003. They adjusted their target portfolio to include primarily major coastal markets, and began to sell the company's other assets, taking advantage of the strong asset sales environment at the time. They focused on fewer markets that met the criteria of their market drivers:

- intellectual and cultural infrastructure,
- highly educated workforce,
- higher average occupancy,
- where EOP could lead the market,
- where EOP could leverage its operating platform,
- where there was sufficient room for EOP to grow.

From 2003 through 2006, the company sold more than US$ 7 billion in properties. EOP sculpted an enviable portfolio of premiere, high-value assets in markets that promised significant and sustainable growth.

4.2   Blackstone merger

Equity Office was not on the market for sale prior to Blackstone's bid. EOP had a fresh restructuring in place, and had narrowed its market focus. Management believed in its strategy, and was operating EOP as a long-term public company. But, EOP also had a strong commitment to its fiduciary responsibility to maximize shareholder value, so it kept the door open to suitors, and management conducted an internal Net Asset Value (NAV) analysis twice a year to ensure it was always fully prepared to accurately assess the company's value.

Beauty contest

EOP had received flirtations from several interested companies over the past year, but the offers were too low to elicit the company's interest. Then, in

November 2006, Blackstone approached EOP with an unsolicited offer of US$ 47.50 per share, a total transaction price of US$ 36 billion. The offer was significantly above the internal NAV estimates, and of such magnitude EOP had to respond.

The management was confident that the Blackstone offer would draw others. After all, Equity Office was a once-in-a-lifetime acquisition. The company had spent the last 10 years acquiring the best office buildings in the best cities in the country. So, it structured the transaction as an auction with a floor. In its merger agreement with Blackstone, EOP intentionally set an exceptionally low break-up fee of US$ 200 million, or 0.91 % of the total transaction value. (The standard break-up fee in an M&A deal is 2.5 % to 3 %.) By keeping the door wide open for other bidders, EOP demonstrated its continuing commitment to steward the public's capital.

Security	Total returns from ... through 2/5/2007 (in %)					
	7/8/97	12/31/02	12/31/03	12/31/04	12/30/05	12/29/06
EOP including dividends	**25.3**	**36.9**	**36.2**	**48.6**	**79.3**	**15.2**
EOP price only	17.1	29.8	30.2	43.2	75.3	15.2
DJIA	6.2	12.6	6.8	8.3	16.5	1.6
S&P 500	6.0	15.7	9.7	9.2	14.5	2.0
NASDAQ	6.9	20.7	7.5	6.5	10.9	2.3
RMZ (price only)	28.0	20.7	33.5	26.3	38.6	9.5

Fig. 7: Equity Office total returns

In mid-January 2007, Vornado Realty Trust, a respected New York-based REIT, along with two partners, countered Blackstone with a US$ 52 per share bid that included 40 % stock. And the largest bidding war in private equity buyout history began. Before Vornado submitted a hard offer, Blackstone upped its offer to US$ 54 per share cash. With the scheduled shareholder vote on Blackstone's offer looming, Vornado lobbed in with a final proposal of US$ 56 per share, 35 % of which was stock.

Leveraged buyout Then, Blackstone upped its offer to US$ 55.50 per share, all cash, and the EOP board's choice was clear. Blackstone offered certainty of closing an all-cash transaction within a very short time frame, as opposed to Vornado's partial stock offer transaction that would not close for six to nine months, and which carried significant risk, including changes in market conditions, and the uncertainty of both Vornado's board approval and a positive shareholder vote. EOP closed the transaction with Blackstone on February 9th, 2007.

Despite Equity Office's inherent value, industry leadership, proven innovation, liquidity, balance sheet and other strengths, EOP was beleaguered throughout much of its life as a public company by the analytic community's consistent undervaluation. The record-high prices being paid for single office assets, and for smaller REITs by private entities, red-flagged the dramatic levels at which analysts were undervaluing the industry, but to no avail. Public NAV persisted below the reality. Spreads were enormous, and as each new REIT transaction closed, it served as a further indictment of the valuation process being used by analysts.

Above all others, the Equity Office transaction with Blackstone amplified this miscalculation of analysts' REIT NAVs. Just one month prior to Blackstone's first offer in November, analysts' average price per share target on EOP ranged in the mid-US$ 30s, dramatically below the closing price of US$ 55.50 per share Blackstone price.

Equity Office's public life ended with a bang, and reflected a strong history of successes and industry breakthroughs. Today's REITs and those that will be created in years to come will benefit from the innovation and through leadership of EOP.

5 Outlook for REITs

The US commercial real estate market has a positive outlook for the next couple of years. There is a dearth of new construction in all sectors, and job growth remains strong. A significant market downturn is not expected until the next recession, which will be around the first half of 2009, barring any unforeseen, catastrophic events.

Positive outlook

There will continue to be solid investor demand for REITs. They have proven themselves as viable cash flows in liquid form, and they offer income stability that is well suited for an aging population. The industry will continue to grow long-term, but will ebb and flow in total industry capitalization, depending on cost of capital and competition. When public/private valuations stabilize, the industry will see much of the real estate that has been brought into the private sector move back into the public market, and this will be yet another validation that real estate is no longer a stand-alone asset class. The privatization of REITs has been part of the industry's maturation process. Like any other industry, if real estate is trading below its intrinsic value, it will move to private ownership.

As perhaps the largest independent REIT shareholder in the US, I, Sam Zell, have a significant investment in the industry. Every day I do not sell my interest in a company, I am deciding it is worth buying, and, as an individual investor, I have never sold a share.

6 Bibliography

[1] Fickes, M., US$ 1 Trillion Milestone, in: Real Estate Portfolio Magazine, May/June 2006.

[2] NAREIT Frequently Asked Questions, "How has Real Estate Financing Changed Over Time?" 2007.

[3] NAREIT, Forty-five @ 45: The 45 events that shaped the course of the REIT Industry, in: Real Estate Portfolio Magazine, September/October 2005.

[4] Emerging Global Labor Market, Demand for Offshore Talent in Services, McKinsey Global Institute, June 2005.

[5] Lohr, S., Outsourcing is Climbing Skills Ladder, in: The New York Times, February 16th, 2006.

6   Funding with German Jumbo Covered Bonds: the example of Hypo Real Estate Group

Robert Grassinger
Andreas Schenk

Table of contents

1   Definition of covered bonds

1.1   Covered bonds and structured covered bonds

**Covered bonds
provide recourse
to an assetpool
and to the issuer**

Covered bonds are debt securities issued by banks since the 18th century in Germany and since the last 10 years in an increasing number of countries in Europe. Basically, a covered bond is a bond issued by a credit institution, i. e., the investor in the security has a claim against the issuer. However, the covered bonds have one essential credit enhancement compared to an unsecured bond of a bank or a corporate bond: The covered bond provides recourse to a pool of assets, the cover pool, which secures or "covers" the bond if the issuer becomes insolvent.

In any situation the volume of the outstanding covered bonds has to be smaller than the volume of the assets in the cover pool. Furthermore, according to the different frameworks the covered bonds have to be overcollateralized, i. e., the amount of assets has to be higher than the amount of the covered bonds outstanding. For example, the German covered bond, the so-called Pfandbrief, requires at least a 2 % overcollateralization.

The assets in the cover pool are also booked on the balance sheet of the credit institution. However, the cover pool has to be segregated from the other assets of the covered bond issuer, i. e., there has to be a clear and transparent definition which assets belong to the cover pool and which assets are not part of the cover pool. The segregation has to be bankruptcy remote as the cover pool provides the additional enhancement to the covered bonds in case the credit institution defaults.

The majority of the European covered bonds are issued on the basis of a specific legislation. The bankruptcy remoteness relies on legal provisions set out in a certain covered bond legislation, a covered bond law. The legislation allows covered bonds issued in one country to be recognized as a common asset class defined by one law and the investors do not have to analyze the legal structure of every single issue on a stand alone basis like, for example, for Mortgage Backed Securities. Figure 1 shows the countries with a specific covered bond legislation in place.

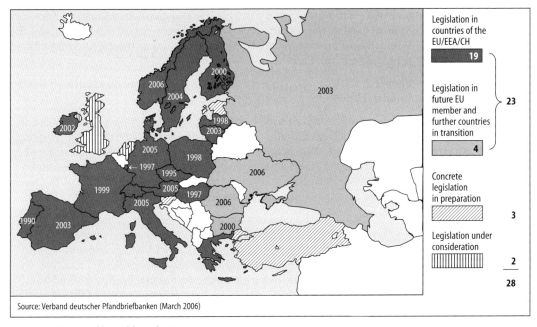

Source: Verband deutscher Pfandbriefbanken (March 2006)

Fig. 1:   Covered bond legislation

There are minimum standards for European covered bonds [1]:

- credit institution as issuer,
- specific legislation (legal basis),
- cover principle (assets matching liabilities),
- specific supervision,
- preferential claim for bondholders in the case of bankruptcy of the issuing institution.

Structured covered bonds

Covered bonds without legal framework are commonly defined as "structured covered bonds". Credit institutions from the United Kingdom (e. g., HBOS plc), the Netherlands (e. g., ABN Amro) and the USA (e. g., Washington Mutual, Bank of America) are examples for issuers of structured covered bonds. The first structured covered bonds were issued out of the UK in 2003. The most recent country joining the covered bond community with structured covered bonds was the USA in 2006.

The structured covered bonds are based on contractual agreements and not on a specific legislation. The main reason for structured covered bonds is that a credit institution is located in a country without a covered bond law in place but the bank wants to participate in the covered bond market.

Structured covered bonds are using Mortgage Backed Securities techniques by pledging or assigning cover assets to Special Purpose Vehicles (SPV) which guarantee the bonds in an event of a default of the issuer. The structured covered bonds provide more flexibility as they are not based on a specific law. Therefore, they can be structured according to the needs of the issuer and the corresponding assets. However, the disadvantage is that structured covered bonds are not one common asset class with a common regulation. Investors have to look at the specific contractual agreements of every issue and the techniques to provide the credit enhancement for a structured covered bond could be very different.

Main differences of covered bonds compared to MBS

The main differences of covered bonds (including structured covered bonds) compared to Mortgage Backed Securities (MBS) are:

- If an investor buys a MBS bond the investor is buying a claim against an SPV. The originator of the assets, i. e., the bank, is perhaps still servicing the loans but there is no recourse to the credit institution. The covered bond investor has a claim against the credit institution. If the credit institution defaults, the investor has an additional claim against the assets in the cover pool which are outside the bankruptcy estate of the issuer.

- The standard MBS pool is a static pool of assets, e. g. mortgage loans. The cover pool for a covered bond is actively managed by the issuer within the rules of the corresponding covered bond framework. The issuer is able to add and remove assets and manage market risk like interest rate and currency risk. As the pool is managed, a covered bond has no prepayment risk, which is a clear distinction from MBS. However, there is no incentive for the covered bond issuer to add "bad" assets to the cover pool and book "good" assets outside the pool. As the cover pool is only separated from the balance sheet of the bank in the case of an issuer default, the covered bond is not transferring any risk from the bank's balance sheet by adding loans to the cover pool. In contrast to covered bonds, if an originator is adding loans to a MBS pool, the bank is clearly transferring the credit risk from the balance sheet to the investors in the MBS bonds.

- The credit quality of an MBS bond is provided by the credit enhancement of the different tranches in an MBS transaction. The credit quality of a covered bond is provided by the legal framework (e. g., the covered bond law including banking regulations and banking supervision) and the conservative eligibility criteria for the cover pool (see following section 1.2).

The European Covered Bond Council summarizes the definition of covered bonds in the following way:

"Covered bonds are debt instruments secured by a cover pool of mortgage loans (property as collateral) or public-sector debt to which investors have a preferential claim in the event of default. While the nature of this preferential claim, as well as other safety features (asset eligibility and coverage, bankruptcy-remoteness and regulation) depends on the specific framework under which a covered bond is issued, it is the safety aspect that is common to all covered bonds" [2].

1.2   Asset classes

Concerning the assets classes in the cover pool there are two different types of asset:

Covered bonds are secured by mortgage loans or public-sector debt

- covered bonds secured by mortgage loans, the so-called "Mortgage Covered Bonds", and

- covered bonds secured by public-sector debt (e. g., loans to municipalities, bonds issued by public-sector entities), the so-called "public-sector covered bonds".

The German Covered Bond Law also allows loans secured by ships as collateral for a so-called Ship Covered Bond (Ship Pfandbrief). However, this asset class is very small compared to the other two asset classes. The other covered bond laws reduce the eligible assets to mortgage loans on the one hand side and public-sector debt on the other hand side.

Every legislation has a set of distinct eligibility criteria which clearly defines the assets eligible for each cover pool. For example, the assets of the German mortgage covered bond (Pfandbrief) have to meet, besides other criteria set out in the Pfandbrief Law, a 60 % Loan-to-property-value (LTV) test.

The market share of public-sector covered bonds decreased compared to mortgage covered bonds in the last couple of years. Figure 2 shows the new issue volume of the two covered bond types 2001 versus 2006.

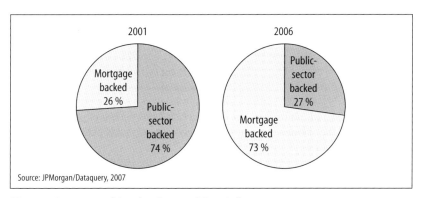

Fig. 2:   Issuance of Jumbo Covered Bonds by asset type

This shift is due to market developments and regulatory changes which had the effect that the supply of public-sector debt eligible for the covered bonds has been decreasing. For example, all bonds issued by German Landesbanks (public-sector banks) were eligible for the public-sector cover pool as the Landesbanks were guaranteed by the state. After this regulation changed in 2005 and the Landesbanks were not state guaranteed any more, one important asset class for the public-sector covered bond disappeared.

Concerning the other asset class, the credit institutions see a much better risk-return profile in the mortgage business and concentrated their business activities in this area.

2　　　Development of the covered bond market

In recent years covered bond market has become the most important segment in privately issued bonds

The history of the covered bond market is very long and dates back more than 200 years. In the past, the main country for covered bond issues had been Germany. This has changed during the last 10 years. Looking at new covered bond issuance, Germany accounted still for nearly 80 % of the market in 2001. In 2006 the German share decreased to 22 %. However, at the same time the volume of new issuance doubled and the covered bond market became a really international market. In 2006, when Washington Mutual issued a structured covered bond also the first issuer outside Europe participated in the covered bond market.

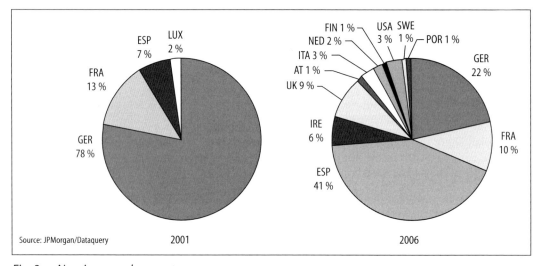

Source: JPMorgan/Dataquery　　　　　2001　　　　　　　　　　　　2006

Fig. 3:　New issuance by country

Due to this internationalization, the covered bond market has clearly developed into the most important segment of privately issued bonds with outstandings amounting of over € 1.8 trillion [3].

Looking at the benchmark issuance of covered bonds compared to other asset classes like sovereigns and agencies, the covered bond market is obviously dominating the new issuance since a couple of years.

What was the crucial factor for the success of the covered bond market?

Covered bond market regarded as AAA-market

The basis for the success and the development of the covered bond market is that the financial market, including the rating agencies, sees the covered bond market as an AAA-market. The reasons for this high quality are the clear, consistent and stable frameworks under which the bonds are issued including the very conservative eligibility criteria. Most of the covered bonds are therefore AAA-rated and attract investors who are looking for a safe investment and bought, e.g., sovereign bonds like US Treasuries or German Bund Futures before they started to invest in covered bonds.

However, these investors, typically international institutional investors like banks, central banks, funds and insurance companies, are also looking for

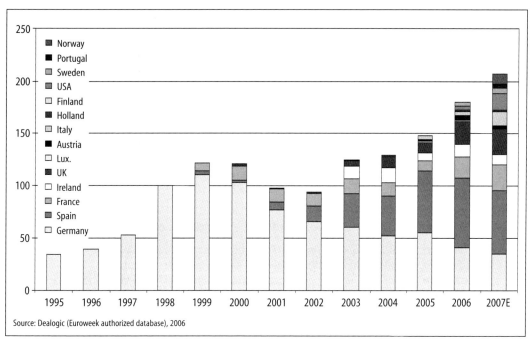

Fig. 4: New issuance of Jumbo Covered Bonds (in € bn)

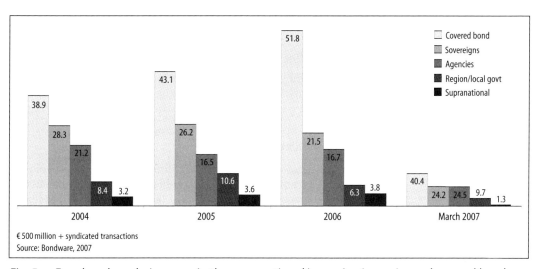

Fig. 5: Euro benchmarks issuance in the supranational/sovereign/agencies and covered bonds universe (in %)

liquidity in the bonds. Liquidity is not a very well defined term in the financial markets and is often used in different connections. Essential for the investors in this respect is that they are able to trade the product after they bought it in the primary market from the issuer. I. e., investors are looking for a developed secondary market with market makers providing bid-ask quotes for the outstanding bonds until maturity. Only if this is the case, investors can use the bonds for an actively managed portfolio and trade, e. g., on a relative value strategy. If such a secondary market is not in place, it could be difficult for investors to sell or buy a bond at a reasonable price at a certain time.

Today the secondary market for Jumbo Covered Bonds is very well developed and established. The reason for this success is the development of the minimum standards for Jumbo Pfandbriefe which was established for the German Pfandbrief market in the mid-1990s. The following section describes the corresponding standards and why these standards were able to develop the domestic German Pfandbrief market to an international covered bond market with investors from all over the world and more and more issuers in Europe and the USA joining the covered bond community.

3   Jumbo Pfandbrief – liquidity is crucial

Jumbo Pfandbriefe provide transparency, reliability and a liquid secondary market

Until 1995 the German Pfandbrief market was dominated by a countless number of smaller issues, so-called private placements. There were no rules in place concerning market making. To increase the liquidity and the transparency of the Pfandbrief market, the German Pfandbrief issuers, the Association of German Pfandbrief banks and several investment banks invented the term "Jumbo Pfandbrief". A Jumbo Pfandbrief is a common Pfandbrief issued under the Pfandbrief law; however, the issue does meet the so-called "Minimum Standards for Jumbo Pfandbriefe". These standards are set to establish a market making system and a liquid secondary market for the Jumbo Pfandbriefe. The first Jumbo Pfandbrief was issued by Frankfurter Hypothekenbank Centralboden in 1995. Since this time, the requirements were adjusted according to the needs of the market and the involved players.

As of August 2006, the minimum standards for Jumbo Pfandbriefe are as follows, section 3 consists mainly of a translation of very official "Minimum Standards" document issued by the Association of German Pfandbrief banks, see FN [4].

" 1. **Minimum issue size**

The minimum issue size of a Jumbo Pfandbrief is € 1 billion. The volume of the initial issue must be at least € 750 million. The issuer is obligated to increase the outstanding total volume of the issue to at least € 1 billion within 180 calendar days after the initial offering.

2. **Format**

Only Pfandbriefe of straight bond format (i. e., fixed coupon payable annually in arrears, bullet redemption) may be offered as Jumbo Pfandbriefe.

3. **Stock market listing**

Jumbo Pfandbriefe must be listed on an organized market in a member state of the European Union or in another member state of the Treaty on the European Economic Area immediately after issue, although not later than 30 calendar days after the settlement date.

4. **Market making**

Each Jumbo Pfandbrief must have at least five market makers who pledge to quote bid-ask (two-way) prices simultaneously for lots of up to € 15 million during usual trading hours (at least 9 a.m. – 5 p.m. CET). The function of market maker may also be performed by the issuing house itself. The market makers undertake to quote prices as long as there is sufficient outstanding volume to maintain a liquid market in the Jumbo Pfandbrief.

The market makers undertake not to exceed the following spread between the bid and ask prices when quoting two-way prices:

Residual life to maturity up to and including four years: five cents, over four up to and including six years: six cents, over six up to and including eight years: eight cents, over eight up to and including 15 years: 10 cents, over 15 up to and including 20 years: 15 cents, over 20 years up to and including 25 years: 25 cents. The maximum bid-ask spread to be quoted is adjusted according to the residual life to maturity of an issue. In the exceptional event of market making being suspended in the situations outlined under recommendation No. 2, this must be immediately communicated to the market by the market maker in an appropriate manner.

5. **Add-ons**

In the event that a Jumbo Pfandbrief is tapped, the amount of the increase should not be less than € 125 million per add-on. In the case of taps and new issues, a maximum of five banking days should separate pricing date and settlement date.

6. **Transfer and buyback**

A subsequent transfer to the name of an investor is inadmissible (restriction on transferability). It is admissible to buy back securities for redemption purposes or trustee administration if the outstanding volume of the issue is not less than € 1 billion at any time. Furthermore, buybacks are limited to half of the outstanding issue volume. The issuer must publicly announce any buyback, the planned volume thereof and the issue marked out for repurchase at least three banking days in advance, and make sure that thorough transparency in the market is assured. After a buyback transaction it is inadmissible to increase such an issue within one year.

7. **Loss of status**

If one of the aforementioned provisions is not met, the issue will lose its Jumbo Pfandbrief status. Jumbo Pfandbriefe that were issued before April 28th, 2004 and have a volume of less than € 1 billion retain the status of a Jumbo notwithstanding number 1 if the other aforementioned provisions are met."

In line with these standards, the Pfandbrief issuers together with the investment banks were able to develop a liquid secondary market for Jumbo Pfandbriefe as the standards provide the transparency and reliability which is so important for institutional investors.

However, the crucial and most discussed standard is no. 4 "market making". Essentially, market making could be understood as the quoting of bid-ask prices and the willingness to trade at these prices at a certain time. Under normal market condition this is not an issue. Also under difficult capital market environments, e. g., after September 11th, 2001, the secondary markets performed well. The market making standard was tested in October 2005 when the news on the new shareholder of the Pfandbrief issuer Allgemeine Hypothekenbank Rheinboden (AHBR) and the possible impacts were discussed in the market.

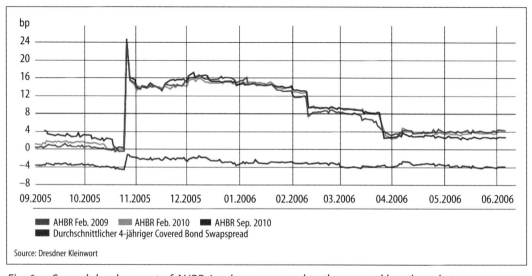

Fig. 6:   Spread development of AHBR Jumbos compared to the covered bond market

Even under difficult market conditions, the secondary market keeps on operating

Figure 6 shows that after the initial crisis the situation stabilized relatively quickly. However, all market participants agreed that the standards for such extraordinary situations could be improved. For these reasons the following recommendations were added to the Minimum Standards for Jumbo Pfandbriefe [5]:

"1. The market makers are to keep separate limits for the issuer's Pfandbriefe.

2. In the event of substantial rating changes or of a considerable deterioration of a Jumbo-issuer's financial situation or of other circumstances that might jeopardize liquid trading of an issuer's Jumbo Pfandbriefe in a similar way, the Market Maker and Issuer Committee (MIC) consisting of representatives of market makers and issuers will immediately convene to discuss and, if applicable, recommend measures aimed at preventing the suspension of market making for the Jumbo Pfandbriefe of the issuer in question or at making the

resumption of market making possible as soon as possible. The MIC will, with due consideration to the circumstances of the particular case, consider widening the bid-ask spread, lowering the single ticket sizes on which bid-ask prices are quoted or other measures that are appropriate and necessary in order for market making to be continued. Measures restricted in time should wherever possible be the subject of recommendations by the MIC."

The fact that an investment bank as market maker for a Jumbo Pfandbrief has separate limits or lines for a Pfandbrief supports the flexibility of the investment bank as the investment bank could take Pfandbriefe on its own book. Furthermore, it is an additional commitment to the market.

The second recommendation goes together with the implementation of the **Market Maker** Market Maker and Issuer Committee. This committee was established to **and Issuer** handle difficult situations like the AHBR crisis in a more coordinated way and **Committee** with a clear communication to the investors and other market participants. Also the discipline of all market participants is expected to increase if the market makers have to answer the questions of the MIC and their behavior is communicated to the market in a defined and coordinated way.

With the new recommendations the Pfandbrief community reacted to the challenges and the Pfandbrief market is prepared to provide the liquidity and transparency the international investors are looking for. As the covered bond market is an international market and uniform standards are an improvement for all market participants, the revised minimum requirements for Jumbo Pfandbriefe have to be discussed as well for other covered bond markets in Europe.

4 Case study on Hypo Real Estate Bank International € 1.5 billion Pfandbrief in February 2006

4.1 Economic rational

For Hypo Real Estate Bank International the Jumbo Pfandbrief market is an efficient tool to fund Pfandbrief eligible assets. If Hypo Real Estate Bank International issued a € 1 billion unsecured bond with a maturity of five years today, the investors would require a spread over the 5-years swap rate of approximately 0.20 %. Hypo Real Estate Bank International's senior unsecured rating is A– by Standard and Poor's, A by Fitch and A1 by Moody's.

For a Jumbo Pfandbrief with the same size and maturity the investors would ask for a spread of approximately –0.05 % (0.05 % below the 5-year swap rate). This advantage of roughly 0.25 % is crucial to be able to compete in the market.

4.2 Preparation and execution of a Jumbo Pfandbrief issue

The preparation of a Jumbo Pfandbrief starts months before the issue date. As **Jumbo** Jumbo Pfandbriefe are bigger than € 1 billion, the collateral pool has to build **Pfandbrief issues** up a corresponding overcollateralization. **might be placed as pot deal or**

Approximately one to two months before an issue the market situation and the **retention deal** best timing is discussed with potential lead managers. The lead managers are investment banks that sell the bonds for the issuer as most of the Pfandbrief issuers do not have an own sales force. Furthermore, the lead managers are responsible for the market making discussed in section 3.

For a € 1.5 billion Jumbo Pfandbrief issue a typical group of investment banks comprises four to six lead managers and six to eight co-lead managers.

Roadshow team: lead managers and issuer
To sell the transaction to the investors, the issuance is prepared by a roadshow. Each roadshow team consists of representatives of the lead managers and the issuer. These teams visit potential investors to explain the issue and current developments regarding the issuing credit institution. Depending on the target investors a typical roadshow lasts one to two weeks. During such a two week roadshow, Hypo Real Estate Bank International was able to visit more than 100 investors in up to 10 countries with two teams traveling at the same time. The meetings with the potential investors are group presentations with two to a dozen investors or private presentations for single investors.

After the roadshow the Pfandbrief issuer decides on the issue size and the pricing of the transaction based on the feedback the investors provided during the roadshow.

Pot or retention deal
For the Pfandbrief issuer there are two ways to place the transaction with the lead managers, either a so-called pot deal or a retention deal.

If the issuer decides to do a retention deal, the lead managers are taking the Jumbo Pfandbrief in predefined shares from the issuer at a fixed price. The placement risk is with the investment banks and the issuer has no execution risk after the Pfandbrief is sold to the syndicate of banks. However, the transaction could be miss-priced and the lead managers are not able to sell the transaction at this price or the issuer is paying to much to the investment banks.

"Pot": determination of marginal price
The second system, the so-called "pot" intends to determine the marginal price for a certain Jumbo Pfandbrief issue. The lead managers are not taking the execution risk of the transaction from the issuer, the bonds are sold in a so-called book building process. After the book is opened, the lead mangers are taking orders from investors and add them to the book (typically an internet based e-book). Before the book building phase begins, the issuer announces a spread range of typically 2 bps to 4 bps in which the transaction will be placed. With their orders the investors are stating which amount they are willing to buy at which spread level.

Depending on the market and the investor demand, a book building process can take between two hours and two days. After the book is closed, the issuer and the investment banks have to allocate the Pfandbrief to the investors. If a transaction is oversubscribed, i. e., the size of the orders is higher than the issue size, the issuer and the investment banks have to allocate the transaction to the investors. Therefore, not every investor is getting the full order amount. Generally, the issuers try to diversify their investor base and therefore smaller orders are considered in a favorable way. If the transaction is oversubscribed, the issuer can also decide to increase the issue size to meet the demand of the market.

4.3 Results of the € 1.5 billion Hypo Real Estate Bank International Jumbo Pfandbrief placement

The € 1.5 billion Pfandbrief issue of Hypo Real Estate Bank International in February 2006 proves that the buyers of Pfandbriefe are institutional investors who are by all means international. Only 36 % of the issue was placed in Germany. Over 15 % were bought by investors in Asia, the rest of the investors were spread over many countries in Europe and also 2 % were bought by investors in the Middle East. This issue was not designed for US investors and the demand for covered bonds from US investors has been very reluctant in the past. However, with the first issuers of structured covered bonds from the USA, the US investors as well are getting more interested in the covered bond market and the number of US investors is increasing, especially if the issuers are able to meet Rule 144A of the Security Act.

Pfandbriefe become increasingly world-wide employed

There was also a similar development in some European countries, when new issuers from new countries started to issue covered bonds, the investors of this country also increased the interest in the covered bond market. For this reason, new countries and issuers were never competitors, but increased the attention to the covered bond market and also the established issuers could improve the diversification of their investor base.

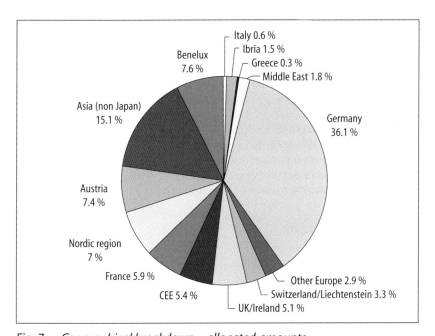

Fig. 7:   Geographical breakdown – allocated amounts

Looking at investor types, the most important buyers are banks (43 %), funds (23 %) and central banks and other typical institutional investors. Only 2.6 % of the transaction was placed to retail customers.

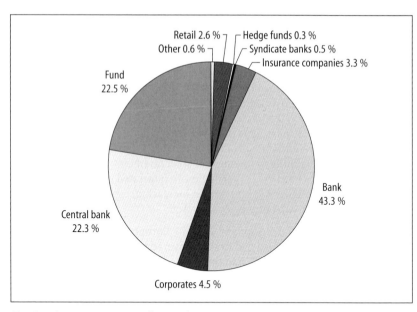

Fig. 8:   *Investor types – allocated amounts*

5   Summary

The Pfandbrief is one of the most important product contribution from Germany

To summarize this overview on funding with the German Jumbo Covered Bond it can be said that the Jumbo Pfandbrief market is an efficient way to fund covered bond eligible assets. The Jumbo market is expanding with an increasing number of covered bond issuers and international institutional investors from all over the world. The Pfandbrief in combination with the Jumbo Pfandbrief standards is one of the most important if not the most important product contribution from Germany to the global financial system, as it was able to establish the biggest market for privately issued bonds with outstandings amounting to over € 1.8 trillion [6].

6   Bibliography

[1] Art. 22 par. 4 UCITS Directive (Directive 2001/108/EC amending Directive 85/611/EEC on Undertakings for Collective Investments in Transferable Securities) and Verband deutscher Pfandbriefemittenten.

[2] http://ecbc.hypo.org/Content/Default.asp?PageID=311, May 20th, 2007.

[3] European Covered Bond Council, European Covered Bond Fact Book, August 2006, p. 17.

[4] Association of German Pfandbrief Banks, www.hypverband.de/d/internet.nsf/0/FB450CD9A5BD2140C12571DB004FCB46/$FILE/nur %20Mindeststandards.pdf, May 27th, 2007.

[5] ib.

[6] European Covered Bond Council, European Covered Bond Fact Book, August 2006, p. 17.

7   German Residential Asset Note Distributor PLC (GRAND) – a case study

Ralf Herfurth
Julian Hester
Sascha Giest

Table of contents

1   Introduction

A benchmark for the European CMBS market

The Grand plc transaction is a benchmark in the German multi-family residential real estate space. It firstly represents the consolidation of the sub-sector as a mainstream asset class in the CMBS market, in a process that saw the Hallam transaction as a pioneer and subsequent transactions like Centaurus and Immeo further testing investor appetite successfully. It also, at the time of writing, represents the largest CMBS ever executed in continental Europe.

Perhaps of more interest to the reader of this case study, Grand plc presented unique structural solutions to certain challenges, some of which are recurrent in the sub-sector, such as the due diligence of title in highly granular portfolios and the presence of properties with hereditary building rights attached to them; other challenges were unique to this very large and complex portfolio, such as the restrictions imposed on the owner on properties acquired from the German railway authority (BEV) and the unusually large number of legal entities involved (29).

In this case study, the background of the transaction will be presented which involved the sale of Germany's then largest private residential landlord and will attempt to explain how the final structure represents an extensive and complex exercise in trying to address legal, tax and regulatory challenges, while providing an acceptable compromise between the needs of management in the daily running of a large complex organization and the requirements of rating agencies and bond investors.

The final result of this huge exercise, as indicated from the oversubscription levels and the fact that today the Grand paper is the most widely held paper in the CMBS market, was an undisputed success.

2   Background of the transaction

The research work for the Grand transaction dates back to 2003 when Viterra, a subsidiary of giant German utility E.on and the largest private residential landlord in Germany at the time, hired Barclays Capital to structure a securitization of one of its smaller portfolios, Frankfurter Siedlungsgesellschaft mbH. Raising large sums of cheap debt against real estate was indispensable in attracting international private equity buyers, a crucial part of E.on's plan to dispose of Viterra. The success of this earlier transaction called Hallam Finance Plc confirmed the viability of securitizations of tenanted residential real estate in Germany.

The largest private equity acquisition in European real estate to date

The auction process for Viterra started in January 2005 and included many of the major international private equity firms involved in the real estate sector. The winning bidder, Deutsche Annington, owned by British private equity firm Terra Firma, bought Viterra in what is still the largest private equity real estate deal in Europe to date.

At Deutsche Annington, Terra Firma implemented a strategy that would become very common for private equity players acquiring large portfolios of residential property in Germany:

- buy large portfolios of under rented properties at a wholesale discount,

- introduce professional property management, spending capex more effectively, reducing vacancies and raising rents where sensible,

- sell units to tenants at a retail-price premium for tenants considering home ownership as an alternative to rising rents and as a defence against the risks presented by a state pension system under pressure due to fiscal constraints and demographic factors (reduction of economically active population).

For years, Deutsche Annington has been successfully implementing this strategy, achieving significant growth on the sales of units to tenants (privatization).

In putting together the winning bid, Terra Firma could count on the synergies and the know-how acquired by their ownership of Deutsche Annington since 2001. The combination of the two entities created one of the largest residential real estate companies in Europe. The acquisition was financed by a combination of an acquisition facility backed by the newly acquired Viterra portfolio and a refinancing of the existing Deutsche Annington business.

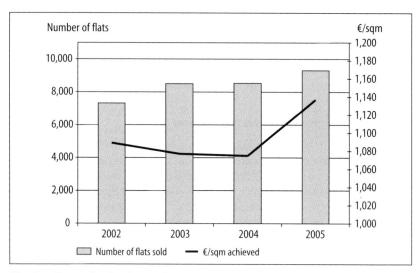

Fig. 1: Deutsche Annington's privatization track record

3   Post acquisition restructuring

Restructuring to realize synergies and enable the securitization

In the months that followed the acquisition, Terra Firma and Deutsche Annington management undertook a large scale integration and restructuring exercise, with the following objectives:

- realizing substantial savings through headcount reduction, integration of IT and administrative functions, increased purchasing power and synergies in the sales program,

- restructuring the group to create a securitization-friendly structure, allowing the acquisition debt, whenever possible, to be pushed down to the level of the assets.

Operations were organized through regional divisions, responsible for local property management. Centralized divisions would be responsible for the sales program and for general management of overheads, including the IT platform.

The corporate legal structure, however, would look very different to the business structure. Over the years, both Viterra and Deutsche Annington had grown through acquisitions, and the most tax efficient way to acquire real estate in Germany is to acquire entities, not the real estate assets directly. Merging two real estate owning companies into one, for example, will cause the surviving entity to pay a 3.5 % real estate transfer tax on the assets being purchased (4.5 % in Berlin). Therefore, in reorganizing the group, there was a tendency to maintain the assets in their previous real estate-owning entities, avoiding unnecessary tax liabilities that would arise from consolidating the assets into a single entity.

Solvent liquidation structure

Furthermore, in order to ensure a certain degree of insolvency remoteness to the assets from potential liabilities encumbering the asset-owning entities, whenever possible the assets were transferred into newly formed limited partnerships, transparent for tax purposes, but providing a certain degree of protection to lenders secured on the real estate assets, similar to what had been used in Hallam Finance Plc.

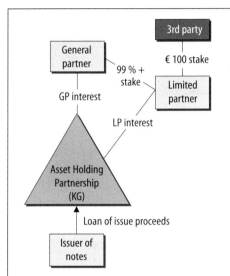

- The General Partner (GP) is the former asset owning entity which transfers its assets to the borrower (Asset Holding Partnership, a KG) without transferring its liabilities.
- Pre-existing liabilities at GP level could in theory cause it to become insolvent.
  - The partnership agreement between the GP and KG provides for a solvent liquidation of the borrower.
  - A solvent liquidation is a process of an orderly disposal of the units.
  - The liquidator is obliged to maximize value to bondholders and equity holders.
  - The liquidator must comply with all existing contracts of the borrower (including contracts with the issuer) and may enter into new contracts to maintain the value of the assets.
  - The liquidation process is not subject to any time restrictions.
  - The liquidator's fees are subordinated to debt service.
- To avoid the theoretical possibility that an insolvency administrator of the GP might set aside such provisions, a third party will hold a share in the limited partner (LP) enabling it to prevent changes to the partnership agreement.

Fig. 2: A typical solvent liquidation structure

Finally, there are tax benefits for entities that intend to hold assets in the long term, and there is trade tax payable by entities that intend to buy and sell assets. It was necessary, therefore, to ensure assets intended for sale were held separately from assets intended for long holds.

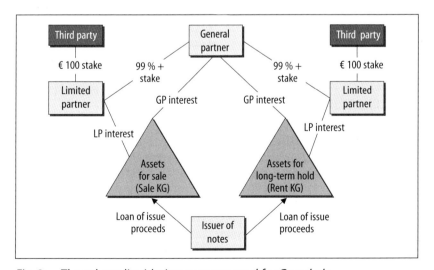

Fig. 3: The solvent liquidation structure used for Grand plc

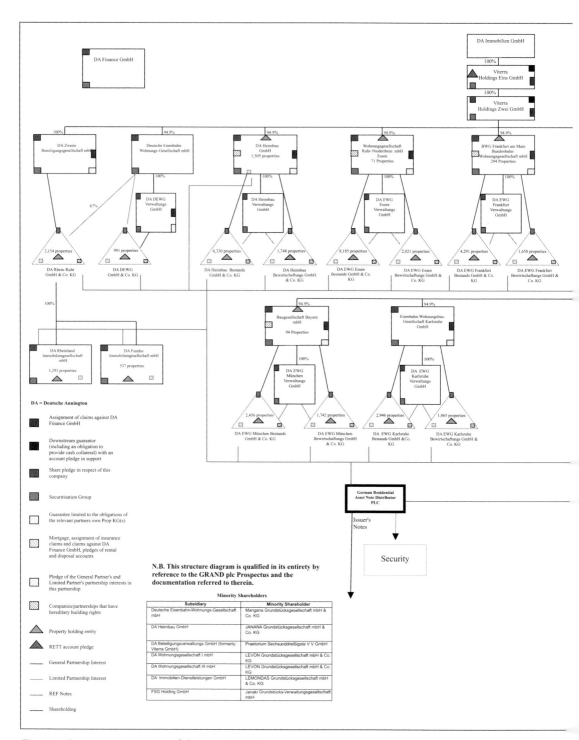

Fig. 4:   Corporate structure of the securitization group

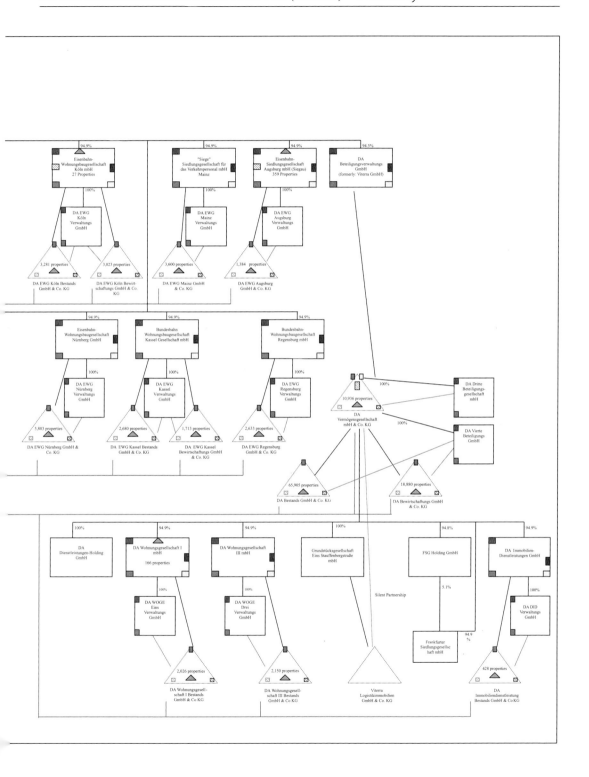

The result was a very complex corporate structure presenting a challenge to management and structurers in devising a bond debt structure that would not hinder the day-to-day running of the company, but that would still provide the adequate protection expected by investors in this asset class.

4   Grand plc transaction

Capital structure and portfolio description

The Grand plc transaction represented the take-out of the financing used to fund the acquisition of Viterra. Figure 5 shows the final capital structure announced in August 2006:

Class	Rating Fitch/S&P/Moody's	Tranche size (€m)	Type	Day 1 LTV (%)	Average life	Expected final maturity	Legal final maturity
Class A	AAA/AAA/Aaa	3,209	FRN	57.20	5.6	July 13th	July 16th
Class B	AAA/AA/Aa2	428	FRN	62.50	5.6	July 13th	July 16th
Class C	AA−/A/A2	869	FRN	73.20	5.6	July 13th	July 16th
Class D	A−/BBB/Baa1	577	FRN	80.20	5.6	July 13th	July 16th
Class E	BBB+/BBB/Baa1	133	Not offered	81.90	5.6	July 13th	July 16th
Class F	BBB/BBB−/Baa3	200	FRN	84.30	5.6	July 13th	July 16th
Total notes		**5,416**		**84.30**	**5.6**	**July 13th**	**July 16th**

Fig. 5:   Original capital structure

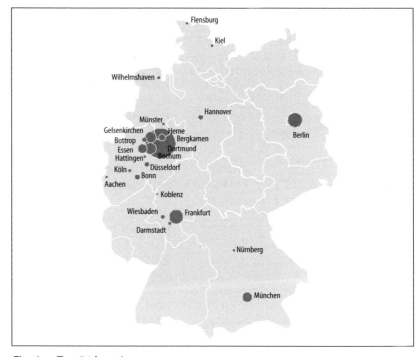

Fig. 6:   Top 24 locations

The €5.4 billion issuance was backed by Viterra and Deutsche Annington, a total of 164,365 residential units, 1,037 commercial units (typically small corner shops attached to the residential blocks) and 38,060 parking spaces. The portfolio was valued at €8.1 billion by Cushman & Wakefield and was geographically well distributed, with concentrations in Berlin, the Ruhr region and the Rhine-Main area.

5 Structural features

5.1 Full coupon pass-through

Unlike typical conduit CMBS transactions, Grand plc represents a so-called agency securitization, where the financing costs of the issuer vehicle are passed on to the borrowers on a one-to-one basis. Hence, the bond capital structure, which represents the borrowing relationship between the issuing vehicle (as borrower) and investors (as lenders) ("issuer level" debt), is replicated in the borrowing relationship between the issuing vehicle (as lender) and the asset owning companies (as borrowers) ("borrower level" debt). In order to ensure that neither a cash surplus nor a cash shortfall is created at the issuer level, it is mandatory that the weighted average cost of debt at issuer level is always exactly the same at borrower level. This condition is only satisfied if any amortization that applied at issuer level is applied in the same way at borrower level.

Mirroring bond and borrower sides

In the Grand transaction amortization can be applied pro rata, sequentially or reverse sequentially across the different classes of notes. In the normal course of business, Grand plc envisages pro rata amortization, so the weighted average cost of debt is always constant. The covenants include a sequential trigger, where an interest cover ratio of less than 1.10x would switch the amortization to sequential priority. In that case, the most senior class of notes outstanding would receive all amortization payments until it is fully repaid. The weighted average cost of debt would escalate in this scenario, as more of the cheaper (senior) debt is repaid. The structure also allows for voluntary prepayments by the sponsor. These prepayments can be applied reverse sequentially, so the weighted average cost of debt is reduced as the more expensive debt gets repaid first.

Therefore, in order to avoid mismatches between weighted average cost of debt and principal amounts at issuer and borrower levels, the amortization features at each level exactly mirror each other.

5.2 Amortization

Deciding on the amortization structure is about finding the right balance between term and maturity risk and, of course, heavily depends on the initial leverage at the start of the transaction. While too little amortization may not bring the leverage at maturity down to a level that is deemed to be safe for refinancing, too much amortization can increase the default risk during the term and might even cause an unnecessary payment default. How much these risks influence the rating outcome depends on the specific analysis of each rating agency and indeed may differ significantly between them.

Balance between amortization and leverage

In the case of Grand plc, a significant amount of amortization was needed over seven years to bring the loan to value ratio down to around 70%, seen to be the suitable maturity level. With a simple amortization structure using LTV covenants or scheduled amortization amounts there would have been a real risk of a payment default occurring once certain "haircuts" (see Glossary) to income were applied.

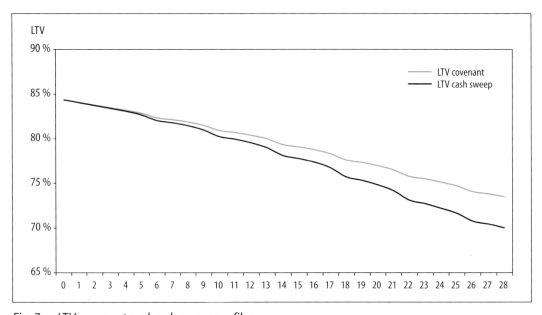

Fig. 7:   LTV covenant and cash sweep profiles

Therefore it was decided to split the amortization into two parts, a covenant and a cash sweep part.

- Under the covenanted amortization curve, quarterly LTV targets were set up decreasing from 84.3% to 73.5% and representing mandatory repayment levels.

- A second amortization curve was also introduced at a slightly steeper level than the first one, decreasing from 84.3% to 70% in year 7, called the cash sweep curve. To the extent that excess cash is available, it had to be used for further amortization until these second targets were met. Any cash remaining after this second step can be distributed as dividends to equity.

In addition, as long as the LTV level is above 80%, all cash is swept into amortization, independent of the LTV curves. This results in an accelerated initial amortization that de-risks the structure faster.

5.3   Release pricing

As it is part of Deutsche Annington's business plan to continue privatizing individual units by selling them to tenants or new owner occupiers, provisions had to be included to make sure the reduction in collateral value resulting from such sales is adequately met by an amortization payment and adverse cherry picking is avoided. For this purpose a schedule was set up including allocated loan amounts for each individual unit in the portfolio. Depending on the LTV level at the time of sale, between 105 % and 115 % of this allocated loan amount has to be repaid in the form of a release price. This approach works fine for most sales given that the assets are typically sold for more than their initial appraisal value in order to generate additional profits. However, in some cases it makes sense to sell selected properties below their appraisal value or even below their allocated loan amount if there are other reasons to part with these properties. To accommodate these sales, a release price shortfall ledger, limited to a total balance of € 10 million each quarter, tracks these sales and is netted against excess proceeds from other sales.

Amortization through the disposal of collateral

5.4   Cross-collateralization

There are a total of 29 borrowers under the original Grand plc transaction (31 after the issuance of further notes in October 2006). Without cross-collateralization, each borrower would represent a separate credit risk and as a consequence the ratings result would suffer. For optimal results it was important to ensure that the entire group could be looked at as a single credit risk. This was achieved by implementation of two interim holding companies above the borrower group. In figure 8 they are called VH1 and VH2. VH2 holds 100 % of the borrower group, and VH1 holds 100 % of VH2. VH1 is in turn held 100 % by Deutsche Annington Immobilien GmbH, the top holding company. In slightly simplified terms, VH1 has granted a pledge over its shares in VH2, which can be enforced if certain global covenants are not met. The

Reduction of credit risk through cross-collateralization

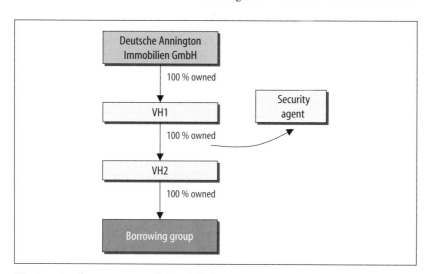

Fig. 8:   Implementation of the global guarantee structure

effect of this is twofold. On the one hand it provides a strong incentive for the sponsor to ensure that any imbalance within the group is corrected before a borrower can get into difficulties, while on the other hand it provides overall security over any remaining equity value in the borrower group.

A useful example is the refinancing of the borrowers' debt at maturity. It should be assumed that all but one of the borrowers can refinance their remaining debt balance without a problem. The one remaining borrower, however, is for some reason unable to do so and therefore threatens to create a loss for the bondholders. In this scenario it would be in the interest of the sponsor to inject sufficient additional equity to fill the gap, as otherwise they would risk that the share pledge over the entire equity value would be enforced and their investment in the entire group would be subject to an enforcement auction. Whilst any proceeds from such enforcement in excess of the remaining debt would go to the sponsor, such a sale is unlikely to yield optimal results. From a bondholder's perspective, however, it presents a means to capture excess value in one part of the borrower group in favor of the other.

5.5   Hyperamortization

Reducing debt service pressure for individual borrowers

In addition to the mere pooling of security and creation of strong incentives for the sponsor to intervene in case of any problems, it was also important to avoid a payment default during the term of the transaction solely based on imbalances between borrowers, which cannot be easily corrected via intra-company transactions. Even if the group's interest coverage remains strong overall, an individual borrower may find itself in a temporary cash shortfall and thereby unable to pay all its interest. Given that the holding structure described above provides effective cross-collateralization, it was possible to implement means for equalization of these shortfalls. An interest shortfall in one borrower can be capitalized, i.e., added to the outstanding debt balance rather than paid in the current period, as long as another borrower makes an additional amortization payment in the same amount and thereby reduces its own debt balance. This process is called hyperamortization. It avoids any commingling of payments between borrowers but at the same time restores all cash flows at the issuer level, where through the additional amortization payment sufficient funds are being received to pay full interest for the current period, while at the borrower level one borrower has slightly increased its debt balance and another one has reduced its balance by the same amount.

5.6   Global covenants

Global covenants level out leverage levels

With cross-collateralization and hyperamortization in place, it is possible to test all covenants on a global basis across all borrowers. An interest cover ratio covenant is in place as an event of default should it drop below 1.05x, and as a sequential amortization trigger at 1.10x. The Loan-to-Value ratio for the above mentioned amortization targets is also tested for the entire group. Once the amortization requirement is established and there are more funds available in the group than required for the debt reduction, it will be the borrower with the then highest individual Loan-to-Value ratio that sweeps all its cash into amortization, then the borrower with the second highest LTV and so on, until the amortization requirement has been satisfied. This selection ensures that, despite the global testing, individual leverage levels are kept close together.

5.7　　Secondary testing

When an event of default occurs and is not being cured within set timeframes, a lender would typically need to seek enforcement action against the collateral pool of borrowers to recover as much of its debt as possible. In the case of Grand plc, the collateral pool is so big that a full enforcement would be a massive task. Most importantly though, it may be unnecessary if the default stems from specific borrowers rather than representing a group-wide problem. For example, the ICR covenant may have been violated because of a few borrowers that significantly underperform, whilst the remaining group's performance is unaffected. By selecting only these troubled borrowers for enforcement action, the remaining group may be able to achieve its covenants and continue operating normally. This process is known as secondary testing, and in order to pass the test and be able to continue to operate the "solvent" part of the group, the sponsor has to "offer" enough entities for enforcement within a specified time limit such that the remaining group passes all global financial covenants.

Selective enforcement preserves the remaining collateral

5.8　　Title insurance

Carrying out due diligence on the borrower's title on all properties as well as on prior ranking encumbrances presents another challenge when large property portfolios are involved. In a typical German residential portfolio, this information may be spread over thousands of individual entries in the land register, or even over tens of thousands in the case of Deutsche Annington. A full due diligence of each individual entry is virtually impossible, given that up to now it is not possible to confirm this information electronically, but instead such a check needs to be done manually. A very viable way to deal with this issue is to test a statistically meaningful sample of properties, which reduces the number of checks to a few hundred rather than thousands, and confirm on this basis the integrity of title and mortgage information. This, however, still leaves a residual risk which the rating agencies need to take into account in their analysis, and this in turn can have a negative impact on the achievable ratings outcome.

Title insurance mitigates due diligence risk

Title insurance, commonplace in the US property market but still something of a novelty to European CMBS, can cover these risks very effectively by providing insurance cover for any title defects or unknown prior-ranking claims. The title insurer would carry out the due diligence effort and provide cover to the security trustee on this basis against the payment of a one-off fee.

Grand plc is the first large-scale European CMBS transaction to make use of this insurance product, provided by First Title Insurance plc. It covers the above mentioned title and prior claims risks, and also covers additional temporary risk stemming from a delay in filing some of the land charges in the collateral pool.

5.9   Class E notes – hereditary building rights

Built-in room for future improvements of the capital structure

Deutsche Annington and its subsidiaries own the vast majority of the units in Grand plc's collateral pool as freehold properties, while for the remaining 8 % they own a long-term hereditary building right ("Erbbaurecht"), comparable to leasehold properties in other jurisdictions. Registration of a land charge on the latter properties requires the consent of the land owner, and is typically subject to negotiations. These negotiations can take a significant amount of time and the outcome is somewhat uncertain. However, even without a registered land charge, it is important to keep in mind that the properties in question form part of the collateral pool and fully contribute to the ongoing rental cash flows. In an enforcement scenario, the lack of a land charge would mean that the lender needs to rely on the value of the pledged shares in the borrower or take the position of an unsecured creditor, instead of taking priority over other unsecured claims as would have been the case if a land charge had been available. The existence of these rights can have timing implications for the enforcement and potentially reduce recovery amounts. Grand plc's day-1 capital structure takes these imperfections into account. However, the structure also includes incentives for Deutsche Annington to continue with their efforts in negotiating the required consents for encumbrance by enabling them to improve Grand plc's capital structure at a later date and thereby reducing the overall cost of debt. Once the consents have been achieved, Class E notes (BBB+/BBB/Baa1) can be redeemed and further Class C notes (AA–/A/A2) can be issued. This can be done in steps of € 50 million notional until all Class E notes have been redeemed. The rating agencies need to affirm the ratings of the notes before such a step can take place.

6   Road shows and outcome

Wide investor base reached

With € 5.4 billion of bonds to be placed, Grand plc represents the largest CMBS transaction to date in continental Europe and as such created enormous investor interest globally. Deutsche Annington and the Lead Managers Barclays Capital and Citigroup formed joint road show teams that travelled to meet investors for individual and group sessions in Amsterdam, Dublin, Duesseldorf, Frankfurt, Hamburg, Lisbon, Madrid, Munich, Oslo, Paris, Stockholm, Vienna and London. In order to meet such a schedule within the timeframe of two weeks, two to three teams were travelling simultaneously to attend 67 one-on-one sessions and a number of group presentations, and investors had the opportunity to take part in site visits and meet Deutsche Annington's management team in Bochum.

7   Asset tap

Inclusion of additional real estate portfolios by issueing further notes

Deutsche Annington is a growing business looking to make further property acquisitions in the future. One important element of the securitization therefore was the ability to add further assets to the collateral pool and on the back of the now enlarged pool issue further notes. To do that, the lead arranger would supply the rating agencies with the necessary property data and due diligence material and add the new collateral to the cash flow model. It is important to note that after the further notes have been issued, the old and the new notes are all secured on the same security pool. Ideally, the new notes should be structured in a way that allows them to have exactly the same characteristics as the old notes and thereby to be fully fungible with the old notes. This pooling of collateral also means that the rating agencies will look at the entire collateral pool again and will affirm the rating of the old notes post issuance of the further notes, and supply a rating for the new notes.

In the case of Grand plc, the company added a further 15,919 properties to the collateral pool, held by two new borrowers. The new borrowers acceded to all relevant agreements and a small supplemental prospectus was issued to explain to investors how the pool had changed. The notional of the new notes totalled € 399,000,000. Figure 9 shows the rating results for the Grand plc further notes.

Class	Rating Fitch/S&P/Moody's	Original Tranche Size (€ million)	Additional Notes (€ million)	Total Tranche Size (€ million)	Original Day-1 LTV (%)	Total Day-1 LTV (%)
Class A	AAA/AAA/Aaa	3,209	236	3,445	57.2 %	57.1 %
Class B	AAA/AA/Aa2	428	32	460	62.5 %	62.4 %
Class C	AA−/A/A2	869	74	943	73.2 %	73.2 %
Class D	A−/BBB/Baa1	577	42	619	80.2 %	80.3 %
Class E	BBB+/BBB/Baa1	133	–	133	81.9 %	81.9 %
Class F	BBB/BBB−/Baa3	200	15	215	84.3 %	84.3 %
Total notes		**5,416**	**399**	**5,815**	**84.3 %**	**84.3 %**

Fig. 9:   Amended capital structure post asset tap

8   Outlook

Grand plc has been a key milestone for the European CMBS market, both in terms of size and structural details, and has pushed the limits of what was previously thought possible in the German multi-family financing market. At the time of writing, the Global market for CMBS is under pressure, and that raises questions about the timing and extent of an eventual recovery, and to what extent the demand for rated CMBS bonds is likely to reach the same levels achieved at the time of the Grand issue. That said, the structuring solutions that enable the ring-fencing of real estate assets for the purpose of issuing securities of varying degrees of credit risk (and hence, return) is likely to remain a valid and constantly evolving financial technology that has the potential to attract significant demand from investors interested in exposure to real estate. In that context, Grand plc is and will remain as relevant as ever.

8   RMBS transactions in Europe: the Belgian example

Piet Hein Schram

Table of contents

1   Introduction

Most memorable transaction

When a securitization professional is asked for his most memorable transaction, in most cases the ranking is either determined by the amount of fees made with a particular transaction or with the amount of publicity a transaction has received, either in the form of press coverage or awards won.

However, for this chapter on Residential Mortgage Backed Securities in Europe, a particular case study based on the number of "firsts" achieved by Delta Lloyd's subsidiary's (Delta Lloyd Bank Belgium or DLBB) first RMBS transaction of October 2006: B-Arena N.V./S.A. Compartment No 1 (B-Arena) has been selected.

Not only was DLBB a first time issuer, the B-Arena transaction was also the first Belgian RMBS transaction to come to market since the two most recent RMBS transactions in 2003 and 2004 and the first securitization transaction to benefit from new legislation implemented in Belgium, enabling a listing of the notes directly on Euronext Brussels and placement with international institutional investors.

Furthermore, B-Arena was also the first European RMBS transaction specifically structured with the aim of achieving regulatory capital relief for the securitized portfolio under both the current regulatory framework and the soon to be implemented Basel II framework. In addition, it was also the first Belgian RMBS transaction that securitized loans backed by mortgages and another form of security: "mandates", a typical Belgian phenomenon where a loan is granted without a fixed mortgage being in place.

Market tightest prints

But most importantly, it was also the first continental European RMBS transaction to achieve pricing on the AAA notes of 10 basis points (bps) during 2006 and achieve market tightest prints on the more junior notes: a truly amazing achievement for a transaction by a first time issuer.

ABN AMRO was appointed sole lead arranger by DLBB in November 2005. Due to the delayed implementation of the new legislation, the B-Arena transaction was finally brought to market at the end of September 2006 and it successfully closed on October 5th, 2006. This case study aims to describe the transaction structure and highlight the key features of the transaction.

2   Transaction objectives

Typically, a mortgage originator intends to realize one or more of the following objectives when undertaking a securitization transaction:

- efficient funding,
- (partial) regulatory capital relief for the securitized portfolio,
- off-balance sheet treatment of the securitized portfolio.

In addition to the objectives of efficient funding and regulatory capital relief, DLBB had two further objectives for their first RMBS transaction:

Objectives of efficient funding and regulatory capital relief

- being the first transaction to come to market following the implementation of the new legislation,

- using the full residential mortgage loan portfolio in order to achieve an efficient transaction size.

As (return on) total assets is not one of the key management criteria within the Delta Lloyd Group, realizing off-balance sheet treatment was not a consideration in deciding on the transaction structure.

3   First transaction under new legislation in Belgium

Apart from a number of RMBS transactions in the end of the 1990s, only two public RMBS transactions had come to market in this millennium: Atomium Mortgage Finance 2003-I B.V. and Diamond Mortgage Finance 2004 N.V. Both transaction structures involved a cumbersome "double SPV" structure to circumvent an uncertainty in the Belgian legislation.

Cumbersome "double SPV" structure

Under Belgian legislation, only an SPV in the form of a so-called "Vennootschap voor Beleggingen in Schuldvorderingen" or an Undertaking for Investment in Receivables (VBS) can purchase a portfolio of receivables without paying transfer taxes. There are two types of VBS:

- **Public:** As a result of the fact that a public VBS has to (at least partly) obtain funds from the public, there are very strict requirements to the reporting and management of a public VBS. In practice this means that it is very difficult to find a trustee willing to undertake the management of a public VBS and provide these cumbersome functions.

- **Institutional:** In case of an institutional VBS, the funding is to be provided by institutional or professional investors acting for their own account. The reporting and management requirements for an institutional VBS are in line with what is normally considered a Special Purpose Vehicle (SPV) in securitization.

"Institutional" character of the VBS was guaranteed

Before the new legislation, there was uncertainty of the criteria a VBS had to meet to ensure it would be (and remain) qualified as an institutional VBS. To address this uncertainty, in Atomium Mortgage Finance 2003-I B.V. and the Diamond Mortgage Finance 2004 N.V., the Belgian institutional VBS attracted funding from a Dutch SPV, which in its turn issued notes into the capital markets. By not having the Belgian VBS issue "public" notes directly into the capital markets, the "institutional" character of the VBS was guaranteed, as the only investor in the Belgian VBS was the Dutch SPV, structured to meet the criteria of an institutional investor.

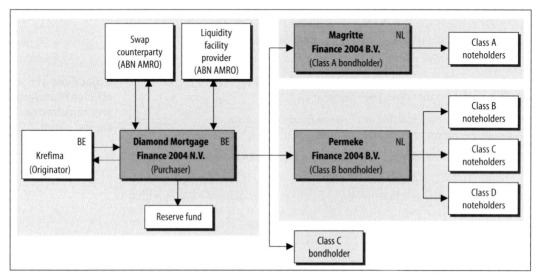

Fig. 1:   Double SPV structure as used in the Diamond Mortgage Finance 2004 N.V. transaction

However, compared to "standard" RMBS transactions, the above double SPV structure is highly inefficient (expensive and difficult to understand for the ultimate capital markets investors) and was considered the main reason for the limited use of RMBS as a funding tool by Belgian mortgage originators. The new legislation was expected to clarify the conditions of qualifying as an institutional VBS when issuing notes listed on an exchange in Belgium and sold directly to capital markets investors.

Legislation only comes into force after formal publication

In Belgium, new legislation only comes into force after formal publication in the "Belgisch Staatsblad", but a draft of the new legislation had been available in the months leading up to the publication. Therefore, in structuring the transaction, legal counsel had already been able to use the draft legislation to design the transaction structure. The Belgian regulator, the "Commissie voor het Bank-, Financie- en Assurantiewezen" (CBFA), had already signed off on the transaction structure based on the draft legislation and the transaction only required formal approval on the day of publication of the new legislation.

Not until the final version of the new legislation in the form of the Royal Decree had been published in the "Belgisch Staatsblad", was it possible to finalize the transaction structure. The B-Arena transaction was announced to the market on September 22nd, 2006, the day the new legislation was made public and came into force.

The B-Arena transaction was announced to the market on September 22nd, 2006

What exactly did the new legislation entail? Under the formerly existing legislation, there was uncertainty whether a VBS would remain to qualify as an institutional VBS if, over time, the original conditions for qualifying as an institutional VBS would no longer be met, e. g., that notes must all be held by professional market parties or "institutional investors". It was unclear whether, if at some point in the future, one of the notes issued by the institutional VBS would be held by the "public", the VBS would lose its status as institutional VBS. Even more important, there was uncertainty whether it would then automatically become a public VBS or lose its status as a VBS altogether with its tax implications.

The new legislation among others provided measures that, if taken by the VBS, would guarantee the "institutional" status of the VBS, irrespective of whether a private investor would be holding any of the notes. These measures included:

- minimum denomination of the Notes of € 250,000,

- notes only to be offered to professional market parties,

- no interest to be paid to the respective noteholder if the directors of the SPV would find out that a note was held by a private person.

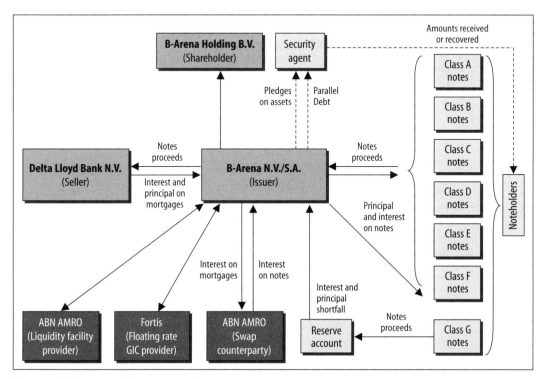

Fig. 2: B-Arena N. V. transaction structure

CBFA formally approved the documentation for the transaction

Following the publication of the actual legislation, the CBFA formally approved the documentation for the transaction and B-Arena became the first Belgian RMBS transaction under the new legislation. The notes have a listing at Euronext Brussels and were directly placed with international capital markets investors without applying the double SPV structure.

Note that in this case study, the ancillary facilities, such as the liquidity facility, interest rate swap and GIC accounts, have not been described in detail as they are considered standard in the industry. All these facilities are provided to the SPV by ABN AMRO Bank.

4   First Belgian RMBS transaction to include "mandates"

The upfront expenses can be significant

The size of a transaction is a key consideration in determining the efficiency of a transaction. Especially in first time issues, such as the B-Arena N.V. transaction, the upfront expenses, such as legal and accounting and rating agency fees, can be significant. The impact of these upfront expenses on the overall cost of funding can be minimized by ensuring a significant transaction size. Given the size of DLBB's mortgage loan portfolio, to achieve a € 1,000 million transaction size, it was important to use the majority of the total available residential mortgage loan portfolio. However, a significant part of the security for the residential mortgage loan portfolio involved a particular Belgian feature, the so-called "mandates". Instead of the mortgage security already being in place, these mandates in essence give the mortgage lender the right to unilaterally create an actual mortgage over the property whenever it is necessary.

In normal circumstances, the borrower and the lender would agree to a mandate under the following conditions:

- The lender has a first ranking mortgage to secure part of the loan (normally around 50 % to 70 % of the loan amount at origination);
- the remaining security would be in the form of a mandate;
- the borrower is/has been performing under his existing loans;
- the moment a borrower gets into arrears, the lender is allowed and expected to convert the mandate into a mortgage and the costs are to be paid by the borrower.

The reason for not taking a mortgage for the full loan amount is based on the following fact: In Belgium a fee of approximately 1.4 % over the mortgaged amount is due upon creation of a mortgage. This fee is not due over the mandate amount (for as long as it is not converted into a mortgage).

Although a mandate can be exercised at any time, the lender will in practice convert the mandate into a mortgage in the name of the lender if a borrower gets into arrears on his loan. Obviously, the mandate can only be converted as long as the borrower or the guarantor owns the relevant underlying property. The mandate would usually contain contractual restrictions on sales of the underlying property and in most cases the mandate is on the same property as the first ranking mortgage.

Transferability of the mandates (in fact, whether the mandate can be exercised to create a mortgage for the benefit of a transferee of the loan) and practical mechanics were topics that involved extensive discussions between legal counsel, DLBB and the rating agencies.

In the perception of a Belgian borrower there is no difference between a mortgage and a mandate. He or she perceives his or her property to be given in security to the lender. As long as the borrower remains current, this is true. However, in case the lender ever has to enforce on the security, there is no guarantee that the mandate can actually be converted into a first ranking mortgage or into the mortgage ranking directly junior to the first ranking mortgage and the lender having first and sequentially lower ranking mortgages.

Theoretically, it is possible that the borrower has granted a second ranking mortgage to another lender which would, in an enforcement situation, rank senior to the mortgage granted under the mandate. However, this is no common practice in Belgium where such behavior is seen as unacceptable. Moreover, the borrower undertakes not to grant a mortgage senior to the "mortgage option" he granted in the mandate. If he were to do so anyway, he would be breaching the negative pledge contained in the mandate.

One of the key considerations when discussing this form of security with the rating agencies, was the fact that over time, the outstanding loan amount secured by the mandate reduces as time elapsed in case of an amortizing mortgage loan. Also the fact that DLBB could demonstrate that it had never incurred a loss as a result of failing to convert a mandate into a valid mortgage, contributed to the discussion.

Ultimately, all three rating agencies accepted most of the arguments brought forward and granted varying amounts of credit to the security in the form of a mandate. This allowed Delta Lloyd Bank to significantly increase the available collateral and the ultimate transaction size.

5   Regulatory capital relief

The CBFA has neither published a framework for the regulatory treatment of securitization transactions nor local guidelines on the translation of the Capital Requirements Directive (European directive implementing the Basel II regulations). Instead, it reviews proposed transactions on a case-by-case basis, taking into consideration the originator's specific situation, the transaction structure and the underlying assets.

Frameworks

DLBB asked the CBFA to review the transaction both in light of the currently existing regulatory framework and the soon to be implemented Basel II framework as its objectives were to achieve regulatory capital relief under both frameworks. In Belgium, the current framework to a large extent already anticipated the implementation of Basel II.

The key considerations in determining the amount of regulatory capital before and after the transaction are:

- the amount of regulatory capital held against the portfolio before the transaction,
- the amount of notes in the transaction retained by the originator,
- the amount of excess spread available in the transaction to cover credit losses.

In addition, the transaction structure is required to meet certain requirements in respect of:

- the call option structure,
- the repurchase obligations of DLBB,
- the arms' length character of the transaction.

Significant risk transfer; implicit support

Under the Capital Requirements Directive (CRD), securitization transactions have to meet a number of further requirements in respect of:

- significant risk transfer,
- implicit support.

§ 538 of the Basel II Accord [1] establishes that *"Banks must apply the securitization framework for determining regulatory capital requirements on exposures arising from traditional and synthetic securitizations or similar structures that contain features common to both. Since securitizations may be structured in many different ways, the capital treatment of a securitization exposure must be determined on the basis of its economic substance rather than its legal form. Similarly, supervisors will look to the economic substance of a transaction to determine whether it should be subject to the securitization framework for purposes of determining regulatory capital"*.

§ 539 of the Basel II Accord provides definitions for traditional and synthetic securitizations. A traditional securitization being *"a structure where the cash flow from an underlying pool of exposures is used to service at least two different stratified risk positions or tranches reflecting different degrees of credit risk. Payments to the investors depend upon the performance of the specified underlying exposures, as opposed to being derived from an obligation of the entity originating those exposures. The stratified/tranched structures that characterise securitizations differ from ordinary senior/subordinated debt instruments in that junior securitization tranches can absorb losses without interrupting contractual payments to more senior tranches, whereas subordination in a senior/subordinated debt structure is a matter of priority of rights to the proceeds of liquidation"*.

The above paragraphs provide a clear indication of how the Belgian regulator would review the B-Arena transaction under the new regulatory framework. To determine whether or not the transaction meets all requirements for regulatory capital relief in respect of significant risk transfer and implicit support, § 554 of the Accord needs to be considered.

§ 554 of the Basel II Accord states:

"An originating bank may exclude securitized exposures from the calculation of riskweighted assets only if all of the following conditions have been met. Banks meeting these conditions must still hold regulatory capital against any securitization exposures they retain.

(a) Significant credit risk associated with the securitized exposures has been transferred to third parties.

(b) The transferor does not maintain effective or indirect control over the transferred exposures. The assets are legally isolated from the transferor in such a way (e. g., through the sale of assets or through subparticipation) that the exposures are put beyond the reach of the transferor and its creditors, even in bankruptcy or receivership. These conditions must be supported by an opinion provided by a qualified legal counsel.

The transferor is deemed to have maintained effective control over the transferred credit risk exposures if it: (i) is able to repurchase from the transferee the previously transferred exposures in order to realise their benefits; or (ii) is obligated to retain the risk of the transferred exposures. The transferor's retention of servicing rights to the exposures will not necessarily constitute indirect control of the exposures.

(c) The securities issued are not obligations of the transferor. Thus, investors who purchase the securities only have claim to the underlying pool of exposures.

(d) The transferee is an SPE and the holders of the beneficial interests in that entity have the right to pledge or exchange them without restriction.

(e) Clean-up calls must satisfy the conditions set out in § 557.

(f) The securitization does not contain clauses that (i) require the originating bank to alter systematically the underlying exposures such that the pool's weighted average credit quality is improved unless this is achieved by selling assets to independent and unaffiliated third parties at market prices; (ii) allow for increases in a retained first loss position or credit enhancement provided by the originating bank after the transaction's inception; or (iii) increase the yield payable to parties other than the originating bank, such as investors and third-party providers of credit enhancements, in response to a deterioration in the credit quality of the underlying pool."

In this respect, the below two paragraphs of the Accord are relevant as well:

Credit enhancement is defined in § 546 of the Accord as *"a contractual arrangement in which the originating) bank retains or assumes a securitization exposure and, in substance, provides some degree of added protection to other parties to the transaction".*

According to § 551, *"Implicit Support arises when a bank provides support to a securitization in excess of its predetermined contractual obligation".* Further, in the Accord, examples of implicit support are *"the purchase of underlying exposures at above market price or an increase in the first loss position according to the deterioration of the underlying exposures".*

Even before the Basel II framework, implicit support was a matter of serious concern by regulators. The assessment as to whether a bank is providing implicit support to its securitization transactions is ultimately a decision to be taken by the regulators, and the Accord provides limited guidance in relation to that. The UK regulator, the FSA, has issued more specific guidelines in respect of securitization transactions.

Although it was not certain whether the Belgian regulator would follow the same route as the FSA in deciding on the final transaction structure for B-Arena N.V. a number of points from the FSA guidelines were addressed in the transaction structure:

- The originating institution (DLBB in this case) will not bear any of the recurring expenses of the scheme.

- The originating institution will not provide temporary finance to cover cash shortfalls arising from delayed payments or non-performance of loans which it administers.

- The originating institution will not enter into swap agreements with the SPV that intentionally bear losses.

- There is absolutely no doubt that the SPV's claim extends solely to the cash collected from the securitized assets.

In which way was all the above incorporated in the B-Arena transaction and more specifically, what made the regulator comfortable that both in respect of implicit support and significant risk transfer, DLBB met the requirements (even though they were not formalized in an official guideline)?

The key considerations in respect of implicit support and significant risk transfer, as highlighted above, are whether the amount of support to a transaction can increase as a result of the performance of the transaction and whether a certain portion of the risk is no longer retained by DLBB.

In the B-Arena transaction structure this is relevant in respect of

- the interest rate swap,

- the amount and timing of availability of excess spread in the transaction and

- the retention by DLBB of the subordinated notes.

Interest rate swap

To ensure that the interest rate swap between the SPV and ABN AMRO (and the back-to-back swap between ABN AMRO and DLBB) do not provide support to the transaction, any mortgage loans in arrears are excluded from the swap payments. As a result, the interest rate swap only swaps payments on the performing part of the underlying portfolio of residential mortgage loans. Any potential shortfall in the payments from ABN AMRO to the SPV can therefore be considered a risk for the noteholders without any support from DLBB.

One key point that was extensively discussed with the regulator was the amount of excess spread that is implicitly guaranteed because of the swap structure. By retaining 10 bps on a quarterly basis from the interest income on the portfolio before the SPV makes any interest payments under the swap to ABN AMRO, the SPV is virtually certain that this amount of credit enhancement will always be available. Ultimately, this is a risk of DLBB as they enter into the back-to-back swap with ABN AMRO and any shortfall between the interest income on the portfolio (after deduction of the excess spread) and the interest payable on the notes results in a loss in the back-to-back swap. One could argue that by providing this guaranteed excess spread, DLBB was not actually transferring any risk to the SPV and therefore to noteholders.

To demonstrate to the CBFA that there is risk transfer taking place, one of the groundbreaking changes compared to existing transaction structures is that the quarterly available excess spread can only be used to cover any credit losses on the portfolio arising in that specific quarter. In "pre Basel II" transactions, excess spread of the future can be used to cover any losses from the past. Obviously, in such structure, any spikes in credit risk are not transferred to the noteholders as basically the originator retains a significant first loss position through the cumulative excess spread. In the B-Arena transaction on the contrary, excess spread can only be used to cover losses of that quarter. If the loss exceeds the amount of available excess spread, the noteholders will lose (part of) their investment.

Timing and availability of excess spread

The downside of having only quarterly excess spread available to cover any losses, is that it became very challenging to achieve (near) investment grade ratings on the subordinated and junior notes. To provide the rating agencies with some additional comfort that losses could be covered from excess spread, an innovative feature was incorporated into the transaction structure: In line with DLBB's business model, upon a loan being declared more than 60 days in arrears, a provisioning would be taken from excess spread and retained by the SPV.

Instead of using excess spread after the loss has materialized, a forward looking provisioning mechanism was implemented that allows the SPV to provision for any potential losses on a mortgage loan at the moment a loan reaches a 60 days in arrears limit. This is in line with the current business principles at DLBB where under the CBFA guidelines, at 60 days arrears, a review of the mortgage loan is done and an estimate made of the potential loss as a result of work out and does not contravene with the Basel II guidelines.

In addition to the above described changes to the transaction structure, DLBB sold a significant part of the two most junior notes to external investors, further demonstrating to the CBFA its intention not to retain all the risks in the transaction. Especially the sale of a portion of the subordinated Class G note (unrated) which is only backed by the existing reserve account, at a spread of 450bps over 3-month-EURIBOR demonstrated the fact that also external parties had confidence in the strength of the underlying portfolio and the transaction structure. For the portion of the Class G note retained by DLBB, a one-to-one deduction of regulatory capital is required under both the existing and the Basel II framework.

Sale of subordinated and junior note

Based on the transaction structure described above and the placement of a portion of the junior and subordinated notes with external investors, the CBFA confirmed the regulatory capital relief realized through the B-Arena transaction.

6   Capital markets placement

Achieve an efficient funding level for the securitized portfolio

As mentioned in section 2, one of the key objectives of DLBB was to achieve an efficient funding level for the securitized portfolio. Until this transaction, the only benchmark transactions from Belgium in the RMBS space were the Atomium Mortgage Finance 2003-I B.V. and the Diamond Mortgage Finance N.V. transactions. However, since 2004, European RMBS spreads have converged significantly. Therefore, DLBB was more ambitious with regard to the pricing levels it was looking to achieve with its B-Arena transaction.

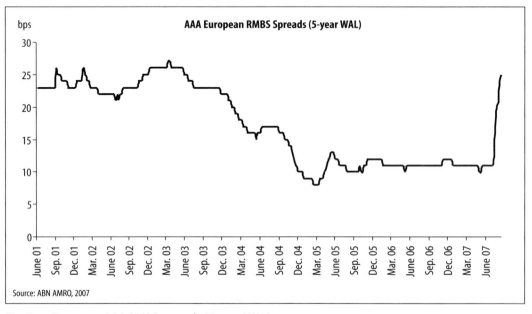

Fig. 3:   European AAA RMBS spreads (5-year WAL)

In the Netherlands, Delta Lloyd is considered one of the benchmark issuers of RMBS transactions, which is reflected in the pricing levels achieved by the Arena program during 2005 and 2006. However, until the B-Arena transaction was put in front of investors, there would be no certainty whether they would see the B-Arena transaction as a Belgian Arena or whether they would see things differently.

To address as many of the potential concerns from investors, DLBB decided to use all three rating agencies (Moody's, Fitch and S&P) instead of Moody's and Fitch only as in the Arena program. Ultimately, the three agencies allocated the following ratings to the transaction:

Transaction Details	Class A notes	Class B notes	Class C notes	Class D notes	Class E notes	Class F notes	Class G notes
Amount in €	920 million	20 million	20 million	18 million	10.5 million	11.5 million	10 million
Rating (S&P/MDY/Fitch)	AAA/Aaa/AAA	AA/Aa3/AA	A/A2/A	BBB/Baa2/BBB	BBB–/NR/BBB–	BB/NR/BB	NR/NR/NR
Interest rate	3-month-EURIBOR + 10 bps	3-month-EURIBOR + 14 bps	3-month-EURIBOR + 20 bps	3-month-EURIBOR + 40 bps	3-month-EURIBOR + 55 bps	3-month-EURIBOR + 160 bps	3-month-EURIBOR + 450 bps
Payment frequency	Quarterly	Quarterly	Quarterly	Quarterly	Quarterly	Quarterly	Quarterly
Issue price	100 %	100 %	100 %	100 %	100 %	100 %	100 %
CE	9.00 %	7.00 %	5.00 %	3.20 %	2.15 %	1.00 %	N. A.
Weighted average life	5 years	5 years	5 years	5 years	5 years	5 years	5 years
Scheduled redemption date	Oct. 2011	Oct. 2011	Oct. 2011	Oct. 2011	Oct. 2011	Oct. 2011	Oct. 2011
Final legal maturity	April 2044	April 2044	April 2044	April 2044	April 2044	April 2044	April 2044
Redemption structure	The Class A notes will only be redeemed upon an amortization event taking place, in which case the margin on the Class A notes will step up by 1 bp. As of the first optional redemption date in October 2011, the notes are expected to be repaid. The Class G notes will be repaid from the monies left in the reserve account.						

Fig. 4: Tranching overview B-Arena N. V.

Innovative feature

In addition, to attract as many bank treasury investors as possible, DLBB decided to structure the most senior AAA rated note as a bullet, as this is the preferred structure by these types of investors given the straightforward repayment profile. An innovative feature introduced in this transaction was a 1 bp step up of the AAA spread in case DLBB decided to start amortizing the class A notes, despite the bullet nature intent. Generally, this 1 bp is seen as the pricing difference between an amortizing note with a weighted average life of five years and a five year bullet note.

The six day road show

To further improve the distribution, Fortis was appointed as second joint lead manager, with the clear intention to give a further impetus to investor interest in Belgium. During the six day road show, DLBB visited all major financial centers across Europe. All in all, over 75 investors attended the meetings, an absolute record considering the relatively limited length of the road show.

To investors, the main attraction of the B-Arena transaction was the diversification opportunity it offered among European RMBS investment opportunities. With very rare asset-backed issuance from Belgium, a well structured prime RMBS transaction from a high-grade issuer proved to be in high demand.

7   Pricing and placement

Normally for RMBS transactions, the spread on the AAA rated notes is considered the benchmark that transactions are compared by. In case of the B-Arena transaction, the Class A notes priced at 10 bps in line with the tightest levels achieved to date in 2006. However, for the Class B to Class G notes, the pricing levels achieved were the tightest ever on continental European RMBS.

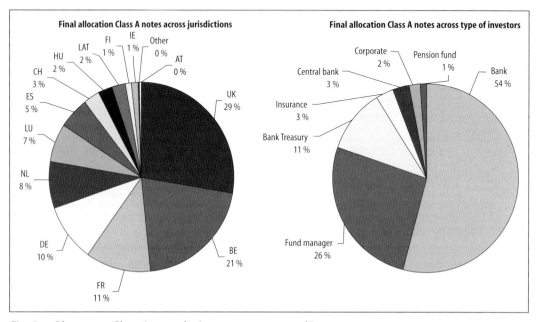

Fig. 5:   Placement Class A notes by investor country and investor type

Not only was the pricing for this first time issuer transaction exceptional, the wide geographical spread of the investor book demonstrated the high level of interest in the transaction across European ABS investors.

Especially the pricing achieved on the BB rated Class F and the unrated Class G notes (160 bps and 450 bps, respectively), are still considered groundbreaking in the RMBS universe. The pricing levels achieved meant that DLBB was in a position to place a significant part of these notes with external investors, allowing for further regulatory capital relief.

8   Conclusion

As highlighted in this case study, meeting an originator's objectives for a RMBS transaction can be extremely challenging especially against the backdrop of an uncertain legal and regulatory framework. In the case of the B-Arena transaction, however, all objectives of DLBB were met. In addition to achieving regulatory capital relief, the actual pricing realized on all classes of notes exceeded all expectations. By incorporating the residential mortgage loans secured by mandates, a € 1,000 million transaction size was realized which contributed to a reduction of the overall start-up expenses.

By announcing the transaction on the day of publication of the new legislation, B-Arena also met the final objective of being the first transaction under the new legislation.

All things considered, the B-Arena transaction was a truly groundbreaking transaction. I sincerely hope this case study highlighted some of the interesting features and demonstrates that even in the "standard" asset class of RMBS, a high degree of innovation and structuring is involved in order to successfully bring a transaction to market.

B-Arena transaction was a truly groundbreaking transaction

9 Bibliography

[1] Basel Committee on Banking Supervision, International Convergence of Capital Measurement and Capital Standards, June 2006, pp. 120–125.

9 CMBS transactions in Europe: segments, structural elements and market development

Martin Damaske

Table of contents

1   Fundamentals of the CMBS market

1.1   Motivation and development of CMBS securitization

As described in chapter C2 of this handbook, Commercial Mortgage Backed Securities (CMBS) are an instrument to refinance commercial property lending.

CMBS versus traditional refinancing
The major difference compared to traditional ways of refinancing through the bank balance sheet and especially covered bonds (Pfandbriefe) is the mitigation of the credit risk through the capital market towards investors. As a result, the primary lending bank does not have to underlie the securitized mortgage loans with equity any more and can reuse it to grant new loans. If the securitization is profitable for the lending bank and it can originate and securitize mortgages quickly, it has the chance to generate a high profit based on a small amount of equity.

Generally speaking, investors like to invest into CMBS notes because they can generate a higher spread compared to other investments, as, for example, covered bonds (Pfandbriefe).

In theory, the borrower should not care how his loan is refinanced or placed on the capital market as long as he receives his liquidity for a low interest. In reality, the way of refinancing has a relevant impact on the borrower because the capital market has specific requirements (for example, transparent information about the borrower, the collateralized property and the features of the loan contract) for an easy and cheap securitization of the mortgage loans.

Shift the credit risk to institutional investors
By pooling different mortgage loans and refinancing them through structured bonds that are specifically designed to meet the risk appetite of investors, securitization is a very powerful tool to mitigate the credit risk from the commercial real estate market onto the shoulders of institutional investors from around the world. A lender's capability to grant mortgage loans is not limited by his maximum amount of equity to underlie the outstanding mortgage volume or maximal ability to carry certain credit risks any more.

In recent years, German and European banks started to use securitization technologies to generate the above mentioned advantages.

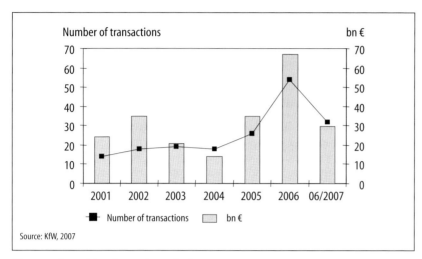

Fig. 1:   *Securitization volume in Germany*

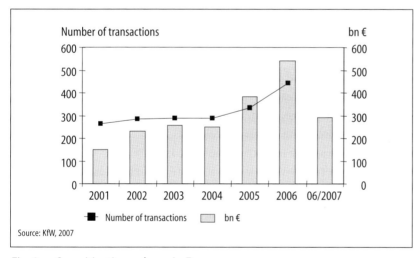

Fig. 2:   *Securitization volume in Europe*

Although the first securitization was already placed in Germany in 1990, the German market started to unfold comparatively late with the first RMBS transaction in 2000.

As figures 1 and 2 visualize, not only the European, but also the German securitization market have experienced a tremendous growth during the last years. Especially in 2005 and 2006, the market volume and the number of transactions achieved record levels. The first six months of 2007 have shown the same positive trend until the market stopped due to the US subprime crisis

Tremendous growth

that expanded into a heavy liquidity crisis effecting major parts of global debt markets.

Although all asset classes were able to benefit from this growth of the market, especially CMBS started to play a more important role during the last few years. Standardized CMBS securitization platforms of several individual banks and German multi-family transactions promoted the named growth of the CMBS segment (see below).

1.2   Segments of the commercial real estate market

Commercial Mortgage Backed Securities (CMBS) are, as the name suggests, backed by one or more properties, representing one or more types of commercial property. The types are usually sectioned into office, retail, industrial, hotel or multi-family properties. Several issues are property-type specific even though overall economic factors, supply and demand, location and accessibility and so forth affect properties and their performance as an investment. Despite this, the five main property types and associated investment considerations will be shortly examined in the following:

Office properties Office properties' values depend tremendously on their state of obsolescence. Hence, office properties are usually classified as Class A, B or C. Their construction periods tend to be longer and they show more volatility than retail or industrial properties, but less than hotel properties.

Before investing into office property, the following should be taken into consideration:

- design structure and flexibility,
- tenant quality and leases,
- management and servicer track record,
- competing properties or business districts,
- proximity to service industry businesses, and
- employment trends in the service sector (e. g., financial and insurance).

Retail properties Retail properties include strip centers next to regional malls and freestanding stores. The major factors for high quality investments are:

- planning restrictions and ownership structure,
- parking availability,
- tenant mix, including presence and quality of anchor tenants,
- management and servicer track record,
- accessibility and proximity to residential developments and major roads,
- area population growth, density and disposable income, and
- forecasts for retail sales growth.

Industrial properties Industrial properties are highly specialized properties which are very often customized to the needs of the respective tenants. When investing in industrial properties, such as storage and distribution warehouses, research and development facilities, light manufacturing and "flex space" buildings adaptable for use as an office, a warehouse, or even a retail center, the following considerations should be taken into account:

- design, such as ceiling heights, floor thickness, column spacing and general flexibility (e. g., for custom fit),
- tenant quality and lease term,
- access to rail, road, air and other transportation possibilities,
- proximity to labor sources,
- proximity to suppliers,
- area employers, and
- employment trends in the manufacturing sector.

Hotel properties are obviously very different from other commercial property types as they show the highest expense-to-income ratios and are nevertheless the most volatile type of property investment. In addition and also in order to cover the high fixed costs, hotel management must successfully re-lease the property on a daily basis. The most important variables to consider for hotel investments are: **Hotel properties**

- source of demand,
- franchise strength and market penetration,
- economic growth,
- seasonality, and
- management.

Multi-family properties are much alike RMBS in terms of portfolio granularity and dependence on tenants' willingness and ability to make rental payments. These transactions exhibit high geographic risks as well as specific building risks and strongly depend on property management and disposal strategies and are exposed to portfolio concentration to a few individual housing estates with potential tenant employment concentration. In addition to the following key variables, investors should also bear regional differences in housing quality in mind: **Multi-family properties**

- refinancing risks,
- highly varying rental performance by city,
- strong varying rent growth even between neighboring cities,
- unclear relationship between market prices for new and existing homes,
- household income, and
- unemployment rates.

1.3   Main types of CMBS transactions

European CMBS are, unlike traditional MBS or ABS, not homogenous asset pools that are automatically suited to statistical analysis. European CMBS appear in numerous shapes and sizes. In addition to this fact, different property types and geographic locations are put together to boost diversification benefits for investors. Each one of the three main types, in which those transactions can be divided into, may include one or more properties depending on the originator's motivation and has got a different risk profile:

Portfolio transactions

Portfolio transactions generally constitute multi-borrower, multi-property collateral pools combining 50 to 100 individual loans and therefore create a strong diversity. Commonly commercial banks originate these transactions in order to transfer risk from their balance sheet to the capital market.

Property transactions

Property transactions (or conduits) refer to multi-borrower loan pools with less than 20 loans and a limited range of properties. In comparison to the American counterpart, European conduits much more resemble the portfolio transaction described above. Depending on whether they are based on only a few tenants or a diversified tenant group, the European conduits can be further divided into two subgroups: Those which rely on only a couple of tenants require not only a property analysis but also a tenant analysis, whereas those conduits relying on a diversified tenant basis in a few properties focus on a property analysis. Investment banks that originate loans to investors or rather to companies holding commercial real estate often undertake conduits. With the objective of producing lower financing costs than in the traditional bank lending market, developers often prefer employing large-loan property exposure CMBS.

Tenant transactions

Tenant transactions (or single-borrower) refer to sale-leaseback, single-borrower, single-property loans and single-borrower, multi-property loans with long tenancies. Single-property transactions can be compared with an investment in a particular property and particular tenant with regard to risk exposure. In spite of risk-sharing, the normal benefits of property diversification, characteristic for most securitizations, are not achieved. Within this transaction type, corporates and governments are often considered as the sole and long-term tenants of properties. Through tenant transactions, they have tried to dispose non-core assets, restructure the balance sheet or they have wanted a source of long-term financing.

1.4   Structural characteristics of European CMBS conduits

In this section the emphasis is laid on CMBS conduits. Compared to tenant transactions, they bring a number of benefits to investors, like greater choice of CMBS assets and therefore improved portfolio diversification and further transaction standardization.

Different maturities provoke critical features

In an ideal world, a conduit might originate loans of a similar maturity. This would either have the effect of a smooth repayment schedule during the life of the transaction or a bullet structure, where either all notes would be paid down sequentially or all tranches are paid down at one bullet day. In reality, the situation is different: The transaction is exposed to balloon repayment of the principal at varying days and/or to unpredictable prepayment of the loans.

The result are critical features of a conduit structure like payment priority between tranches (especially in regards to prepayments), interest rate hedging, liquidity facilities and limiting interest payment to available funds. In the recent past, European transactions have varied widely in approaching those factors. Now, with the rising number of conduits, there is also a strong tendency of standardized structures for dealing with those risks. In recent transactions the following trends have occurred:

Prepayment occurred especially in the last years thanks to low interest rates which allowed borrowers to refinance at cheaper levels and restructure the repayment terms. Investors suffer in various terms from early repayments. They complain about reinvestment risks when spreads tightened or wasted efforts and additional costs while analyzing a deal when early prepayment occurs. With a sequential distribution, i.e., senior notes first, a further undesirable consequence is the increase of the average funding costs and the uneven placement of the burden on the senior note holders. To mitigate this inconvenience, a modified form of pro rata distribution of principle has become acceptable. Under these structures, prepayments are distributed to all tranches according to their size or a prescribed ratio. In general, most modified pro rata payment structures incorporate portfolio performance and minimum outstanding triggers, which switch back to sequential payment when there is a credit concern.

Diminishing risks of prepayment

Since junior notes yield a higher coupon than senior, the average funding costs increase while loans prepay and notes are paid down in sequential order. This may result in compression of the margin between the portfolio yield and the funding cost to the extent that it is not possible to meet the interest cost of the outstanding notes. As a result, some transactions incorporate a cap on payment of interest to junior notes. Available Funds Caps (AFC) are mostly applied only to double-B tranches. The structures differ if interest is deferred or extinguished.

There are different ways to mitigate interest rate risk in CMBS transactions. Of course, it is never entirely eliminated as the structure bears the costs of unwinding any swap on default of an asset. As most commercial property loans have fixed rates to match underlying rents, a fixed/floating swap is required. A basis swap is necessary as payment timing and floating rate benchmarks differ. Further issues concerning the interest rate hedging include whether a swap is placed on issuer or borrower level, what liquidity support is required for making swap payments and who bears the cost of terminating a swap on default or prepayment of a loan.

Diminishing interest rate risk

Liquidity facilities are used to meet payment timing differences, equalize temporary loan delinquency and, as mentioned before, maintain payments where necessary under hedge agreements. Interesting points concerning liquidity facilities include: minimizing costs through efficient structuring, availability of liquidity to service junior notes and appropriate measures to avoid advancing liquidity against debts. In the past, most conduits set an initial liquidity facility which may reduce pro rata when notes have been paid down to a certain level until it reaches a certain floor amount. Liquidity may also be trenched to ensure that a sufficient level is available to the most senior tranches. Full liquidity provision for all notes would make the costs prohibitive high. Therefore some delinquency risk is left with junior noteholders. If a loan is defaulted and it becomes obvious during the following foreclosure process that a full recovery is not possible, liquidity should not be advanced. An appraisal mechanism can be used to reduce the available amount by the liquidity facility.

Liquidity facilities

Usually, it is reduced by a level equal to the excess of outstanding note principal plus fees plus unpaid interest, etc., over current collateral value.

2   European CMBS market

2.1   Volumes and market structure

Besides the tremendous growth of European securitization volume across all asset classes, the CMBS even outperformed this growth again.

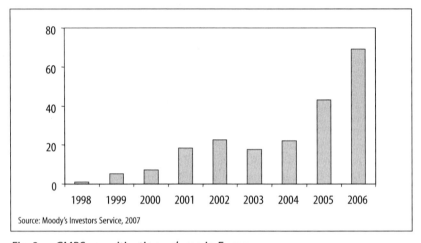

Fig. 3:   CMBS securitization volume in Europe

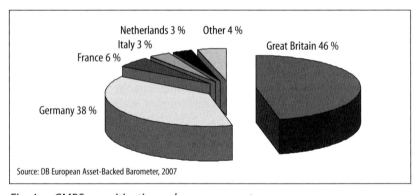

Fig. 4:   CMBS securitization volume per country

UK market versus German market   As in the years before, the highest volume of CMBS was originated in the UK market in 2006 again. However, compared to 2005 the share of UK deals dropped by 20 % due to the fact that the German CMBS volume really boosted up to second position in Europe. The tendency continued: In the first six months of 2007, CMBS was the most important asset class in Germany and for the first time outstripped the UK market.

These numbers show that German lenders of commercial mortgages totally changed their business model from the former pure lend-and-hold strategy by amending a big portion of lend-and-sell strategy for mortgage loans within the last five years.

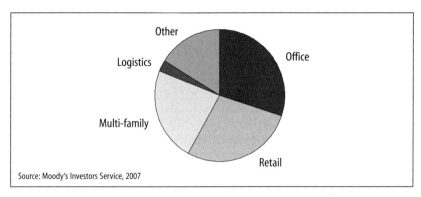

Source: Moody's Investors Service, 2007

Fig. 5:   *Asset types in the European CMBS securitization market*

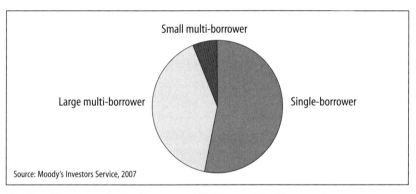

Source: Moody's Investors Service, 2007

Fig. 6:   *Structures in the European CMBS securitization market*

The three most important property types in European CMBS transactions are office, retail and multi-family. Especially the last mentioned property type increased strongly due to the development of private equity investments into German multi-family housing portfolios that were leveraged by huge bank loans which were securitized later on.

A typical aspect of CMBS transactions is that one institution securitizes the cash flow of one large property, for example, a shopping center (single-borrower – single-property). CMBS is the only asset class in the securitization market dominated by single-borrower transactions.

Single-borrower transactions dominate

More and more banks use standardized platforms for CMBS transactions to grant smaller participants access to the capital market. Because of the pooling of smaller volumes, which are granted to many different participants, these transactions are multi-borrower transactions.

2.2   Structural developments of CMBS

As mentioned above, CMBS strongly feature differences concerning their structure and require a different analysis approach. Nevertheless, some fundamental credit views apply for all transaction types.

Influences of location   The main determinant of current and long-term property performance is location. It involves both the country and the local market area plus the city. In European CMBS, the geographic location defines on the one hand the relative position within the commercial property cycle. On the other hand it affects the legal and regulatory environments and valuation rigor to which the mortgage loan and property are subject, too. Regional economy, employment, planning and demographic trends are decisive concerning the success of any property location. Hence, these factors influence its ability to attract stable tenants on a regular basis.

Debt Service Coverage Ratio   The sustainability of cash flows, which commercial property generates, is the second most important performance factor. For any property investment, the first year net cash flow figure can be obtained. It represents the EBITDA of the property or the Net Operating Income, in short NOI, minus capital

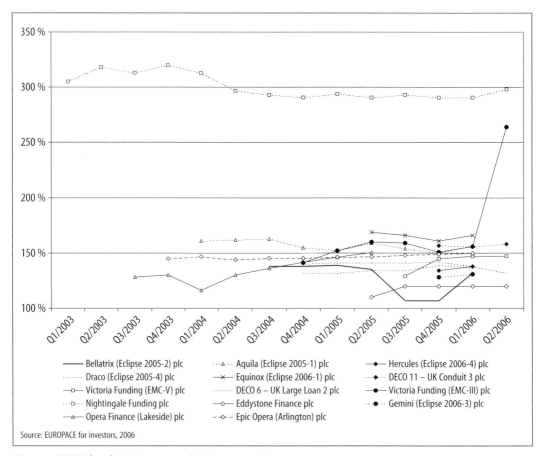

Fig. 7:   *DSCR levels in European CMBS transactions*

expenses (e. g., tenant improvements). This figure must be compared with the required debt service under the loan and result in the Debt Service Coverage Ratio (DSCR) and the Interest Coverage Ratio (ICR). The DSCR is regarded as being the most important performance figure concerning the monitoring by investors on a regular basis. Rating agencies use common approaches like standard amortization schedules and own assumptions on future interest and capitalization rates to calculate the DSCR. Because there exists no standard across Europe with regard to the different rental and capital value growth rates, investors have to distinguish between them by jurisdiction.

The Loan-to-Value ratio (LTV) is the third key credit metric. Its function is to quantify the property value relative to the debt financing and it is denoted as the prime indicator on the recovery value upon a loan default. In spite of the importance of this figure it has to be taken into account that LTV can cause varying degrees of error on, e. g., the quality of appraisal in the related country, the elapse of time since the most recent or initial appraisal, relative illiquidity of the commercial real estate market and the presence of comparable transaction data. Often, the LTV is disabled to estimate future increases or rather decreases in property value because of its state, which is not marked-to-market. Therefore the explanatory power of LTV is low respecting the salability of a property upon the default of a loan and consequently investors must rely on their own view on the likelihood of a significant decline in realizable value.

Loan-to-Value

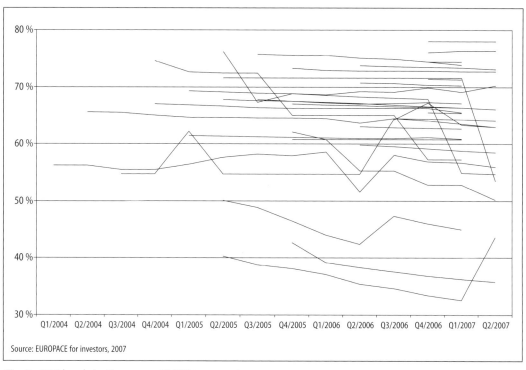

Source: EUROPACE for investors, 2007

Fig. 8: LTV levels in European CMBS transactions

Eminently important for portfolios that consist of smaller properties is the valuation of the properties. Concerning this matter, a consistent valuation practice is essential for the reliability of the LTV in its role as an indicator of recovery value upon loan default. The type and quality of property, future outlook for such properties and the industries to which they are exposed over the near and long run are characteristics which always have to be checked in this framework. Concerning large, unique or illiquid properties investors should pay more attention to the credit quality of the tenant and the lease terms to which they are contractually bound.

Major risks of single asset transactions
In a single asset transaction, two major risks affect the property. The first one is the concentrated tenant default which is associated with the credit quality of the tenant and furthermore with its position within the industry in which it competes. The second one is the tenant non-renewal. This risk often depends on market rents and the presence of new, competitive properties built in relative proximity to the existing building.

Sale-leasebacks
Sale-leasebacks constitute a special case of single-borrower transactions. Their solely basis is the rental cash flow from a single occupying entity flowing through to the investor. In face of this situation, the underlying property has often been highly customized for the tenant concerning European transaction. Furthermore, there hardly exist alternative tenants.

2.3   Performance

There have not been any defaults in European CMBS transactions up to now, either due to young transactions or a good general market development within the last five to seven years when the CMBS securitization was established in Europe. Compared to US transactions, which also developed very well during the last years, European deals have even lower delinquencies.

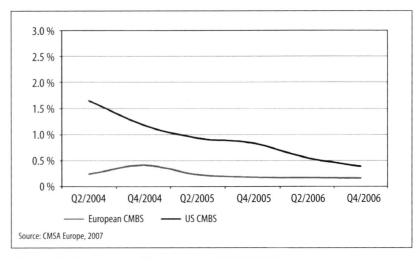

Fig. 9:   Delinquencies of European and US CMBS in comparison

Compared to RMBS transactions, European CMBS deals have lower delinquencies. This has an obvious reason: The possibility of tenants not paying their mortgages in RMBS deals with thousands of borrowers is much higher than in single-borrower deals or CMBS deals with a much lower number of underlying properties. Additionally, the property manager reacts much faster and tries to recover an office building if one tenant does not pay. But if there is a real problem in a CMBS deal, the loss will be much higher than in RMBS deals.

Lower delinquencies of CMBS deals

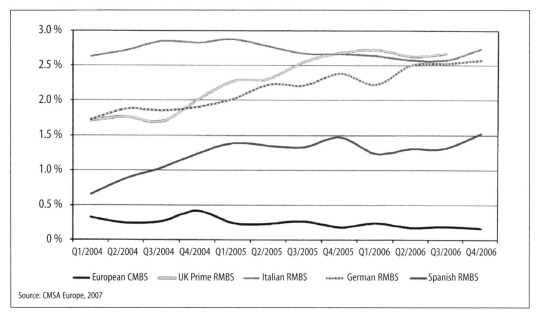

Fig. 10: Delinquencies of European and US CMBS in comparison

3   European CMBS: trends and outlook

In 2006, the CMBS market has seen a new record issuance with 84 transactions of over € 65 billion, which is up approximately 60 % from 2005 issuances. AAA-spreads have been within a stable range of 17 to 24 basis points according to Barclays Capital. Although investor demand was already strong in 2006, Barclays forecasts an increase of 44 % for 2007 which would allow a further increase in issuance up to the 100 billion barrier. Further strong issuance of the established CMBS conduit programs was expected in 2007 as well as a few number of new European conduit programs.

Prospering CMBS market

The first half of 2007 went exactly into this direction until the US subprime crisis stopped the entire global ABS market and lead to one of the heaviest liquidity crises in the bond market that is to be expected to heal firstly in Q1/2008 – perhaps Q2/2008. It is absolutely astonishing that one segment of the ABS market (US residential subprime mortgages) was able to stop the entire securitization industry due to counter transparent risk diversification mechanisms via multi-leveraged structures (arbitrage ABCP programs, SIVs,

CDOs, etc.) and – as in all crises – a rapid and exaggerated loss in confidence into the market. It is absolutely astonishing and approved by many market participants that there is a huge mismatch between missing liquidity combined with rapid growth in credit risk spreads on the one hand, and still good credit quality within the ABS deals on the other hand.

In terms of performance, delinquencies and losses on European CMBS have been good relative to other European ABS sectors. The CMBS sector has still not seen any default at note level yet and this trend is expected to remain almost stable in 2008, although individual transactions are expected to bring up first losses in a normal range.

In the long-run, there should be two trends in terms of CMBS collateral: increased granularity (especially for German multi-family CMBS) and more multi-jurisdictional issuance. The increase in multi-borrower, multi-property transactions is mostly due to transactions relating to multi-family property portfolios. Multi-jurisdictional transactions were from conduit programs and contain collateral from two or more countries. The increased focus on continental Europe can be explained by the increased competition among UK conduit lenders. The percentage of multi-jurisdictional transactions of total issuance was much higher in the past, especially in 2002, with a number of large, synthetic transactions. Barclays therefore notes the re-emergence of synthetic structure types.

Calls for transparency   With regard to standardization and transparency, the long lasting industry discussion around the publication of investor reports is supposed to be resolved – and is in the current crisis one of the biggest issues from a regulators point of view. All major conduit issuers are expected to remove passwords from their websites and make investor reports available to regulatory data providers. The next step will be to convince servicers and trustees to use a standardized reporting template such as the European Investor Reporting Package by CMSA, the Commercial Mortgage Association. This would contribute to a further increasing transparency of performance data on CMBS and the underlying collateral and thus help investors with their performance monitoring and investment decisions.

Outlook remains strong   In terms of the fundamental economic drivers for CMBS which are the GDP (Gross Domestic Product) and the interest rates, these are expected to remain at a level not to cause a decline in demand for commercial property in the letting and investment markets in Europe. Based on each country's sectoral rental income and capital value growth forecasts, Barclays recommended avoiding exposures to sectors with lesser rent and value growth prospects such as UK industrials, shopping centers and French industrials. The outlook for the fundamentals of the European CMBS market remains strong. The one and only question is: When will the irrational liquidity crisis in the ABS market end?

10 Insurance wrapped receivables financing – a suggestion for real estate assets

Patrick Trutwein
Volker Helms

Table of contents

1   Introduction

Insurance wrapped receivables financing as an opportunity for real estate markets

While insurance wrapped receivables financing predominantly saw its recent growth in trade related import-export transactions, its characteristics suggest viable solutions for real estate capital markets. In particular, the structural and risk-mitigating features make it worthwhile to explore the concept as an idea for at least four types of real estate related businesses:

- financing backed by real estate receivables portfolios in sub-investment grade regions with limited or no transparency,

- project risk insurance in politically instable countries,

- funding of receivables portfolios held by suppliers of technical equipment used during the construction period,

- financing for development companies with outstanding receivables to an array of awarding authorities and other large clients.

This chapter aims to present the key aspects of insurance wrapped receivables financing (as already successfully done in trade finance), to provide some suggestions and inspire thought in the context of real estate capital markets.

2   Key elements and definitions of receivables financing

In today's financial industry, countless forms of receivables financing are offered by a great variety of service providers: banks, forfeiters, factoring companies, securitization houses, financial arms/subsidiaries of corporations, specialized entities or broker-like institutions solely focused on receivables financing.

Definitions of key words

Given this vast spectrum of applications, it is noted that structures can be fairly similar, but the terminology used often is not. Hence, the most relevant terms shall be defined for the purpose of more clarity throughout this chapter:

Receivable:	Payment obligation arising from an underlying commercial transaction.
Seller:	The originator of the receivables, e. g., via sale of a certain product.
Obligor:	The buyer of respective goods, owing a form of (recurring) cash payment.
Purchaser:	In this case the bank or entity the receivables are sold to.
Insurer:	The insurance company insuring the receivables against non-payment by the obligor also referred to as the underwriter.
Advance rate:	The percentage rate that is applied to the face value of a receivable or pool of receivables, in order to determine the amount the seller receives from the purchaser.

Receivables financing can occur without the true sale of the receivables to the purchaser. A bank or another financing entity may advance funds without a transfer of ownership. In these cases, the receivables will serve as collateral for the financing and will most likely be pledged for the benefit of the financing entity.

3   Receivables financing in practice: relevance, application areas and characteristics

Any financial institution of the size and scope of an international player will have several areas or locations where receivables are used to provide or enhance financing. The most traditional form might be the advancing of funds to an exporter (i. e., the seller) covered by an assignment of the proceeds from the export receivables. If the obligor had a bank issuing a letter of credit on his behalf, then the bank will rely on the issuing bank's credit rating for the purpose of determining the underlying risk. If furthermore the letter of credit has a deferred payment term, then the performance risk of producing and exporting the goods as well as their acceptance by the obligor is limited. The remaining pure payment risk of the issuing bank replaces the payment risk of the obligor. Whenever banks are documenting their payment guarantee by accepting or issuing a promissory note, they give way to forfeiting, the trading of usually short and medium-term bank debt related to or financing underlying trade.

Institutional background

Trade financing has obviously developed a variety of new products and has also implemented new technologies as they became available. In its core, however, trade financing is what it always has been: A form of receivables financing by advancing funds before payment by the obligor, and thus providing liquidity for transactions.

While traditional trade financing is generally applied on a transactional basis or involving a single seller (supplier finance) or a single obligor (vendor financing), securitizations have developed to address portfolios of different asset classes. The underlying receivables may be trade or finance related (e.g., import-export driven or pools of mortgages), and if large and suitable enough, can be securitized and traded in capital markets. However, with securitizations come certain requirements that the sellers can often not meet, or, only at a relatively high price.

A niche can be determined that starts when a seller is generating export receivables that are too large in number to be efficiently handled on a transactional basis. On the other hand, volumes might not be large enough and/ or the characteristics of receivables might not be suitable for a securitization. In contrast, receivables financing solutions have been tailored to meet the seller's objectives. The most commonly used structure is the insured receivables purchase facility which, as mentioned above, might also be found to be a useful tool in real estate financing.

Various opportunities for applications

Receivables financing facilities can be as small as US$ 20 million or can have a size of US$ 500 million or more. The number of obligors can vary from single digit to several hundred names. For securitizations, volumes of several billions and obligors in the thousands are not uncommon and securitizations may also be suitable for smaller portfolios and/or in cases where fewer obligors are involved. However, they tend to use domestic receivables rather than exports and they are typically addressing the flow of a large number of smaller individual amounts in order to avoid concentration risk. Furthermore, they are often able to use historic data as to dilutions and defaults, in order to determine advance rates and also to obtain required ratings.

Receivables financing facilities do have a strong commercial aspect and almost always include, or are even limited to, export receivables. Sales of commercial goods and services do have a different cycle. Seasonal aspects as to the demand and production of goods become relevant. Purchase orders in a particular year do mean little for the next year's demand for these goods. Portfolios of mortgages, consumer loans or credit cards are either long term in nature or provide a high likelihood for stable volumes or flows for the coming years. Not so much for commercial activities, and, if we add the cross-border aspect to the equation it becomes more obvious. Why do export receivables change a portfolio intended for securitization? There are a number of reasons: sales to overseas customers are less predictable, since the seller competes with other multinational companies and buyers can also source from local providers of goods. Cycles of offer and demand, trade barriers, exchange rates, etc., all affect projections for future sales. The same applies to dilutions and the credit risk for any particular foreign obligor. Finally, country risks add another layer of complexity.

A portfolio of trade receivables and export receivables can still be securitized. But the particularities of these portfolios will likely be punished by the more generalist approach of the securitization. While securitizations may have their advantages in large and homorganic pools of receivables, in the case of export receivables the opposite holds true. The low transparency, less predictability and increased uncertainty will result in lower advance rates and/or increased cost. These trade portfolios, however, do offer a series of advantages, and banks specialized in trade finance know that. For this reason specialized banks design insured receivables purchase facilities where a seller's trade or export portfolio preserves its value. These facilities offer specific benefits, because the particularities of these receivables are enhancing the structure, resulting in higher advance rates and lower all-in costs while at the same time all major advantages of a securitization are offered as well.

Design of trade and export receivables

The typical seller that has a sizable volume of trade and export receivables is able to breakdown his annual sales or projected sales by country and by obligor. Average payment terms or historic data will permit the seller to calculate the actual Days Sales Outstanding (DSO). A company's balance sheet often does not lead to the DSO number relevant for the objectives of the seller. For example: A seller reports outstanding receivables of US$ 100 million at December 31st. Sales for that year were US$ 400 million. The static DSO would toss out 90 days. It would be a mistake to assume that the seller has the potential for a securitization or Receivables Purchase Facility of US$ 100 million. A breakdown by obligors might reveal the following:

Obligor	Country	Sales in US$	Payment terms
A	A	100 million	30 days
B	B	100 million	60 days
C	C	50 million	30 days
D	D	50 million	60 days
E	E	10 million	90 days
F	F	90 million	advance payment

According to the above table and without considering seasonal factors, the potential facility amount based on average unpaid receivables would only be US$ 40 million. Without entering the pro's and con's of a securitization, it can be assumed that in this case the seller is no longer compelled to follow the requirements and pay the associated costs of a securitization. Instead, a US$ 40 million insured receivables purchase facility could be implemented with the resulting effects as described in section 6.

4   Advantages of insurance companies

Regulators require banks to analyze, approve, document, report and monitor its exposure at any time. Two different kinds of exposure are relevant: counterparty exposure resulting from funded operations, and potential exposure in connection with committed lines of credit.

Purchases of receivables by banks

This means that if a bank finances a company, then its exposure is directly with the seller as counterparty. Receivables of the seller may be pledged as collateral to secure the financing, in this case receivables serving merely as general collateral possibly required the bank's credit department and usually considered as a risk mitigant. This collateral could also ease the eventual syndication of the loan and even prompt the bank to raise internal counterparty ratings. But this form of collateral does not affect the bank's exposure with any of the obligors that comprise the pledged receivables.

On the other hand, if the bank purchases the receivables, then the obligors become the main source of repayment. The bank might have recourse to the seller in cases that have to be defined and that will be discussed further. But the ability and willingness of the obligors to make payments are now the main focus of the bank. In cases where the seller only sells to a limited number of obligors, the bank might be able to assign individual credit limits per obligor depending on the financial information available and the resulting approvals of its credit department. In addition, exposures to individual obligors will also increase the respective country risk the bank has with the country of origin of each buyer. In any event, the monitoring and reporting of the exposure will depend on the usage, i. e., the volumes of receivables bought from the seller, in its aggregate, until the obligor starts paying.

Problem environment: cyclical nature and seasonality

For the purpose of the seller, there has to be transparency regarding the amount of receivables the bank will be purchasing at any point during the availability of the facility, both per obligor and per country, and also the maximum size of the facility will have to be set up front. And that is where the problem environment can be identified. Because of the cyclical nature of the business and the seasonality of sales, the seller will rarely be able to predict the exposures that will result from its commercial activity during the next 12 months. Regardless, the seller is looking for a commitment from the bank as to each of his potential obligors. The less accurate the forecast is and the more flexibility in terms of sales volumes covered the seller is requesting, the large the amount of limits the bank will have to reserve. However, as can be seen from the example in section 3, the facility size may be for US$ 40 million, but the composition of obligor limits that comprise these US$ 40 million may and will vary throughout the lifetime of the facility. In other words, the seller is looking to obtain a commitment from the bank where the aggregate of the individual counterparty limits is larger than the intended facility size. The simple solution would be a larger facility size, but even if the bank is willing to adjust certain up-front fees, the issue with the reporting of committed lines of credit still remains. And committed lines of credit cost any bank economical capital. In return, banks charge commitment fee for amounts that are committed, but not drawn during a specific time period. Finally, the seller will have to pay a higher price.

Higher flexibility of insurance companies

Insurers, however, have a different way of reporting and are regulated differently. Insurers can underwrite any number of obligors and can assign for each obligor an individual maximum limit. What the facility size is for a bank, the insurer calls it policy limit or maximum limit of liability. The insurer, its re-insurers as well as the regulators are aware of the fact that the aggregate amounts of individual limits are larger than the policy limit. In fact, it is the other way around, i. e., the insurer limits its maximum liability by determining the policy limit. The insurance regulators also count on the fact that the insurer relies on principles of probability. Insurance companies know that it is mathematically less likely that a larger number of the obligors will default at the same time, making it virtually impossible that the seller would ever claim for the entire amount of the policy limit. And for specific large individual limits and for concentration risk in a specific sector, industry or country, re-insurers come into the picture and share the risk. The insurer's cost for underwriting the individual obligor limits is the risk premium. The risk premium is calculated either on individual limits or on sales volume. In both cases, the risk premium reflects the calculated probability of default plus the insurer's profit.

However, while insurers seem to have higher flexibility in extending limits, they also face an important disadvantage: Whenever a potential (but committed) limit for a single obligor is exhausted, the insurer is unable to underwrite this name, for example, for another seller. The same applies to re-insurers. Once a specific name is maxed out, there is no more capacity. As a result, the insurer and/or re-insurer might reconsider its premium calculation upon renewal of the policy.

5   Implementing receivables financing

The relationship manager or senior investment banker will detect an opportunity to "monetize" a client's assets. If receivables play a role then both the securitization group and the structured trade and export finance specialist will be contacted. Depending on whether the ideal solution for the particular client appears to be a securitization or a receivables purchase facility, follow-up visits or calls with the relevant group will be set up in order to precisely determine the situation the client is facing and to formulate different proposals or options for the client's consideration. If the structured financer feels that any kind of receivables financing could be of interest, the first contact with the relevant credit officer (or officers) is established in order to present the client with an array of viable alternatives.

Considering client's needs

These alternatives may include taking clean risk of the seller whether resulting in connection with recourse or through any other combination of factors. Depending on the seller's portfolio of receivables, the structured financer might also contemplate clean risk of certain or all obligors. Other alternatives include making use of existing methods of risk enhancement including the use of letters of credit that are issued by the obligor and confirmed in favor of the seller. While any of these structures are also offered by the structured financer both in form of a tailored solution or as one tranche of a multi-tranche facility, for the purpose of this chapter the determination is assumed that an insured receivables purchase facility is the ideal solution to be offered to the client.

5.1   Seller has existing trade credit insurance

Previous experiences in credit insurance trades

The next step will depend on the fact whether the seller is already making use of trade credit insurance. Many companies have an existing trade credit insurance program, essentially for the sole benefit as a risk mitigation tool. The seller's internal credit department or collection area has established internal comfort levels of acceptable risk for any or all of the following:

- maximum outstanding per obligor,
- maximum payment terms,
- maximum country limit,
- maximum outstanding to a particular sector/industry.

Trade credit insurance will help to lower any of these potential limitations to growth by insuring the seller against the risk of non-payment of the obligor. Reasons covered range from non-acceptance of goods to default/ bankruptcy to country events like moratorium, currency inconvertibility and expropriation.

Even in the absence of any form of financing, trade credit insurance is a very common, traditional and complex tool of risk control. Creditors, rating agencies, auditors and of course shareholders appreciate the intelligent use of this product.

If the seller has existing trade credit insurance, then the structured financer will incorporate the particular aspects of the insurance policy into its Insured Receivables Finance Program. Usually, there is limited or no need to ask the respective underwriter for adjustments in connection with our Program.

5.2   Seller does not have an insurance program

External assistance

In this case the structured financer will suggest the seller to contact a broker specialized in trade credit insurance. The broker will assist the seller in obtaining the most competitive quotes depending on the desired cover and specifics of the insurance policy. A few brokers are also familiar with the structured financer's insured receivables purchase facilities and might therefore also advice the seller of certain additional features or benefits such insurance policy might incorporate. Otherwise, the structured financer can assist in the interpretation of all-in advantages of different insurance quotations.

The process of implementing the right trade credit insurance policy is done in parallel with the documentation of the insured receivables purchase facility.

6   Balanced benefits

Figure 1 illustrates the three main benefits of the Insured Receivables Purchase Facility:

Institutional background

- **Liquidity**
  The sale of receivables will immediately convert the amount reported as account receivable into cash. Working capital requirements are substantially lowered, as well as the financing cost of other debt of the seller.

- **Risk mitigation**
  As explained above, the trade credit insurance has is own, unique advantages.

- **Balance sheet**
  Because most of the described transactions have a true-sale effect, the off-balance sheet implications are critical: Receivables converted into cash will be used to pay down the most expensive debt of the seller. As a result, all relevant ratios improve (DSO, operational efficiency, liquidity ratios, debt ratios, equity ratios). In turn, improvements of ratios (e. g., debt to EBITDA) will result in better ratings and lower borrowing costs for the remaining debt.

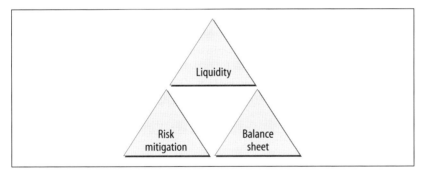

Fig. 1:   Balanced benefits

While every single transaction inevitably comes with all three benefits, each client's main motivation for implementing an insured receivables purchase program varies. For some sellers the risk mitigation part plays the most important role. Others, especially those sellers with elevated financing cost, appreciate the liquidity aspect of the deal. A few clients are most interested in the effects the transaction has on their balance sheet. The majority of sellers wishes a combination of two of the three main features.

7   Structures of transactions

Three general features: true sale, bankruptcy remoteness and trust

Since each transaction has some unique features and/or deal characteristics, the number of structures is unlimited. For simplicity reasons, this chapter is limited to the following three basic and recurring features:

- **True sale**
  For the purpose of off-balance sheet treatment it is critical for the seller that the sale of receivables is registered as a true sale. This includes the respective UCC filings of ownership interest in favor of the buyer, the legal opinion of the seller's counsel and, most importantly, the auditor following suit and recognizing the off-balance sheet effect (see figure 2).

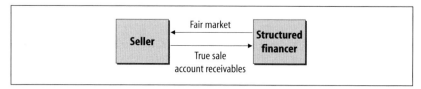

Fig. 2:   True sale

- **Bankruptcy remoteness**
  The buyer, i. e., the bank, might in addition insist on using a Qualified Special Purpose Entity (QSPE). This special purpose entity is bankruptcy remote and the true sale takes place between the seller and the QSPE as the first buyer. The bank then purchases the receivables from the QSPE or provides lending to this entity. In the latter case the bank will file to register a security interest. The financial strength of the seller usually determines whether banks suggest the use of the QSPE, in order to avoid being challenged as a preferred creditor in the case of bankruptcy of the seller (see figure 3).

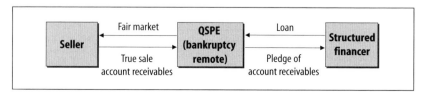

Fig. 3:   Bankruptcy remoteness combined with lending relationship

- **Trust**
  In some cases a trust structure is established to adequately reflect the nature of the risk, i. e., expected repayment from obligors or insurance, instead of from the seller, which a bank might already have direct exposure to. The trust is not owned or controlled by either the buyer or the seller and therefore exposure of the bank vis-à-vis the trust does not add on to existing gross exposure of the seller. In this case structure follows form and is reflective of the true risk exposure of the transaction, i. e., the reliance on servicer quality and the insurance policy (figure 4 shows a complex deal structure involving all of the three features mentioned).

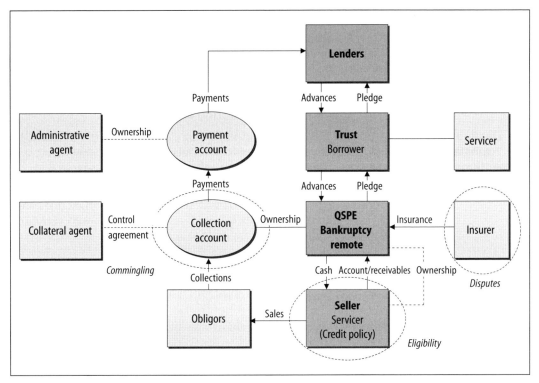

Fig. 4:   Complex deal structure with QSPE and trust

8   Insurance policies

Trade credit insurance policies are not set in stone. Different underwriters use different policy wordings and also have some characteristics that have an effect on the value of such policy to both the seller as well as the purchaser, i. e., the bank as the insured. The main difference is between cancelable limits and non-cancelable limits. In the case of cancelable limits, the insurance company can inform the seller and the insured of any reduction in coverage with a 30-day notification period. On the other hand, non-cancelable limits are in place for the entire policy period and can not be changed to the insured's disadvantage.

Cancelable limits vs. non-cancelable limits

Another differentiating characteristic is the way the insurance premium is assessed. Some underwriters charge a fixed amount in function of the approved limits; others calculate the premium due on the basis of actual sales (insured sales).

For sellers with a widespread portfolio, the insurance company might not go through an individual analysis of each obligor, but rather rely on the seller's experience with the obligor(s) and the seller's internal credit and collection procedures. Discretionary credit limits are approved, i. e., the seller can grant the limits itself up to a certain amount and while observing some rules.

Finally, the policy wording can be more or less "insurer-friendly". The number and nature of exclusions and the claim filing procedures might have an effect on the true quality of a trade credit insurance policy. As always, the insurer is just another provider of financial services competing for the seller's business. Therefore, everything is negotiable.

9   Operating and monitoring activities

Dealing with substantial operational risk

The structured finance team as entire team dedicated to operate receivables purchase facilities. After the team is finished with the documentation and implementation of a transaction, the seller can start selling its receivables.

Depending on the complexity of a deal and of the creditworthiness of the seller, operational risk can be substantial. It is therefore important that banks have an experienced team and solid procedures in place which will control and mitigate any operational risk completely.

On a daily, weekly or monthly basis, the seller presents a list of receivables it intends to sell. The purchaser will compare the list with the insurance policy and with available limits taking into account past utilizations and payments received.

The purchaser accepts the sale and credits the funds to the seller's account. The purchase has taken place. Now the seller conducts its collection in line with the normal course of business. In most cases the obligor does not know that the seller has sold any receivables or that it now owes the face value of the receivable to the purchaser. The seller will, however, ask the obligors to pay the amounts due into an account at his or her consulting bank. Upon receipt of the funds, the seller will inform the purchaser and the cycle is closed. The seller has now new availability for the sale of new receivables with this particular obligor.

The transaction goes on uninterrupted until the end of the facility period and might be extended seamlessly beyond. During the facility period, the seller can ask the insurer to add, increase and/or decrease obligors, individual and country limits.

10   Risk and return

Risk management and returns

Irrespective of the underlying transaction, one universal principle of capital markets will always apply to insurance wrapped receivables financings: A group of lenders is effectively advancing funds, in expectation of an attractive return and avoiding losses on their capital invested. The more complex the deal, the more sophisticated and thorough the due diligence on risk issues has to be. Basically, there are three layers of repayment lenders can gain comfort from.

Although a group of lenders primarily finances receivables, various unacceptable risk characteristics (e.g., no transparency, no payment history, poor credit quality of the seller) require that any form of support has to be based on the credit enhancement, i.e., the insurance policy.

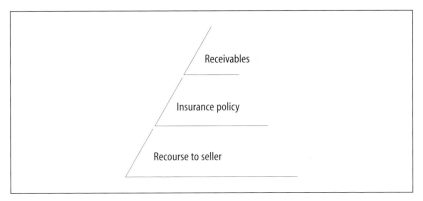

Fig. 5:   Risk layers

Apart from efforts to negotiate very tight, guarantee-like terms for the insurance policy the following features can ideally be employed to further minimize the risk of incurring losses: **Features to minimize risk**

- Ring fenced structures which ensure that a security interest is not consolidated in case of a bankruptcy by the seller.

- Due diligence on the operational and credit processes of the seller.

- Funding "haircuts" (see Glossary) corresponding to payment exclusions and deductibles under the insurance policy.

- Preferably short term funding commitments as well as clearly termination events allowing regular re-consideration.

- Reducing dispute risk between seller and obligors by clear deal documentation.

Ultimately, the goal is obviously not to be left empty handed if one layer breaks away. **Consequences if layer breaks away**

- *Payment default of obligors,* mitigated by insurance policy, adequate documentation and sufficient haircuts.

- *Default of servicer: Mitigants:* Lender's right to change servicer and terminate facility in this case. Security package/structure allowing an independent wind-down of facility.

- *Refusal to pay by insurer* (e. g., protesting eligibility of receivables). *Mitigant:* Tightened documentation regarding exclusions and reps/warranties, and over-collateralization of receivables.

- *Operational risks that can be substantial (e. g., misbooking of receivables), have to be mitigated by clearly defined servicer agreements.*

- *Commingling risk:* All payments from obligors, made to a collection account have to separate from other payment flows. *Mitigants:* Separate collection account of *daily* settlement of the account sub-servicer agreements.

Insurance backing remains conditional

In conclusion, an insurance backing always remains conditional by nature given the fact that eligibility of specific receivables is not reviewed and confirmed/declined by the insurers until they receive a reimbursement claim (unlike an unconditional irrevocable bank guarantee). Typically the main exclusions are:

- *Fraudulent, dishonest, or criminal acts,* omissions, material mis-representations and breaches of warranties or covenants (notification agreements, adherence to standard credit procedures), breaches of law/regulations by the seller.

- *Disputes* between the seller and obligors until resolved between the parties or by a court of law.

- *Insolvency of the insured* or the originators, with the exception of losses on receivables purchased by the insured prior to the occurrence of such insolvency.

Given the cited risks, it is crucial to address some key aspects within complex structures for insurance wrapped receivables financing.

11   Syndication

Reducing risk due to syndication

After the above mentioned risk aspects have been addressed accordingly, the syndication phase of the transaction can start. Because of the structured character of the deal and its complexity it is not always clear who the interested risk takers are. If banks are approached, the most likely contact is the syndication area of that institution as well as the relevant relationship manager. The bank that has limited credit appetite for the seller, but wishes to enhance its business and relationship might find the ideal solution in an insured receivables purchase facility. The risk to the seller is rather limited or has been completely eliminated and an insurance company has taken its place.

The very same reasoning can, however, reduce the support a relationship manager is able to add to the approval of such deal. The fact that counterparty limits of the respective insurer are used will alert the relationship/credit area for the insurance counterparty. There, however, certain structural/operational risk aspects might again call for involvement of the seller's relationship manager. After all, a large part of the transactional success is based on the accuracy of information provided by the seller as well as the continuous servicing of the seller vis-à-vis the obligor's final payment.

For the structured financer participation in these transactions from conduits and funds is interesting. These entities deal with complex structures frequently and are very well qualified to fully appreciate the various risk mitigating features of the deal. Likewise, since these entities obtain funding in the commercial paper market they are usually not shy to commit significant amounts to a given transaction.

12   Vision

For years, insurance wrapped receivables financing has been used in traditional trade financing. Some banks have successfully grown this product and are able to offer structures that meet major corporate finance objectives of their clients.

Insured receivables purchase facilities and real estates

The authors believe that the risk mitigating aspects and their respective features, components and structures found in insured receivables purchase facilities can be adopted for real estate capital markets and that viable solutions are within reach.

11   Strategies to hedge interest rate and foreign exchange exposure

Patrick Butz
Gavan Duemke

Table of contents

1   Introduction

Undesired risks in real estate financings Investing in real estate often carries substantial interest rate risk for the debt capital deployed and if done abroad may carry additional foreign exchange rate risk for the equity capital involved. This assumes local currency debt is being sourced for the project, which is usually done to avoid currency risk on the debt piece of the financing.

Real estate investors usually seek real estate specific risk-return profiles and preponderantly do not want to expose their capital to interest rate or foreign exchange risk-return profiles. Additionally, most banks – and bond holders in case of a securitization – seek to expose their capital to the risk-return profile linked to the borrower credit. Again, interest rate risks or foreign exchange risk-return profiles are not usually part of their desired asset allocation. Most real estate investment fund managers therefore find themselves in a position where both their debt and equity holders may ask for the removal of these undesirable risks that go hand in hand with investing in real estate assets. Just a word of caution at this stage: Contrary to the common belief in continental Europe, fixed rate loans do not solve the interest rate risk problem involved.

2   Case study

The following case study details how to quantify such risks, in terms of their IRR impact, if they remain unhedged. Basic but effective hedging strategies and their IRR impact are compared and a suitable hedging strategy for the underlying financing is developed.

2.1   Assumptions

A EUR-denominated fund purchases a CHF-denominated single asset in Switzerland. The total acquisition cost is CHF 400 million with a closing date of the financing of January 1st, 2008. The floating rate 3-month-CHF-LIBOR financing with a margin of 100 basis points (bps) is provided by a Swiss-based lender. The project is leveraged at 85 % with the asset generating a quarterly

CHF-denominated net income of CHF 5 million and a projected 1 % annual capital growth. The most aggressive exit strategy proposes selling the asset after about three years and worst case, the holding period will be around five years. The performance of the fund is measured in IRR and EUR-denominated equity will be injected at the start of the project only.

2.2 Types of risk involved

The project obviously exposes the EUR-denominated investors to a Swiss real estate risk-return profile, which is what investors desire. However, investors face two additional and unwanted risks: **Interest rate and foreign exchange risks**

- Interest Rate (IR) risk: If 3-month-CHF-LIBOR increases over the life of the project, net income will be eroded and the project IRR will fall.

- Foreign Exchange (FX) risk: If CHF weakens to the EUR, the amount of EUR that can be repatriated to investors will drop and the project IRR will fall.

Both IRR risks can be quantified via standard deviation analysis; the calculations performed assume a 95 % confidence interval. This effectively means there is only a 2.5 % chance that the outcome might be better than the predicted best case IRR prediction and a 2.5 % chance that the outcome might be worse than the predicted worst case IRR prediction. Future 3-month-CHF-LIBOR rates and EUR-CHF exchange rates calculated on this basis are shown in figures 1 and 2.

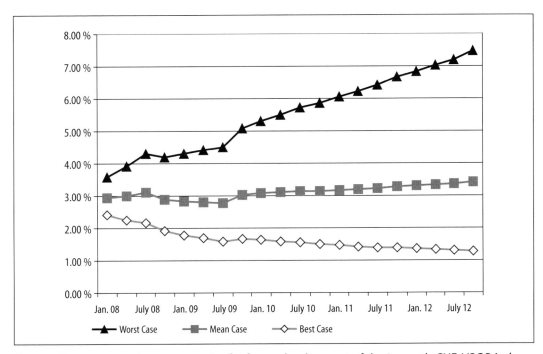

Fig. 1:   *Best, mean and worst scenarios for future development of the 3-month-CHF-LIBOR index*

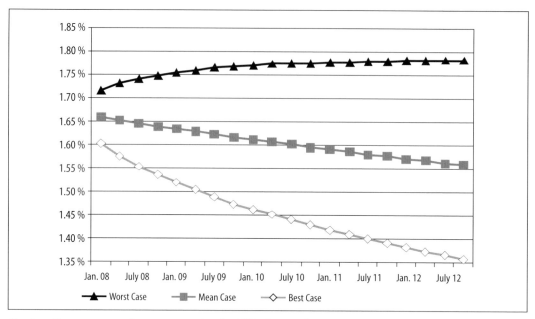

Fig. 2:   Best, mean and worst scenarios for EUR-CHF exchange rates

Best case if unhedged   Figure 3 shows the best case projected IRR if neither the IR nor the FX risk are hedged. The financing could yield an IRR of around 30% to the equity holders. This assumes most favorable (two standard deviation) movements of CHF interest rates and the EUR-CHF exchange rate in favor of the investors. Measuring the CHF-denominated IRR yields around 26%, which means the project, is mainly sensitive to IR movements. Obviously, having both "risks" move extremely in the investors' favor is a highly unlikely scenario but the numbers help to understand the upside potential and sensitivity of the project.

Quarter	Rates (%)	Incl. margin (%)	Interest (CHF)	Equity (CHF)	Rental income (CHF)	CHF cash flows	FX rates (%)	EUR cash flows
1	2.41	3.41	−2,900,665	−60,000,000	5,000,000	−57,900,665	1.602	−36,150,330
2	2.25	3.25	−2,764,414		5,000,000	2,235,586	1.575	1,419,790
3	2.17	3.17	−2,696,947		5,000,000	2,303,053	1.553	1,482,923
4	1.91	2.91	−2,470,991		5,000,000	2,529,009	1.537	1,645,584
5	1.78	2.78	−2,366,978		5,000,000	2,633,022	1.520	1,732,286
6	1.68	2.68	−2,281,520		5,000,000	2,718,480	1.505	1,806,457
7	1.59	2.59	−2,204,633		5,000,000	2,795,367	1.490	1,875,872
8	1.67	2.67	−2,272,563		5,000,000	2,727,437	1.474	1,850,736
9	1.63	2.63	−2,235,904		5,000,000	2,764,096	1.463	1,889,624
10	1.59	2.59	−2,199,504		5,000,000	2,800,496	1.453	1,927,820
11	1.55	2.55	−2,165,187		5,000,000	2,834,813	1.441	1,966,970
12	1.50	2.50	−2,125,309		5,000,000	2,874,691	1.430	2,010,546
13	1.46	2.46	−2,093,365		5,000,000	2,906,635	1.420	2,047,507
14	1.43	2.43	−2,064,298		5,000,000	2,935,702	1.410	2,082,069
15	1.40	2.40	−2,036,328		5,000,000	2,963,672	1.401	2,116,129
16	1.38	2.38	−2,021,159		5,000,000	2,978,841	1.391	2,141,123
17	1.35	2.35	−1,996,425		5,000,000	3,003,575	1.382	2,172,829
18	1.32	2.32	−1,972,736		5,000,000	3,027,264	1.374	2,203,641
19	1.29	2.29	−1,949,980		5,000,000	3,050,020	1.365	2,233,879
20	1.28	2.28	−1,939,941	80,404,020	5,000,000	83,464,079	1.357	61,495,171

Loan amount:	CHF 340,000,000	**IRR 30.39 %**
Fixed rate:	3.098 %	
Equity:	CHF 60,000,000	
Annual value increase:	1.000 %	

Fig. 3: IR and FX risk unhedged – best case

Figure 4 shows the worst case project performance if both CHF interest rates and the EUR-CHF exchange rate move in a direction unfavorable (two standard deviations) to investors. In that case the IRR would hover around the 2%-mark. IR again contributes to the vast majority of that number with FX being a minor contributor. Just a word of caution: 2 % might not seem that bad and prompt abandoning the idea of hedging altogether, depending on what the fund's hurdle rate is. If both investors and the lender allow such a thinking, it should be kept in mind that the main reason for the most negative project IRR still being around 2 % is the favorable interest rate differential between EUR and CHF. Interest rate parity helps the project IRRs when exiting the financing. The reverse would be true for higher yielding currencies, for instance, the current situation between euro and pound sterling. In this case, the project IRR could easily become negative.

Worst case if unhedged

End	Rates (%)	Incl. margin (%)	Interest (CHF)	Equity (CHF)	Rental income (CHF)	CHF cash flows	FX rates (%)	EUR cash flows
1	3.58	4.58	−3,889,291	−60,000,000	5,000,000	−58,889,291	1.716	−34,309,263
2	3.93	4.93	−4,188,321		5,000,000	811,679	1.731	469,024
3	4.29	5.29	−4,498,826		5,000,000	501,174	1.741	287,904
4	4.19	5.19	−4,411,668		5,000,000	588,332	1.747	336,807
5	4.31	5.31	−4,510,096		5,000,000	489,904	1.753	279,389
6	4.42	5.42	−4,602,841		5,000,000	397,159	1.759	225,765
7	4.51	5.51	−4,686,374		5,000,000	313,626	1.763	177,848
8	5.10	6.10	−5,182,293		5,000,000	−182,293	1.767	−103,161
9	5.32	6.32	−5,368,468		5,000,000	−368,468	1.770	−208,123
10	5.51	6.51	−5,536,333		5,000,000	−536,333	1.774	−302,411
11	5.71	6.71	−5,702,962		5,000,000	−702,962	1.774	−396,175
12	5.87	6.87	−5,839,925		5,000,000	−839,925	1.775	−473,261
13	6.05	7.05	−5,996,203		5,000,000	−996,203	1.776	−560,940
14	6.23	7.23	−6,148,973		5,000,000	−1,148,973	1.777	−646,537
15	6.41	7.41	−6,301,236		5,000,000	−1,301,236	1.778	−731,783
16	6.66	7.66	−6,510,169		5,000,000	−1,510,169	1.779	−848,886
17	6.85	7.85	−6,668,375		5,000,000	−1,668,375	1.780	−937,350
18	7.03	8.03	−6,821,438		5,000,000	−1,821,438	1.781	−1,022,931
19	7.20	8.20	−6,973,174		5,000,000	−1,973,174	1.781	−1,107,671
20	7.47	8.47	−7,195,738	80,404,020	5,000,000	78,208,282	1.782	43,882,265

Loan amount:	CHF 340,000,000			**IRR 2.33 %**
Fixed rate:	3.098 %			
Equity:	CHF 60,000,000			
Annual value increase:	1.000 %			

Fig. 4:   IR and FX risk unhedged – worst case

Mean case if unhedged Figure 5 shows the project performance based on current market pricing. This assumes that neither interest rates nor exchange rates – themselves a function of interest rates – change over the life of the entire project. Obviously, this is unrealistic but helps to understand the mean IRR performance of the project. The predicted mean performance of around 18 % IRR illustrates how substantial the IRR volatility of the project is: in the best case, the financing could gain around 12 % simply due to favorable IR and FX moves; the worst case would be an IRR loss of 16 %. This variation around the mean is certainly not acceptable to most debt and equity holders if their intention is to invest in real estate rather than the IR or FX market.

End	Rates (%)	Incl. margin (%)	Interest (CHF)	Equity (CHF)	Rental income (CHF)	CHF cash flows	FX rates (%)	EUR cash flows
1	2.95	3.95	−3,358,618	−60,000,000	5,000,000	−58,358,618	1.658	−35,191,834
2	3.00	4.00	−3,402,574		5,000,000	1,597,426	1.651	967,433
3	3.10	4.10	−3,483,877		5,000,000	1,516,123	1.645	921,712
4	2.88	3.88	−3,299,779		5,000,000	1,700,221	1.639	1,037,163
5	2.84	3.84	−3,264,149		5,000,000	1,735,851	1.634	1,062,592
6	2.81	3.81	−3,236,081		5,000,000	1,763,919	1.628	1,083,289
7	2.77	3.77	−3,208,189		5,000,000	1,791,811	1.623	1,104,352
8	3.04	4.04	−3,430,632		5,000,000	1,569,368	1.615	971,504
9	3.08	4.08	−3,464,073		5,000,000	1,535,927	1.611	953,340
10	3.11	4.11	−3,489,595		5,000,000	1,510,405	1.607	939,833
11	3.13	4.13	−3,514,598		5,000,000	1,485,402	1.601	927,622
12	3.15	4.15	−3,523,704		5,000,000	1,476,296	1.595	925,403
13	3.17	4.17	−3,544,174		5,000,000	1,455,826	1.590	915,441
14	3.19	4.19	−3,564,684		5,000,000	1,435,316	1.586	905,220
15	3.22	4.22	−3,584,713		5,000,000	1,415,287	1.581	895,241
16	3.27	4.27	−3,632,330		5,000,000	1,367,670	1.576	867,701
17	3.30	4.30	−3,654,683		5,000,000	1,345,317	1.572	855,963
18	3.32	4.32	−3,675,424		5,000,000	1,324,576	1.567	845,132
19	3.35	4.35	−3,695,650		5,000,000	1,304,350	1.563	834,517
20	3.41	4.41	−3,747,754	80,404,020	5,000,000	81,656,266	1.559	52,380,695

Loan amount:	CHF 340,000,000	**IRR 18.47 %**
Fixed rate:	3.098 %	
Equity:	CHF 60,000,000	
Annual value increase:	1.000 %	

Fig. 5:   IR and FX risk unhedged – mean case

2.3   Hedging interest rate risk

The analysis of both IR and FX risk has demonstrated that the main risk for investors to be concerned about is IR risk. Running IRR numbers on a hedging strategy that removes IR risk but keeps FX risk may provide more insights into the dynamics at work. For now a fairly simplistic hedging strategy is assumed and an interest rate swap is used to hedge the project's IR risk. This materializes in the figures below as a constant interest rate. The only variables that produce IRR volatility therefore are changing FX rates.

The importance of hedging IR risk

Figure 6 illustrates a best case IRR of around 21 %, offset by a worst case performance of roughly 16 % in figure 7 indicating much less IRR volatility than when remaining unhedged. The mean again hovers around the 18%-mark (see figure 8). Compared to staying unhedged, the project now gains around 8 % IRR less if markets move in the investors' favor. However, that downside is offset for investors by losing around 14 % less compared to what would happen if the project remained unhedged.

Hedging IR risk exclusively

Quarter	Rates (%)	Interest (CHF)	Equity (CHF)	Rental income (CHF)	CHF cash flows	FX rates (%)	EUR cash flows
1	4.10	−3,483,300	−60,000,000	5,000,000	−58,483,300	1.602	−36,514,099
2	4.10	−3,483,300		5,000,000	1,516,700	1.575	963,235
3	4.10	−3,483,300		5,000,000	1,516,700	1.553	976,594
4	4.10	−3,483,300		5,000,000	1,516,700	1.537	986,891
5	4.10	−3,483,300		5,000,000	1,516,700	1.520	997,849
6	4.10	−3,483,300		5,000,000	1,516,700	1.505	1,007,862
7	4.10	−3,483,300		5,000,000	1,516,700	1.490	1,017,804
8	4.10	−3,483,300		5,000,000	1,516,700	1.474	1,029,175
9	4.10	−3,483,300		5,000,000	1,516,700	1.463	1,036,864
10	4.10	−3,483,300		5,000,000	1,516,700	1.453	1,044,074
11	4.10	−3,483,300		5,000,000	1,516,700	1.441	1,052,381
12	4.10	−3,483,300		5,000,000	1,516,700	1.430	1,060,773
13	4.10	−3,483,300		5,000,000	1,516,700	1.420	1,068,402
14	4.10	−3,483,300		5,000,000	1,516,700	1.410	1,075,679
15	4.10	−3,483,300		5,000,000	1,516,700	1.401	1,082,958
16	4.10	−3,483,300		5,000,000	1,516,700	1.391	1,090,169
17	4.10	−3,483,300		5,000,000	1,516,700	1.382	1,097,202
18	4.10	−3,483,300		5,000,000	1,516,700	1.374	1,104,054
19	4.10	−3,483,300		5,000,000	1,516,700	1.365	1,110,853
20	4.10	−3,483,300	80,404,020	5,000,000	81,920,720	1.357	60,358,045

Loan amount:	CHF 340,000,000	Equity:	CHF 60,000,000	**IRR 21.04 %**
Fixed rate incl. margin:	4.098 %	Annual value increase:	1.000 %	
Fixed rate:	3.098 %			

Fig. 6:   IR hedged, FX unhedged – best case

Quarter	Rates (%)	Interest (CHF)	Equity (CHF)	Rental income (CHF)	CHF cash flows	FX rates (%)	EUR cash flows
1	4.10	−3,483,300	−60,000,000	5,000,000	−58,483,300	1.716	−34,072,730
2	4.10	−3,483,300		5,000,000	1,516,700	1.731	876,415
3	4.10	−3,483,300		5,000,000	1,516,700	1.741	871,284
4	4.10	−3,483,300		5,000,000	1,516,700	1.747	868,277
5	4.10	−3,483,300		5,000,000	1,516,700	1.753	864,963
6	4.10	−3,483,300		5,000,000	1,516,700	1.759	862,166
7	4.10	−3,483,300		5,000,000	1,516,700	1.763	860,073
8	4.10	−3,483,300		5,000,000	1,516,700	1.767	858,310
9	4.10	−3,483,300		5,000,000	1,516,700	1.770	856,686
10	4.10	−3,483,300		5,000,000	1,516,700	1.774	855,191
11	4.10	−3,483,300		5,000,000	1,516,700	1.774	854,781
12	4.10	−3,483,300		5,000,000	1,516,700	1.775	854,595
13	4.10	−3,483,300		5,000,000	1,516,700	1.776	854,020
14	4.10	−3,483,300		5,000,000	1,516,700	1.777	853,460
15	4.10	−3,483,300		5,000,000	1,516,700	1.778	852,955
16	4.10	−3,483,300		5,000,000	1,516,700	1.779	852,557
17	4.10	−3,483,300		5,000,000	1,516,700	1.780	852,134
18	4.10	−3,483,300		5,000,000	1,516,700	1.781	851,788
19	4.10	−3,483,300		5,000,000	1,516,700	1.781	851,422
20	4.10	−3,483,300	80,404,020	5,000,000	81,920,720	1.782	45,965,294

Loan amount:	CHF 340,000,000	Equity:	CHF 60,000,000	**IRR 15.73 %**
Fixed rate incl. margin:	4.098 %	Annual value increase:	1.000 %	
Fixed rate:	3.098 %			

Fig. 7:   IR hedged, FX unhedged – worst case

Quarter	Rates (%)	Interest (CHF)	Equity (CHF)	Rental income (CHF)	CHF cash flows	FX rates (%)	EUR cash flows
1	4.10	−3,483,300	−60,000,000	5,000,000	−58,483,300	1.658	−35,267,020
2	4.10	−3,483,300		5,000,000	1,516,700	1.651	918,544
3	4.10	−3,483,300		5,000,000	1,516,700	1.645	922,062
4	4.10	−3,483,300		5,000,000	1,516,700	1.639	925,212
5	4.10	−3,483,300		5,000,000	1,516,700	1.634	928,440
6	4.10	−3,483,300		5,000,000	1,516,700	1.628	931,462
7	4.10	−3,483,300		5,000,000	1,516,700	1.623	934,792
8	4.10	−3,483,300		5,000,000	1,516,700	1.615	938,901
9	4.10	−3,483,300		5,000,000	1,516,700	1.611	941,406
10	4.10	−3,483,300		5,000,000	1,516,700	1.607	943,750
11	4.10	−3,483,300		5,000,000	1,516,700	1.601	947,168
12	4.10	−3,483,300		5,000,000	1,516,700	1.595	950,730
13	4.10	−3,483,300		5,000,000	1,516,700	1.590	953,719
14	4.10	−3,483,300		5,000,000	1,516,700	1.586	956,546
15	4.10	−3,483,300		5,000,000	1,516,700	1.581	959,390
16	4.10	−3,483,300		5,000,000	1,516,700	1.576	962,251
17	4.10	−3,483,300		5,000,000	1,516,700	1.572	965,006
18	4.10	−3,483,300		5,000,000	1,516,700	1.567	967,715
19	4.10	−3,483,300		5,000,000	1,516,700	1.563	970,377
20	4.10	−3,483,300	80,404,020	5,000,000	81,920,720	1.559	52,550,337

Loan amount:	CHF 340,000,000		Equity:	CHF 60,000,000		**IRR 18.30 %**
Fixed rate incl. margin:	4.098 %		Annual value increase:	1.000 %		
Fixed rate:	3.098 %					

Fig. 8:   IR hedged, FX unhedged – mean case

An interesting point to mention is that the "expected" cost of removing the 14 % downside risk is the drop of the project's mean IRR from – to be accurate – 18.48 % to 18.30 %. In other words, the cost of protecting against a drop in IRR of 23 % is negligible. This number does take into account the loss of 8 % upside potential.

2.4   Hedging interest rate and foreign exchange risk

Why hedging FX?

Although the main IRR volatility is being introduced by changes in interest rates, investors, or regulators, may insist on hedging FX risk as well. Figure 9 shows the project's IRR if both IR and FX risks are removed. Again, the hedging strategy assumes the IR risk being hedged via a swap and additionally the FX risk is being hedged via a series of forwards. It should be noted that both instruments are obligations rather than options and therefore are inflexible.

Fixed rate loans

The hedging of the IR risk most closely resembles using a fixed rate loan. For the most part, fixed rate loans do not exist in commercial real estate in Europe. Banks that provide fixed rate loans need to hedge themselves internally, often using a simple interest rate swap to hedge a specific IR exposure in order to provide a fixed rate loan to a borrower. Economically, a fixed rate loan equals a floating rate loan with a swap. In practice, however, a fixed rate loan carries several major economic disadvantages for the borrower. Discussing these is not subject of this chapter; however, non-existing two-way breakage, illiquid

Quarter	Rates (%)	Interest (CHF)	Equity (CHF)	Rental income (CHF)	CHF cash flows	FX rates (%)	EUR cash flows
1	4.10	−3,483,300	−60,000,000	5,000,000	−58,483,300	1.658	−35,267,020
2	4.10	−3,483,300		5,000,000	1,516,700	1.651	918,544
3	4.10	−3,483,300		5,000,000	1,516,700	1.645	922,062
4	4.10	−3,483,300		5,000,000	1,516,700	1.639	925,212
5	4.10	−3,483,300		5,000,000	1,516,700	1.634	928,440
6	4.10	−3,483,300		5,000,000	1,516,700	1.628	931,462
7	4.10	−3,483,300		5,000,000	1,516,700	1.623	934,792
8	4.10	−3,483,300		5,000,000	1,516,700	1.615	938,901
9	4.10	−3,483,300		5,000,000	1,516,700	1.611	941,406
10	4.10	−3,483,300		5,000,000	1,516,700	1.607	943,750
11	4.10	−3,483,300		5,000,000	1,516,700	1.601	947,168
12	4.10	−3,483,300		5,000,000	1,516,700	1.595	950,730
13	4.10	−3,483,300		5,000,000	1,516,700	1.590	953,719
14	4.10	−3,483,300		5,000,000	1,516,700	1.586	956,546
15	4.10	−3,483,300		5,000,000	1,516,700	1.581	959,390
16	4.10	−3,483,300		5,000,000	1,516,700	1.576	962,251
17	4.10	−3,483,300		5,000,000	1,516,700	1.572	965,006
18	4.10	−3,483,300		5,000,000	1,516,700	1.567	967,715
19	4.10	−3,483,300		5,000,000	1,516,700	1.563	970,377
20	4.10	−3,483,300	80,404,020	5,000,000	81,920,720	1.559	52,550,337

Loan amount:	CHF 340,000,000	Equity:	CHF 60,000,000	**IRR 18.30 %**
Fixed rate:	4.098 %	Annual value increase:	1.000 %	
Fixed rate incl. margin:	3.098 %	Possible swap breakage:	CHF 23,200,000	

Fig. 9:   Fully hedged with swap and forwards

indices, inflated pricing and a non-fit with the financing are just a few of the issues. Ignoring all of the significant economic disadvantages of a fixed rate loan for now, investors who hedged the IR risk of this investment with an interest rate swap (or a fixed rate loan) have one major problem: It carries an obligation to remain in the financing until maturity, in this example a period of five years. If the asset is sold earlier, after year 3 as is proposed for this project, the swap (or fixed rate loan) could be subject to substantial breakage payments that would impact the IRR.

The risk of being over-hedged
Figure 10 illustrates such a scenario. The hypothetical investors managed to attract an interesting offer for the asset after year 3; a buyer is offering a price which is CHF 10 million above the projected 1 % annual asset value increase and that would generate a project IRR of 25 %, which is very attractive given the expected mean project IRR of around 18 % after five years. The major problem the investors may be facing is illustrated in figure 11. In the event of falling interest rates between entering the financing and accepting the attractive offer after year 3, breakage will have to be paid in order to exit the

Quarter	Rates (%)	Interest (CHF)	Equity (CHF)	Rental income (CHF)	CHF cash flows	FX rates (%)	EUR cash flows
1	4.10	−3,483,300	−60,000,000	5,000,000	−58,483,300	1.658	−35,267,020
2	4.10	−3,483,300		5,000,000	1,516,700	1.651	918,544
3	4.10	−3,483,300		5,000,000	1,516,700	1.645	922,062
4	4.10	−3,483,300		5,000,000	1,516,700	1.639	925,212
5	4.10	−3,483,300		5,000,000	1,516,700	1.634	928,440
6	4.10	−3,483,300		5,000,000	1,516,700	1.628	931,462
7	4.10	−3,483,300		5,000,000	1,516,700	1.623	934,792
8	4.10	−3,483,300		5,000,000	1,516,700	1.615	938,901
9	4.10	−3,483,300		5,000,000	1,516,700	1.611	941,406
10	4.10	−3,483,300		5,000,000	1,516,700	1.607	943,750
11	4.10	−3,483,300		5,000,000	1,516,700	1.601	947,168
12	4.10	−3,483,300	82,120,400	5,000,000	83,637,100	1.595	52,427,192

Loan amount:	CHF 340,000,000	Possible swap breakage:	CHF 23,200,000	**IRR 25.05 %**
Equity:	CHF 60,000,000	Extra premium on sale:	CHF 10,000,000	
Annual value increase:	1.000 %			

Fig. 10: Fully hedged with swap and forwards – exit after three years and no swap breakage payable

Quarter	Rates (%)	Interest (CHF)	Equity (CHF)	Rental income (CHF)	CHF cash flows	FX rates (%)	EUR cash flows
1	4.10	−3,483,300	−60,000,000	5,000,000	−58,483,300	1.658	−35,267,020
2	4.10	−3,483,300		5,000,000	1,516,700	1.651	918,544
3	4.10	−3,483,300		5,000,000	1,516,700	1.645	922,062
4	4.10	−3,483,300		5,000,000	1,516,700	1.639	925,212
5	4.10	−3,483,300		5,000,000	1,516,700	1.634	928,440
6	4.10	−3,483,300		5,000,000	1,516,700	1.628	931,462
7	4.10	−3,483,300		5,000,000	1,516,700	1.623	934,792
8	4.10	−3,483,300		5,000,000	1,516,700	1.615	938,901
9	4.10	−3,483,300		5,000,000	1,516,700	1.611	941,406
10	4.10	−3,483,300		5,000,000	1,516,700	1.607	943,750
11	4.10	−3,483,300		5,000,000	1,516,700	1.601	947,168
12	4.10	−3,483,300	58,920,400	5,000,000	60,437,100	1.595	37,884,473

Loan amount:	CHF 340,000,000	Possible swap breakage:	CHF 23,200,000	**IRR 12.61 %**
Equity:	CHF 60,000,000	Extra premium on sale:	CHF 10,000,000	
Annual value increase:	1.000 %			

Fig. 11: Fully hedged with swap and forwards – exit after three years and worst case swap breakage payable

swap two years earlier, as it was initially contracted for five years. The same would apply to a fixed rate loan. This breakage payment could be as significant as CHF 23.2 million if interest rates fall by two standard deviations. Investors have to hand out a very significant amount of cash and the breakage costs would obviously ruin the handsome 25 % IRR calculated on the exciting sales price the prospective buyer is willing to pay. In fact the project IRR would fall from 25 % to about half, roughly 13 %, when the breakage payment is taken into account.

Hedging strategy has to be in line with the business plan
This is why both, a swap or a fixed rate loan, are wholly unsuitable to hedge the IR risks in this financing. Breaking the FX contract after a strengthening of CHF versus EUR would subject investors to breakage payments on the FX forward contracts as well; however, as the impact of such breakage would be rather minor compared to the magnitude of IR breakage, they are disregarded here to keep the example focussed.

2.5   Partially hedging interest rate and foreign exchange risk

Remaining partially unhedged
The above breakage cost problems may lead investors to adopt a partial hedging strategy. The idea is to hedge the first three years with IR swaps and FX forward contracts and leave the last two years unhedged as investors are uncertain if they were even to remain in the financing for those years. Often both debt and equity holders would not allow this – but for the sake of this example, this freedom is assumed to be granted. Figures 12, 13 and 14 illustrate the IRR impact of such a decision. In the best case, the project IRR hovers around the 25%-mark; in the worst case around 8 %. The expected performance if IR and FX rates remained unchanged (in line with the level at which rates trade today rather than the one they will trade in the future) would be roughly 18 %.

The chosen strategies and their suitability for the hypothetical investors shall be summerized at this stage:

IR and FX unhedged for five years:
Best case: 30 %
Worst case: 2 %
Mean: 18 %
Downside from mean: 16 %

IR hedged and FX unhedged for five years:
Best case: 21 %
Worst case: 16 %
Mean: 18 %
Downside from mean: 2 % (this is an unrealistically low number as it assumes – counter to the business plan – that the project will not be exited after three years and therefore disregards any breakage costs; the true number can be found in the next example as that takes into account potential breakage)

IR and FX hedged:
Fully hedged: 25 % (if remaining in project for five years)
Early exit: 13 % (if remaining in project for three years, assuming an extra CHF 10 million profit upon sale and worst case swap breakage payable)
Downside from fully hedged case: 12 %

Quarter	Rates (%)	Incl. margin (%)	Interest (CHF)	Equity (CHF)	Rental income (CHF)	CHF cash flows	FX rates (%)	EUR cash flows
1	3.10	4.10	−3,483,300	−60,000,000	5,000,000	−58,483,300	1.658	−35,267,020
2	3.10	4.10	−3,483,300		5,000,000	1,516,700	1.651	918,544
3	3.10	4.10	−3,483,300		5,000,000	1,516,700	1.645	922,062
4	3.10	4.10	−3,483,300		5,000,000	1,516,700	1.639	925,212
5	3.10	4.10	−3,483,300		5,000,000	1,516,700	1.634	928,440
6	3.10	4.10	−3,483,300		5,000,000	1,516,700	1.628	931,462
7	3.10	4.10	−3,483,300		5,000,000	1,516,700	1.623	934,792
8	3.10	4.10	−3,483,300		5,000,000	1,516,700	1.615	938,901
9	3.10	4.10	−3,483,300		5,000,000	1,516,700	1.611	941,406
10	3.10	4.10	−3,483,300		5,000,000	1,516,700	1.607	943,750
11	3.10	4.10	−3,483,300		5,000,000	1,516,700	1.601	947,168
12	3.10	4.10	−3,483,300		5,000,000	1,516,700	1.595	950,730
13	1.46	2.46	−2,093,365		5,000,000	2,906,635	1.420	2,047,507
14	1.43	2.43	−2,064,298		5,000,000	2,935,702	1.410	2,082,069
15	1.40	2.40	−2,036,328		5,000,000	2,963,672	1.401	2,116,129
16	1.38	2.38	−2,021,159		5,000,000	2,978,841	1.391	2,141,123
17	1.35	2.35	−1,996,425		5,000,000	3,003,575	1.382	2,172,829
18	1.32	2.32	−1,972,736		5,000,000	3,027,264	1.374	2,203,641
19	1.29	2.29	−1,949,980		5,000,000	3,050,020	1.365	2,233,879
20	1.28	2.28	−1,939,941	80,404,020	5,000,000	83,464,079	1.357	61,495,171

Loan amount:	CHF 340,000,000		Equity:	CHF 60,000,000		**IRR 24.98 %**
Fixed rate:	3.098 %		Annual value increase:	1.000 %		
First three years:	hedged with swap and forwards		Years 4 and 5:	unhedged		

Fig. 12: Fully hedged in year 1 to 3 – unhedged in years 4 and 5 – best case

Quarter	Rates (%)	Incl. margin (%)	Interest (CHF)	Equity (CHF)	Rental income (CHF)	CHF cash flows	FX rates (%)	EUR cash flows
1	3.10	4.10	−3,483,300	−60,000,000	5,000,000	−58,483,300	1.658	−35,267,020
2	3.10	4.10	−3,483,300		5,000,000	1,516,700	1.651	918,544
3	3.10	4.10	−3,483,300		5,000,000	1,516,700	1.645	922,062
4	3.10	4.10	−3,483,300		5,000,000	1,516,700	1.639	925,212
5	3.10	4.10	−3,483,300		5,000,000	1,516,700	1.634	928,440
6	3.10	4.10	−3,483,300		5,000,000	1,516,700	1.628	931,462
7	3.10	4.10	−3,483,300		5,000,000	1,516,700	1.623	934,792
8	3.10	4.10	−3,483,300		5,000,000	1,516,700	1.615	938,901
9	3.10	4.10	−3,483,300		5,000,000	1,516,700	1.611	941,406
10	3.10	4.10	−3,483,300		5,000,000	1,516,700	1.607	943,750
11	3.10	4.10	−3,483,300		5,000,000	1,516,700	1.601	947,168
12	3.10	4.10	−3,483,300		5,000,000	1,516,700	1.595	950,730
13	6.05	7.05	−5,996,203		5,000,000	−996,203	1.776	−560,940
14	6.23	7.23	−6,148,973		5,000,000	−1,148,973	1.777	−646,537
15	6.41	7.41	−6,301,236		5,000,000	−1,301,236	1.778	−731,783
16	6.66	7.66	−6,510,169		5,000,000	−1,510,169	1.779	−848,886
17	6.85	7.85	−6,668,375		5,000,000	−1,668,375	1.780	−937,350
18	7.03	8.03	−6,821,438		5,000,000	−1,821,438	1.781	−1,022,931
19	7.20	8.20	−6,973,174		5,000,000	−1,973,174	1.781	−1,107,671
20	7.47	8.47	−7,195,738	80,404,020	5,000,000	78,208,282	1.782	43,882,265

Loan amount:	CHF 340,000,000		Equity:	CHF 60,000,000		**IRR 7.99 %**
Fixed rate:	3.098 %		Annual value increase:	1.000 %		
First three years:	hedged with swap and forwards		Years 4 and 5:	unhedged		

Fig. 13: Fully hedged in year 1 to 3 – unhedged in years 4 and 5 – worst case

Quarter	Rates (%)	Incl. margin (%)	Interest (CHF)	Equity (CHF)	Rental income (CHF)	CHF cash flows	FX rates (%)	EUR cash flows
1	3.10	4.10	−3,483,300	−60,000,000	5,000,000	−58,483,300	1.658	−35,267,020
2	3.10	4.10	−3,483,300		5,000,000	1,516,700	1.651	918,544
3	3.10	4.10	−3,483,300		5,000,000	1,516,700	1.645	922,062
4	3.10	4.10	−3,483,300		5,000,000	1,516,700	1.639	925,212
5	3.10	4.10	−3,483,300		5,000,000	1,516,700	1.634	928,440
6	3.10	4.10	−3,483,300		5,000,000	1,516,700	1.628	931,462
7	3.10	4.10	−3,483,300		5,000,000	1,516,700	1.623	934,792
8	3.10	4.10	−3,483,300		5,000,000	1,516,700	1.615	938,901
9	3.10	4.10	−3,483,300		5,000,000	1,516,700	1.611	941,406
10	3.10	4.10	−3,483,300		5,000,000	1,516,700	1.607	943,750
11	3.10	4.10	−3,483,300		5,000,000	1,516,700	1.601	947,168
12	3.10	4.10	−3,483,300		5,000,000	1,516,700	1.595	950,730
13	3.17	4.17	−3,544,174		5,000,000	1,455,826	1.590	915,441
14	3.19	4.19	−3,564,684		5,000,000	1,435,316	1.586	905,220
15	3.22	4.22	−3,584,713		5,000,000	1,415,287	1.581	895,241
16	3.27	4.27	−3,632,330		5,000,000	1,367,670	1.576	867,701
17	3.30	4.30	−3,654,683		5,000,000	1,345,317	1.572	855,963
18	3.32	4.32	−3,675,424		5,000,000	1,324,576	1.567	845,132
19	3.35	4.35	−3,695,650		5,000,000	1,304,350	1.563	834,517
20	3.41	4.41	−3,747,754	80,404,020	5,000,000	81,656,266	1.559	52,380,695

Loan amount:	CHF 340,000,000		Equity:	CHF 60,000,000	**IRR 17.96%**
Fixed rate:	3.098%		Annual value increase:	1.000%	
First three years:	hedged with swap and forwards		Years 4 and 5:	unhedged	

Fig. 14: Fully hedged in year 1 to 3 – unhedged in years 4 and 5 – mean case

IR and FX hedged for three years:
Best case: 25%
Worst case: 8%
Mean: 18%
Downside from mean: 10%

2.6   Interim conclusion

As investors care about removal of IRR volatility that is caused by non-real estate specific risk, the numbers that count most in evaluating hedging strategies are both the mean IRR and the potential downside from the mean. Given that there is a high likelihood of exiting the investment after year 3, the above numbers indicate that the mean project IRR in any hedging strategy will range around the 18%-mark. Downside risk from the mean varies between 16% and 10%. The 2% of the second strategy (IR only hedged) are unrealistic as this number disregards breakage risk and therefore has to be neglected.

At this stage, the most favorable strategy would be to hedge both the FX and IR exposure for three years and stay fully exposed on the potentially remaining two years.

2.7 Flexible hedging strategies

Hedging with options

It can be concluded that in the first three years, unwanted IR and FX risk can be eliminated by fixing the interest rates with a swap and entering into forwards to set future exchange rates. In the last two years of the financing where according to the business plan an early sale might take place, IR and FX risk management are more challenging. On the one hand, downside should be eliminated, and on the other hand, flexibility is required so that there is no danger of incurring breakage payments. Whenever flexibility is required, the strategy of choice should be an options based hedge as options offer the right to a predefined worst case rate which can be exercised by the options holder. If future market conditions offer more favorable levels, the option will expire worthless. Options can never become a liability and can be sold to the market at any time, for instance, if the financing is exited early. The downside of an option is that the buyer will have to pay a premium (option cost) to purchase it.

IR hedging with an interest rate cap

There are a number of options strategies to hedge interest rate exposure. The most common and liquid instrument is a cap. The holder of a cap is paying the floating rate up to a certain ceiling rate, the strike rate of the option. In case the floating rate rises above the strike rate the cap seller would pay the interest difference between the strike rate and the floating rate; the lower the strike rate, the higher the premium payable. A cap with a strike rate equal to a swap with the same underlying economic details (index, calculation periods, notional amount) is called at-the-money. Purchasing a cap below the at-the-money rate would effectively mean that interest is partly paid up-front which does not make much sense from an IRR point of view. The cap strike should be chosen to be as high as the business plan allows the interest payments to become without violating any covenants, e.g., interest cover ratio or debt service cover ratio. In this example the cap strike is set to be 3.5 %.

Financing of the premium

The premium for this cap can be calculated to be CHF 2.6 million. In order to achieve IRR efficiency, investors are seeking to avoid upfront payments and therefore might consider financing the cap premium over the lifetime of the project, however, since the business plan requires flexibility after year 3, the cap premium should be fully paid by the beginning of the fourth year. For the sake of operational efficiency, the swap premium payment can be netted with any swap payments; i.e., the cap premium is embedded into the swap rate. Rather than paying a premium of CHF 2.6 million the cap premium can be financed by an increase in the swap rate of 26.5 basis points, which equals the present value of the cap premium.

FX hedging with foreign exchange options

The same dynamics apply to the hedging of the FX exposure. The potential early exit after year 3 requires flexibility which can be attained by purchasing FX options. The strike rate is a defined future exchange rate. Now the CHF repatriation after the first quarter in year 3 is taken as an example in this example calculations. The option strike rate is set to be equal to the forward rate of 1.5903 for the end of this quarter. A high EUR-CHF exchange rate creates less euros for the same amount of Swiss francs. In case the market rate rises above the strike, the option can be exercised and a rate of 1.5903 is guaranteed. If on the other hand the exchange rate falls below 1.5903, the CHF an be exchanged in the market and the option expires worthless. As such, once the premium is paid an option cannot become a liability at any time; it will always be an asset and can be sold to the market if not required any more. The premium of an option is dependent on a number of factors including the time to expiry, notional amount and the volatility of the underlying asset. In this example, the option for the repatriation of the CHF 80,404,020 (equity plus assumed profit upon asset sale) is by far the one with the highest premium (CHF 1,875,000). The option premium for the hedging of the interim cash flows is around CHF 2.3 million. The premiums for the FX options are paid up-front.

IRR analysis of a mixed swap, forward and options hedge

Figures 15, 16 and 17 illustrate the IRR impact on the same financing where the first three years are hedged with a swap and a string of forwards and in years 4 and 5 with a cap and a string of FX options. As mentioned above, the cap premium is embedded in to the swap rate so that only the FX option premium is paid up-front.

Quarter	Floating (%)	Rate (%)	Incl. margin (%)	Interest (CHF)	Equity (CHF)	Rental income (CHF)	CHF cash flows	FX strike	Best rate	Rate (%)	EUR cash flows
1		3.25	4.25	−3,612,760	−62,333,937	5,000,000	−60,946,698	1.658		1.658	−36,752,516
2		3.25	4.25	−3,612,760		5,000,000	1,387,240	1.651		1.651	840,140
3		3.25	4.25	−3,612,760		5,000,000	1,387,240	1.645		1.645	843,358
4		3.25	4.25	−3,612,760		5,000,000	1,387,240	1.639		1.639	846,239
5		3.25	4.25	−3,612,760		5,000,000	1,387,240	1.634		1.634	849,192
6		3.25	4.25	−3,612,760		5,000,000	1,387,240	1.628		1.628	851,956
7		3.25	4.25	−3,612,760		5,000,000	1,387,240	1.623		1.623	855,001
8		3.25	4.25	−3,612,760		5,000,000	1,387,240	1.615		1.615	858,759
9		3.25	4.25	−3,612,760		5,000,000	1,387,240	1.611		1.611	861,051
10		3.25	4.25	−3,612,760		5,000,000	1,387,240	1.607		1.607	863,194
11		3.25	4.25	−3,612,760		5,000,000	1,387,240	1.601		1.601	866,321
12		3.25	4.25	−3,612,760		5,000,000	1,387,240	1.595		1.595	869,579
13	1.46	1.46	2.46	−2,093,365		5,000,000	2,906,635	1.590	1.420	1.420	2,047,507
14	1.43	1.43	2.43	−2,064,298		5,000,000	2,935,702	1.586	1.410	1.410	2,082,069
15	1.40	1.40	2.40	−2,036,328		5,000,000	2,963,672	1.581	1.401	1.401	2,116,129
16	1.38	1.38	2.38	−2,021,159		5,000,000	2,978,841	1.576	1.391	1.391	2,141,123
17	1.35	1.35	2.35	−1,996,425		5,000,000	3,003,575	1.572	1.382	1.382	2,172,829
18	1.32	1.32	2.32	−1,972,736		5,000,000	3,027,264	1.567	1.374	1.374	2,203,641
19	1.29	1.29	2.29	−1,949,980		5,000,000	3,050,020	1.563	1.365	1.365	2,233,879
20	1.28	1.28	2.28	−1,939,941	80,404,020	5,000,000	83,464,079	1.559	1.357	1.357	61,495,171

Loan amount:	CHF 340,000,000	Cap strike:	3.500 %			**23.09 %**
Fixed rate 3-year swap:	2.9850 %	Cap premium:	CHF 2,600,000			
Swap PV01:	CHF 98,000	3-year swap rate incl. premium	3.250 %			
Equity:	CHF 60,000,000					
Annual value increase:	1.000 %	FX option premium:	CHF 2,333,937.45			

Fig 15:   Swap/forward hedge years 1 to 3, options hedge in years 4 and 5 – best case

Quarter	CHF-LIBOR (%)	Rate (%)	Incl. margin (%)	Interest (CHF)	Equity (CHF)	Rental income (CHF)	CHF cash flows	FX strike	Worst rate	Rate (%)	EUR cash flows
1		3.25	4.25	−3,612,760	−62,333,937	5,000,000	−60,946,698	1.658		1.658	−36,752,516
2		3.25	4.25	−3,612,760		5,000,000	1,387,240	1.651		1.651	840,140
3		3.25	4.25	−3,612,760		5,000,000	1,387,240	1.645		1.645	843,358
4		3.25	4.25	−3,612,760		5,000,000	1,387,240	1.639		1.639	846,239
5		3.25	4.25	−3,612,760		5,000,000	1,387,240	1.634		1.634	849,192
6		3.25	4.25	−3,612,760		5,000,000	1,387,240	1.628		1.628	851,956
7		3.25	4.25	−3,612,760		5,000,000	1,387,240	1.623		1.623	855,001
8		3.25	4.25	−3,612,760		5,000,000	1,387,240	1.615		1.615	858,759
9		3.25	4.25	−3,612,760		5,000,000	1,387,240	1.611		1.611	861,051
10		3.25	4.25	−3,612,760		5,000,000	1,387,240	1.607		1.607	863,194
11		3.25	4.25	−3,612,760		5,000,000	1,387,240	1.601		1.601	866,321
12		3.25	4.25	−3,612,760		5,000,000	1,387,240	1.595		1.595	869,579
13	6.05	3.50	4.50	−3,825,000		5,000,000	1,175,000	1.590	1.776	1.590	738,854
14	6.23	3.50	4.50	−3,825,000		5,000,000	1,175,000	1.586	1.777	1.586	741,044
15	6.41	3.50	4.50	−3,825,000		5,000,000	1,175,000	1.581	1.778	1.581	743,248
16	6.66	3.50	4.50	−3,825,000		5,000,000	1,175,000	1.576	1.779	1.576	745,464
17	6.85	3.50	4.50	−3,825,000		5,000,000	1,175,000	1.572	1.780	1.572	747,598
18	7.03	3.50	4.50	−3,825,000		5,000,000	1,175,000	1.567	1.781	1.567	749,697
19	7.20	3.50	4.50	−3,825,000		5,000,000	1,175,000	1.563	1.781	1.563	751,759
20	7.47	3.50	4.50	−3,825,000	80,404,020	5,000,000	81,579,020	1.559	1.782	1.559	52,331,144

Loan amount:	CHF 340,000,000	Cap strike:	3.500%		**15.72%**
Fixed rate 3-year swap:	2.9850%	Cap premium:	CHF 2,600,000		
Swap PV01:	CHF 98,000	3-year swap rate incl. premium	3.250%		
Equity:	CHF 60,000,000				
Annual value increase:	1.000%	FX option premium:	CHF 2,333,937.45		

Fig 16: Swap/forward hedge years 1 to 3, options hedge in years 4 and 5 – worst case

IR and FX hedged, options strategy in years 4 and 5:

Best case: 23%
Worst case: 16%
Mean: 17%
Downside from mean: 1%

This strategy combines the advantages of the strategies discussed so far. The downside from mean of 1% is very low. The IRR difference in the 95% confidence interval is only 7% and provides predictability to investors. Compared to the fully hedged scenario, the mean IRR is only 2% lower. These 2% loss in mean IRR "bought" the flexibility to sell the asset without breakage costs at any time in years 4 and 5.

Again it shall be assumed that there would be the same buyer who is offering the attractive price of CHF 10 million above the assumed asset value and that would generate a project IRR of 25%. Swap or forward breakage would not be a problem any more. Quite the opposite, the options can be sold in the market generating additional cash. This hedging strategy would allow the investors to realize an attractive 25% IRR after year 3.

Quarter	CHF-LIBOR (%)	Rate (%)	Incl. margin (%)	Interest (CHF)	Equity (CHF)	Rental income (CHF)	CHF cash flows	FX strike	Mean rate	Rate (%)	EUR cash flows
1		3.25	4.25	−3,612,760	−60,000,000	5,000,000	−58,612,760	1.658		1.658	−35,345,088
2		3.25	4.25	−3,612,760		5,000,000	1,387,240	1.651		1.651	840,140
3		3.25	4.25	−3,612,760		5,000,000	1,387,240	1.645		1.645	843,358
4		3.25	4.25	−3,612,760		5,000,000	1,387,240	1.639		1.639	846,239
5		3.25	4.25	−3,612,760		5,000,000	1,387,240	1.634		1.634	849,192
6		3.25	4.25	−3,612,760		5,000,000	1,387,240	1.628		1.628	851,956
7		3.25	4.25	−3,612,760		5,000,000	1,387,240	1.623		1.623	855,001
8		3.25	4.25	−3,612,760		5,000,000	1,387,240	1.615		1.615	858,759
9		3.25	4.25	−3,612,760		5,000,000	1,387,240	1.611		1.611	861,051
10		3.25	4.25	−3,612,760		5,000,000	1,387,240	1.607		1.607	863,194
11		3.25	4.25	−3,612,760		5,000,000	1,387,240	1.601		1.601	866,321
12		3.25	4.25	−3,612,760		5,000,000	1,387,240	1.595		1.595	869,579
13	3.17	3.17	4.17	−3,544,174		5,000,000	1,455,826	1.590	1.590	1.590	915,441
14	3.19	3.19	4.19	−3,564,684		5,000,000	1,435,316	1.586	1.586	1.586	905,220
15	3.22	3.22	4.22	−3,584,713		5,000,000	1,415,287	1.581	1.581	1.581	895,241
16	3.27	3.27	4.27	−3,632,330		5,000,000	1,367,670	1.576	1.576	1.576	867,701
17	3.30	3.30	4.30	−3,654,683		5,000,000	1,345,317	1.572	1.572	1.572	855,963
18	3.32	3.32	4.32	−3,675,424		5,000,000	1,324,576	1.567	1.567	1.567	845,132
19	3.35	3.35	4.35	−3,695,650		5,000,000	1,304,350	1.563	1.563	1.563	834,517
20	3.41	3.41	4.41	−3,747,754	80,404,020	5,000,000	81,656,266	1.559	1.559	1.559	52,380,695

Loan amount:	CHF 340,000,000	Cap strike:	3.500 %		**17.31 %**
Fixed rate 3-year swap:	2.9850 %	Cap premium:	CHF 2,600,000		
Swap PV01:	CHF 98,000	3-year swap rate incl. premium	3.250 %		
Equity:	CHF 60,000,000				
Annual value increase:	1.000 %	FX option premium:	CHF 2,333,937.45		

Fig 17: Swap/forward hedge years 1 to 3, options hedge in years 4 and 5 – mean case

The advantage in comparison to the strategy which implements hedges only for the first three years is self evident when looking at the downside from mean. Remaining unhedged in year 4 and 5 results in a downside from mean of 10 %. The difference between best and worst case is a steep 17 %. It is unlikely that investors are willing to accept such a high volatility.

Fixed income derivatives for hedging undesired risks in real estate financings

The majority of all IR and FX risks associated with real estate investments can be hedged with the use of swaps, caps, forwards and FX options. The liquidity is high and trading costs upon entry and exit are relatively low. There is, however, a huge number of fixed income derivatives on offer. Under certain circumstances it might be useful to use other instruments. Cross currency swaps (combination of swap and string of forwards) are used to hedge debt taken out in the home currency. A swaption (option to enter into a swap in the future) can be used to pre-hedge an upcoming financing and the use of cancellable swaps (swaps which can be cancelled at predefined dates) can be used for IR hedging if the desired strike has to be very low. Exotic derivatives add additional and unpredictable risks and cannot be traded efficiently. Exotic derivatives can be considered to be unsuitable to hedge most real estate financing.

3 Conclusion

Real estate investments often carry substantial IR and FX risks which impose volatility on the project IRR. It is therefore necessary to hedge against these unwanted additional risks. A hedge has to serve the requirements of the business plan and an unsuitable hedging strategy can be as inefficient as not hedging at all. IR and FX risks are most effectively hedged with swaps and forwards, respectively. Fixed rate loans are an inefficient – in most cases – combination of a floating rate loan and a swap. If the business plan requires flexibility (e. g., because the asset might be sold early), it is necessary to hedge with options. Optionality does not come for free and a premium is payable to purchase an option. There is a variety of fixed income derivatives on offer but the majority of all financings can be hedged with swaps, caps, forwards and FX options. In certain circumstances it makes sense to use other strategies, e. g., debt taken out in home currency, hedge traded prior to funding. Exotic derivatives introduce additional uncertainties, do not trade efficiently and can largely be considered to be unsuitable to hedge IR and FX risks associated with real estate financings.

12 Private to public: A case study on the IPO of GAGFAH as exit onto the German public market without a REIT structure

Fabian Brämisch
Mark Mietzner

Table of contents

1   Introduction

Biggest real estate IPO in Germany   The European real estate market has been substantially growing in the last three years and the number of real estate IPOs doubled within the 2004 and 2006 period compared to the previous decade. Especially Germany, the biggest European real estate market, attracted considerable attention in this time period. In September 2004, the private equity investor Fortress acquired one of the biggest German real estate companies, GAGFAH, for € 3.5 billion. Thereafter, the new owner restructured the company and acquired other large real estate companies like NILEG (in 2005) and WOBA (in 2006). At the end of 2006, Fortress decided to issue GAGFAH's stocks in Germany's biggest real estate IPO. For several reasons GAGFAH's IPO was a milestone: First, the IPO size was remarkable compared to previous European equity offerings. Second, in contrast to the company acquired by Fortress in 2004 the financial investor issued stocks of a real estate company. Especially, this attracted substantial attention of institutional investors. Furthermore, GAGFAH's IPO can be regarded as a signal for subsequent real estate IPOs. Therefore, this chapter focuses on Germany's largest real estate IPO by analyzing initial and aftermarket performance.

2   Transformation from private to public equity: overview of the European real estate IPO market

Motivation of going public   When a company wants to sell common stocks to the public for the first time and hereby gets listed on a stock exchange this process is usually referred to as an Initial Public Offering (IPO). The stocks may either be existing or new shares issued by the company. The proceeds of the equity offering may be used to finance a company's investment projects or will be received by the selling shareholders.

The decision to go public is the culmination of a long-term strategic plan that has to be prepared and monitored carefully, especially for real estate private equity investors that seek exit possibilities for their investments. In general, the major benefits of an IPO include the possibility to raise external financing whenever needed; enjoy lower financing costs due to higher available information and to allow current investors to retrieve their investments.

Research on real estate IPOs shows that real estate companies are motivated to go public by

- exploiting favorable market conditions,
- raising capital in expectation of increased financing requirements or
- protecting themselves against industry consolidation.

In particular, studies reveal that property companies use the capital markets to raise capital in advance of expected growth in the real estate sector which suggests that real estate IPOs are rather a function of financing needs than pure market timing.

However, going public is costly and may not be appropriate for all firms, even when they are in need of additional financing. The dilution of the ownership structure, an increase in public monitoring and direct financial costs, such as filing costs of prospectus and subsequent federal filings as well as underwriting fees, have to be taken into consideration when considering an IPO decision.

Despite some demerits of going public, figure 1 clearly documents a strong increase of listings of real estate companies in Europe which has experienced outstanding performance since 2003. The FTSE/EPRA Europe total return index delivered a price appreciation of 284 % between 2003 and 2006 which equals a compound annual growth rate of 34 %. In contrast, the compounded annual growth rate between 1994 and 2003 amounts 5 % [1]. Furthermore,

Hot IPO market

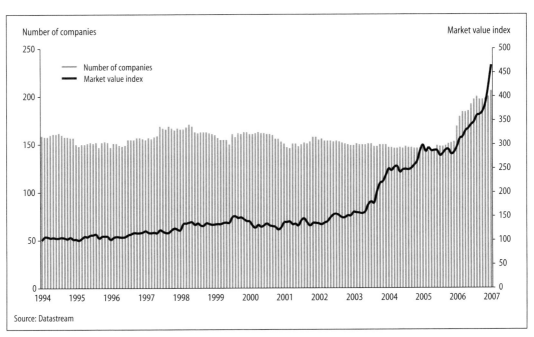

Fig. 1: Development of European real estate share market between 1994 and 2007

figure 1 shows the increase of listed European real estate companies which rose by 34 % from 149 to 200 between 2003 and 2006.

Nevertheless, the European listed real estate universe is still relatively small in absolute and relative terms when compared to other industries. The percentage of wealth tied in listed real estate companies relative to the value of the total investible real estate universe in Europe amounted to 2.83 % as of October 2006. This number is marginal compared to the ratios observable in North America, US (9.67 %) or Asia (9.24 %). As diverse as the market maturity between the continents appears to be, it is even more pronounced across Europe. Some of Europe's more mature property share markets, such as UK, France or Sweden, boast securitized equity levels of more than 5 %, whereas other major real estate markets, such as Germany, only have a small listed real estate universe [2].

This evidence suggests that Europe's real estate capital markets in general and several submarkets in particular should catch up with the international peers over the next few years. Indeed, this trend has already commenced: Between 2004 and 2006, 76 property companies conducted initial public offerings which is more than double the number of property IPOs between 1994 and 2003.

The recent growth in listed real estate companies has been fuelled by several factors. Among the most often cited reasons that might explain the current hot IPO market are:

- the growing investors' interest in real estate stocks due to its favorable risk-return characteristics,
- the introduction of REITs in Germany and the UK as well as
- changing financing needs.

To sum up, the listed property market is bound to experience further growth with an increasing number of companies conducting an IPO. In this context, the chapter will provide insights into the largest real estate IPO in German history including its initial and aftermarket performance.

3   The Initial Public Offering of GAGFAH

3.1   Historical background

First privatization attempts GAGFAH AG was founded in Berlin in 1918 by several employees' associations. 35 years thereafter, in 1953, the company was acquired by the German Federal Insurance Agency for Employees (Bundesversicherungsanstalt für Angestellte – BfA) which was then integrated into the German Social Security Insurance Authority. In June 1996, the German parliament, the Bundestag, decided that the BfA would have to sell GAGFAH to provide additional funding for the surcharged pension system. The privatization was intended to attenuate employees' increasing contributions to the pension insurance fund. At that time, GAGFAH's real estate portfolio encompassed about 72,000 apartments and the estimated value of GAGFAH's real estate portfolio – based on GAGFAH's own calculations – amounted to DM 2 billion. In contrast, politicians and agents of the Federal Audit Office expected the privatization proceeds to range from DM 4.5 billion to DM 10 billion.

Some parties represented in the German parliament disagreed with the decision to sell GAGFAH to strategic or financial investors as a privatization option. On February 26th, 1997, the Social Democratic Party of former German Chancellor Gerhard Schröder suggested the establishment of a public limited company (Deutsche Wohnimmobilien AG) as an umbrella organization for the government's various investments. According to those plans, the company should have been privatized via an initial public offering later on. In detail, they argued that GAGFAH could function as such a holding company for two reasons: First, GAGFAH possessed a major residential portfolio. Second, the company's rental method was subject to common public interest.

However, consultants of the Bankgesellschaft Berlin asserted that privatization proceeds via an IPO were lower compared to a sale to strategic investors. Therefore, the government established a real estate tendering process with 12 bidders representing 30 interested parties. Participants of this tender offer process were national corporations, such as Veba and Thyssen, as well as international companies, e. g., the Nomura Group or NatWest. Nomura submitted an offer of DM 4.5 billion for GAGFAH and – in summer 1998 – the final version of the contract of sale was submitted to the Secretary of Labor, whose approval was mandatory by law. Due to the upcoming elections, the Secretary of Labor hesitated to support the GAGFAH sale. After the elections, the period of commitment ended and in November 1998, Nomura resubmitted an offer of DM 3.9 billion due to its firm-specific as well as general economic changes [3]. Finally, the German government decided to refuse the offer and asserted the reduced purchase price as a reason.

Second property tendering process

In autumn 2003, the government initiated a second property tendering process, which was supervised by the investment bank division of Sal. Oppenheim jr. & Cie. The bidders in the second tendering process deviated significantly from the first round. Especially there was a remarkable interest of private equity investors. Binding offers were submitted by six investors: Cerberus, Fortress, Blackstone, Terra Firma, HSH Nordbank and Corpus. The offer prices ranged from € 2.9 billion to € 3.3 billion resulting in a head-to-head match between Fortress and Terra Firma Capital Partners Ltd. In contrast, GAGFAH's owner (BfA) stated a value of € 1,6 billion for GAGFAH's equity and a debt amount between € 1.3 billion and € 1.4 billion in its financial statement [4]. Finally, in July 2004, the highest offer prevailed and the government accepted Fortress' bid to purchase the company for € 3.5 billion. The equity stake amounted to € 2.12 billion [5] and Fortress had to take over a total of € 1.38 billion of the debt accumulated by GAGFAH.

At that time, the company owned a portfolio of 82,000 apartments, which were located in 120 cities throughout Germany. In addition, the company managed approximately 28,000 units for third parties. After the change in the ownership structure, GAGFAH realigned its strategy; moving from managing real estate to trading it [6]. GAGFAH intended to expand its real estate business and expected to sell approximately 1,500 units in 2005. Furthermore, the company announced to give up its project development unit until 2007 and to increase its real estate portfolio by 18,000 units [7].

In 2003, GAGFAH's revenues amounted to € 507 million and remained almost stable in the year thereafter [8]. The net profit assessed to € 53 million (in 2003) and increased substantially to € 58.7 million in 2004. Consequently, GAGFAH's return on equity increased from 8.4 % in 2003 to 8.5 % in 2005. The return on assets was 5.1 % (in 2003: 4.9 %).

The acquisition of GAGFAH by Fortress – structure of the transaction and its funding
Fortress acquired GAGFAH basically via two investment vehicles: GAG ACQ. Ireland Ltd, Dublin and UC ACQ. Ireland, Dublin. In a first step, both investment funds purchased approximately 97 % of GAGFAH's shares by September 30th, 2004. Thereafter, the investor secured the company's remaining shares from the former majority shareholder; except one single "golden share" which was retained by the BfA. As a part of the acquisition, the purchaser agreed to adopt the existing debt of GAGFAH of € 1.32 billion. The unleveraged company was acquired for € 2.12 billion, whereas the funds used in connection with this acquisition were provided by equity investments of € 800 million [9]. In contrast, GAGFAH S.A.'s prospectus showed an increase in interest expenses in 2005. The reason can be found in the integration of the two investment vehicles and their existing debt of € 1.49 billion, which is related to the financing of the transaction [10]. Concluding from these findings, the two investment vehicles were initially capitalized by equity contributions totaling € 800 million from Fortress and used debt of € 1.49 billion to acquire GAGFAH's stocks. Relating the purchase price of € 2.29 billion to earnings before interest, taxes, depreciation and amortization, yields a value of $6.3 \times \text{EBITDA}_{\text{LTM-2004}}$.

Position	2004 € million	Maturity	Spreads/ interest rates	EBITDA$_{\text{LTM}}$ multiple	In %
Investment vehicles debt	1,488	8	3.19	6.3x	65 %
Total senior debt	1,488	8	3.19	6.3x	65 %
Total debt	**1,488**	**8**	**3.19**	**6.3x**	**65 %**
Sponsor equity	800			3.4x	35 %
Total equity	**800**			**3.4x**	**35 %**
Total sources	**2,288**			**9.7x**	**100 %**
Source: Own illustration, GAGFAH S.A. (2006)					

Fig. 2:   Source of funds

On July 12th, 2005, GAGFAH S.A., which was formerly known as NLG Acquisition Holdings S.C.A., was established as a corporate limited partnership by shares in Luxembourg. Six weeks thereafter (August 30th, 2005), GAGFAH changed its objectives and became a securitization company. One year later, on September 29th, 2006, the enterprise organization changed to that of a stock corporation.

Acquisition of NILEG and WOBA
On August 31st, 2005 and September 2nd, 2005, Fortress acquired the NILEG Holding from NORD/LB via NLG Acquisition GmbH for € 1.54 billion. The acquisition of NILEG was presumably financed by € 1.15 billion of the borrowings under the global loan shown in GAGFAH S.A.'s financial statement as of December 31st, 2005 [11]. In addition, on April 5th, 2006, GAGFAH acquired via Blitz 06-652 GmbH, a German limited liability company, Dresdner

WOBA GMBH for € 1.7 billion [12]. Since the investment vehicle's equity was increased by € 261.5 million prior to the acquisition of WOBA, the transaction was financed by 15.4 % of equity at least.

GAGFAH S.A. proceeded to acquire the investment vehicles as well as GAGFAH Acquisition 1 GmbH. In contrast to the WOBA and NILEG, Acquisition 1 GmbH's object clause was to purchase new residential portfolios. For that purpose, the company acquired a portfolio of 4,400 apartment units from LEG NRW in Dezember 2005. The transaction amounted to a total value of € 136 million. In December 2007, GAGFAH S.A.'s corporate structure can be divided into four units:

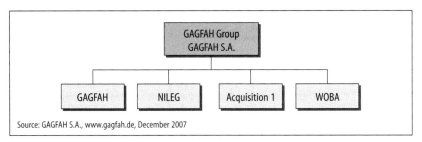

Source: GAGFAH S.A., www.gagfah.de, December 2007

Fig. 3: GAGFAH's company structure

3.2 GAGFAH's equity story and value creation strategies

From the perspective of potential investors, the firm's offering prospectus provides the major source of strategic, competitive and financial information at the time of the IPO. The offering prospectus becomes the primary source of information to investors, particularly individual investors and small institutional investors not participating in the road show process. In the case of GAGFAH, two teams visited seven locations and met with 60 investors in one-on-one meetings. Additionally, 192 investors participated in 12 group meetings [13]. Both, the IPO prospectus and the road show meetings are designed to convince investors of the company's equity story that shall help investors understand
Reaching the investors

- the pricing of the IPO, i. e., whether the shares are underpriced or overpriced and

- the firm's business model whose key elements will be discussed in the following.

With regard to rents, it is essential to exploit the rent increase potential from an under-rented portfolio while maintaining or improving tenant stability and quality of accommodation within the existing German rent law boundaries. GAGFAH sees a high potential for selected modernizations of units in disrepair to facilitate lease-up and rent increases. At the time of the IPO, GAGFAH's portfolio was characterized by an average monthly rent of € 4.76 per sqm, based on an average unit size of 60 sqm. This leads to an average monthly rent per unit of € 285 which is on average 9 % below market levels. At the upper end is Hamburg with 27 % theoretical upside potential and at the lower end is Freiburg with only 2 % downside potential [14].
Rent increase and vacancy reductions

However, creating value via massive rent increases is limited since the market forces of demand and supply also apply for the real estate business and exaggerated rent increases will lead to a drop in demand, resulting in increased vacancy rates. Also legal reasons forbit a massive rent increase in Germany over a short period of time. 20 % maximum incease in three years. High vacancy rates have significant impact on the overall return of a portfolio since the company is not only suffering from the vacancy loss but also has to cover running expenses like property tax, basic heating costs, etc. that can normally be rolled over to the respective tenant. As of June 30th, 2006, the average vacancy rate of GAGFAH was 6.2 % of which two thirds can be found in the WOBA portfolio in Dresden, compared to a relatively low vacancy rate of 4.3 % for all residential rental apartments in Germany [15].

Cost synergies through economies of scale

Increasing operating efficiencies via exploiting cost synergies is another important aspect of value creation for financial investors. Fortress plans to benefit from GAGFAH's size, geographic footprint and centralized corporate infrastructure resulting in significant ongoing cost savings through economies of scale. The company intends to decrease costs for repairs, maintenance and capital expenditures by reducing general and administrative expenses via already initiated cost saving initiatives as well as taking advantage of its purchasing power. According to GAGFAH's IPO prospectus, first efficiency gains via improved cost controlling had been realized and have resulted in an overall cost reduction of 35 % within one and a half years [16].

Earnings accretive acquisitions

Next to the above mentioned organic growth strategies, residential real estate companies can also rely on earnings accretive acquisitions for wealth creation purposes. GAGFAH accomplishes this goal by specializing on smaller-sized as well as large portfolio acquisitions in Germany. Through its operational capability and capacity, the company will be able to integrate and operate further residential property acquisitions at low marginal costs and to realize sustainable ongoing cost savings.

Figure 4 shows an illustrative example of an earnings accretive acquisition for GAGFAH. The calculation is based on an assumed capital raising for the acquisition of 28,000 residential units valued at € 50,000 each. The resulting investment volume of € 1.4 billion is in line with GAGFAH's plans to double its residential portfolio within five years. The cost of financing was incorporated at 100 basis points (bps) over GAGFAH's current cost of debt to reflect a rising interest rate environment [17].

Synthetic REIT structure

GAGFAH's corporate structure had to be designed in such a way that it was and still is able to attract investors. Therefore, the company intended to pay out a substantial part of its Funds From Operations (FFO) as dividends in a tax efficient way that can compete with the newly introduced G-REITs. The solution is to build a synthetic REIT structure which orients to the regulatory payout requirements of REIT regimes that qualify for tax-exempt status on corporate level, paying out 80 % to 90 % of their taxable income. This could be accomplished by locating GAGFAH's headquarter in Luxembourg which provides the opportunity to benefit from a regulatory environment with low tax rates and allowed GAGFAH to target a payout ratio of circa 80 % going forward. The advantage of a headquarter in Luxembourg lies in the high

Acquisition (€ million)		Impact (€ million)	
Purchased assets	1,400	Issue new shares	
Equity invested	350	17.5 m @ € 20 per share	350
Equity in %	25%		
Debt in %	75%	Shares at H1 2006 (m)	225
		Annualized FFO at H1 2006 (m)	157
Asset yield (unleveraged)	5.3%	Annualized FFO per share (€)	0.70
Cost of financing	4.6%		
		New number of shares (m)	243
NOI	74.20	New FFO	181
Cost of financing	−48.30	New FFO per share (€)	0.75
FFO pre-tax	25.90	**Increase in FFO per share**	**7%**
Levered yield	7.4%	**Increase in FFO per share (€)**	**0.05**
Tax rate	10%		
FFO post-tax	23.31		
Leveraged net yield	6.7%		
Source: Deutsche Bank, 2007			

Fig. 4:   *Illustrative example of an earnings accretive acquisition*

discrepancies of tax rates within Europe. Since the firm's FFO paid out to GAGFAH's investors are taxed at moderate levels, set by the Luxembourgian tax law, the payout cash flows qualify as normal dividends which will be taxed on investor level via the half-income system. In contrast, dividends paid out by German REITs are not regarded as dividends and have to be fully taxed on investor level. Thus, the Luxembourg model might be a competitive alternative to the G-REIT.

3.3   Fortress' exit

Fortress' exit

Since GAGFAH's equity offering was comparatively large for a European real estate sector IPO, it attracted considerable attention. Fortress mentioned that the entire order book was filled within one day; indicating the great demand in GAGFAH's shares [18]. Market experts name as one of the main reasons for the strong demand for GAGFAH shares the lack of other German residential companies to invest in and the involvement of Fortress, which is known for its professionalism and high returns. Referring to the ownership structure of the IPO, not only domestic investors were interested in the German real estate group, but also US investors, who received around 50% of the shares issued, and retail investors, who achieved 1.8% of GAGFAH's shares [19]. The great interest that was spent on the company's shares led to a shortening of the bookbuilding period from October 18th to October 20th, 2006 [20]. Finally, 19.96% or 44.9 million (including an exercise of the full Greenshoe Option) of GAGFAH S.A.'s shares have been listed on the Frankfurt Stock Exchange (FWB) on October 19th, 2006. The offer price was set at € 19, representing the upper end of the bookbuilding range and gave GAGFAH a market value of nearly € 4.3 billion, making it the biggest German-listed real estate company, ahead of IVG Immobilien and the second largest IPO in the year 2006 in Germany.

Fortress retained a 71.36 % stake in the company and received the proceeds and proposed to provide the opportunity to the company to get access to new funds for financing its growth process [21]. However, an increase of capital was not planned and the proceeds from GAGFAH's IPO accrued to Fortress, amounting to €853 million. [22]. Even if GAGFAH planned to finance future acquisitions by a seasoned equity offering, Fortress would not increase its capital.

Exercise of greenshoe option and freefloat
Greenshoe options typically allow underwriters to sell up to 15 % more shares than the original number set by the issuer, if demand conditions warrant such action. A greenshoe option can provide additional price stability to a security issue because the underwriter has the ability to increase supply and smooth out price fluctuations if demand surges. Deutsche Bank AG, Goldman Sachs International, Dresdner Bank AG and Morgan Stanley Bank AG, on behalf of the underwriters, fully exercised the call-option which Fortress had granted in connection with the IPO of GAGFAH to purchase up to 2.1 million additional shares of the company from the selling shareholders at the IPO offer price of €19 per share. The company's free float has thereby increased to 44.9 million shares, or 19.95 % which was for Fortress the minimum required issuance ratio in order to produce a sufficient free float to qualify GAGFAH for a listing on the MDAX midcap index. On December 18th, 2006, Deutsche Börse decided a change in its equity indices MDAX and SDAX and included GAGFAH in the MDAX. In exchange, Fielmann was removed and put back to the SDAX. GAGFAH was admitted on the basis of the so-called fast-entry rule, because the company is ranked 40th or higher in terms of both market capitalization and trading volume.

First trading day
On the first trading day, GAGFAH shares closed at €23.60, an increase of 24 %. However, according to the estimates of available equity-research reports, GAGFAH was trading at a €13 to €14 Net Asset Value (NAV) per share, which represents a 78 % premium to the NAV and makes the company look highly overvalued at that date. Whether the high valuation level was justified, will be analyzed in the following IPO performance analysis of GAGFAH.

3.4   Initial and aftermarket performance

Stock performance of GAGFAH
Between October 20th, 2006, the date of GAGFAH's IPO, and November 2006 the share price increased to its maximum value of €25.4. However, at the end of 2007, the company's share price closed at €11.7 which is more than 38 % below the initial public offering price of €19, representing a decline in market capitalization of more than €1.6 billion. Compared to the DIMAX, which was adjusted for the GAGFAH's stock performance, figure 5 clearly shows that the majority of German real estate securities outperformed GAGFAH in the beginning. However, with the outcome of the subprime crisis, the market turned down as well, closing nearly 20 % below its level of October 2006.

Whether these performance patterns are consistent with previous findings on IPO performance will be discussed in the following.

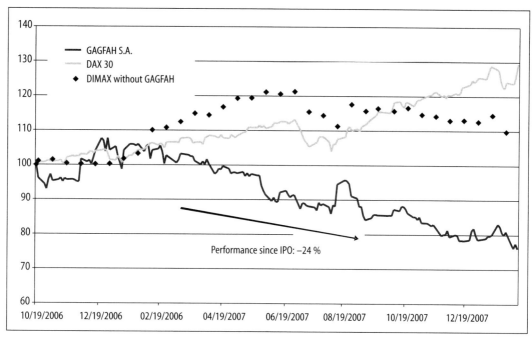

Fig. 5:   Stock performance of GAGFAH

Much of the scholarly research on emerging publicly traded firm valuations has focused on the well-recognized phenomenon of underpricing, where the short-term post-IPO equity price is significantly higher than the initial IPO price, thus generating high abnormal returns on the first trading day. Studies show that especially relatively immature real estate markets experience lower levels of underpricing than the more mature markets in the UK, US and Hong Kong [23]. The big exception is Australia, which is one of the most mature REIT markets in the world. Research shows that Australia has very low underpricing levels that can be attributed to low valuation uncertainty because of the high interest of institutional investors for real estate company IPOs, transparent property markets and a strict regulatory framework [24].

Underpricing phenomena

In terms of issue size and aftermarket standard deviation, a positive correlation with the overall underpricing level has been identified. Larger issue sizes are likely to be managed more professionally and hence likely to experience less underpricing.

In contrast, the relationship of debt and underpricing levels are negatively correlated, meaning that highly leveraged companies generate only moderate first day returns. The negative relation between underpricing and debt ratios might explain that growth firms are less able to access the debt market due to their higher risk profile and instead turn to the equity markets. Investors are assumed to be aware of these company characteristics and thus require a higher underpricing due to the higher risk [25].

Another empirical finding is a significant relation between property type as well as specialization level with the underpricing phenomena. Diversified companies generate lower initial returns than their specialized peers which might be attributable to the companies' investment strategy which attempts to reduce systematic risk.

Aftermarket performance Findings on long-term or aftermarket performance of real estate IPOs are not as clear as the underpricing phenomena. Findings indicate that property IPOs underperform the benchmark over a 36-month period after the IPO. In particular, development companies outperform their investment peers over the first 16 months before this trend reverses and development companies significantly underperform the investment companies over the following 20 months [26]. However, there are other studies that are not in line with these findings. As diverse as the evidence appears, the opposing results might be due to differing measurement periods. In general, the findings indicate that the property companies outperform the market over a short-run period of 100 to 200 days and then underperform the benchmark. However, with a negative performance of 24 % during the first 126 trading days, this does not hold true for GAGFAH. A more in depth analysis of the IPO performance of the 10 largest German real estate IPOs that took place in 2006 will be conducted in the following and will be compared and discussed in the light of the previously mentioned evidence of anomalous behavior of equity offerings.

Data and methodology The sample is comprised of 10 initial public offerings of Germany real estate companies in 2006. To evaluate the aftermarket performance – meaning the performance after the first trading day – a buy-and-hold return (BAHR) measure is used. Returns are calculated for two intervals: the initial return period (one day), defined as the percentage change between the offer price and the closing price of the first trading day and the aftermarket period, defined as the six months after the IPO exclusive of the initial return period. The initial return period is defined to be month 0, and the aftermarket period includes the following six months where months are defined as successive 21-trading-day periods relative to the IPO date. Thus, month 1 consists of event days 2 to 22, month 2 consists of event days 23 to 43 etc. [27].

In order to identify abnormal performance figures, the primarily calculated returns are corrected for a benchmark return. The abnormal initial return is taken as the difference between the first day return and the benchmark return for the corresponding day. The monthly aftermarket benchmark-adjusted returns are calculated as the monthly raw return on a stock minus the monthly benchmark return for the corresponding 21-trading-day period. The benchmark used is the FTSE/EPRA Germany Index which is structured in such a way that it can be considered to represent general trends in German real estate stocks. The index series is designed to reflect the stock performance of companies engaged in specific aspects of the German real estate markets as perceived by institutional investors.

Results The following figure shows the abnormal initial return and the abnormal BAHR of the 10 largest initial public offerings of German real estate companies that took place in 2006. The size of the bubbles represents each company's respective issuing volume. For categorization reasons, the figure has been

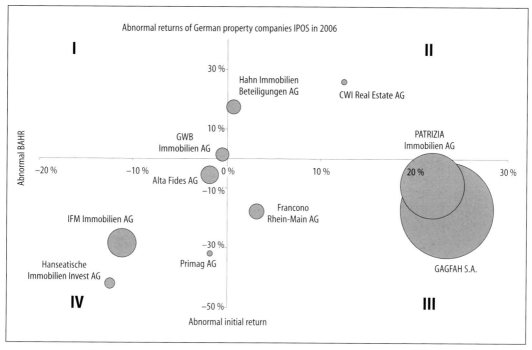

Fig. 6:   IPO performance of German real estate companies in 2006

subdivided into four different quadrants, which will be discussed in the following.

Quadrant I

The only company in quadrant I is GWB Immobilien AG. However, with an abnormal initial return of –0.48 % and an abnormal BAHR of 1.30 %, the performance of the company is almost equal to the return of the benchmark FTSE/EPRA Germany. GWB is a leading player in the German niche market of the real estate industry. The company has specialized in administrating and building commercial real estates and retail centers. Founded in 1992, the firm has 16 employees and can profit from long-term market knowledge and long standing relations between management and key customers. The company's clear story line and its focus on retail centers and specialized retail in Germany's midsize towns shows potential for the future. Although the firm's fundamentals look promising, the company could not outperform the market. This may be attributed to the company's small issuing volume of € 17,625,000 and a free float of only around 30 %.

Quadrant II

Quadrant II represents all companies that have outperformed the benchmark and have achieved positive first day as well as positive BAHR returns. Evidently, CWI Real Estate AG, whose principal activity is trading of residential property, has generated the highest overall return. The company buys, sells, and lets out real estates by taking advantage from special circumstances to generate value for its investors. This includes in particular the acquisition of properties from banks, official receivers and other investors. Trying to sell the remaining housing units after a successful privatization process to current tenants, (inter-)national real estate investors find in CWI Real Estate AG an exclusive partner to buy the remaining units, as long as the investment criteria of the company is met. Thus, the convincing equity story of CWI group fills an attractive niche position by unitizing existing residential portfolio and selling it with profit to investors. The firm's emission volume of only € 3,400,000 seems to be disqualifying investment criteria for institutional investors. However, the company's first trading day was only six days after the successful IPO of GAGFAH and might therefore have benefited from the positive market conditions and at least explain the high abnormal first day return.

The single other company that has achieved overall positive abnormal returns is Hahn Immobilien Beteiligungen AG. For the past 25 years, the Hahn group has specialized in investments in large-scale retail properties. With a rental space of 1.4 million sqm under management spread out over 150 locations and a total volume of investments of around € 2 billion, the Hahn Group ranks as one of Germany's market leaders for the asset management of large-scale retail real estate. The company went public in October 2006 and its IPO raised capital of € 20,000,000. Since Hahn Immobilien could not benefit from the momentum of the GAGFAH IPO like CWI Real Estate AG, the group's abnormal first day return is only 1.85 %. However, with a free float of 19 % and a market capitalization of € 174,150,000, (as of May 31st, 2007), Hahn Immobilien Beteiligungen is more than four times larger than the CWI group and thus more attractive for institutional investors. The company's BAHR is 10.89 %.

Quadrant III The two largest IPOs, PATRIZIA Immobilien AG and GAGFAH S.A. can be found in Quadrant III. They have raised € 402,700,000 and € 852,900,000, respectively. They also have by far the highest abnormal initial returns, 23.24 % and 24.21 %, respectively which undermines the big-is-beautiful hypothesis. As it is the case with GAGFAH S.A., PATRIZIA Immobilien AG had no problems to place its 21.77 million shares (including the full exercise of the greenshoe option) on the equity capital market at an offer price of € 18.50. However, during the six-month-aftermarket period, the shares were trading at € 21.13 which equals a BAHR of –9.05 %. The BAHR of –17.27 % of GAGFAH also underperformed the benchmark index by far.

Quadrant IV The fourth quadrant shows all companies that have negative returns only. Four (Alta Fides AG, IFM Immobilien AG, Primag AG and the Hanseatische Immobilien Invest – HII AG) out of 10 real estate IPOs were not able to generate wealth for their investors. HII has by far the worst performance with an abnormal first day return of –12.36 % and an abnormal BAHR of –42.15 %. The company is mainly active in the area of housing real estate in Northern Germany and pursues a strategy of residential privatization and brokerage business. The strategy is supplemented by package trading and the housing real estate stocking. These four business segments might allow on the one hand for a relatively low-risk business model, on the other hand raise questions about a convincing equity story. In addition, the competition has intensified in the acquisition of housing real estate, particularly with packages of 200 residential units or more. The small issuing volume of € 10,530,000 and a free float of 27.5 % might be other explaining factors of the company's underperformance.

To sum up, the analysis shows that five out of 10 initial public offerings of German real estate companies in 2006 could generate a positive abnormal initial return. Since the sample size is far too small to derive a statistical significant conclusion, the analysis is not representative for the German real estate IPO market in general. However, 2006 was the most active year in terms of equity real estate equity issuance and it can be noticed that 50 % of the 10 largest IPOs were underpriced. Regarding the abnormal six-month BAHRs, only three companies came up with positive figures. On average, the companies generated a positive abnormal initial return of 3.42 % and abnormal BAHR of –10.36 %.

4   Final remarks

Summary

The decision of the private equity investor Fortress to issue GAGFAH's stocks in Germany's biggest real estate IPO constitutes Fortress' exit two years after they acquired the real estate company. However, shareholders that acquired GAGFAH shares on its IPO had lost more than 38 % of their investment by the end of 2007. Considering cash flows and share holdings, the private equity investor received considerable returns. The results of our IPO analysis show the IPOs of GAGFAH and PATRIZIA Immobilien have initial abnormal returns of approximately 20 %. While the initial market reaction was positive, market performance for the six months after the IPO was lower than the benchmark. This low market performance represents a negative signal for the German real estate market. This view may be confirmed by the finding that only three out of ten IPOs have positive buy-and-hold returns.

5   Bibliography

[1] EPRA, FTSE EPRA/NAREIT Global Real Estate Index – Monthly Bulletin, Schiphol, October 2006.

[2] EPRA, FTSE EPRA/NAREIT Global Real Estate Index – Monthly Bulletin, Schiphol, October 2006, pp. 4–5.

[3] Börsen-Zeitung, Privatisierung der GAGFAH politisch ausgehebelt: Auf Druck der BfA Verkaufsverfahren beendet – Chance auf Senkung der Rentenbeiträge vertan, April 24th, 1999.

[4] Börsen-Zeitung, Verkauf der GAGFAH geht in die heiße Phase: Sechs Interessenten bieten 2,9 bis 3,3 Mrd. Euro, May 8th, 2004.

[5] Börsen-Zeitung, Fortress übernimmt GAGFAH für 3,5 Mrd. Euro und hat Börsenpläne: Terra Firma zieht den Kürzeren – Sozialklauseln tangieren Erwerber in der Kalkulation nicht – "Vom Wohnungs-verwalter zum Wohnungshändler" – Weitere Akquisitionen, July 16th, 2004.

[6] Financial Times Deutschland, Wohnungsfirma GAGFAH soll bis 2007 an die Börse, April 1st, 2005.

[7] Süddeutsche Zeitung, GAGFAH forciert Börsenpläne, April 1st, 2005.

[8] Börsen-Zeitung, Fortress übernimmt GAGFAH für 3,5 Mrd. Euro und hat Börsenpläne, op. cit.

[9] ib.

[10] GAGFAH S.A., GAGFAH S.A. – IPO prospectus, 2006.

[11] ib.

[12] GAGFAH S.A., Homepage der GAGFAH, www.gagfah.de, December 18th, 2006.

[13] Deutsche Bank, GAGFAH S.A. – Initial public offering – transaction review, 2006, p. 6.

[14] GAGFAH, GAGFAH S.A. – IPO prospectus, 2006, p. 150.

[15] GAGFAH, GAGFAH S.A. – IPO prospectus, 2006, p. 71.

[16] GAGFAH, GAGFAH S.A. – IPO prospectus, 2006, p. 76.

[17] Deutsche Bank, GAGFAH – company research, 2006, p. 19.

[18] Financial Times Deutschland, GAGFAH stößt auf gute Nachfrage, October 13th, 2006.

[19] Frankfurter Allgemeine Zeitung, GAGFAH weckt Appetit auf Immobilienaktien, October 20th, 2006.

[20] Financial Times Deutschland, GAGFAH stößt auf gute Nachfrage, October 13th, 2006.

[21] Financial Times Deutschland, GAGFAH-Wohnungen sollen in MDax, August 4th, 2006.

[22] ib.

[23] Londerville, J., Canadian Real Estate Investment Trusts: A Review of the IPO Literature and Preliminary Analysis of Canadian REIT IPO Pricing, in: Canadian Journal of Administrative Sciences, Vol. 19, No. 4, 2002, p. 367.

[24] Dimovski, W./Brooks, R., The Pricing of Property Trust IPOs in Australia, in: Journal of Real Estate Finance and Economics, Vol. 32, No. 2, 2006, pp. 194-195.

[25] Brounen, D./Eichholtz, P., Initial Public Offerings: Evidence from the British, French and Swedish Property Share Markets, in: Journal of Real Estate Finance and Economics, Vol. 24, No. 1/2, 2002, pp. 108–109.

[26] Gerbich, M./Levis, M./Venmore-Rowland, P., Property Investment and Property Development Firm Performance around Initial Public Offerings and Rights Offerings: U.K. Evidence, in: Journal of Real Estate Finance and Economics, Vol. 18, No. 2, 1999, p. 222.

[27] Ritter, J. R., The Long-Run Performance of Initial Public Offerings, in: The Journal of Finance, Vol. 46, No. 1, 1991, p. 7.

13   Public to private: evidence from the US

Jeffrey A. Barclay

Table of contents

1   Introduction

Remarkable volume and size of privatizations in the US

The privatization of publicly-traded commercial real estate companies in the US since 2005 has been remarkable for both the volume and size of transactions. The public-to-private phenomena reflected an unprecedented fusion of disparate elements of the capital market coming together. The primary drivers of this activity have been the increased appetite for real estate on the part of both large institutional investors and a small group of global investment managers. The appetite was encouraged by the mis-pricing of assets in the public market relative to private market valuations and the marriage of public and private real estate, facilitated by the availability of plentiful and cheap debt capital until the deterioration of credit conditions beginning in the second half of 2007.

Mis-pricing driven by different valuation metrics

The pricing differential was fundamentally driven by intrinsically different valuation metrics applied by the private and public markets. Large, private institutional investors and global investment management firms were able to place a premium on management teams and development projects on public platforms. On the other hand, public market analysts struggled to account for the intrinsic value of either development projects or management teams. As a result, private buyers were comfortable placing a higher valuation on public companies. Other factors also influenced valuation, including the ability of private market investors to use low-cost debt more effectively at higher levels of leverage even though they did not necessarily apply a lower cost of equity. On the other hand, public companies were limited in their ability to use leverage. In addition, while public market investors continued to rely on measures of value such as NAV and measures of return such as FFO and FAD – the calculation of which often ignores components of substantial value – private market investors applied more traditional real estate metrics, including the valuation of development pipelines and the ability to engage in active sales to buyers with even higher pricing models. In some cases, valuing management itself made a difference.

As to the public companies themselves, some management teams were either **Flexibility of** eager to cash out or no longer willing to run public companies, or both, **private formats** preferring instead the flexibility and relative independence of private formats. In those cases where boards of directors were very supportive of going private, managements were even more likely to solicit interest from investors, either directly or through Wall Street.

Depending on the objectives of the capital source, the investment manager and the target company, the transactions that took place during this period can be viewed as being based either on a going-concern strategy, on a liquidation strategy, or on some combination thereof. The choice of business model has depended on the combined objectives of both the investment management firm leading the transaction and the target company's management.

2 Background

Private and public markets for the ownership of income producing assets co-exist in many industries. Indeed, the rise of private equity has been a hallmark of the growing sophistication of the capital markets, both in the US and throughout the world [1]. Public-to-private transactions in the commercial real estate asset class may therefore be viewed as simply a subset of this activity, and indeed the dynamics, rationale and many of the participants reflect and resemble those outside real estate. But some elements appear to be peculiar to the real estate investment industry; in some cases they may be (merely) reflective of larger trends, in others sui generis.

The private market for real estate first developed in the 1970s, when US **Change in US** pension laws were amended to permit the ownership of commercial real **pension laws in** estate and investment managers responded by creating separate account and **the 1970s** commingled fund vehicles. Public equity ownership of institutional-quality commercial real estate began even earlier, in the 1960s, but only became a major component of the capital markets much later, as a direct response to and outgrowth of the US real estate depression of the early 1990s.

It is widely known that the modern REIT industry in the US was born in **S-11 or** response to an acute capital shortage. Private operators, developers, managers **Chapter 11** and owners were facing massive foreclosures as equity and debt capital, mostly in private hands, refused to invest in or refinance commercial real estate after sustaining substantial losses. A familiar expression dating back to the early 1990s was that real estate companies had a choice between "S-11" the document required to be filed with the Securities and Exchange Commission to go public, or "Chapter 11" one of the sections of US law pertaining to bankruptcy. Thus, in addition to the limitations on their activities imposed by the REIT regulations, including the nature of acceptable income, acting as a dealer, etc., certain additional structural limitations were imposed to mitigate of risk. The most notable was a relatively low level of total (corporate combined with asset-level) debt.

Turning to the capital markets, the REIT concept of ownership really began in **KIMCO-IPO** earnest with the IPO of KIMCO Realty in November 1992. Public ownership **in 1992** grew rapidly in the 1990s and steadily as private real estate companies, under the direction of a new generation of real estate investment bankers, tapped public markets, using a number of innovative techniques, including the UPREIT structure, corporate-level financing of real estate rather than asset-level mortgage debt, and an entirely new set of investment measures [2]. These included NAV, FFO, and FAD, to name a few [3]. With the passage of the REIT Modernization Act of 1999, REITs were permitted to own up to 100 % of the stock of a Taxable REIT Subsidiary (TRS) that could now provide non-customary services to REIT tenants. Since then, the market capitalization of US REITs has increased manifold with a number of REITs included in the widely followed S&P 500 benchmark.

3   Public-to-private transactions since 2005

Public-to-private trend in 2007

Equity investors in US commercial real estate have utilized both private (i. e., direct) and public ownership vehicles for decades, but a trend in public-to-private transactions – which began in 2005 – reached an unprecedented level in 2007, with Equity Office Properties (EOP) at US$ 40 billion, Archstone Smith (ASN) at US$ 22 billion and Hilton Hotels (HLT) at US$ 27 billion going private within months of each other. The institutional investors and investment managers in each case – Blackstone and Lehman Brothers/Tishman Speyer – had a mix of strategic and opportunistic motivations for pursuing the go-private transactions.

	2001	2002	2003	2004	2005	2006	2007
Total M&A deals	10	9	8	13	14	24	15
Total M&A activity (US$, equity)	9.95	2.88	3.49	20.40	22.98	61.95	52.49
Total privatizations	2	2	3	8	11	13	12
Total privatizations (US$, equity)	1.43	0.72	1.53	7.72	17.10	41.93	48.87
Average premium	10.6 %	14.9 %	24.1 %	20.2 %	21.0 %	20.7 %	25.0 %
Source: ING Clarion and Company Filings							

Fig. 1:   Volume of public-to-private transactions (2001–2007)

The volume of privatization was particularly intense during 2005 to 2007 with an approximate cumulative value of US$ 108 billion of public assets converting to private hands. This compares to an annual average of US$ 2.3 billion in privatization transactions during 2000 and 2005 and represented a massive increase in volume and scale. At the same time, the average premium to the closing share price also increased from 10.5 % in 2001 to 25 % in 2007. Clearly, institutional capital, investment managers as well as the capital markets had both come to agreement on the undervaluation of real estate assets in public markets and the higher returns these could generate on the private market.

Desire to unlock value

A study of the conditions that enabled this trend, including why and how such transactions have been consummated, should provide an understanding of why it began and support a view as to how long it may last. Fundamentally, it has been the desire to create or unlock value – either through a strategic alliance or through rapid fire dispositions – that have guided these transactions.

4   Institutional investor objectives

As any other private equity transaction, the rationale for public-to-private in real estate depends on the motives of those who benefit from it. The participants in real estate include institutional investors, who represent the vast majority of the capital. They also include the public companies themselves, led by managements and governed by boards of directors. And finally, they include a handful of investment management firms, in most cases divisions of large (often global) financial institutions.   **Benefits for going private**

With the growing acceptance of real estate as an asset class and its manifold benefits to a mixed asset portfolio, large institutions began to increase or add to their existing allocations from the late 1990s as the technology bubble wreaked havoc on broader equities. Experience over time has shown that adding commercial real estate not only diversifies away some portfolio risk, but also helps to manage asset-liability programs more efficiently given the cash flow rich basis of real estate investment. Moreover, the stellar performance of real estate generated pressure on these large institutions to add to their portfolios. In fact, the largest US pension funds, such as CalPERS, the New York State Common Retirement Fund, and TIAA-CREF are now measured in the hundreds of billions in total assets, implying real estate exposure in the tens of billions assuming an allocation in the typical range of 3 % to 10 % of total assets.

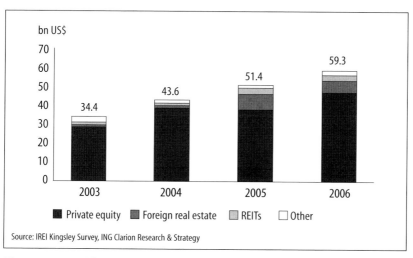

Fig. 2:   Capital flows to real estate

The desire to add commercial real estate to institutional portfolios became a critical driver for the privatizations that followed. Capital flows in the US are estimated to have increased 15 % in 2006, according to IREI's Plan Sponsor Survey. Approximately 80 % of the US$ 59.3 billion of capital estimated to have flowed into real estate in 2006 was channeled into direct asset-owning vehicles, while only 5 % of capital went to REITs implying that there was a substantial volume of capital looking for private commercial real estate. For institutional   **Substantial capital looking for private real estate in 2006** capital therefore, privatization represented an opportunity to gain access to an asset class with well-known diversification capacities in scale. Often the challenge for the large institutions has been putting capital to work on a scale where returns can justify the cost of investing in real estate. The large size of transactions in 2005 to 2007 provided the ideal opportunity for these large institutional investors to deploy capital efficiently, rapidly and to managers with which they have had considerable experience with.

5   Target company objectives

Enhancement of shareholder value?

What did privatization offer to the target company? From a strategic and operational perspective, privatization needed to be handled in a manner that kept in mind the fiduciary duty of the boards of directors and whether the transaction enhanced shareholder value – the ultimate goal for management and the board of directors of these companies.

Strategically, going private has allowed the formerly public real estate company to shed an onerous regulatory framework, focus on long-term value generation and appreciate and align management more closely with the capital sources. From an operational perspective, going private has permitted a higher level of leverage (and therefore, presumably, higher levered returns) and opportunistically to harvest asset sales. Each objective is discussed below.

Operating in a less regulated environment

One objective has been to operate in a less regulated environment where management's focus can be on creating long-term value. Operating as a public company requires adherence to regulatory and reporting requirements. Public real estate companies have severe limitations on asset sales and must remain committed to meeting dividend and FFO-expectations on a quarterly basis. A private platform, on the other hand, has no such responsibility and can invest/divest without any concern for short-term cash flow or a detrimental impact on earnings. Private investors' investment horizon tends to be much longer than that of public companies: The IRR becomes the focus, rather than meeting quarterly divided payments.

Alignment of interest by going private

Management teams in public companies are often faced with the classic agency issue – should the management team work for the benefit of the shareholders, the bondholders or itself? Going private effectively rids the management team of the agency problem [4]. Investors and management on a private platform are closely linked by a tight alignment of interests. With fewer restrictions and competing interests, a private company is able to focus on the principal goal of achieving the highest total return. One of the greatest frustrations of top quality REIT management teams has been the inability of public market analysts to distinguish between the best run and the merely run-of-the-mill companies [5].

Higher leverage as key benefit

From the operational perspective, the key benefits of a private platform include the ability to use higher levels of leverage to generate higher returns. REITs are limited in how much leverage they can use as their credit ratings by the major ratings agencies are determined partly by their debt strategy. In order to maintain an investment-grade rating, REITs target a debt-plus-preferred-stock

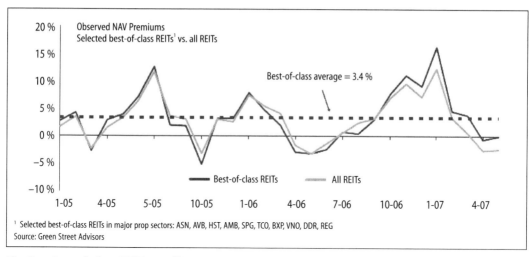

Fig. 3: Best-of-class REITs vs. all REITs

to gross asset ratio in the 40 % to 50 % range. Increases in debt levels may have a substantial impact on a REIT's credit rating.

On the other hand, private companies commonly have leverage levels of 70 % to 90 % of cost or value (and in some cases, and for periods of time, even higher), thereby permitting larger transactions and enhanced returns. Cheap debt and mezzanine borrowings help private buyers obtain this leverage. The use of leverage, whether judicious or injudicious, therefore can significantly enhance returns and thus provide an immediate incentive for public-private transactions. Private platforms thus allow management teams to focus on both strategic and opportunistic acquisitions with the goal of enhancing value.

Another operational benefit of going private is to harvest gains on an opportunistic basis. Private equity investors can also enhance returns by opportunistic sales of assets given the focus on a total return strategy versus meeting dividend payouts on a quarterly basis. There are severe restrictions on such sales in a public company because of regulatory requirements to meet a high dividend payout ratio. However, such sales can immediately create value on a private platform in the form of higher total returns. For example, in the Equity Office Properties (EOP) transaction, a key strategy for both bidders was to sell off large pieces of the portfolio to realize large and immediate gains.

Harvest gains on an opportunistic basis

It is important to place these motivations in the context of the maturation of the US REIT market, which has evolved from a small, close-knit group of entrepreneurs to a set of large, professionally run public companies. When making the decision to go private, they have been faced with the choice of either retiring from active management or aligning with a larger investment manager with all the requisite resources to grow their business further. More often than not, these management teams have chosen to re-align and enjoy the benefits of a larger platform.

6   Investment manager objectives

Finally, there are the objectives of the investment manager, often the executor of the transaction. The business of managing financial assets has been one of the most successful in history, by every measure: from growth in assets to return on equity. Large national and global financial institutions, often banks, insurance companies or merged entities of both, have created large and highly sophisticated groups of asset managers, often called investment or fund managers more or less interchangeably, to serve the needs of the growing institutions described above.

Growth in Assets Under Management

One objective for such managers is to grow Assets Under Management (AUM) – in fact the business model of many investment managers calls for growth in AUM. The privatization and subsequent transfer of assets to a proprietary platform immediately raises AUM and by implication the fees collected.

Enhance the investment performance

A second objective is to enhance investment performance. Strategically, acquiring a portfolio of assets can help an investment manager position for long-term growth while also harnessing short-term performance by selectively disposing of assets.

Burnish/add to real estate portfolio in cases of underweight

A third objective for large multi-asset investment managers has been to burnish or add to their real estate portfolio in cases when they are underweight the asset class in an efficient and cost-effective manner. Many multi-strategy platforms have participated in recent privatizations because they were underweight real estate as an asset class. In all three cases, the motivation for the investment manager is to increase the value of its business, through both higher fee income and a higher multiple on its income.

Diversification and expansion of platform

Investment managers can accomplish the objectives above via two principal strategies. One strategy may be called a "diversification and expansion of platform" objective where the end goal of the investment manager is to gain access not only to the assets of the public company but the management team and platform with the ultimate goal of delivering long-term value. Such an objective can also be considered to be strategic in aim with the goal of the investor not so much in the realization of immediate value through break up and sale of assets but in long-term farming and harvesting.

Desire to unlock value

The other objective behind privatization of public real estate companies has been the desire to unlock value though the individual sale of assets that command a higher price. The goal behind such take out privatizations is typically not strategic in nature but on the shorter horizon of generating the highest returns possible. Such an objective may be characterized as an absolute return goal which relies heavily on light covenant, usually floating rate, high Loan-to-Value debt and groups of buyers of the disaggregated assets who can actively "work" them. Such an absolute return strategy works best in a benign credit environment where the risk premium attached to real estate is lower than the historical norm.

In both instances, the goal of the investment manager is to generate higher returns than would have been possible in the public markets for the reasons that have already been discussed. Moreover, as real estate in the US became more aggressively priced in the private markets, investors believed that they could grow their portfolios more rapidly and efficiently by buying under-priced REITs. The familiar expression was that real estate was cheaper on Wall Street than it was on Main Street.

7 Observations from a case study: Gables Residential Trust

In 2005, a large European/global investment manager initiated a privatization that opened the floodgates of the go-private transactions that followed. The investment manager took private a large, established apartment company: Gables Residential Trust owned and managed a diverse and high-quality portfolio of assets across the US. The acquisition of Gables provided an efficient strategy for the investment manager to remedy its underweight to the residential sector and also retain a high-quality management team. The premium paid for the transaction (approximately 18%) was below the average premium paid for privatizations that year (21%) and reflected the undervaluation by public market analysts which failed to adequately value Gables' extensive development pipeline. The investment manager's confidence in paying the premium reflected not only its ability to more accurately asses the real estate, but also its recognition of the value of the management team embedded in Gables – epitomizing the clear objectives that have been mentioned above.

Undervaluation by public market analysts

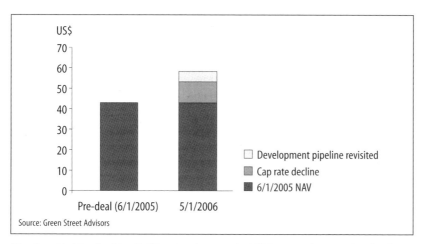

Fig. 4: Gables Residential Trust – changes in NAV pre and post privatization

In an initial analysis by Green Street Advisors in 2005, a highly regarded independent research firm, the enterprise value of Gables Residential Trust was placed at US$ 36 per share. The investment manager, however, additionally priced the development pipeline of the company and thus felt comfortable paying an 18%-premium over the NAV with the knowledge that it would be able to benefit from the gain in value and the significant development pipeline. In April 2006, Green Street placed an enterprise value of US$ 58.25 per share on the company. This 35% increase in valuation within one year effectively validated the investment manager's strategic decision to take the company private.

Valuing the development pipeline

The transaction was unique for the time since there were few known bidders and sources of institutional capital: The investment manager had to hope its assumptions on future growth would be shared by other sources of capital. The speed of bidding also compressed the due diligence period.

8   Expectations for the future

Unique set of factors facilitates going private process   The volume of privatizations that transformed the real estate markets in 2005 to 2007 were facilitated by a unique set of factors that allowed investors and investment managers to pursue both strategic (i. e., platform) and opportunistic (i. e., liquidation) acquisitions to suit their end objectives. A benign capital market environment was a critical enabling factor, as was the anticipation that cash flows from real estate assets would more than offset the higher levels of debt assumed by the privatized entity.

Going forward, much will depend on the state of the capital markets, especially the debt markets. Stricter underwriting standards and tighter loan covenants from the second half of 2007 suggest that highly leveraged buyouts will be much rarer than during 2005 to 2007. The transactions focused on liquidation strategies will likely take a back seat to more strategic, long-term alliances (such as Blackstone/Hilton) as the real estate market cools. It is equally possible for private companies to turn to the public markets to expand and grow – reflecting the fact that the transactions are always a function of the most efficient allocation of capital.

Sovereign Wealth Funds as new source of capital   The addition of new and alternative sources of capital – in the form of Sovereign Wealth Funds (SWFs) – with their long-term investment horizons and patience in achieving maximum value, may once again lead to another phase of privatizations. As is the case in the private equity world, investor demand will drive the direction of the next phase of the public-private cycle enabled by global investment managers.

9   Bibliography

[1] The rise of private equity buyouts in the 1980s spawned a series of books and firms most famous of which was "Barbarians at the Gate" chronicling the takeover of RJR Nabisco by Kohlberg, Kravis and Roberts (KKR).

[2] According to NAREIT, there were 95 IPOs for an aggregate equity investment of US$16.5 billion during 1993 to 1994.

[3] UPREIT = Umbrella Partnership REIT, NAV = Net Asset Value, FFO = Funds From Operations, FAD = Funds Available for Distribution.

[4] There is plenty of literature on the agency issue – seminal works include Jensen and Meckling (1976) and Denis, Denis and Sarin (1997).

[5] Kirby, M. (Green Street Advisors, Inc.), Heard on the Beach, June 1st, 2007.

F   Glossary

Fabian Brämisch
Julia Gentgen

ABCP (Asset Backed Commercial Paper)

An Asset Backed Commercial Paper (ABCP) is short-term debt, generally limited to a tenor of no more than 270 days and is exempt from the registration requirements of the Securities Act of 1933. The proceeds of ABCP issuance are primarily used to obtain interests in various assets. Some common assets financed through ABCP conduits include trade receivables, consumer debt receivables, auto and equipment loans and leases, and Collateralized Debt Obligations (CDOs). The arbitrage business (short- vs. long-term financing) of off-balance ABCP programs is regarded as the systemic reason for the 2007 subprime crisis as individual mortgage customers were connected with institutional money market via intermediating investment banks.

Adjusted Fund From Operation (AFFO) (see also FFO)

Adjusted Fund From Operation (AFFO) is a measure of REIT performance that is widely used by many analysts with concerns about quality of earnings as measured by Funds From Operations (FFO). The most common adjustment to FFO is an estimate of certain recurring capital expenditures needed to keep the property portfolio competitive in its marketplace. For this reason, some analysts also consider AFFO as a measure of REITs' ability to pay its shareholders dividend distribution.

Alpha

The term Alpha is most commonly used with mutual funds and describes the difference between a fund's actual return and its expected return, given the level of risk it takes, as measured by beta. A fund with a positive alpha has done better than expected, while a fund with a negative alpha has underperformed.

Alpha strategy

In designing a portfolio, trustees and investment staff often use their own estimates or data from consultants to forecast the rates of return and volatilities that they might expect in each asset class. Most of these estimates are based on averages from a historical index that represents the asset class. Portable alpha conjures up images of highly complex and sophisticated financial engineering techniques. Entire investment conferences are formed to explain the idea, its structural aspects, and its practical benefits. Simplified, portable alpha is a technique to outperform an index in any asset class in which more traditional methods for outperforming are unlikely to work or are difficult to implement.

Arbitrage

Arbitrage is a concept in valuing and pricing derivative securities. In its purest sense, arbitrage is riskless. If a return greater than the risk-free rate can be earned by holding a portfolio of assets that produces a certain riskless return, then an arbitrage opportunity exists. Thus, arbitrage opportunities arise when assets are mispriced. However, per-transaction profits tend to be small, and they can be consumed entirely by transaction costs. Accordingly, most arbitrage is performed by institutions that have very low transaction costs and that can generate revenue even in a small profit margin environment by doing a large volume of transactions. Arbitrageurs will continue trading until they affect supply and demand enough to bring asset prices to efficient (no-arbitrage) levels.

ARIMA model

Auto Regressive Integrated Moving Average: ARIMA models are the most general class of models for forecasting a time series which can be stationarized by transformations such as differencing and logging. The most simple way to think of ARIMA models is as fine-tuned versions of random-walk and random-trend models: The fine-tuning consists of adding lags of the differenced series and/or lags of the forecast errors to the prediction equation, as needed to remove any last traces of autocorrelation from the forecast errors. Lags of the differenced series appearing in the forecasting equation are called "auto-regressive" terms, lags of the forecast errors are called "moving average" terms, and a time series which needs to be differenced to be made stationary is said to be an "integrated" version of a stationary series. Random-walk and random-trend models, autoregressive models, and exponential smoothing models (i. e., exponential weighted moving averages) are all special cases of ARIMA models.

ARMA model

An ARMA model is a forecasting model or process in which both auto-regression analysis and moving average methods are applied to a well-behaved time series data. ARMA assumes that the time series is stationary and fluctuates more or less uniformly around a time-invariant mean. Non-stationary series need to be differenced one or more times to achieve stationarity. ARMA models are considered inappropriate for impact analysis or for data that incorporates random "shocks".

Arranger

The term arranger is most commonly used in Europe and describes the bank that handles structuring and syndications.

Asset Backed Security (ABS)

An Asset Backed Security is a financial instrument which is secured by a pool of assets. Conceptually, the structure is similar to a Mortgage Backed Security (MBS). Since MBS are backed by mortgages, ABS are backed by non-mortgage assets such as auto loans, credit card receivables, etc. In the US, government guarantees ensure that MBS typically entail no credit risk. ABS do not have such guarantees and therefore entail credit risk. However, due to diversification of the underlying assets and credit enhancement, this risk type tends to be modest. With regard to prepayment risk, ABS are also better off than MBS, since people are more likely to refinance their homes than their credit-card debt in the case of falling interest rates. ABS are appealing to issuers because the structure allows them to get assets off their balance sheets which frees up capital for further receivables. In addition, ABS make it possible for issuers whose unsecured debt is below investment grade to sell investment grade or higher rated debt. To create an ABS, the issuer creates a Special Purpose Vehicle (SPV) to which he sells the assets. In turn, the SPV sells securities (the ABS) to investors in order to refinance the purchase of the assets. In order to protect investors from any defaults due to, e. g., bankruptcy of the issuer, the asset sale is structured as a non-recourse true sale. Further, investors receive a perfected interest in the asset's cash flows, which means that the cash flows are senior to any existing or future third party claims in the event of bankruptcy. Lastly, the non-consolidation rule ensures that the assets of the SPV can not be consolidated with the issuer's assets in the event of bankruptcy. These safeguards allow the issuing company to remove the assets from its balance sheet. Nevertheless, the company continues to service the assets, i. e., collecting interest and principal payments, pursuing delinquencies, etc. For investors, ABS offer a good alternative to investing in highly rated debt, since ABS offer at least similar liquidity and the diversified structure of the underlying assets reduces credit risk. The final structure (different tranches with different credit ratings) of ABS is subject to investor demand and the nature of the underlying asset.

Backstop facility

A backstop facility is a payment assumption by a higher-rated party if the primary debtor cannot meet its obligations, also called Letter of Credit.

Balloon mortgage

A balloon mortgage is a mortgage which does not fully amortize over the term of the note, thus leaving a balance due at maturity. The final payment is called balloon or bullet payment because of its large size. Balloon mortgages are more common in commercial real estate than in residential real estate. A normal structured balloon mortgage looks as follows: The borrower is obliged to make monthly mortgage payments based on a 30-year amortization schedule, and has the choice at the end, e. g., of a 5-year term to either pay off the remaining balance or reset the mortgage. Thus, he benefits from a low monthly payment, like someone with a 30-year loan, but must pay off the loan at the end of the specified term. In general, balloon mortgages have a lower interest rate, and can be easier to qualify for than a traditional 30-year fixed mortgage. There is, however, a risk to consider. At the time, the balloon payment is due, one has to refinance the mortgage, sell the property or convert the balloon mortgage to a traditional mortgage at the current interest rates.

Basis Points (BPs)

A basis point is the smallest measure used in quoting yields on bills, notes, and bonds. One basis point is 0.01 %, or one one-hundredth of a percent of yield. It is commonly used to denote the change in a financial instrument, or the difference (spread) between two interest rates. Although it may be used in any case where percentages are used, it is used for convenience when quantities in percentage points are small. However, since certain loans and bonds may commonly be quoted in relation to some index or underlying security, they will often be quoted as a spread over (or under) the index. For example, a loan that bears interest of 0.50 % above LIBOR is said to be 50 basis points over LIBOR or EURIBOR.

Beauty contest

When a company is considering doing an IPO, the company's executives typically interview a number of investment banks to determine which ones would have the best concept in managing the offering and provide ongoing research reports once the company is public. The parade of investment bankers through a company's offices is known as the beauty contest.

Beta

Beta is a risk metric that is employed primarily in the equity markets. It measures the systematic risk of a single instrument or an entire portfolio. William Sharpe (1964) first used the term beta when introducing the Capital Asset Pricing Model (CAPM). Beta records how volatile and risky investing in an individual stock is compared with the risk of the equity market as a whole. Beta measures how much the individual stock's excess return, defined as the difference between the stock actual performance and the risk-free rate, varies in comparison with movement in the excess return of the market as a whole (usually represented by the market's benchmark index). If the market's excess return rises by 1 % and the stock's excess return rises during the same period by the same 1 % then the stock's beta is 1. The higher the beta the riskier the stock, reflected in its greater required return. A stock with a beta of more than 1 tends to be riskier than the market. A stock with a beta of less than 1 is less risky compared to the market. High beta stocks tend to be in cyclical sectors such as real estate and consumer durables. Low beta stocks, also known as defensive stocks, tend to be in non-cyclical sectors such as food retailing and public utilities.

Bid-ask spread

The bid-ask spread is an indication of the market liquidity for a security/asset. It is the difference between the price that dealers are willing to pay for a security/asset (the bid) and the price at which dealers are willing to sell a security/asset (the ask). If trading activity in a particular security/asset declines, the bid-ask spread will widen (increase), and the issue is considered to be less liquid.

Book building

Book building refers to an exercise by an investment bank, which is lead-managing a new issue to ascertain the likely levels of demand for a security at different prices. It is designed to prevent an issue being undersubscribed because of a large discrepancy between the issue price and the price at which the security starts trading on the secondary market.

Bottom-up approach to investing

The bottom-up approach to investing is an investment strategy which begins by searching for outstanding performance among individual securities or tranches of securities before considering the impact of macro-level economic trends. This approach assumes that an investment in an individual asset will perform well, even if the industry does not perform well.

Bullet loan

Bullet loans are loans that become due and payable in a lump sum when the loan matures at bullet maturity. No principal repayments are being required over the duration of the loan. Prepayments often incur a penalty fee.

Callable bond (redeemable bond)

A callable bond is a bond that can be redeemed (i. e., have its principal repaid) prior to maturity, according to conditions stated at the time of issue. These contractual provisions are detailed in an indenture, also called the deed of trust, which identifies a trustee who holds the indenture, supervises principal and interest payments, and represents bondholders in the event of default. Generally, the issuer of such a bond will "call" the bond if market interest rates fall below the coupon, allowing the company to reissue the debt at the lower market rate. For most callable bonds there is an initial period in which the bond cannot be called. In addition, a premium may be paid to the bondholder when the bond is called.

Call option

A call option is an agreement that gives an investor the right but not the obligation to buy a stock, bond, commodity, or other instrument at a specified price within a specific time period.

Capitalization rate

The capitalization rate (cap rate) is defined as the net operating income for the year divided by the appraised value of the property. It is used as a measure and/or benchmark for a property's value based on current performance. Cap rates also serve as an indicator of investor expectations. A going-in cap rate is the capitalization rate applied to the first year's income. A reversionary or going-out cap rate is the capitalization rate applied to the expected ultimate sale price/value of a building, after a holding period of several years. Typically, this ratio is about 50 basis points higher than a going-in cap rate.

CAPM

The Capital Asset Pricing Model (CAPM) is an economic theory that describes the relationship between risk and expected return and serves as a model for the pricing of risky securities. The CAPM asserts that the only risk that is priced by rational investors is systematic risk, because it cannot be eliminated by diversification. On the other side, there is also unsystematic risk, also called the diversifiable risk, residual risk, or company-specific risk, the risk that is unique to a company such as a strike, the outcome of unfavorable litigation, or a natural catastrophe. The CAPM says that the expected return of a security or a portfolio is equal to the rate on a risk-free security plus a risk premium.

CBO

A Collateralized Bond Obligation (CBO) is an investment-grade bond backed by a pool of junk bonds usually consisting of tiers with different degrees of risk and interest rates.

CFA standards

The CFA Institute Code of Ethics and Standards of Professional Conduct are designed to achieve the mission to lead the investment profession globally by setting high standards of education, integrity, and professional excellence. High ethical standards are critical to maintaining the public's trust in financial markets and in the investment profession. Since their creation in the 1960s, the Code and Standards have promoted the integrity of CFA Institute members and served as a model for measuring the ethics of investment professionals globally, regardless of job function, cultural differences, or local laws and regulations.

Clearinghouse

A clearinghouse is a financial services company that provides clearing and settlement services for financial transactions, usually on a futures exchange. The clearinghouse is responsible for settling trading accounts as well as clearing trades. Other functions include making sure that underlying financial instruments or commodities are actually delivered to fulfill futures contracts, maintaining the margin accounts, and reporting trading data. The clearinghouse acts as third party to all futures and options contracts, i. e., by acting as the opposite side either the buy or the sell side. Thus, the clearinghouse acts as the buyer to every seller and the seller to every buyer, thereby greatly reducing counter party risk.

CLO

A Collateralized Loan Obligation (CLO) is a debt security that is backed by commercial loans.

Closed-end fund

A closed-end fund is a vehicle with a fixed amount of authorized share capital. New shares may not be created on demand. Closed-end funds are also known as closed-end publicly quoted funds in the US and investment trusts in the UK. All participants are treated pro rata and discretion usually resides with the sponsor or advisor. New shares are rarely issued after the fund is launched; shares are not normally redeemable for cash or securities until the fund liquidates. Typically, an investor can acquire shares in a closed-end fund by buying shares on a secondary market from a broker or a market maker as opposed to an open-end fund where all transactions eventually involve the fund company creating new shares on the fly in exchange for either cash or securities or redeeming shares for cash or securities.

Co-integration

Unlike correlation, co-integration refers not to co-movements in returns, but to co-movements in raw asset prices (or exchange rates or yields). If spreads are mean reverting, asset prices are tied together in the long term by some common stochastic trend. Asset prices behaving like this are called to be co-integrated. Since the seminal work of Engle and Granger (1987), co-integration has become the prevalent tool of time series econometrics. Co-integration has emerged as a technique for investigating common trends in multivariate time series, and provides a methodology for modeling both long-run and short-run dynamics in a system.

Collateral

Collateral are assets that are used to secure an obligation. Traditionally, banks require corporate borrowers of loans to use their company assets as security which is nowadays called secured lending or asset-based lending. Collaterals can take many forms such as properties, inventory, equipment, receivables, etc. A more recent development is using collateral to secure repurchase agreements and derivative transactions where the party who owes an obligation to another posts the collateral. In the case of default of the obligation party, the secured party may seize the collateral. However, arrangements requiring the posting of collateral can even be two-sided obligations, such as a swap or foreign exchange forward, meaning that both parties post the collateral according to the value of their total obligation. In a typical collateral arrangement, the obligations are marked-to-market. If any change in the obligation has occurred, the collateral is adjusted, i. e., when market value has risen, the securing party posts additional collateral et vice versa for the case of fallen values. The need for additional collateral is called a margin call.

Collateralized Debt Obligation (CDO)

Collateralized Debt Obligations (CDOs) are securitized interests in pools of generally non-mortgage assets. The assets which are the collateral usually comprise loans or debt instruments. CDO investors bear the credit risk of the collateral. However, via multiple tranches of securities that are issued by the CDO, investors can choose from various maturity and credit risk characteristics. These tranches are categorized according to their degree of credit risk depending on the seniority of the claim, as well as the creditworthiness of the underlying pool of debt securities. A CDO has a sponsoring organization that includes banks, other financial institutions or investment managers. They establish a Special Purpose Vehicle (SPV) to hold collateral and issue securities. CDOs can be structured in many different ways. Today, most CDOs are managed deals with the portfolio manager as sponsor. In managed CDO deals, portfolio managers actively manage the collateral of the CDO, leaving the investor unclear about the specific assets that will serve as collateral. Thus, investors of managed CDO face besides credit risk also the risk of poor management.

Collateralized Mortgage Obligation (CMO)

A Collateralized Mortgage Obligation (CMO) is a type of Mortgage Backed Security (MBS). Unlike a mortgage pass-through, in which all investors participate proportionately in the net cash flows from the mortgage collateral, with a CMO, different bond classes are issued, which participate in different components, called tranches, of the net cash flows. The CMOs are issued by a special purpose entity that is set up by the holder of the loans. The new entity purchases a group of mortgages using the proceeds of an offering of securities collateralized by the mortgages (CMOs). The trust uses the underlying cash flow of the collateral to fund the debt service on the CMOs. The CMOs are priced based on their own maturity and rate of return rather than that of the underlying mortgages. Because CMOs are backed by MBS with fixed maturities, they significantly reduce prepayment risk. Investors in CMOs accept lower interest rates in return for more predictable payments.

Comfort letter

A letter written by the issuer's accounting firm stating the procedures the accountants used to verify the accuracy of numbers included in the Registration Statement. This letter gives "comfort" to the underwriters that the accountants have checked the numbers provided by the issuer in the Registration Statement. This letter is part of the underwriter's due diligence defense in case of a later law suit.

Commercial Mortgage Backed Securities (CMBS)

Commercial Mortgage Backed Securities (CMBS) are securities backed by mortgages on commercial properties such as multifamily apartment buildings, office towers, industrial buildings, hotels, and retail shopping malls. Commercial mortgage securities are usually collateralized by fixed-rate mortgages that are locked out from prepaying for 5 to 10 years but may also have floating-rate bonds collateralized by shorter-term prepayable mortgages. The pool of securities has a multi-class structure starting with investment-grade bonds that are rated triple-A extending all the way down to unrated junior class bonds. If any mortgage loan defaults, losses are allocated to the lowest rated bonds and recoveries are credited to the senior-level investment-grade bonds. This allocation of loss enables the entire collateral loan pool to be sold to a variety of investors.

Commercial paper

The most widely understood and accepted definition of "commercial paper" relates to the mortgage industry when a mortgage company issues a particular type of bond. Commercial paper is a short-term security issued by a company in order to finance short-term costs or increase short-term operating capital. Because commercial paper maturities do not exceed nine months and proceeds typically are used for current transactions, the notes are exempt from registration as securities at the exchange commissions. Due to its low risk, the returns, however, are low. Commercial papers are a way for large companies to borrow money from other large companies without actually borrowing it in a conventional sense, but rather by selling a short-term security.

Commingling risk

A commingling risk describes a SPV's asset shortfall risk resulting from loss or commingling at the level of the originator, other creditors, or debtors. This also includes the risk that assets may be off-set against originator liabilities, e. g., positive account balances against loan debt.

Common stock

When a company issues both common and preferred stock, both have ownership rights; however, only common shares have voting rights, while preferred shares normally have prior claim on dividends and, in the event of liquidation, assets. Common stock holders therefore assume greater risk, but also exert greater control and may gain greater rewards.

Conduit

The term conduit is typically used when referring to the commercial paper issuing vehicle of an Asset Backed Commercial Paper program (ABCP program). Conduits are usually nominally capitalized Special Purpose Vehicles (SPVs), owned by management companies that are independent from the sponsor and structured to be bankruptcy remote. Typically, ABCP conduits contract with various agents to obtain services in connection with the administration and operation of a program. Typical agents involved in an ABCP program are the administrative agent, the issuing and paying agent, the collateral agent, the referral agent, and the manager. While ABCP programs share certain features with term securitizations, they may differ in the following ways:

- Conduits' investments in assets can be revolving and fluctuate in size.

- Conduits may invest in various asset types, thereby creating diversified portfolios.

- Conduits frequently fund long-term assets by issuing short-term liabilities, relying on liquidity support for potential repayment shortfalls caused by asset and liability timing mismatches.

- In conduits, there is no scheduled amortization of assets and liabilities since the additional issuance of commercial papers may be used to, and in most cases is expected to, maintain the conduit's investment in assets.

Coupon

A coupon is the contractual interest obligation a bond or debenture issuer covenants to pay to its debt holders. Coupons are typically paid semi-annually, but some bonds pay annual, quarterly or monthly coupons. Coupons continue to be paid until the bond's maturity date, at which time one final coupon is paid along with the bond's par value.

Covenants

Covenants are a series of restrictions in loan agreements which dictate, to varying degrees, how borrowers can operate and how they can carry themselves financially. Among the most important covenants are the Loan-to-Value ratio (LTV) and the Debt Service Coverage Ratio (DSCR). The LTV is the key in determining the amount of capital that can be obtained to finance a given property. LTV relates the principle portion of a mortgage to the appraised value of a property. The lender will determine an LTV based on factors such as financial history of the business, credit scores, length of loan, etc. After which, the lender will multiply the LTV by the appraised property value to determine the maximum loan amount that can be given to a borrower. The DSCR approaches the mortgage picture from an entirely different angle than the LTV. Where the LTV determines the loan amount based on the value of the property, the DSCR is based upon the cash flow, which is calculated by adding non-cash expenses back to net income, of the property and/or borrower. The debt service is usually taken as an annual figure that includes both repayments of principle and interest payments for a given year.

Credit Default Swap (CDS)

A Credit Default Swap (CDS) is the simplest type of credit derivative. Basic CDS contracts are similar to an insurance. They allow one party to buy protection against a company or country defaulting or restructuring debt over a certain period of time. The buyer of the default protection pays an annual fee in basis points based on a notional amount to the contract seller. If a default occurs, the protection buyer can hand over the defaulted bonds to the contract seller and receive their par value. The contracts can also be cash settled with no transfer of bonds. CDS spreads are similar to regular corporate bond spreads in reflecting the market's view of default risk. Most commonly traded is a 5-year contract, but maturities range from one year to 10 years.

Credit enhancement

Credit enhancement encompasses a variety of methods to reduce credit risk of an obligation. Most of the time credit enhancements are incorporated into over-the-counter derivatives, corporate or securitized debt or other instruments. There are several techniques of credit enhancement. The first method is collateralization, where one or more parties agree to post collateral whose level may vary over time in order to reflect the market value of different parties' obligation. Further, in a third party loan guaranty a parent or third party company is contractually bound to meet obligations in the case of default. Lastly, credit insurance generally provides compensation in the event that a party defaults. Other techniques may sometimes also be referred to as credit enhancement such as netting agreements, credit downgrade triggers, etc.

Credit facility

A credit facility is a type of loan structured for companies that are issued by banks. Specific types of credit facilities are: revolving credit, term loans, committed facilities, Letters of Credit and most retail credit accounts. Credit facilities are often implemented in conjunction with equity issuance in form of initial or secondary public offerings. A key consideration for any company is how it will incorporate debt in its capital structure, at the same time it must consider the parameters of its equity financing. The company must look at its capital structure as a whole, determining how much capital it needs immediately and over time, and the combination of equity and debt that it will use to fulfill those requirements.

Credit rating

Credit ratings measure a borrower's creditworthiness and provide an international framework for comparing the credit quality of issuers and rated debt securities. Rating agencies allocate three kinds of ratings: issuer credit ratings, long-term debt, and short-term debt. Issuer credit ratings are amongst the most widely watched. They measure the creditworthiness of the borrower including its capacity and willingness to meet financial needs. The top credit rating issued by the main agencies – Standard & Poor's, Moody's and Fitch IBCA – is AAA or Aaa. However, these ratings are reserved for a few sovereign and corporate issuers only. Ratings are divided into two broad groups – investment grade which includes all ratings of Baa (Moody's) or BBB (Standard & Poor's) or better and speculative (junk) grade which includes all ratings of Ba (Moody's) or BB (Standard & Poor's) or worse. D symbolizes in default.

Cross-collateralization

Cross-collateralization depicts a practice of using assets as backup or secondary collateral for debt other than the debt they are primarily pledged for. Thus, any deficiency in income or loss on the sale of one property can be made up by the income, or sale of another property. A network of cross-collateralization may facilitate an increase in borrowing or a reduction in borrowing cost.

Default

Default describes the failure to do a required (debt) payment in accordance to a predetermined payment schedule or to comply with other predetermined conditions of an obligation or agreement.

Delinquency

Delinquency represents payment in arrears by an asset pool debtor. There are three main categories of delinquencies: 30 days late, up to 60 days late, and up to 90 days late.

Derivative

A derivative instrument (or simply derivative) is a financial instrument which derives its value from the value of some other financial instrument or variable. Examples of derivatives include futures, options, forwards and swaps. For example, a forward contract can be derived from the spot currency market and the spot markets for borrowing and lending. In the past, derivative instruments tended to be restricted only to those products which could be derived from spot markets. However, today the term seems to be used for any product that can be derived from any other. Exchange-traded derivatives are standardized and backed by a clearinghouse. Derivative instruments are categorized in various ways. One is the distinction between linear and non-linear derivatives. The former have payoff diagrams which are linear or almost linear. The latter has payoff diagrams that are highly non-linear that is always due to the derivative either being an option or having an option embedded in its structure. A somewhat arbitrary distinction is between vanilla and exotic derivatives. (Plain) vanilla derivatives tend to be simple and more common, whereas exotic derivatives are more complicated and specialized. There is no definitive rule for distinguishing one from the other, so the distinction is mostly a matter of custom.

DIMAX

The E&G DIMAX is a composite index for the real estate sector in Germany introduced by bank house Ellwanger & Geiger in 1998 (E&G DIMAX). The criteria to be listed in the DIMAX are to generate a minimum of 75 % of revenue and earning from real estate business which can be leasing activity, facilities management, real estate commerce, development or real estate consulting.

Disintermediation

Disintermediation means the removal of intermediaries, or middlemen, such as bankers and brokers from lending and other financial transactions. Disintermediation is often the result of improved communication and data processing technology, and reduces costs by eliminating layers of commissions and fees. For example, a company can raise funds more efficiently, and from a wider group of investors, by issuing bonds than it can from taking many individual loans.

Diversification

Diversification explains the investment concept that risk within a portfolio can be reduced by increasing the number of individual investments within that portfolio. A portfolio that is invested in multiple instruments whose returns are uncorrelated will have an expected simple return which is the weighted average of the individual instruments' returns. Its volatility will be less than the weighted average of the individual instruments' volatilities. Geography, property type, property size, property age, length of lease terms, or other variables may diversify a real estate portfolio.

Duration

Duration is an indication of the percentage change in the price of a security relative to a change in interest rates, measured in years. It is also called the Macaulay duration. It provides a measure of the price volatility of the security, i.e., the greater the duration, the greater the price volatility relative to a change in interest rates. Positive duration means that the price of a security moves in the opposite direction of a change in interest rates; conversely, negative duration means that the price moves in the same direction as a change in interest rates. For example: A bond has a duration of three years. This means, that the bond's value will decline approximately by 3 % for each 1 % increase in interest rate. This bond is less risky than a bond with a duration of 10 years. Typically, duration of bonds will be positive, whereas shorting fixed income instruments or paying fixed for floating on an interest rate swap have negative durations.

Efficient frontier

The efficient frontier represents combinations of securities portfolios that maximize expected return for any level of expected risk, or that minimizes expected risk for any level of expected return. The efficient frontier was pioneered by Harry Markowitz. The graphical depiction is an efficient set of portfolios which represents the boundary of the set of feasible portfolios that have the maximum return for a given level of risk. Any portfolios above the frontier cannot be achieved. Any below the frontier are dominated by Markowitz's efficient portfolios.

EPRA

EPRA is the abbreviation for European Public Real Estate Association. Based in Amsterdam, EPRA is an organization that represents the interests of the major listed European property management companies and supports the development and market presence of European public property companies. The well-known international index named after it, the EPRA index, tracks the performance of the largest European and North American listed property companies.

EREIT

REITs are called EREITs in the US, if they invest almost exclusively in real estate, as opposed to mortgages or construction loans on real estate. The term stands for Equity Real Estate Investment Trust. EREITs are considered as a less risky investment than REITs that specialize in loans, since they have more control over the properties in the portfolio. However, even EREITs can become more risky by using borrowed funds to purchase properties.

Equity swap

In an equity swap, the return on a stock, a portfolio, or a stock index is paid each period by one party in return for a fixed-rate or floating-rate payment. The return can be the capital appreciation or the total return including dividends on the stock, portfolio, or index. In order to reduce equity risk, a portfolio manager might enter into a 1-year quarterly pay S&P 500 index swap and agree to receive a fixed rate. The percentage increase in the index each quarter is netted against the fixed rate to determine the payment to be made. If the index return is negative, the fixed-rate payer must also pay the percentage decline in the index to the portfolio manager. Uniquely among swaps, equity swap payments can be floating on both sides and the payments are not known until the end of the quarter.

EURIBOR

EURIBOR (Euro Interbank Offered Rate) is the benchmark rate of the large euro money market which has emerged since 1999. It is sponsored by the European Banking Federation, which represents the interests of 4,500 banks in 24 member states of the European Union and in Iceland, Norway and Switzerland and by the Financial Markets Association. EURIBOR is the rate at which Euro Interbank term deposits are offered by one to another prime bank. It is published at 11.00 a.m. CET for spot value. The choice of banks quoting for EURIBOR is based on market criteria. These banks are of first class credit standing. They have been selected to ensure that the diversity of the euro money market is adequately reflected, thereby making EURIBOR an efficient and representative benchmark.

Exchange rate risk

Exchange rate risk arises from the uncertainty about the value of foreign currency cash flows to an investor in terms of his home-country currency. While a US Treasury bill may be considered quite low risk or even risk-free to US-based investors, the value of the T-bill to a European investor will be reduced by a depreciation of the US dollar's value relative to the euro.

Exchange Traded Fund (ETF)

An Exchange Traded Fund (ETF) is an investment vehicle which issues and trades shares representing an underlying basket of assets, typically the constituents of a major share market index. ETFs allow small investors to diversify their risk over a broad spread of investments, tracking an index, while offering the flexibility of trading like a share. In particular, an ETF can be bought and sold throughout the trading day, not just once a day as is the case for most mutual funds. Like a share, an ETF can also be sold short.

Fiduciary

The term "fiduciary" describes a relationship that implies a position of trust or confidence wherein one person is usually entrusted to hold or manage property or money for another. It also describes the faithful relationship owed by an attorney to a client or by a broker (and salesperson) to a principal. The fiduciary owes complete allegiance to the client. Among the obligations that a fiduciary owes to his or her principal are the duties of loyalty, obedience and full disclosure; the duty to use skill, care and diligence; and the duty to account for all monies.

First loss piece

The first loss piece is the debt class with the lowest payment priority in a senior or subordinated debt structure. It is also called an "equity piece".

Foreclosure

Foreclosure involves a lawsuit in which a bank, a mortgage company, or another creditor seeks to take an owner's property to satisfy a debt. The bank or lender may actually take the property, or have the property sold to pay off the debt. A property usually goes into the process of foreclosure if payments are more than 90 days past due.

Forward

A forward contract is a bilateral contract that obligates one party to buy and the other party to sell a specific quantity of an asset, at a set price, on a specific date in the future. Typically, neither party to the contract pays anything to get into the contract. If the expected future price of the asset increases over the life of the contract, the right to buy at the contract price will have a positive value, and the obligation to sell will have an equal negative value. If the future price of the asset falls below the contract price, the result is opposite and the right to sell (at an above-market price) will have the positive value. The parties may enter into the contract as a speculation on the future price. More often, a party seeks to enter into a forward contract to hedge a risk it already has. The forward contract is used to eliminate uncertainty about the future price of an asset it plans to buy or sell at a later date. Unlike futures, forwards are not contracts with standard fixed terms. They are tailor-made between the buyer and seller for each deal and are traded over-the-counter (OTC) rather than on an exchange.

Funds From Operations (FFO) (see also AFFO)

Fund From Operations (FFO) is the most commonly accepted and reported measure of REIT operating performance. It is a ratio intended to highlight the amount of cash generated by a company's real estate portfolio relative to its total operating cash flow. FFO is equal to net income, excluding gains (or losses) from debt restructuring and sales of property, plus depreciation and amortization.

Futures

A future is an undertaking to buy or sell a standard quantity of a financial asset or commodity at a future date at a fixed price. Futures resemble forwards, but are standardized contracts (i. e., every futures contract has standardized terms that dictate the size, the unit of price quotation, the delivery date and contract months) and must be traded on a recognized exchange. Price movements are expressed in ticks (the smallest unit of price quotation). Delivery of a future is rare. As the delivery date draws near, most investors close out their positions by undertaking an equal and opposite trade. The markets for futures bring together hedgers who wish to protect themselves against the rise or fall of prices, and speculators who are trying to benefit from such movements. A clearinghouse acts as the counter party in every transaction to protect against default risk, so the buyer and seller do not have to deal directly with each other. Futures have developed as a method for establishing forward purchase prices and managing price instability caused by seasonal factors in agricultural markets. Today, interest rate and stock index futures attract the greatest volume.

Goodwill

Goodwill is created when a firm purchasing another business pays more than the fair market value of the business's assets if they were purchased individually. If the excess purchase price cannot be attributed to patents, brands, copyrights, or other intangible assets, it is recorded as goodwill. Goodwill reflects the factors that enable a company to earn an above average rate of return such as strong management, manufacturing efficiency, and customer approval. The process of accounting for goodwill is different from the process for other intangible assets. According to US GAAP, goodwill is not amortized, but is subject to an annual impairment review. Each year, a company must estimate the fair market value of its goodwill. If the fair market value is less than the carrying value on the balance sheet, the goodwill is said to be impaired. If impairment occurs, the carrying value of the goodwill account is reduced to its fair market value and an impairment charge is recorded on the income statement.

Grace period

The additional penalty-free period of time a lender provides for a borrower as an extension to make a payment on a loan is called a "grace period".

Greenshoe option

The greenshoe option is often referred to as the overallotment during an Initial Public Offering (IPO). An amount of shares, generally no greater than 15 % of the original shares issued, that is reserved for issuance at the underwriter's option at the original price. This is used by the underwriter to cover some, if not all, of the short position the brokerage firm(s) may have created in pursuit of maintaining a stable market by meeting aftermarket demand once the stock has begun to trade. The shares get issued at the IPO price which goes to the issuer, less fees. The difference between the IPO price and the price the firm sold those shares to the aftermarket buyers is earned by the underwriter. The term comes from the Green Shoe Company, which was the first to have this option.

Haircut

The difference between the market value of an asset and the perceived value by the lender. The lending side requires this safety cushion for the risk that the asset's value turns out to be lower than the market value in case of liquidation.

Hybrid mortgage

A hybrid mortgage is an instrument that is used to secure hybrid debt. Typically, a mortgage with an interest rate below current market rate which also provides for a meaningful participation (usually 50 % or more) in both net cash flow and gain on sale or refinance of the secured asset. Some hybrid mortgages have an option to convert to equity investments in the future. Others retain their participation in the operating performance of the property and also participate in the proceeds from sale or refinance.

Initial Public Offering (IPO)

An Initial Public Offering (IPO) is the issuance of stock, or equity, through an underwriter for purchase on the open market by investors. An IPO is made when a private company "goes public" to raise capital (also referred to as "flotation").

Interest rate cap

An interest rate cap is an over-the-counter (OTC) derivative that protects the holder from rises in short-term interest rates by making a payment to the holder when an underlying interest rate (the "index" or "reference" interest rate) exceeds a specified strike rate (the "cap rate"). Caps are purchased for a premium and typically have expirations between one and seven years. They may make payments to the holder on a monthly, quarterly or semi-annual basis, with the period generally set equal to the maturity of the index interest rate. Each period, the payment is determined by comparing the current level of the index interest rate with the cap rate. If the index rate exceeds the cap rate, the payment is based upon the difference between the two rates, the length of the period, and the contract's notional amount. Otherwise, no payment is made for that period. Caps are frequently purchased by issuers of floating rate debt who wish to protect themselves from the increased financing costs that would result from a rise in interest rates. To reduce the up-front cost of such protection, a long cap may be combined with a short floor to form a collar.

Interest rate floor

Interest rate floors compare to interest rate caps in the same way that puts compare to calls. They are over-the-counter (OTC) derivatives that protect the holder from declines in short-term interest rates by making a payment to the holder when an underlying interest rate (the "index" or "reference" interest rate) falls below a specified strike rate (the "floor rate"). Each period, the payment is determined by comparing the current level of the index interest rate with the floor rate. If the index rate is below the floor rate, the payment is based upon the difference between the two rates, the length of the period, and the contract's notional amount. Otherwise, no payment is made for that period. Floors are used by purchasers of floating rate debt who wish to protect themselves from the loss of income that would result from a decline in interest rates. End users may also short a floor against a cap to construct an inexpensive or costless collar.

In the money

A call option is said to be "in the money" when it has a strike price below the current price of the underlying commodity or security on which the option has been written. Likewise when a put option has a strike price above the current price it is said to be in the money.

IPD

IPD is a global information business, dedicated to the supply of independent market indices and portfolio benchmarks to the property industry. Benchmarks and indices rely on records of detailed financial and descriptive information on individual buildings, leases and tenants of properties owned by investors, managed by portfolio managers, and occupied by businesses and government.

Issuer

An issuer is a corporation, an investment trust or a public entity, which initially emits securities to investors.

Jumbo bond

Bond issues with high nominal volume are called Jumbo bonds; their size is usually around € 1 billion.

Junior debt

Junior debt or subordinated debt has a lower priority than senior debt or is even unsecured, meaning that it is served after senior claims are satisfied.

Junk bonds

Based on their credit ratings, corporate bonds can be divided into investment grade bonds and junk bonds. The dividing line is the BBB rating (Standard & Poor's), which is the lowest credit rating considered to be investment grade. Below BBB, bonds are considered as "junk". Other names for junk bonds are below investment grade, speculative grade and high yield bonds. The lower-rated debt typically offers a higher yield, making speculative bonds attractive investment vehicles for certain types of financial portfolios and strategies. Many pension funds and other investors (banks, insurance companies), however, are prohibited in their by-laws from investing in bonds which have ratings below a particular level. Junk bonds became ubiquitous in the 1980s as a financing mechanism in mergers and acquisitions and leveraged buyouts where these bonds were used to help closing the financing gap for an acquisition. High yield bonds can also be repackaged into Collateralized Debt Obligations (CDOs), thereby raising the credit rating of the senior tranches above the rating of the original debt. The senior tranches of high yield CDOs can thus meet the minimum credit rating requirements of pension funds and other institutional investors despite the significant risk in the original high yield debt.

Lead manager

A lead manager is the institution which the borrower mandated to raise money via a bond, loan or share issue. The lead manager guarantees the liquidity of the deal, arranges the syndication of the issue and undertakes a major underwriting and distribution commitment. For bonds or loans, the lead manager forms a syndicate of co-lead managers, co-managers and underwriters. For share issues, the underwriters guarantee to sell a certain number of shares at a certain price. The names of the managers appear on the bottom of the front page of the prospectus, with the lead manager's name in the uppermost left.

Letter of Credit (LoC)

A Letter of Credit (LoC) is an agreement of a bank on behalf of its customer that the bank will honor drafts or other demands of payment from third parties upon compliance with conditions specified in the Letter of Credit. Letters of Credit have become an alternative form of partial lease guarantees whereby the bank issuing the Letter of Credit agrees to pay the landlord a specified sum of money if the tenant should default on its payments under the lease.

LIBOR (London Interbank Offered Rate)

LIBOR is one of the most important short-term (one year or less) money market rates at which banks lend funds to each other. LIBOR terms are usually for one, two, three or six months or one year where 3-month LIBOR is one of the most widely used interest rates in the fixed-income universe. It is often the base rate for bond issues from corporations and countries, both fixed and floating rate notes. The coupon on floating rate notes is often a fixed number of basis points above 3-month LIBOR. The 3-month LIBOR is also the key rate for the floating rate leg of interest rate swaps. Eurodollar futures, the most traded futures in the world, are based on 3-month LIBOR.

Lock-in period

There are two definitions for the lock-in period:

- The lock-in period can either be the period of time in which a mortgagor cannot refinance a mortgage without paying a penalty to the lender.

- The lock-in period is the time period, usually 30 to 60 days; a mortgage lender agrees to hold the borrowers mortgage rate constant at the rate quoted when the application was taken. It is not the same as a loan commitment although some commitments may contain a lock-in provision. This protects the borrower against rate increases if interest rates rise before the loan closing takes place. Lenders may charge a flat fee or a percentage of the mortgage loan, or add a fraction of a percentage point to the loan's interest rate.

LTV (see also covenants)

The Loan-to-Value (LTV) is the ratio of loan amount over property value. Property value may be stated as market value, bank assessment value, and collateral eligibility value, e. g., under the German Pfandbrief Act. Principal repayments lower the LTV over the loan life. The lower the LTV, the lower is the risk.

Margin

The term margin has several meanings. First, margin can encompass an adjustment, expressed in basis points, which is added to or subtracted from a reference interest rate (e. g., 6-month LIBOR) to establish the coupon of a floating rate or short-term money market security. Secondly, the margin can be a measure of return on floating rate notes calculated with reference to some interest rate such as LIBOR. Lastly, margins can be cash deposits required for each futures contract to serve as a good faith deposit guaranteeing that both parties to the agreement will perform the transaction some time in the future.

Market capitalization

Market capitalization (also: market cap) is the total market value of a firm. It is defined as the product of the company's stock price per share and the total number of shares outstanding. The market cap should not be confused with the float, which is the amount of shares in circulation. A company's market cap can greatly exceed the float, especially in the case of a new publicly traded company. Fully diluted market cap includes convertible preferred stock, convertible debentures, warrants, options and other securities with equity conversion features.

Mark-to-market

The term "mark-to-market" means an adjustment of estimated value or cash flows to reflect current market levels. In a falling or weak market, this is likely to create a downward adjustment of current value based on lower expected future income streams if rental rates on existing leases are greater than rental rates being charged for new leases in the market (i. e., if there are several above-market leases in a building that are "burning off"). The opposite holds true in a strong or rising market.

Mezzanine

Mezzanine or subordinated debt is a type of cash flow lending without a first lien against the company's assets. Mezzanine pieces are often used as acquisition capital in combination with straight debt and/or equity.

Modern Portfolio Theory (MPT)

The Modern Portfolio Theory (MPT) is an approach to quantify risk and return in a portfolio of assets. It emphasizes the portfolio rather than individual assets, and in particular, how assets perform (or affect risk) in relation to each other. Developed in 1959 by Harry M. Markowitz, MPT is the foundation for present-day principles of investment diversification. MPT refers to a set of models and techniques that are used to construct efficient portfolios. A portfolio is "efficient" when it offers the highest expected future return for a selected level of risk, or equivalently the lowest risk for a given return. For particular sets of assets, there are multiple efficient portfolios. The efficient portfolio an investor chooses depends on the investor's willingness to increase portfolio risk (volatility) in exchange for a higher expected return.

Monoline insurer

A monoline insurer is an insurance company that only insures a single type of risk (in ABS deals that is usually securitization risk). The insurer's rating becomes in this case the tranche rating, as the insurer acts as tranche guarantor.

Mortgage Backed Security (MBS)

A Mortgage Backed Security (MBS) is a securitized interest in a pool of mortgages and can be seen as a bond. But instead of paying investors fixed coupons and principal, it pays out the cash flows from the pool of mortgages. The simplest form of mortgage-backed security is a mortgage pass-through which passes all principal and interest payments (less a servicing fee) from the pool of mortgages directly to investors each month. The servicing fee is a fixed percent of outstanding principal, say 0.25 % on an annual basis. The fee is subtracted from interest payments to investors. If a pool of mortgages has an average mortgage rate of 8.50 % and the servicing fee is 0.25 % p.a., then investors in the pool receive an average yield of 8.25 % p.a. Although the mortgage payments are scheduled and fixed from one month to the next, cash flows to the holder of a mortgage pass-through are not fixed since mortgage holders have the option of prepaying their mortgages. When the prepayment option is exercised, the principal prepayment is passed to investors in the pass-through. This accelerates the cash flows to the investors, who receive the principal payments early but never receive the future interest payments that would have been made on that principal. The rate at which fixed-rate mortgagors prepay is influenced by many factors. A significant factor is the level of interest rates. Mortgage holders tend to prepay mortgages so they can refinance when mortgage rates drop. By acting in their own best interest, they act to the detriment of the investors holding the mortgage pass-through. Mortgage holders tend to return principal to investors when reinvestment rates are unattractive. They tend to not do so when reinvestment rates are attractive. The originator may sell the rights to service the mortgages to a third party. There is a market for such servicing rights. Prepayments introduce uncertainty into the cash flows of a mortgage pass-through.

(German) Mortgage-backed bond (Pfandbrief)

German mortgage-backed bonds (Pfandbrief) are long-term bonds that are used to finance building loans. Mortgage-backed bonds are similar to bonds in form, and are issued by mortgage banks, ship mortgage banks, and public-sector credit institutions. A trustee ensures that mortgage bonds are always backed by mortgages of the same amount that carry at least the same interest rate. As a rule, mortgage bonds have a long maturity, in some cases over 25 years. The holder of a mortgage bond can not redeem it before the end of the term agreed upon. The borrower must begin repaying the principal at the latest when one-third of the maturity has elapsed. The redemption value of mortgage bonds may not exceed their face value. Mortgage backed bonds are traded on the exchange in the official market (Amtlicher Markt) segment. Different to MBS, the refinanced receivable remains on the balance of the financing mortgage bank, whereas MBS are usually outsourced to SPVs.

Municipal bond

A bond issued by a state, city or local government, generally to fund infrastructure projects such as roads, sewer systems, and schools, is called a municipal bond. Interest on municipal bonds is generally exempt from federal tax, as well as from state tax if purchased by a resident of the issuing state, and local tax if purchased by a resident of the issuing city or locality. For this reason, yields on municipal bonds are often lower than for corporate bonds or treasuries. Municipal bonds are also considered a safer investment than corporate bonds, since state and local governments are judged less likely to default.

Mutual fund

A mutual fund is a fund administered by a professional investment management firm that raises money from many small investors and uses the pooled cash to purchase stocks, bonds, or other financial assets in accordance with a stated set of objectives. The investors are buying shares in the fund and, by extension, in each of its underlying securities. In this way, they benefit from greater diversification without having to research or buy many individual financial instruments. In return for directing the fund, the investment manager collects a fee.

NAREIT

NAREIT stands for the National Association of Real Estate Investment Trusts, a trade organization focused on REITs. For investors, NAREIT publishes information and performance data related to REITs. This NAREIT data can also be useful to other real estate investors as a proxy for the current attractiveness of specific real estate sectors. For REIT managers, NAREIT publishes guidelines on performance reporting. For accountants, NAREIT provides commentary on REIT-specific accounting issues. NAREIT also lobbies policy makers at the national and state level on matters related to REITs. NAREIT is headquartered in Washington D. C.

NCREIF

The National Council of Real Estate Investment Fiduciaries (NCREIF) is an association of real estate professionals who serve on working committees, sponsor research articles, seminars and symposiums and produce the NCREIF Property Index. The index reports quarterly and annual returns consisting of income and appreciation components. The index is based on data collected from the voting members of NCREIF. Specific property-type indices include apartment, office, retail, R&D/office and warehouse.

Net Asset Value (NAV)

Net Asset Value (NAV) is the current real estate value or equity, net of debt. In common practice, current real estate value is considered to be the most recent appraised value, or if prior to the initial appraisal following acquisition, the asset's acquisition cost adjusted for capital expenditures and additional contributions or distributions. The NAV per share is the current value of a property company's asset, including its real estate, less debt, divided by shares outstanding. The shares may trade at a premium (share price higher than NAV) or at a discount (share price lower than NAV) to the actual NAV of the funds' assets.

Net Present Value Coverage Ratio (NPVCR)

The Net Present Value Coverage Ratio (NPVCR) is a measure that is helpful in Cash Flow Related Lending (CRL) analyses. The NPVCR enables the analyst to determine the maximum lending volume of a single project by calculating the present value of future loan payments. A ratio greater than one means that future earnings will be greater than the outstanding loan amount at the end of the investment horizon and vice versa for a ratio less than one.

Non-performing loan (NPL)

A non-performing loan (NPL) is a loan that is past due and unpaid for more than 90 days (usually equally to three dates of payment). The broad definition of the term is also encompassing sub-performing loans and watch list loans. A sub-performing loan is already defaulted but has not met the 3-month threshold; a watch list loan is still performing, but has a certain probability of default in the near future and an internal bank rating of B- and worse.

Non-recourse debt

Non-recourse debt is constituted as a loan (debt) that is secured by a pledge of collateral, typically real estate, but for which the borrower is not personally liable. Thus, in the event of default by the borrower, non-recourse debt limits the lender's remedies to a foreclosure of the mortgage. As a result, the lender waives any personal liability by the borrower. If a property is insufficient to cover the outstanding loan balance at maturity (e. g., if real estate prices have dropped), the lender is not obliged to pay the difference. Therefore, non-recourse debt is typically limited to 80 % or 90 % Loan-to-Value ratios, so that the property itself provides overcollateralization of the loan. Non-recourse debt is typically used to finance commercial real estate and similar projects with high capital expenditures, long loan periods, and uncertain revenue streams. Non-recourse debt is usually carried on a company's balance sheet as a liability, and the collateral is carried as an asset. Most commercial real estate in the US is financed long term by non-recourse debt. Most real estate in other parts of the world is financed with full or partial recourse to the borrower.

Off-balance

Off-balance sheet exposures refer to the business activities of a bank that generally do not involve booking assets (loans) and taking deposits. Off-balance sheet activities normally generate fees, but produce liabilities or assets that are deferred or contingent and thus, do not appear on the institution's balance sheet until or unless they become actual assets or liabilities.

Open-end fund

A fund that does not have a finite life and that continually (usually at the end of each calendar quarter) accepts new investor capital and continually consummates new property investments is called "open-end". Individual properties typically are sold from time to time by managers of open-end funds. Typically, investors in open-end funds may liquidate their units over a certain prescribed time frame, assuming the fund sponsor is able to meet liquidation requests through cash flow or property sales.

Option

An option gives the buyer or holder the right, but not the obligation, to buy or sell an underlying financial asset or commodity. Unlike futures, where the buyer has to fulfill the contract, an option gives the choice of whether to exercise or not. An option contract specifies a future date on or before which it can be exercised. This date is known as the expiry date. The price of an option – the "strike" or "exercise" price – is the price at which it can be exercised. Options are very flexible instruments. They allow investors to benefit from favorable price movements while limiting the consequence of unfavorable price movements. Options holders have to pay a "premium" for this protection as with any insurance contract. There are two kinds of options. A "call", which gives the holder the right to buy the underlying instrument at a set exercise price, and a "put", which gives the holder the right to sell the underlying instrument at a set strike price. More than one option transaction can be combined to create a spread. These strategies usually involve the simultaneous purchase and sale of options with different prices, or expiry dates, within the same class. American style options can be exercised at any time before the expiry date, whereas European style options can be exercised only at the specific expiry date and not before.

Out of the money

An option is described as being out of the money when the current price of the underlying is below the strike or exercise price for a call, and above the strike price for a put. Options can also be described as being deep out of the money when they are likely to expire out of the money.

Overcollateralization

Overcollateralization is the amount, if any, by which the aggregate outstanding principal balance of the collateral exceeds the aggregate outstanding principal balance of the securities backed by such collateral. Overcollateralization is used as a form of credit enhancement in certain asset-backed transactions.

Over-the-counter (OTC)

Some financial or commodities instruments are traded on established exchanges. Examples include most highly-capitalized stocks, which trade on exchanges such as the New York Stock Exchange (NYSE), and futures, which trade on futures exchanges such as the Eurex. These instruments are called exchange traded. An instrument is traded over-the-counter (OTC) if it trades in some context other than a formal exchange. Most debt instruments are traded OTC with investment banks making markets in specific issues. If someone wants to buy or sell a bond, they call the bank that makes a market in that bond and ask for quotes. Many derivative instruments, including forwards, swaps and most exotic derivatives, are also traded OTC. In these markets, large financial institutions serve as derivatives dealers, customizing derivatives for the needs of clients.

Pass-through securities

A pass-through security is a security representing pooled debt obligations repackaged as shares that passes income from debtors through an intermediary to investors. The most common type of pass-through is a mortgage-backed certificate, many of which are government-guaranteed, in which homeowners' principal and interest payments pass from the originating bank or savings and loan through a government agency or investment bank to investors, net of service charges. Pass-throughs representing other types of assets, such as auto loans or student loans, are also widely marketed. Such securities can be structured as straight pass-through, partially modified pass-through or modified pass-through securities:

- Straight pass-through: Pays principal and interest to the investor as and when received from the underlying mortgage loan pool.

- Partially modified pass-through: Pays certain sums whether or not such sums have been paid by the pool's mortgagors.

- Modified pass-through: Involves a guaranty of all scheduled principal and interest payments to investors whether or not such payments have been paid by the mortgagors.

Preferred stock

Preferred stock is a form of hybrid security that blends aspects of stocks and bonds. Unlike common stock, whose dividend varies with the corporation's fortunes, preferred stock pays a fixed dividend. This is subordinate to other claims on the corporation, so the corporation cannot pay dividends on preferred stock unless it is current in meeting all claims of debtors, tax authorities, employees, etc. However, preferred dividends are superior to the claims of common stockholders, who can only receive a dividend when preferred dividends are also paid in full.

Preliminary prospectus

A preliminary prospectus or private placement memorandum includes all of the information that will be included in the final prospectus but is subject to amendment. It is identified by the red printing on the front cover, hence the colloquial name of "red herring" or, more briefly, "the red". Despite the name, there is no implication that the document is in any way diversionary (as the common use of the term "red herring" might suggest). It is a valuable marketing tool for securities transactions because it allows investors to make some preliminary assessment of the utility of the particular security for meeting their investment goals.

Prepayment risk

Prepayment risk is the risk that homeowners will pay off their mortgages early; for instance, to refinance when interest rates fall. Prepayment risk is a concern primarily for investors in Mortgage Backed Securities, since the return of an MBS will increase or decrease in relation to the frequency and predictability of prepayments. Prepayments also shorten the life of an MBS.

Private placement

A private placement is a direct private offering of securities to a limited number of investors. Private placements are easier and less costly than public offerings, since no registration or prospects are required. Both equity and debt securities can be privately placed. Private equity tends to be issued by corporations in start-up, leveraged buy-out or distressed situations. Privately placed debt is more often issued by established and financially stable corporations to institutional investors such as life insurance companies. Privately placed securities are transferable, but they are not intended to be actively traded. Private placements are attractive to long-term investors because they should, in theory, offer modestly higher returns than comparable publicly traded securities. In addition, private placements should offer a liquidity premium since there is no organized trading platform for such securities. Further, the issuer's savings on the costs of issuance are generally shared with investors.

Prospectus

A prospectus is essentially an invitation or offer to the public to subscribe for or buy the securities of a company. A prospectus must contain all relevant information about the company making the issuance, and must be filed with the relevant authorities. The final prospectus is commonly called "the black" to differentiate it from the preliminary prospectus which had been distinguished by red lettering on the cover to avoid confusion between the preliminary and final prospectus.

Put option

The holder of a put option owns the right, but is not obliged, to sell a certain underlying security to the option seller in a predefined quantity, to a fixed price and on the date of expiration.

Rating service

A servicer that evaluates securities by judging the ability of the rated company to meet the debt obligation consistently and timely. Basis for the rating is the data obtained from the balance sheet. Changes in the rating can influence the borrowing costs of the pertinent company considerably.

Real Estate Investment Trust (REIT)

A corporation or trust formed for the ownership of real estate which is owned in share units by investors. In the US, these shares may be traded either publicly, if registered with the stock exchange, or privately. Unlike an ordinary corporation, a REIT is not taxed on corporate level. In return, REITs are required to distribute 90 % of their income, which may be taxable on investor level. The REIT structure was designed to provide a similar structure for investment in real estate as mutual funds provide for investment in stocks. REITs offer the benefits of high liquidity, diversification, and the sharing of investments in larger, non-residential properties such as hotels, malls, and industrial facilities. They can also offer the opportunity to invest in a specific real estate market or region. REITs can be classified as equity, mortgage or hybrid. The key statistics to look at in a REIT are its Net Asset Value and Adjusted Funds From Operations. REIT legislation differs slightly all over the world, e. g., in terms of income distribution, the obligation to go public or fiscal benefits.

Real Estate Operating Company (REOC)

A Real Estate Operating Company (REOC) is defined as an entity having at least 50 % of its assets invested in real estate, engaged in the ownership and operation of real estate in the ordinary course of its business, and participating in the active management of that real estate. A REOC is similar to a REIT the difference being that a REOC will reinvest its earnings rather than distributing them to shareholders like REITs do. Also, REOCs are more flexible than REITs in terms of what types of real estate investments they can make. As REOCs reinvest earnings rather than distribute dividends to shareholders, they do not get the same benefits of lower corporate taxation that are common REIT characteristics.

Recourse

Recourse is the ability of a lender to claim money from a defaulting borrower in addition to the property pledged as collateral. There are three different forms of recourse:

- Limited recourse is a financing arrangement where the lender can require the borrower to repay only in special conditions that are spelled out in the loan agreement itself, and otherwise must look to the collateral as a source of repayment. Borrowers may have to pay more for limited recourse financing.

- Non-resource is a loan where the lender's source of repayment is the cash flow generated by a project financed by the loan or the collateral securing the loan. The non-recourse form of financing commonly is used in factoring of accounts receivable. The lender fully assumes the credit risk. If the borrower defaults, the lender's only recourse is to foreclose on the collateral backing the loan; the borrower is not liable personally for repayment. In a non-recourse mortgage loan, for example, the lender must look to the collateral, rather than the borrower, as the ultimate source of repayment.

- Full recourse means that the borrower agrees to fully reimburse the lender personally for not paying back principal and interest of a loan, e. g., by amortizing loans granted for a real estate portfolio purchase where the cash flow of the portfolio is not able – due to bankruptcy or lease termination of tenants – to fully pay interest and principal.

Reserve

A reserve is the amount of the collateral less the loan amount. Furthermore, reserves act as a backup for potential future needs in difficult market situations.

Reverse mortgage

A reverse mortgage is a non-recourse loan made to older homeowners, generally not less than 62 years of age, secured by a lien on the related mortgaged property, that does not require a scheduled monthly payment of principal or interest prior to maturity. Instead, accrued interest at the applicable mortgage rate is added to the outstanding amount of the related mortgage loan, and the entire outstanding amount is payable in a lump sum at maturity.

Risk-free return

The risk-free return equals a theoretical interest rate that would be achieved on a completely risk-free investment. The 3-month Treasury bill serves as a close approximation, since it is virtually risk-free.

Risk premium

A risk premium is the reward that someone receives for holding a risky investment rather than a risk-free one.

RMBS

Residential Mortgage Backed Securities (RMBS) comprise a large amount of pooled residential mortgages, including Home Equity Loans (HEL) and subprime mortgages. RMBS investors have the claim on interest and principal payments from the debtors of residential mortgages.

Road show

A road show is a tour by executives of a going-public company where they travel to various cities to meet with underwriters and analysts and make presentations regarding their company and IPO. The road show takes place during the marketing period before the registration statement becomes effective.

Securitization

Securitization is the financing or refinancing of income yielding assets by packing them into a tradable form through an issue of securities. There are three principal types of securitization: true-sale, synthetic and whole business. In a true-sale securitization, a company – the originator or seller – sells a pool of its assets to a Special Purpose Vehicle (SPV). To finance the purchase of the assets, the SPV issues debt instruments (e. g., bonds) into the capital markets. The debt instruments are referred to as Asset Backed Securities (ABS) because the purchased assets typically represent the principal source of cash to service the debt instruments. In a synthetic securitization, the originator does not sell any assets, but transfers the risk of loss associated with certain of its assets to an SPV or bank against payment of a premium or a fee. Whole business securitization is essentially a secured loan granted by a SPV to the originator.

Senior debt

Senior debt is the capital piece that has priority for repayment in case of liquidation of the asset or company.

Sharpe ratio

The Sharpe ratio is a way of deciding whether returns are produced by intelligent investment decisions or by accepting excess risk. It measures the return of an investment compared with investments in government bonds, which are regarded as virtually risk free because the government in theory always repays its debts. The Sharpe ratio is calculated by subtracting the rate of return on government securities from the rate of return on a portfolio, and then dividing the difference by the standard deviation of the portfolio's returns.

Short Term Investment Fund (STIF)

A Short Term Investment Fund (STIF) is a type of fund that invests in short-term investments of high quality and low risk. The goal of this type of fund is to protect capital with low-risk investments while achieving a return that beats a relevant benchmark such as a Treasury bill index. Short Term Investment Funds comprise cash, bank notes, corporate notes, government bills and various safe short-term debt instruments. These types of funds are usually used by investors who are temporarily parking funds before moving them to another investment that will provide higher returns. These funds traditionally have low management fees, usually well below 1 % a year.

SICAV

An abbreviation for the Société d'Investissement à Capital Variable. The SICAV is an open-end investment structure under French, Luxembourgish, Swiss and Italian law with the purpose to invest the variable capital from investors into securities. The investor has the right to redeem his or her share anytime.

SIIC

Société d'Investissements Immobiliers Cotée (SIIC): At the end of 2003, France introduced the fiscal status of SIIC, which has been directly inspired by international REITs. Most French property companies have now adopted SIIC status. All companies are free of direct tax, on their current profits and on capital gains. French companies had to pay an exit tax (16.5 % of the unrealized capital gains) in order to gain SIIC status. In exchange, they were allowed to use their latent fiscal losses against the capital gains. All companies are committed to distribution, from 85 % (France) to 100 % (Netherlands) of the current results (after depreciation). French SIICs also have to distribute 50 % of the capital gains. French SIICs still depreciate their assets, which reduces the net attributable profits. None has been using that ability to artificially minimize the distribution.

Special Purpose Vehicle (SPV)

A Special Purpose Vehicle (SPV) is a separate legal entity to which a corporation transfers the financial assets for Asset Backed Security issues. It is important to note that a legal transfer of assets is made to the SPV. This shields the assets from the claims of the corporation's general creditors, making it possible for the ABS issue to receive a higher credit rating than the corporation as a whole. Because the assets are sold to the SPV, they are highly unlikely to be subject to any claims arising from the bankruptcy of the corporation, and the SPV is termed a bankruptcy remote entity.

Spread

The term "spread" has several different meanings:

- The spread can be the difference in a price quotation between the "bid", the price at which a dealer is willing to buy, and the "ask", the price at which a dealer is willing to sell a specific asset or security. A large spread is usually an indicator for market illiquidity.

- "Spread" can also be used to express the difference in yields between two fixed income securities of the same quality but different maturities, or of different quality but the same maturities.

- Often "spread" refers to the difference in yields between a bond and a reference government bond, which is regarded as relatively risk-free.

- A futures spread is the difference in prices between delivery months in the same or different markets.

- "Spread" can also refer to the difference between borrowing and lending rates by which a financial intermediary makes profits.

Structured finance

Structured finance is a broad term used to describe a sector of finance that was created to help transfer risk using complex legal and corporate entities. Structured finance affords issuers and underwriters the opportunity to efficiently access the capital markets to finance any type of borrowing, including mortgage loans, consumer loans, auto loans, student loans, business loans and commercial loans. Lenders, borrowers, businesses and individuals all benefit from reduced interest rates and lower transaction costs.

Subordination clause

A subordination clause is a clause in which the holder of a mortgage permits a subsequent mortgage to take priority. Subordination is the act of yielding priority. This clause provides that if a prior mortgage is paid off or renewed, the junior mortgage will continue in its subordinate position and will not automatically become a higher or first mortgage. A subordination clause is usually standard in a junior mortgage, because the junior mortgagee gets a higher interest rate and is often not concerned about the inferior mortgage position.

Sub-performing loan

A loan that is making payments, perhaps even the full principal and interest payments required in the mortgage note, but with a debt coverage ratio that would be unacceptable if underwritten at this time. Many investors also classify a loan as sub-performing even if monthly payments are current if the Loan-to-Value ratio (LTV) or other primary value indicator suggests that the loan is unlikely to be able to pay off in full at maturity.

Subprime

A classification of borrowers that have a bad or short credit history. A credit scoring system determines the loan terms for which a borrower qualifies. As credit risk is higher, the interest rate is consequently also higher. The value of US subprime mortgages is estimated at US$ 1.3 trillion, with over 7.5 million such mortgages outstanding. Over 320,000 foreclosures were initiated during each of the first two quarters of 2007, most of which were related to subprime loans, versus a typical level of 225,000 over the past six years. Approximately 16% of subprime loans with Adjustable Rate Mortgages (ARM) are 90-days into default or in foreclosure proceedings as of October 2007, roughly triple the rate of 2005.

Swap

A swap is an exchange of cash flows between two counterparties designed to offset interest rate or currency risk and to match their assets to their liabilities. There are interest rate swaps (the larger category) or cross currency swaps. For example, a company may have costs which it must pay in euro while its revenues are in US dollars. Another company may have the opposite requirement. A bank, in exchange for a fee, arranges a currency swap which meets both requirements. The same is true of interest rate swaps, which allow two parties to exchange fixed rate for floating rate risk to their mutual advantage. A key point is that parties to a swap do not exchange principal, or the underlying fixed amount of debt, but just cash flow, or the interest payments.

Synthetic REIT

A synthetic REIT is an entity with real estate holdings that, without formally operating as a REIT, fulfills the constitutive formal requirements. Therefore, synthetic REIT is an indirect investment in real estate with the same advantages as a direct REIT. However, management is more flexible since it is not obliged to comply with the REIT legislature.

Top-down approach to investing

An investment strategy is described as "top-down approach", when an investor first looks at large-scale trends in the general economy and afterwards selects those industries and companies that are likely to benefit from those trends. For example, an investor who thinks that the general economic environment is favorable for real estate might further examine which specific real estate financial vehicles are most appropriate, then review and assess specific transactions that meet investor's requirements.

Tranche

A tranche is one of the classes of debt securities issued as part of a single bond or instrument, from the French word "tranche", meaning slice. Securities are often issued in tranches to meet different investor objectives for portfolio diversification. Typically, lower-rated tranches have higher coupons and longer lives, since they receive interest payments (the coupon) but no principal payments until the higher-rated tranches have been retired or paid off.

Treasury bill (T-bill)

Treasury bills (or T-bills) are treasury securities that have a maturity of a year or less at the time of issuance. Unlike longer-term treasuries, T-bills pay no coupons. Instead, they make a single payment of par value at maturity. Consequently, T-bills are issued at a discount to par, so an investor who holds a T-bill to maturity earns the difference between the par value and discounted value at which the instrument was purchased. Treasury bills play an important role in the local money market because most banks are required to hold them as part of their reserve requirements and because central bank open market operations undertaken in the process of implementing monetary policy are usually conducted in the T-bill market.

True Sale Initiative (TSI)

The True Sale Initiative (TSI) is a group of 13 German and international banks which aim at professionalism and development of the German securitization market.

Underwriter

An underwriter is an intermediary between the issuer of a bond or stock and the public financial markets. The underwriter, most often an investment bank, works with the issuer to determine the financial structure of the securities and to set an offering price. The underwriter then buys the securities from the issuer and sells it to investors. In return for assuming sales and administrative responsibilities, the underwriter receives underwriting fees from the issuer, as well as any profit from securities sold above the offering price. If the market price falls below the offering price, however, the underwriter may have to sell remaining shares at a loss.

UPREIT

An Umbrella Partnership Real Estate Investment Trust (UPREIT) is a REIT that owns a controlling interest in an entity that owns real estate. The umbrella partnership is also referred to as an Operating Partnership (OP), since all or most of the operations take place at the partnership level. It usually consists of the following:

The general partner of the OP is a REIT (usually publicly traded) that issues one share of stock for each general partner and limited partnership unit it holds in the OP; and other holders of limited partnership units, commonly referred to as OP units, have the right to exchange their OP units for shares of the stock in the REIT at any time on a one-for-one basis. Such exchanges for stock are taxable at the time exchanged and therefore all gains taxes are deferred until the OP unit holder decides to sell all or part of the units held. If the holder retains the units in their estate, the gains taxes can be eliminated completely.

Volatility

Volatility equates to the variability of returns from an investment. It is an acceptable substitute for risk. The greater the volatility, the greater is the risk that an investment will not turn out as hoped because its market price happens to be on the downswing of a bounce at the time that it needs to be cashed in. The problem is that future volatility is hard to predict and measures of past volatility can, themselves, be variable, depending on how frequently returns are measured (e. g., weekly or monthly) and for how long. Therefore, putting expectations of future volatility into predictive models is of limited use, but resorting to using past levels of volatility is equally limited.

Warrant

A warrant is a type of financial instrument attached to a security that has a separate life and value. A warrant allows the investor to purchase ordinary shares at a fixed price over a period of time or to perpetuity. The price of the shares is usually higher than the market price at the time of issue. A warrant is freely transferable and can be traded separately. Warrants are usually issued by companies for their own shares, or the shares of a subsidiary. Covered warrants are issued by banks, for the shares of other companies, or for use as a trading instrument.

Waterfall

A waterfall is a term used to describe the cash flow pay-out priority of a Commercial Mortgage Backed Security (CMBS). The cash flow from the pool of mortgages typically pays principal plus interest to the highest-rated tranche, while paying only interest on the lower-rated tranches (the coupon payment having been stipulated at the time of issue). After all of the certificates from the highest-rated tranche have been retired or paid down, the cash flow then is dedicated to paying principal as well as interest to the next highest-rated tranche. While all tranches receive interest or coupon payments, principal is paid to each tranche in sequence until each successively-rated tranche is paid down, in accord with the sequence stipulated in the prospectus at the time of issue. Since lower-rated tranches receive principal payments only after higher-rated tranches are paid down, they typically have longer average lives, i. e., are paid off later. The "waterfall" analogy refers to the visual image of a champagne waterfall, in which the flow of champagne (cash) first fills up the highest tier, then spills into the next tier, etc.

Winner's curse

Winner's curse refers to the tendency that in a bidding contest or in some types of auctions, the winner is the bidder with the highest (over-optimistic) estimate of value. This explains the high frequency of negative returns to acquiring firms in takeovers with multiple bidders.

Yield curve

The yield curve is the graphical representation of the yields of a set of bonds or other instruments with the same credit risk and currency, but with different maturities. The yield is plotted along the vertical axis and time to maturity on the horizontal axis. There are many different yield curves, including government benchmark curves, deposit curves, swap curves, and credit curves. Benchmark curves consist of securities that meet certain criteria for liquidity, size, price, availability, turnover rate and other characteristics. These securities set standards for the market against which other issues can be measured. A yield curve is not static and can change quickly at any time. Expectations of higher inflation, which may cause longer-term debt prices to fall more than short-term prices, may have immediate effect on the yield curve. The normal yield curve is positive, rising from left to right, because yields on longer maturities are higher than on short maturities to reflect the greater risk of lending money for a longer time. An inverted, or negative, yield curve slopes downwards from left to right, with short-term yields higher than long-term yields. This is because investors may be expecting a reduction in inflation in the longer term or there may be expectations of sharply reduced supply of bonds, both of which will depress yields.

Yield-to-maturity (YTM)

The Yield-to-maturity (YTM) is the rate of return expected on a bond if it is held until maturity and is a key consideration when comparing bond investments, assuming all coupon and principal payments are received as scheduled. The YTM is calculated by taking into account its coupon, current market price and time to maturity. Expressed as an annualized rate of return, the YTM assumes all coupons from the bonds will be reinvested at the same rate. The principal repayment due on maturity, plus the present inflation-adjusted value of all future coupon payments should, in theory, equal the current market price of a bond.

Zero-coupon bonds

A zero-coupon bond is a bond that pays no coupon but is issued at a deep discount to face value and pays the par value at maturity. The difference between the issue and redemption price creates a capital gain that boosts the effective yield close to market levels. As it does not pay a coupon, investors do not run the risk of reinvesting interest paid at a lower rate if interest rates fall during the life of the bond. There may also be tax advantages to an investor from taking a one-off capital gain rather than a stream of income from coupon payments. Zero-coupon securities are frequently used to plan for a specific investment goal. For example, parents knowing their child will enter college in 10 years can buy a "zero" that will mature in 10 years, and thus be assured of having money available for tuition.

Zinsschranke (interest deduction ceiling)

The interest deduction ceiling (German: Zinsschranke) – limits the tax deductibility of interest payments in Germany, and will mean that interest of more that € 1 million a year will reduce taxable corporate income only to the extent that this interest does not exceed a certain proportion of taxable profits. The precise ratio has not been finalized, but a rate of 30 % is under discussion. Interest expenses not deductible under this regime will be carried forward to future years and the rule will cover all kinds of interest expenses – whether they are paid to third party banks or to shareholders.

Sources

1. www.acera.org
2. www.albion-intl.com
3. www.allbusiness.com
4. www.anzbank.com.au
5. www.architecture411.com
6. www.armencomp.com
7. www.a-trade.com
8. www.bloombergwire.net
9. www.bnzmarkets.co.nz
10. www.bondstrade.com
11. www.bt-finance.net
12. www.bursamalaysia.com
13. www.businessweek.com
14. www.cananews.com
15. www.cfainstitute.org
16. www.clenow.net
17. www.cmacapital.com
18. www.cmbs.org
19. www.consumersresearchcncl.org
20. www.contingencyanalysis.com
21. www.darenmiller.com
22. www.deutsche-euroshop.de
23. www.dividendcapital.com
24. www.docloan.com
25. www.duke.edu/~rnau/
26. www.euribor.org
27. epp.eurostat.ec.europa.eu
28. www.exchange-data.com
29. www.financegates.com
30. www.fmcommercial.com
31. www.fmsinc.org
32. www.freshfields.com
33. www.gerdau.com.br
34. www.hantecforex.com
35. www.harperrisk.com
36. www.hedgefundprofiler.com
37. www.homeproperties.com
38. www.wfn.ipohome.com
39. www.iposyndicate.com
40. www.juliekershner.com
41. www.kbsh.ca
42. www.kerrhometeam.com
43. www.landonthe.net
44. www.lendersquotes.com
45. www.mccarystevens.com
46. www.midmarketplace.com
47. www.mjxam.com
48. www.myspx.com
49. www.nareim.org
50. www.netinvestmentadvisor.com
51. www.northstarfg.com
52. www.nysscpa.org
53. pages.stern.nyu.edu/~igiddy/
54. www.propertyoz.com.au
55. www.qtc.qld.gov.au
56. www.reitstreet.com
57. www.rentlaw.com
58. glossary.reuters.com
59. www.rheinhyp-bank.de
60. pages.ripco.net/~lees/
61. www.riskglossary.com
62. www.santaclaritahomeguide.com
63. www.sc.com.my
64. www.schorkreport.com
65. www.schweser.com
66. www.sebfrey.com
67. www.semper-financial.com
68. www.spreaderx.com
69. www.teamcaa.org
70. www.teccoach.com
71. www.thestreet.com
72. www.tpw.com
73. www.treasurer.ca.gov
74. www.sp.uconn.edu
75. www.westerntech.com
76. www.womenswallstreet.com
77. www.worldbank.org

Index